D0758893

THE LOEB CLASSICAL LIBRARY

FOUNDED BY JAMES LOEB

EDITED BY

G. P. GOOLD

PHILO

IV

LCL 261

PREFACE

text of this standard edition should be preserved, has been followed in this volume with modification.

A mild regret has also been expressed that no account of the MSS. has been given. It is perhaps a pity that this was not attempted in the General Introduction. In apology it may be said that, leaving out of consideration excerpts and quotations, which form a considerable part of the evidence for the text, the MSS. used by Cohn and Wendland, few of which are earlier than the thirteenth century and none earlier than the eleventh or tenth, amount to more than twenty in the six volumes and vary greatly with the different treatises ; and that Cohn has declared at the end of his survey that no single MS. or family of MSS. stands out in such a way that anything more than an eclectic recension of Philo's text is possible.[a]

I cannot conclude without again expressing the greatness of the debt I owe to Leisegang's index. True, there are a good many words absent, on which one would be glad to be able to investigate Philo's usage, and of the words dealt with I have sometimes found examples omitted, so that one has to be cautious in drawing negative conclusions from it. Still, on the whole, it is an admirable piece of work, and not only the present translator but all future editors of Philo will have in their hands an instrument which Mangey and Wendland would have given much to possess.

F. H. C.

February 1932.

---

[a] Prolegomena to Vol. I, p. xli.

ON THE CONFUSION OF TONGUES
(DE CONFUSIONE LINGUARUM)

ANALYTICAL INTRODUCTION

THE text of this treatise is Gen. xi. 1-9, which is given in full in the first section.

Philo begins by stating the objections which the sceptical critics had brought against the story. They had said that the project of building a tower to reach heaven was really the same as the Homeric myth of the Aloeidae (2-4), and had pointed out the absurdity of the idea (5). Secondly they had said that the story of the confusion of tongues was much the same as the fable that all animals originally understood each other's language and lost the privilege by presumption (6-8), and though the story in Genesis was a little more rational, still the idea that the multiplication of languages would serve to prevent co-operation in sin was absurd (9-13). Philo will leave the literalists to answer these criticisms as they can. His own answer is to give an allegorical interpretation of the whole story (14-15).

By " one lip and one voice " Moses is indicating a " symphony " of evils, which is seen not only in the multitude, but in the individual (16), where it sometimes takes the form of the external calamities of fortune (16-20), but still more in the passions which beset the soul (21-22), of which the deluge story is an allegory (23-25), as also the alliance against Abraham (26), and the attack of the whole people of Sodom upon the angel visitors (27-28). The illustration which follows leads to a meditation on the word " lip " ($\chi\epsilon\hat{\iota}\lambda os$) [a] which also means " edge." Moses met Pharoah on the " lip " of the river. The Egyptians lay dead on the " lip " of the sea (29-36), and since " lip " means speech, we may see in this death the silencing of convicted falsehood (37-38), though here a caution is needed. There are many unskilled in refuting falsehood and they can only do so with God's help (39).

The " symphony " of evil suggests the " symphony " of good, and this appears in the words of the patriarchs " we are men of peace, sons of one man." The one man is the Divine Logos, and only those who acknowledge him are men of peace, while the opposite creed of polytheism breeds discord (40-43). Yet this peace is also a war against the symphony of evil. This thought leads to an exposition of Jeremiah xv. 10, particularly of the description by the prophet of himself as a " man of war " (43-51), and hence to the " symphony " gained by the Captains who fought against Midian (52-57), and the highest of all symphonies, when Israel would " do and hear," that is would do God's will even before they heard the commandment (58-59). [b]

The next verse of the text is " as they march from the east (or " rising ") they *found* a plain in the land of Shinar (interpreted as shaking off) and *dwelt* there." " Rising " and " shaking off " being applicable to good and ill lead to illustrations from other texts where these words occur (60-74). " Finding " suggests that the wicked actually seek evil (75), and

[a] The word is the *motif* running through the whole treatise.
[b] For a closer account of the connexion of thought in §§ 52-57 see note on § 57.

" dwelling there " suggests the contrast (illustrated from sayings of Abraham, Isaac, Jacob and Moses) of the good man regarding himself as only a sojourner in the body (76-82).

We now come to the building of the city and tower. The third verse is " come let us make bricks and bake them with fire." By " brick-making " is meant the analysing and shaping of evil-minded thoughts (83-90), and we are reminded that such brick-making is also imposed upon the Israel-soul, when once it is in bondage to Egypt (91-93). This last thought gives rise to a very loosely connected meditation on the vision of the Divine granted to the liberated Israel in Ex. xxiv.[a] and the interpretation of its details (94-100). The " baking with fire " signifies the solidarity which sophistical argument gives to their vices, and so too we have " their brick became a stone " (101-102). But on the other hand the " asphalt became clay,[b] " that is, God subverts their evil designs, before they attain the safety ($\dot{\alpha}\sigma\phi\dot{\alpha}\lambda\epsilon\iota\alpha$) of " asphalt " (103-104). Two thoughts on " asphalt " follow suggesting that its " safety " is rather the safety of bodily than of spiritual things (105-106).

" Let us build ourselves a city and tower whose head shall reach to heaven." Our souls are cities and the fool summons all his senses and passions to help him build his city with its tower or acropolis to his taste (107-112). When the tower seeks to rise to heaven, it signifies the impious attempt of theological falsities (especially the denial of providence) to attack celestial truths (113-115). On the next words " let us make our name " Philo bursts into

---

[a] Partly induced by the occurrence of the words " brick " or " plinth " in the narrative.   [b] See note on § 102.

invective against the madness of the wicked in actually flaunting their wickedness (116-118). It is true indeed that they have an inkling that there is a divine judgement awaiting them as they shew by the next words " before we are scattered abroad " (119-121). But this is only in the background of their thoughts. In general they are of Cain's lineage and believe in the self-sufficiency of man, the folly of which Philo denounces in his usual way, and this self-sufficiency gives a second meaning to the words " its head shall reach to heaven " (122-128). But this tower will be overthrown even as Gideon overthrew the tower of Penuel (turning away from God), not in war but when he returned in peace—the true peace (129-132). By a third interpretation " heaven " may mean " mind," and the attempt to reach it be the attempt to exalt sense above mind (133).

The words " the Lord came down to see the city and the tower " call for the usual protest against anthropomorphism, and Philo again emphasizes the truth that God's Potencies are everywhere, while His essential nature is not in space at all (134-139). The intention of Moses in using the phrase is to shew us by God's example the need of close examination before we dogmatize, and the superiority of sight to hearsay (140-141). As for the phrase the " sons of men," some may scoff at it as a pleonasm, but the true meaning is that these builders are not, like the pious, " sons of God " (141-145), nor yet sons of " one man," [a] that is the Logos (146-147). Sonship in fact is often in the scriptures used in this spiritual sense (148-149). The next words, " behold they are all one race and one lip," give rise to the

[a] See § 41.

thought that there may easily be unison in the worst disharmony (150-151), while in " they have begun to do this " " this " is the impiety against heaven which crowns their misdeeds to men. They only " began," for heaven is inviolable and blasphemies recoil upon the blasphemer (152-154), yet they are treated as though they succeeded, which is indicated by the words " the tower which they built " (155). (At this point Philo interpolates a curious piece of literalism ; not only is it a physical impossibility to build such a tower, but anyone who attempted it would be blasted by the heat of the sun) (156-157). That the punishment entailed by the accomplished sin falls upon the undertaken sin is shewn in Balaam's fate (158-159), and the law which refuses sanctuary to him who has attempted murder (160). (Incidentally this law is given the spiritual meaning that the mind which believes God to be the author of evil as well as good and thus throws the responsibility for its own sins upon Him, is essentially unholy) (161). The next words, " nothing shall fail them of all they attempt," teach us that the greatest punishment God can give is to give the sinner opportunity without restraint, and this is illustrated (as in *Quod Det.* 141 ff.) by Cain's word " that I should be let free is the greater indictment (or punishment) " (162-167).

When we come to the words " let us go down and confound their tongues " we have first to explain the plural in God's mouth, of which he gives other examples (168-169). He then puts forward, as in *De Op.* 75, the theory (based on the *Timaeus*) that God committed certain tasks to his lieutenants, the Potencies and the spiritual beings called " Angels " (170-175). As man also has free will and is therefore capable of sin God shared the work of man's creation with His ministers, that He Himself should not be the cause of evil (176-179). So too He calls upon His subordinates (here definitely called Angels)[a] to bring the punishment of " confusion " upon the impious (180-182). As for the word " confusion " (σύγχυσις) we may accept the philosophic usage in which it stands for a mixing so complete that the original properties of the ingredients are destroyed, in contrast to μίξις where the ingredients are merely juxtaposed, and κρᾶσις where though chemically combined they can still be analysed (183-188). Thus σύγχυσις of the impious means that their powers are so annihilated that neither separately nor in combination they can work mischief (189). The literalist interpretation that the story merely describes the differentiation of languages may not be untrue, but it is inadequate. Had such differentiation been intended we should have expected some such term as separation or distribution rather than confusion, and moreover differentiation of function, as we see in the human organism, is beneficial rather than the reverse (190-195). That σύγχυσις implies destruction in this passage is confirmed by the words which follow, " the Lord dispersed them thence," for dispersion conveys a similar idea (196). The dispersion of the wicked will imply the reassembling of the good whom they had dispersed, in fact establish the " symphony " of virtues in the place of the " symphony " of evil. Viewed in this double light of " destruction " and " dispersion " the name σύγχυσις well describes the fool whose life is as worthless as it is unstable[b] (197-end).

[a] See note on § 182.　　　　[b] See note on § 198.

ΠΕΡΙ ΣΥΓΧΥΣΕΩΣ ΔΙΑΛΕΚΤΩΝ

1 I. Περὶ μὲν δὴ τούτων ἀρκέσει τὰ εἰρημένα.
σκεπτέον δὲ ἑξῆς οὐ παρέργως, ἃ περὶ τῆς τῶν
διαλέκτων συγχύσεως φιλοσοφεῖ· λέγει γὰρ ὧδε·
" καὶ ἦν πᾶσα ἡ γῆ χεῖλος ἕν, καὶ φωνὴ μία
πᾶσι. καὶ ἐγένετο ἐν τῷ κινῆσαι αὐτοὺς ἀπὸ
ἀνατολῶν, εὗρον πεδίον ἐν τῇ γῇ Σενααρ καὶ
κατῴκησαν ἐκεῖ. καὶ εἶπεν ἄνθρωπος τῷ πλησίον·
δεῦτε πλινθεύσωμεν πλίνθους καὶ ὀπτήσωμεν αὐτὰς
πυρί. καὶ ἐγένετο αὐτοῖς ἡ πλίνθος εἰς λίθον, καὶ
ἄσφαλτος ἦν αὐτοῖς ὁ πηλός.[1] καὶ εἶπον· δεῦτε
οἰκοδομήσωμεν ἑαυτοῖς πόλιν καὶ πύργον, οὗ ἡ
κεφαλὴ ἔσται ἕως τοῦ οὐρανοῦ, καὶ ποιήσωμεν
ἑαυτῶν ὄνομα πρὸ τοῦ διασπαρῆναι ἐπὶ πρόσωπον
πάσης τῆς γῆς. καὶ κατέβη κύριος ἰδεῖν τὴν πόλιν
καὶ τὸν πύργον ὃν ᾠκοδόμησαν οἱ υἱοὶ τῶν ἀνθρώπων. καὶ εἶπε κύριος· ἰδοὺ γένος ἓν καὶ χεῖλος
ἓν πάντων· καὶ τοῦτο ἤρξαντο ποιῆσαι, καὶ νῦν
οὐκ ἐκλείψει ἐξ αὐτῶν πάντα ὅσα ἂν ἐπιθῶνται
ποιεῖν· δεῦτε καὶ καταβάντες συγχέωμεν ἐκεῖ
αὐτῶν τὴν γλῶσσαν, ἵνα μὴ ἀκούσωσιν ἕκαστος
τὴν φωνὴν τοῦ πλησίον. καὶ διέσπειρεν αὐτοὺς
κύριος ἐκεῖθεν ἐπὶ πρόσωπον πάσης τῆς γῆς, καὶ

---

[1] Wend. conjectures ⟨ἡ⟩ ἄσφαλτος . . [ὁ] πηλός from 103;
but see note there (App. p. 555).

ON THE CONFUSION OF TONGUES

I. Enough has been said on these matters. The [1] next question which demands our careful consideration is the confusion of tongues and the lessons of wisdom taught by Moses thereon. For he says as follows.

" And all the earth was one lip and there was one voice to all. And it came to pass as they moved from the east, they found a plain in the land of Shinar and dwelt there. And a man said to his neighbour, Come, let us make bricks and bake them with fire. And the brick became as stone to them and the clay was asphalt to them. And they said, ' Come, let us build for ourselves a city and a tower, whose head shall be unto heaven, and let us make our name before we are scattered abroad, on the face of all the earth.' And the Lord came down to see the city and the tower which the sons of men built. And the Lord said, ' Behold, they have all one race and one lip, and they have begun to do this, and now nothing shall fail from them of all that they attempt to do. Come and let us go down and confuse their tongue there, that they may not understand each the voice of his neighbour.' And the Lord scattered them abroad thence on the face of all the earth, and they

ἐπαύσαντο οἰκοδομοῦντες τὴν πόλιν καὶ τὸν πύργον.
διὰ τοῦτο ἐκλήθη τὸ ὄνομα αὐτῆς[1] σύγχυσις, ὅτι
ἐκεῖ συνέχεε κύριος τὰ χείλη πάσης τῆς γῆς, καὶ
ἐκεῖθεν διέσπειρεν αὐτοὺς κύριος ἐπὶ πρόσωπον
πάσης τῆς γῆς.''

2
[405]   II. | Οἱ μὲν δυσχεραίνοντες τῇ πατρίῳ πολιτείᾳ,
ψόγον καὶ κατηγορίαν αἰεὶ τῶν νόμων μελετῶντες,
τούτοις καὶ τοῖς παραπλησίοις ὡς ἂν ἐπιβάθραις
τῆς ἀθεότητος αὐτῶν, οἱ δυσσεβεῖς, χρῶνται φάσ-
κοντες· ἔτι νῦν σεμνηγορεῖτε περὶ τῶν διατεταγ-
μένων ὡς τοὺς ἀληθείας κανόνας αὐτῆς περιεχόντων; ἰδοὺ γὰρ αἱ ἱεραὶ λεγόμεναι βίβλοι παρ᾽
ὑμῖν καὶ μύθους περιέχουσιν, ἐφ᾽ οἷς εἰώθατε γελᾶν,
3 ὅταν ἄλλων διεξιόντων ἀκούητε. καίτοι τί δεῖ
τοὺς πολλαχόθι τῆς νομοθεσίας ἐσπαρμένους ἀναλέγεσθαι ὥσπερ σχολὴν ἄγοντας καὶ ἐνευκαιροῦν-
τας διαβολαῖς, ἀλλ᾽ οὐ μόνον τῶν ἐν χερσὶ καὶ
4 παρὰ πόδας ὑπομιμνήσκειν;   εἷς μὲν οὖν
ἐστιν ὁ ἐοικὼς τῷ συντεθέντι ἐπὶ τῶν Ἀλωειδῶν,
οὓς ὁ μέγιστος καὶ δοκιμώτατος τῶν ποιητῶν
Ὅμηρος διανοηθῆναί φησι τρία τὰ περιμήκιστα
τῶν ὀρῶν ἐπιφορῆσαι καὶ ἐπιχῶσαι ἐλπίσαντας
τὴν εἰς οὐρανὸν ὁδὸν τοῖς ἀνέρχεσθαι βουλομένοις
εὐμαρῆ διὰ τούτων ἔσεσθαι πρὸς αἰθέριον ὕψος
ἀρθέντων· ἔστι δὲ τὰ περὶ τούτων ἔπη τοιαῦτα·

Ὄσσαν ἐπ᾽ Οὐλύμπῳ μέμασαν θέμεν, αὐτὰρ ἐπ᾽
Ὄσσῃ
Πήλιον εἰνοσίφυλλον, ἵν᾽ οὐρανὸς ἀμβατὸς εἴη,
Ὄλυμπος δὲ καὶ Ὄσσα καὶ Πήλιον ὀρῶν ὀνόματα.

---

[1] αὐτῆς] so LXX and the majority of MSS.: Wend. αὐτοῦ;
but cf. 196 τὴν κακίας πόλιν with 198 κακίας ὄνομα σύγχυσις.

ceased building the city and the tower. Therefore the name of the city was called ' Confusion,' because the Lord confounded there the lips of the whole earth, and the Lord scattered them thence over the face of the whole earth " (Gen. xi. 1-9).

II. Persons who cherish a dislike of the institutions 2 of our fathers and make it their constant study to denounce and decry the Laws find in these and similar passages openings[a] as it were for their godlessness. " Can you still," say these impious scoffers, " speak gravely of the ordinances as containing the canons of absolute truth ? For see your so-called holy books contain also myths, which you regularly deride when you hear them related by others. And 3 indeed," they continue, " it is needless to collect the numerous examples scattered about the Law-book, as we might had we leisure to spend in exposing its failings. We have but to remind you of the instances which lie at our very feet and ready to our hand."

One of these we have here, which re- 4 sembles the fable told of the Aloeidae, who according to Homer the greatest and most reputed of poets planned to pile the three loftiest mountains on each other in one heap, hoping that when these were raised to the height of the upper sky they would furnish an easy road to heaven for those who wished to ascend thither. Homer's lines on this subject run thus :

> They on Olympus Ossa fain would pile,
> On Ossa Pelion with its quivering leaves,
> In hope thereby to climb the heights of heaven.[b]

Olympus, Ossa and Pelion are names of mountains.

---

[a] Or, more literally, "means of approach to"; cf. De Agr. 56. [b] Od. xi. 315, 318.

5   πύργον δὲ ὁ νομοθέτης ἀντὶ τούτων
εἰσάγει πρὸς τῶν τότε ἀνθρώπων κατασκευαζόμε-
νον θελησάντων ὑπ' ἀνοίας ἅμα καὶ μεγαλαυχίας[1]
οὐρανοῦ ψαῦσαι. πῶς γὰρ οὐ[2] φρενοβλάβεια δεινή;
καὶ γὰρ εἰ τὰ τῆς συμπάσης μέρη γῆς ἐποικο-
δομηθείη προκαταβληθέντι βραχεῖ θεμελίῳ καὶ
ἀνεγερθείη τρόπον κίονος ἑνός, μυρίοις τῆς αἰ-
θερίου σφαίρας ἀπολειφθήσεται διαστήμασι, καὶ μάλιστα κατὰ τοὺς ζητητικοὺς τῶν φιλοσόφων, οἳ
τοῦ παντὸς κέντρον εἶναι τὴν γῆν ἀνωμολόγησαν.

6   III. ἕτερος δέ τις συγγενὴς τούτῳ
περὶ τῆς τῶν ζῴων ὁμοφωνίας πρὸς μυθοπλαστῶν
ἀναγράφεται· λέγεται γάρ, ὡς ἄρα πάνθ' ὅσα ζῷα
χερσαῖα καὶ ἔνυδρα καὶ πτηνὰ τὸ παλαιὸν ὁμόφωνα
ἦν, καὶ ὅνπερ τρόπον ἀνθρώπων Ἕλληνες μὲν
Ἕλλησι, βαρβάροις δὲ βάρβαροι νῦν οἱ ὁμόγλωττοι
διαλέγονται, τοῦτον τὸν τρόπον καὶ πάντα πᾶσι
περὶ ὧν ἢ δρᾶν ἢ πάσχειν τι συνέβαινεν ὡμίλει,
ὡς καὶ ἐπὶ ταῖς κακοπραγίαις συνάχθεσθαι[3] κἂν
εἴ πού τι λυσιτελὲς ἀπαντῴη, συνευφραίνεσθαι.

7 τάς τε γὰρ ἡδονὰς καὶ ἀηδίας ἀλλήλοις ἀνα-
φέροντα διὰ τοῦ ὁμοφώνου συνήδετο καὶ συναηδί-
[406] ζετο, | κἀκ τούτου τὸ ὁμοιότροπον καὶ ὁμοιοπαθὲς
εὑρίσκετο, μέχριπερ κορεσθέντα τῆς τῶν παρόντων ἀγαθῶν ἀφθονίας, ὃ πολλάκις γίνεσθαι φιλεῖ,
πρὸς τὸν τῶν ἀνεφίκτων ἔρωτα ἐξώκειλε καὶ περὶ
ἀθανασίας ἐπρεσβεύετο γήρως ἔκλυσιν καὶ τὴν εἰς

---

[1] MSS. μεγαλουργίας.   [2] MSS. πᾶσα γὰρ οὖν.
[3] MSS. συνέχεσθαι.

For these the lawgiver substitutes a 5 tower which he represents as being built by the men of that day who wished in their folly and insolent pride to touch the heaven. Folly indeed; surely dreadful madness! For if one should lay a small foundation and build up upon it the different parts of the whole earth, rising in the form of a single pillar, it would still be divided by vast distances from the sphere of ether, particularly if we accept the view of the philosophers who inquire into such problems, all of whom are agreed that the earth is the centre of the universe.[a] III. Another 6 similar story is to be found in the writings of the mythologists, telling of the days when all animals had a common language. The tale is that in old days all animals, whether on land or in water or winged, had the same language, and just as among men to-day Greeks talk with Greeks and barbarians with barbarians if they have the same tongue, so too every creature conversed with every other, about all that happened to be done to them or by them, and in this way they mourned together at misfortunes, and rejoiced together when anything of advantage came their way. For since community 7 of language led them to impart to each other their pleasures and discomforts, both emotions were shared by them in common. As a result they gained a similarity of temperament and feeling until surfeited with the abundance of their present blessings they desired the unattainable, as so often happens, and wrecked their happiness thereon. They sent an embassy to demand immortality, asking that they might be exempted from old age and allowed to

[a] See App. p. 553.

αἰεὶ νεότητος ἀκμὴν αἰτούμενα, φάσκοντα καὶ τῶν
παρ' αὑτοῖς ἐν ἤδη ζῴων τὸ ἑρπετόν, ὄφιν, τετυ-
χηκέναι ταύτης τῆς δωρεᾶς· ἀποδυόμενον γὰρ τὸ
γῆρας πάλιν ἐξ ὑπαρχῆς ἀνηβᾶν· ἄτοπον δ' εἶναι
ἢ τὰ κρείττω τοῦ χείρονος ἢ ἑνὸς τὰ πάντα
8 λειφθῆναι. δίκην μέντοι τοῦ τολμήματος ἔδωκε τὴν
προσήκουσαν· ἑτερόγλωττα γὰρ εὐθὺς ἐγένετο, ὡς
ἐξ ἐκείνου μηκέτ' ἀλλήλων ἐπακοῦσαι δυνηθῆναι
χάριν τῆς ἐν ταῖς διαλέκτοις εἰς ἃς ἡ μία καὶ
κοινὴ πάντων ἐτμήθη, διαφορᾶς.

9 IV. Ὁ δ' ἐγγυτέρω τἀληθοῦς προσάγων τὸν
λόγον τὰ ἄλογα τῶν λογικῶν διέζευξεν, ὡς ἀνθρώποις μόνοις μαρτυρῆσαι τὸ ὁμόφωνον. ἔστι
δέ, ὥς γέ φασι, καὶ τοῦτο μυθῶδες. καὶ μὴν τήν[1]
γε φωνῆς εἰς μυρίας διαλέκτων ἰδέας τομήν, ἣν
καλεῖ γλώττης σύγχυσιν, ἐπὶ θεραπείᾳ λέγουσιν
ἁμαρτημάτων συμβῆναι, ὡς μηκέτ' ἀλλήλων ἀκροώ-
μενοι κοινῇ συναδικῶσιν, ἀλλὰ τρόπον τινὰ [ἄλλοι]
ἀλλήλοις κεκωφωμένοι * * *[2] κατὰ συμπράξεις
10 ἐγχειρῶσι τοῖς αὐτοῖς. τὸ δὲ οὐκ ἐπ' ὠφελείᾳ
φαίνεται συμβῆναι· καὶ γὰρ αὖθις οὐδὲν ἧττον
κατὰ ἔθνη διῳκισμένων καὶ μὴ μιᾷ διαλέκτῳ
χρωμένων γῆ καὶ θάλαττα πολλάκις ἀμυθήτων
κακῶν ἐπληρώθη. οὐ γὰρ αἱ φωναί, ἀλλὰ αἱ
ὁμότροποι τῆς ψυχῆς πρὸς τὸ ἁμαρτάνειν ζηλώσεις
11 τοῦ συναδικεῖν αἴτιαι· καὶ γὰρ οἱ ἐκτετμημένοι

---

[1] mss. τῆς.
[2] The translation follows Mangey in assuming that μὴ
alone has been omitted in the mss. Wend. (*Rhein. Mus.* liii.
p. 18) thought that this made the last part of the sentence
too much a mere repetition of the first part. He suggested
καθ' ⟨ἑαυτὸν ἕκαστος ἐργάζηται, ἀλλὰ μὴ⟩.

14

enjoy the vigour of youth for ever. They pleaded that one of their fellow-creatures, that mere reptile the serpent, had already obtained this boon, since he shed his old age and renewed his youth afresh, and it was absurd that the superior beings should fare worse than the inferior, or all than the one. How- 8 ever, for this audacity they were punished as they deserved. For their speech at once became different, so that from that day forward they could no longer understand each other, because of the difference of the languages into which the single language which they all shared had been divided.

IV. Now Moses, say the objectors, brings his 9 story nearer to reality and makes a distinction between reasoning and unreasoning creatures, so that the unity of language for which he vouches applies to men only. Still even this, they say, is mythical. They point out that the division of speech into a multitude of different kinds of language, which Moses calls " Confusion of tongues," is in the story brought about as a remedy for sin, to the end that men should no longer through mutual understanding be partners in iniquity, but be deaf in a sense to each other and thus cease to act together to effect the same purposes. But no good result appears to have 10 been attained by it. For all the same after they had been separated into different nations and no longer spoke the same tongue, land and sea were constantly full of innumerable evil deeds. For it is not the utterances of men but the presence of the same cravings for sin in the soul which causes combination in wrongdoing. Indeed men who have lost their 11

γλῶτταν νεύμασι καὶ βλέμμασι καὶ ταῖς ἄλλαις
τοῦ σώματος σχέσεσι καὶ κινήσεσιν οὐχ ἧττον
τῆς διὰ λόγων προφορᾶς ἃ ἂν θελήσωσιν ὑπο-
σημαίνουσι· χωρὶς τοῦ καὶ ἔθνος ἓν πολλάκις οὐχ
ὁμόφωνον μόνον ἀλλὰ καὶ ὁμόνομον καὶ ὁμοδίαιτον
τοσοῦτον ἐπιβῆναι κακίας, ὥστε τοῖς ἀνθρώπων
ἁπάντων ἁμαρτήμασιν ἰσοστάσια δύνασθαι πλημ-
12 μελεῖν· ἀπειρίᾳ τε διαλέκτων μυρίοι πρὸς τῶν
ἐπιτιθεμένων οὐ προϊδόμενοι τὸ μέλλον προκατ-
ελήφθησαν, ὡς ἔμπαλιν ἐπιστήμῃ τοὺς ἐπικρεμασ-
θέντας ἴσχυσαν φόβους τε καὶ κινδύνους ἀπώσασθαι·
ὥστε λυσιτελὲς μᾶλλον ἢ βλαβερὸν εἶναι τὴν ἐν
διαλέκτοις κοινωνίαν, ἐπεὶ καὶ μέχρι νῦν οἱ καθ'
ἑκάστην χώραν, καὶ μάλιστα τῶν[1] αὐτοχθόνων, δι'
οὐδὲν οὕτως ὡς διὰ τὸ ὁμόγλωσσον ἀπαθεῖς κακῶν
13 διατελοῦσι. κἂν εἰ μέντοι τις ἀνὴρ πλείους ἀνα-
μάθοι διαλέκτους, εὐδόκιμος εὐθὺς παρὰ τοῖς ἐπι-
σταμένοις ἐστὶν ὡς ἤδη φίλιος ὤν, οὐ βραχὺ
γνώρισμα κοινωνίας ἐπιφερόμενος τὴν ἐν τοῖς
[407] ὀνόμασι | συνήθειαν, ἀφ' ἧς τὸ ἀδεὲς εἰς τὸ μηδὲν
ἀνήκεστον παθεῖν ἔοικε πεπορίσθαι. τί οὖν ὡς
κακῶν αἴτιον τὸ ὁμόγλωττον ἐξ ἀνθρώπων ἠφάνιζε,
δέον ὡς ὠφελιμώτατον ἱδρῦσθαι;
14 V. Τοὺς δὴ ταῦτα συντιθέντας καὶ κακοτεχ-
νοῦντας ἰδίᾳ μὲν διελέγξουσιν οἱ τὰς προχείρους
ἀποδόσεις τῶν ἀεὶ ζητουμένων ἐκ τῆς φανερᾶς

---

[1] Perhaps, as Wend. conjectures, ⟨τὴν⟩ τῶν.

[a] The thought seems to be that the confusion of languages
did but divide nation from nation, and a single evil nation
can do all the mischief.

tongue by mutilation do by means of nods and glances and the other attitudes and movements of the body indicate their wishes as well as the uttered word can do it. Besides a single nation in which not only language but laws and modes of life are identical often reaches such a pitch of wickedness that its misdeeds can balance the sins of the whole of mankind.[a] Again multitudes through ignorance of other 12 languages have failed to foresee the impending danger, and thus been caught unawares by the attacking force, while on the contrary such a knowledge has enabled them to repel the alarms and dangers which menaced them. The conclusion is that the possession of a common language does more good than harm—a conclusion confirmed by all past experience which shews that in every country, particularly where the population is indigenous, nothing has kept the inhabitants so free from disaster as uniformity of language. Further the acquisition of 13 languages other than his own at once gives a man a high standing with those who know and speak them. They now consider him a friendly person, who brings no small evidence of fellow-feeling in his familiarity with their vocabulary, since that familiarity seems to render them secure against the chance of meeting any disastrous injury at his hands. Why then, they ask, did God wish to deprive mankind of its universal language as though it were a source of evil, when He should rather have established it firmly as a source of the utmost profit ?

V. Those who take the letter of the law in its 14 outward sense and provide for each question as it arises the explanation which lies on the surface, will no doubt refute on their own principles the authors

τῶν νόμων γραφῆς[1] * * * ἀφιλονείκως, οὐκ ἀντι-
σοφιζόμενοί ποθεν, ἀλλ' ἑπόμενοι τῷ τῆς ἀκολουθίας εἱρμῷ προσπταίειν οὐκ ἐῶντι, ἀλλὰ κἄν, εἴ
τινα ἐμποδὼν εἴη, ῥᾳδίως ἀναστέλλοντι, ὅπως αἱ
τῶν λόγων διέξοδοι γίνωνται ἄπταιστοι.

15 φαμὲν τοίνυν ἐκ τοῦ "τὴν γῆν εἶναι πᾶσαν χεῖλος ἓν
καὶ φωνὴν μίαν" κακῶν ἀμυθήτων καὶ μεγάλων
συμφωνίαν δηλοῦσθαι, ὅσα τε πόλεις πόλεσι καὶ
ἔθνεσιν ἔθνη καὶ χώραις χῶραι ἀντεπιφέρουσι, καὶ
ὅσα μὴ μόνον εἰς ἑαυτοὺς ἀλλὰ καὶ εἰς τὸ θεῖον
ἀσεβοῦσιν ἄνθρωποι· καίτοι ταῦτα πληθῶν ἐστιν
ἀδικήματα. σκεπτόμεθα δ' ἡμεῖς καὶ ἐφ' ἑνὸς
ἀνδρὸς τὸ ἀδιεξήγητον τῶν κακῶν πλῆθος, καὶ
μάλισθ' ὅταν τὴν ἀνάρμοστον καὶ ἐκμελῆ καὶ
16 ἄμουσον ἴσχῃ[2] συμφωνίαν.   VI. τὰ μὲν
δὴ τυχηρὰ τίς οὐκ οἶδεν, ὅταν πενία καὶ ἀδοξία
σώματος νόσοις ἢ πηρώσεσι συνενεχθῶσι, καὶ
πάλιν ταῦτα ψυχῆς ἀρρωστήμασιν ἔκφρονος ὑπὸ
μελαγχολίας ἢ μακροῦ γήρως ἤ τινος βαρείας

---

[1] The sentence as it stands cannot be translated. Wend.,
who places the lacuna after ἀφιλονείκως and inserts ⟨ταμιευό-
μενοι⟩, is no doubt right in assuming that a participle must be
supplied. But if one word has been lost, it is not improbable
that others have been lost. With his reading the whole
sentence is an elaborate compliment to the literalists, which
is not paralleled elsewhere, though occasionally, as in § 190, a
certain amount of respect for them is shown. But the overwhelming argument against his view is φαμὲν τοίνυν, which
cannot make an antithesis to ἰδίᾳ μὲν but presupposes a δέ
clause. Cf. De Somn. i. 102 ταῦτα μὲν δὴ καὶ τὰ τοιαῦτα πρὸς
τοὺς τῆς ῥητῆς πραγματείας σοφιστὰς . . εἰρήσθω, λέγωμεν δὲ
ἡμεῖς ἑπόμενοι τοῖς ἀλληγορίας νόμοις τὰ πρέποντα περὶ τούτων.
φαμὲν τοίνυν λόγον σύμβολον ἱμάτιον εἶναι. Philo in my
view is describing his own method and says that he will not

of these insidious criticisms. But we shall take the
line of allegorical interpretation not in any contentious spirit, nor seeking some means of meeting
sophistry with sophistry. Rather we shall follow the
chain of logical sequence,[a] which does not admit of
stumbling but easily removes any obstructions and
thus allows the argument to march to its conclusion
with unfaltering steps.　　　　　We suggest then 15
that by the words "the earth was all one lip and one
voice" is meant a consonance of evil deeds great
and innumerable, and these include the injuries
which cities and nations and countries inflict and
retaliate, as well as the impious deeds which men
commit, not only against each other, but against the
Deity. These indeed are the wrongdoings of multitudes. But we consider also the vast multitude of
ills which are found in the individual man, especially
when the unison of voices within him is a disharmony
tuneless and unmusical.　　　　　VI. Who does 16
not know the calamities of fortune when poverty and
disrepute combine with disease or disablement in the
body, and these again are mixed with the infirmities
of a soul rendered distracted by melancholy or

---

[a] The words which follow suggest that he means that
each deduction from the text is logical, rather than that he
takes each point of the narrative successively.

---

enter into direct conflict with the unbelievers, but show that the
passage, if logically treated on the allegorical method, makes
a reasonable whole.　What the words lost are, one can only
conjecture. It would be enough perhaps to insert ⟨ἀκριβοῦντες,
ἡμεῖς δὲ⟩, sc. διελέγξομεν.　But perhaps it is more likely that
there were some words describing the allegorical method,
ending with an homoioteleuton to γραφῆς, e.g. ⟨ἀκριβοῦντες,
ἡμεῖς δὲ ἀλληγοροῦντες διερμηνεύσομεν τὸ ἐγκείμενον ἐν τῇ γραφῇ⟩.
Cf. De Sobr. 23.　　　　　　　　　　　　　[2] MSS. σχοίη.

ἄλλης κακοδαιμονίας γεγενημένης ἀνακραθῶσι;
17 καὶ γὰρ ἓν μόνον τῶν εἰρημένων βιαίως ἀντι-
στατῆσαν ἱκανὸν ἀνατρέψαι καὶ καταβαλεῖν καὶ
τὸν λίαν ὑπέρογκόν ἐστιν· ὅταν δὲ ἀθρόα ὥσπερ
προστάξει μιᾷ κατὰ τὸν αὐτὸν χρόνον ἑνὶ πάντα
σωρηδὸν ἐπιθῆται[1] τὰ σώματος, τὰ ψυχῆς, τὰ
ἐκτός, τίνα οὐχ ὑπερβάλλει σχετλιότητα;   πεσόν-
των γὰρ δορυφόρων ἀνάγκη καὶ τὸ δορυφορούμενον
18 πίπτειν. δορυφόροι μὲν οὖν σώματος πλοῦτος,
εὐδοξία, τιμαί, ὀρθοῦντες αὐτὸ καὶ εἰς ὕψος αἴροντες
καὶ γαῦρον ἀποδεικνύντες, ὡς τἀναντία, ἀτιμία,
ἀδοξία, πενία, πολεμίων τρόπον καταράττουσι.
19 πάλιν τε δορυφόροι ψυχῆς ἀκοαὶ καὶ ὄψεις ὄσφρησίς
τε καὶ γεῦσις καὶ ξύμπαν τὸ αἰσθήσεως στῖφος,
ἔτι μέντοι ὑγίεια καὶ ἰσχὺς δύναμίς τε καὶ ῥώμη·
τούτοις γὰρ ὥσπερ ἑστῶσι καὶ κραταιῶς ἐρη-
ρεισμένοις εὐερκέσιν οἴκοις ὁ νοῦς ἐμπεριπατῶν
καὶ ‹ἐν›διαιτώμενος ἀγάλλεται πρὸς μηδενὸς ταῖς
ἰδίαις ὁρμαῖς χρῆσθαι κωλυόμενος, ἀλλ' εὐμαρεῖς
καὶ λεωφόρους ἀναπεπταμένας ἔχων τὰς διὰ πάν-
20 των ὁδούς.   τὰ δὲ | τοῖς δορυφόροις τούτοις ἐχθρὰ
[408] ἀντικάθηται, πήρωσις αἰσθητηρίων καὶ νόσος, ὡς
ἔφην, οἷς ἡ διάνοια συγκατακρημνισθῆναι πολλάκις ἐμέλλησε.   καὶ τὰ μὲν τυχηρὰ
ταῦτα ἀργαλέα σφόδρα καὶ σχέτλια ἐξ ἑαυτῶν,
πρὸς δὲ τὴν ‹τῶν› ἐκ προνοίας σύγκρισιν κουφό-
21 τερα πολλῷ. VII. τίς οὖν ἡ τῶν ἑκουσίων κακῶν
συμφωνία, πάλιν ἐν μέρει σκοπῶμεν· τριμεροῦς
ἡμῶν τῆς ψυχῆς ὑπαρχούσης τὸ μὲν νοῦς καὶ λόγος,

---

[1] MSS. ἐπιθεῖναι.

---

[a] Cf. De Ebr. 201 ff.

senility, or any other grievous misfortune ? For **17**
indeed a single item of this list is enough to upset
and overthrow even the very stoutest, if it brings
its force to bear upon him. But when the ills of body
and soul and the external world unite and in serried
mass, as though obedient to a single commanding
voice, bear down at the same moment upon their
lone victim, what misery is not insignificant beside
them ? When the guards fall, that which they
guard must fall too. Now the guards *a* of the body **18**
are wealth and reputation and honours, who keep it
erect and lift it on high and give it a sense of pride,
just as their opposites, dishonour, disrepute and
poverty are like foes who bring it crashing to the
ground. Again the guards of the soul are the powers **19**
of hearing and sight and smell and taste, and the
whole company of the senses and besides them health
and strength of body and limb and muscle. For
these serve as fortresses well-walled and stayed on
firm foundations, houses within which the mind can
range and dwell rejoicing, with none to hinder it from
following the urges of its personality, but with free
passage everywhere as on easy and open high roads.
But against these guards also are posted hostile **20**
forces, disablement of the sense-organs and disease,
as I have said, which often bid fair to carry the
understanding over the precipice in their arms.
While these calamities of fortune which
work independently of us are full of pain and misery,
they are far outweighed in comparison with those
which spring from our deliberate volition. VII. Let **21**
us turn, then, to where the voice of unison is the voice
of our self-caused ills and consider it in its turn. Our
soul, we are told, is tripartite, having one part assigned

τὸ δὲ θυμός, τὸ δὲ ἐπιθυμία κεκληρῶσθαι λέγεται.
κηραίνει δὲ καθ' αὑτό τε ἕκαστον ἰδίᾳ καὶ πρὸς
ἄλληλα πάντα κοινῇ, ἐπειδὰν ὁ μὲν νοῦς ὅσα
ἀφροσύναι καὶ δειλίαι ἀκολασίαι τε καὶ ἀδικίαι
σπείρουσι θερίσῃ, ὁ δὲ θυμὸς τὰς ἐκμανεῖς καὶ
παραφόρους λύττας καὶ ὅσα ἄλλα ὠδίνει κακὰ
τέκῃ, ἡ δὲ ἐπιθυμία τοὺς ὑπὸ νηπιότητος ἀεὶ
κούφους ἔρωτας καὶ τοῖς ἐπιτυχοῦσι σώμασί τε
καὶ πράγμασι προσιπταμένους ἐπιπέμψῃ παντα-
22 χόσε· τότε γὰρ ὥσπερ ἐν σκάφει ναυτῶν, ἐπιβατῶν,
κυβερνητῶν κατά τινα φρενοβλάβειαν ἐπ' ἀπωλείᾳ
τούτου συμφρονησάντων καὶ οἱ ἐπιβουλεύσαντες
αὐτῇ νηὶ οὐχ ἥκιστα συναπώλοντο. βαρύτατον γὰρ
κακῶν καὶ σχεδὸν ἀνίατον μόνον ἡ πάντων τῶν
ψυχῆς μερῶν πρὸς τὸ ἁμαρτάνειν συνεργία, μηδενὸς
οἷα ἐν πανδήμῳ συμφορᾷ δυνηθέντος ὑγιαίνειν, ἵνα
τοὺς πάσχοντας ἰᾶται, ἀλλὰ καὶ τῶν ἰατρῶν ἅμα
τοῖς ἰδιώταις καμνόντων, οὓς ἡ λοιμώδης νόσος
ἐφ' ὁμολογουμένῃ συμφορᾷ πιέσασα κατέχει.
23   τοῦ παθήματος τούτου ⟨σύμβολον⟩ ὁ
μέγας ἀναγραφεὶς παρὰ τῷ νομοθέτῃ κατακλυσμός
ἐστι, " τῶν τε ἀπ' οὐρανοῦ καταρρακτῶν " τοὺς
κακίας αὐτῆς λάβρῳ φορᾷ χειμάρρους ἐπομβρούντων καὶ " τῶν ἀπὸ γῆς," λέγω δὲ τοῦ σώματος,
" πηγῶν " ἀναχεουσῶν τὰ πάθους ἑκάστου ῥεύματα
πολλὰ ὄντα καὶ μεγάλα, ἅπερ εἰς ταὐτὸν τοῖς
προτέροις συνιόντα καὶ ἀναμιγνύμενα κυκᾶταί τε
καὶ τὸ δεδεγμένον ἅπαν τῆς ψυχῆς στροβεῖ χωρίον

---

[a] Or "a succession of desires" (ἀεί meaning "from time
to time").

[b] For this translation of the frequently recurring phrase
σώματα καὶ πράγματα, various versions of which have been

22

to the mind and reason, one to the spirited element and one to the appetites. There is mischief working in them all, in each in relation to itself, in all in relation to each other, when the mind reaps what is sown by its follies and acts of cowardice and intemperance and injustice, and the spirited part brings to the birth its fierce and raging furies and the other evil children of its womb, and the appetite sends forth on every side desires ever [a] winged by childish fancy, desires which light as chance directs on things material and immaterial.[b] For then, as though on 22 a ship crew, passengers and steersmen had conspired through some madness to sink it, the first to perish with the boat are those who planned its destruction. It stands alone as the most grievous of mischiefs and one almost past all cure—this co-operation of all the parts of the soul in sin, where, as when a nation is plague-stricken, none can have the health to heal the sufferers, but the physicians share the sickness of the common herd who lie crushed by the pestilential scourge, victims of a calamity which none can ignore. We have a symbol of this dire 23 happening in the great deluge described in the words of the lawgiver, when the " cataracts of heaven "[c] poured forth the torrents of absolute wickedness in impetuous downfall and the " fountains from the earth," [d] that is from the body (Gen. vii. 11), spouted forth the streams of each passion, streams many and great, and these, uniting and commingling with the rainpour, in wild commotion eddied and swirled continually through the whole region of the soul

given in previous volumes, see note on *Quis Rerum* 242 (App.).
  [c] E.V. " windows of heaven."
  [d] LXX. ἀπὸ τῆς ἀβύσσου. E.V. " from the great deep."

24 δίναις ἐπαλλήλοις. " ἰδὼν " γάρ φησι " κύριος ὁ
θεός, ὅτι ἐπληθύνθησαν αἱ κακίαι τῶν ἀνθρώπων
ἐπὶ τῆς γῆς, καὶ πᾶς τις διανοεῖται ἐν τῇ καρδίᾳ
ἐπιμελῶς τὰ πονηρὰ πάσας τὰς ἡμέρας " ἔγνω
τὸν ἄνθρωπον, λέγω δὲ τὸν νοῦν, μετὰ τῶν περὶ
αὐτὸν ἑρπετῶν τε καὶ πτηνῶν καὶ τῆς ἄλλης ἀλόγου
τῶν ἀτιθάσων θηρίων πληθύος ἐφ' οἷς ἀνίατα
ἠδικήκει τίσασθαι· ἡ δὲ τιμωρία κατακλυσμός.
25 ἦν γὰρ ἔφεσις ἁμαρτημάτων καὶ πολλὴ τοῦ ἀδικεῖν
μηδενὸς κωλύοντος φορά, ἀλλὰ προσαναρρηγνυ-
μένων ἀδεῶς ἁπάντων εἰς χορηγίας ἀφθόνους τοῖς
πρὸς τὰς ἀπολαύσεις ἑτοιμοτάτοις, καὶ μήποτ'
εἰκότως· οὐ γὰρ ἔν τι μέρος διέφθαρτο τῆς ψυχῆς,
ἵνα τοῖς ἄλλοις ὑγιαίνουσι σῴζεσθαι δύναιτο, ἀλλ'
οὐδὲν ἄνοσον οὐδὲ ἀδιάφθαρτον αὐτῆς κατελείπετο·
[409] | ἰδὼν γὰρ ὅτι πᾶς τις, φησί, διανοεῖται [πᾶς]
λογισμός, οὐχὶ μόνος εἷς, τὴν ἁρμόττουσαν ὁ
ἀδέκαστος δικαστὴς ἐπήγαγε τιμωρίαν.

26 VIII. Οὗτοί εἰσιν οἱ ἐπὶ τῆς ἁλμυρᾶς φάραγγος
ὁμαιχμίαν πρὸς ἀλλήλους θέμενοι¹—κοῖλον γὰρ καὶ
τραχὺ καὶ φαραγγῶδες τὸ κακιῶν ⟨καὶ⟩ παθῶν
χωρίον, ἁλμυρὸν τῷ ὄντι καὶ πικρὰς φέρον ὠδῖνας
—ὧν ὁ σοφὸς Ἀβραὰμ τὸ ἐνώμοτον καὶ ἔνσπονδον
οὔθ' ὅρκων οὔτε σπονδῶν ἐπάξιον εἰδὼς καθαιρεῖ·
λέγεται γὰρ ὅτι " πάντες οὗτοι συνεφώνησαν ἐπὶ
τὴν φάραγγα τὴν ἁλυκήν· αὕτη ἡ θάλασσα τῶν
27 ἁλῶν." ἢ οὐχ ὁρᾷς τοὺς ἐστειρωμένους
σοφίαν καὶ τυφλοὺς διάνοιαν, ἣν ὀξυδερκεῖν εἰκὸς

---

¹ Wend. and Mangey punctuate with a full stop before
κοῖλον, thus apparently making ὠδῖνας to be the antecedent
of ὧν.

24

which formed their meeting-place. " For the Lord **24**
God," it runs, " seeing that the wickednesses of men
were multiplied on the earth, and that every man
carefully purposed in his heart evil things every day,"
determined to punish man, that is the mind, for
his deadly misdeeds, together with the creeping and
flying creatures around him and the other unreasoning multitude of untamed beasts [a] (Gen. vi. 5-6).
This punishment was the deluge. For the deluge **25**
was a letting loose of sins, a rushing torrent of
iniquity where there was naught to hinder, but all
things burst forth without restraint to supply abundant opportunities to those who were all readiness to
take pleasure therein. And surely this punishment
was suitable. For not one part only of the soul had
been corrupted, so that it might be saved through
the soundness of others, but nothing in it was left
free from disease and corruption. For " seeing," as the
scripture says, that " everyone," that is every thought
and not one only, " purposed," the upright judge
awarded the penalty which the fault deserved.

VIII. These are they who made a confederacy at **26**
the salt ravine. For the place of vices and passions
is hollow and rough and ravine-like ; salt indeed,
and bitter are the pangs which it brings. The
covenant of alliance which they swore was destroyed
by wise Abraham, for he knew that it had not the
sanctity of oaths or covenant-rites. Thus we read
" all these joined their voices to come to the salt-
ravine ; this is the salt sea " (Gen. xiv. 3).
Observe further those who were barren of wisdom **27**
and blind in the understanding which should naturally be sharp of sight, their qualities veiled under

[a] See App. p. 553.

ἦν, Σοδομίτας κατὰ γλῶτταν, ἀπὸ νεανίσκου ἕως
πρεσβυτέρου πάνθ' ὁμοῦ τὸν λεὼν ἐν κύκλῳ τὴν
οἰκίαν τῆς ψυχῆς περιθέοντας, ἵνα τοὺς ξενωθέντας
ἱεροὺς καὶ ὁσίους λόγους αὐτῇ, φρουροὺς καὶ
φύλακας ὄντας, αἰσχύνωσι καὶ διαφθείρωσι, καὶ
μηδένα τὸ παράπαν μήτε τοῖς ἀδικοῦσιν ἐναντιοῦσθαι μήτε τοῦ τι ποιεῖν ἄδικον ἀποδιδράσκειν
28 ἐγνωκότα; οὐ γὰρ οἱ μέν, οἱ δ' οὔ, " πᾶς δ'," ὥς
φησιν, " ὁ λαὸς περιεκύκλωσαν ἅμα τὴν οἰκίαν,
νέοι τε καὶ πρεσβῦται " κατὰ τῶν θείων καὶ ἱερῶν
λόγων[1] συνομοσάμενοι, οὓς καλεῖν ἔθος ἀγγέλους.

29   IX. ἀλλ' ὅ γε θεοπρόπος Μωυσῆς
θράσει πολλῷ ῥέοντας αὐτοὺς ὑπαντιάσας ἐφέξει,
κἂν τὸν θρασύτατον καὶ δεινότατον εἰπεῖν ἐν
ἑαυτοῖς βασιλέα λόγον προστησάμενοι μιᾷ ῥύμῃ
κατατρέχωσι, συναύξοντες τὰ οἰκεῖα καὶ ποταμοῦ
τρόπον πλημμύροντες· " ἰδοὺ " γάρ φησιν " ὁ τῆς
Αἰγύπτου βασιλεὺς ἐπὶ τὸ ὕδωρ ἀφικνεῖται. σὺ
δὲ στήσῃ συναντῶν αὐτῷ ἐπὶ τὸ χεῖλος τοῦ ποτα-
30 μοῦ." οὐκοῦν ὁ μὲν φαῦλος ἔξεισιν ἐπὶ τὴν τῶν
ἀδικημάτων καὶ παθῶν ἀθρόων φοράν, ἅπερ ὕδατι
ἀπεικάζεται· ὁ δὲ σοφὸς πρῶτον μὲν κτᾶται γέρας
παρὰ τοῦ ἑστῶτος ἀεὶ θεοῦ συγγενὲς αὐτοῦ τῇ
ἀκλινεῖ καὶ ἀρρεπεῖ πρὸς πάντα δυνάμει λαβών·
31 εἴρηται γὰρ " σὺ δὲ αὐτοῦ στῆθι μετ' ἐμοῦ," ἵνα
ἐνδοιασμὸν καὶ ἐπαμφοτερισμόν, ἀβεβαίου ψυχῆς
διαθέσεις, ἀποδυσάμενος τὴν ὀχυρωτάτην καὶ βεβαιοτάτην διάθεσιν, πίστιν, ἐνδύσηται. ἔπειτα δὲ

---

[1] MSS. θείων ἔργων καὶ λόγων (the correction seems to me somewhat conjectural).

<hr>

ᵃ See App. p. 553.

their name of Sodomite [a]—how the whole people from the young men to the eldest ran round and round the house of the soul to bring dishonour and ruin on those sacred and holy Thoughts which were its guests, its guardians and sentinels; how not a single one is minded to oppose the unjust or shrink from doing injustice himself. For we read that not merely some 28 but the "whole people surrounded the house, both young and old" (Gen. xix. 4), conspiring against the divine and holy Thoughts,[b] who are often called angels.[c]   IX. But Moses the prophet of God 29 shall meet and stem the strong current of their boldness, though, setting before them as their king their boldest and most cunning eloquence, they come rushing with united onset, though they mass their wealth of water and their tide is as the tide of a river. "Behold," he says, "the King of Egypt comes to the water, but thou shalt stand meeting him at the edge of the river" (Ex. vii. 15). The fool, then, will 30 go forth to the rushing flood of the iniquities and passions, which Moses likens to a river. But the wise man in the first place gains a privilege vouchsafed to him from God, who ever stands fast, a privilege which is the congener of His power which never swerves and never wavers. For it was said to 31 him "Stand thou here with me" (Deut. v. 31), to the end that he should put off doubt and hesitation, the qualities [d] of the unstable mind, and put on that surest and most stable quality, faith. This is his

---

[b] This translation is given in despair. In this particular allegory of the soul, the λόγοι no doubt take the form of thoughts, but the use is far wider. As manifestations of the Divine Logos the angels suggest not only spiritual influences, as in *De Sobr.* 65, but also spiritual beings, as in § 174.

[c] *i.e.* in scripture, *cf.* § 174.   [d] Or "dispositions."

ἑστώς, τὸ παραδοξότατον, ὑπαντᾷ· " στήσῃ " γάρ
⟨φησιν⟩ " ὑπαντιάζων"· καίτοι τὸ μὲν ὑπαντᾶν ἐν
κινήσει, κατὰ δ' ἠρεμίαν τὸ ἵστασθαι θεωρεῖται.
32 λέγει δὲ οὐ τὰ μαχόμενα, τὰ δὲ τῇ φύσει μάλιστα
ἀκολουθοῦντα· ὅτῳ γὰρ ἠρεμεῖν πέφυκεν ἡ γνώμη
καὶ ἀρρεπῶς ἱδρῦσθαι, συμβαίνει πᾶσιν ἀνθίστασ-
θαι τοῖς σάλῳ καὶ κλύδωνι χαίρουσι καὶ τὸν γαληνιά-
σαι δυνάμενον χειροποιήτῳ χειμῶνι κυμαίνουσιν.

33
[410]   X. εὖ μέντοι γε ἔχει παρὰ | τὸ χεῖλος
τοῦ ποταμοῦ τὴν ἐναντίωσιν συνίστασθαι· χείλη
δὲ στόματος μέν ἐστι πέρατα, φραγμὸς δέ τις
γλώττης, δι' ὧν φέρεται τὸ τοῦ λόγου ῥεῦμα, ὅταν
34 ἄρξηται κατέρχεσθαι. λόγῳ δὲ καὶ οἱ μισάρετοι
καὶ φιλοπαθεῖς[1] συμμάχῳ χρῶνται πρὸς τὴν τῶν
ἀδοκίμων δογμάτων εἰσήγησιν καὶ πάλιν οἱ σπου-
δαῖοι πρός τε τὴν τούτων ἀναίρεσιν καὶ πρὸς τὸ
τῶν ἀμεινόνων καὶ ἀψευδῶς ἀγαθῶν κράτος ἀνανт-
35 αγώνιστον. ὅταν μέντοι πάντα κάλων ἀνασείσαν-
τες ἐριστικῶν δογμάτων ὑπ' ἐναντίας ῥύμης λόγων
ἀνατραπέντες ἀπόλωνται, τὸ ἐπινίκιον δικαίως καὶ
προσηκόντως ὁ σοφὸς ᾆσμα χορὸν ἱερώτατον
36 στησάμενος ἐμμελῶς ᾄσεται· " εἶδε " γάρ φησιν
" Ἰσραὴλ τοὺς Αἰγυπτίους " οὐχ ἑτέρωθι " τεθνεῶ-
τας " ἀλλὰ παρὰ " τὸ χεῖλος τοῦ ποταμοῦ,[2] "
θάνατον λέγων οὐ τὴν ἀπὸ σώματος ψυχῆς διάκρισιν, ἀλλὰ τὴν ἀνοσίων δογμάτων καὶ λόγων
φθοράν, οἷς ἐχρῶντο διὰ στόματος καὶ γλώττης
καὶ τῶν ἄλλων φωνητηρίων ὀργάνων.

---

[1] mss. φιλομαθεῖς.
[2] Presumably a slip for τῆς θαλάσσης.

first privilege—to stand ; but secondly—strange
paradox—he " meets." For " thou shalt stand
meeting " says the text, though " meet " involves
the idea of motion and " stand " calls up the thought
of rest. Yet the two things here spoken of are not 32
really in conflict, but in most natural sequence to
each other. For he whose constitution of mind and
judgement is tranquil and firmly established will be
found to oppose all those who rejoice in surge and
tumult and manufacture the storm to disturb his
natural capacity for calmness.   X. It is 33
well indeed that the opponents should meet on the
lip or edge of the river. The lips are the boundaries
of the mouth and a kind of hedge to the tongue and
through them the stream of speech passes, when it
begins its downward flow. Now speech is an ally 34
employed by those who hate virtue and love the
passions to inculcate their untenable tenets, and also
by men of worth for the destruction of such doctrines
and to set up beyond resistance the sovereignty of
those that are better, those in whose goodness there
is no deceit. When, indeed, after they have let out 35
every reef of contentious sophistry, the opposing
onset of the sage's speech has overturned their bark
and sent them to perdition, he will, as is just and fit,
set in order his holy choir to sing the anthem of
victory, and sweet is the melody of that song. For 36
Israel, it says, saw the Egyptians dead on the edge
of the sea (Ex. xiv. 30)—not elsewhere. And when
he says " dead " he does not mean the death which
is the separation of soul and body, but the destruction of unholy doctrines and of the words which
their mouth and tongue and the other vocal organs
gave them to use.   Now the death of 37

37 λόγου δὲ θάνατός ἐστιν ἡσυχία, οὐχ ἣν οἱ ἐπιεικέ-
στεροι ποιούμενοι σύμβολον αἰδοῦς μετέρχονται—
δύναμις γὰρ καὶ ἥδε ἐστὶν ἀδελφὴ τῆς ἐν τῷ λέγειν
ταμιευομένη μέχρι καιροῦ τὰ λεκτέα—, ἀλλ᾽ ἣν
οἱ ἐξησθενηκότες καὶ ἀπειρηκότες διὰ τὴν τῶν
ἐναντίων ἰσχὺν ὑπομένουσιν ἄκοντες λαβὴν[1] οὐδεμίαν
38 ἔθ᾽ εὑρίσκοντες. ὧν τε γὰρ ἂν ἐφάψωνται, διαρρεῖ,
καὶ οἷς ἂν ἐπιβῶσιν, οὐχ ὑπομένει, ὡς πρὶν ἢ
στῆναι πίπτειν ἀναγκάζεσθαι, ὥσπερ ἡ ἕλιξ, τὸ
ὑδρηρὸν ὄργανον, ἔχει· κατὰ γὰρ μέσον αὐτὸ γεγόνασι βαθμοί τινες, ὧν ὁ γεωπόνος, ὅταν ἐθελήσῃ
ποτίσαι τὰς ἀρούρας, ἐπιβαίνει μέν, περιολισθαίνει
δ᾽ ἀναγκαίως· ὑπὲρ δὴ τοῦ μὴ πίπτειν συνεχῶς
πλησίον ἐχυροῦ τινος ταῖς χερσὶ περιδράττεται, οὗ
ἐνειλημμένος τὸ ὅλον σῶμα ἀπηώρηκεν αὑτοῦ·
⟨ὥστε⟩ ἀντὶ μὲν ποδῶν χερσίν, ἀντὶ δὲ χειρῶν
ποσὶ χρῆσθαι· ἵσταται μὲν γὰρ ἐπὶ χειρῶν, δι᾽ ὧν
εἰσιν αἱ πράξεις, πράττει δ᾽ ἐν ποσίν, ἐφ᾽ ὧν εἰκὸς
39 ἵστασθαι.   XI. πολλοὶ δ᾽ οὐ δυνάμενοι
τὰς πιθανὰς τῶν σοφιστῶν εὑρέσεις ἀνὰ κράτος
ἑλεῖν τῷ μὴ σφόδρα περὶ λόγους διὰ τὴν ἐν τοῖς
ἔργοις συνεχῆ μελέτην γεγυμνάσθαι κατέφυγον ἐπὶ
τὴν τοῦ μόνου σοφοῦ συμμαχίαν καὶ βοηθὸν αὐτὸν
ἱκέτευσαν γενέσθαι· καθὰ καὶ τῶν Μωυσέως γνω-
ρίμων τις ἐν ὕμνοις εὐχόμενος εἶπεν· "ἄλαλα
γενέσθω τὰ χείλη τὰ δόλια." πῶς δ᾽ ἂν ἡσυχάσαι,
εἰ μὴ πρὸς μόνου τοῦ καὶ τὸν λόγον αὐτὸν ἔχοντος
ὑπήκοον ἐπιστομισθείη;

[1] mss. βλάβην.

---

[a] Or "arguments," εὕρεσις being the technical term in
rhetoric for collecting material for speech.   See on De
Mig. 35.

words is silence, not the silence which well-behaved people cultivate, regarding it as a sign of modesty, for that silence is actually a power, sister to the power of speech, husbanding the fitting words till the moment for utterance comes. No, it is the undesired silence to which those whom the strength of their opponent has reduced to exhaustion and prostration must submit, when they find no longer any argument ready to their hand. For what they 38 handle dissolves in their hands, and what they stand on gives way beneath them, so that they must needs fall before they stand. You might compare the treadmill which is used for drawing water. In the middle are some steps and on these the labourer, when he wants to water the fields, sets his feet but cannot help slipping off, and to save himself from continually falling he grasps with his hands some firm object nearby and holding tight to it uses it as a suspender for his whole body. And so his feet serve him for hands and his hands for feet, for he keeps himself standing with the hands which we use for work, and works with his feet, on which he would naturally stand. XI. Now there are many who 39 though they have not the capacity to demolish by sheer force the plausible inventions [a] of the sophists, because their occupation has lain continuously in active life and thus they are not trained in any high degree to deal with words, find refuge in the support of the solely Wise Being and beseech Him to become their helper. Such a one is the disciple of Moses who prays thus in the Psalms: " Let their cunning lips become speechless " (Ps. xxx. [xxxi.] 19). And how should such lips be silent, unless they were bridled by Him who alone holds speech itself as His vassal ?

40 Τὰς μὲν οὖν εἰς τὸ ἁμαρτάνειν συνόδους ἀμεταστρεπτὶ φευκτέον, τὸ δὲ ἔνσπονδον πρὸς τοὺς
[411] φρονήσεως καὶ | ἐπιστήμης ἑταίρους βεβαιωτέον.
41 παρὸ καὶ τοὺς λέγοντας " πάντες ἐσμὲν υἱοὶ ἑνὸς
ἀνθρώπου, εἰρηνικοί ἐσμεν " τεθαύμακα τῆς εὐαρ-
μόστου συμφωνίας· ἐπεὶ καὶ πῶς οὐκ ἐμέλλετε,
φήσαιμ' ἄν, ὦ γενναῖοι, πολέμῳ μὲν δυσχεραίνειν,
εἰρήνην δὲ ἀγαπᾶν, ἕνα καὶ τὸν αὐτὸν ἐπιγεγραμ-
μένοι πατέρα οὐ θνητὸν ἀλλ' ἀθάνατον, ἄνθρωπον
θεοῦ, ὃς τοῦ ἀιδίου λόγος ὢν ἐξ ἀνάγκης καὶ αὐτός
42 ἐστιν ἄφθαρτος; οἱ μὲν γὰρ πολλὰς ἀρχὰς τοῦ
κατὰ ψυχὴν γένους συστησάμενοι, τῷ πολυθέῳ
λεγομένῳ κακῷ προσνείμαντες ἑαυτούς, ἄλλοι πρὸς
ἄλλων τιμὰς τραπόμενοι ταραχὰς καὶ στάσεις
ἐμφυλίους τε καὶ ξενικὰς ἐδημιούργησαν[1] τὸν ἀπ'
ἀρχῆς γενέσεως ἄχρι τελευτῆς βίον πολέμων ἀκη-
43 ρύκτων καταπλήσαντες. οἱ δὲ ἑνὶ γένει
χαίροντες καὶ ἕνα πατέρα τὸν ὀρθὸν τιμῶντες
λόγον, τὴν εὐάρμοστον καὶ πάμμουσον συμφωνίαν
ἀρετῶν τεθαυμακότες, εὔδιον καὶ γαληνὸν βίον
ζῶσιν, οὐ μὴν ἀργὸν καὶ ἀγενῆ τινα, ὡς ἔνιοι
νομίζουσιν, ἀλλὰ σφόδρα ἀνδρεῖον καὶ λίαν ἠκονημένον κατὰ τῶν σπονδὰς λύειν ἐπιχειρούντων καὶ
σύγχυσιν ὁρκίων αἰεὶ μελετώντων· τοὺς γὰρ εἰρη-
ναίους φύσει πολεμικοὺς εἶναι συμβέβηκεν ἀντι-
καθημένους καὶ ἀνθεστῶτας τοῖς τὸ εὐσταθὲς τῆς
44 ψυχῆς ἀνατρέπουσι. XII. μαρτυρεῖ δέ
μου τῷ λόγῳ πρῶτον μὲν ἡ ἑκάστου τῶν φιλαρέτων
διάνοια διακειμένη τὸν τρόπον τοῦτον, ἔπειτα δὲ

---

[1] MSS. ἐδημιουργήσαντο.

[a] This conception of the Logos recurs in §§ 62 and 146.

Let us flee, then, without a backward glance from **40**
the unions which are unions for sin, but hold fast to
our alliance with the comrades of good sense and
knowledge. And therefore when I hear those who **41**
say " We are all sons of one man, we are peaceful "
(Gen. xlii. 11), I am filled with admiration for the
harmonious concert which their words reveal. " Ah !
my friends," I would say, " how should you not hate
war and love peace—you who have enrolled yourselves as children of one and the same Father, who
is not mortal but immortal—God's Man,[a] who being
the Word of the Eternal must needs himself be imperishable ? " Those whose system includes many **42**
origins for the family of the soul, who affiliate themselves to that evil thing called polytheism, who take
in hand to render homage some to this deity, some
to that, are the authors of tumult and strife at home
and abroad, and fill the whole of life from birth to
death with internecine wars. But those **43**
who rejoice in the oneness of their blood and honour
one father, right reason, reverence that concert of
virtues, which is full of harmony and melody, and
live a life of calmness and fair weather. And yet
that life is not, as some suppose, an idle and ignoble
life, but one of high courage, and the edge of its
spirit is exceeding sharp to fight against those
who attempt to break treaties and ever practise the
violation of the vows they have sworn. For it is the
nature of men of peace that they prove to be men of
war, when they take the field and resist those who
would subvert the stability of the soul.

XII. The truth of my words is attested first by the **44**
consciousness of every virtue-lover, which feels what
I have described, and secondly by a chorister of the

καὶ τοῦ προφητικοῦ θιασώτης χοροῦ, ὃς καταπνευσθεὶς ἐνθουσιῶν ἀνεφθέγξατο· " ὦ μῆτερ,
ἡλίκον με ἔτεκες, ἄνθρωπον μάχης καὶ ἄνθρωπον
ἀηδίας πάσης τῆς γῆς; οὐκ ὠφείλησα,[1] οὐδὲ
ὠφείλησάν μοι, οὐδὲ ἡ ἰσχύς μου ἐξέλιπεν ἀπὸ
45 καταρῶν αὐτῶν." ἀλλ' οὐ πᾶς σοφὸς πᾶσι φαύλοις
ἐχθρός ἐστιν ἄσπονδος, οὐ τριηρῶν ἢ μηχανημάτων
ἢ ὅπλων ἢ στρατιωτῶν παρασκευῇ πρὸς ἄμυναν
46 χρώμενος, ἀλλὰ λογισμοῖς[2];   ὅταν γὰρ
τὸν ἐν τῇ ἀπολέμῳ εἰρήνῃ συνεχῆ καὶ ἐπάλληλον
ἀνθρώπων ἁπάντων ἴδιον καὶ κοινόν, μὴ κατὰ ἔθνη
καὶ χώρας ἢ πόλεις καὶ κώμας αὐτὸ μόνον, ἀλλὰ
καὶ κατ' οἰκίαν καὶ ἕνα ἕκαστον τῶν ἐν μέρει
συγκροτούμενον πόλεμον θεάσηται, τίς ἐστιν ὅ γε
μὴ παραινῶν,[3] κακίζων, νουθετῶν, σωφρονίζων, οὐ
μεθ' ἡμέραν μόνον ἀλλὰ καὶ νύκτωρ, τῆς ψυχῆς
αὐτῷ ἠρεμεῖν μὴ δυναμένης διὰ τὸ μισοπόνηρον
47 φύσει; πάντα γὰρ ὅσα ἐν πολέμῳ δρᾶται κατ'
εἰρήνην· συλῶσιν, ἁρπάζουσιν, ἀνδραποδίζονται,
[412] λεηλατοῦσι, | πορθοῦσιν, ὑβρίζουσιν, αἰκίζονται,
φθείρουσιν, αἰσχύνουσι, δολοφονοῦσιν, ἄντικρυς, ἢν
48 ὦσι δυνατώτεροι, κτείνουσι. πλοῦτον γὰρ ἢ δόξαν
ἕκαστος αὐτῶν σκοπὸν προτεθειμένος ἐπὶ τοῦτον
ὥσπερ βέλη τὰς τοῦ βίου πράξεις ἁπάσας ἀφιεὶς
ἰσότητος ἀλογεῖ, τὸ ἄνισον διώκει, κοινωνίαν ἀποστρέφεται, μόνος τὰ πάντων ἔχειν ἀθρόα ἐσπούδακε,
μισάνθρωπος καὶ μισάλληλός ἐστιν, ὑποκρινόμενος

---

[1] For the question between ὠφείλησα . . . ὠφείλησάν μοι
and ὠφέλησα . . . ὠφέλησάν με here and in § 50 see App. p. 553.
[2] mss. χρώμενος ἐπιλογισμοῖς.   [3] mss. παροῦσι.

[a] See App. p. 553.
[b] Or " is organized." See on De Agr. 35.

prophetic company, who possessed by divine inspiration spoke thus : " O my mother, how great didst thou bear me, a man of combat and a man of displeasure in all the earth ! I did not owe, nor did they owe to me, nor did my strength fail from their curses " (Jer. xv. 10 [a]). Yes, is not every wise man **45** the mortal foe of every fool, a foe who is equipped not with triremes or engines, or body-armour or soldiers for his defence, but with reasonings only ?

For who, when he sees that war, which **46** amid the fullest peace [a] is waged [b] among all men continuously, phase ever succeeding phase, in private and public life, a war in which the combatants are not just nations and countries, or cities and villages, but also house against house and each particular man against himself, who, I say, does not exhort, reproach, admonish, correct by day and night alike, since his soul cannot rest, because its nature is to hate evil ? For all the deeds of war are done in peace. Men **47** plunder, rob, kidnap, spoil, sack, outrage, maltreat, violate, dishonour and commit murder sometimes by treachery, or if they be stronger without disguise. Every man sets before him money or reputation as **48** his aim, and at this he directs all the actions of his life like arrows against a target. He takes no heed of equity, but pursues the inequitable.[c] He eschews thoughts of fellowship, and his eager desire is that the wealth of all should be gathered in his single purse. He hates others, whether his hate be returned or not.[d] His benevolence is hypocrisy. He is hand

[c] Or "equality . . . inequality."
[d] Or "hates both mankind and his neighbour." That is to say, Philo perhaps uses μισάλληλος, which, properly speaking, can only be used, and indeed seems elsewhere to be only used, in the plural, somewhat loosely.

εὔνοιαν, κολακείας νόθης ἑταῖρος ὤν, φιλίας γνησίου
πολέμιος, ἀληθείας ἐχθρός, ὑπέρμαχος ψεύδους,
βραδὺς ὠφελῆσαι, ταχὺς βλάψαι, διαβαλεῖν προ-
χειρότατος, ὑπερασπίσαι μελλητής, δεινὸς φενακίσαι, ψευδορκότατος, ἀπιστότατος, δοῦλος ὀργῆς,
εἴκων ἡδονῇ, φύλαξ κακῶν, φθορεὺς ἀγαθῶν.

49   XIII. ταῦτα καὶ τὰ τοιαῦτα τῆς
ᾀδομένης καὶ θαυμαζομένης εἰρήνης περιμάχητα
κειμήλια, ἅπερ ἡ ἑκάστου τῶν ἀφρόνων ἀγαλματο-
φοροῦσα διάνοια τέθηπε καὶ προσκυνεῖ. ἐφ᾽ οἷς
εἰκότως καὶ πᾶς σοφὸς ἄχθεται, καὶ πρός γε τὴν
μητέρα καὶ τιθήνην ἑαυτοῦ, σοφίαν, εἴωθε λέγειν·
" ὦ μῆτερ, ἡλίκον με ἔτεκες," οὐ δυνάμει σώματος,
ἀλλὰ τῇ πρὸς ⟨τὸ⟩ μισοπόνηρον ἀλκῇ, ἄνθρωπον ἀηδίας καὶ μάχης, φύσει μὲν εἰρηνικόν, διὰ
δὲ τοῦτο καὶ πολεμικὸν κατὰ τῶν αἰσχυνόντων τὸ
50 περιμάχητον κάλλος εἰρήνης. " οὐκ ὠφείλησα, οὐδὲ
ὠφείλησάν μοι." οὔτε γὰρ αὐτοὶ τοῖς ἐμοῖς ἀγαθοῖς
ποτε ἐχρήσαντο, οὔτε ἐγὼ τοῖς ἐκείνων κακοῖς,
ἀλλὰ κατὰ τὸ Μωυσέως γράμμα " ἐπιθύμημα
οὐδενὸς αὐτῶν ἔλαβον," σύμπαν τὸ τῆς ἐπιθυμίας
αὐτῶν γένος θησαυρισαμένων παρ᾽ ἑαυτοῖς ὡς
51 μέγιστον ὄφελος ὑπερβάλλον βλάβος. " οὐδὲ ἡ
ἰσχύς μου ἐξέλιπεν ἀπὸ τῶν ἀρῶν ἃς ἐτίθεντό μοι,"
δυνάμει δὲ κραταιοτάτῃ τῶν θείων ἐνειλημμένος
δογμάτων οὐδὲ[1] κακούμενος[2] ἐκάμφθην, ἀλλὰ ἐρρω-

---

[1] MSS. οὔτε, which is quite impossible. Wend., who retains
it in the text, notes " write οὐ, or place a lacuna after
ἐκάμφθην." It seems to me that, as the words are a para-
phrase of οὐδὲ ἡ ἰσχὺς κτλ. of the quotation, the easier
correction to οὐδὲ is reasonable.

[2] MSS. ἐκκακούμενος.

and glove with canting flattery, at open war with genuine friendship ; an enemy to truth, a defender of falsehood, slow to help, quick to harm, ever forward to slander, backward to champion the accused, skilful to cozen, false to his oath, faithless to his promise, a slave to anger, a thrall to pleasure, protector of the bad, corrupter of the good.

XIII. These and the like are the much-coveted 49 treasures of the peace which men admire and praise so loudly—treasures enshrined in the mind of every fool with wonder and veneration. But to every wise man they are, as they should be, a source of pain, and often will he say to his mother and nurse, wisdom, " O mother, how great didst thou bear me ! " Great, not in power of body, but in strength to hate evil, a man of displeasure and combat, by nature a man of peace, but for this very cause also a man of war against those who dishonour the much-prized loveliness of peace. " I did not owe nor did they owe to 50 me," for neither did they use the good I had to give, nor I their evil, but, as Moses wrote, " I received from none of them what they desired "[a] (Num. xvi. 15). For all that comes under the head of their desire they kept as treasure to themselves, believing that to be the greatest blessing which was the supreme mischief. " Nor did my strength fail from the curses 51 which they laid upon me," but with all my might and main I clung to the divine truths ; I did not bend under their ill-treatment, but used my strength

[a] E.V. " I have not taken one ass from them." The verse in the LXX. goes on οὐδὲ ἐκάκωσα οὐδένα αὐτῶν, which shows that οὐδενός is, as it is taken in the translation, masculine. Philo's interpretation, however (σύμπαν τὸ τῆς ἐπιθυμίας γένος), suggests, perhaps, that he took it as neuter, " I did not receive their desire for anything."

μένως ὠνείδισα τοῖς ἐξ ἑαυτῶν μὴ καθαιρομένοις·
52 "ἔθετο" γὰρ "ἡμᾶς ὁ θεὸς εἰς ἀντιλογίαν τοῖς
γείτοσιν ἡμῶν," ὡς καὶ ἐν ὕμνοις που λέλεκται,
πάντας τοὺς ὀρθῆς γνώμης ἐφιεμένους. ἀλλ' οὐκ
ἀντιλογικοὶ φύσει γεγόνασιν, ὅσοι τὸν ἐπιστήμης
καὶ ἀρετῆς ζῆλον ἔσχον ἀεί, τοῖς γείτοσι ψυχῆς
ἀντιφιλονεικοῦντες, ἐλέγχοντες μὲν τὰς συνοίκους
ἡδονάς, ἐλέγχοντες δὲ τὰς ὁμοδιαίτους ἐπιθυμίας,
δειλίας τε καὶ φόβους, τὸ παθῶν καὶ κακιῶν στῖφος
δυσωποῦντες, ἐλέγχοντες μέντοι καὶ πᾶσαν αἴσθησιν, περὶ μὲν ὧν εἶδον ὀφθαλμούς, περὶ ὧν δὲ
ἤκουσαν ἀκοάς, ὀσμάς τε περὶ ἀτμῶν καὶ γεύσεις
περὶ χυμῶν, ἔτι δὲ ἁφὰς περὶ τῶν κατὰ τὰς προσπιπτούσας τῶν ἐν τοῖς σώμασι δυνάμεων ἰδιότητας, καὶ μὲν δὴ[1] τὸν προφορικὸν λόγον περὶ ὧν
[413] διεξελθεῖν | ἔδοξε;   τίνα γὰρ ἢ πῶς ἢ
53 διὰ τί ἡ αἴσθησις ᾔσθετο ἢ ὁ λόγος διηρμήνευσεν
ἢ τὸ πάθος διέθηκεν, ἄξιον ἐρευνᾶν μὴ παρέργως
54 καὶ τῶν σφαλμάτων διελέγχειν ἕκαστον. ὁ δὲ
μηδενὶ τούτων ἀντιλέγων, ἅπασι δὲ ἑξῆς συνεπι-
νεύων ἑαυτὸν λέληθεν ἀπατῶν καὶ ἐπιτειχίζων
ψυχῇ βαρεῖς γείτονας, οἷς ἄμεινον ὑπηκόοις ἢ ἄρ-
χουσι χρῆσθαι· ἡγεμονεύοντες μὲν γὰρ πολλὰ
πημανοῦσι καὶ μεγάλα βασιλευούσης παρ' αὐτοῖς
ἀνοίας, ὑπακούοντες δὲ τὰ δέονθ' ὑπηρετήσουσι
πειθηνίως οὐκέθ' ὁμοίως ἀπαυχενίζοντες.
55 οὕτως μέντοι τῶν μὲν ὑπακούειν μαθόντων, τῶν

---

[1] καὶ μὲν δή] so mss. and Wend., but this combination of
particles seems to me hardly possible.

---

[a] Cf. De Gig. 46 τοὺς ἐξ ἑαυτῶν μὴ πεφυκότας νουθετεῖσθαι.
  Lit. "the things belonging to the peculiarities of the

to reproach those who refused to effect their own purification.[a] For " God has set us up for a contra- 52 diction to our neighbours," as is said in a verse of the Psalms (Ps. lxxix. [lxxx.] 7) ; us, that is all who desire right judgement. Yes, surely they are by nature men of contradiction, all who have ever been zealous for knowledge and virtue, who contend jealously with the " neighbours " of the soul ; who test the pleasures which share our home, the desires which live at our side, our fears and faintings of heart, and put to shame the tribe of passions and vices. Further, they test also every sense, the eyes on what they see, the ears on what they hear, the sense of smell on its perfumes, the taste on its flavours, the touch on the characteristics which mark the qualities of substances as they come in contact with it.[b] And lastly they test the utterance on the statements which it has been led to make.   For what 53 our senses perceive, or our speech expresses, or our emotion causes us to feel, and how or why each result is attained, are matters which we should scrutinize carefully and expose every error that we find. He who contradicts none of these, but assents to all 54 as they come before him, is unconsciously deceiving himself and raising up a stronghold of dangerous neighbours to menace the soul, neighbours who should be dealt with as subjects, not as rulers. For if they have the mastery, since folly is their king, the mischief they work will be great and manifold ; but as subjects they will render due service and obey the rein, and chafe no more against the yoke.

And, when these have thus learnt the 55

powers in bodies " (τῶν κατὰ τὰς ἰδιότητας being practically equivalent to τῶν ἰδιοτήτων). See further App. p. 554.

PHILO

δ' οὐκ ἐπιστήμῃ μόνον ἀλλὰ καὶ δυνάμει τὴν ἀρχὴν
λαβόντων πάντες οἱ δορυφόροι καὶ ὑπέρμαχοι ψυχῆς
συμφρονήσουσι λογισμοὶ καὶ τῷ πρεσβυτάτῳ τῶν
ἐν αὐτοῖς προσελθόντες ἐροῦσιν· '' οἱ παῖδές σου
εἰλήφασι τὸ κεφάλαιον τῶν ἀνδρῶν τῶν πολεμιστῶν
τῶν μεθ' ἡμῶν, οὐ διαπεφώνηκεν αὐτῶν οὐδὲ εἷς,''
ἀλλ' ὥσπερ τὰ μουσικῆς ὄργανα ἄκρως ἡρμοσμένα
πᾶσι τοῖς φθόγγοις, οὕτως ἡμεῖς πάσαις ταῖς
ὑφηγήσεσι συνηχήσαμεν, ἐκμελὲς ἢ ἀπῳδὸν οὐδὲν
οὔτε¹ ῥῆμα εἰπόντες οὔτ' ἔργον διαπραξάμενοι, ὡς
τὸν ἕτερον τῶν ἀμούσων χορὸν πάντα ἄφωνον καὶ
νεκρὸν ἀποδεῖξαι γελασθέντα τὴν τῶν σωματικῶν
τροφὸν² Μαδιὰμ καὶ τὸν ἔκγονον αὐτῆς δερμάτινον
56 ὄγκον Βεελφεγὼρ ὄνομα ὑμνοῦντα.³ γένος γάρ
ἐσμεν '' τῶν ἐπιλέκτων τοῦ '' τὸν θεὸν ὁρῶντος
'' Ἰσραήλ,'' ὧν '' διεφώνησεν οὐδὲ εἷς,'' ἵνα τὸ
τοῦ παντὸς ὄργανον, ὁ κόσμος πᾶς, ταῖς ἁρμονίαις
57 μουσικῶς μελῳδῆται.   διὰ τοῦτο καὶ
Μωυσῆς τῷ πολεμικωτάτῳ λόγῳ, ὃς καλεῖται
Φινεές, γέρας εἰρήνην φησὶ δεδόσθαι, ὅτι ζῆλον
τὸν ἀρετῆς λαβὼν καὶ πόλεμον πρὸς κακίαν ἀρά-

---

¹ mss. οὐδέ.
² τροφὸν Mangey: mss. and Wend. τροφήν. See App.
p. 554.
³ I have adopted ὑμνοῦντα (originally suggested by G. H. W.)
for the ὑπνοῦντα of mss. and Wend., who defends it as an
antithesis to ὁρῶντος in the next sentence. For a discussion
of the text of the whole sentence see App. p. 554.

lesson of obedience, and those have assumed the command which not only knowledge but power has given them, all the thoughts that attend and guard the soul will be one in purpose and approaching Him that ranks highest among them will speak thus : " Thy servants have taken the sum of the men of war who were with us, and there is no discordant voice " (Num. xxxi. 49).[a] "We," they will continue, " like instruments of music where all the notes are in perfect tune, echo with our voices all the lessons we have received. We speak no word and do no deed that is harsh or grating, and thus we have made a laughing-stock of all that other dead and voiceless choir, the choir of those who know not the muse, the choir which hymns Midian, the nurse of things bodily, and her offspring, the heavy leathern weight whose name is Baal-Peor. For we are the ' race of **56** the Chosen ones of that Israel ' who sees God, ' and there is none amongst us of discordant voice ' " (Ex. xxiv. 11),[b] that so the whole world, which is the instrument of the All, may be filled with the sweet melody of its undiscording harmonies.   And **57** therefore too Moses tells us how peace was assigned as the prize of that most warlike reason, called Phinehas (Num. xxv. 12), because, inspired with zeal for virtue and waging war against vice, he ripped

---

[a] For Philo's treatment of this text see *De Ebr.* 114 ff. and note.

[b] LXX. LXX. καὶ τῶν ἐπιλέκτων τοῦ Ἰσραὴλ οὐ διεφώνησεν οὐδὲ εἷς, E.V. " and on the elders of Israel he laid not his hand." Here clearly διαφωνεῖν means "to perish," and so perhaps in Num. xxxi. 49. rather than "failed to answer his name." Philo probably understood this, but for the purpose of his musical allegory gives the word its literal meaning.

PHILO

μενος ὅλην ἀνέτεμε γένεσιν, ἑξῆς[1] τοῖς βουλομένοις,
διακύψασι καὶ διερευνησαμένοις ἀκριβῶς ὄψει πρὸ
ἀκοῆς σαφεστέρῳ χρησαμένοις μάρτυρι, πιστεῦσαι,
ὅτι γέμει τὸ θνητὸν ἀπιστίας, ἐκ μόνου τοῦ
58 δοκεῖν ἠρτημένον.   θαυμάσιος μὲν οὖν ἡ
λεχθεῖσα συμφωνία, θαυμασιωτάτη δὲ καὶ πάσας
τὰς ἁρμονίας ὑπερβάλλουσα ἡ κοινὴ πάντων, καθ'
ἣν ὁ λαὸς ἅπας ὁμοθυμαδὸν εἰσάγεται λέγων·
" πάντα ὅσα εἶπεν ὁ θεός, ποιήσομεν καὶ ἀκουσό-
59 μεθα"· οὗτοι γὰρ οὐκέτι ἐξάρχοντι πείθονται λόγῳ,
ἀλλὰ τῷ τοῦ παντὸς ἡγεμόνι θεῷ, δι' ὃν πρὸς τὰ
[414] ἔργα φθάνουσι μᾶλλον ἢ τοὺς | λόγους ἀπαντῶν-
τες· τῶν γὰρ ἄλλων ἐπειδὰν ἀκούσωσι πραττόντων
οὗτοι, τὸ παραδοξότατον, ὑπὸ κατοκωχῆς ἐνθέου
πράξειν φασὶ πρότερον, εἶτα ἀκούσεσθαι, ἵνα μὴ
διδασκαλίᾳ καὶ ὑφηγήσει δοκῶσιν, ἀλλὰ ἐθελουργῷ
καὶ αὐτοκελεύστῳ διανοίᾳ πρὸς τὰ καλὰ τῶν ἔργων
ὑπαντᾶν· ἐργασάμενοι δὲ ἀκούσεσθαί φασιν, ὅπως
ἐπικρίνωσι τὰ πραχθέντα, εἰ λόγοις θείοις καὶ ἱεραῖς
παραινέσεσι συνᾴδει.
60 XIV. Τοὺς δὲ συνομοσαμένους ἐπ' ἀδικήμασιν
" ἀπὸ ἀνατολῶν " φησι " κινήσαντας εὑρεῖν πεδίον
ἐν τῇ γῇ Σενααρ κἀκεῖ κατοικῆσαι," φυσικώτατα·

---

[1] Perhaps ἑξῆς ⟨δὲ⟩. Wend. places a lacuna before ἑξῆς,
Cohn after it, corrected to ἐξ ἧς. Neither gives any suggestion as to what this lacuna contained. My reasons for
thinking that there is no such lacuna are given in note *a*
below.

---

a The course of the thought, as I understand, is this. By
close examination, particularly of the senses (§§ 52, 53), we
obtain a mastery of them, and thus reach the harmony of
which the Captains of Num. xxxi. spoke (§ 55). This involves

open all created being; how in their turn [a] that prize is given to those who, after diligent and careful scrutiny, following the more certain testimony of sight, rather than hearing, have the will to accept the faith that mortality is full of unfaith and clings only to the seeming. **58** Wonderful then indeed is the symphony of voices here described, but most wonderful of all, exceeding every harmony, is that united universal symphony in which we find the whole people declaring with one heart, " All that God hath said we will do and hear " (Ex. xix. 8). Here the precentor whom they follow is no longer **59** the Word, but God the Sovereign of all, for whose sake [b] they become quicker to meet the call to action than the call of words. For other men act after they have heard, but these under the divine inspiration say—strange inversion—that they will act first and hear afterwards, that so they may be seen to go forward to deeds of excellence, not led by teaching or instruction, but through the self-acting, self-dictated instinct of their own hearts. And when they have *done*, then, as they say, they will *hear*, that so they may judge their actions, whether they chime with the divine words and the sacred admonitions.

XIV. Now those who conspired for iniquities, **60** " moved," we are told, " from the ' east ' (or ' rising ') and found a plain in the land of Shinar and dwelt

the conviction of the untrustworthiness of all created things, and thus brings the Captains into line with Phinehas, whose ripping up of the " woman " γένεσις meant the same thing. Thus the prize of true peace goes first to Phinehas, but also in their turn (ἑξῆς) to the Captains. Historically, of course, they are linked with Phinehas, who was their leader in the war against Midian.

[b] Or "through whom." See note on § 127.

διττὸν γὰρ εἶδος τῆς κατὰ τὴν ψυχὴν ἀνατολῆς,
τὸ μὲν ἄμεινον, τὸ δὲ χεῖρον, ἄμεινον μέν, ὅταν
ἡλιακῶν ἀκτίνων τρόπον ἀνάσχῃ τὸ ἀρετῶν φέγγος, χεῖρον δ', ὅταν αἱ μὲν ἐπισκιασθῶσι, κακίαι
61 δὲ ἀνάσχωσι. παράδειγμα τοῦ μὲν προτέρου τόδε·
" καὶ ἐφύτευσεν ὁ θεὸς παράδεισον ἐν Ἐδὲμ κατὰ
ἀνατολάς," οὐ χερσαίων φυτῶν, ἀλλ' οὐρανίων
ἀρετῶν, ἃς ἐξ ἀσωμάτου τοῦ παρ' ἑαυτῷ φωτὸς
ἀσβέστους εἰσαεὶ γενησομένας ὁ φυτουργὸς ἀν-
62 έτειλεν.   ἤκουσα μέντοι καὶ τῶν Μωυσέως ἑταίρων τινὸς ἀποφθεγξαμένου τοιόνδε λό-
γιον· " ἰδοὺ ἄνθρωπος ᾧ ὄνομα ἀνατολή" καινο-
τάτη γε πρόσρησις, ἐάν γε τὸν ἐκ σώματος καὶ
ψυχῆς συνεστῶτα λέγεσθαι νομίσῃς· ἐὰν δὲ τὸν
ἀσώματον ἐκεῖνον, θείας ἀδιαφοροῦντα εἰκόνος,
ὁμολογήσεις ὅτι εὐθυβολώτατον ὄνομα ἐπεφημίσθη
63 τὸ ἀνατολῆς[1] αὐτῷ· τοῦτον μὲν γὰρ πρεσβύτατον
υἱὸν ὁ τῶν ὅλων ἀνέτειλε πατήρ, ὃν ἑτέρωθι πρωτό-
γονον ὠνόμασε, καὶ ὁ γεννηθεὶς μέντοι, μιμούμενος τὰς τοῦ πατρὸς ὁδούς, πρὸς παραδείγματα
ἀρχέτυπα ἐκείνου βλέπων ἐμόρφου τὰ εἴδη.

64   XV. Τοῦ δὲ χείρονος ἀνατολῆς εἴδους ὑπόδειγμα
τὸ λεχθὲν ἐπὶ τοῦ βουλομένου τὸν ἐπαινούμενον
ὑπὸ θεοῦ καταράσασθαι· πρὸς γὰρ ἀνατολαῖς εἰσάγεται κἀκεῖνος οἰκῶν, αἵτινες ὁμωνυμοῦσαι ταῖς
προτέραις ἐναντιότητα καὶ μάχην πρὸς αὐτὰς
65 ἔχουσιν· " ἐκ Μεσοποταμίας " γάρ φησι " μετε-
πέμψατό με Βαλάκ, ἐξ ὀρέων ἀπὸ ἀνατολῶν, λέγων·

---

[1] Or perhaps ἀνατολή.

[a] E.V. " branch " (margin, " bud ").

there " (Gen. xi. 2). How true to nature! For there are two kinds of " rising " in the soul, the better and the worse. The better is when the beam of the virtues rises like the rays of the sun; the worse when virtues pass into the shadow and vices rise above the horizon. We have an example of the former in these 61 words: " And God planted a pleasaunce in Eden towards the sun-rise " (Gen. ii. 8). That garden was not a garden of the plants of the soil, but of heavenly virtues, which out of His own incorporeal light the Planter brought to their rising, never to be extinguished. I have heard also an oracle 62 from the lips of one of the disciples of Moses, which runs thus: " Behold a man whose name is the rising " *a* (Zech. vi. 12), strangest of titles, surely, if you suppose that a being composed of soul and body is here described. But if you suppose that it is that Incorporeal one, who differs not a whit from the divine image, you will agree that the name of " rising " assigned to him quite truly describes him. For that man is the eldest son, whom the Father of 63 all raised up, and elsewhere calls him His first-born, and indeed the Son thus begotten followed the ways of his Father, and shaped the different kinds, looking to the archetypal patterns which that Father supplied.

XV. Of the worse kind of rising we have an 64 example in the description of him who wished to curse one who was praised by God. For he too is represented as dwelling at the " rising," and this rising though it bears the same name as the other is in direct conflict with it. " Balak," we read, 65 " sent for me from Mesopotamia from the mountains from the rising saying, ' Come hither, curse for me

45

δεῦρο ἄρασαί μοι ὃν μὴ ἄραται ὁ θεός.'' ἑρμη-
[415] νεύεται δὲ Βαλὰκ ἄνους, εὐθυβολώτατα· πῶς | γὰρ
οὐκ ἄνοια δεινὴ τὸ ὂν ἐλπίσαι ἀπατᾶσθαι καὶ
γνώμην αὐτοῦ τὴν βεβαιοτάτην ἀνθρώπων σοφί-
66 σμασι παρατρέπεσθαι; διὰ τοῦτο καὶ Μεσοποταμίαν
οἰκεῖ καταπεποντωμένης ὥσπερ ἐν μεσαιτάτῳ
ποταμοῦ βυθῷ τῆς διανοίας αὐτοῦ καὶ μὴ δυναμένης ἀνανήξασθαι καὶ ἀνακύψαι· τοῦτο δὲ τὸ
πάθος ἀνατολὴ μὲν ἀφροσύνης, κατάδυσις δὲ
67 εὐλογιστίας ἐστίν.   οἱ τὴν ἀσύμφωνον
οὖν ἁρμοζόμενοι συμφωνίαν ἀπὸ ἀνατολῶν κινεῖσθαι
λέγονται. πότερον ἄρα γε τῶν ⟨κατ' ἀρετὴν ἢ
τῶν⟩ κατὰ κακίαν; ἀλλ' εἰ μὲν τῶν κατ' ἀρετήν,
παντελὴς ὑπογράφεται διάζευξις· εἰ δὲ τῶν κατὰ
κακίαν, ἡνωμένη τις κίνησις, καθάπερ ἐπὶ χειρῶν
ἔχει, οὐκ ἰδίᾳ κατὰ ἀπάρτησιν, ἀλλ' ἐν ἁρμονίᾳ
68 τινὶ τῷ ὅλῳ σώματι συγκινουμένων. ἀρχὴ γὰρ
καὶ ἀφορμὴ φαύλῳ πρὸς τὰς παρὰ φύσιν ἐνεργείας
τὸ κακίας χωρίον·   ὅσοι δὲ μετανάσται
μὲν ἀρετῆς ἐγένοντο, ταῖς δ' ἀφροσύνης ἐχρήσαντο
ἀφορμαῖς, οἰκειότατον εὑρόντες οἰκοῦσι τόπον, ὃς
Ἑβραίων μὲν γλώττῃ Σεναάρ, Ἑλλήνων δὲ ἐκ-
69 τιναγμὸς καλεῖται· σπαράττεται γὰρ καὶ κλονεῖται
καὶ τινάττεται πᾶς ὁ τῶν φαύλων βίος, κυκώμενος
ἀεὶ καὶ ταραττόμενος καὶ μηδὲν ἴχνος ἀγαθοῦ
γνησίου θησαυριζόμενος ἐν ἑαυτῷ. καθάπερ γὰρ
τῶν ἀποτιναττομένων ὅσα μὴ ἑνώσει διακρατεῖται
πάντα ἐκπίπτει, τοῦτόν μοι δοκεῖ καὶ ἡ τοῦ
συμπεπνευκότος ἐπὶ τῷ ἀδικεῖν ἐκτετινάχθαι τὸν

ᵃ Lit. "the things of virtue . . . of vice."

46

him whom God does not curse ' " (Num. xxiii. 7, 8).
Now Balak is by interpretation " foolish," and the
interpretation is most true. For surely it were the
pitch of folly to hope that the Existent should be
deceived, and that His surest purpose should be
upset by the devices of men ? And this is the reason 66
why Balaam also dwells in " Mid-river-land," for his
understanding is submerged in the midmost depths
of a river, unable to swim its way upward and lift its
head above the surface. This condition is the rising
of folly and the setting of reasonableness.

Now these makers of a music whose harmony is dis- 67
harmony, moved, we are told, " from the rising."
Is it the rising of virtue that is meant, or the rising
of vice ? [a] If the former, the movement suggested is
one of complete severance. But if it is the latter, it
is what we may call an united movement, as when
we move our hands, not apart or in isolation, but in
connexion and accordance with the whole body. For 68
the place where vice is located serves as the initial
starting-point to the fool for those activities which
defy nature.   Now all who have wan-
dered away from virtue and accepted the starting-
points of folly, find and dwell in a most suitable place,
a place which in the Hebrew tongue is called Shinar
and in our own " shaking out." For all the life of 69
the fools is torn and hustled and shaken, ever in
chaos and disturbance, and keeping no trace of
genuine good treasured within it. For just as things
which are shaken off all fall out, if not held fast
through being part of a unified body,[b] so too I think,
when a man has conspired for wrongdoing, his soul

[b] For the Stoic conception of ἕνωσις see note on *Quod
Det.* 49.

τρόπον ψυχή· πᾶσαν γὰρ ἰδέαν ἀρετῆς ἀπορρίπτει,
ὡς μήτε σκιὰν μήτε εἴδωλον αὐτῆς[1] ἐμφαίνεσθαι τὸ
70 παράπαν.   XVI. τὸ γοῦν φιλοσώματον
γένος τῶν Αἰγυπτίων οὐκ ἀπὸ τοῦ ὕδατος, ἀλλ'
" ὑπὸ τὸ ὕδωρ " φεῦγον, τουτέστιν ὑπὸ τὴν τῶν
παθῶν φοράν, εἰσάγεται, καὶ ἐπειδὰν ὑποδράμῃ
τὰ πάθη, τινάττεται καὶ κυκᾶται, τὸ μὲν εὐσταθὲς
καὶ εἰρηναῖον ἀποβάλλον ἀρετῆς, τὸ δὲ ταραχῶδες
ἐπαναιρούμενον κακίας· λέγεται γὰρ ὅτι " ἐξετίναξε
τοὺς Αἰγυπτίους κατὰ μέσον τῆς θαλάσσης φεύγον-
71 τας ὑπὸ τὸ ὕδωρ."   οὗτοί εἰσιν οἱ μηδὲ
τὸν Ἰωσὴφ εἰδότες, τὸν ποικίλον τοῦ βίου τῦφον,
ἀλλ' ἀποκεκαλυμμένοις χρώμενοι τοῖς ἁμαρτήμασιν, οὐδὲ ἴχνος ἢ σκιὰν καὶ εἴδωλον καλοκἀγαθίας
72 ταμιευσάμενοι· " ἀνέστη " γάρ φησι " βασιλεὺς
ἕτερος ἐπ' Αἴγυπτον," ὃς οὐδὲ τὸ πανύστατον καὶ
νεώτατον αἰσθητὸν ἀγαθὸν " ᾔδει τὸν Ἰωσήφ,"
ὅστις οὐ μόνον τελειότητας ἀλλὰ καὶ προκοπάς,
οὐδὲ ἐνάργειαν τὴν οἵαν δι' ὁράσεως ἀλλὰ καὶ
διδασκαλίαν τὴν δι' ἀκοῆς ἐγγινομένην ἀνῄρει
λέγων· " δεῦρο ἄρασαί μοι τὸν Ἰακώβ, καὶ δεῦρο
ἐπικατάρασαί μοι τὸν Ἰσραήλ," ἴσον τῷ ἐλθέ,
ἀμφότερα κατάλυσον, ὅρασίν τε καὶ ἀκοὴν ψυχῆς,
ἵνα μηδὲν ἀληθὲς καὶ γνήσιον καλὸν μήτε ἴδῃ μήτε
ἀκούσῃ· ὁράσεως μὲν γὰρ Ἰσραήλ, Ἰακὼβ δὲ
73 ἀκοῆς σύμβολον.   ὁ μὲν δὴ τῶν τοιούτων
[416] νοῦς ἀπορρίπτει πᾶσαν τὴν ἀγαθοῦ | φύσιν τρόπον
τινὰ τινασσόμενος, ἔμπαλιν δ' ὁ τῶν ἀστείων,
ἀμιγοῦς καὶ ἀκράτου μεταποιούμενος τῆς τῶν

---

[1] mss. αὐτῇ.

a See App. p. 554.

48

is subject to a " shaking out," for it casts away every form of good so that no shadow or semblance of it can be seen at all. XVI. We have example 70 in the Egyptians, the representatives of those who love the body, who are shewn to us as flying not from the water, but " under the water," that is under the stream of the passions, and when they are submerged^a therein they are shaken and wildly disordered; they cast away the stability and peacefulness of virtue and take upon them the confusion of vice. For we are told, " that he shook off the Egyptians in the midst of the sea, fleeing under the water " (Ex. xiv. 27).

These are they who know not even 71 Joseph, the many-sided pride of worldly life, and give way to their sins without veil or disguise, husbanding no vestige or shadow or semblance of honourable living. For there rose up, we are told, another King 72 over Egypt, who " knew not " even " Joseph " (Ex. i. 8)—the good that is, which is given by the senses, the last and latest in the scale of goods. It is this same King who would destroy not only all perfection but all progress; not only the clear vision such as comes of sight, but the instruction also that comes of hearing. He says, " Come hither, curse me Jacob, and come hither, send thy curses upon Israel " (Num. xxiii. 7), and that is equivalent to " Put an end to them both, the soul's sight and the soul's hearing, that it may neither see nor hear any true and genuine excellence." For Israel is the type of seeing, and Jacob of hearing. The 73 mind of such as these is in a sense shaken and casts forth the whole nature of good, while the mind of the virtuous in contrast claims as its own the Idea of the good, an Idea pure and unalloyed, and shakes and

ἀγαθῶν ἰδέας, ἀποτινάττει καὶ ἀποβάλλει τὰ φαῦλα[1]·

74 θέασαι γοῦν[2] τὸν ἀσκητὴν οἷά φησιν· '' ἄρατε τοὺς θεοὺς τοὺς ἀλλοτρίους τοὺς μεθ' ὑμῶν ἐκ μέσου ὑμῶν, καὶ καθαρίσασθε καὶ ἀλλάξατε τὰς στολὰς ὑμῶν, καὶ ἀναστάντες ἀναβῶμεν εἰς Βαιθήλ,'' ἵνα, κἂν Λάβαν ἔρευναν αἰτῆται, ἐν ὅλῳ τῷ οἴκῳ μὴ εὑρεθῇ τὰ εἴδωλα, ⟨ἀλλὰ⟩ πράγματα ὑφεστηκότα καὶ ὄντως ὑπαρκτά, ἐστηλιτευμένα ἐν τῇ τοῦ σοφοῦ διανοίᾳ, ὧν καὶ τὸ αὐτομαθὲς γένος Ἰσαὰκ κληρονομεῖ· τὰ γὰρ ὑπαρκτὰ μόνος οὗτος παρὰ τοῦ πατρὸς λαμβάνει.

75 XVII. Παρατήρει δ' ὅτι οὔ φησιν ἐλθεῖν αὐτοὺς εἰς τὸ πεδίον ἐν ᾧ κατέμειναν, ἀλλὰ εὑρεῖν ἀναζητήσαντας πάντως καὶ σκεψαμένους τὸ ἐπιτηδειότατον ἀφροσύνῃ[3] χωρίον· τῷ γὰρ ὄντι πᾶς ἄφρων οὐ παρ' ἑτέρου λαμβάνει ἑαυτῷ τὰ δὲ κακὰ ζητῶν ἀνευρίσκει, μὴ μόνοις[4] ἀρκούμενος τούτοις ἐφ' ἅπερ ἡ μοχθηρὰ φύσις δι' ἑαυτῆς βαδίζει, ἀλλὰ καὶ προστιθεὶς τὰ ἐκ τοῦ κακοτεχνεῖν τέλεια γυμνάσ-

76 ματα. καὶ εἴθε μέντοι πρὸς ὀλίγον ἐνδιατρίψας αὐτοῖς χρόνον μετανίστατο. νυνὶ δὲ καὶ καταμένειν ἀξιοῖ· λέγεται γὰρ ὅτι εὑρόντες τὸ πεδίον κατῴκησαν ὡς ἐν πατρίδι, οὐχ ὡς ἐπὶ ξένης παρῴκησαν. ἧττον γὰρ ἦν δεινὸν συντυχόντας ἁμαρτήμασιν ὀθνεῖα αὐτὰ καὶ ὥσπερ ἀλλοδαπὰ νομίσαι, ἀλλὰ μὴ οἰκεῖα καὶ συγγενῆ ὑπολαβεῖν εἶναι· παρεπιδημήσαντες γὰρ κἂν ἀπέστησαν αὖθις, κατοικήσαντες δὲ βεβαίως καταμένειν εἰσάπαν ἔμελλον.

77 διὰ τοῦτο οἱ κατὰ Μωυσῆν σοφοὶ πάντες εἰσάγονται

---

[1] MSS. φύλλα.   [2] MSS. οὖν.
[3] MSS. ἀφροσύνης, which perhaps retain in the sense of '' the folly-spot best suited to them.''   [4] μόνον MSS.

casts off what is worthless. Thus mark how the Man 74
of Practice speaks : " Take away the alien gods who
are with you from the midst of you, and purify yourselves and change your raiment and let us rise up
and go up to Bethel " (Gen. xxxv. 2, 3), so that, even
though Laban demand a search, no idols may be
found in all the house (Gen. xxxi. 35) but veritable
substantial realities *a* graven, as though on stone, on
the heart of the wise, realities which are the heritage of
the self-taught nature, Isaac. For Isaac alone receives
from his father the " real substance " (Gen. xxv. 5).

XVII. Again observe that he does not say that 75
they *came* to the plain in which they stayed, but that
only after full search and exploration they *found* the
spot which was the fittest for folly. For indeed every
fool does not just take to him what another gives,
but he seeks for evil and discovers it. He is not
content with the evils only to which depravity proceeds in its natural course, but adds the perfected
efforts of the artist in wickedness. And would that 76
he might only stay for a while among them and then
change his habitation, but as it is he determines to
abide there. For they " found," we are told, " the
plain and dwelt there," as though it were their
fatherland. They did not sojourn there as on a
foreign soil. For it were a less grievous thing if when
they fell in with sins, they should count them strangers
and outlanders as it were, instead of holding them
to be of their own household and kin. For were it a
passing visit they would have departed in course of
time ; their dwelling there was a sure evidence of a
permanent stay. This is why all whom 77
Moses calls wise are represented as sojourners.

a See note on *De Mig.* 94.

παροικοῦντες· αἱ γὰρ τούτων ψυχαὶ στέλλονται
μὲν ἀποικίαν οὐδέποτε[1] τὴν ἐξ οὐρανοῦ, εἰώθασι
δὲ ἕνεκα τοῦ φιλοθεάμονος καὶ φιλομαθοῦς εἰς τὴν
78 περίγειον φύσιν ἀποδημεῖν. ἐπειδὰν οὖν ἐνδια-
τρίψασαι σώμασι τὰ αἰσθητὰ καὶ θνητὰ δι' αὐτῶν
πάντα κατίδωσιν, ἐπανέρχονται ἐκεῖσε πάλιν, ὅθεν
ὡρμήθησαν τὸ πρῶτον, πατρίδα μὲν τὸν οὐράνιον
χῶρον ἐν ᾧ πολιτεύονται, ξένην δὲ τὸν περίγειον
ἐν ᾧ παρῴκησαν νομίζουσαι· τοῖς μὲν γὰρ ἀποικίαν
στειλαμένοις ἀντὶ τῆς μητροπόλεως ἡ ὑποδεξαμένη
δήπου πατρίς, ἡ δ' ἐκπέμψασα μένει τοῖς ἀπο-
δεδημηκόσιν, εἰς ἣν καὶ ποθοῦσιν ἐπανέρχεσθαι. |
79 τοιγαροῦν εἰκότως Ἀβραὰμ ἐρεῖ τοῖς νεκροφύλαξι
[417] καὶ ταμίαις τῶν θνητῶν, ἀναστὰς ἀπὸ τοῦ νεκροῦ
βίου καὶ τύφου· " πάροικος καὶ παρεπίδημός εἰμι
ἐγὼ μεθ' ὑμῶν," αὐτόχθονες δὲ ὑμεῖς, κόνιν καὶ
χοῦν ψυχῆς προτιμήσαντες, προεδρίας ἀξιώσαντες
80 ὄνομα[2] Ἐφρών, ὃς ἑρμηνεύεται χοῦς. εἰκότως δὲ
καὶ ὁ ἀσκητὴς Ἰακὼβ τὴν ἐν σώματι παροικίαν
ὀλοφύρεται λέγων· " αἱ ἡμέραι τῶν ἐτῶν τῆς ζωῆς
μου, ἃς παροικῶ, μικραὶ καὶ πονηραὶ γεγόνασιν·
οὐκ ἐξίκοντο εἰς ἡμέρας τῶν πατέρων μου ἃς
81 παρῴκησαν." τῷ δ' αὐτοδιδάκτῳ καὶ λογίῳ
ἐχρήσθη τοιόνδε· " μὴ καταβῇς εἰς " τὸ πάθος
" Αἴγυπτον, κατοίκησον δ' ἐν τῇ γῇ ἣν ἄν σοι
εἴπω," τῇ ἀδείκτῳ καὶ ἀσωμάτῳ φρονήσει, " καὶ
παροίκει ἐν τῇ γῇ ταύτῃ," τῇ δεικνυμένῃ καὶ

---

[1] mss. δή (δέ) ποτε.
[2] Perhaps as Mangey ⟨τὸν⟩ ὄνομα.

---

[a] The LXX of course intended no such distinction between
κατοίκει and παροίκει, or between the land of the first half and
that of the second half of the verse.

Their souls are never colonists leaving heaven for a new home. Their way is to visit earthly nature as men who travel abroad to see and learn. So when they have stayed awhile in their bodies, and beheld through them all that sense and mortality has to shew, they make their way back to the place from which they set out at the first. To them the heavenly region, where their citizenship lies, is their native land ; the earthly region in which they became sojourners is a foreign country. For surely, when men found a colony, the land which receives them becomes their native land instead of the mother city, but to the traveller abroad the land which sent him forth is still the mother to whom also he yearns to return. We shall not be surprised, then, to find Abraham, when he rose from the life of death and vanity, saying to the guardians of the dead and stewards of mortality, " I am a stranger and so-journer with you " (Gen. xxiii. 4). " You," he means, " are children of the soil who honour the dust and clay before the soul and have adjudged the precedence to the man named Ephron, which being interpreted is ' clay.' " And just as natural are the words of the Practiser Jacob, when he laments his sojourn in the body. " The days of the years of my life, the days which I sojourn, have been few and evil, they have not reached to the days of my fathers which they sojourned " (Gen. xlvii. 9). Isaac, too, the self-taught had an oracle vouchsafed to him thus, " Go not down into Egypt," that is passion, " but dwell in the land which I say to thee " (that is in the wisdom which has no material body, and none can shew it to another), " and sojourn in this land " [a]

αἰσθητῇ οὐσίᾳ, πρὸς τὸ δεῖξαι ὅτι παροικεῖ μὲν ὁ
σοφὸς ὡς ἐν ξένῃ σώματι αἰσθητῷ, κατοικεῖ δ'
ὡς ἐν πατρίδι νοηταῖς ἀρεταῖς, ἃς λαλεῖ ὁ θεὸς
82 ἀδιαφορούσας λόγων θείων. Μωυσῆς δὲ " γειώρας "
φησίν " εἰμὶ ἐν γῇ ἀλλοτρίᾳ," διαφερόντως οὐ
μόνον ξένην τὴν ἐν σώματι μονὴν ὡς οἱ μέτοικοι
νομίζων, ἀλλὰ καὶ ἀλλοτριώσεως ἀξίαν οὐκ ἔμπαλιν
οἰκειώσεως ὑπολαμβάνων.

83 XVIII. Τὸ δ' ὁμόφωνον καὶ ὁμόγλωττον οὐκ ἐν
τοῖς ὀνόμασι καὶ ῥήμασι μᾶλλον ἢ ἐν τῇ τῶν ἀδίκων
πράξεων κοινωνίᾳ βουλόμενος ὁ φαῦλος ἐπιδεί-
ξασθαι πόλιν ἄρχεται καὶ πύργον, ὡς ἀκρόπολιν
τυράννῳ, κακίᾳ κατασκευάζειν, καὶ τοὺς θιασώτας
πάντας παρακαλεῖ τοῦ ἔργου μετασχεῖν τὴν ἁρμότ-
84 τουσαν προευτρεπισαμένους ὕλην· " ἴτε " γάρ φησι
" πλινθεύσωμεν πλίνθους καὶ ὀπτήσωμεν αὐτὰς
πυρί," ἴσον τῷ νῦν ἐστιν ἡμῖν συμπεφορημένα καὶ
συγκεχυμένα τὰ πάντα τῆς ψυχῆς, ὡς ἐναργῆ
85 τύπον μηδένα μηδενὸς εἴδους προφαίνεσθαι. ἁρμόττει δ' ὥσπερ ἀνείδεόν τινα καὶ ἄποιον οὐσίαν
τό τε πάθος καὶ τὴν κακίαν παραλαβόντας εἰς τὰς
ἁρμοττούσας ποιότητας καὶ τὰ προσεχέστατα μέχρι
τῶν ἐσχάτων ἀεὶ τεμεῖν εἴδη πρός τε ἐναργεστέραν
κατάληψιν αὐτῶν καὶ τὴν σὺν ἐμπειρίᾳ χρῆσίν τε
καὶ ἀπόλαυσιν, ἣ πλείους ἡδονὰς καὶ τέρψεις ἔοικεν

---

[a] The fanciful thought is as follows: What we speak is
words not things. Therefore when God "speaks a land"
(meaning virtues), those virtues are God's words. He has
this much excuse that εἴπω followed by the things spoken
of is doubtful Greek.

[b] προσεχής (next) frequently means (the species) next to
the genus, *i.e.* primary. Here each εἶδος is προσεχές to the
next above it.

(Gen. xxvi. 2, 3), that is in that form of existence which may be shewn and is perceived by the senses. The purpose of this is to shew him that the wise man does but sojourn in this body which our senses know, as in a strange land, but dwells in and has for his fatherland the virtues known through the mind, which God " speaks " and which thus are identical with divine words.[a] But Moses says, " I am an out- 82 lander in the alien land " (Ex. ii. 22). Thus he uses stronger terms. His tenancy of the body is not to him merely that of the foreigner as immigrant settlers count it. To alienate himself from it, never to count it as his own, is, he holds, to give it its due.

XVIII. Now the wicked man wishes to display 83 his unity of voice and speech through fellowship in unjust deeds rather than in actual words, and there- fore begins to build a city and a tower which will serve for the hold of vice, as a citadel for a despot. He exhorts all those who form his company to take their share in the work, but first to prepare the suitable material. " Come," he says, " let us make bricks 84 and bake them with fire " (Gen. xi. 3). The meaning of this is as follows. At present we have all the contents of the soul in inextricable confusion, so that no clear form of any particular kind is discernible. Our right course is to take the passion and vice, 85 which at present is a substance devoid of form and quality, and divide it by continuous analysis into the proper categories and the subdivisions in regular descending order[b] till we reach the ultimate ; thus we shall obtain both a clearer apprehension of them and that experienced use and enjoyment which is calculated to multiply our pleasure and delight.

86 ἐντίκτειν. πάριτε οὖν οἱ λογισμοὶ πάντες βουλευτῶν τινα τρόπον εἰς τὸ ψυχῆς συνέδριον, ὅσοι ⟨πρὸς⟩ τὸν δικαιοσύνης καὶ πάσης ἀρετῆς συγκατατάττεσθε ὄλεθρον, καὶ πεφροντισμένως δια-
87 σκεψώμεθα, ὡς ἐπιθέμενοι κατορθώσωμεν· τῆς μέντοι κατορθώσεως ἔσονται θεμέλιοι κραταιότατοι οἵδε, ἄμορφα μορφῶσαι τύποις καὶ σχήμασι καὶ περιγραφαῖς ἕκαστον ἰδίᾳ διακρῖναι, μὴ κραδαι-
[418] νόμενα¹ καὶ χωλαίνοντα, ἀλλὰ | πεπηγότα βεβαίως, τῇ τοῦ τετραγώνου σχήματος οἰκειούμενα φύσει—ἀκράδαντον γὰρ τοῦτό γε—, ἵνα πλίνθου τινὰ τρόπον ἀκλινῶς ἐρηρεισμένα βεβαίως καὶ τὰ ἐπ-
88 οικοδομούμενα δέχηται. XIX. τούτων πᾶς ὁ ἀντίθεος νοῦς, ὃν φαμὲν Αἰγύπτου, τοῦ σώματος, εἶναι βασιλέα, δημιουργὸς ἀνευρίσκεται· καὶ γὰρ τοῦτον εἰσάγει Μωυσῆς τοῖς ἐκ πλίνθου κατα-
89 σκευαζομένοις χαίροντα οἰκοδομήμασιν. ἐπειδὰν γάρ τις τὴν ὕδατος καὶ γῆς τὴν μὲν ὑγράν, τὴν δ' αὖ στερεὰν οὐσίαν, διαλυομένας καὶ φθειρομένας, ἀνακερασάμενος τρίτον μεθόριον ἀμφοῖν ἀπεργάσηται, ὃ καλεῖται πηλός, τέμνων κατὰ μοίρας τοῦτον οὐ παύεται σχήματα περιτιθεὶς ἑκάστῳ τῶν τμημάτων τὰ οἰκεῖα, ὅπως εὐπαγέστερά τε καὶ εὐφορώτερα γένηται· ῥᾳδίως γὰρ οὕτως ἔμελλε τὰ κατασκευαζόμενα τελειοῦσθαι.
90 τοῦτ' ἀπομιμούμενοι τὸ ἔργον οἱ μοχθηροὶ τὰς φύσεις, ὅταν τὰς ἀλόγους καὶ πλεοναζούσας τῶν παθῶν ὁρμὰς ταῖς ἀργαλεωτάταις κακίαις ἀνακεράσωνται, τέμνουσι τὸ κραθὲν εἰς εἴδη καὶ

¹ MSS. κραδαίνοντα.

Forward then, come as senators to the 86
council-hall [a] of the soul, all you reasonings which are
ranged together for the destruction of righteousness
and every virtue, and let us carefully consider how
our attack may succeed. The firmest foundations 87
for such success will be to give form to the formless
by assigning them definite shapes and figures and to
distinguish them in each case by separate limitations,
not with the uncertain equilibrium of the halting,
but firmly planted, assimilated to the nature of the
square—that most stable of figures—and thus rooted
brick-like in unwavering equilibrium they will form
a secure support for the superstructure.

XIX. Every mind that sets itself up against God, the 88
mind which we call " King of Egypt," that is of the
body, proves to be a maker of such structures. For
Moses describes Pharoah as rejoicing in buildings
constructed of brick. This is natural, for when the 89
workman has taken the two substances of earth and
water, one solid and the other liquid, but both in
the process of dissolution or destruction, and by
mixing them has produced a third on the boundary
line between the two, called clay, he divides it up
into portions and without interruption gives each of
the sections its proper shape. He wishes thus to
make them firmer and more manageable [b] since this,
he knows, is the easiest way to secure the completion
of the building. This process is copied by the natur- 90
ally depraved, when they first mix the unreasoning
and exuberant impulses of passion with the gravest
vices, and then divide the mixture into its kinds,

[a] Or " council," the soul being looked upon as a collective
body ; cf. De Mig. 60.
[b] Or " more capable of sustaining the structure."

διαπλάττουσι καὶ σχηματίζουσιν οἱ βαρυδαίμονες,
δι' ὧν ὁ τῆς ψυχῆς ἐπιτειχισμὸς μετέωρος ἀρθή-
σεται, τὴν αἴσθησιν εἰς ὅρασιν καὶ ἀκοήν, ἔτι δὲ
γεῦσιν ὄσφρησίν τε καὶ ἁφήν, τὸ δὲ πάθος εἰς
ἡδονὴν καὶ ἐπιθυμίαν φόβον τε καὶ λύπην, τό τε
κακιῶν γένος εἰς ἀφροσύνην, ἀκολασίαν, δειλίαν,
ἀδικίαν καὶ ὅσα ἄλλα ἀδελφὰ καὶ συγγενῆ τούτοις.

91   XX. ἤδη δὲ καὶ προσυπερβάλλοντές
τινες οὐ μόνον τὰς αὑτῶν ψυχὰς ἐπὶ ταῦτα ἤλειψαν,
ἀλλὰ καὶ τοὺς ἀμείνους καὶ γένους ὄντας ὁρατικοῦ
βιασάμενοι κατηνάγκασαν πλινθουργεῖν καὶ πόλεις
οἰκοδομεῖν ὀχυρὰς τῷ βασιλεύειν δοκοῦντι νῷ,
βουλόμενοι τοῦτο ἐνδείξασθαι, ὅτι δοῦλον μὲν τὸ
ἀγαθὸν κακοῦ πάθος τ' εὐπαθείας δυνατώτερον,
φρόνησις δὲ καὶ πᾶσα ἀρετὴ ἀφροσύνης καὶ κακίας
ἁπάσης ὑπήκοον, ὡς ὑπηρετεῖν ἐξ ἀνάγκης ἅττ' ἂν
92 προστάττῃ τὸ δεσπόζον. ἰδού, γάρ φησι, καὶ ὁ
ψυχῆς ὀφθαλμὸς ὁ διαυγέστατος καὶ καθαρώτατος
καὶ πάντων ὀξυωπέστατος, ᾧ μόνῳ τὸν θεὸν ἔξεστι
καθορᾶν, ὄνομα Ἰσραήλ, ἐνδεθείς ποτε τοῖς σωματικοῖς Αἰγύπτου δικτύοις ἐπιταγμάτων βαρυ-
τάτων ἀνέχεται, ὡς πλίνθον καὶ πᾶν τὸ γεῶδες
ἐργάζεσθαι μετὰ ἀργαλεωτάτων καὶ ἀτρυτοτάτων
πόνων· ἐφ' οἷς εἰκότως ὀδυνᾶται καὶ στένει, τοῦτο
μόνον ὡς ἐν κακοῖς τεθησαυρισμένος κειμήλιον,
93 ἐκδακρῦσαι τὰ παρόντα· λέγεται γὰρ ὑγιῶς ὅτι
" κατεστέναξαν οἱ υἱοὶ Ἰσραὴλ ἀπὸ τῶν ἔργων."
τίς δ' οὐκ ἂν τῶν εὖ φρονούντων τὰ τῶν πολλῶν
ἀνθρώπων ἰδὼν ἔργα καὶ τὰς ὑπερβαλλούσας
σπουδάς, αἷς ἢ πρὸς ἀργυρισμὸν ἢ δόξαν ἢ τὴν ἐν

ᵃ See App. p. 554.

sense into sight and hearing, and again into taste and smell and touch ; passion into pleasure and lust, and fear and grief; vices in general into folly, profligacy, cowardice, injustice, and the other members of that fraternity and family*—the materials which moulded and shaped, to the misery and sorrow of their builders, will form the fort which towers aloft to menace the soul. XX. Ere now, 91 too, there have been those who went to a further extreme, and not only worked up their own souls to do thus, but have violently forced their betters, the children of the race that has vision, to make bricks under duress and build strong cities (Ex. i. 11) for the mind which thinks itself their sovereign. They wished in this way to shew that good is the slave of evil and passion stronger than the higher emotions, that prudence and every virtue are subject to folly and all vice, and thus must render obedience to every command of the despotic power. " Behold," says the 92 enemy, " the eye of the soul so translucent, so pure, so keen of vision, the eye which alone is permitted to look on God, the eye whose name is Israel, is imprisoned after all in the gross material nets of Egypt and submits to do the bidding of an iron tyranny, to work at brick and every earthy substance with labour painful and unremitting." It is but natural that Israel should sorrow and groan because of them ; for the one solitary thing which he still treasures as a jewel amid his sufferings is that he can weep sore for his present state. There is sound wis- 93 dom in the words, " The children of Israel groaned because of their tasks " (Ex. ii. 23). Which of the wisely-minded, when he sees the tasks which many men endure and the extravagance of the zeal which

59

ἡδοναῖς ἀπόλαυσιν εἰώθασι χρῆσθαι, σφόδρα κατ-
ηφῆσαι καὶ πρὸς τὸν μόνον σωτῆρα θεὸν ἐκβοῆσαι,
[419] ἵνα τὰ | μὲν ἐπικουφίσῃ, λύτρα δὲ καὶ σῶστρα
καταθεὶς τῆς ψυχῆς εἰς ἐλευθερίαν αὐτὴν ἐξέληται·
94 τίς οὖν ἐλευθερία βεβαιοτάτη; τίς; ἡ τοῦ μόνου
θεραπεία σοφοῦ, καθάπερ μαρτυροῦσιν οἱ χρησμοί,
ἐν οἷς εἴρηται " ἐξαπόστειλον τὸν λαόν, ἵνα με
95 θεραπεύῃ." ἴδιον δὲ τῶν τὸ ὂν θερα-
πευόντων οἰνοχόων μὲν ἢ σιτοποιῶν ἢ μαγείρων
ἔργα ἢ ὅσα ἄλλα γεώδη[1] μήτε διαπλάττειν μήτε
συντιθέναι σώματα πλίνθου τρόπον, ἀναβαίνειν δὲ
τοῖς λογισμοῖς πρὸς αἰθέριον ὕψος, Μωυσῆν, τὸ
θεοφιλὲς γένος, προστησαμένους ἡγεμόνα τῆς ὁδοῦ·
96 τότε γὰρ τὸν μὲν τόπον, ὃς δὴ λόγος ἐστί,[2] θεά-
σονται, ᾧ ὁ ἀκλινὴς καὶ ἄτρεπτος θεὸς ἐφέστηκε,
" τὰ δ'[3] ὑπὸ τοὺς πόδας αὐτοῦ, τὸ ὡσεὶ ἔργον
πλίνθου[4] σαπφείρου καὶ ὡς ἂν εἶδος στερεώματος
τοῦ οὐρανοῦ," τὸν αἰσθητὸν κόσμον, ὃν αἰνίττεται

---

[1] Mangey suggests inserting after γεώδη: ⟨ἐπιτηδεύειν⟩
(rather μήτε ἐπιτηδεύειν). This would avoid the zeugma of
associating διαπλάττειν w'th the ἔργα οἰνοχόων.

[2] ὃς δὴ λόγος ἐστί] this is my conjecture for the ὃς δῆλός
ἐστι of all mss. and editions. It is based (1) on De Som.
i. 62, where Philo discussing the three senses in which τόπος
is used declares that one of these is the Divine Logos and
that this is the sense in which it is used in this passage,
Ex. xxiv. 10 (the same idea that τόπος = λόγος appears in
De Op. 20 and De Som. i. 117): (2) on the sequel in § 97,
where the identification of the τόπος ᾧ ὁ θεὸς ἐφέστηκε with
the λόγος is clearly implied. The simple alteration of the
somewhat pointless δῆλος to δὴ λόγος makes this identification,
which otherwise comes in very abruptly, perfectly clear.
The use of δή with the relative constantly recurs in Philo.

[3] Wend. τά θ'—evidently wrongly. The δέ is required to
balance the μέν and to mark the antithesis between the Logos
and the Sensible World.

they commonly put forth to win money or glory or the enjoyment which pleasure give, would not in the exceeding bitterness of his heart cry aloud to God the only Saviour to lighten their tasks and provide a price of the soul's salvation to redeem it into liberty? What then is the liberty which is really 94 sure and stable? Aye, what? It is the service of the only wise Being, as the oracles testify, in which it is said, "Send forth the people that they may serve me" (Ex. viii. 1). But it is the 95 special mark of those who serve the Existent, that theirs are not the tasks of cupbearers or bakers or cooks, or any other tasks of the earth earthy, nor do they mould or fashion material forms like the brick-makers, but in their thoughts ascend to the heavenly height, setting before them Moses, the nature beloved of God, to lead them on the way. For then 96 they shall behold the place [a] which in fact is the Word, where stands God [b] the never changing, never swerving, and also what lies under his feet like "the work of a brick of sapphire, like the form of the firmament of the heaven" [c] (Ex. xxiv. 10), even the world of our senses, which he indicates in this mystery. For it 97

---

[a] LXX. εἶδον τὸν τόπον οὗ εἱστήκει ὁ θεὸς τοῦ Ἰσραήλ. E.V. "They saw the God of Israel."

[b] So, as the sequel shows, rather than "the place on which He stands." This use of ἐφέστηκε with the dative may be paralleled, e.g. ἐπέστη τοῖς κατὰ τὸ Ῥηγίον τόποις, Polybius ix. 7. 10. Perhaps, however, read ἐνέστηκε. In De Som. i. 62 we have the οὗ εἱστήκει of the LXX.

[c] Or perhaps Philo may have taken the words to mean "like a kind of basis for the heaven." Though in De Op. 36 he makes στερέωμα = the heaven, his identification of it here with the αἰσθητὸς κόσμος points to the latter interpretation.

---

[d] πλίνθου] SO LXX.: MSS. λίθου.

97 διὰ τούτων. εὐπρεπὲς γὰρ τοῖς ἑταιρείαν πρὸς
ἐπιστήμην θεμένοις ἐφίεσθαι μὲν τοῦ τὸ ὂν ἰδεῖν,
εἰ δὲ μὴ δύναιντο, τὴν γοῦν εἰκόνα αὐτοῦ, τὸν
ἱερώτατον λόγον, μεθ' ὃν καὶ τὸ ἐν αἰσθητοῖς
τελειότατον ἔργον, τόνδε τὸν κόσμον· τὸ γὰρ
φιλοσοφεῖν οὐδὲν ἦν ἄλλο ἢ ταῦτα σπουδάζειν
98 ἀκριβῶς ἰδεῖν.   XXI. τὸν δὲ αἰσθητὸν
κόσμον ὡς ἂν ὑποπόδιον θεοῦ φησιν εἶναι διὰ τάδε·
πρῶτον μὲν ἵν' ἐπιδείξῃ, ὅτι οὐκ ἐν τῷ γεγονότι
τὸ πεποιηκὸς αἴτιον, ἔπειτα δ' ὑπὲρ τοῦ παραστῆσαι, ὅτι οὐδ' ὁ κόσμος ἅπας ἀφέτῳ καὶ ἀπελευ-
θεριαζούσῃ κινήσει κέχρηται, ἀλλ' ἐπιβέβηκεν ὁ
κυβερνήτης θεὸς τῶν ὅλων οἰακονομῶν[1] καὶ πηδα-
λιουχῶν σωτηρίως τὰ σύμπαντα, οὔτε ποσὶν οὔτε
χερσὶν οὔτε ἄλλῳ τῶν ἐν γενέσει κεχρημένος μέρει
τὸ παράπαν οὐδενὶ κατὰ τὸν ἀληθῆ λόγον—" οὐ
γὰρ ὡς ἄνθρωπος ὁ θεός ”—, ἀλλὰ τὸν ἕνεκα αὐτὸ
μόνον διδασκαλίας εἰσαγόμενον ἡμῶν τῶν ἑαυτοὺς
ἐκβῆναι μὴ δυναμένων, ἀλλ' ἀπὸ τῶν ἡμῖν αὐτοῖς
συμβεβηκότων τὰς περὶ τοῦ ἀγενήτου καταλήψεις
99 λαμβανόντων.   παγκάλως δ' ἔχει τὸ ἐν
παραβολῆς εἴδει φάναι τὸν κόσμον ὡς εἶδος πλίνθου·
δοκεῖ μὲν γὰρ ἑστάναι καὶ βεβηκέναι ὡς ἐκείνη
κατὰ τὰς τῆς αἰσθητῆς ὄψεως προσβολάς, κέχρηται
[420] δὲ ὠκυτάτῃ | κινήσει καὶ τὰς ἐν μέρει πάσας παρα-
100 θεούσῃ. καὶ γὰρ μεθ' ἡμέραν ἡλίου καὶ νύκτωρ
σελήνης φαντασίαν ὡς ἑστώτων οἱ σώματος ὀφθαλμοὶ λαμβάνουσι· καίτοι τίς οὐκ οἶδεν, ὅτι ⟨τὸ⟩ τῆς
περὶ αὐτοὺς φορᾶς τάχος ἀνανταγώνιστόν ἐστιν,
εἴ γε τὸν σύμπαντα οὐρανὸν μιᾷ περιπολοῦσιν

----

[1] mss. οἰκονομῶν.

well befits those who have entered into comradeship with knowledge to desire to see the Existent if they may, but, if they cannot, to see at any rate his image, the most holy Word, and after the Word its most perfect work of all that our senses know, even this world. For by philosophy nothing else has ever been meant, than the earnest desire to see these things exactly as they are. XXI. But when he speaks of the world of our senses as God's footstool, it is for these reasons. First to shew that not in creation is to be found the cause which made it ; secondly to make it plain that even the whole world does not move at its own free unshackled will, but is the standing-ground of God who steers and pilots in safety all that is. And yet to say that He uses hands or feet or any created part at all is not the true account. For God is not as man (Num. xxiii. 19). It is but the form employed merely for our instruction because we cannot get outside ourselves, but frame our conceptions of the Uncreated from our own experience. It is a fine saying when by way of illustration he speaks of the world as an appearance of brick.[a] It does seem to stand fast and firm like a brick as we judge it when our outward sight comes in contact with it,[b] but its actual movement is exceeding swift, outstripping all particular movements. To our bodily eyes the sun by day and the moon by night present the appearance of standing still. Yet we all know that the rapidity of the course on which they are carried is unapproached, since they traverse the whole heaven in a single day.

---

[a] See App. p. 555.
[b] So rather than the " impression produced upon our sight."
Cf. ἡ ὄψις προσβάλλουσα, Quod Deus 78.

ἡμέρᾳ; οὕτως μέντοι καὶ αὐτὸς ὁ σύμπας οὐρανὸς
ἑστάναι δοκῶν περιδινεῖται κύκλῳ, τῆς κινήσεως
τῷ ἀειδεῖ καὶ θειοτέρῳ καταλαμβανομένης[1] τῷ κατὰ
διάνοιαν ὀφθαλμῷ.

101 XXII. Πυροῦντες δὲ τὰς πλίνθους εἰσάγονται
συμβολικῶς, τὰ πάθη καὶ τὰς κακίας θερμῷ καὶ
κινητικωτάτῳ λόγῳ κραταιούμενοι, ὡς μὴ πρὸς
τῶν σοφίας δορυφόρων ποτὲ καθαιρεθεῖεν, οἷς τὰ
πρὸς ἀνατροπὴν αὐτῶν αἰεὶ μηχανήματα συγ-
102 κροτεῖται. διὸ καὶ ἐπιλέγεται '' ἐγένετο αὐτοῖς ἡ
πλίνθος εἰς λίθον.'' τὸ γὰρ μανὸν καὶ κεχυμένον
τῆς μὴ σὺν λόγῳ φορᾶς εἰς ἀντίτυπον καὶ στερεὰν[2]
φύσιν πιληθὲν καὶ πυκνωθὲν λόγοις δυνατοῖς καὶ
ἀποδείξεσιν ἐχυρωτάταις μετέβαλεν, ἀνδρωθείσης
τρόπον τινὰ τῆς τῶν θεωρημάτων καταλήψεως,
ἥτις ἐν ἡλικίᾳ διαρρεῖ παιδικῇ διὰ τὴν τῆς ψυχῆς
ὑγρότητα μήπω δυναμένης τοὺς ἐνσφραγιζομένους
πήττειν καὶ διαφυλάττειν χαρακτῆρας.

103 '' [3]Καὶ ἡ ἄσφαλτος ἦν αὐτοῖς πηλός,'' οὐκ ἔμπαλιν
ὁ πηλὸς ἄσφαλτος· δοκοῦσι μὲν γὰρ οἱ φαῦλοι τὰ
ἀσθενῆ κραταιοῦσθαι κατὰ τῶν ἀμεινόνων καὶ τὰ
διαλυόμενα καὶ ῥέοντα ἐξ αὐτῶν πήττειν, ἵν' ἐπ'
ἐχυροῦ βάλωσι καὶ τοξεύσωσιν ἀρετήν· ὁ δ' ἵλεως
καὶ πατὴρ τῶν καλῶν οὐκ ἐφήσει τὸ δεδμημένον[4]

---

[1] mss. καταλαμβανόμενος.   [2] mss. ἀντιτύπου καὶ στερεᾶς.
[3] Wend. prints τὸ γὰρ μανὸν . . . χαρακτῆρας as a parenthesis,
and treats καὶ ἡ ἄσφαλτος ἦν αὐτοῖς πηλός as a continuation
of the text introduced by διὸ καὶ ἐπιλέγεται. But the words
introduce a totally different thought from that which is given
in §§ 101 and 102. Philo, as often, cites the text without any
λέγεται or φησί.

So too also the whole heaven itself appears to stand still but actually revolves, and this motion is apprehended by the eye which is itself invisible and closer akin to the divine—the eye of the understanding.

XXII. When they are described as using fire with 101 their bricks, it is a symbolical way of saying that they hardened and strengthened their passions and vices by the heat and high pressure of argument, to prevent their ever being demolished by the guards of wisdom, who are ever forging engines to subvert them. And therefore we have the addition, " their 102 brick became stone to them " (Gen. xi. 3). For the looseness and incoherence of the talk which streams along unsupported by reason turns into a solid and resisting substance, when it gains density and compactness through powerful reasonings and convincing demonstrations. The power of apprehending conclusions grows, so to speak, to manhood, whereas in its childhood it is fluid through the humidity of the soul, which is unable as yet to harden and thus retain the impressions which are stamped upon it.

" And the asphalt was clay[a] to them " (ibid.). Not 103 the reverse, their clay was asphalt. The wicked may seem to make the weak cause strong against the better, and to harden the loose stuff which exudes from the weak, to obtain a firm footing from which to shoot their bolts against virtue. But the Father of excellence in His loving-kindness will not suffer the

[a] See App. p. 555.

---

[4] mss. and all editions δεδεμένον. But "bound" is hardly sense. Mangey translates "substructiones," Stein "Gebilde," Yonge "buildings," which suggest that they all took it from δέμω. But this is surely impossible. Possibly we might read δεμόμενον or τόδε τὸ μανὸν.

ἐκνικᾶν[1] εἰς ἀδιάλυτον ἀσφάλειαν, ῥεούσης σπουδῆς μὴ ὑφεστὼς ἔργον ὡς πλαδῶντα πηλὸν ἀναδείξας.[2]

104 εἰ μὲν γὰρ ὁ πηλὸς ἐγένετο[3] ἄσφαλτος, μέχρι παντὸς ἂν ἴσως τὸ ἐν συνεχεῖ ῥύσει γεῶδες αἰσθητὸν εἰς ἀσφαλῆ καὶ ἀμετάβλητον δύναμιν ἐξενίκησεν· ἐπεὶ δὲ τοὐναντίον ἡ ἄσφαλτος εἰς πηλὸν μετέβαλεν, οὐκ ἀθυμητέον· ἐλπὶς γάρ, ἐλπὶς τὰ βέβαια τῆς κακίας ἐρείσματα κράτει θεοῦ

105 διακοπῆναι.   τοιγαροῦν ὁ δίκαιος καὶ ἐν τῷ μεγάλῳ καὶ ἐπαλλήλῳ τοῦ βίου κατακλυσμῷ, μήπω δυνάμενος δίχα αἰσθήσεως ψυχῇ μόνῃ τὰ ὄντα ὄντως ὁρᾶν, " τὴν κιβωτόν," λέγω δὲ τὸ σῶμα, " ἔνδοθέν τε καὶ ἔξωθεν ἀσφάλτῳ " κατα- χρίσει βεβαιούμενος τὰς δι' αὐτοῦ φαντασίας καὶ ἐνεργείας· λωφήσαντος δὲ τοῦ κακοῦ καὶ τῆς φορᾶς ἐπισχούσης ἐξελεύσεται χρησάμενος ἀσωμάτῳ

106 διανοίᾳ πρὸς τὴν ἀληθείας ἀντίληψιν.   ὁ μὲν γὰρ ἀστεῖος ἀπὸ γενέσεως ἀρχῆς φυτευθεὶς καὶ προσαγορευθεὶς τρόπος, ὄνομα Μωυσῆς, ὁ τὸν κόσμον ὡς ἄστυ καὶ πατρίδα οἰκήσας ἅτε κοσμο- πολίτης γενόμενος, ἐνδεθείς ποτε τῷ ἐπαληλιμ- μένῳ ὡς ἂν[4] " ἀσφαλτοπίσσῃ " σώματι καὶ δοκοῦντι

[421] τὰς πάντων ⟨τῶν⟩ | ὑποκειμένων ἐν αἰσθήσει φαν- τασίας ἀσφαλῶς δέχεσθαί τε καὶ κεχωρηκέναι,

---

[1] MSS. ἐκείνων.   [2] MSS. ἀναδεῖξαι.
[3] MSS. γίνεται.   [4] MSS. ἐν.

[a] The word is used here and in § 106 to preserve the obvious play between ἀσφαλής and ἄσφαλτος.

[b] The antithesis intended is that while the Noah-mind in its lower stages, when the sensible world is so absorbing, finds in the ark of the body a source of strength, which it will discard when the stress is past, the higher Moses-mind, which receives the Stoic name of ἀστεῖος from the first, never

platform to reach the condition of cement which defies dissolution, but makes the unsubstantial result of their fluid industry to be but as sloppy clay. For 104 if the clay had become asphalt, what is now a piece of earth in constant flux and perceived only by the outward sense might have won its way in complete triumph to power fast-cemented [a] and irremovable. But since the reverse has come to pass and the asphalt has changed to clay, we must not lose heart, for there is hope, aye hope, that the stout supports of vice may fall beneath the axe of God's might.   So it was with just Noah. In 105 the great ceaseless deluge of life, while he is as yet unable to behold existences as they really are through the soul alone apart from sense, he will " coat the ark," I mean the body, " with asphalt within and without " (Gen. vi. 14), thus strengthening the impressions and activities of which the body is the medium. But when the trouble has abated and the rush of the waters stayed, he will come forth and employ his understanding, free from the body, for the apprehension of truth.   [b] On the other 106 hand the mind called Moses, that goodly plant, given the name of goodly at his very birth (Ex. ii. 2), who in virtue of his larger citizenship took the world for his township and country, weeps bitterly (Ex. ii. 6) in the days when he is imprisoned in the ark of the body bedaubed as with " asphalt-pitch " (Ex. ii. 3), which thinks to receive and contain, as with cement, impressions of all that is presented through sense. He

rests contented with it, but recognizes from the first, that the " asphalt " which serves the body, can never give the real " safety." See further, App. p. 555.

κατακλαίει μὲν τὴν ἔνδεσιν ἀσωμάτου φύσεως
πιεσθεὶς ἔρωτι, κατακλαίει δὲ καὶ τὸν πλάνητα καὶ
τετυφωμένον τῶν πολλῶν ἄθλιον νοῦν, ὃς ψευδοῦς
δόξης ἐκκρεμασθεὶς ᾠήθη τι παρ' ἑαυτῷ βέβαιον
καὶ ἀσφαλὲς ἢ συνόλως παρά τινι τῶν γενομένων
ἄτρεπτον ἱδρῦσθαι, τοῦ παγίως καὶ κατὰ τὰ αὐτὰ
καὶ ὡσαύτως ἔχοντος ἐστηλιτευμένου παρὰ μόνῳ
τῷ θεῷ.

107 XXIII. Τὸ δὲ "δεῦτε καὶ οἰκοδομήσωμεν
ἑαυτοῖς πόλιν καὶ πύργον, οὗ ἡ κεφαλὴ ἔσται ἕως
τοῦ οὐρανοῦ" τοιοῦτον ὑποβάλλει νοῦν· πόλεις ὁ
νομοθέτης οὐχὶ ταύτας μόνον οἴεται εἶναι τὰς ἐπὶ
γῆς δημιουργηθείσας, ὧν εἰσιν ὗλαι λίθοι καὶ ξύλα,
ἀλλὰ καὶ ἃς ἄνθρωποι περιφέρουσι ταῖς ψυχαῖς
108 ἑαυτῶν ἐνιδρυμένας. εἰσὶ δ' αὗται μέν, ὡς εἰκός,
ἀρχέτυποι ἅτε θειοτέρας κατασκευῆς λαχοῦσαι,
ἐκεῖναι δὲ μιμήματα ὡς ἂν ἐκ φθαρτῆς οὐσίας
συνεστῶσαι. διττὸν δὲ πόλεως εἶδος, τὸ μὲν
ἄμεινον, τὸ δὲ χεῖρον, ἄμεινον μὲν τὸ δημοκρατίᾳ
χρώμενον ἰσότητα τιμώσῃ πολιτείᾳ, ἧς ἄρχοντές
εἰσι νόμος καὶ δίκη—θεοῦ δὲ ὕμνος ἡ τοιάδε—,[1]
χεῖρον δὲ τὸ κιβδηλεῦον αὐτήν, ὡς τὸ παράσημον
καὶ παρακεκομμένον ἐν νομίσμασιν, ὀχλοκρατία,
ἣ θαυμάζει τὸ ἄνισον, ἐν ᾗ ἀδικία καὶ ἀνομία
109 καταδυναστεύουσιν. ἐγγράφονται δ' οἱ μὲν ἀστεῖοι

---

[1] I cannot think that the phrase θεοῦ δὲ ὕμνος ἡ τοιάδε is
right. And Cohn's and Wend.'s suggestions of (1) εὐνομωτάτη
δ', (2) θεοῦ δ' ὕπαδος, (3) εὐδόκιμος seem to me quite wild.
The only variants in the mss. are ἤτοι ᾄδεται and ἡ τοιαιδέτε
for ἡ τοιάδε. From this I conjecture θεοῦ δ' ⟨ἐν⟩ ὕμνο⟨ι⟩ς ἡ
τοιάδε ᾄδεται, i.e. such a soul-city or such a πολιτεία is called in
the Psalms God's (city). I understand Philo to be alluding
to the use of the phrase "the city of God" in Ps. xlvi. 4 and

weeps for his captivity, pressed sore by his yearning for a nature that knows no body. He weeps also for the mind of the multitude, so erring, so vanity-ridden, so miserable—the mind which clings to false opinion and thinks that itself, or any created being at all, possesses aught that is firm, fast-cemented and immutably established, whereas all that is fixed and permanent in circumstances and condition is graven as on stone in the keeping of God alone.

XXIII. The words, " Come, let us build for our- 107 selves a city and a tower whose head shall be unto heaven," suggest such thoughts as these. The lawgiver thinks that besides those cities which are built by men's hands upon the earth, of which the materials are stones and timber, there are others, even those which men carry about established in their souls. Naturally these last are models or archetypes, for 108 the workmanship bestowed upon them is of a more divine kind, while the former are copies composed of perishing material. Of the soul-city there are two kinds, one better, .the other worse. The better adopts as its constitution democracy,[a] which honours equality and has law and justice for its rulers—such a one is as a melody which sings God's praises. The worse, which corrupts and adulterates the better, as the false counterfeit coin corrupts the currency, is mob-rule, which takes inequality for its ideal, and in it injustice and lawlessness are paramount. The 109

[a] For Philo's conception of democracy see note on *Quod Deus* 176.

---

lxxxvii. 3. To interpret the phrase as meaning a just soul or a just condition of civic life is as natural for him as for a Christian to apply it to the Church. Philo regularly quotes the Psalms with the words ἐν ὕμνοις, as *e.g.* above 52, *De Som.* ii. 242 ἐπεὶ καὶ ἐν ὕμνοις ᾄδεται. See also App. p. 555.

69

τῷ τῆς προτέρας πολιτεύματι, τῶν δὲ φαύλων ἡ
πληθὺς τὴν ἑτέραν καὶ χείρω διέζωσται, πρὸ
εὐκοσμίας ἀκοσμίαν καὶ σύγχυσιν πρὸ εὐσταθοῦς
110 καταστάσεως ἀγαπῶσα.   συνεργοῖς δὲ ὁ
ἄφρων ἀξιοῖ πρὸς τὸ ἁμαρτάνειν οὐκ ἀρκούμενος
αὑτῷ μόνῳ χρῆσθαι, καὶ προτρέπει μὲν ὄρασιν,
προτρέπει δὲ ἀκοήν, παρακαλεῖ δὲ πᾶσαν αἴσθησιν
ἀνυπερθέτως αὑτῷ συντετάχθαι, φερούσης ἑκάστης
τὰ πρὸς ὑπηρεσίαν ἐπιτήδεια πάντα· ἐπαίρει μέντοι
καὶ παραθήγει καὶ τὸ ἄλλο ἀτίθασον ἐκ φύσεως
τῶν παθῶν στῖφος, ἵνα ἄσκησιν καὶ μελέτην προσ-
111 λαβὸν ἀνύποιστον γένηται. τούτους οὖν καλέσας
τοὺς συμμάχους ὁ νοῦς[1] φησιν· " οἰκοδομήσωμεν
ἑαυτοῖς πόλιν," ἴσον τῷ ὀχυρωσώμεθα τὰ οἰκεῖα
καὶ φραξώμεθα δυνατῶς, ὡς μὴ πρὸς τῶν κατα-
τρεχόντων εὐμαρῶς ἁλισκώμεθα[2]· διέλωμεν καὶ δια-
νείμωμεν ὥσπερ κατὰ φυλὰς καὶ δήμους ἑκάστας
τῶν ἐν ψυχῇ δυνάμεων προσκληρώσαντες τὰς μὲν
112 λογικῇ, τὰς δὲ ἀλόγῳ μερίδι· ἄρχοντας ἑλώμεθα
τοὺς ἱκανοὺς πλοῦτον, δόξαν, τιμάς, ἡδονὰς ἀφ'
ὧν ἂν δύνωνται περιποιεῖν ἁπάντων· τὴν πενίας
καὶ ἀδοξίας αἰτίαν δικαιοσύνην τιθεμένους ἐκποδὼν
γράφωμεν νόμους, οἳ τὸ τοῦ κρείττονος συμφέρον
βεβαιώσουσι τοῖς πλέον ἑτέρων αἰεὶ φέρεσθαι δυνα-
113 μένοις. " πύργος " δ' ὡς ἂν ἀκρόπολις κατ-
[422] εσκευάσθω τῇ | τυράννῳ κακίᾳ βασίλειον ὀχυρώ-
τατον, ἧς οἱ μὲν πόδες ἐπὶ γῆς βαινέτωσαν, ἡ δὲ
κεφαλὴ πρὸς οὐρανὸν φθανέτω τοσοῦτον ὑπὸ
114 μεγαλαυχίας ὕψος ἐπιβᾶσα.   τῷ γὰρ

---

[1] I conjecture ὁ ἄνους. See App. p. 555.
[2] mss. ἁλισκοίμεθα.

---

[a] Lit. " have girded themselves with."

good have their names entered on the burgess-roll of the former type of state, but the multitude of the wicked are embraced under[a] the second and baser type, for they love disorder rather than order, confusion rather than fixedness and stability.

The fool not content with using himself alone thinks 110 fit to use fellow-workers in sin. He calls upon the sight and the hearing and invokes every sense to range itself beside him without delay, each bringing all the instruments that are needed for the service. And further he spurs and incites that other company, the company of the passions, to put their untutored nature under training and practice and thus render themselves resistless. These allies, then, the 111 mind summons, saying, " Let us build ourselves a city," which means, " Let us fortify our resources and fence them in with strength, that we may not fall easy victims to the onset of the foe. Let us mete out and distribute the several powers of the soul as by wards and tithings, allotting some to the reasoning and some to the unreasoning portion. Let us 112 choose for our magistrates such as are able to provide wealth, reputation, honours, pleasures, from every source available to them. Let us enact laws which shall eject from our community the justice whose product is poverty and disrepute—laws which shall assure the emoluments of the stronger to the succession of those whose powers of acquisition are greater than others. And let a tower be built[b] as a 113 citadel, as a royal and impregnable castle for the despot vice. Let its feet walk upon the earth and its head reach to heaven, carried by our vaulting ambition to that vast height."   For in fact 114

[b] Or (if the perfect is to be emphasized) " stand complete."

ὄντι οὐ μόνον ἐπὶ τῶν ἀνθρωπείων ἀδικημάτων
ἵσταται, μετατρέχει δὲ καὶ τὰ ὀλύμπια τοὺς
ἀσεβείας καὶ ἀθεότητος λόγους προτείνουσα, ἐπειδὰν ἢ ὡς οὐκ ἔστι τὸ θεῖον διεξίῃ, ἢ ὡς ὂν τὸ
προνοεῖ, ἢ ὡς ὁ κόσμος οὔποτε γενέσεως ἔλαβεν
ἀρχήν, ἢ ὡς γενόμενος ἀστάτοις αἰτίαις ὡς ἂν
τύχῃ φέρεται, ποτὲ μὲν πλημμελῶς, ποτὲ δὲ οὐχ
ὑπαιτίως, καθάπερ ἐπὶ πλοίων καὶ τεθρίππων εἴωθε
115 γίνεσθαι· φιλεῖ γὰρ ἔστιν ὅτε χωρὶς ἡνιόχων τε καὶ
κυβερνητῶν ὅ τε πλοῦς καὶ ὁ δρόμος εὐθύνεσθαι·
προνοίας δ' οὐ τὸ ὀλιγάκις, ἀλλὰ τῆς μὲν ἀνθρωπίνης πολλάκις, τῆς δὲ θείας ἀδιαστάτως αἰεὶ
κατορθοῦν, ἐπεὶ τὸ διαμαρτάνειν ἀλλότριον ἀνωμολόγηται θείας δυνάμεως.   κατασκευά-
ζουσι μέντοι συμβολικῶς ὡσανεὶ πύργον τὸν περὶ
κακίας λόγον οἱ φρενοβλαβεῖς, τί βουλόμενοι ἢ
ὄνομα αὐτῶν ὑπολείπεσθαι τὸ δυσώνυμον; XXIV.
116 λέγουσι γάρ· '' ποιήσωμεν ἑαυτῶν ὄνομα.'' ὦ περιτ-
τῆς καὶ κεχυμένης ἀναισχυντίας. τί φατε; νυκτὶ
καὶ βαθεῖ σκότῳ τὰ ἑαυτῶν ἀδικήματα συγκρύπτειν
ὀφείλοντες καὶ προκάλυμμα αὐτῶν, εἰ καὶ μὴ τὴν
ἀληθῆ, τὴν γοῦν προσποίητον αἰδῶ πεποιῆσθαι ἢ
χάριτος ἕνεκα τῆς πρὸς τοὺς ἐπιεικεστέρους ἢ
διαδύσεως τῶν ἐφ' ὁμολογουμένοις ἁμαρτήμασι
τιμωριῶν, τοσοῦτον τῆς τόλμης ἐπιβαίνετε, ὥστε
οὐ μόνον[1] πρὸς φῶς καὶ λαμπρότατον ἥλιον ἐναυγά-
ζεσθε[2] μήτε τὰς ἀνθρώπων τῶν ἀμεινόνων ἀπειλὰς
μήτε τὰς ἀπαραιτήτους ἐκ θεοῦ δίκας τοῖς οὕτως

---

[1] mss. μόνον οὐ.
[2] mss. ἐναυγάζεσθαι, which might be kept as depending
on ἀξιοῦτε.

[a] See note on *De Ebr.* 199.

that tower not only has human misdeeds for its base, but it seeks to rise to the region of celestial things, with the arguments of impiety and godlessness in its van. Such are its pronouncements,[a] either that the Deity does not exist, or that it exists but does not exert providence, or that the world had no beginning in which it was created, or that though created its course is under the sway of varying and random causation, sometimes leading it amiss, though sometimes no fault can be found. For this last an analogy is often seen in ships and chariots. For the course of **115** the one on the water and of the other on land often goes straight without helmsman or charioteer. But providence demands, they say, more than a rare and occasional success. Human providence frequently achieves its purpose, the divine should do so always and without exception, since error is admitted to be inconsistent with divine power.[b]

Further, when these victims of delusion build up under the symbol of a tower their argument of vice, what is their object but to leave a record of their ill-savoured name ? XXIV. For they say, " let us make **116** our name." What monstrous and extravagant shamelessness ! What is this you say ? You ought to be hiding your misdeeds in night and profound darkness, and to have taken, if not true shame, at least the simulation of it to veil them, whether to keep the goodwill of the more decent sort, or to escape the punishments which wait on open sins. Instead, to such a pitch of impudent hardihood have you come, that you not only let the full sunlight shine upon you and fear neither the threats of better men, nor the inexorable judgements of God, which

[b] See App. p. 556.

ἀνοσιουργοῖς ἀπαντωμένας καταδείσαντες, ἀλλὰ
καὶ πανταχόσε φήμας ἀγγέλους τῶν οἰκείων ἀδικημάτων περιπέμπειν ἀξιοῦτε, ὡς μηδεὶς ἀμύητος
μηδ' ἀνήκοος γένοιτο τῶν ὑμετέρων, ὦ σχέτλιοι
117 καὶ παμμίαροι, τολμημάτων.   ὀνόματος
οὖν ποίου γλίχεσθε; ἢ τοῦ τοῖς πραττομένοις
οἰκειοτάτου; ἆρ' οὖν ἕν ἐστι μόνον; γένει μὲν
ἴσως ἕν, μυρία δὲ τοῖς εἴδεσιν, ἅ, κἂν ἡσυχάζητε,
ἑτέρων λεγόντων ἀκούσεσθε· προπέτεια τοίνυν ἐστὶ
μετὰ ἀναισχυντίας, ὕβρις μετὰ βίας, βία μετὰ
ἀνδροφονίας, σὺν μοιχείαις φθοραί, σὺν ἀμέτροις
ἡδοναῖς ἀόριστος ἐπιθυμία, μετὰ θράσους ἀπόνοια,
μετὰ πανουργίας ἀδικία, κλοπαὶ μετὰ ἁρπαγῆς,
σὺν ψευδολογίαις ψευδορκίαι, μετὰ παρανομιῶν
ἀσέβειαι. ταῦτα καὶ τὰ παραπλήσια τῶν τοιούτων
118 ἔστ' ὀνόματα. καλὸν γ' ἐναυχῆσαι κἀπισεμνύνε-
σθαι δόξαν θηρωμένους τὴν ἀπὸ τούτων, ἐφ' οἷς
εἰκὸς ἦν ἐγκαλύπτεσθαι.   καὶ μὴν ἔνιοι
μέγα φρονοῦσιν ἐπὶ τούτοις, ὡς ἄμαχόν τινα ἰσχὺν
[423] ἐκ τοῦ τοιοῦτοι[1] | νομισθῆναι παρὰ πᾶσι καρπωσά-
μενοι, οὓς τοῦ πολλοῦ θράσους ἡ ὀπαδὸς τοῦ θεοῦ
δίκη τίσεται καίτοι τάχα τὸν οἰκεῖον οὐ μαντευο-
μένους μόνον, ἀλλὰ καὶ προορωμένους ὄλεθρον·
φασὶ γάρ· "πρὶν διασπαρῆναι," φροντίσωμεν ὀνό-
119 ματός τε καὶ δόξης. οὐκοῦν, εἴποιμ' ἂν αὐτοῖς,
ὅτι σκεδασθήσεσθε γινώσκετε; τί οὖν ἁμαρτάνετε;
ἀλλὰ μήποτε τὸν τρόπον τῶν ἀφρόνων διασυνίστησιν, οἳ καίτοι μεγίστων ἐπικρεμαμένων οὐκ

---

[1] mss. τοιοῦτον. Mangey and Wend. τοιούτους. But the
ordinary usage of Greek demands the nominative when
referring to the subject of the main verb, and this is usually,
if not always, followed by Philo, e.g. ἀδικοῦντες 120.

confront the authors of such unholy deeds, but you also deliberately send to every part rumours to report the misdeeds of which you yourselves are guilty, that none may fail to learn and hear the story of your shameless crimes. O wretched, utter miscreants !

What sort of name, then, do you desire ? Is it the 117 name that best befits your deeds ? Is it one name only ? One general name perhaps, but a thousand specific ones, which you will hear from the lips of others even if your own are silent. Recklessness with shamelessness, insolence with violence, violence with murder, seductions with adulteries, unbridled lust with unmeasured pleasures, desperation with foolhardiness, injustice with knavery, thefts with robbery, perjuries with falsehoods, impieties with lawbreakings, these and the like are the names for such deeds as yours. It is indeed a fine cause for pride 118 and boasting, when you pursue so eagerly the repute which these names give, names at which you should in all reason hide your heads for shame.

With some indeed their pride in these names comes from the belief that they have gained invincible strength by the fact that all men think them such, and these God's minister Justice will punish for their great audacity. Though perhaps they have not merely a presentiment, but a clear foresight of their own destruction. For they say, " before we are dispersed " (Gen. xi. 4) let us take thought for our name and glory. Do you then know, I would say to 119 them, that you will be scattered ? Why then do you sin ? But surely it bespeaks the mind of fools that they do not shrink from iniquity, though the gravest

ἀδήλως ἀλλ' ἐκ τοῦ φανεροῦ πολλάκις τιμωριῶν
ἀδικεῖν ὅμως οὐκ ὀκνοῦσι· γνωριμώταται δ' εἰσὶν
αἱ τιμωρίαι ἀδηλοῦσθαι νομισθεῖσαι, ἃς ἐκ θεοῦ
120 κατασκήπτειν συμβέβηκε. πάντες γὰρ οἱ φαυλότατοι λαμβάνουσιν ἐννοίας περὶ τοῦ μὴ λήσειν τὸ
θεῖον ἀδικοῦντες μηδὲ τὸ δίκην ὑφέξειν εἰσάπαν
121 ἰσχῦσαι διακρούσασθαι· ἐπεὶ πόθεν ἴσασιν, ὅτι
σκεδασθήσονται; καὶ μὴν λέγουσι "πρὶν ἡμᾶς
διασπαρῆναι"· ἀλλὰ τὸ συνειδὸς ἔνδοθεν ἐλέγχει
καὶ σφόδρα ἐπιτηδεύοντας ἀθεότητα κεντεῖ, ὡς
ἄκοντας εἰς συναίνεσιν ἐπισπάσασθαι περὶ τοῦ
τὰ κατ' ἀνθρώπους πάντα πρὸς ἀμείνονος φύσεως
ἐφορᾶσθαι καὶ δίκην ἐφεστάναι τιμωρὸν ἀδέκαστον,
ἀσεβῶν πράξεις ἐχθραίνουσαν ἀδίκους καὶ λόγους
122 τοὺς συνηγόρους αὐταῖς.   XXV. ἀλλ'
εἰσὶν ἀπόγονοι πάντες οὗτοι τῆς αἰεὶ μὲν ἀπο-
θνῃσκούσης, μηδέποτε δὲ τεθνηκυίας μοχθηρίας,
ἧς Κάιν ἐστιν ὄνομα. ἢ οὐχὶ καὶ ὁ Κάιν υἱὸν
γεννήσας, ὃν Ἐνὼχ ἐκάλεσεν, ὁμώνυμον αὐτῷ
[καὶ] κτίζων εἰσάγεται πόλιν καὶ τρόπον τινὰ τὰ
γενητὰ καὶ θνητὰ οἰκοδομῶν ἐπὶ τῇ τῶν θειοτέρας
123 κατασκευῆς λαχόντων ἀνατροπῇ; ὁ γὰρ Ἐνὼχ
ἑρμηνεύεται χάρις σου· τῶν δ' ἀνοσίων ἕκαστος
διάνοιαν μὲν ἡγεῖται χαρίζεσθαι ἑαυτῷ τάς τε
καταλήψεις καὶ διανοήσεις, ὀφθαλμοὺς δὲ τὸ
βλέπειν καὶ ἀκούειν ὦτα καὶ μυκτῆρας ὀσφραίνεσθαι, καὶ τὰς ἄλλας αἰσθήσεις τὰ οἰκεῖα ἑαυταῖς,
ἔτι μέντοι καὶ τὰ φωνῆς ὄργανα τὸ λέγειν, θεὸν δὲ

ᵃ This conception of wickedness as being in one sense
immortal, though at the same time a perpetual process of
dying to the true life, is Philo's interpretation of the sign
given to Cain that no one should kill him (Gen. iv. 15),

penalties often menace them, openly and not obscurely. The punishments of God's visitation may be thought to be hidden from our sight, but they are really well known. For all, however wicked, receive 120 some general notions to the effect that their iniquity will not pass unseen by God, and that they cannot altogether evade the necessity of being brought to judgement. Otherwise how do they know that they 121 will be scattered ? They certainly do say, " before we are dispersed." But it is the conscience within which convicts them and pricks them in spite of the exceeding godlessness of their lives, thus drawing them on reluctantly to assent to the truth that all human doings are surveyed by a superior being and that there awaits them an incorruptible avenger, even justice, who hates the unjust deeds of the impious and the arguments which advocate those deeds.

XXV. But all these are descended from the depravity 122 which is ever dying and never dead, whose name is Cain.[a] Is not Cain, when he had begotten a son whom he called Enoch, described as founding a city to bear his son's name (Gen. iv. 17), and thus in a sense raising a building of created and mortal things to subvert those to which has fallen the honour to be the work of a diviner architect ? For Enoch is by 123 interpretation " thy gift," and each of the unholy thinks that his understanding gives him his apprehension and reflections, that his eyes give him sight, his ears hearing, his nostrils smell, and the other senses the functions that belong to themselves severally, and again that the vocal organs give him speech, but God, he thinks, is either not the cause in any sense

coupled with the absence of any mention of his death in Genesis. *Cf. Quod Det.* 177, *De Fuga* 60.

ἢ μὴ συνόλως ἢ μὴ ὡς πρῶτον αἴτιον [ὄν].[1]

124 διὰ τοῦτο καὶ ὧν ἐγεωπόνησε τὰς ἀπαρχὰς[2] ἑαυτῷ
ταμιεύεται, καρποὺς δὲ αὐτὸ μόνον αὖθις προσ-
ενεγκεῖν θεῷ λέγεται καίτοι παραδείγματος ὑγιοῦς
ἐγγὺς ἑστῶτος· ὁ γὰρ ἀδελφὸς αὐτοῦ τὰ πρωτότοκα, οὐ τὰ δεύτερα τῆς ποίμνης ἔκγονα ἱερουργεῖ,
τὰς τῶν γινομένων πρεσβυτέρας αἰτίας κατὰ τὸ
πρεσβύτατον τῶν αἰτίων ὁμολογῶν συνίστασθαι.

125 τῷ δ' ἀσεβεῖ τοὐναντίον δοκεῖ, αὐτοκράτορα μὲν
εἶναι τὸν νοῦν ὧν βουλεύεται, αὐτοκράτορα δὲ καὶ
τὴν αἴσθησιν ὧν αἰσθάνεται· δικάζειν γὰρ ἀνυπαιτίως καὶ ἀψευδῶς τὴν μὲν τὰ σώματα, τὸν δὲ
126 πάντα.   τούτων δὲ τί | ἂν γένοιτο ἐπιληπτότερον
[424] ἢ μᾶλλον ὑπὸ τῆς ἀληθείας ἐλεγχόμενον; ἢ οὐχὶ
καὶ ὁ νοῦς πολλάκις ἐπὶ μυρίων ὅσων ἠλέγχθη
παρανοῶν, καὶ αἱ αἰσθήσεις ἅπασαι ψευδομαρ-
τυριῶν ἑάλωσαν οὐ παρ' ἀλόγοις δικασταῖς, οὓς
εἰκὸς ἀπατᾶσθαι, ἀλλ' ἐν τῷ τῆς φύσεως αὐτῆς
127 δικαστηρίῳ, ἣν οὐ θέμις δεκάζεσθαι; καὶ μὴν
σφαλλομένων γε τῶν καθ' ἡμᾶς αὐτοὺς περί τε
νοῦν καὶ αἴσθησιν κριτηρίων ἀνάγκη τἀκόλουθον
ὁμολογεῖν, ὅτι ὁ θεὸς τῷ μὲν τὰς ἐννοίας, τῇ δὲ
τὰς ἀντιλήψεις ἐπομβρεῖ, καὶ ἔστιν οὐ τῶν καθ'
ἡμᾶς μερῶν χάρις τὰ γινόμενα, ἀλλὰ τοῦ δι' ὃν
καὶ ἡμεῖς γεγόναμεν δωρεαὶ πᾶσαι.

128 XXVI. τὸν φιλαυτίας κλῆρον παραλαβόντες παῖδες
παρὰ πατρὸς συναυξῆσαι γλίχονται μέχρις οὐρανοῦ,
ἕως ἂν ἡ φιλάρετός τε καὶ μισοπόνηρος δίκη

---

[1] Or perhaps ὄντα.   [2] mss. ἀρχὰς.

[a] See App. p. 556.
[b] Or "to whom also we owe our very being." δι' ὃν seems

or not the first cause.   And therefore 124
Cain retained in his own keeping the firstlings of the
fruits of his husbandry and offered, as we are told,
merely the fruits at a later time, although he had
beside him a wholesome example. For his brother
brought to the altar the first-born younglings of the
flock, not the after-born, thus confessing that even
the causes which come higher in the chain of causation[a] owe their existence to the Cause which is highest
and first of all. The impious man thinks the opposite, 125
that the mind has sovereign power over what it
plans, and sense over what it perceives. He holds
that the latter judges material things and the former
all things, and that both are free from fault or error.
And yet what could be more blameworthy or more 126
clearly convicted of falsehood by the truth than these
beliefs ? Is not the mind constantly convicted of
delusion on numberless points, and all the senses
judged guilty of false witness, not before unreasoning
judges who may easily be deceived, but at the bar
of nature herself whom it is fundamentally impossible
to corrupt ? And surely if the means of judgement 127
within us, supplied by mind and sense, are capable
of error, we must admit the logical consequence,
that it is God who showers conceptions on the mind
and perceptions on sense, and that what comes into
being is no gift of any part of ourselves, but all are
bestowed by Him, through whom we too have been
made.[b]   XXVI. Having received from 128
their father self-love as their portion, his children
desire to add to it and raise it heaven high, until
Justice who loves virtue and hates evil comes to the

here to differ little from δι' οὗ. It thinks of God as the
cause rather than as the maker.

παρελθοῦσα καθέλῃ τὰς πόλεις, ἃς ἐπετείχισαν
ψυχῇ τῇ ταλαίνῃ, καὶ τὸν πύργον, οὗ τοὔνομα ἐν
τῇ τῶν κριμάτων[1] ἀναγραφομένῃ βίβλῳ δεδήλωται.
129 ἔστι δὲ ὡς μὲν Ἑβραῖοι λέγουσι Φανουήλ, ὡς δὲ
ἡμεῖς ἀποστροφὴ θεοῦ· τὸ γὰρ κατεσκευασμένον
ὀχύρωμα διὰ τῆς τῶν λόγων πιθανότητος οὐδενὸς
ἕνεκα ἑτέρου κατεσκευάζετο ἢ τοῦ μετατραπῆναι
καὶ μετακλιθῆναι διάνοιαν ἀπὸ τῆς τοῦ θεοῦ τιμῆς·
130 οὗ τί ἂν γένοιτο ἀδικώτερον; ἀλλὰ πρός γε τὴν
τοῦ ὀχυρώματος τούτου καθαίρεσιν ὁ πειρατὴς τῆς
ἀδικίας καὶ φονῶν[2] αἰεὶ κατ' αὐτῆς εὐτρέπισται, ὃν
Ἑβραῖοι καλοῦσι Γεδεών, ὃς ἑρμηνεύεται πειρα-
τήριον· " ὤμοσε " γάρ φησι " Γεδεὼν τοῖς ἀνδράσι
Φανουὴλ λέγων· ἐν τῷ με ἐπιστρέφειν μετ' εἰρήνης
131 τὸν πύργον τοῦτον κατασκάψω." πάγκαλον καὶ
πρεπωδέστατον αὔχημα μισοπονήρῳ ψυχῇ κατὰ
ἀσεβῶν ἠκονημένη τὸ βεβαιοῦσθαι καθαιρήσειν
πάντα λόγον ἀποστρέφειν διάνοιαν ὁσιότητος ἀνα-
πείθοντα. καὶ πέφυκεν οὕτως ἔχειν· ὅταν γὰρ ὁ
νοῦς ἐπιστρέψῃ, τὸ ἀποκλῖνον καὶ ἀποστρεφόμενον
132 αὐτοῦ πᾶν[3] λύεται. τούτου δὲ καιρός ἐστι τῆς
καθαιρέσεως, τὸ παραδοξότατον, ᾗ φησιν, οὐ
πόλεμος, ἀλλ' εἰρήνη· διανοίας γὰρ εὐσταθείᾳ καὶ
ἠρεμίᾳ, ἣν εὐσέβεια γεννᾶν πέφυκεν, ἀνατρέπεται
πᾶς λόγος, ὃν ἐδημιούργησεν ἀσέβεια.
133 πολλοὶ καὶ τὰς αἰσθήσεις πύργου τινὰ τρόπον ἐπὶ
τοσοῦτον ἤγειραν, ὡς ἅψασθαι τῶν οὐρανοῦ περά-
των· οὐρανὸς δὲ συμβολικῶς ὁ νοῦς ἡμῶν ἐστι,

---

[1] Perhaps a slip for κριτῶν.

[2] MSS. φρονῶν.   [3] MSS. πάλιν.

---

[a] This is of course what the LXX. means by ἐπιστρέφειν.

aid. She razes to the ground the cities which they fortified to menace the unhappy soul, and the tower whose name is explained in the book of Judges. That name is in the Hebrew tongue Penuel, but in 129 our own "turning from God." For the stronghold which was built through persuasiveness of argument was built solely for the purpose of diverting and deflecting the mind from honouring God. And what greater sin against justice could there be than this ? But there stands ready armed for the destruction of 130 this stronghold the robber who despoils injustice and ever breathes slaughter against her, whom the Hebrews call Gideon, which is interpreted the "Robbers' Hold." Gideon swore, we read, to the men of Penuel saying, "When I return with peace I will demolish this tower" (Jud. viii. 9). A grand 131 boast, most fitting to the evil-hating soul whose edge has been made sharp against the impious, that it receives the strength to pull down every argument which would persuade the mind to turn away from holiness. And the words are true to nature, for when the mind "returns," [a] all in it that was starting aside or turning away is brought to nothing. And the fit 132 time for destruction of this, though clean contrary to expectation, is, as Gideon says, not war but peace. For it is through that stability and tranquillity of understanding, which it is the nature of piety to engender, that every argument is overturned which impiety has wrought. Many too have 133 exalted their senses, as though they were a tower, so that they touch the boundaries of heaven, that is symbolically our mind, wherein range and dwell

Philo perhaps gives it the sense of "turns round," "is converted."

καθ' ὃν αἱ ἄρισται καὶ θεῖαι φύσεις περιπολοῦσιν.
οἱ δὲ ταῦτα τολμῶντες αἴσθησιν μὲν διανοίας προ-
κρίνουσιν, ἀξιοῦσι δὲ καὶ διὰ τῶν αἰσθητῶν τὰ
νοητὰ πάντα ἑλεῖν ἀνὰ κράτος, εἰς μὲν δούλων τάξιν
τὰ δεσπόζοντα, εἰς δὲ ἡγεμόνων τὰ φύσει δοῦλα
μεθαρμόσασθαι βιαζόμενοι.

134
[425]

XXVII. | Τὸ δέ, " κατέβη κύριος ἰδεῖν τὴν πόλιν
καὶ τὸν πύργον " τροπικώτερον πάντως ἀκουστέον·
προσιέναι γὰρ ἢ ἀπιέναι ἢ κατιέναι ἢ τοὐναντίον
<ἀν>έρχεσθαι ἢ συνόλως τὰς αὐτὰς τοῖς κατὰ μέρος
ζῴοις σχέσεις καὶ κινήσεις ἴσχεσθαι καὶ κινεῖσθαι
τὸ θεῖον ὑπολαμβάνειν ὑπερωκεάνιος καὶ μετα-
135 κόσμιος, ὡς ἔπος εἰπεῖν, ἐστὶν ἀσέβεια. ταῦτα δὲ
ἀνθρωπολογεῖται παρὰ τῷ νομοθέτῃ περὶ τοῦ μὴ
ἀνθρωπομόρφου θεοῦ διὰ τὰς τῶν παιδευομένων
ἡμῶν, ὡς πολλάκις ἐν ἑτέροις εἶπον, ὠφελείας.
ἐπεὶ τίς οὐκ οἶδεν ὅτι τῷ κατιόντι τὸν μὲν ἀπολεί-
136 πειν, τὸν δὲ ἐπιλαμβάνειν τόπον ἀναγκαῖον; ὑπὸ
δὲ τοῦ θεοῦ πεπλήρωται τὰ πάντα, περιέχοντος, οὐ
περιεχομένου, ᾧ πανταχοῦ τε καὶ οὐδαμοῦ συμβέβηκεν εἶναι μόνῳ· οὐδαμοῦ μέν, ὅτι καὶ χώραν
καὶ τόπον αὐτὸς τοῖς σώμασι συγγεγέννηκε, τὸ δὲ
πεποιηκὸς ἐν οὐδενὶ τῶν γεγονότων θέμις εἰπεῖν
περιέχεσθαι, πανταχοῦ δέ, ὅτι τὰς δυνάμεις αὐτοῦ
διὰ γῆς καὶ ὕδατος ἀέρος τε καὶ οὐρανοῦ τείνας
μέρος οὐδὲν ἔρημον ἀπολέλοιπε τοῦ κόσμου, πάντα
δὲ συναγαγὼν διὰ πάντων ἀοράτοις ἔσφιγξε δεσ-

those divine forms of being which excel all others. They who do not shrink from this give the preference to sense rather than understanding. They would use perceptible things to subdue and capture the world of things intelligible, thus forcing the two to change places, the one to pass from mastery to slavery, the other from its natural servitude to dominance.

XXVII. The words, " the Lord came down to see 134 the city and the tower " (Gen. xi. 5), must certainly be understood in a figurative sense. For to suppose that the Deity approaches or departs, goes down or goes up, or in general remains stationary or puts Himself in motion, as particular living creatures do, is an impiety which may be said to transcend the bounds of ocean or of the universe itself. No, as I 135 have often said elsewhere, the lawgiver is applying human terms to the superhuman God, to help us, his pupils, to learn our lesson. For we all know that when a person comes down he must leave one place and occupy another. But God fills all things ; He 136 contains but is not contained. To be everywhere and nowhere is His property and His alone. He is nowhere, because He Himself created space and place coincidently with material things, and it is against all right principle to say that the Maker is contained in anything that He has made. He is everywhere, because He has made His powers extend through earth and water, air and heaven, and left no part of the universe without His presence, and uniting all

PHILO

μοῖς, ἵνα μή ποτε λυθείη, οὗ χάριν μελετήσας ὦ[1]
137 * * *. τὸ μὲν γὰρ ὑπεράνω τῶν δυνάμεων ὂν
ἐπινοεῖται περιττεύειν, οὐ * * * κατὰ τὸ εἶναι
μόνον[2]· τούτου δύναμις δέ, καθ' ἣν ἔθηκε καὶ
διετάξατο τὰ πάντα, κέκληται μὲν ἐτύμως θεός,
ἐγκεκόλπισται δὲ τὰ ὅλα καὶ διὰ τῶν τοῦ παντὸς
138 μερῶν διελήλυθε. τὸ δὲ θεῖον καὶ ἀόρατον καὶ
ἀκατάληπτον καὶ πανταχοῦ ὂν ὁρατόν τε καὶ καταληπτὸν οὐδαμοῦ πρὸς ἀλήθειάν ἐστιν * * * " ὧδε
στὰς ἐγὼ πρὸ τοῦ σέ,"[3] δείκνυσθαι καὶ καταλαμβάνεσθαι δοκῶν, πρὸ πάσης δείξεως καὶ φαντασίας
139 ὑπερβαλὼν τὰ γεγονότα. τῶν οὖν μεταβατικῆς
κινήσεως ὀνομάτων οὐδὲν ἐφαρμόττει τῷ κατὰ
τὸ εἶναι θεῷ, τὸ ἄνω, τὸ κάτω, τὸ ἐπὶ δεξιά, τὸ
ἐπ' εὐώνυμα, τὸ πρόσω, τὸ κατόπιν· ἐν οὐδενὶ
γὰρ τῶν λεχθέντων ἐπινοεῖται, ὡς οὐδ' ἂν μετα-
140 τρεπόμενος ἐναλλάττοι χωρία.   λέγεται δ'
οὐδὲν ἧττον κατελθὼν ἰδεῖν, ὁ προλήψει πάντα οὐ
γενόμενα μόνον ἀλλὰ καὶ πρὶν γενέσθαι σαφῶς
κατειληφώς, προτροπῆς ἕνεκα καὶ διδασκαλίας, ἵνα

---

[1] I have not attempted to translate these corrupt words
which appear in Mangey's edition as οὗ χάριν μελίσας ᾄσω
(" on account of which I will celebrate it in song "!) Wend.
suggested θεοῦ χάρισιν συνημμένα with no lacuna. But this
bears little resemblance to the text. I suggest οὗ χάριν
⟨ἐ⟩μελ⟨λ⟩ε τῆς ἀσω⟨μάτου⟩, followed by some such words as
οὐσίας πληροῦσθαι. This will fit the argument well. God is
everywhere, because His binding things with invisible bonds
necessarily (ἔμελλε) involves His filling all things with
His being. Wend.

[2] Wend. suggests ⟨οὐκ⟩ ἐπινοεῖται περὶ τόπον, οὐ κατα-
⟨λαμβανόμενον, εἰ μὴ κατὰ⟩ τὸ εἶναι μόνον. As an alternative
I suggest ἐπινοεῖται πέρα τοῦ εἶναί που κατὰ τὸ εἶναι μόνον (" is
conceived of as transcending the idea of being in any particular place and in terms of existence only "). See App. p. 556.

84

with all has bound them fast with invisible bonds, that they should never be loosed. . . . That aspect 137 of Him which transcends His Potencies cannot be conceived of at all in terms of place, but only as pure being, but that Potency of His by which He made and ordered all things, while it is called God in accordance with the derivation of that name,[a] holds the whole in its embrace and has interfused itself through the parts of the universe. But this divine nature 138 which presents itself to us, as visible and comprehensible and everywhere, is in reality invisible, incomprehensible and nowhere. . . . And so we have the words " Here I stand before thou wast " (Ex. xvii. 6). " I seem," He says, " the object of demonstration and comprehension, yet I transcend created things, preceding all demonstration or presentation to the mind."[b] None of the terms, then, which express move- 139 ment from place to place, whether up or down, to right or to left, forward or backward, are applicable to God in His aspect of pure being. For no such term is compatible with our conception of Him, so that He must also be incapable of displacement or change of locality.   All the same Moses 140 applies the phrase " came down and saw " to Him, who in His prescience had comprehended all things, not only after but before they came to pass, and he did so to admonish and instruct us, that the absent,

---

[a] See App. p. 556.   [b] See note on De Sac. 67.

[3] This sentence has been completely confused in the MSS. Wend. reconstructs it as follows: τὸ δὴ θεῖον ὁρατόν τε καὶ καταληπτὸν καὶ πανταχοῦ φαντασιαζόμενον ἀόρατον καὶ ἀκατάληπτον καὶ οὐδαμοῦ πρὸς ἀλήθειάν ἐστιν ὡς ἀψευδέστατον ἐκεῖνον εἶναι τὸν χρησμόν, ἐν ᾧ λέλεκται (cf. De Mig. 183), and this seems to be the general sense. In the next words στὰς should probably be ἕστηκα.

μηδεὶς ἀνθρώπων οἷς οὐ πάρεστιν, ἀβεβαίῳ χρώμενος εἰκασίᾳ, μακρὰν ἀφεστὼς προπιστεύῃ, ἀλλ'
ἄχρι τῶν πραγμάτων ἐλθὼν καὶ διακύψας εἰς
ἕκαστα καὶ ἐπιμελῶς αὐτὰ αὐγασάμενος· ὄψιν γὰρ
ἀπλανῆ πρὸ ἀκοῆς ἀπατεῶνος ἄξιον μάρτυρα
141 τίθεσθαι. οὗ χάριν καὶ παρὰ τοῖς ἄριστα πολι-
[426] τευομένοις ἀναγέγραπται νόμος | ἀκοὴν[1] μὴ μαρ-
τυρεῖν, ὅτι φύσει τὸ δικαστήριον αὐτῆς πρὸς τὸ
δεκάζεσθαι ταλαντεύει· καὶ Μωυσῆς μέντοι φησὶν
ἐν τοῖς ⟨ἀπ⟩αγορευτικοῖς· " οὐ παραδέξῃ ἀκοὴν
ματαίαν," οὐχὶ μόνον τοῦτο λέγων, ⟨μὴ⟩[2] παραδέχεσθαι ψευδῆ λόγον ἢ εὐήθη δι' ἀκοῆς, ἀλλὰ καὶ
ὅτι πρὸς τὴν σαφῆ τῆς ἀληθείας κατάληψιν μακρὸν
ὅσον ὄψεως ὑστερίζουσα διελέγχεται γέμουσα
ματαιότητος ἀκοή.
142   XXVIII. Ταύτην φαμὲν αἰτίαν εἶναι τοῦ λέγεσθαι " τὸν θεὸν καταβεβηκέναι τὴν πόλιν καὶ τὸν
πύργον θεάσασθαι." οὐ παρέργως δὲ πρόσκειται
" ὃν ᾠκοδόμησαν οἱ υἱοὶ τῶν ἀνθρώπων." ἴσως
γὰρ ἄν τις εἴποι τῶν οὐκ εὐαγῶν ἐπιχλευάζων
ἅμα· καινὸν[3] ἡμᾶς ἀναδιδάσκει μάθημα ὁ νομοθέτης, ὅτι πύργους καὶ πόλεις οὐχ ἕτεροί τινες,
ἀλλὰ παῖδες ἀνθρώπων ἀνοικοδομοῦνται. τίς γὰρ
τά γ' οὕτως ἐμφανῆ καὶ περίοπτα καὶ τῶν λίαν
143 ἐξεστηκότων ἀγνοεῖ; ἀλλὰ μὴ τὸ πρόχειρον τοῦτο
καὶ κατημαξευμένον ἐν τοῖς ἱερωτάτοις χρησμοῖς
ἀναγεγράφθαι ⟨νομίσῃς⟩, ἀλλ' ὅπερ ἀποκεκρυμ-
μένον ἰχνηλατεῖται διὰ τῶν ἐμφανῶν ὀνομάτων.

---

[1] mss. ἀκοῇ. See App. p. 556.
[2] Wend. prints a lacuna after λέγων with note that Cohn
suggests ⟨ὅτι οὐ θέμις⟩.   Mangey ⟨μὴ⟩.
[3] Heinemann suggests ἀναγκαῖον for ἅμα καινὸν.

who are at a long distance from the facts, should never form conclusions hastily or rely on precarious conjectures, but should come to close quarters with things, inspect them one by one and carefully envisage them. For the certitude of sight must be held as better evidence than the deceitfulness of hearing. And therefore among those who live under 141 the best institutions a law has been enacted against giving as evidence what has been merely heard, because hearing's tribunal has a natural bias towards corrupt judgement. In fact Moses says in his prohibitions, "Thou shalt not accept vain hearing" (Ex. xxiii. 1), by which he does not merely mean that we must not accept a false or foolish story on hearsay, but also that as a means of giving a sure apprehension of the truth, hearing is proved to lag far behind sight and is brimful of vanity.

XXVIII. This is the reason we assign for the 142 words "God came down to see the city and the tower," but the phrase which follows, "which the sons of men built" (Gen. xi. 5), is no idle addition, though perhaps some profane person might say with a sneer, "a novel piece of information this which the lawgiver here imparts to us, namely that it is the sons of men and not some other beings who build cities and towers." "Who," he would continue, "even among those who are far gone in insanity, does not know facts so obvious and conspicuous?" But you must suppose that it is not this obvious and 143 hackneyed fact which is recorded for us in our most holy oracles, but the hidden truth which can be traced under the surface meaning of the words.

144   τί οὖν ἐστι τοῦτο; οἱ πολλοὺς ἐπι-
γραφόμενοι τῶν ὄντων ὡσανεὶ πατέρας καὶ τὸ
πολύθεον εἰσηγούμενοι στῖφος ἀπειρίαν ὁμοῦ καὶ
πολυμιγίαν τῶν πραγμάτων καταχέαντες καὶ τὸ
ψυχῆς τέλος ἡδονῇ παραδόντες δημιουργοὶ τῆς
εἰρημένης πόλεως καὶ τῆς κατ’ αὐτὴν ἀκροπόλεως,
εἰ δεῖ τἀληθὲς εἰπεῖν, γεγόνασι, τὰ ποιητικὰ τοῦ
τέλους τρόπον οἰκοδομημάτων συναύξοντες, τῶν
ἐκ πόρνης ἀποκυηθέντων οὐδέν, ὥς γ’ οἶμαι,
διαφέροντες, οὓς ὁ νόμος ἐκκλησίας ἀπελήλακε
θείας εἰπών· “ οὐκ εἰσελεύσεται ἐκ πόρνης εἰς
ἐκκλησίαν κυρίου,” ὅτι, καθάπερ περὶ πολλὰ τέλη
πλανώμενοι τοξόται καὶ μηδενὸς εὐστόχως ἐφ-
ιέμενοι σκοποῦ, μυρίας ἀρχὰς καὶ αἰτίας τῆς τῶν
ὄντων ὑποθέμενοι γενέσεως ψευδωνύμους πάσας
τὸν ἕνα ποιητὴν καὶ πατέρα τῶν ὅλων ἠγνόησαν.

145   οἱ δὲ ἐπιστήμῃ κεχρημένοι τοῦ ἑνὸς
υἱοὶ θεοῦ προσαγορεύονται δεόντως, καθὰ καὶ
Μωυσῆς ὁμολογεῖ φάσκων· “ υἱοί ἐστε κυρίου τοῦ
θεοῦ ” καὶ “ θεὸν τὸν γεννήσαντά σε ” καὶ “ οὐκ
αὐτὸς οὗτός σου πατήρ;” ἕπεται μέντοι τοῖς οὕτω
τὴν ψυχὴν διατεθεῖσι μόνον τὸ καλὸν ἀγαθὸν εἶναι
νομίζειν, ὅπερ τῷ τέλει τῆς ἡδονῆς πρὸς ἐμπειρο-
πολέμων ἀνδρῶν ἀντιτειχίζεται πρὸς ἀνατροπὴν
146 καὶ καθαίρεσιν ἐκείνου. | κἂν μηδέπω μέντοι τυγ-
[427] χάνῃ τις ἀξιόχρεως ὢν υἱὸς θεοῦ προσαγορεύε-
σθαι, σπουδαζέτω κοσμεῖσθαι κατὰ τὸν πρωτό-
γονον αὐτοῦ λόγον, τὸν ἀγγέλων πρεσβύτατον, ὡς
ἂν ἀρχάγγελον, πολυώνυμον ὑπάρχοντα· καὶ γὰρ
ἀρχὴ καὶ ὄνομα θεοῦ καὶ λόγος καὶ ὁ κατ’ εἰκόνα

---

   [a] An obvious reference to Stoics and Epicureans.

What then is this truth? Those who **144** ascribe to existing things a multitude of fathers as it were and by introducing their miscellany of deities have flooded everything with ignorance and confusion, or have assigned to pleasure the function of being the aim and end of the soul, have become in very truth builders of the city of our text and of its acropolis. They pile up as in an edifice all that serves to produce that aim or end and thus differ not a whit to my mind from the harlot's offspring, whom the law has banished from God's congregation with the words " he that is born of a harlot shall not enter the congregation of the Lord " (Deut. xxiii. 2). For like bowmen, whose shots roam from mark to mark and who never take a skilful aim at any single point, they assume a multitude of what they falsely call sources and causes to account for the origin of the existing world and have no knowledge of the one Maker and Father of all.   But they who **145** live in the knowledge of the One are rightly called " Sons of God," as Moses also acknowledges when he says, " Ye are sons of the Lord God " (Deut. xiv. 1), and " God who begat thee " (*ibid*. xxxii. 18), and " Is not He Himself thy father? " (*ibid*. 6). Indeed with those whose soul is thus disposed it follows that they hold moral beauty to be the only good, and this serves as a counterwork engineered by veteran warriors to fight the cause which makes Pleasure the end and to subvert and overthrow it.[a] But if there **146** be any as yet unfit to be called a Son of God, let him press to take his place under God's First-born, the Word, who holds the eldership among the angels, their ruler as it were. And many names are his, for he is called, " the Beginning," and the Name of

ἄνθρωπος καὶ ὁ ὁρῶν, Ἰσραήλ, προσαγορεύεται.

147   διὸ προήχθην ὀλίγῳ πρότερον ἐπαινέσαι τὰς ἀρετὰς τῶν φασκόντων ὅτι " πάντες ἐσμὲν υἱοὶ ἑνὸς ἀνθρώπου"· καὶ γὰρ εἰ μήπω ἱκανοὶ θεοῦ παῖδες νομίζεσθαι γεγόναμεν, ἀλλά τοι τῆς ἀειδοῦς εἰκόνος αὐτοῦ, λόγου τοῦ ἱερωτάτου· θεοῦ γὰρ

148 εἰκὼν λόγος ὁ πρεσβύτατος. καὶ πολλαχοῦ μέντοι τῆς νομοθεσίας υἱοὶ πάλιν Ἰσραὴλ καλοῦνται, τοῦ ὁρῶντος οἱ ἀκούοντες, ἐπειδὴ μεθ' ὅρασιν ἀκοὴ δευτερείοις τετίμηται καὶ τὸ διδασκόμενον τοῦ χωρὶς ὑφηγήσεως ἐναργεῖς τύπους τῶν ὑποκειμέ-

149 νων λαμβάνοντος αἰεὶ δεύτερον.   ἄγαμαι καὶ τῶν ἐν βασιλικαῖς βίβλοις ἱεροφαντηθέντων, καθ' ἃς[a] οἱ πολλαῖς γενεαῖς ὕστερον ἀκμάσαντες καὶ βιώσαντες ⟨ἀν⟩υπαιτίως υἱοὶ τοῦ τὸν θεὸν ὑμνή-σαντος Δαβὶδ ἀναγράφονται, οὗ περιόντος οὐδ' οἱ πρόπαπποι τούτων ἦσαν ἴσως[1] γεγενημένοι· ψυχῶν γὰρ ἀπαθανατιζομένων ἀρεταῖς, οὐ φθαρτῶν σωμά-των ἐστὶ γένεσις, ἣν ἐπὶ τοὺς καλοκἀγαθίας ἡγεμόνας ὡσανεὶ γεννητὰς καὶ πατέρας ἀναφέρεσθαι συμβαίνει.

150 XXIX. Κατὰ δὲ τῶν ἐπ' ἀδικίαις σεμνυνομένων εἶπε κύριος· " ἰδοὺ γένος ἓν καὶ χεῖλος ἓν πάντων," ἴσον τῷ ἰδοὺ μία οἰκειότης καὶ συγγένεια, καὶ πάλιν ἁρμονία καὶ συμφωνία ἡ αὐτὴ πάντων ὁμοῦ, μηδενὸς ἠλλοτριωμένου τὴν γνώμην μηδ' ἀπ-ᾴδοντος, καθάπερ ἔχει καὶ ἐπ' ἀνθρώπων ἀμούσων· τὸ γὰρ φωνητήριον αὐτοῖς ὄργανον πᾶσι τοῖς φθόγγοις ἔστιν ὅτε δι' ὅλων ἐκμελὲς καὶ ἀπῳδὸν

---

[1] MSS. πιστῶς.

[a] i.e. in § 41.   [b] See App. p. 557.

God, and His Word, and the Man after His image, and " he that sees," that is Israel. And 147 therefore I was moved a few pages above[a] to praise the virtues of those who say that " We are all sons of one man " (Gen. xlii. 11). For if we have not yet become fit to be thought sons of God yet we may be sons of His invisible image, the most holy Word. For the Word is the eldest-born image of God. And 148 often indeed in the law-book we find another phrase, " sons of Israel," hearers, that is, sons of him that sees, since hearing stands second in estimation and below sight, and the recipient of teaching is always second to him with whom realities present their forms clear to his vision and not through the medium of instruction. I bow, too, in admiration 149 before the mysteries revealed in the books of Kings, where it does not offend us to find described as sons of God's psalmist David those who lived and flourished many generations afterwards (1 Kings xv. 11 ; 2 Kings xviii. 3),[b] though in David's lifetime probably not even their great-grandparents had been born. For the paternity we find ascribed to the standard-bearers of noble living, whom we think of as the fathers who begat us, is the paternity of souls raised to immortality by virtues, not of corruptible bodies.

XXIX. But of those who glory in their iniquities, 150 the Lord said "behold there is one race and one lip of them all" (Gen. xi. 5), that is, behold they are one connexion of family and fellowship of race, and again all have the same harmony and fellowship of voice ; there is none whose mind is a stranger to the other nor his voice discordant. It is so also with men who have no gift of music. Sometimes their vocal organ, though every note is entirely tuneless and

οὐ μετρίως καθέστηκε, πρὸς ἀναρμοστίαν ἄκρως
ἡρμοσμένον καὶ πρὸς τὸ ἀσύμφωνον συμφωνίαν
151 μόνον ἄγον. καὶ ἐπὶ τῆς πολίτιδος τὸ κατα-
σκευαστὸν[1] τὸ παραπλήσιον ἰδεῖν ἔστιν· αἵ τε[2] γὰρ
ἀμφημεριναὶ καὶ διάτριτοι καὶ τεταρταΐζουσαι παρὰ
παισὶν ἰατρῶν λεγόμεναι περίοδοι μεθ' ἡμέραν τε
καὶ νύκτωρ περὶ τὰς αὐτὰς ὥρας κατασκήπτουσι
152 τὴν εἰς αὐτὰ[1] καὶ τάξιν φυλάττουσαι.
[428]   Τὸ δὲ " καὶ τοῦτο ἤρξαντο | ποιῆσαι " μετ' οὐ
μετρίου σχετλιασμοῦ λέλεκται, διότι τοῖς ῥᾳδιουρ-
γοῖς οὐ τὰ πρὸς τοὺς ὁμοφύλους μόνον συγχεῖν
δίκαια ἐξήρκεσεν, ἀλλ' ἤδη καὶ τῶν ὀλυμπίων ἐπι-
βαίνειν ἐτόλμησαν, ἀδικίαν μὲν σπείραντες, ἀσέ-
153 βειαν δὲ θερίσαντες. ὄφελος δὲ τοῖς ἀθλίοις οὐδέν·
οὐ γὰρ ὥσπερ ἀδικοῦντες ἀλλήλους πολλὰ ὧν
ἂν ἐθελήσωσιν ἀνύτουσιν ἔργοις βεβαιούμενοι τὰ
βουλαῖς ἀγνώμοσιν ἐπιλογισθέντα, οὕτως καὶ ἀ-
σεβοῦντες· ἀζήμια γὰρ καὶ ἀπήμονα τὰ θεῖα, τοῦ
δὲ πλημμελεῖν εἰς αὐτὰ οἱ δυσκάθαρτοι τὰς ἀρχὰς
εὑρίσκονται μόνον, πρὸς δὲ τὸ τέλος φθάνουσιν
154 οὐδέποτε. διὸ καὶ λέγεται τοῦτο· " ἤρξαντο
ποιῆσαι." κορεσθέντες ⟨γὰρ⟩ οἱ τοῦ παρανομεῖν
ἄπληστοι τῶν πρὸς τὰ ἐν γῇ καὶ θαλάττῃ καὶ ἀέρι,
ἃ φθαρτῆς φύσεως ἔλαχε, κακῶν ἐπὶ τὰς ἐν
οὐρανῷ θείας φύσεις μετατάξασθαι διενοήθησαν,
ἅς τι[3] τῶν ὄντων ἔξω τοῦ κακηγορεῖν ἔθος ἐστὶ
διαθεῖναι τὸ παράπαν οὐδέν· καὶ αὐτὸ μέντοι τὸ
βλασφημεῖν οὐ τοῖς κακηγορουμένοις ἐπιφέρει τινὰ
ζημίαν, ἃ τῆς ἰδίου φύσεως οὔποτ' ἐξίσταται, ἀλλὰ
155 τοῖς καταιτιωμένοις συμφορὰς ἀνηκέστους. οὐκ

─────────

[1] See App. p. 557.   [2] MSS. ἔτι.

92

highly unmelodious, is supremely harmonized to produce disharmony, with a consonance which it turns to mere dissonance. And the same studied regularity 151 may be noticed in fever. For the recurrences which are called in the medical schools quotidian, or tertian, or quartan, make their visitation about the same hour of the day or night and maintain their relative order.

The words "And they have begun to do this" 152 (Gen. xi. 6), express strong scorn and indignation. They mean that the miscreants, not content with making havoc of the justice due to their fellows, went further. They dared to attack the rights of heaven, and having sown injustice, they reaped impiety. Yet the wretches had no profit of it. For while in 153 wronging each other they achieved much of what they wished and their deeds confirmed what their senseless scheming had devised, it was not so with their impiety. For the things that are God's cannot be harmed or injured, and when these reprobates turn their transgressions against them, they attain but to the beginning and never arrive at the end. Therefore we have these words, "They have *begun* 154 to do." For when, insatiate in wrongdoing, they had taken their fill of sins against all that is of earth and sea and air whose allotted nature is to perish, they bethought them to turn their forces against the divine natures in heaven. But on them nothing that exists can usually have any effect save evil speech, though indeed even the foul tongue does not work harm to those who are its objects (for they still possess their nature unchanged), but only brings disasters beyond cure on the revilers. Yet that they 155

---

[3] So Mangey: mss. ἅ ἐστι: Wend. conjectures, but does not print, ἃς [ἐστι] τῶν κακῶν. See App. p. 558.

ἐπειδὴ μέντοι μόνον ἤρξαντο πρὸς τὸ τέλος ἐλθεῖν
ἀδυνατήσαντες ἀσεβείας, διὰ τοῦτ' αὐτοὺς οὐχ ὡς
διαπραξαμένους ἕκαστα ὧν διενοήθησαν αἰτιατέον·
οὗ χάριν καὶ τετελειωκέναι φησὶ τὸν πύργον αὐτοὺς
οὐ τελειώσαντας, ἐπειδὰν λέγῃ· " κύριος κατέβη
ἰδεῖν τὴν πόλιν καὶ τὸν πύργον," οὐχ ὃν οἰκο-
δομῆσαι μέλλουσιν, ἀλλ' ὃν " ᾠκοδόμησαν " ἤδη.

156   XXX. τίς οὖν πίστις τοῦ μὴ τετε-
λεσιουργῆσθαι τὴν κατασκευήν; ἡ ἐνάργεια πρώτη·
γῆς γὰρ ὁτιοῦν μέρος ἀμήχανον οὐρανοῦ ψαῦσαι
διὰ τὴν ἔμπροσθεν[1] αἰτίαν, ὅτιπερ οὐδὲ κέντρον
περιφερείας ἅπτεται· δευτέρα[2] δ', ὅτι ὁ αἰθήρ, ἱερὸν
πῦρ, φλόξ ἐστιν ἄσβεστος, ὡς καὶ αὐτὸ δηλοῖ
τοὔνομα παρὰ τὸ αἴθειν, ὃ δὴ καίειν ἐστὶ κατὰ
157 γλῶτταν, εἰρημένον. μάρτυς δὲ μία μοῖρα τῆς
οὐρανίου πυρᾶς ἥλιος, ὃς τοσοῦτον γῆς ἀφεστὼς
ἄχρι μυχῶν τὰς ἀκτῖνας ἐπιπέμπων αὐτήν τε καὶ
τὸν ἀπ' αὐτῆς ἀνατείνοντα μέχρι τῆς οὐρανίου
σφαίρας ἀέρα φύσει ψυχρὸν ὄντα τῇ μὲν ἀλεαίνει,
τῇ δὲ καταφλέγει· τὰ μὲν γὰρ ὅσα ἢ μακρὰν
ἀφέστηκεν αὐτοῦ τῆς φορᾶς ἢ ἐγκάρσια παρα-
βέβληται ἀλεαίνει μόνον, τὰ δ' ἐγγὺς ἢ ἐπ' εὐθείας
ὄντα καὶ προσανακαίει βίᾳ. εἰ δὲ ταῦθ' οὕτως
ἔχει, τοὺς ἀναβαίνειν τολμῶντας ἀνθρώπους οὐκ
ἀναγκαῖον ἦν ἐμπεπρῆσθαι κεραυνωθέντας, ἀτελοῦς
αὐτοῖς τῆς μεγαλουργηθείσης ἐπινοίας γενομένης;
158 τοῦτ' ἔοικεν αἰνίττεσθαι διὰ τῶν αὖθις λεγομένων·

---

[1] Wend. suggests τὴν ἔμπροσθεν ⟨λεχθεῖσαν⟩. The reference
is to § 5.   [2] mss. δεύτερον.

only began and were unable to reach the end of their impiety is no reason why they should not be denounced as they would had they carried out all their intentions. Therefore he speaks of their having completed the tower, though they had not done so. " The Lord," he says, " came down to see the city and tower which they had built " already, not which they intended to build (Gen. xi. 5).

XXX. What proof then have we that the structure 156 was not already completed ? First, self-evident facts. No part of the earth can possibly touch the heaven for the reason already mentioned, namely that it is just as impossible as it is for the centre to touch the circumference. Secondly, because the aether, that holy fire, is an unquenchable flame, as its very name shews, derived as it is from $a\check{i}\theta\epsilon\iota\nu$, which is a special term [a] for " burn." This is attested by a single part 157 of the heavenly expanse of fire, namely the Sun, which, in spite of its great distance, sends its rays to the corners of the earth, and both earth and the naturally cold extent of air, which divides it from the sphere of heaven, is warmed or consumed by it as the case may be. For to all that is at a long distance from its course or lies at an angle to it, it merely gives warmth, but all that is near it or directly under it it actually destroys with the force of its flames. If this is so, the men who ventured on the ascent could not fail to be blasted and consumed by the fire, leaving their vaulting ambition unfulfilled. That it was unfulfilled [b] seems to be suggested by 158 Moses in the words which follow. " They ceased,"

---

[a] See note on § 27.

[b] $\tau o\hat{v}\tau o$ can only refer to $\dot{a}\tau\epsilon\lambda o\hat{v}s$, not to the curiously literalistic arguments given in the preceding section.

" ἐπαύσαντο " γάρ φησιν " οἰκοδομοῦντες τὴν πόλιν καὶ τὸν πύργον," οὐ δήπου τελειώσαντες, | [429] ἀλλὰ τελεσιουργῆσαι κωλυθέντες διὰ τὴν ἐπιγενομένην σύγχυσιν.

Οὐ μὴν ἐκπεφεύγασι τὴν τῶν διαπράξεων αἰτίαν οἱ πρὸς τῷ βουλεύσασθαι καὶ ἐγκεχειρηκότες.

159 XXXI. τὸν γοῦν οἰωνόμαντιν καὶ τερατοσκόπον περὶ τὰς ἀβεβαίους εἰκασίας ματαιάζοντα—καὶ γὰρ μάταιος[1] ἑρμηνεύεται Βαλαάμ—φησὶν ὁ νόμος τῷ ὁρῶντι καταράσασθαι καίτοι διὰ τῶν λόγων εὐφήμους ποιησάμενος εὐχάς, σκοπῶν οὐ τὰ λεχθέντα ἃ προμηθείᾳ θεοῦ μετεχαράττετο οἷα δόκιμον ἀντὶ κιβδήλου νόμισμα, τὴν δὲ διάνοιαν, ἐν ᾗ τὰ βλάψοντα πρὸ τῶν ὠφελησόντων[2] ἀνεπολεῖτο. ἔστι δὲ φύσει πολέμια ταῦτα, στοχασμὸς ἀληθείᾳ καὶ ματαιότης ἐπιστήμῃ καὶ ἡ δίχα[3] ἐνθουσιασμοῦ μαντεία νηφούσῃ σοφίᾳ.

160 καὶ ἂν ἐξ ἐνέδρας μέντοι τις ἐπιχειρήσας ἀνελεῖν τινα μὴ δυνηθῇ κτεῖναι, τῇ τῶν ἀνδροφόνων οὐδὲν ἧττον ὕποχος δίκῃ καθέστηκεν, ὡς ὁ γραφεὶς περὶ τούτων δηλοῖ νόμος· " ἐὰν " γάρ φησι " τὶς ἐπιθῆται τῷ πλησίον ἀποκτεῖναι αὐτὸν δόλῳ καὶ καταφύγῃ, ἀπὸ[4] τοῦ θυσιαστηρίου λήψῃ αὐτὸν θανατῶσαι"· καίτοι ἐπιτίθεται μόνον, οὐκ ἀνῄρηκεν, ἀλλ' ἴσον ἡγήσατο ἀδίκημα τῷ κτεῖναι τὸ βουλεῦσαι τὸν φόνον· οὗ χάριν οὐδ' ἱκέτῃ γενομένῳ δέδωκεν ἀμνηστίαν, ἀλλὰ καὶ ἐξ ἱεροῦ ἐκέλευσεν ἀπάγειν

---

[1] Mangey may be right in suggesting μάταιος ⟨λαὸς⟩, the interpretation of the name given in *De Cher.* 32.

[2] MSS. βλάψαντα . . . ὠφελησάντων.

[3] So MSS.: Mangey and Wend. διά, quite untenably, I think. The index gives no example where ἐνθουσιασμός is

he says, " building the city and the tower " (Gen. xi. 8), obviously not because they had finished it, but because they were prevented from completing it by the confusion that fell upon them.

Yet as the enterprise was not only planned but undertaken, they have not escaped the guilt which would attend its accomplishment. XXXI. We have 159 a parallel in Balaam, that dealer in auguries and prodigies and in the vanity of unfounded conjectures, for the name Balaam is by interpretation " vain." The law-book declares that he cursed the Man of Vision, though in words he uttered prayers of blessing, for it considers not what he actually said, words restamped under God's providence, like a true coin substituted for the false, but his heart, in which he cherished thoughts of injury rather than of benefit. There is a natural hostility between conjecture and truth, between vanity and knowledge, and between the divination which has no true inspiration and sound sober wisdom. And indeed if a 160 man makes a treacherous attempt against another's life, but is unable to kill him, he is none the less liable to the penalty of the homicide, as is shewn by the law enacted for such cases. " If," it runs, " a man attacks his neighbour to kill him by guile and flees to refuge, thou shalt take him from the altar to put him to death " (Ex. xxi. 14). And yet he merely " attacks " him and has not killed him, but the law regards the purpose of murder as a crime equal to murder itself, and so, even though he takes sanctuary, it does not grant him the privileges of sanctuary, but bids him be taken even from the

---

used in this depreciating sense. The δίχα ἐνθουσιασμοῦ μαντεία repeat οἰωνόμαντις.   [4] MSS. ἐπί.

97

161 τὸν ἀνιέρῳ γνώμῃ χρησάμενον. ἀνίερος δὲ οὐ
ταύτῃ μόνον, ὅτι κατὰ ψυχῆς τῆς αἰεὶ ζῆν δυναμένης ἀρετῶν κτήσει τε καὶ χρήσει τὸν διὰ προσβολῆς κακίας φόνον ἐβούλευσεν, ἀλλὰ καὶ ὅτι θεὸν
τῆς ἀνοσιουργοῦ τόλμης αἰτιᾶται· τὸ γὰρ " καταφύγῃ " τοιοῦτον ὑποβάλλει νοῦν, διότι πολλοὶ τὰ
καθ' ἑαυτῶν ἀποδιδράσκειν ἐθέλοντες ἐγκλήματα
καὶ ῥύεσθαι τῶν ἐφ' οἷς ἠδίκησαν ἀξιοῦντες ἑαυτοὺς
τιμωριῶν τὸ οἰκεῖον ἄγος τῷ κακοῦ μὲν μηδενὸς
ἀγαθῶν δ' ἁπάντων αἰτίῳ προσβάλλουσι θεῷ. διὸ
καὶ ἀπ' αὐτῶν βωμῶν τοὺς τοιούτους ἀπάγειν
ὅσιον εἶναι ἐνομίσθη.

162 Δίκην δ' ὑπερβάλλουσαν κατὰ τῶν ἐπ' ἀθεότητι
λόγους οἰκοδομουμένων καὶ συγκροτούντων ὁρίζει,
ἣν ἴσως τινὲς τῶν ἀφρόνων οὐ βλάβην, ἀλλ'
ὠφέλειαν ὑποτοπήσουσιν· " οὐ γὰρ ἐκλείψει "
φησίν " ἀπ' αὐτῶν πάντα ὅσα ἂν ἐπιθῶνται ποιεῖν."
ὦ τῆς ἀπεριγράφου καὶ ἀμέτρου κακοδαιμονίας,
πάνθ' οἷς ἂν ὁ φρενοβλαβέστατος ἐπιθῆται νοῦς,
ὑποχείρια εἶναι καὶ ὑπήκοα, καὶ μηδέν, ⟨μὴ⟩ μέγα
μὴ μικρόν, ὑστερίζειν τὸ παράπαν, ἀλλ' ὡσπερεὶ
[430] φθάνοντα προαπαντᾶν πρὸς τὰς | χρείας ἑκάστας.

163 XXXII. ψυχῆς ταῦτα φρονήσεως χηρευούσης
ἐστὶν ἐπίδειξις μηδὲν τῶν εἰς τὸ ἁμαρτάνειν
ἐχούσης ἐμποδών. εὔξαιτο γὰρ ἂν ὁ μὴ σφόδρα
ἀνιάτως ἔχων τὰ ἐξ ὑποθέσεως τοῦ νοῦ πάντ'
ἐπιλιπεῖν αὐτῷ, ἵνα μὴ τῷ κλέπτειν ἢ μοιχεύειν ἢ
ἀνδροφονεῖν ἢ ἱεροσυλεῖν ἤ τινι τῶν ὁμοιοτρόπων
ἐπιτιθέμενος εὐοδῇ, μυρία δ' εὑρίσκῃ τὰ κωλυ-

98

holy place, because the purpose he has harboured is unholy. Its unholiness does not merely consist in 161 this, that it plans death to be dealt by the arm of wickedness against the soul which might live for ever by the acquisition and practice of virtue, but in that it lays its abominable audacity to the charge of God. For the words " flee to refuge " lead us to the reflexion that there are many who, wishing to shirk all charges to which they are liable and claiming to escape the penalties of their misdeeds, ascribe the guilty responsibility,[a] which really belongs to themselves, to God who is the cause of nothing evil, but of all that is good. And therefore it was held no sacrilege to drag such as these from the very altar.

The punishment which he decrees against those 162 who " build " up and weld together arguments for godlessness is indeed extreme, though perhaps some foolish people will imagine it to be beneficial rather than injurious. " Nothing shall fail from them of all that they attempt to do," it says (Gen. xi. 6). What a misery, transcending limitation and measurement, that everything which the mind in its utter infatuation attempts should be its obedient vassal not backward in any service whether great or small, but hastening as it were to anticipate its every need. XXXII. This is a sign of a soul lacking good sense, 163 which finds no obstacle in all that lies between it and its sin. For he who is not far gone in mortal error would pray that all the promptings of his mind's purposes should fail him, so that when he attempts to commit theft or adultery, or murder or sacrilege, or any similar deed, he should not find an easy path,

---

[a] ἄγος implies guilt which demands, and is felt to demand, expiation.

σιεργήσοντα. κωλυθεὶς[1] μὲν γὰρ τὴν μεγίστην
νόσον, ἀδικίαν, ἀποβάλλει, σὺν ἀδείᾳ δ' ἐπεξελθὼν
164 ταύτην ἀναδέξεται. τί οὖν ἔτι τὰς τῶν τυράννων
τύχας ὡς μακαρίων[2] ζηλοῦτε καὶ θαυμάζετε, δι'
ἃς εὐπετῶς ἕκαστα ἐπεξίασιν, ὧν ἂν ὁ ἐκλελυτ-
τηκὼς κἀκτεθηριωμένος τέκῃ νοῦς, καὶ ἐν ἑαυτοῖς
δέον ἐπιστένειν, εἴ γε ἀπορίᾳ καὶ [ἡ] ἀσθένεια
κακοῖς λυσιτελές, ὡς περιουσία καὶ ἰσχὺς ἀγαθοῖς
165 ὠφελιμώτατον;   εἰς δέ τις τῶν ἀφρόνων
ᾐσθημένος, εἰς ὅσην κακοδαιμονίας ὑπερβολὴν ἄγει
ἡ τοῦ διαμαρτάνειν ἐκεχειρία, μετὰ παρρησίας
εἶπε· '' μείζων ἡ αἰτία μου τοῦ ἀφεθῆναι.'' παγ-
χάλεπον γὰρ ἀχαλίνωτον ἐαθῆναι ψυχὴν ἀτίθασον
οὖσαν ἐξ ἑαυτῆς, ἣν μόλις ἡνίαις μετ' ἐπανατάσεως
166 μαστίγων ἔστι κατασχόντα πραῦναι. διόπερ λόγιον
τοῦ ἵλεω θεοῦ μεστὸν ἡμερότητος ἐλπίδας χρηστὰς
ὑπογράφον τοῖς παιδείας ἐρασταῖς ἀνήρηται τοιόνδε·
'' οὐ μή σε ἀνῶ, οὐδ' οὐ μή σε ἐγκαταλίπω·''
τῶν γὰρ τῆς ψυχῆς δεσμῶν χαλασθέντων, οἷς δι-
εκρατεῖτο, ἡ μεγίστη παρέπεται συμφορά, κατα-
λειφθῆναι ὑπὸ θεοῦ, ὃς τοῖς ὅλοις δεσμοὺς τὰς
ἑαυτοῦ δυνάμεις περιῆψεν ἀρρήκτους, αἷς τὰ πάντα
167 σφίγξας ἄλυτα εἶναι βεβούληται. λέγει μέντοι
καὶ ἑτέρωθι, ὅτι '' πάνθ' ὅσα δεσμῷ καταδέδεται,
καθαρά ἐστιν,'' ἐπειδὴ τῆς ἀκαθάρτου φθορᾶς

---

[1] mss. κώλυσις.
[2] So Wend.: mss. ὦ μακάριοι, and so Mangey. I do not
feel sure that Wend. is right. Philo is fond of these Platonic
forms of address, and ὦ μακάριοι, like ὦ θαυμάσιε, conveys a
note of expostulation, which is suitable enough here.

---

[a] See App. p. 558.
[b] Or perhaps '' punishment,'' as Philo understands the

but rather a host of obstacles to hinder its execution.
For if he is prevented, he is rid of that supreme
malady, injustice, but if he carries out his purpose
in security that malady will be upon him. Why then 164
do you continue to envy and admire the fortunes of
tyrants,[a] which enable them to achieve with ease all
that the madness and brutal savagery of their minds
conceive, and hold them blessed, when rather our
hearts should bewail them, since poverty and
bodily weakness are a positive benefit to the bad,
just as abundance of means and strength are most
useful to the good ?   One of the foolish 165
who saw to what a pitch of misery free licence
to sin leads said boldly, "That I should be let free is
the greater indictment[b]" (Gen. iv. 13). For it is a
terrible thing that the soul, so wild as it is by nature,
should be suffered to go unbridled, when even under
the rein and with the whip in full play it can hardly
be controlled and made docile. And therefore the 166
merciful God has delivered an oracle full of loving-
kindness which has a message of good hope to the
lovers of discipline. It is to this purport. " I will
not let thee go nor will I abandon thee " (Josh. i. 5).
For when the bonds of the soul which held it fast are
loosened, there follows the greatest of disasters, even
to be abandoned by God who has encircled all things
with the adamantine chains of His potencies and willed
that thus bound tight and fast they should never be
unloosed. Further in another place he says, " All 167
that are bound with a bond are clean " (Num. xix. 15),
for unbinding is the cause of destruction which is

word. The text has been expounded in the same sense in
Quod Det. 141. E.V. " My punishment is greater than I
can bear."

αἴτιον ἡ διάλυσις. μηδέποτ' οὖν ἰδών τινα τῶν
φαύλων οἷς ἂν ἐπιθῆται πᾶσιν εὐμαρῶς ἐπεξιόντα
θαυμάσῃς ὡς κατορθοῦντα, ἀλλὰ τοὐναντίον ὡς
ἀποτυγχάνοντα οἰκτίζου, ὅτι ἀφορίᾳ μὲν ἀρετῆς,
κακίας δὲ εὐφορίᾳ χρώμενος διατελεῖ.

168 XXXIII. Σκέψασθαι δ' οὐ παρέργως ἄξιον, τίν'
ἔχει λόγον τὸ εἰρημένον ἐκ προσώπου τοῦ θεοῦ·
" δεῦτε καὶ καταβάντες συγχέωμεν ἐκεῖ αὐτῶν
τὴν γλῶτταν." φαίνεται γὰρ διαλεγόμενός τισιν
ὡς ἂν συνεργοῖς αὐτοῦ, τὸ δ' αὐτὸ καὶ πρότερον
ἐπὶ τῆς τἀνθρώπου κατασκευῆς ἀναγέγραπται·
169 " εἶπε " γάρ φησι " κύριος ὁ θεός· ποιήσωμεν
ἄνθρωπον κατ' εἰκόνα ἡμετέραν καὶ καθ' ὁμοίω-
σιν " τοῦ " ποιήσωμεν " πλῆθος ἐμφαίνοντος· καὶ
πάλιν " εἶπεν ὁ θεός· ἰδού, γέγονεν Ἀδὰμ ὡς εἷς
[431] ἡμῶν, τῷ γινώσκειν καλὸν καὶ πονηρόν"· | τὸ γὰρ
" ὡς εἷς ἡμῶν " οὐκ ἐφ' ἑνός, ἀλλ' ἐπὶ πλειόνων
170 τίθεται. λεκτέον οὖν ἐκεῖνο πρῶτον, ὅτι οὐδὲν
τῶν ὄντων ἰσότιμον ὑφέστηκε θεῷ, ἀλλ' ἔστιν εἷς
ἄρχων καὶ ἡγεμὼν καὶ βασιλεύς, ᾧ πρυτανεύειν
καὶ διοικεῖν μόνῳ θέμις τὰ σύμπαντα. τὸ γὰρ

οὐκ ἀγαθὸν πολυκοιρανίη, εἷς κοίρανος ἔστω,
εἷς βασιλεὺς

οὐκ ἐπὶ πόλεων καὶ ἀνθρώπων λέγοιτ' ἂν ἐν δίκῃ
μᾶλλον ἢ ἐπὶ κόσμου καὶ θεοῦ· ἑνὸς γὰρ ἕνα
ποιητήν τε καὶ πατέρα πάλιν καὶ δεσπότην ἀναγ-
171 καῖον εἶναι. XXXIV. τούτου δὴ προ-
διομολογηθέντος ἀκόλουθον ἂν εἴη συνυφαίνειν τὰ
ἁρμόζοντα. τίν' οὖν ἐστι, σκοπῶμεν· εἷς ὢν ὁ
θεὸς ἀμυθήτους περὶ αὐτὸν ἔχει δυνάμεις ἀρωγοὺς

---

[a] *Iliad*, ii. 204, 205.

unclean. Never then, when you see any of the wicked accomplishing with ease whatsoever he attempts, admire him for his success, but contrariwise pity him for his ill-luck, for his is a life of continual barrenness in virtue and fruitfulness in vice.

XXXIII. We should give careful consideration to 168 the question of what is implied by the words which are put into the mouth of God. " Come and let us go down and confuse their tongue there " (Gen. xi. 7). For it is clear that He is conversing with some persons whom He treats as His fellow-workers, and we find the same in an earlier passage of the formation of man. Here we have " The Lord God 169 said 'let us make man in our own image and likeness'" (Gen. i. 26); where the words " let us make " imply plurality. And once more, " God said, ' behold Adam has become as one of us by knowing good and evil '" (Gen. iii. 22); here the " us " in " as one of us " is said not of one, but of more than one. Now we must 170 first lay down that no existing thing is of equal honour to God and that there is only one sovereign and ruler and king, who alone may direct and dispose of all things. For the lines :

> It is not well that many lords should rule;
> Be there but one, one king,[a]

could be said with more justice of the world and of God than of cities and men. For being one it must needs have one maker and father and master.

XXXIV. Having reached agreement on 171 this preliminary question our next step will be to gather the relevant considerations into a coherent argument. Let us consider what these are. God is one, but He has around Him numberless Potencies,

καὶ σωτηρίους τοῦ γενομένου πάσας, αἷς ἐμφέρονται
καὶ αἱ κολαστήριοι· ἔστι δὲ καὶ ἡ κόλασις οὐκ
ἐπιζήμιον, ἁμαρτημάτων οὖσα κώλυσις καὶ ἐπαν-
172 όρθωσις. διὰ τούτων τῶν δυνάμεων ὁ ἀσώματος
καὶ νοητὸς ἐπάγη κόσμος, τὸ τοῦ φαινομένου τοῦδε
ἀρχέτυπον, ἰδέαις ἀοράτοις συσταθείς, ὥσπερ οὗτος
173 σώμασιν ὁρατοῖς. καταπλαγέντες οὖν τινες τὴν
ἑκατέρου τῶν κόσμων φύσιν οὐ μόνον ὅλους
ἐξεθείωσαν, ἀλλὰ καὶ τὰ κάλλιστα τῶν ἐν αὐτοῖς
μερῶν, ἥλιον καὶ σελήνην καὶ τὸν σύμπαντα
οὐρανόν, ἅπερ οὐδὲν αἰδεσθέντες θεοὺς ἐκάλεσαν.
ὧν τὴν ἀπόνοιαν[1] κατιδὼν Μωυσῆς φησι· " κύριε,
κύριε, βασιλεῦ τῶν θεῶν " ⟨εἰς⟩ ἔνδειξιν τῆς παρ'
174 ὑπηκόους ἄρχοντος διαφορᾶς.   ἔστι δὲ
καὶ κατὰ τὸν ἀέρα ψυχῶν ἀσωμάτων ἱερώτατος
χορὸς ὀπαδὸς τῶν οὐρανίων· ἀγγέλους τὰς ψυχὰς
ταύτας εἴωθε καλεῖν ὁ θεσπιῳδὸς λόγος· πάντ' οὖν
τὸν στρατὸν ἑκάστων[2] ἐν ταῖς ἁρμοττούσαις διακεκοσμημένον τάξεσιν ὑπηρέτην καὶ θεραπευτὴν
εἶναι συμβέβηκε τοῦ διακοσμήσαντος ἡγεμόνος, ᾧ
ταξιαρχοῦντι κατὰ δίκην καὶ θεσμὸν ἕπεται·
λιποταξίου γὰρ οὐ θέμις ἁλῶναί ποτε τὸ θεῖον
175 στράτευμα. βασιλεῖ δὲ ταῖς ἑαυτοῦ δυνάμεσιν
ἐμπρεπὲς ὁμιλεῖν τε καὶ χρῆσθαι πρὸς τὰς τῶν
τοιούτων πραγμάτων ὑπηρεσίας, οἷσπερ ἁρμόττει
μὴ ὑπὸ μόνου πήγνυσθαι θεοῦ. χρεῖος μὲν γὰρ

---

[1] mss. ἐπίνοιαν.
[2] Mangey suggests ἑκατέρων, Wend. ἐκείνων.   See App.
p. 558.

---

[a] See App. p. 558.
[b] Cf. Deut. iv. 19, which Philo probably has in mind.

which all assist and protect created being, and among them are included the powers of chastisement. Now chastisement is not a thing of harm or mischief, but a preventive and correction of sin. Through these 172 Potencies the incorporeal and intelligible world was framed, the archetype of this phenomenal world, that being a system of invisible ideal forms, as this is of visible material bodies. Now the nature of 173 these two worlds has so struck with awe the minds of some, that they have deified not merely each of them as a whole,[a] but also their fairest parts, the sun, the moon and the whole sky,[b] and have felt no shame in calling them gods. It was the delusion of such persons that Moses saw, when he says " Lord, Lord, King of the Gods "[c] (Deut. x. 17), to shew the difference between the ruler and the subjects.

There is, too, in the air a sacred company of unbodied 174 souls, commonly called angels in the inspired pages, who wait upon these heavenly powers. So the whole army composed of the several contingents, each marshalled in their proper ranks, have as their business to serve and minister to the word of the Captain who thus marshalled them, and to follow His leadership as right and the law of service demand. For it must not be that God's soldiers should ever be guilty of desertion from the ranks.[d] Now the King may fitly 175 hold converse with his powers and employ them to serve in matters which should not be consummated by God alone. It is true indeed that the Father of

[c] Very inaccurately quoted for ὁ κύριος ὁ θεὸς ὑμῶν, οὗτος θεὸς τῶν θεῶν.

[d] For the leading ideas of the following sections, viz. God as the cause of good alone and His employment of subordinates, see notes on De Op. 72, and De Agr. 128, with the references to Plato there given.

οὐδενός ἐστιν ὁ τοῦ παντὸς πατήρ, ὡς δεῖσθαι τῆς
ἀφ' ἑτέρων, εἰ ἐθέλοι δημιουργῆσαι, ⟨συμπράξεως⟩,[1]
τὸ δὲ πρέπον ὁρῶν ἑαυτῷ τε καὶ τοῖς γινομένοις
ταῖς ὑπηκόοις δυνάμεσιν ἔστιν ἃ διαπλάττειν
ἐφῆκεν, οὐδὲ ταύταις εἰσάπαν αὐτοκράτορα δοὺς
τοῦ τελεσιουργεῖν ἐπιστήμην,[2] ἵνα μή τι πλημ-
μεληθείη τῶν ἀφικνουμένων εἰς γένεσιν.

176 XXXV. ταῦτα μὲν οὖν ἀναγκαῖον ἦν προτυπῶσαι·
ὧν δὲ χάριν, ἤδη λεκτέον· ἡ μὲν φύσις τῶν ζῴων
εἴς τε ἄλογον καὶ λογικὴν μοῖραν, ἐναντίας ἀλλή-
[432] λαις, ἐτμήθη τὸ πρῶτον, | ἡ δ' αὖ λογικὴ πάλιν
εἴς τε τὸ φθαρτὸν καὶ ἀθάνατον εἶδος, φθαρτὸν
μὲν τὸ ἀνθρώπων, ἀθάνατον δὲ τὸ ψυχῶν ἀσωμάτων, αἳ κατά τε ἀέρα καὶ οὐρανὸν περιπολοῦσι.

177 κακίας δὲ ἀμέτοχοι μέν εἰσιν αὗται, τὸν ἀκήρατον
καὶ εὐδαίμονα κλῆρον ἐξ ἀρχῆς λαχοῦσαι καὶ
τῷ συμφορῶν ἀνηνύτων οὐκ ἐνδεθεῖσαι χωρίῳ,
σώματι, ἀμέτοχοι δὲ καὶ ⟨αἱ⟩ τῶν ἀλόγων, παρόσον ἀμοιροῦσαι διανοίας οὐδὲ τῶν ἐκ λογισμοῦ
συμβαινόντων ἑκουσίων ἀδικημάτων ἁλίσκονται.

178 μόνος δὲ σχεδὸν ἐκ πάντων ὁ ἄνθρωπος ἀγαθῶν
καὶ κακῶν ἔχων ἐπιστήμην αἱρεῖται μὲν πολλάκις
τὰ φαυλότατα, φεύγει δὲ τὰ σπουδῆς ἄξια, ὥστ'
αὐτὸν[3] μάλιστα ἐπὶ τοῖς ἐκ προνοίας ἁμαρτήμασι

179 καταγινώσκεσθαι.   προσηκόντως οὖν τὴν
τούτου κατασκευὴν ὁ θεὸς περιῆψε καὶ τοῖς ὑπ-
άρχοις αὐτοῦ λέγων· '' ποιήσωμεν ἄνθρωπον,'' ἵνα
αἱ μὲν τοῦ ἀνθρώπου[4] κατορθώσεις ἐπ' αὐτὸν ἀνα-

---

[1] The insertion is perhaps unnecessary, as ὑπηρεσίας (which
Mangey suggested in preference to συμπράξεως) might possibly be understood from the previous sentence.
[2] Wend. suggests ἐξουσίαν, cf. § 181. If alteration is required, I should prefer ἐπιστασίαν. Cf. De Cher. 24.

All has no need of aught, so that He should require the co-operation of others, if He wills some creative work, yet seeing what was fitting to Himself and the world which was coming into being, He allowed His subject powers to have the fashioning of some things, though He did not give them sovereign and independent knowledge for completion of the task, lest aught of what was coming into being should be miscreated.   XXXV. This outline was 176 needed as premises.   Now for the inferences. Living nature was primarily divided into two opposite parts, the unreasoning and reasoning, this last again into the mortal and immortal species, the mortal being that of men, the immortal that of unbodied souls which range through the air and sky. These 177 are immune from wickedness because their lot from the first has been one of unmixed happiness, and they have not been imprisoned in that dwelling-place of endless calamities—the body. And this immunity is shared by unreasoning natures, because, as they have no gift of understanding, they are also not guilty of wrongdoing willed freely as a result of deliberate reflection.   Man is practically the only 178 being who having knowledge of good and evil often chooses the worst, and shuns what should be the object of his efforts, and thus he stands apart as convicted of sin deliberate and aforethought.

Thus it was meet and right that when man was 179 formed, God should assign a share in the work to His lieutenants, as He does with the words " let *us* make men," that so man's right actions might be attribut-

---

[3] MSS. ὡς ταῦτα or ὡς ταύτῃ.

[4] So Wend. and Mangey: MSS. νοῦ, which might be defended as equivalent to the ψυχὴ λογική below.

PHILO

φέρωνται μόνον, ἐπ' ἄλλους δὲ αἱ ἁμαρτίαι. θεῷ
γὰρ τῷ πανηγεμόνι ἐμπρεπὲς οὐκ ἔδοξεν εἶναι τὴν
ἐπὶ κακίαν ὁδὸν ἐν ψυχῇ λογικῇ δι' ἑαυτοῦ δημιουρ-
γῆσαι· οὗ χάριν τοῖς μετ' αὐτὸν ἐπέτρεψε τὴν
τούτου τοῦ μέρους κατασκευήν. ἔδει γὰρ καὶ τὸ
ἀντίπαλον τῷ ἀκουσίῳ, τὸ ἑκούσιον, εἰς τὴν τοῦ
παντὸς συμπλήρωσιν κατασκευασθὲν ἀναδειχθῆναι.

180 XXXVI. τοῦτο μὲν δὴ ταύτῃ λελέχθω.
προσήκει δὲ κἀκεῖνο λελογίσθαι, ὅτι μόνων ἀγαθῶν
ἐστιν ὁ θεὸς αἴτιος, κακοῦ δὲ οὐδενὸς τὸ παράπαν,
ἐπειδὴ καὶ τὸ πρεσβύτατον τῶν ὄντων καὶ τελειότατον ἀγαθὸν αὐτὸς ἦν. ἐμπρεπέστατον[1] δὲ τὰ
οἰκεῖα τῇ ἑαυτοῦ φύσει δημιουργεῖν ἄριστα τῷ
ἀρίστῳ,[2] τὰς μέντοι κατὰ πονηρῶν κολάσεις διὰ
181 τῶν ὑπ' αὐτὸν βεβαιοῦσθαι. μαρτυρεῖ δέ μου τῷ
λόγῳ καὶ τὸ εἰρημένον ὑπὸ τοῦ τελειωθέντος ἐξ
ἀσκήσεως τόδε· " ὁ θεὸς ὁ τρέφων με ἐκ νεότητος,
ὁ ἄγγελος ὁ ῥυόμενός με ἐκ πάντων τῶν κακῶν."
ὁμολογεῖ γὰρ καὶ οὗτος ἤδη, ὅτι τὰ μὲν γνήσια
τῶν ἀγαθῶν, ἃ φιλαρέτους τρέφει ψυχάς, ἐπὶ θεὸν
ἀναφέρεται μόνον ὡς αἴτιον, ἡ δὲ τῶν κακῶν μοῖρα
ἀγγέλοις ἐπιτέτραπται πάλιν, οὐδὲ ἐκείνοις ἔχουσι
τὴν τοῦ κολάζειν αὐτοκράτορα ἐξουσίαν, ἵνα
μηδενὸς τῶν εἰς φθορὰν τεινόντων ἡ σωτήριος
182 αὐτοῦ κατάρχῃ φύσις. διὸ λέγει· " δεῦτε καὶ
καταβάντες συγχέωμεν." οἱ μὲν γὰρ ἀσεβεῖς
τοιαύτης ἐπάξιοι δίκης τυγχάνειν, ἵλεως καὶ εὐερ-
γέτιδας καὶ φιλοδώρους αὐτοῦ δυνάμεις οἰκειοῦσθαι
τιμωρίαις. εἰδὼς μέντοι τῷ γένει τῶν ἀνθρώπων
ὠφελίμους ὑπαρχούσας δι' ἑτέρων αὐτὰς ὥρισεν·

[1] MSS. ἐμπρεπέστατα.
[2] MSS. τῶν ἀρίστων or τὸν ἄριστον.

able to God, but his sins to others. For it seemed to be unfitting to God the All-ruler that the road to wickedness within the reasonable soul should be of His making, and therefore He delegated the forming of this part to His inferiors. For the work of forming the voluntary element to balance the involuntary had to be accomplished to render the whole complete.

XXXVI. So much for this point, but 180 it is well to have considered this truth also, that God is the cause of good things only and of nothing at all that is bad, since He Himself was the most ancient of beings and the good in its most perfect form. And it best becomes Him that the work of His hands should be akin to His nature, surpassing in excellence even as He surpasses, but that the chastisement of the wicked should be assured through His underlings. My thoughts are attested also by the words 181 of him who was made perfect through practice, " the God who nourisheth me from my youth ; the angel who saveth me from all evils " (Gen. xlviii. 15, 16). For he, too, hereby confesses that the truly good gifts, which nourish virtue-loving souls, are referred to God alone as their cause, but on the other hand the province of things evil has been committed to angels (though neither have they full and absolute power of punishment), that nothing which tends to destruction should have its origin in Him whose nature is to save. Therefore he says, " Come and 182 let us go down and confound them." The impious indeed deserve to have it as their punishment, that God's beneficent and merciful and bountiful powers should be brought into association with works of vengeance. Yet, though knowing that punishment was salutary for the human race, He decreed that it

ἔδει γὰρ τὸ μὲν ἐπανορθώσεως ἀξιωθῆναι, τὰς δὲ
πηγὰς τῶν ἀεννάων αὐτοῦ χαρίτων ἀμιγεῖς κακῶν
[433] | οὐκ ὄντων μόνον ἀλλὰ καὶ νομιζομένων φυλαχθῆναι.
183 XXXVII. Τίς δέ ἐστιν ἡ σύγχυσις, ἐρευνητέον.
πῶς οὖν ἐρευνήσομεν; οὕτως, ὥς γ᾽ ἐμοὶ φαίνεται·
πολλάκις οὓς πρότερον οὐκ ᾔδειμεν, ἀπὸ τῶν συγ-
γενῶν καί τινα πρὸς αὐτοὺς ἐχόντων ἐμφέρειαν
ἐγνωρίσαμεν· οὐκοῦν καὶ πράγματα τὸν αὐτὸν
τρόπον, ἃ μὴ ῥᾴδιον ἐξ ἑαυτῶν καταλαμβάνεσθαι,
δῆλα γένοιτ᾽ ἂν κατὰ τὴν τῶν οἰκείων αὐτοῖς
184 ὁμοιότητα. τίνα οὖν ἐστι συγχύσει πράγματα
ὅμοια; ἡ μῖξις, ὥσπερ ὁ παλαιὸς λόγος, καὶ
κρᾶσις· ἀλλ᾽ ἡ μὲν μῖξις ἐν ξηραῖς, ἡ δὲ κρᾶσις ἐν
185 ὑγραῖς οὐσίαις δοκιμάζεται. μῖξις μὲν οὖν σωμάτων διαφερόντων ἐστὶν οὐκ ἐν κόσμῳ παράθεσις,
ὥσπερ ἂν εἴ τις σωρὸν ποιήσειε κριθὰς καὶ πυροὺς
καὶ ὀρόβους καὶ ἄλλ᾽ ἄττα εἴδη τῶν σπαρτῶν εἰς
ταὐτὸ εἰσενεγκών, κρᾶσις δ᾽ οὐ παράθεσις, ἀλλὰ
τῶν ἀνομοίων μερῶν εἰς ἄλληλα εἰσδυομένων δι᾽
ὅλων ἀντιπαρέκτασις, ἔτι δυναμένων ἐπιτεχνήσει
τινὶ διακρίνεσθαι τῶν ποιοτήτων, ὡς ἐπὶ οἴνου καὶ
186 ὕδατός φασι γίνεσθαι· συνελθούσας μὲν γὰρ τὰς
οὐσίας ἀποτελεῖν κρᾶσιν, τὸ δὲ κραθὲν οὐδὲν ἧττον
ἀναπλοῦσθαι πάλιν εἰς τὰς ἐξ ὧν ἀπετελέσθη
ποιότητας· σπόγγῳ γὰρ ἡλαιωμένῳ τὸ μὲν ὕδωρ
ἀναλαμβάνεσθαι, τὸν δ᾽ οἶνον ὑπολείπεσθαι· μήποτε

ᵃ Philo here seems to assign the work of punishment
to the lower division of the ministers rather than to the
Potencies, though elsewhere he treats it as belonging to the
Kingly Potency indicated by the name of ὁ Κύριος, *e.g.*
De Abr. 144, 145. Here the "angels" have the whole
province of evil assigned to them, whether to save from it,
as with Jacob, or to inflict it.

should be exacted by others.[a] It was meet that while mankind was judged to deserve correction, the fountains of God's ever-flowing gifts of grace should be kept free not only from all that is, but from all that is deemed to be, evil.

XXXVII. We must now inquire what is meant by 183 " confusion." What should be our method ? The following in my opinion. We often obtain a knowledge of persons whom we have not known before from their kinsfolk or those who bear some resemblance to them. And so in the same way things which in themselves are not easy to apprehend may reveal their nature through their likeness to their congeners. [b] What things then resemble confusion ? 184 " Mechanical mixture," to use the old philosophical term, and " chemical mixture." The first presents itself for examination in dry substances, the latter in liquid. Mechanical mixture of different bodies 185 occurs when they are juxtaposed in no regular order, as when we collect barley and wheat and pulse or any other kind of grain and pile them together. Chemical mixture is not juxtaposition, but the mutual coextension and complete interpenetration of dissimilar parts, though their various qualities can still be distinguished by artificial means, as is said to be the case with water and wine. These substances 186 if united do produce, we are told, a chemical mixture, but all the same that mixture can be resolved [c] into the different qualities out of which it was composed. A sponge dipped in oil will absorb the water and leave the wine. Probably the explanation is that

---

[b] See App. p. 558 on this and the following sections.
[c] See App. p. 558.

ἐπειδήπερ ἐξ ὕδατος ἡ σπογγιᾶς γένεσίς ἐστι, τὸ
μὲν οἰκεῖον, ὕδωρ, πέφυκεν ἀναλαμβάνεσθαι πρὸς
αὐτῆς ἐκ τοῦ κράματος, τὸ δ' ἀλλότριον ὑπολεί-
187 πεσθαι, ὁ οἶνος.   σύγχυσις δέ ἐστι φθορὰ
τῶν ἐξ ἀρχῆς ποιοτήτων πᾶσι τοῖς μέρεσιν ἀντι-
παρεκτεινομένων εἰς διαφερούσης μιᾶς[1] γένεσιν, ὡς
ἐπὶ τῆς ἐν ἰατρικῇ τετραφαρμάκου συντέτευχε·
κηρὸς γὰρ καὶ στέαρ καὶ πίττα ῥητίνη τε, οἶμαι,
συνελθόντα ταύτην ἀποτελεῖ, συντεθείσης δὲ ἀμήχανον ἔτι[2] τὰς ἐξ ὧν συνετέθη διακριθῆναι δυνάμεις,
ἀλλ' ἑκάστη μὲν αὐτῶν ἠφάνισται, πασῶν δ' ἡ
φθορὰ μίαν ἐξαίρετον ἄλλην ἐγέννησε δύναμιν.
188 ὅταν δ' ἀπειλῇ σύγχυσιν τοῖς ἀσεβέσι λογισμοῖς ὁ
θεός, οὐ μόνον ἑκάστης κακίας τό τε εἶδος καὶ τὴν
δύναμιν ἀφανισθῆναι κελεύει, ἀλλὰ καὶ τὸ συν-
ερανισθὲν ἐξ αὐτῶν, ἵνα μήτε τὰ μέρη καθ' ἑαυτὰ
μήθ' ἡ πάντων σύνοδός τε καὶ συμφωνία περι-
βάληταί τινα ἰσχὺν ἐπὶ καθαιρέσει τῆς ἀμείνονος
189 μοίρας. οὗ χάριν φησί· " συγχέωμεν ἐκεῖ αὐτῶν
τὴν γλῶτταν, ἵνα μὴ ἀκούσωσιν ἕκαστος τὴν φωνὴν
τοῦ πλησίον," ὅπερ ἴσον ἐστὶ τούτῳ· κωφὸν
ἕκαστον ἐργασώμεθα τῶν κακίας μερῶν, ὡς μήτε
ἰδίαν ἀφιὲν[3] ⟨φωνὴν⟩ μήτε συνηχοῦν ἑτέρῳ βλάβης
190 αἴτιον γίνηται.   XXXVIII. ταῦτα μὲν
ἡμεῖς, οἱ δὲ τοῖς ἐμφανέσι καὶ προχείροις μόνον
[434] ἐπακολουθοῦντες οἴονται νυνὶ γένεσιν | διαλέκτων
Ἑλληνικῶν τε καὶ βαρβάρων ὑπογράφεσθαι· οὓς

---

[1] mss. μίαν.   [2] mss. ἐπὶ.   [3] mss. ἀφιέναι.

---

[a] See App. p. 558.
[b] Lit. "another single special power." This use of
δύναμις which suggests both "nature" and "value" cannot
be translated by any single or at least any singular word.

since the sponge is produced out of water, it tends to absorb out of the mixture the substance which is akin to it, the water, and leave the foreign substance, the wine. But confusion is the annihila- 187 tion *a* of the original varieties or qualities, which become coextensive through all the parts and thus produce a single and quite different quality. An example of this is the quadruple drug used in medicine. This is produced, I believe, by the combination of wax, tallow, pitch and resin, but, when the compound has been formed, it is impossible to analyse or separate the properties which went to form it. Each of them has been annihilated, and from this loss of identity in each has sprung another single something with properties peculiar to itself.*b* But 188 when God threatens impious thoughts with confusion He does not order merely the annihilation of the specific nature and properties of each separate vice. The order applies also to the aggregate to which they have contributed. He means that neither their separate parts, nor yet their united body and voice, shall be invested with strength to destroy the better element. And therefore he says, " Let us confound 189 their tongue there, that each of them may not understand the voice of his neighbour " (Gen. xi. 7), and this is equivalent to " let us make each part of vice mute that it may not by its separate utterance nor yet in unison with the others be the cause of mischief."

XXXVIII. This is our explanation, 190 but those who merely follow the outward and obvious think that we have at this point a reference to the origin of the Greek and barbarian languages. I

For this use of ἐξαίρετος *cf. De Op.* 62, where the senses have each their ἐξαίρετος ὕλη.

οὐκ ἂν αἰτιασάμενος—ἴσως γὰρ ἀληθεῖ καὶ αὐτοὶ
χρῶνται λόγῳ—παρακαλέσαιμ' ἂν μὴ ἐπὶ τούτων
στῆναι, μετελθεῖν δὲ ἐπὶ τὰς τροπικὰς ἀποδόσεις,
νομίσαντας τὰ μὲν ῥητὰ τῶν χρησμῶν σκιάς τινας
ὡσανεὶ σωμάτων εἶναι, τὰς δ' ἐμφαινομένας δυνά-
191 μεις τὰ ὑφεστῶτα ἀληθείᾳ πράγματα. δίδωσι
μέντοι πρὸς τοῦτ' ἀφορμὰς τὸ εἶδος τοῖς μὴ τυφλοῖς
διάνοιαν ὁ νομοθέτης αὐτός, ὥσπερ ἀμέλει καὶ ἐφ'
ὧν νῦν ἐστιν ὁ λόγος· τὸ γὰρ γινόμενον σύγχυσιν
προσεῖπε.   καίτοι γε εἰ διαλέκτων γένεσιν αὐτὸ μόνον ἐδήλου, κἂν ὄνομα εὐθυβολώτερον
ἐπεφήμισεν ἀντὶ συγχύσεως διάκρισιν· οὐ γὰρ
συγχεῖται τὰ τεμνόμενα, διακρίνεται δ' ἔμπαλιν,
καὶ ἔστιν οὐ μόνον ἐναντίον ὄνομα ὀνόματι, ἀλλ'
192 ἔργον ἔργῳ. σύγχυσις μὲν γάρ, ὡς ἔφην, ἐστὶ
φθορὰ τῶν ἁπλῶν δυνάμεων εἰς συμπεφορημένης
μιᾶς γένεσιν, διάκρισις δὲ ἑνὸς εἰς πλείω τομή,
καθάπερ ἐπὶ γένους καὶ τῶν κατ' αὐτὸ εἰδῶν ἔχειν
συντέτευχεν. ὥστε εἰ μίαν οὖσαν φωνὴν ἐκέλευσε
τέμνειν ὁ σοφὸς εἰς πλειόνων διαλέκτων τμήματα,
προσεχεστέροις ἂν καὶ κυριωτέροις ἐχρήσατο τοῖς
ὀνόμασι, τομὴν ἢ διανέμησιν ἢ διάκρισιν ἤ τι
ὁμοιότροπον εἰπών, οὐ τὸ μαχόμενον αὐτοῖς,
193 σύγχυσιν. ἀλλ' ἔστιν ἡ σπουδὴ διαλῦσαι τὸ κακίας
στῖφος, τὰς ὁμολογίας αὐτῆς ἀκυρῶσαι, τὴν κοινωνίαν ἀνελεῖν, τὰς δυνάμεις ἀφανίσαι καὶ διαφθεῖραι,
τὸ τῆς ἀρχῆς κράτος, ὃ δειναῖς ὠχυρώσατο παρα-

---

[a] Or more literally "the destruction of the simple uncom-
pounded natures, to produce a single compounded nature."
[b] *i.e.* Moses, not God. Philo often calls God ὁ μόνος
σοφός, but not ὁ σοφός. The command is thought of as
emanating from Moses, because the language in which it is
clothed is his.

would not censure such persons, for perhaps the truth is with them also. Still I would exhort them not to halt there, but to press on to allegorical interpretations and to recognize that the letter is to the oracle but as the shadow to the substance and that the higher values therein revealed are what really and truly exist. Indeed the lawgiver himself gives 191 openings for this kind of treatment to those whose understanding is not blinded, as he certainly does in the case now under discussion, when he calls what was then taking place a "confusion."

Surely if he had merely meant that different languages then originated, he would have applied a more correct term and called it "separation" rather than "confusion." For when things are divided they are not "confused," but quite the contrary, "separated." And the contradiction is not merely one of name but of fact. Confusion—the process of fusing 192 together—is, as I have said, the annihilation of the individual properties, and the production thereby of a single whole with its own properties,[a] whereas separation is the division of one into several, as in the case of genus and the species, which form the genus. And therefore if the Sage's[b] command was to divide speech, the single whole, by section into several languages, he would have used more apposite and exact terms such as dissection or distribution or separation, and not their opposite, confusion. But 193 his purpose and desire is to break up the company of vice, to make her agreements of none effect, to do away with her fellowship, to annihilate and destroy her powers, to overthrow the might of her queenship which by her abominable transgressions she had

194 νομίαις, καθελεῖν.   οὐχ ὁρᾷς ὅτι καὶ τῶν ψυχῆς ὁ πλάστης μερῶν οὐδὲν οὐδενὶ εἰς τὴν τοῦ ἑτέρου κοινωνίαν ἤγαγεν; ἀλλ' ὀφθαλμοὶ μὲν οὐκ ἂν ἀκούσειαν, ὦτα δὲ οὐκ ἂν θεάσαιτο, χυλὸς δὲ ἐνστόμιος¹ οὐκ ἂν ὄσφροιτο, οὐδ' ἂν γεύσαιντο ῥῖνες, ὅ τ' αὖ λόγος οὐδὲν ἂν τῶν κατὰ τὰς αἰσθήσεις πάθοι, οὐδ' ἔμπαλιν ῥῆξαι φωνὴν δύναιτ' ἂν

195 αἴσθησις. ἔγνω γὰρ ὁ τεχνίτης, ὅτι τὸ μὴ ἀκούειν ἕκαστον τούτων τῆς τοῦ πλησίον φωνῆς λυσιτελές ἐστιν, ἀλλὰ τὰ μὲν τῆς ψυχῆς μέρη ταῖς οἰκείαις δυνάμεσιν ἀσυγχύτοις χρῆσθαι πρὸς τὴν τῶν ζῴων ὠφέλειαν καὶ τὴν πρὸς ἄλληλα κοινωνίαν ἀφ-ῃρῆσθαι,² τὰ δὲ τῆς κακίας εἰς ⟨σύγ⟩χυσιν καὶ φθορὰν ἀχθῆναι παντελῆ, ἵνα μήτε συμφωνήσαντα μήτε καθ' ἑαυτὰ ὄντα ζημία τοῖς ἀμείνοσι γένηται.

196 Παρὸ καὶ λέγει· "διέσπειρεν αὐτοὺς κύριος ἐκεῖθεν," ἐν ἴσῳ τῷ ἐσκέδασεν, ἐφυγάδευσεν, ἀφανεῖς ἐποίησε· τὸ γὰρ σπείρειν ⟨ἀγαθῶν, κακῶν δὲ αἴτιον τὸ διασπείρειν⟩, ὅτι τὸ μὲν ἐπιδόσεως καὶ αὐξήσεως καὶ γενέσεως ἑτέρων ἕνεκα συμ-βαίνει, τὸ δ' ἀπωλείας καὶ φθορᾶς. βούλεται δὲ ὁ

[435] φυτουργὸς θεὸς σπείρειν μὲν ἐν τῷ παντὶ | καλο-κἀγαθίαν, διασπείρειν δὲ καὶ ἐλαύνειν ἐκ τῆς τοῦ κόσμου πολιτείας τὴν ἐπάρατον ἀσέβειαν, ἵν' ἤδη ποτὲ παύσωνται τὴν κακίας πόλιν καὶ τὸν ἀθεό-τητος πύργον οἰκοδομοῦντες μισάρετοι τρόποι.

197 τούτων γὰρ σκεδασθέντων οἱ πάλαι πεφευγότες τὴν τυραννίδα τῆς ἀφροσύνης ἑνὶ κηρύγματι κάθοδον

---

¹ So Wend.; cf. *De Ebr.* 190: mss. ἐνστοματίας or ἐν στόματι. The latter does not seem impossible.
² mss. καὶ εἰ . . . ἀφῄρηται.

made so strong.   Observe that he who **194**
fashioned the living being, brought none of its parts
into fellowship with any other. The eyes cannot
hear, nor the ears see ; the palatal juices cannot
smell, nor the nostrils taste ; nor again can speech
have any of the sensations which the senses produce,
just as on the other hand the senses have no power
of utterance. For the great Contriver knew that it **195**
was well for them that none should hear the voice of
his neighbour. He willed rather in the interests of
animal life, that each part of the living organism
should have the use of its own particular powers
without confusion with others, and that fellowship of
part with part should be withdrawn from them, while
on the other hand the parts of vice should be brought
into confusion and complete annihilation, so that
neither in unison nor separately by themselves should
they become a source of injury to their betters.

That is why he adds—The Lord dispersed them **196**
thence (Gen. xi. 8), that is He caused them to be
scattered, to be fugitives, to vanish from sight. For
while sowing is the cause of good, dispersing or
sowing broadcast is the cause of ill. The purpose of
the first is to improve, to increase, to create something else ; the purpose of the second is to ruin and
destroy. But God the Master-planter wills to sow
noble living throughout the All, and to disperse and
banish from the Commonwealth of the world the
impiety which He holds accursed. Thus the evil
ways which hate virtue may at last cease to build
the city of vice and the tower of godlessness. For **197**
when these are scattered, those who have been living
in exile for many a day under the ban of folly's
tyranny, shall receive their recall under a single

117

εὑρήσουσι, γράψαντός τε καὶ βεβαιώσαντος ⟨θεοῦ⟩
τὸ κήρυγμα, ὡς δηλοῦσιν οἱ χρησμοί, ἐν οἷς
διείρηται ὅτι '' ἐὰν ᾖ ἡ διασπορά σου ἀπ' ἄκρου
τοῦ οὐρανοῦ ἕως ἄκρου τοῦ οὐρανοῦ, ἐκεῖθεν
198 συνάξει σε ''· ὥστε τὴν μὲν ἀρετῶν συμφωνίαν
ἐμπρεπὲς ἁρμόζεσθαι θεῷ, τὴν δὲ κακιῶν[1] διαλύειν
τε καὶ φθείρειν. οἰκειότατον δὲ κακίας ὄνομα
σύγχυσις· οὗ πίστις ἐναργὴς πᾶς ἄφρων, λόγοις
καὶ βουλαῖς καὶ πράξεσιν ἀδοκίμοις καὶ πεφορη-
μέναις χρώμενος.

[1] MSS. κακίαν.

[a] *i.e.* the two ideas which have been connected with
σύγχυσις are φθορά and διασπορά. The first of these is here

proclamation, even the proclamation enacted and ratified by God, as the oracles shew, in which it is declared that " if thy dispersion be from one end of heaven to the other he shall gather thee from thence " (Deut. xxx. 4). Thus it is a work well-befitting to 198 God to bring into full harmony the consonance of the virtues, but to dissipate and destroy the consonance of vices. Yes, confusion is indeed a most proper name for vice, and a standing evidence of this is every fool, whose words and purposes and deeds alike are worthless and unstable.[a]

expressed by ἀδόκιμος which often means something not merely worthless but cast away as such. The second is expressed by πεφορημένος. But see App. p. 559.

ON THE MIGRATION OF ABRAHAM

(DE MIGRATIONE ABRAHAMI)

ANALYTICAL INTRODUCTION

THE subject of this treatise is Gen. xii. 1-4 and 6. This naturally falls into two divisions, of which the first contains the words of God to Abraham. This again is analysed as follows :

I. (a) The command to depart from country, kindred and father's house.

(b) To the land which I will shew thee (this constitutes the first promise or gift to Abraham).

(c) And I will make thee a great nation (Second Gift).

(d) And I will bless thee (Third Gift).

(e) And I will magnify thy name (Fourth Gift).

(f) And thou shalt be blessed (Fifth Gift).

(g) I will bless them that bless thee, and curse them that curse thee.

And in thee shall all the nations of the earth be blessed (the gifts to others through Abraham.)

In the second part we deal successively with the statements.

(a) He went as God spake to him.

(b) And Lot went with him.

(c) And Abraham was seventy-five years old, when he went forth out of Haran.

(d) And Abraham travelled through the land to

the length of it, to the place Shechem t
high oak.

" Land " means spiritually body, " kinsf
senses (2-4), while " father's house " is speech,
this last is illustrated by the way in which the I
itself is spoken of as God's house (4-6). Thu
command is to alienate ourselves from these
so to " depart " to higher realities (7-12). Bi
examples of this departing follow : Abraham
Lot, the Exodus of Israel from Egypt (13-15), a
connexion with this Philo propounds the idea
when we read of Joseph's body being placed
coffin in Egypt, and later of his bones being tak
Canaan at the Exodus, we have an allegory o
spiritual burial of the lower qualities, and the sur
of the higher qualities of the mixed or Joseph
(16-17). An enumeration of these higher qualiti
shewn in the story of Joseph follows (18-23),
from this we pass back to the theme of " depart
as shewn in the order of Moses to make the Pas
" with speed " (24-25), and (with a difference *a*) i
injunction in Gen. xxxi. 3 to Jacob to turn back t
father's land, which must be understood in the
of wisdom (26-30). The last words of that pas
" I will be with thee," lead to a meditation on
independent of our efforts is the Divine presenc
inspiration, which Philo illustrates from his
experience in literary composition (31-35), w
we pass almost insensibly to the consideration o
words of the First Gift, " The land which I will
thee." After some thoughts about the "
shewn," *i.e.* the perfect good, " the person who s
i.e. the wise man, and the " Shewer," *i.e.* God (3

a For the difference see note on § 26.

Philo points out that the shewing is in the future, thus calling for Abraham's faith. He illustrates it further from the words of Deut. xxxiv. 4, " I shewed it to thine eyes but thou shalt not possess it," and this points to the thought that possession of the perfect good is more than seeing it (43-46). And yet seeing is higher than hearing, and thus God's words are said in certain places to be seen rather than heard, a noteworthy usage when we remember that hearing in the ordinary sense is even less than the other senses capable of being associated with sight (47-52).

We pass on to the Second Gift. " I will make thee a great nation." Here nation can be taken to mean " multitude of qualities." " Great " shews something more, namely that the qualities grow to their full stature (53-55). A great nation is elsewhere defined as one which draws nigh to God (56-59). Indeed, mere quantity or multitude is often spoken of as an evil thing, which is vanquished by the little and good (59-63). The many-footed is called an abomination in Leviticus. This reminds us that the footless which crawls on its belly, is equally an abomination (64-65). And thence he digresses for the moment to suggest that the breast stands for the spirited element, as the belly stands for desire, and it is when both these are exscinded as in the sacrificial directions of Lev. viii., and reason is left supreme, that we get both multitude and greatness (65-68). From another point of view the many-footed and the footless are respectively the polytheist and the atheist (69).

The Third Gift is " I will bless thee " (εὐλογήσω). Looking at the composition of the word, Philo takes this to mean " I will give thee excellent Logos." Now Logos is both thought and speech, and this last

125

leads him to the idea that mastery of language is needed by the sage and that otherwise he will be unable to hold his own against the sophist (70-75). This is illustrated first from the case of Cain and Abel and then from that of Moses, and there follows a commentary on Exodus iv. 10-16 in which " Aaron thy brother " is shewn to represent the speech or eloquence which rejoices when it finds clear conceptions to express (76-81). It is this use of language in the service of truth which is shewn by the story of Moses with Aaron's rod outdoing the Egyptian magicians (82-85).[a]

The Fourth Gift is " I will magnify thy name." Here " name " is interpreted as equivalent to what we seem. The seeming indeed is worthless without the being, but true happiness consists in both (86-88). The need of obedience to established custom is a necessary consequence, and here Philo takes the opportunity to define his attitude to the literal Law, Sabbath, Circumcision, Feast-days. Though these have their soul, namely the spiritual interpretation, they have also their body, and the body is the house of the soul, and must not be set at nought (89-94). The same lesson is taught by the " lesser substance " bequeathed by Abraham to the children of the concubines who, though of less account, were still children (94). So too Leah accounted herself blessed, because women will count her such, and by women are meant those comparatively earth-bound souls whose esteem is nevertheless valuable (95-96). This leads to an illustration from the work entrusted by Moses to the women—the senses, that is—but the senses also must have their due if happiness is to be

[a] Much of this part reproduces parts of *Quod Det.*

had (97-100). This thought is further developed from Isaac's prayer that Jacob may have the wealth of earth as well as of heaven, and from Aaron's robe on which the sensible world is figured by the bells whose sound was to be audible when he entered the Holy Place (101-104). So the sensible must second the music of the mental in the great Choir, and the three-fold phrase of Ex. xxi., the "needful," the "raiment," and the "fellowship," means that the sensible and the mental must be so blended that we shall find in the first the sacrament of the second (104-105).

Yet in the three next sections Philo swings round to the other point of view. The Fifth Gift is "Thou shalt be blessed." Here he reads εὐλογητός (meet to be blessed), for the εὐλογημένος (subject to blessing) of our texts, and thence deduces, in spite of all that has been said, that true blessedness is to him who is worthy of it rather than to him who is so reputed by men (106-108).

In the next words, "I will bless them who bless thee, and curse them who curse thee," we go on to shew what the Abraham mind can do for others. It stands to reason that to praise the praiseworthy is in itself a praiseworthy act, if done in sincerity. But this is an important exception, and thus the blessing of Israel by Balaam, splendid as it is, only brought on him God's curse (109-115). Conversely, curses which are meant to benefit, such as the rebukes of those who have charge of the young, bring blessings on those who speak them. All depends on the intention (115-117).

The next words "And in thee shall all the tribes of the earth be blessed" shew that the blessing con-

ferred by the Abraham spirit is not to be limited to
those who know its value. In one sense indeed the
words may be applied to the individual himself. The
perfect mind will sanctify all its tribes, that is, all
its faculties (118-119). But in the wider sense the
righteous man both by his influence and prayers is a
pillar of society. We see this in God's words to Moses
(I will be merciful to them for thy word) ; in the
willingness to spare Sodom, if only a few righteous
could be found there ; most of all in the story of Noah,
who victorious over the deluge of moral decay, founded
the line of Israel, which, though obscured at times,
will be brought to the light again, when that season
comes of which God spoke to Sarah (120-126).

The second part of the treatise begins with the
words : " And Abraham went as the Lord spake."
Philo interprets this to mean that his way of going was
in accordance with God's word, *i.e.* his life was in
accordance with God's laws (127-132). And he
proceeds to ask what the " end " and the " reward "
of such " going " is. The true end and reward is to
be able to recognize that the only thing we can know
is our own ignorance (133-135). This leads to a
denunciation of speculation about the universe
instead of self-examination (136-138). A rambling
discussion of some texts follows (139-142).[a] And
then in contrast to the " going " of Abraham, we have
the weaklings who lag behind and are " cut off " as
the " weary " part of Israel was by Amalek (143-144),
though indeed there is a better kind of weariness
which is typified by Leah (144-145). The treatment
of this part concludes with the thought which has
been fully developed in *Quod Deus*, that the true path

[a] For such thread of thought as there is see note.

of the soul is, as Aristotle taught, along the Mean (146-147).

" Lot went with him." As Lot means " turning away," we see that this was a companionship not to imitate but to hinder, and this is proved by his later disaster and Abraham's separation from him (148-150). That this separation did not take place at once shews that the Abraham soul has still much to learn. The hindrance which is caused by such conflicting companionship is symbolized by the " mixed multitude," which went up from Egypt and caused Israel to wander for forty years (150-155). (Incidentally we hear of this multitude weeping and this leads to a short digression on good and bad tears (155-157).) While some refuse all intercourse with this mixed multitude others make alliance with it, as Joseph, ever the man of compromise, did when he was accompanied by the Egyptians to his father's funeral (158-163). Some illustrations of good fellow-travelling (συμπορεύεσθαι) are now given. Abraham's comrades in war ; Isaac going with Abraham to the sacrifice, signifying the union of natural gifts with effort (164-167).[a] And while it is natural that higher minds should be drawn up to God, as Aaron and his fellow priests were, Moses will cry " Unless thou journey with me (συμπορεύῃ) bring me not up hence," for God must be our fellow-traveller (168-172). Abraham, too, "journeyed with the angels." For though in the imperfect state the Logos leads us, the perfected will walk at his side (173-175).

" Abraham was seventy-five years old when he went forth out of Haran." What do these words mean ? We remember that originally he went from

[a] See further note on § 167.

Chaldea to Haran. Now Chaldea is astrology, which conceives of the universe as a whole where all the parts work in harmony with each other (176-179). So far Moses agrees with it : it is when the astrologers ignore God and His creative goodness that he disagrees (180-183). And when he shews Abraham as leaving Chaldea for Haran, that is, for the place of the senses, which is also the house of the mind, he is bidding us discard astrological speculations for the Socratic study of ourselves (184-189). And when we have done this we may leave Haran also, to contemplate God Himself, just as Saul had to be taken from the " baggage " before he could grasp the kingship (189-197).

" Seventy-five years old." Seventy is the number of the higher mind and reason (198-202), five of the senses (203-206), and both these are proved by many texts (203-206). The combination indicates an intermediate and necessary stage in the soul's progress (207). And so Rebecca bids Jacob even in his hour of triumph fly to Haran, for compromise with the senses is often necessary for a time (208-213). Yet Jacob also will ultimately leave Haran and " make a house for himself," that is, " the fear of God " which won, according to Ex. i. 21 "'their houses' for the midwives " (214-215).

" He travelled through the land to the length of it to the place Shechem, to the high oak." " Travelled through" shews us the course of the soul in its search for wisdom, a search which must cover the whole land *i.e.* whole of ethical philosophy (216-220). In Shechem, which means " shouldering," and in the oak, we find a symbol of the solid labour which such travelling entails (221-223). But we remember that in Genesis we have a man Shechem, who represents evil labour, the seducer of Dinah. Or rather, the would-be seducer. For to Philo's mind the spiritual Dinah being Virtue can never be corrupted, and the treatise ends with the thought that the vengeance of her brothers and defenders will overtake the seducer with his purpose unattained (224-end).

ΠΕΡΙ ΑΠΟΙΚΙΑΣ

1   I. " Καὶ εἶπε κύριος τῷ Ἀβραάμ· ἄπελθε ἐκ τῆς
γῆς σου καὶ ἐκ τῆς συγγενείας σου καὶ ἐκ τοῦ οἴκου
τοῦ πατρός σου εἰς τὴν γῆν, ἥν σοι δείξω· καὶ
ποιήσω σε εἰς ἔθνος μέγα καὶ εὐλογήσω σε καὶ
μεγαλυνῶ τὸ ὄνομά σου, καὶ ἔσῃ εὐλογητός. καὶ
εὐλογήσω τοὺς εὐλογοῦντάς σε, καὶ τοὺς καταρωμένους σε καταράσομαι, καὶ ἐνευλογηθήσονται ἐν σοὶ
2 πᾶσαι αἱ φυλαὶ τῆς γῆς.''   βουληθεὶς ὁ
θεὸς τὴν ἀνθρώπου ψυχὴν καθῆραι πρῶτον αὐτῇ
δίδωσιν ἀφορμὴν εἰς σωτηρίαν παντελῆ τὴν ἐκ
τριῶν χωρίων μετανάστασιν, σώματος, αἰσθήσεως,
λόγου τοῦ κατὰ προφοράν· τὴν μὲν γὰρ γῆν σώματος, τὴν δὲ συγγένειαν αἰσθήσεως, τὸν δὲ τοῦ
πατρὸς οἶκον λόγου συμβέβηκεν εἶναι σύμβολον.
3 διὰ τί; ὅτι τὸ μὲν σῶμα καὶ ἐκ γῆς ἔλαβε τὴν
σύστασιν καὶ ἀναλύεται πάλιν εἰς γῆν—μάρτυς δὲ
Μωυσῆς, ὅταν φῇ· '' γῆ εἶ, καὶ εἰς γῆν ἀπελεύσῃ·''
καὶ γὰρ παγῆναί φησιν αὐτὸ χοῦν εἰς ἀνθρωπείαν
μορφὴν τοῦ θεοῦ διαπλάσαντος, ἀνάγκη δὲ τὸ
λυόμενον εἰς τὰ δεθέντα λύεσθαι—, αἴσθησις δὲ
συγγενὲς καὶ ἀδελφόν ἐστι διανοίας, ἄλογον λογικῆς,
ἐπειδὴ μιᾶς ἄμφω μέρη ψυχῆς ταῦτα, πατρὸς δὲ
οἶκος ὁ | λόγος, ὅτι πατὴρ μὲν ἡμῶν ὁ νοῦς σπείρων

ON THE MIGRATION OF ABRAHAM

I. " And the Lord said unto Abraham, Depart out 1 of thy land, and out of thy kindred, and out of thy father's house, into the land which I shall shew thee ; and I will make thee a great nation and will bless thee and will make thy name great, and thou shalt be blessed. And I will bless them that bless thee, and them that curse thee I will curse, and in thee shall all the tribes of the earth be blessed " (Gen. xii. 1-3).

God begins the carrying out of His will 2 to cleanse man's soul by giving it a starting-point for full salvation in its removal out of three localities, namely, body, sense-perception, and speech. " Land" or " country " is a symbol of body, " kindred " of sense-perception, " father's house " of speech. How so ? Because the body took its substance out of 3 earth (or land) and is again resolved into earth. Moses is a witness to this, when he says, " Earth thou art and into earth shalt thou return " (Gen. iii. 19) ; indeed he also says that the body was clay formed into human shape by God's moulding hand, and what suffers solution must needs be resolved into the elements which were united to form it. Sense-perception, again, is of one kin and family with understanding, the irrational with the rational, for both these are parts of one soul. And speech is our " father's house," " father's " because Mind is our

133

PHILO

εἰς ἕκαστον τῶν μερῶν τὰς ἀφ' ἑαυτοῦ δυνάμεις
καὶ διανέμων εἰς αὐτὰ τὰς ἐνεργείας ἐπιμέλειάν
τε καὶ ἐπιτροπὴν ἀνημμένος ἁπάντων, οἶκος δέ,
ἐν ᾧ διαιτᾶται, τῆς ἄλλης¹ ὑπεξῃρημένος οἰκίας ὁ
λόγος· καθάπερ γὰρ ἀνδρὸς ἑστία, καὶ νοῦ λόγος
4 ἐνδιαίτημα. ἑαυτὸν γοῦν καὶ ὅσα ἂν ἐνθυμήματα
τέκῃ, ὥσπερ ἐν οἴκῳ τῷ λόγῳ διαθεὶς καὶ δια-
κοσμήσας ἐπιδείκνυται.   μὴ θαυμάσῃς
δέ, εἰ νοῦ τὸν λόγον ἐν ἀνθρώπῳ κέκληκεν οἶκον·
καὶ γὰρ τὸν τῶν ὅλων νοῦν, τὸν θεόν, οἶκον ἔχειν
5 φησὶ τὸν ἑαυτοῦ λόγον. οὗ τὴν φαντασίαν ὁ
ἀσκητὴς λαβὼν ἄντικρυς ὁμολογεῖ ὅτι " οὐκ ἔστι
τοῦτο ἀλλ' ἢ οἶκος θεοῦ," ἴσον τῷ ὁ τοῦ θεοῦ οἶκος
οὐκ ἔστι τοῦτο τῶν εἰς δεῖξιν ἐρχομένων ἢ συνόλως
πιπτόντων ὑπ' αἴσθησιν, οὐκ ἔστιν, ἀλλ' ἀόρατος,
ἀειδής, ψυχῇ μόνον ὡς ψυχῇ καταλαμβανόμενος.
6 τίς ἂν οὖν εἴη πλὴν ὁ λόγος ὁ πρεσβύτερος τῶν
γέ ἐσιν εἰληφότων, οὗ καθάπερ οἴακος ἐνειλημμένος ὁ τῶν ὅλων κυβερνήτης πηδαλιουχεῖ τὰ
σύμπαντα, καὶ ὅτε ἐκοσμοπλάστει χρησάμενος
ὀργάνῳ τούτῳ πρὸς τὴν ἀνυπαίτιον τῶν ἀποτελου-
μένων σύστασιν ;

¹ mss. ὅλης, which perhaps might be retained in the sense of the "homestead as a whole."

ᵃ Or "chamber," *cf. Il.* vi. 490 and elsewhere, where οἶκος is clearly the inner part of the house. For the thought that while mind has a wider range, its most intimate home is speech, *cf.* the explanation of τὸν ἔγγιστα as speech in *De Ebr.* 71.

ᵇ Or "this is not the House of God, only (yet) there is a House of God." Mr. Whitaker defended his translation by suggesting that Philo is following the occasional use of ἀλλ' ἤ in the lxx for "certainly," *e.g.* 2 Chron. xix. 3. But the explanation which follows seems to me to point to the alternative translation given above, and in this case the use
134

father, sowing in each of the parts of the body the faculties that issue from itself, and assigning to them their workings, being in control and charge of them all; house—because mind has speech for its house [a] or living-room, secluded from the rest of the homestead. It is Mind's living-place, just as the hearthside is man's. It is there that Mind displays in 4 orderly form itself and all the conceptions to which it gives birth, treating it as a man treats a house.

And marvel not at Moses having given to speech the title of Mind's house in man ; for indeed he says that God, the Mind of the universe, has for His house His own Word. It was the vision of 5 this Word that the Self-trainer received when he emphatically declares " This is assuredly not the House of God " [b] (Gen. xxviii. 17), as much as to say " The House of God is not this that is all round me, consisting of things at which we can point or that fall under sense-perception generally, no, not such is God's House, but invisible, withdrawn from sight, and apprehended only by soul as soul.[c] Who, then, can 6 that House be, save the Word who is antecedent to all that has come into existence ? the Word, which the Helmsman of the Universe grasps as a rudder to guide all things on their course ? Even as, when He was fashioning the world, He employed it as His instrument, that the fabric of His handiwork might be without reproach.

of ἀλλ' ἤ would be something like that in Deut. iv. 12 (quoted in 48). In *De Som.* i. 185 we have another way of taking the verse.

[c] Or " soul in the true sense of the word." Philo means that he is not using the word in the wider sense of the whole soul or life of the animal, but for the mind or dominant principal. See App. p. 560.

7 II. Ὡς μὲν τοίνυν γῆν μὲν τὸ σῶμα, συγγένειαν
δὲ τὴν αἴσθησιν, οἶκον δὲ πατρὸς τὸν λόγον αἰνίττεται, δεδηλώκαμεν. τὸ δὲ " ἄπελθε ἐκ τούτων "
οὐκ ἔσθ᾽[1] ὅμοιον τῷ διαζεύχθητι κατὰ τὴν οὐσίαν,
ἐπεὶ θάνατον ἦν διαγορεύοντος ἡ πρόσταξις, ἀλλ᾽
ἴσον τῷ τὴν γνώμην ἀλλοτριώθητι, πρὸς μηδενὸς
8 περισχεθεὶς αὐτῶν ὑπεράνω στῆθι πάντων· ὑπήκοοί
σού εἰσι, μηδέποτε ὡς ἡγεμόσι χρῶ· βασιλεὺς
ὢν ἄρχειν ἀλλὰ μὴ ἄρχεσθαι πεπαίδευσο, πάντα
τὸν αἰῶνα γίνωσκε σεαυτόν, ὡς καὶ Μωυσῆς
πολλαχοῦ διδάσκει λέγων " πρόσεχε σεαυτῷ "·
οὕτως γὰρ ὧν τε ὑπακούειν καὶ οἷς ἐπιτάττειν
9 προσῆκεν αἰσθήσῃ.   ἄπελθε οὖν ἐκ τοῦ
περὶ σεαυτὸν γεώδους, τὸ παμμίαρον, ὦ οὗτος,
ἐκφυγὼν δεσμωτήριον, τὸ σῶμα, καὶ τὰς ὥσπερ
εἰρκτοφύλακας ἡδονὰς καὶ ἐπιθυμίας αὐτοῦ παντὶ
σθένει καὶ πάσῃ δυνάμει, μηδὲν τῶν εἰς κάκωσιν
παρείς, ἀλλὰ πάντα ἀθρόα συλλήβδην ἐπανατεινά-
10 μενος.   ἄπελθε κἀκ τῆς συγγενοῦς αἰσ-
θήσεως· νυνὶ μὲν γὰρ κέχρηκας ἑκάστῃ σεαυτὸν
καὶ γέγονας ἀλλότριον τῶν δεδανεισμένων ἀγαθὸν
ἀποβεβληκὼς τὸ ἴδιον. οἶδας δέ, κἂν πάντες ἡσυχάζωσιν, ὡς ὀφθαλμοί σε ἄγουσι καὶ ὦτα καὶ ἡ
ἄλλη τῆς συγγενείας πληθὺς ἅπασα πρὸς τὰ φίλα
11 ἑαυτοῖς. ἐὰν δὲ ἐθελήσῃς κομίσασθαι | τὰ σαυτοῦ
[438]   δάνεια καὶ τὴν ἰδίαν κτῆσιν περιβαλέσθαι μηδὲν

———
[1] mss. οὐκέθ᾽.

II. We have now shewn how Moses uses " earth " 7
to represent the body, " kindred " to represent sense-
perception, " thy father's house " to represent
speech. The words " Depart out of these " are not
equivalent to " Sever thyself from them absolutely,"
since to issue such a command as that would be to
prescribe death. No, the words import " Make thyself a stranger to them in judgement and purpose ;
let none of them cling to thee ; rise superior to them
all ; they are thy subjects, never treat them as 8
sovereign lords ; thou art a king, school thyself once
and for all to rule, not to be ruled ; evermore be coming to know thyself, as Moses teaches thee in many
places, saying " Give heed to thyself " (Ex. xxiv. 12),
for in this way shalt thou perceive those to whom
it befits thee to shew obedience and those to whom
it befits thee to give commands.   Depart, 9
therefore, out of the earthly matter that encompasses
thee : escape, man, from the foul prison-house, thy
body, with all thy might and main, and from the
pleasures and lusts that act as its jailers ; every terror
that can vex and hurt them, leave none of them
unused ; menace the enemy with them all united and
combined.   Depart also out of sense- 10
perception thy kin. For at present thou hast made
a loan of thyself to each sense, and art become the
property of others, a portion of the goods of those
who have borrowed thee, and hast thrown away the
good thing that was thine own. Yes, thou knowest,
even though all men should hold their peace, how
eyes draw thee, and ears, and the whole crowd of
thine other kinsfolk, towards what they themselves
love. But if thou desire to recover the self that thou 11
hast lent and to have thine own possessions about

αὑτῆς διαζεύξας ἢ ἀλλοτριώσας μέρος, εὐδαίμονος
μεταποιήσῃ βίου, χρῆσιν καὶ ἀπόλαυσιν οὐκ
ὀθνείων ἀλλ' οἰκείων ἀγαθῶν εἰς ἀεὶ καρπούμενος.

12 ἀλλὰ μετανάστηθι κἀκ τοῦ κατὰ
προφορὰν λόγου, ὃν πατρὸς οἶκον ὠνόμασεν, ἵνα μὴ
ῥημάτων καὶ ὀνομάτων ἀπατηθεὶς κάλλεσι τοῦ
πρὸς ἀλήθειαν κάλλους, ὅπερ ἐστὶν ἐν τοῖς δηλουμένοις πράγμασι, διαζευχθῇς. ἄτοπον γὰρ ἢ σκιὰν
σωμάτων ἢ μίμημα ἀρχετύπων φέρεσθαι πλέον·
σκιᾷ μὲν δὴ καὶ μιμήματι ἔοικεν ἑρμηνεία, σώμασι
δὲ καὶ ἀρχετύποις αἱ τῶν διερμηνευομένων φύσεις
πραγμάτων, ὧν τὸν ἐφιέμενον τοῦ εἶναι μᾶλλον ἢ
τοῦ δοκεῖν χρὴ περιέχεσθαι διοικιζόμενον ἀπ'
13 ἐκείνων.   III. ἐπειδὰν γοῦν ὁ νοῦς ἄρξηται γνωρίζειν ἑαυτὸν καὶ τοῖς νοητοῖς ἐνομιλεῖν
θεωρήμασιν, ἅπαν τὸ κλινόμενον τῆς ψυχῆς πρὸς
τὸ αἰσθητὸν εἶδος ἀπώσεται, ὃ κέκληται παρ'
Ἑβραίοις Λώτ. οὗ χάριν ὁ σοφὸς εἰσάγεται λέγων
ἄντικρυς· "διαχωρίσθητι ἀπ' ἐμοῦ·" συνοικεῖν γὰρ
ἀμήχανον τὸν ἀσωμάτων καὶ ἀφθάρτων ἔρωτι
κατεσχημένον τῷ πρὸς τὰ αἰσθητὰ καὶ θνητὰ
14 ῥέποντι. παγκάλως οὖν ὁ ἱεροφάντης μίαν τῆς
νομοθεσίας ὅλην ἱερὰν βίβλον Ἐξαγωγὴν ἀνέγραψεν
οἰκεῖον ὄνομα εὑράμενος τοῖς περιεχομένοις χρη-
σμοῖς· ἅτε γὰρ παιδευτικὸς ὢν καὶ πρὸς νουθεσίαν
καὶ σωφρονισμὸν ἑτοιμότατος τῶν οἵων τε νουθετεῖσθαι καὶ σωφρονίζεσθαι πάντα τῆς ψυχῆς τὸν

thee, letting no portion of them be alienated and fall into other hands, thou shalt claim instead a happy life, enjoying in perpetuity the benefit and pleasure derived from good things not foreign to thee but thine own. Again, quit speech also, " thy 12 father's house," as Moses calls it, for fear thou shouldst be beguiled by beauties of mere phrasing, and be cut off from the real beauty, which lies in the matter expressed. Monstrous it is that shadow should be preferred to substance or a copy to originals. And verbal expression is like a shadow or copy, while the essential bearing of the matters conveyed by words resembles substance and originals ; and it behoves the man, whose aim it is to be rather than to seem, to dissociate himself from the former and hold fast to the latter. III. So we find 13 that when the Mind begins to know itself and to hold converse with the things of mind, it will thrust away from it that part of the soul which inclines to the province of sense-perception, the inclining which among the Hebrews is entitled " Lot." Hence the wise man is represented as saying outright, " Separate thyself from me " (Gen. xiii. 9). For it is impossible for one who is possessed by love for all that is incorporeal and incorruptible to dwell together with one who leans towards the objects of sense-perception doomed to die. Right well, then, did the Sacred 14 Guide inscribe one entire sacred book of the Law-giving " Exagoge " or " Leading out," for the name thus found was appropriate to the oracles contained in it. For being well qualified to train men and fully furnished for the admonition and correction of those who were capable of admonition and correction, he contemplates the task of taking out all the population

λεὼν ἀπὸ τῆς Αἰγυπτίας χώρας, τοῦ σώματος, καὶ
τῶν οἰκητόρων αὐτῆς ἐξελεῖν διανοεῖται, χαλεπώ-
τατον καὶ βαρύτατον ἄχθος ἡγούμενος ὁρατικὴν
διάνοιαν πρὸς σαρκὸς ἡδονῶν πιεσθῆναι καὶ ἐπιτάγμασιν ὑπηρετεῖν, ἅττ᾽ ἂν αἱ ἀνηλεεῖς προστάττωσιν
15 ἐπιθυμίαι. τούτους μὲν οὖν στενάξαντας καὶ
πολλὰ ἐκδακρύσαντας τὴν σωματικὴν εὐθηνίαν καὶ
τὰς τῶν ἐκτὸς ἀφθόνους περιουσίας—λέγεται γὰρ
ὅτι " ἐστέναξαν οἱ υἱοὶ Ἰσραὴλ ἀπὸ τῶν ἔργων "—
ὑφηγησαμένου τοῦ ἵλεω θεοῦ τὰ περὶ τὴν ἔξοδον ὁ
προφήτης αὐτοῦ ῥύεται.

16   Εἰσὶ δ᾽ οἳ μέχρι τῆς τελευτῆς τὰς πρὸς σῶμα
σπονδὰς ἔθεντο καὶ ὥσπερ λάρνακι ἢ σορῷ ἢ ὅπως
ὀνομάζειν ἑτέρως φίλον τῷδε ἐνετάφησαν. ὧν τὰ
μὲν ὅσα φιλοσώματα καὶ φιλοπαθῆ μέρη λήθῃ
παραδοθέντα κατορύττεται· εἰ δέ πού τι φιλάρετον
παρανέβλαστε, μνήμαις ἀνασῴζεται, δι᾽ ὧν τὰ
17 καλὰ ζωπυρεῖσθαι πέφυκε.   IV. τὰ γοῦν
ὀστᾶ Ἰωσήφ, λέγω δὴ τὰ μόνα ὑπολειφθέντα τῆς
τοσαύτης ψυχῆς ἀδιάφθορα καὶ ἀξιομνημόνευτα
εἴδη, περιποιεῖται ὁ ἱερὸς λόγος, ἄτοπον ἡγούμενος
[439] καθαρὰ | μὴ καθαροῖς συνεζεῦχθαι.   τὰ
18 δ᾽ ἀξιομνημόνευτα ταῦτα ἦν· τὸ πιστεῦσαι ὅτι
" ἐπισκέψεται ὁ θεὸς " τὸ ὁρατικὸν γένος καὶ οὐ

---

^a " Things outside the body " (see note on *Quod Det.* 7)
interpret the " inhabitants of Egypt " in § 14, as " the things
of the body " interpret Egypt.

^b For the interpretation of these " works " or tasks as
slavery to the passions and the like *cf. De Conf.* 93.

^c Here begins the digression about Joseph which continues
to the end of § 24. The opening words of § 16 are a meditation on Gen. l. 26 " And Joseph died (ἐτελεύτησε, *cf.* μέχρι τῆς
τελευτῆς) and was buried, and they laid him in a *coffin* (σορῷ),
in *Egypt.*" The lesson deduced is that the compromising

of the soul right away from Egypt, the body, and away from its inhabitants ; deeming it a most sore and heavy burden that an understanding endowed with vision should be under the pressure of the pleasures of the flesh, and should submit to such injunctions as its merciless cravings may lay upon it. These, indeed, groaned over and greatly bewailed 15 their bodily well-being, and the lavish abundance of things outside the body,[a] which was theirs, for we read that " the children of Israel groaned by reason of their works [b] " (Ex. ii. 23). When they do this, the gracious God instructs His prophet regarding their coming out, and His prophet delivers them.

[c] But some make a truce with the body and main- 16 tain it till their death, and are buried in it as in a coffin or shell or whatever else you like to call it. All the body-loving and passion-loving portions of these are laid in the grave and consigned to oblivion. But if anywhere by the side of these there grows up a virtue-loving tendency, it is saved from extinction by memories, which are a means of keeping alive the flame of noble qualities. IV. So the Holy 17 Word, deeming it unfitting that pure things should have impure things associated with them, provides for the safe-keeping of Joseph's bones, by which I mean the only relics of such a soul as were left behind untouched by corruption and worthy of perpetual memory (Gen. l. 25).[d] Those of the 18 latter kind were these ; Joseph's confidence that " God will visit " the race that has vision (Gen. l. 24),

Joseph-nature is " buried in the body " and forgotten, but it may have higher things or " bones ". These are remembered and serve to kindle excellence in others.
[d] See App. p. 560.

PHILO

παραδώσει μέχρι παντὸς αὐτὸ ἀμαθίᾳ, τυφλῇ
δεσποίνῃ, τὸ διακρῖναι τά τε θνητὰ τῆς ψυχῆς καὶ
τὰ ἄφθαρτα καὶ τὰ μὲν ὅσα περὶ τὰς σώματος
ἡδονὰς καὶ τὰς ἄλλας παθῶν ἀμετρίας θνητὰ ὄντα
Αἰγύπτῳ καταλιπεῖν, περὶ δὲ τῶν ἀφθάρτων
σπονδὴν[1] ποιήσασθαι, ὅπως μετὰ τῶν ἀναβαινόντων
εἰς τὰς ἀρετῆς πόλεις διακομισθῇ, καὶ ὅρκῳ τὴν
19 σπονδὴν ἐμπεδώσασθαι.   τίνα οὖν τὰ
ἄφθαρτα; ἡ πρὸς ἡδονὴν ἀλλοτρίωσις τὴν λέγου-
σαν· συνευνασθῶμεν καὶ τῶν ἀνθρωπείων ἀπο-
λαύσωμεν ἀγαθῶν, ἡ μετὰ καρτερίας ἀγχίνοια, δι'
ἧς τὰ τῶν κενῶν δοξῶν νομιζόμενα ἀγαθὰ ὡς
ἂν ἐνύπνια ὄντα * * *[2] διακρίνει καὶ διαστέλλει,
ὁμολογῶν τὰς μὲν ἀληθεῖς καὶ σαφεῖς τῶν πραγμάτων συγκρίσεις εἶναι κατὰ θεόν, τὰς δὲ ἀδήλους
καὶ ἀσαφεῖς φαντασίας κατὰ τὸν πλάνητα καὶ
τύφου μεστὸν μήπω κεκαθαρμένων ἀνθρώπων βίον
ταῖς διὰ σιτοπόνων καὶ μαγείρων καὶ οἰνοχόων
20 τέρψεσι χαίροντα, τὸ μὴ ὑπήκοον, ἀλλ' ἄρχοντα
Αἰγύπτου πάσης, τῆς σωματικῆς χώρας, ἀνα-
γραφῆναι, τὸ αὐχεῖν ἐπὶ τῷ γένος εἶναι Ἑβραίων,
οἷς ἔθος ἀπὸ τῶν αἰσθητῶν ἐπὶ τὰ νοητὰ μετανίστασθαι—περάτης γὰρ ὁ Ἑβραῖος ἑρμηνεύεται—,
τὸ σεμνύνεσθαι ὅτι " ὧδε οὐκ ἐποίησεν οὐδέν "—τὸ
γὰρ μηδὲν τῶν ἐνταῦθα σπουδαζομένων[3] παρὰ τοῖς
φαύλοις ἐργάσασθαι, διαμισῆσαι δὲ καὶ ἀποστραφῆ-

[1] mss. σπονδήν.
[2] Wend. conjectures ⟨τῶν ἀληθῶς ὄντων⟩. I am not sure
that it is necessary to suppose any lacuna.
[3] mss. σπουδαζόντων.

[a] See App. p. 560, on § 17.
[b] An allusion to the description of Potiphar in the lxx
(Gen. xxxix. 1) as chief cook.
142

and will not utterly hand it over to Ignorance, that blind task-mistress ; his discernment between the mortal and the incorruptible portions of the soul and his leaving behind to Egypt those which had to do with bodily pleasures and other forms of unrestrained passion, while concerning the incorruptible parts he made an agreement, that they should accompany those who went up to the cities of virtue, and should be conveyed thither, and had the agreement secured by an oath.   What, then, are the un- 19 corrupted parts ?[a]   His having nothing to do with Pleasure when she says, " Let us lie together " (Gen. xxxix. 7) and enjoy the good things of mankind : the shrewdness coupled with the resoluteness which enabled him to recognize the products of empty fancies which many accounted to be good, and to distinguish them as mere dreams from those which are really so ; and to confess that the true and certain interpretations of things are given under God's guidance (Gen. xl. 8), while the doubtful imaginations that have no certainty follow the rule and line of the erring and deluded life of men who have not undergone purification, a life that finds its joy in the delights provided by bakers and cooks[b] and butlers. Other traits of incorruption were these : he was pro- 20 claimed not the subject, but the ruler of all Egypt, the domain of the body (Gen. xli. 41) : he was proud to own himself a member of the Hebrew race (Gen. xl. 15), whose wont it is, as the name " Hebrew " or " Migrant " indicates, to quit the objects of sense-perception and go after those of Mind : he gloried in the fact that " here he had done nothing " (*ibid.*), for to have performed no single act such as the worthless people there admired, but to have utterly

21 ναι πάντα οὐ μετρίως ἐπαινετόν—, τὸ ἐμπαίζειν
ἐπιθυμιῶν καὶ πάντων παθῶν ἀμετρίαις, τὸ φοβεῖσθαι τὸν θεόν, εἰ καὶ μηδέπω γέγονεν ἀγαπᾶν ἱκανός,
τὸ ζωῆς ἐν Αἰγύπτῳ μεταποιεῖσθαι τῆς ἀληθοῦς—
(V.) ὃ δὴ θαυμάσας ὁ ὁρῶν, καὶ γὰρ ἄξιον ἦν κατα-
πλαγῆναι, φησί· " μέγα μοί ἐστιν, εἰ ἔτι ὁ υἱός μου
Ἰωσὴφ ζῇ," ἀλλὰ μὴ κεναῖς δόξαις καὶ τῷ νεκρο-
22 φορουμένῳ σώματι συντέθηκε—, τὸ ὁμολογεῖν ὅτι
" τοῦ θεοῦ ἐστι," τῶν δ' εἰς γένεσιν ἐλθόντων
οὐδενός, τὸ γνωριζόμενον τοῖς ἀδελφοῖς πάντας
τοὺς φιλοσωμάτους κινῆσαι καὶ σαλεῦσαι τρόπους
ἑστάναι παγίως ἐπὶ τῶν ἰδίων οἰομένους δογμάτων
καὶ ἀνὰ κράτος ἀπώσασθαι, τὸ φάναι μὴ πρὸς
ἀνθρώπων ἀπεστάλθαι, ὑπὸ δὲ τοῦ θεοῦ κεχειρο-
τονῆσθαι πρὸς τὴν τοῦ σώματος καὶ τῶν ἐκτὸς
23 ἔννομον ἐπιστασίαν.   πολλὰ δὲ καὶ ἄλλα
τούτοις ὁμοιότροπα τῆς ἀμείνονος καὶ ἱερωτέρας
ὄντα τάξεως, Αἴγυπτον τὸν σωματικὸν οἶκον οἰκεῖν
οὐκ ἀνέχεται οὐδ' ἐνθάπτεται σορῷ τὸ παράπαν,
[440] ἔξω δὲ παντὸς τοῦ θνητοῦ | κεχωρηκότα παρέπε-
24 ται[1] θεσμοθέτῃ λόγῳ Μωυσῇ ποδηγετοῦντι· τροφεὺς
γὰρ καὶ τιθηνὸς οὗτος ἀστείων ἔργων, λόγων,
βουλευμάτων, ἅ, κἂν τοῖς ἐναντίοις ἀνακραθῇ ποτε
διὰ τὴν ὑποσύγχυτον τοῦ θνητοῦ πολυμιγίαν, οὐδὲν
ἧττον διακρίνει[2] παρελθών, ἵνα μὴ μέχρι παντὸς τὰ

---

[1] Wend. and Mangey put a comma after ἐπιστασίαν and
correct ἀνέχεται, ἐνθάπτεται, παρέχεται of the mss. to the
corresponding infinitives. See App. p. 560.
[2] mss. διακρίνεται. See App. p. 561.

---

[a] See App. p. 560.
[b] The thought of the body as a dead thing from the first,
which the soul supports, has been more fully developed in
Leg. All. iii. 69 f. Cf. also De Agr. 25.

hated and eschewed them all, was conduct that called 21
for no slight praise : he derided lusts and all passions
and their gross excesses (Gen. xxxix. 14, 17) :[a] he
feared God (Gen. xlii. 18) even though he was not
yet ready to love Him : when in Egypt he claimed
as his own the life that is real life, (V.) a claim which
caused Israel to marvel in just amazement, and to
cry, "It is a great matter in my eyes if my son Joseph
still *lives*" (Gen. xlv. 28), and has not shared the
death of vain opinions, and of the body the corpse
he carries with him :[b] he confesses that he is God's 22
(Gen. l. 19),[c] not the property of any created being :
when making himself known to his brethren he thrust
perforce from his presence, shaken and tottering, all
those frames of mind that make the body their
delight and think that their own doctrines afford them
a firm standing (Gen. xlv. 1 f.) : he declared that
he had not received his commission at the hands of
men, but had been appointed by God (Gen. xlv. 7 f.)
to be duly constituted controller of the body and of
things outside the body.[d]   And these are 23
but a few of the traits indicative of the better and
holier standing, which utterly refuse to dwell in
Egypt the bodily tenement, are never buried in a
coffin at all, but, having passed out of all that is
mortal, follow the guiding steps of Moses, the Law-
giving Word. For Moses is the nursing-father who 24
rears with fostering care noble deeds, words, designs,
which, albeit often mingled with their opposites owing
to the chaos and confusion which besets mortality,
he none the less comes forward and separates from

---

[c] E.V. "Am I in the place of God?"
[d] Again, as in § 15, the two lower goods serve to interpret
"Lord of all his *house* and ruler of all the *land of Egypt*."

καλοκἀγαθίας σπέρματα καὶ φυτὰ ἀφανισθέντα
οἴχηται.

25 Καὶ προτρέπεται μάλα ἐρρωμένως ἀπολιπεῖν τὴν
παντὸς ἀτόπου χρηματίζουσαν μητέρα, μὴ μέλ-
λοντας καὶ βραδύνοντας, ἀλλ᾽ ὑπερβάλλοντι τάχει
χρωμένους· φησὶ γὰρ μετὰ σπουδῆς δεῖν θύειν τὸ
Πάσχα, τὸ δέ ἐστιν ἑρμηνευθὲν διάβασις, ἵν᾽
ἀνενδοιάστῳ γνώμῃ καὶ προθυμίᾳ συντόνῳ χρώμενος ὁ νοῦς τήν τε ἀπὸ τῶν παθῶν ἀμεταστρεπτὶ
ποιῆται διάβασιν καὶ τὴν πρὸς τὸν σωτῆρα θεὸν
εὐχαριστίαν, ὃς εἰς ἐλευθερίαν οὐ προσδοκήσαντα
26 αὐτὸν ἐξείλετο.   VI. καὶ τί θαυμάζομεν,
εἰ τὸν ὑπηγμένον κράτει πάθους ἀλόγου προτρέπει
μὴ ἐνδιδόναι μηδὲ τῇ ῥύμῃ τῆς ἐκείνου φορᾶς
κατασυρῆναι, βιάσασθαι δὲ ἀντισχόντα κἄν, εἰ μὴ
δύναιτο, ἀποδρᾶναι; δευτέρα γὰρ ἔφοδος εἰς
σωτηρίαν τοῖς ἀμύνεσθαι μὴ δυναμένοις δρασμός
ἐστιν· ὁπότε καὶ τὸν ἀγωνιστὴν φύσει καὶ μηδέποτε
παθῶν δοῦλον γεγενημένον, ἀεὶ δὲ ἀθλοῦντα τοὺς
πρὸς ἕκαστον αὐτῶν ἄθλους, οὐκ ἐᾷ μέχρι παντὸς
τοῖς παλαίσμασι χρήσασθαι, μή ποτε τῷ συνεχεῖ
τῆς εἰς ταὐτὸ συνόδου χαλεπὴν ἀπ᾽ ἐκείνων κῆρα
ἀναμάξηται· πολλοὶ γὰρ ἤδη καὶ ἀντιπάλου κακίας
27 ἐγένοντο μιμηταί, ὡς ἀρετῆς ἔμπαλιν ἕτεροι. διὸ
λόγιον ἐχρήσθη τοιόνδε· "ἀποστρέφου εἰς τὴν γῆν
τοῦ πατρός σου καὶ εἰς τὴν γενεάν σου, καὶ ἔσομαι

―――――

ᵃ The thought of §§ 26-30 seems to be that while ordinary
souls, typified by Israel leaving Egypt, must shun outward
temptations, because they will prove too strong for them,
even the Jacob-souls, who have proved their superiority, will
do well to detach themselves and become immersed in that

146

the rest, that the germs and shoots of moral excellence may not permanently be obliterated and lost.

Moses also urges the Israelites to quit right stoutly 25 her who bears the name of mother of every monstrous thing, with no slow or lingering steps, but with exceeding speed; for he bids them with haste to sacrifice the Passover (Ex. xii. 11), which means " a passing over," to the intent that the Mind with resolute purpose and unfailing eagerness may carry out both its passing away from the passions without turning back, and its thanksgiving to God its Saviour, Who brought it forth into liberty when it looked not for it. VI. And what is there to wonder at 26 in his urging the mind, that had been brought under the control of irrational passion, not to give in, nor to be swept down by the violence of that passion's current, but to resist with all its might, and, should it fail, even to run away? For flight remains as an alternative way of reaching safety for those who are not able to repel the danger. See how Moses deals with one who was by nature a sturdy fighter and had never become the slave of passions, but was always engaged in the conflict with each one of them?[a] Even him he forbids to keep up his wrestlings to the end, lest one day, by perpetually meeting them, he should contract from them a pernicious taint: for many before now have proved imitators of an opponent's vice, as others on the other hand have imitated his virtue. For this reason a Divine intimation was 27 vouchsafed to him to this effect: " Turn back to the land of thy father and thy kindred, and I will be with thee " (Gen. xxxi. 3); as much as to say " Thou

higher wisdom represented by Isaac, which is beyond all worldly thoughts.

147

μετὰ σοῦ," ἴσον τῷ γέγονας μὲν ἀθλητὴς τέλειος
καὶ βραβείων καὶ στεφάνων ἠξιώθης ἀγωνο-
θετούσης ἀρετῆς καὶ προτεινούσης ἆθλά σοι τὰ
νικητήρια· κατάλυσον δὲ ἤδη τὸ φιλόνεικον, ἵνα μὴ
πάντοτε πονῇς, ἀλλὰ καὶ τῶν πονηθέντων ἀπόνασ-
28 θαι δυνηθῇς. τοῦτο δὲ ἐνταυθοῖ καταμένων οὐδέποτε εὑρήσεις τοῖς αἰσθητοῖς ἔτι συνοικῶν καὶ ταῖς
σωματικαῖς ἐνδιατρίβων ποιότησιν, ὧν Λάβαν
ἐστὶν ἔξαρχος—ὄνομα δὲ ποιότητος τοῦτ' ἐστίν—,
ἀλλὰ μετανάστην χρὴ γενέσθαι εἰς τὴν πατρῴαν
γῆν τὴν ἱεροῦ λόγου καὶ τρόπον τινὰ τῶν ἀσκητῶν
πατρός· ἡ δ' ἐστὶ σοφία, τῶν φιλαρέτων ψυχῶν
29 ἄριστον ἐνδιαίτημα. ἐν ταύτῃ τῇ χώρᾳ καὶ γένος
ἐστί σοι τὸ αὐτομαθές, τὸ αὐτοδίδακτον, τὸ νηπίας
καὶ γαλακτώδους τροφῆς ἀμέτοχον, τὸ χρησμῷ
θείῳ καταβαίνειν εἰς Αἴγυπτον κεκωλυμένον καὶ
τῆς σαρκὸς ἐντυγχάνειν δελεαζούσαις ἡδοναῖς,
30 ἐπίκλησιν Ἰσαάκ. οὗ τὸν κλῆρον παραλαβὼν ἐξ
ἀνάγκης ἀποθήσῃ τὸν πόνον· αἱ γὰρ ἀφθονίαι τῶν
[441] ἑτοίμων καὶ κατὰ χειρὸς ἀγαθῶν | ἀπονίας αἴτιαι.
πηγὴ δέ, ἀφ' ἧς ὀμβρεῖ τὰ ἀγαθά, ἡ τοῦ φιλοδώ-
ρου θεοῦ σύνοδός ἐστιν· οὗ χάριν ἐπισφραγιζόμενος
τὰ τῶν εὐεργεσιῶν φησιν· " ἔσομαι μετὰ σοῦ."
31   VII. Τί οὖν ἂν ἐπιλίποι καλὸν τοῦ
τελεσφόρου [παντὸς] παρόντος θεοῦ μετὰ χαρίτων
τῶν παρθένων αὐτοῦ θυγατέρων, ἃς ἀδιαφθόρους
καὶ ἀμιάντους ὁ γεννήσας πατὴρ κουροτροφεῖ; τότε
μελέται μὲν καὶ πόνοι καὶ ἀσκήσεις ἡσυχάζουσιν,

---

^a Perhaps an allusion to Gen. xxi. 8 " and the child grew
and was weaned " (ἀπεγαλακτίσθη).

hast proved thyself a perfect athlete, and been awarded prizes and crowns with Virtue presiding and holding forth to thee the meed of victory : but now it is time for thee to have done with strife, lest thou be ever toiling, and have no power to reap the fruits of thy toil. This thou wilt never find while thou re- 28 mainest where thou art, dwelling still with the objects of sense-perception, and spending thy days surrounded by bodily existence in its varied aspects, whose head and chief is Laban, bearing a name meaning variety of character. Nay, thou must change thine abode and betake thee to thy father's land, the land of the Word that is holy and in some sense father of those who submit to training : and that land is Wisdom, abode most choice of virtue-loving souls. In this 29 country there awaiteth thee the nature which is its own pupil, its own teacher, that needs not to be fed on milk as children are fed,[a] that has been stayed by a Divine oracle from going down into Egypt (Gen. xxvi. 2) and from meeting with the ensnaring pleasures of the flesh. That nature is entitled Isaac. When 30 thou hast entered upon his inheritance, thou canst not but lay aside thy toil ; for the perpetual abundance of good things ever ready to the hand gives freedom from toil. And the fountain from which the good things are poured forth is the companionship of the bountiful God. He shews this to be so when to set His seal upon the flow of His kindnesses, He says " I will be with thee." VII. What 31 fair thing, then, could fail when there was present God the Perfecter, with gifts of grace, His virgin daughters, whom the Father that begat them rears up uncorrupted and undefiled ? Then are all forms of studying, toiling, practising at rest ; and without

PHILO

ἀναδίδοται δὲ ἄνευ τέχνης φύσεως προμηθείᾳ πάντα
32 ἀθρόα πᾶσιν ὠφέλιμα.   καλεῖται δ᾽ ἡ
φορὰ τῶν αὐτοματιζομένων ἀγαθῶν ἄφεσις, ἐπειδήπερ ὁ νοῦς ἀφεῖται τῶν κατὰ τὰς ἰδίας ἐπιβολὰς
ἐνεργειῶν καὶ ὥσπερ τῶν ἑκουσίων ἠλευθέρωται
διὰ τὴν πληθὺν τῶν ὑομένων καὶ ἀδιαστάτως
33 ἐπομβρούντων. ἔστι δὲ ταῦτα θαυμασιώτατα φύσει
καὶ περικαλλέστατα. ὧν μὲν γὰρ ἂν ὠδίνῃ δι᾽
ἑαυτῆς ἡ ψυχή, τὰ πολλὰ ἀμβλωθρίδια, ἠλιτόμηνα·
ὅσα δὲ ἂν ἐπινίφων ὁ θεὸς ἄρδῃ, τέλεια καὶ ὁλόκληρα
34 καὶ πάντων ἄριστα γεννᾶται.   τὸ ἐμαυτοῦ πάθος, ὃ μυριάκις παθὼν οἶδα, διηγούμενος οὐκ
αἰσχύνομαι· βουληθεὶς ἔστιν ὅτε κατὰ τὴν συνήθη
τῶν κατὰ φιλοσοφίαν δογμάτων γραφὴν ἐλθεῖν καὶ
ἃ χρὴ συνθεῖναι ἀκριβῶς εἰδώς,[1] ἄγονον καὶ στεῖραν
εὑρὼν τὴν διάνοιαν ἄπρακτος ἀπηλλάγην, τὴν μὲν
κακίσας τῆς οἰήσεως, τὸ δὲ τοῦ ὄντος κράτος
καταπλαγείς, παρ᾽ ὃν[2] τὰς τῆς ψυχῆς ἀνοίγνυσθαί
35 τε καὶ συγκλείεσθαι μήτρας συμβέβηκεν. ἔστι δὲ
ὅτε κενὸς ἐλθὼν πλήρης ἐξαίφνης ἐγενόμην ἐπι-
νιφομένων καὶ σπειρομένων ἄνωθεν ἀφανῶς τῶν
ἐνθυμημάτων, ὡς ὑπὸ κατοχῆς ἐνθέου κορυβαντιᾶν
καὶ πάντα ἀγνοεῖν, τὸν τόπον, τοὺς παρόντας,
ἐμαυτόν, τὰ λεγόμενα, τὰ γραφόμενα. ἔσχον γὰρ
ἑρμηνείαν,[3] εὕρεσιν, φωτὸς ἀπόλαυσιν, ὀξυδερκε-
στάτην ὄψιν, ἐνάργειαν τῶν πραγμάτων ἀριδηλο-

---

[1] mss. ἰδών.   [2] mss. οὖ.
[3] mss. σχεδὸν γὰρ ἑρμηνεύει, which Wend. prints, though
pronouncing it corrupt: Markland suggested ἔσχον γὰρ
ἑρμηνείας ῥεῦσιν. See App. p. 561.

interference of art by contrivance of Nature there come forth all things in one outburst charged with benefit for all.   And the harvest of spon- 32 taneous good things is called " Release," [a] inasmuch as the Mind is released from the working out of its own projects, and is, we may say, emancipated from self-chosen tasks, by reason of the abundance of the rain and ceaseless shower of blessings. And these 33 are of a most marvellous nature and passing fair. For the offspring of the soul's own travail are for the most part poor abortions, things untimely born ; but those which God waters with the snows of heaven come to the birth perfect, complete and peerless.

I feel no shame in recording my own 34 experience, a thing I know from its having happened to me a thousand times. On some occasions, after making up my mind to follow the usual course of writing on philosophical tenets, and knowing defi- nitely the substance of what I was to set down, I have found my understanding incapable of giving birth to a single idea, and have given it up without accomplishing anything, reviling my understanding for its self-conceit, and filled with amazement at the might of Him that is to Whom is due the opening and closing of the soul-wombs. On other 35 occasions, I have approached my work empty and suddenly become full, the ideas falling in a shower from above and being sown invisibly, so that under the influence of the Divine possession I have been filled with corybantic frenzy and been unconscious of anything, place, persons present, myself, words spoken, lines written. For I obtained language, ideas, an enjoyment of light, keenest vision, pellucid dis-

[a] See App. p. 561.

τάτην, οἷα γένοιτ' ἂν δι' ὀφθαλμῶν ἐκ σαφεστάτης
δείξεως.

36 VIII. Τὸ μὲν οὖν δεικνύμενον τὸ ἀξιόρατον καὶ
ἀξιοθέατον καὶ ἀξιέραστόν ἐστι, τὸ τέλειον ἀγαθόν,
ὃ καὶ τὰς τῆς ψυχῆς πικρίας πέφυκε μεταβάλλον
γλυκαίνειν, ἡδυσμάτων συμπάντων παράρτυμα
κάλλιστον, δι' οὗ καὶ τὰ μὴ τρέφοντα τροφὴ γίνεται
σωτήριος· λέγεται γὰρ ὅτι " ἔδειξεν αὐτῷ κύριος
ξύλον, καὶ ἐνέβαλεν αὐτὸ εἰς τὸ ὕδωρ," τὸν κεχυμένον καὶ πλαδῶντα καὶ πικρίας γέμοντα νοῦν, ἵνα
37 γλυκανθεὶς ἡμερωθῇ. τὸ δὲ ξύλον τοῦτο οὐ μόνον
τροφήν, ἀλλὰ καὶ ἀθανασίαν ἐπαγγέλλεται· τὸ γὰρ
ξύλον τῆς ζωῆς ἐν μέσῳ τῷ παραδείσῳ φησὶ
πεφυτεῦσθαι, τὴν ἀγαθότητα δορυφορουμένην ὑπὸ
τῶν κατὰ μέρος ἀρετῶν[1] καὶ τῶν κατ' αὐτὰς πρά-
[442] ξεων· αὕτη | γὰρ τὸν μεσαίτατον καὶ ἄριστον ἐν
38 ψυχῇ κεκλήρωται τόπον.   ὁ δὲ ὁρῶν
ἐστιν ὁ σοφός· τυφλοὶ γὰρ ἢ ἀμυδροὶ τὰς ὄψεις οἵ
γε ἄφρονες. διὰ τοῦτο καὶ τοὺς προφήτας ἐκάλουν
πρότερον τοὺς βλέποντας· καὶ ὁ ἀσκητὴς ἐσπού-
δασεν ὦτα ὀφθαλμῶν ἀντιδοὺς ἰδεῖν ἃ πρότερον
ἤκουε, καὶ τυγχάνει τοῦ καθ' ὅρασιν κλήρου τὸν ἐξ
39 ἀκοῆς ὑπερβάς. εἰς γὰρ τὸν ὁρῶντα Ἰσραὴλ
μεταχαράττεται τὸ μαθήσεως καὶ διδασκαλίας
νόμισμα, οὗπερ ἐπώνυμος ἦν Ἰακώβ, δι' οὗ καὶ τὸ
ὁρᾶν γίνεται φῶς τὸ θεῖον, ἀδιαφοροῦν ἐπιστήμης,
ἢ τὸ τῆς ψυχῆς διοίγνυσιν ὄμμα καὶ πρὸς τὰς ὤτων
τηλαυγεστέρας καὶ ἀριδηλοτέρας[2] ἄγει καταλήψεις.

---

[1] mss. ἀγαθῶν.
[2] mss. τηλαυγεστάτας καὶ ἀριδηλοτάτας. The alternative
(Mangey) is to retain the superlatives and correct ὤτων to
νοητῶν or ὄντων.

152

tinctness of objects, such as might be received through
the eyes as the result of clearest shewing.[a]

VIII. Now the thing shewn is the thing worthy to 36
be seen, contemplated, loved, the perfect good, whose
nature it is to change all that is bitter in the soul
and make it sweet, fairest seasoning of all spices,
turning into salutary nourishment even foods that do
not nourish. So we read "The Lord shewed him a tree,
and he cast it into the water" (Ex. xv. 25), that is
into the flabby, flaccid mind teeming with bitterness,
that its savagery might be sweetened away. This 37
tree offers not nourishment only but immortality also,
for we are told that the Tree of Life has been planted
in the midst of the Garden (Gen. ii. 9), even Goodness
with the particular virtues and the doings which
accord with them to be its bodyguard. For it is
Virtue that has obtained as its own the central and
most honourable place in the soul. Such 38
is that which is shewn, and he that sees it is the wise
man, for fools are blind or dim-sighted. That is why
in former times they called the prophets seers (1 Sam.
ix. 9) ; and the Trainer of self was eager to exchange
ears for eyes, and to see what before he heard, and,
going beyond the inheritance which has hearing as
its source, he obtains that of which sight is the ruling
principle. For the current coin of learning and teach- 39
ing from which Jacob took his title is reminted into
the seeing Israel. Hereby comes to pass even the
seeing of the Divine light, identical with knowledge,
which opens wide the soul's eye, and leads it to
apprehensions distinct and brilliant beyond those

[a] The concluding word "shewing" serves to bridge over
transition from this meditation on the Spontaneous Blessings
to the discussion of the First Gift to Abraham, i.e. "the
land which I will shew thee."

ὥσπερ γὰρ διὰ μουσικῆς τὰ κατὰ μουσικὴν καὶ διὰ
πάσης τέχνης τὰ ἐν ἑκάστῃ καταλαμβάνεται, οὕτω
40 καὶ διὰ σοφίας τὸ σοφὸν θεωρεῖται. σοφία δὲ οὐ
μόνον φωτὸς τρόπον ὄργανον τοῦ ὁρᾶν ἐστιν, ἀλλὰ
καὶ αὐτὴν ὁρᾷ. αὕτη θεοῦ τὸ ἀρχέτυπον [ἡλίου]
φέγγος, οὗ μίμημα καὶ εἰκὼν ἥλιος.   ὁ
δὲ δεικνὺς ἕκαστα ὁ μόνος ἐπιστήμων θεός· ἄνθρωποι μὲν γὰρ τῷ δοκεῖν ἐπίστασθαι λέγονται μόνον
ἐπιστήμονες· ὁ δὲ θεός τῷ εἶναι ἧττον ἢ πέφυκε
λέγεται· νικῶνται γὰρ ὑπὸ τῶν τοῦ ὄντος δυνάμεων
41 οἱ περὶ αὐτὸν ἅπαντες ἅπαξ λόγοι. τὴν δὲ σοφίαν
αὐτοῦ διασυνίστησιν οὐ μόνον ἐκ τοῦ τὸν κόσμον
δεδημιουργηκέναι, ἀλλὰ καὶ ἐκ τοῦ τὴν ἐπιστήμην
τῶν γεγονότων ἱδρυκέναι βεβαιότατα παρ' ἑαυτῷ·
42 λέγεται γὰρ ὅτι " εἶδεν ὁ θεὸς τὰ πάντα ὅσα
ἐποίησεν," οὐκ ἴσον τῷ ὄψιν ἑκάστοις προσέβαλεν,
ἀλλ' εἴδησιν καὶ γνῶσιν καὶ κατάληψιν ὧν ἐποίησεν
εἶχεν. ⟨οὐ⟩ τοίνυν[1] εὐπρεπὲς ὑφηγεῖσθαι καὶ
διδάσκειν καὶ δεικνύναι τὰ καθ' ἕκαστα τοῖς ἀγνοοῦ-
σιν ὅτι μὴ τῷ ἐπιστήμονι, ὅστις οὐχ ὡς ἄνθρωπος

---

[1] mss. ὧν ἐποίησεν. εἶχε τοίνυν, which Mangey retained,
changing ὅτι μὴ to ἀλλὰ μή. See App. p. 562.

---

[a] i.e. the Israel-soul, the seer, first sees the light, i.e. knowledge, and this in its turn enables the soul's eye to see the
objects of knowledge, and so knowledge (or wisdom) is the
"instrument" of sight (§ 40). ἀδιαφοροῦν agrees with φῶς,
not with τὸ ὁρᾶν.

gained by the ears.[a] For as the application of the
principles of music [b] is apprehended through the
science of music, and the practice of each science
through that science, even so only through wisdom
comes discernment of what is wise. But wisdom is **40**
not only, after the manner of light, an instrument of
sight, but is able to see its own self besides. Wisdom
is God's archetypal luminary and the sun is a copy
and image of it.   But he that shews each
several object is God, who alone is possessed of perfect knowledge. For men are only said to have knowledge because they seem to know ; whereas God is so
called because He *is* the possessor of knowledge
though the phrase does not adequately express this
nature ; for all things whatever that can be said
regarding Him that is fall far short of the reality of
His powers. He gives clear proof of His wisdom not **41**
only from His having been the Artificer of the universe, but also from His having made the knowledge
of the things that had been brought into existence
His sure possession. For we read " God saw all **42**
things that He had made " (Gen. i. 31). This does
not just mean that He set His eyes on each of them,
but that He had insight [c] and knowledge and apprehension of the things which He had made. It follows
then that to give teaching and guidance on each
several thing, in fact to " shew " them, to the
ignorant is proper only for the One who knows, seeing
that He has not, as a man has, been profited by

---

[b] That τὰ κατά means the " practical application " is
brought out more clearly in *Quod Det.* 114, where we have
τὰ καθ' ἑκάστην (sc. ἀρετὴν) ἐνεργήματα.

[c] See App. p. 562.

ὑπὸ τέχνης ὠφέληται, ἀλλ' αὐτὸς ἀρχὴ καὶ πηγὴ
τεχνῶν καὶ ἐπιστημῶν ἀνωμολόγηται.

43 IX. Παρατετηρημένως δὲ οὐ τὸν ἐνεστῶτα, ἀλλὰ
τὸν μέλλοντα τῇ ὑποσχέσει χρόνον προδιώρισται,
εἰπὼν οὐχ ἣν δείκνυμι ἀλλ' '' ἣν σοι δείξω,'' εἰς
μαρτυρίαν πίστεως ἣν ἐπίστευσεν ἡ ψυχὴ θεῷ, οὐκ
ἐκ τῶν ἀποτελεσμάτων ἐπιδεικνυμένη τὸ εὐχάρι-
44 στον, ἀλλ' ἐκ προσδοκίας τῶν μελλόντων· ἀρτηθεῖσα
γὰρ καὶ ἐκκρεμασθεῖσα ἐλπίδος χρηστῆς καὶ ἀνεν-
δοίαστα νομίσασα ἤδη παρεῖναι τὰ μὴ παρόντα διὰ
τὴν τοῦ ὑποσχομένου βεβαιότητα[1] πίστιν, ἀγαθὸν |
[443] τέλειον, ἆθλον εὕρηται· καὶ γὰρ αὖθις λέγεται, ὅτι
'' ἐπίστευσεν Ἀβραὰμ τῷ θεῷ,'' καὶ Μωυσεῖ δὲ
ὁμοίως πᾶσαν ἐπιδειξάμενος τὴν γῆν φησιν, ὅτι
'' ἔδειξα τοῖς ὀφθαλμοῖς σου, κἀκεῖ οὐκ εἰσελεύσῃ.''
45 μὴ μέντοι νομίσῃς ἐπὶ καθαιρέσει τοῦ πανσόφου,
ὡς ὑπολαμβάνουσιν ἔνιοι τῶν ἀπερισκέπτων, τοῦτο
εἰρῆσθαι· καὶ γὰρ εὔηθες τοὺς δούλους οἰηθῆναι
πρὸ τῶν φίλων τοῦ θεοῦ τὴν ἀρετῆς χώραν διανέμε-
46 σθαι. ἀλλὰ πρῶτον ἐκεῖνό σοι βούλεται παραστῆσαι,
ὅτι ἕτερος νηπίων καὶ ἕτερος τελείων χῶρός ἐστιν,
ὁ μὲν ὀνομαζόμενος ἄσκησις, ὁ δὲ καλούμενος σοφία,
ἔπειτα ὅτι τὰ κάλλιστα τῶν ἐν τῇ φύσει ὁρατὰ
μᾶλλόν ἐστιν ἢ κτητά· κτήσασθαι μὲν γὰρ τὰ
θειοτέρας μοίρας λαχόντα πῶς ἔνεστιν ; ἰδεῖν δ'
οὐκ ἀδύνατον, ἀλλ' οὐχ ἅπασιν, ἔστι δ' αὐτὸ μόνον[2]
τῷ καθαρωτάτῳ καὶ ὀξυωπεστάτῳ γένει, ᾧ τὰ

---

[1] mss. βεβαιοτάτην.   [2] mss. ἐπὶ δ' αὐτῷ μόνῳ.

---

[a] Or, as Mangey, " referring to the death of."

science and its lore, but is acknowledged to be Himself the Source and Fountain-head of science and knowledge in all their forms.

IX. There is a deliberate intention when his words **43** take the form of a promise and define the time of fulfilment not as present but future. He says not " which I am shewing " but " which I will shew thee " (Gen. xii. 1). Thus he testifies to the trust which the soul reposed in God, exhibiting its thankfulness not as called out by accomplished facts, but by expectation of what was to be. For the soul, clinging in **44** utter dependence on a good hope, and deeming that things not present are beyond question already present by reason of the sure stedfastness of Him that promised them, has won as its meed faith, a perfect good ; for we read a little later " Abraham believed God " (Gen. xv. 6). To Moses, too, He says in like manner, when He had shewn to him all the Land, " I shewed it to thine eyes, but thou shalt not enter in " (Deut. xxxiv. 4). You must not think that **45** this was said, as some unconsidering people suppose, to humiliate*a* the all-wise leader ; for indeed it is folly to imagine that the servants of God take precedence of His friends in receiving their portion in the land of virtue. No, what he wishes to bring home to you **46** first of all is that children have one place and full-grown men another, the one named training, the other called wisdom : secondly, that the fairest things in nature are objects of sight rather than of possession. For how is it possible to become possessed of things whose allotted place is nearer to the Divine ? Yet to see them is within the bounds of possibility : though not for all. It is exclusively for the purest and most keen-eyed class, on whom the Father of all

ἴδια ἐπιδεικνύμενος ὁ τῶν ὅλων πατὴρ ἔργα μεγί-
47 στην πασῶν χαρίζεται δωρεάν.   θεωρη-
τικοῦ γὰρ τίς ἀμείνων βίος ἢ μᾶλλον οἰκειούμενος
λογικῷ; διὰ τοῦτο καὶ τῆς τῶν θνητῶν ζῴων
φωνῆς κριτήριον ἐχούσης ἀκοὴν τοὺς τοῦ θεοῦ
λόγους οἱ χρησμοὶ φωτὸς τρόπον ὁρωμένους μη-
νύουσι· λέγεται γὰρ ὅτι " πᾶς ὁ λαὸς ἑώρα τὴν
φωνήν," οὐκ ἤκουεν, ἐπειδήπερ οὐκ ἀέρος πλῆξις
ἦν διὰ τῶν στόματος καὶ γλώττης ὀργάνων τὸ
γινόμενον, ἀλλὰ φέγγος ἀρετῆς τὸ περιαυγέστατον,
λογικῆς ἀδιαφοροῦν πηγῆς, ὃ καὶ ἑτέρωθι μηνύεται
τὸν τρόπον τοῦτον· " ὑμεῖς ἑωράκατε, ὅτι ἐκ τοῦ
οὐρανοῦ λελάληκα πρὸς ὑμᾶς," οὐχὶ ἠκούσατε, διὰ
48 τὴν αὐτὴν αἰτίαν. ἔστι δ' ὅπου τὰ ἀκουστὰ τῶν
ὁρατῶν καὶ ἀκοὴν ὁράσεως διακρίνει λέγων·
" φωνὴν ῥημάτων ὑμεῖς ἠκούσατε, καὶ ὁμοίωμα οὐκ
εἴδετε ἀλλ' ἢ φωνήν," ἄγαν περιττῶς· τὴν μὲν γὰρ
εἰς ὄνομα καὶ ῥῆμα καὶ συνόλως τὰ τοῦ λόγου μέρη
τεμνομένην ἀκουστὴν εἰκότως εἶπεν—ὑπὸ γὰρ ἀκοῆς
δοκιμάζεται—, τὴν δὲ μὴ ῥημάτων μηδ' ὀνομάτων ἀλλὰ θεοῦ φωνήν, ὁρωμένην τῷ τῆς ψυχῆς
49 ὄμματι, ὁρατὴν δεόντως εἰσάγει. προειπὼν δὲ τὸ
" ὁμοίωμα οὐκ εἴδετε " ἐπιφέρει " ἀλλ' ἢ φωνήν,"
ἣν πάντως εἴδετε—τὸ γὰρ προσυπακουόμενον
τοῦτ' ἂν εἴη—· ὥσθ' οἱ μὲν τοῦ θεοῦ λόγοι ὅρασιν
ἔχουσι τὴν ἐν ψυχῇ κριτήριον, ἀκοὴν δ' οἱ εἰς
ὀνομάτων καὶ ῥημάτων ἰδέας μεριζόμενοι.
50 καινὸς δ' ὢν ἐν ἅπασι τὴν ἐπιστήμην καὶ τοῦτ'

---

[a] Philo connects the " voice of words " with the grammatical use of ῥήματα for verbs and supposes the verse to
mean " ordinary human voice you hear, but God's voice
you see."

things, by shewing to them His own works, bestows an all-surpassing gift. For what life is 47 better than a contemplative life, or more appropriate to a rational being ? For this reason, whereas the voice of mortal beings is judged by hearing, the sacred oracles intimate that the words of God are seen as light is seen ; for we are told that " all the people saw the Voice " (Ex. xx. 18), not that they heard it ; for what was happening was not an impact on air made by the organs of mouth and tongue, but virtue shining with intense brilliance, wholly resembling a fountain of reason, and this is also indicated elsewhere on this wise : " Ye have seen that I have spoken to you out of Heaven " (Ex. xx. 22), not " ye heard," for the same cause as before. In one 48 place the writer distinguishes things heard from things seen and hearing from sight, saying, " Ye heard a voice of words, and saw no similitude but only a voice " (Deut. iv. 12), making a very subtle distinction, for the voice dividing itself into noun and verb and the parts of speech in general[a] he naturally spoke of as " audible," for it comes to the test of hearing : but the voice or sound that was not that of verbs and nouns but of God, seen by the eye of the soul, he rightly represents as " visible." And after first 49 saying " Ye saw no similitude " he adds " but only a Voice," evidently meaning the reader to supply in thought " which you did see." This shews that words spoken by God are interpreted by the power of sight residing in the soul, whereas those which are divided up among the various parts of speech[b] appeal to hearing. Fresh and original as is the 50 insight which he shews in all cases, there is a special

[b] See App. p. 562.

PHILO

ἰδίως καὶ ξένως κεκαινούργηκεν εἰπὼν ὁρατὴν
εἶναι τὴν φωνήν, τὴν μόνην σχεδὸν τῶν ἐν ἡμῖν
οὐχ ὁρατὴν ὑπεξῃρημένης διανοίας· τὰ μὲν γὰρ
[444] κατὰ | τὰς ἄλλας αἰσθήσεις πάνθ' ὁρατά, τὰ χρώ-
ματα, οἱ χυλοί, οἱ ἀτμοί, τὰ θερμά, τὰ ψυχρά, τὰ
λεῖα, τὰ τραχέα, τὰ μαλακὰ καὶ σκληρά, ᾗ σώματα.
51   τί δέ ἐστι τοῦτο, σαφέστερον ἐρῶ· ὁ
χυλὸς ὁρατός ἐστιν, οὐχ ᾗ χυλός, ἀλλ' ᾗ μόνον
σῶμα, τὸ γὰρ ᾗ χυλὸς εἴσεται ἡ γεῦσις· καὶ ὁ
ἀτμός, ᾗ μὲν ἀτμός, ὑπὸ ῥινῶν ἐξετασθήσεται, ᾗ δὲ
σῶμα, καὶ πρὸς ὀφθαλμῶν· καὶ τὰ ἄλλα ταύτῃ
52 δοκιμασθήσεται. φωνὴ δὲ οὔθ' ὡς ἀκουστὸν οὔθ'
ὡς σῶμα, εἰ δὴ καὶ σῶμά ἐστιν, ὁρατὸν εἶναι
πέφυκεν, ἀλλὰ δύο ταῦτα τῶν ἐν ἡμῖν ἀόρατα, νοῦς
καὶ λόγος. ἀλλὰ γὰρ οὐχ ὅμοιον τὸ ἡμέτερον
ἠχεῖον[1] τῷ θείῳ φωνῆς ὀργάνῳ· τὸ μὲν γὰρ ἡμέτερον ἀέρι κίρναται καὶ πρὸς τὸν συγγενῆ τόπον
καταφεύγει, τὰ ὦτα, τὸ δὲ θεῖον ἀκράτου[2] καὶ
ἀμιγοῦς ἐστι λόγου, φθάνοντος μὲν ἀκοὴν διὰ
λεπτότητα, ὁρωμένου δὲ ὑπὸ ψυχῆς ἀκραιφνοῦς διὰ
τὴν ἐν τῷ βλέπειν ὀξύτητα.
53 X. Οὐκοῦν μετὰ τὴν ἀπόλειψιν τῶν θνητῶν
πρώτην ὁ θεὸς χαρίζεται τῇ ψυχῇ δωρεάν, ὡς ἔφην,
ἐπίδειξιν καὶ θεωρίαν τῶν ἀθανάτων, δευτέραν ⟨δὲ⟩
τὴν εἰς πλῆθος ὁμοῦ καὶ μέγεθος τῶν ἀρετῆς
δογμάτων ἐπίδοσιν· λέγει γάρ· " καὶ ποιήσω σε εἰς
ἔθνος μέγα," διὰ μὲν τοῦ ἔθνους τὸ πλῆθος, διὰ δὲ

---

[1] MSS. ἠχεῖ (ἠχῇ) ἐν or ἤχημα.
[2] MSS. (and, strange to say, all editions) ἀκρατοῦς, a word impossible in this context.

---

[a] The thought seems to be that, while none of our sensa-

160

and unusual originality in this instance in his saying
that the voice is visible, practically the only thing in
us, if understanding be left out of consideration,
which is not visible : for the objects of the senses
other than the eyes are all of them, colours, savours,
perfumes, things warm, things cold, things smooth,
things rough, things soft and hard, visible as bodies.

What this means I will state more 51
clearly. The savour is visible, not as a savour, but
only as a body, for as savour, it is the taste that will
know it ; and the odour, as odour, will be assayed by
the nostrils, but as body, by the eyes also ; and the
rest will be subject to the same double test.[a] But
it is not the nature of voice to be visible whether we
regard it as something audible or as body, if body
indeed it is ;[b] but of our properties these two are
invisible, mind and speech. The truth is that our 52
sound-producer is not similar to the Divine organ of
voice ; for ours mingles with air and betakes itself
to the place akin to it, the ears ; but the Divine is
an organ of pure and unalloyed speech, too subtle
for the hearing to catch it, but visible to the soul
which is single in virtue of its keenness of sight.

X. So then, the first boon which God vouchsafes 53
to the soul after it has relinquished mortal things is,
as I have said, the shewing of things immortal and
the power to contemplate them ; and the second,
progress in the principles of virtue, alike as regards
number and " greatness " : for He says, " And I
will make thee to become a great nation," implying
by the word " nation " their number, and by the

tions are visible, those of taste, smell, and touch are produced
by visible objects.

[b] According to the Stoics φωνή is a body, but Philo does
not unreservedly accept this.

161

τοῦ μεγάλου τὴν πρὸς τὸ ἄμεινον αὔξησιν παραλαμ-
54 βάνων. τὴν δὲ τοῦ ποσοῦ καθ' ἑκάτερον εἶδος, τό
τε ἐν μεγέθει καὶ τὸ ἐν πλήθει, παραύξησιν διασυνίστησι καὶ ὁ τῆς Αἰγύπτου βασιλεύς· '' ἰδοὺ '' γάρ
φησι '' τὸ γένος τῶν υἱῶν Ἰσραὴλ μέγα πλῆθος,''
ἐπειδή γε ἀμφότερα τῷ ὁρατικῷ τοῦ ὄντος γένει
προσμαρτυρεῖ, ὡς πληθύν τε καὶ μέγεθος κτησαμένῳ, τὰ περὶ τὸν βίον καὶ λόγον κατορθώματα.
55 οὐ γάρ, ὅπερ ἄν τις τὸν ἐν τοῖς ὀνόμασιν εἱρμὸν
διαφυλάττων, πολὺ πλῆθος, ἀλλὰ μέγα εἶπεν, εἰδὼς
τὸ πολὺ καθ' αὑτὸ ἀτελὲς μέγεθος, εἰ μὴ προσλάβοι
δύναμιν νοήσεως καὶ ἐπιστήμης. τί γὰρ ὄφελος
πολλὰ μὲν θεωρήματα παραλαμβάνειν, ἕκαστον δὲ
αὐτῶν εἰς τὸ ἁρμόττον μέγεθος μὴ συναυξῆσαι;
οὐδὲ γὰρ ἀγρὸς τέλειος, ᾧ μυρία μὲν ὅσα ἐνυπάρχει
φυτὰ χαμαίζηλα, τέλειον δὲ μηδὲν ἔρνος γεωργικῇ
τέχνῃ συνανέβλαστεν ἤδη καρποτοκεῖν δυνάμενον.
56   τοῦ δὲ μεγέθους καὶ πλήθους τῶν
καλῶν ἀρχὴ καὶ τέλος ἡ ἀδιάστατος περὶ θεοῦ
μνήμη καὶ ἡ κατάκλησις τῆς ἀπ' αὐτοῦ συμμαχίας
πρὸς τὸν ἐμφύλιον καὶ συγκεχυμένον καὶ συνεχῆ
τοῦ βίου πόλεμον· λέγει γάρ· '' ἰδοὺ λαὸς σοφὸς καὶ
ἐπιστήμων τὸ ἔθνος τὸ μέγα τοῦτο· ὅτι ποῖον ἔθνος
μέγα, ᾧ ἐστι θεὸς ἐγγίζων ὡς κύριος ὁ θεὸς ἡμῶν
57 ἐν πᾶσιν οἷς ἂν αὐτὸν ἐπικαλεσώμεθα ; ''
[445] οὐκοῦν ὅτι καὶ πρὸς βοήθειαν δύναμις | ἀρωγὸς
εὐτρεπὴς ἐφεδρεύει παρὰ θεῷ καὶ αὐτὸς ὁ ἡγεμὼν

---

[a] Lit. '' growth to something better.''
[b] See App. p. 562.

word " great " their improvement in quality.[a] How 54
great their advance was in either respect, alike in
" greatness " and in number, is made evident by the
words of the King of Egypt, " Lo the race of the
children of Israel is a great multitude " (Ex. i. 9).
There he bears witness to the race that has eyes to
see Him that ıs, that it has acquired both multitude
and greatness, high achievement, that is, both in
conduct of life and in principle.[b] For he did not say, 55
as a man strictly observing the association of noun
and epithet would say, " much multitude," but " a
great multitude," knowing that " much " is but an
incomplete greatness, if it stands by itself without
the addition of the power to understand and know.
For what advantage is there in receiving (from our
teachers) the results of study in plenty, unless we go
on to develop each of them to its fitting stature ?
For a field, too, is but an imperfect one which contains any number of plants only a little above the
ground, but in which no fully formed growth has shot
up aided by skilful tillage and able now to yield fruit.

The greatness and large number of the 56
good and noble has for its beginning and end the
perpetual recollection of God, and the calling down
of the aid that comes from Him, to counter the intestine warfare of life, unbroken in its bewildering
irregularity, for it says : " Lo this great nation is a
wise and understanding people : for what kind of
great nation is there, which has God drawing nigh to
it, as the Lord our God in all things in which we call
upon Him ? " (Deut. iv. 6 f.).   So far it 57
has been shewn that there is waiting ready and
equipped at God's side strong help to come to our
succour, and that the Sovereign Ruler will Himself

ἐγγυτέρω πρόσεισιν ἐπ᾽ ὠφελείᾳ τῶν ἀξίων ὠφε-
λεῖσθαι, δεδήλωται. XI. τίνες δ᾽ οἱ τούτων ἐπάξιοι
τυγχάνειν εἰσίν; ἢ δῆλον ὅτι οἱ σοφίας καὶ ἐπι-
58 στήμης ἐρασταὶ πάντες; οὗτοι γάρ εἰσιν ὁ σοφὸς
καὶ ἐπιστήμων, ὃν εἶπε, λεώς, ὧν ἕκαστος μέγας
εἰκότως ἐστίν, ἐπειδὴ μεγάλων ὀρέγεται, ἑνὸς δὲ
καὶ λίαν ὑπερβαλλόντως, τοῦ μὴ διαζευχθῆναι θεοῦ
τοῦ μεγίστου, ἀλλὰ τὴν πρόσοδον αὐτοῦ συνεγ-
γίζοντος σταθερῶς ἄνευ καταπλήξεως ὑπομεῖναι.
59 οὗτος ὁ ὅρος ἐστὶ τοῦ μεγάλου λεώ,[1] τὸ τῷ θεῷ
συνεγγίζειν ἢ " ᾧ θεὸς συνεγγίζει."   ὁ
μὲν δὴ κόσμος καὶ ὁ κοσμοπολίτης σοφὸς πολλῶν
καὶ μεγάλων ἀγαθῶν ἀναπέπλησται, ὁ δὲ ἄλλος
ἀνθρώπων ὅμιλος πλείοσι μὲν κέχρηται κακοῖς,
ἀγαθοῖς δὲ ἐλάττοσι· σπάνιον γὰρ ἐν πεφυρμένῳ
60 καὶ συγκεχυμένῳ βίῳ τὸ καλόν. διόπερ ἐν χρησμοῖς ᾄδεται· " οὐχ ὅτι πολυπληθεῖτε παρὰ πάντα
τὰ ἔθνη, προείλετο κύριος ὑμᾶς καὶ ἐξελέξατο—
ὑμεῖς γάρ ἐστε ὀλιγοστοὶ παρὰ πάντα τὰ ἔθνη—,
ἀλλὰ παρὰ τὸ ἀγαπᾶν κύριον ὑμᾶς." εἰ γάρ τις
βουληθείη τὸν ὄχλον μιᾶς ψυχῆς ὥσπερ κατὰ ἔθνη
διανεῖμαι, πολλὰς μὲν ἂν εὕροι τάξεις ἀκοσμούσας,
ὧν ἡδοναὶ ἢ ἐπιθυμίαι ἢ λῦπαι ἢ φόβοι ἢ πάλιν
ἀφροσύναι καὶ ἀδικίαι καὶ αἱ τούτων συγγενεῖς καὶ
ἀδελφαὶ[2] ταξιαρχοῦσι, μίαν δὲ αὐτὸ μόνον εὖ δια-
κεκοσμημένην, ἧς ὁ ὀρθὸς λόγος ἀφηγεῖται.
61 παρὰ μὲν οὖν ἀνθρώποις τὸ ἄδικον πλῆθος πρὸ
ἑνὸς τοῦ δικαίου προτετίμηται, παρὰ δὲ τῷ θεῷ τὸ
σπάνιον ἀγαθὸν πρὸ μυρίων ἀδίκων· ᾧ καὶ παρ-

---

[1] mss. θεοῦ.
[2] Perhaps, as Wend. suggests, ἀδελφαὶ ⟨κακίαι⟩.

draw near for the benefit of those who are worthy
to receive His benefits.   XI. But who are they that
are worthy to obtain these ?   Is it not clear that all
the lovers of wisdom and knowledge are so ?   For 58
these are the wise and understanding people which
was spoken of, each member of which is with good
reason great, since he reaches out after great things ;
and after one most eagerly, never to be severed from
God, the supremely Great, but without dismay sted-
fastly to abide His approach as He draws near.   This 59
is the defining mark of the people that is " great,"
to draw nigh to God, or to be that " to which God
draws nigh."   Now the world and the
wise man, the world-citizen,[a] is filled full of good
things many and great, but the remaining mass of
men experiences evil things in greater number, but
fewer good things ; for in the medley and confusion
of human life that which is fair and goodly is rare and
scanty.   And for this reason the sacred oracles con- 60
tain this utterance : " Not because ye are numerous
beyond all the nations did the Lord prefer and choose
you out : for ye surpass all the nations in fewness ;
but because the Lord loveth you " (Deut. vii. 7 f.).
For were a man to desire to distribute, as it were into
nations, the crowd contained in a single soul, many
disorderly companies would he find, commanded by
pleasures or desires or griefs or fears or again by
follies and wrongdoings, and the nearest kinsfolk
of these, but one only well-ordered, of which right
reason is the captain.   Now, in the judge- 61
ment of men the multitude of the unjust is preferred
to the single just ; but in God's judgement the few
good to the myriad unjust ; and He charges the just

[a] See note on *De Op.* 3.

αγγέλλει μηδέποτε τοιούτῳ συναινέσαι πλήθει· " οὐκ
ἔσῃ " γάρ φησι " μετὰ πολλῶν ἐπὶ κακίᾳ." ἆρ'
οὖν μετ' ὀλίγων χρή; μετ' οὐδενὸς μὲν οὖν φαύ-
λου· εἷς δ' ὢν ὁ φαῦλος πολύς ἐστι κακίαις, ᾧ
συντάσσεσθαι μεγίστη ζημία· τοὐναντίον γὰρ ἀνθ-
ίστασθαι καὶ πολεμεῖν ἀκαταπλήκτῳ χρωμένους
62 δυνάμει προσήκει. " ἐὰν " γάρ φησιν " ἐξέλθῃς
εἰς πόλεμον ἐπὶ τοὺς ἐχθρούς σου καὶ ἴδῃς ἵππον,"
τὸ ὑπέραυχον καὶ σκιρτητικὸν πάθος ἀφηνιάζον,
" καὶ ἀναβάτην," τὸν ἐποχούμενον αὐτῷ φιλοπαθῆ
νοῦν, " καὶ λαὸν πλείονά σου," τοὺς ζηλωτὰς τῶν
εἰρημένων φαλαγγηδὸν ἐπιόντας, " οὐ φοβηθήσῃ
ἀπ' αὐτῶν"· εἷς γὰρ ὢν ἑνὶ τῷ πάντων ἡγεμόνι
χρήσῃ συμμάχῳ, " ὅτι κύριος ὁ θεός σου μετὰ
63 σοῦ." τούτου γὰρ ἡ σύνοδος καθαιρεῖ πολέμους,
εἰρήνην ἀνοικοδομεῖ, τὰ πολλὰ καὶ συνήθη κακὰ
ἀνατρέπει, τὸ σπάνιον καὶ θεοφιλὲς γένος ἀνασῴζει,
ᾧ πᾶς ὁ γενόμενος ὑπήκοος μισεῖ καὶ βδελύττεται
64 τὰ τῶν γεωδεστέρων στίφη.   XII. " ἃ
γὰρ πολυπληθεῖ " φησί " ποσὶν ἐν πᾶσι τοῖς
ἑρπετοῖς τοῖς ⟨ἕρπουσιν⟩ ἐπὶ τῆς γῆς, οὐ φάγεσθε,
[446] ὅτι βδελύγματά ἐστιν." | ἀλλ' οὐ μίσους ἐστὶν
ἐπαξία ψυχὴ μὴ καθ' ἓν μέρος ἀλλὰ κατὰ πάντα ἢ
τὰ πλεῖστα βαίνουσα ἐπὶ τὴν γῆν καὶ τὰ σώματος
περιλιχνεύουσα καὶ συνόλως εἰς τὰς οὐρανοῦ θείας
65 περιόδους ἀνακῦψαι μὴ δυναμένη; καὶ μὴν ὥσπερ
τὸ πολύπουν, οὕτως καὶ τὸ ἄπουν ἐν ἑρπετοῖς
ψεκτόν, τὸ μὲν διὰ τὴν λεχθεῖσαν αἰτίαν, τὸ δ' ὅτι

166

never to agree with such a multitude : for He says " Thou shalt not be with many to engage in wickedness " (Ex. xxiii. 2). Should we then be so with few ? Nay, not with any bad man : and the bad man, one though he be, is made manifold by wickednesses, and to range oneself by his side is a very great disaster : on the contrary it behoves us to shew a vigour free from terror and resist him and be at war with him. For it says " If thou go out to war against thine enemies and see horse and rider," that is passion, the insolent, the restive, the unruly, and the passion-loving mind mounted on it, " and a people more numerous than thou art," even the devoted followers of these leaders advancing in serried mass " thou shalt not be afraid of them." One as thou art thou shalt have One fighting on thy side, even the Ruler of all, as it says, " for the Lord Thy God is with thee " (Deut. xx. 1). This companionship brings wars to an end, builds up peace, overthrows the host of evil things to which we grow accustomed, rescues the scanty band of those beloved of God, every loyal adherent of which loathes and hates the battalions of the earth-bound. XII. For it says : " Whatsoever hath many feet among all creeping things that creep upon the earth, ye shall not eat, for they are an abomination " (Lev. xi. 42). Now, is not a soul deserving of hatred which moves over the ground not on one part of itself but on all or most parts, even licking with a relish the things of the body, and altogether incapable of lifting its eyes to the holy revolutions of heaven ? And further among creeping things just as that which has many feet is disallowed, so too is that which has no feet, the former for the reason just given, the latter be-

ὅλον δι' ὅλων πέπτωκεν ἐπὶ γῆν, ὑπ' οὐδενὸς ἀλλ'
οὐδ' ἐπὶ τὸ βραχύτατον ἐξαιρόμενον· πάντα γὰρ
τὸν πορευόμενον ἐπὶ κοιλίαν ἀκάθαρτον εἶναί φησι,
τὸν τὰς τῆς γαστρὸς ἡδονὰς μεταδιώκοντα αἰνιτ-
66 τόμενος.   ἔνιοι δὲ προσυπερβάλλοντες οὐ
μόνον τῷ τῆς ἐπιθυμίας ἐχρήσαντο γένει, ἀλλὰ
καὶ τὸ ἀδελφὸν αὐτῇ πάθος, τὸν θυμόν, προσεκτή-
σαντο, βουληθέντες ὅλον τὸ τῆς ψυχῆς ἄλογον
ἐκζωπυρῆσαι μέρος, τὸν δὲ νοῦν διαφθεῖραι· τὸ γὰρ
εἰρημένον λόγῳ μὲν ἐπὶ ὄφεως, ἔργῳ δὲ ἐπὶ παντὸς
ἀλόγου καὶ φιλοπαθοῦς ἀνθρώπου χρησμὸς ὡς
ἀληθῶς ἐστι θεῖος· " ἐπὶ τῷ στήθει καὶ τῇ κοιλίᾳ
πορεύσῃ." περὶ μὲν γὰρ τὰ στέρνα ὁ θυμός, τὸ δὲ
67 ἐπιθυμίας εἶδος ἐν κοιλίᾳ. πορεύεται δὲ ὁ ἄφρων
δι' ἀμφοτέρων, θυμοῦ τε καὶ ἐπιθυμίας, ἀεὶ μηδένα
διαλείπων χρόνον, τὸν ἡνίοχον καὶ βραβευτὴν νοῦν
ἀποβαλών· ὁ δ' ἐναντίος τούτῳ θυμὸν μὲν καὶ
ἐπιθυμίαν ἐκτέτμηται, κυβερνήτην δὲ ἐπιγέγραπται
λόγον θεῖον, καθὰ καὶ Μωυσῆς ὁ θεοφιλέστατος, ὅς,
ὅταν τὰς ὁλοκαύτους τῆς ψυχῆς ἱερουργῇ θυσίας,
" τὴν μὲν κοιλίαν ἐκπλυνεῖ," τουτέστιν ὅλον τὸ
ἐπιθυμίας εἶδος ἐκνίψεται, τὸ δὲ " στηθύνιον ἀπὸ
τοῦ κριοῦ τῆς τελειώσεως ἀφελεῖ," σύμπαντα
δήπου τὸν πολεμικὸν θυμόν, ἵνα τὸ λοιπὸν μέρος
καὶ ἄμεινον τῆς ψυχῆς, τὸ λογικόν, μηδενὸς ἀντι-
σπῶντος ἔτι καὶ μεθέλκοντος ἐλευθέροις καὶ εὐγε-
νέσι τῷ ὄντι χρήσηται πρὸς τὰ καλὰ πάντα ὁρμαῖς.
68   οὕτως γὰρ εἷς τε πλῆθος καὶ μέγεθος

cause it lies its full length sprawling upon the earth, lifted out of it by nothing even to the smallest extent : for it says that all that goeth upon the belly is unclean (*ibid.*), indicating by this figure the man who is in pursuit of the pleasures of the belly.

But some, exceeding all bounds, in their determination to kindle into activity all the irrational portion of the soul, and to destroy the mind, have not only indulged all that comes under the head of desire, but taken to them also its brother passion, fierce spirit. For that which was said, " Upon thy breast and thy belly shalt thou go " (Gen. iii. 14), in the literal sense applies to the serpent, but is really a truly Divine oracle applying to every irrational and passion-loving man ; for the breast is the abode of fierce spirit, and desire dwells in the belly. The fool's whole course through every moment of his journey depends on this pair, fierce spirit and desire ; since he has got rid of mind, who is the charioteer and monitor. The man of the opposite character has exscinded fierce spirit and desire, and chosen as his patron and controlling guide the Divine Word. Even so Moses, best beloved of God, when offering the whole burnt sacrifices of the soul, will " wash out the belly " (Lev. viii. 21), that is, will cleanse away desire in every shape, but " the breast from the ram of consecration he will take away " (Lev. viii. 29). This means, we may be sure, the warlike spirit in its completeness ; and the object of taking it away is that the better portion of the soul, the rational part, that is left, may exercise its truly free and noble impulses towards all things beautiful, with nothing pulling against it any longer and dragging it in another direction.

In these circumstances it will improve both in number **68**

ἐπιδώσει· λέγεται γάρ· '' ἕως τίνος παροξυνοῦσιν ὁ
λαὸς οὗτος ; καὶ ἕως τίνος οὐ πιστεύσουσί μοι ἐν
πᾶσι τοῖς σημείοις οἷς ἐποίησα ἐν αὐτοῖς ; πατάξω
αὐτοὺς θανάτῳ καὶ ἀπολῶ αὐτούς, καὶ ποιήσω σὲ
καὶ τὸν οἶκον τοῦ πατρός σου εἰς ἔθνος μέγα καὶ
πολὺ ἢ τοῦτο·'' ἐπειδὰν γὰρ ὁ θυμῷ καὶ ἐπιθυμίᾳ
χρώμενος πολὺς ὅμιλος καταλυθῇ τῆς ψυχῆς,
πάντως εὐθὺς ὁ τῆς λογικῆς φύσεως διεξηρτημένος
69 ἀνίσχει καὶ ἀνατέλλει.   ὥσπερ δὲ τὸ
πολύπουν καὶ ἄπουν, ἐναντία ὄντα ἐν τῷ γένει τῶν
[447] ἑρπετῶν, ἀκάθαρτα | ἀναγράφεται, οὕτως καὶ ἡ
ἄθεος καὶ πολύθεος ἀντίπαλοι ἐν ψυχῇ δόξαι
βέβηλοι. σημεῖον δέ· ἀμφοτέρας ὁ νόμος ἐκκλησίας ἱερᾶς ἀπελήλακε, τὴν μὲν ἄθεον θλαδίαν καὶ
ἀποκεκομμένον εἴρξας ἐκκλησιάζειν, τὴν δὲ πολύθεον τὸν ἐκ πόρνης ὁμοίως κωλύσας ἀκούειν ἢ
λέγειν· ἄθεος μὲν γὰρ ὁ ἄγονος, πολύθεος δὲ ὁ ἐκ
πόρνης τυφλώττων περὶ τὸν ἀληθῆ πατέρα καὶ διὰ
τοῦτο πολλοὺς ἀνθ' ἑνὸς γονεῖς ἐπιγραφόμενος.[1]
70 XIII. Δύο μὲν αὗται δωρεαὶ προείρηνται, θεω-
ρητικοῦ τε ἐλπὶς βίου καὶ πρὸς πλῆθος καὶ μέγεθος
τῶν καλῶν ἐπίδοσις. τρίτη δ' ἐστὶν εὐλογία, ἧς
ἄνευ βεβαιώσασθαι τὰς προτέρας χάριτας οὐκ ἔστι·
λέγει γάρ· '' καὶ εὐλογήσω σε,'' τουτέστιν ἐπαινετὸν λόγον δωρήσομαι· τὸ γὰρ εὖ πάντως ἐπ'

---

[1] MSS. αἰνιττόμενος.   See App. p. 562.

[a] Cf. De Ebr. 213.

and greatness : for it is said : " How long shall the
people provoke ? and how long shall they refuse to
trust Me in all the signs which I wrought among
them ? I will smite them with death and will destroy
them, and I will make thee and thy father's house
a nation great and numerous beyond this one "
(Num. xiv. 11 f.). For, in the soul when once the
great concourse is broken up, in which fierce spirit
and desire prevail, there rises and springs up without fail another concourse, even that which wholly
depends on the rational nature.   Now 69
just as the creature with many feet and that
without feet, opposite species in the genus of creeping
things, are proclaimed unclean, so also atheism and
polytheism, mutually antagonistic doctrines in the
soul, are alike profane. Here is the indication of
this : the Law has expelled both of these doctrines
from the sacred assembly, atheism, by debarring a
eunuch from membership of it ;[a] polytheism, by likewise forbidding the son of a harlot to be a listener or
speaker in it (Deut. xxiii. 1 f.). For the sterile man
is godless ; and the son of a whore is a polytheist,
being in the dark about his real father, and for this
reason ascribing his begetting to many, instead of
to one.

XIII. Two gifts have been already spoken of, which 70
are these, a hope held out of a life of contemplation,
and progress towards abundance and "greatness" of
things fair and beautiful. A third gift is " blessing "
or excellence of reason and speech, and apart from
this it is not possible to make the former gracious
gifts secure. He says " And I will bless thee," *i.e.*
" I will endow thee with excellent reason and speech."
" Blessing " or " eulogy " is a word compounded of

PHILO

71 ἀρετῆς· λόγος δὲ ὁ μὲν πηγῇ ἔοικεν, ὁ δὲ ἀπορροῇ, πηγῇ μὲν ὁ ἐν διανοίᾳ, προφορὰ δὲ ἡ διὰ στόματος καὶ γλώττης ἀπορροή. ἑκάτερον δὲ εἶδος λόγου βελτιωθῆναι πολὺς πλοῦτος, διάνοιαν μὲν εὐλογιστίᾳ πρὸς πάντα μικρὰ καὶ μείζω χρωμένην, προφορὰν δὲ ὑπὸ παιδείας ὀρθῆς ἡνιοχουμένην.

72 πολλοὶ γὰρ λογίζονται μὲν τὰ βέλτιστα, ὑπὸ δὲ ἑρμηνέως κακοῦ προὐδόθησαν, λόγου, μουσικὴν τὴν ἐγκύκλιον οὐκ ἐκπονήσαντες· οἱ δὲ ἔμπαλιν ἑρμηνεῦσαι μὲν ἐγένοντο δυνατώτατοι, βουλεύσασθαι δὲ φαυλότατοι, καθάπερ οἱ λεγόμενοι σοφισταί· τούτων γὰρ ἀχόρευτος μὲν καὶ ἄμουσος ἡ διάνοια, πάμμουσοι δὲ αἱ διὰ τῶν φωνητηρίων ὀργάνων

73 διέξοδοι. χαρίζεται δὲ ὁ θεὸς τοῖς ὑπηκόοις ἀτελὲς οὐδέν, πλήρη δὲ καὶ τέλεια πάντα· διὸ καὶ νῦν τὴν εὐλογίαν οὐχ ἑνὶ λόγου τμήματι, τοῖς δὲ μέρεσιν ἀμφοτέροις ἐπιπέμπει δικαιῶν τὸν εὐεργετούμενον καὶ ἐνθυμεῖσθαι τὰ βέλτιστα καὶ ἐξαγγέλλειν τὰ νοηθέντα δυνατῶς· ἡ γὰρ τελειότης δι' ἀμφοῖν, ὡς ἔοικε, τοῦ τε ὑποβάλλοντος τὰ ἐνθυμήματα καθαρῶς καὶ τοῦ διερμηνεύοντος αὐτὰ

74 ἀπταίστως. ἢ οὐχ ὁρᾷς τὸν Ἄβελ—ὄνομα δέ ἐστι τὰ θνητὰ πενθοῦντος καὶ τὰ ἀθάνατα εὐδαιμονίζοντος—, ὡς ἀνεπιλήπτῳ μὲν κέχρηται διανοίᾳ, τῷ δὲ μὴ γεγυμνάσθαι περὶ λόγους ἥττηται πρὸς δεινοῦ παλαῖσαι Κάιν[1] τέχνῃ μᾶλλον ἢ ῥώμῃ περι-

1 MSS. καί.

---

a For Philo's use of εὐλογιστία in connexion with εὐλογεῖν see note on De Sobr. 18.

172

" well " and " logos." Of these, " well " connotes **71**
nothing but excellence: "logos" has two aspects, one
resembling a spring, the other its outflow; "logos" in
the understanding resembles a spring, and is called
" reason," while utterance by mouth and tongue is
like its outflow, and is called " speech." That each
species of logos should be improved is vast wealth, the
understanding having good reasoning *a* at its command
for all things great and small, and utterance being
under the guidance of right training. For many **72**
reason excellently, but find speech a bad interpreter
of thought and are by it betrayed, through not having
had a thorough grounding in the ordinary subjects of
culture. Others, again, have shewn great ability in
expounding themes, and yet been most evil thinkers,
such as the so-called sophists ; for the understanding
of these men is wholly untrained by the Muses, whose
united voice is heard in the output of the vocal organs.
But God bestows on those who obey Him no im- **73**
perfect boon. All His gifts are full and complete.
And so, in this case also, He does not send the blessing
or " logos-excellence " in one division of logos, but
in both its parts, for He holds it just that the recipient
of His bounty should both conceive the noblest conceptions and give masterly expression to his ideas.
For perfection depends, as we know, on both divisions
of logos, the reason which suggests the ideas with
clearness, and the speech which gives unfailing
expression to them.   Do you not notice **74**
Abel, whose name stands for one to whom things
mortal are a grief and things immortal are full of
happiness, how, though he has the advantage of a
faultless understanding, yet through lack of training
in speaking he is worsted by Cain, a clever wrestler

173

75 γενέσθαι δυναμένου; διὸ καὶ θαυμάζων τῆς περὶ
τὴν φύσιν εὐμοιρίας τὸν τρόπον αἰτιῶμαι τοσοῦτον,
ὅτι προκληθεὶς εἰς ἅμιλλαν λόγων ἧκεν ἀγωνιού-
μενος, δέον ἐπὶ τῆς συνήθους ἠρεμίας στῆναι πολλὰ
χαίρειν φράσαντα τῷ φιλονείκῳ, εἰ δ᾽ ἄρα ἐβούλετο
πάντως διαγωνίσασθαι, μὴ πρότερον κονίσασθαι ἢ
[448] τοῖς | τεχνικοῖς παλαίσμασιν ἐνασκηθῆναι· τῶν γὰρ
ἀγροικοσόφων οἱ τὰ πολιτικὰ κεκομψευμένοι μάλι-
76 στά πως εἰώθασι περιεῖναι.   XIV. διὸ καὶ
Μωυσῆς ὁ πάνσοφος παραιτεῖται μὲν εἰς τὴν τῶν
εὐλόγων καὶ πιθανῶν ἐπίσκεψιν ἐλθεῖν, ἀφ᾽ οὗ τὸ
ἀληθείας φέγγος ἤρξατο ὁ θεὸς ἐναστράπτειν αὐτῷ
διὰ τῶν ἐπιστήμης καὶ σοφίας αὐτῆς ἀθανάτων
λόγων, ἄγεται δὲ οὐδὲν ἧττον πρὸς τὴν θέαν αὐτῶν
οὐχ ἕνεκα τοῦ πλειόνων ἔμπειρος γενέσθαι πραγμάτων—ἀποχρῶσι γὰρ αἱ περὶ θεοῦ καὶ τῶν ἱερω-
τάτων αὐτοῦ δυνάμεων ζητήσεις τῷ φιλοθεάμονι—,
ἀλλ᾽ ὑπὲρ τοῦ περιγενέσθαι τῶν ἐν Αἰγύπτῳ
σοφιστῶν, οἷς αἱ[1] μυθικαὶ πιθανότητες πρὸ τῆς τῶν
77 ἀληθῶν ἐναργείας τετίμηνται. ὅταν μὲν οὖν τοῖς
τοῦ πανηγεμόνος ἐμπεριπατῇ πράγμασιν ὁ νοῦς,
οὐδενὸς ἑτέρου προσδεῖται πρὸς τὴν θεωρίαν,
ἐπειδὴ τῶν νοητῶν μόνη διάνοια ὀφθαλμὸς ὀξυ-
ωπέστατος· ὅταν δὲ καὶ τοῖς κατὰ αἴσθησιν ἢ πάθος
ἢ σῶμα, ὧν ἐστιν ἡ Αἰγύπτου χώρα σύμβολον,
δεήσεται καὶ τῆς περὶ λόγους τέχνης ὁμοῦ καὶ
78 δυνάμεως.   οὗ χάριν ἐπάγεσθαι τὸν
Ἀαρὼν αὐτῷ διείρηται, τὸν προφορικὸν λόγον·
" οὐκ ἰδοὺ " φησίν " Ἀαρὼν ὁ ἀδελφός σου ; "

[1] MSS. ὅσαι.

174

able to prevail by skill rather than strength ? Where- 75
fore, admiring as I do his character for its rich natural
endowment, I find fault with him in so far as, when
challenged to a contest of words, he came forward to
engage in it, whereas he ought to have maintained
his wonted quietude, totally disregarding his quarrelsome brother ; and, if he was quite bent on fighting
it out, not to have entered the lists until he had had
some practice in scientific grips and tricks ; for village
sages usually get the worst of it when they encounter
those who have acquired the cleverness of the town.

XIV. That is why Moses, the man of all 76
wisdom, though he excuses himself from investigating
well-worded and specious arguments, from the time
that God began to flash into him the light of truth by
means of the undying words of the very self of Knowledge and Wisdom (Ex. iv. 10), yet is led none the
less to look into them, not for the sake of gaining
acquaintance with a greater number of subjects—for
the lover of contemplation finds researches touching
God and His most holy powers all-sufficing—but with
a view to getting the better of the sophists in Egypt,
for whom specious sounding fables are of more value
than the clear evidence of realities.   Yes, whensoever 77
the mind is moving amid matters concerned with the
Ruler of all, it needs no extraneous help in its study,
inasmuch as for objects of intellectual apprehension
unaided mind is an eye of keenest sight : but when it
is occupied besides with matters affected by sense-
perception or passion or the body, of which the land of
Egypt is a symbol, it will need alike the art of speaking
and ability in exercising it.   For the sake 78
of this he was enjoined to call to his aid Aaron, the
logos in utterance.   " Lo," saith He, " is not Aaron

175

μιᾶς γὰρ ἀμφοῖν τῆς λογικῆς φύσεως μητρὸς οὔσης
ἀδελφὰ δήπου τὰ γεννήματα. " ἐπίσταμαι, ὅτι
λαλήσει·" διανοίας μὲν γὰρ τὸ καταλαμβάνειν,
προφορᾶς δὲ τὸ λαλεῖν ἴδιον. " λαλήσει " φησίν
" αὐτός σοι·" τὰ γὰρ ἐν αὐτῷ ταμιευόμενα μὴ
δυνάμενος ὁ νοῦς ἀπαγγεῖλαι τῷ πλησίον ἑρμηνεῖ
79 χρῆται λόγῳ πρὸς τὴν ὧν πέπονθε δήλωσιν. εἶτ'
ἐπιλέγει· " ἰδοὺ αὐτὸς ἐξελεύσεται εἰς συνάντησίν
σοι," ἐπειδὴ τῷ ὄντι ὁ λόγος τοῖς ἐνθυμήμασιν
ὑπαντῶν, ῥήματα καὶ ὀνόματα προστιθεὶς χαράττει
τὰ ἄσημα, ὡς ἐπίσημα ποιεῖν. καὶ " ἰδών σε "
φησί " χαρήσεται ἐν αὐτῷ·" γήθει γὰρ ὁ λόγος
καὶ εὐφραίνεται,[1] ὅταν μὴ ἀμυδρὸν ᾖ τὸ ἐνθύμημα,
διότι τηλαυγοῦς ὄντος ἀπταίστῳ καὶ εὐτρόχῳ
διερμηνεύσει χρῆται κυρίων καὶ εὐθυβόλων καὶ
γεμόντων πολλῆς ἐμφάσεως εὐπορῶν ὀνομάτων·
80 XV. ἐπειδὰν γοῦν ἀδηλότερά πως ᾖ τὰ νοήματα,
κατὰ κενοῦ βαίνει καὶ ὀλισθὼν πολλάκις μέγα
πτῶμα ἔπεσεν, ὡς μηκέτι ἀναστῆναι δύνασθαι.
" καὶ ἐρεῖς πρὸς αὐτὸν καὶ δώσεις τὰ ῥήματά μου
εἰς τὸ στόμα αὐτοῦ," ἴσον τῷ ὑπηχήσεις αὐτῷ τὰ
ἐνθυμήματα, ἃ ῥημάτων καὶ λόγων ἀδιαφορεῖ
81 θείων· ἄνευ γὰρ τοῦ ὑποβολέως οὐ φθέγξεται ὁ
λόγος, ὑποβολεὺς δὲ λόγου νοῦς, ὡς νοῦ θεός.
" καὶ αὐτός σοι προσλαλήσει πρὸς τὸν λαόν, καὶ
αὐτὸς ἔσται σου στόμα· σὺ δὲ αὐτῷ ἔσῃ τὰ πρὸς

---

[1] mss. εὐφορεῖ.

<hr/>

[a] Or "express." ἀπαγγελία is often used in rhetoric as
a synonym for ἑρμηνεία. See on § 35.

[b] See App. p. 563.

[c] Or "in himself" (ἐν αὐτῷ). See App. p. 563.

[d] The phrase ῥημάτων καὶ λόγων must not be confused with
the common collocation ῥ. καὶ ὀνομάτων (" verbs and nouns ")

thy brother ? " For the logical nature being the one
mother of them both, its offspring are of course
brothers. " I know that he will speak " (He continues). For it is the property of understanding to
apprehend, and of utterance to speak. " He," saith
He, " will speak for thee." For the mind, unable to
report[a] the thoughts stored up in it, employs speech
which stands hard by as an interpreter, for the making
known of its experiences. Then He adds, " Lo, it is 79
he that shall come out to meet thee " : for it is indeed
a fact that speech meeting the mind's conceptions,
and wedding the parts of speech to them, mints them
like uncoined gold, and gives the stamp of expression
to what was unstamped and unexpressed before.[b]
And saith He, " On seeing thee he will rejoice in it[c]"
(Ex. iv. 14) : for speech does exult and is glad,
when the conception is not indistinct, because it finds
that the wording which issues from its rich store of
terms apt and expressive and full of vividness is
fluent and unhalting when the thought is luminous.
XV. And similarly when the ideas to be expressed are 80
in any way deficient in clearness, speech is stepping
on empty air and is apt to slip and have a bad fall
and be unable to get up again. " And thou shalt speak
to him and shall put My words into his mouth." This
is equivalent to saying " Thou shalt suggest to him
the thoughts," for " thoughts " are nothing else than
God's " words " or speech.[d] For without the prompter 81
speech will give forth no utterance, and mind is the
prompter of speech, as God is of mind. " And he
shall speak to the people for thee, and he shall be thy
mouth, and thou shalt be his Godward things "

for speech in general. Here the ῥημάτων echoes the ῥήματα of
the quoted text, and is then interpreted by λόγων (speech).

τὸν θεόν"· ἐμφαντικώτατα τό τε " προσλαλήσει
σοι " φάναι, οἷον διερμηνεύσει τὰ σά, καὶ ὅτι
[449] " ἔσται σου | στόμα"· διὰ γὰρ γλώττης καὶ στό-
ματος φερόμενον τὸ τοῦ λόγου νᾶμα συνεκφέρει
τὰ νοήματα. ἀλλ' ὁ μὲν λόγος ἑρμηνεὺς διανοίας
πρὸς ἀνθρώπους, ἡ δὲ διάνοια γίνεται τῷ λόγῳ τὰ
πρὸς τὸν θεόν, ταῦτα δέ ἐστιν ἐνθυμήματα, ὧν
82 μόνος ὁ θεὸς ἐπίσκοπος.   ἀναγκαῖον οὖν
ἐστι τῷ μέλλοντι πρὸς ἀγῶνα σοφιστικὸν ἀπαντᾶν
ἐπιμεμελῆσθαι λόγων ἐρρωμένως οὕτως, ὡς μὴ
μόνον ἐκφεύγειν τὰ παλαίσματα, ἀλλὰ καὶ ἀντεπι-
τιθέμενον ἀμφοτέροις, τέχνῃ τε καὶ δυνάμει, περι-
83 εἶναι. ἢ οὐχ ὁρᾷς τοὺς ἐπαοιδοὺς καὶ φαρμακευτὰς
ἀντισοφιστεύοντας τῷ θείῳ λόγῳ καὶ τοῖς παραπλησίοις τολμῶντας ἐγχειρεῖν, οὐχ οὕτως ἐπὶ τῷ τὴν
ἰδίαν ἐπιστήμην ἀποφῆναι περιβόητον, ὡς ἐπὶ τῷ
διασῦραι καὶ χλευάσαι τὰ γινόμενα; καὶ γὰρ τὰς
βακτηρίας εἰς δρακόντων μεταστοιχειοῦσι φύσεις,
καὶ τὸ ὕδωρ εἰς αἵματος χρόαν μετατρέπουσι, καὶ
τῶν βατράχων τὸ ὑπολειφθὲν ἐπῳδαῖς ἀνέλκου-
σιν ἐπὶ γῆν, καὶ πάντα οἱ κακοδαίμονες τὰ πρὸς
τὸν οἰκεῖον ὄλεθρον συναύξοντες ἀπατᾶν δοκοῦντες
84 ἀπατῶνται. πρὸς οὓς πῶς ἐνῆν ἀπαντῆσαι μὴ τὸν
ἑρμηνέα διανοίας λόγον, Ἀαρὼν ἐπίκλησιν, ἑτοι-
μασάμενον; ὃς νῦν μὲν εἴρηται στόμα,[1] αὖθις δὲ

----

[1] mss. σόφισμα.

----

[a] The sense of the section is that human thoughts being
in the charge of or inspired by God may be called God's
words, and thus the mind which conceives them is " the Godward things," *i.e.* stands in the relation of God to the mouth.

(Ex. iv. 15 f.). Very vivid are his expressions. Not only does he say " he shall speak to them for thee," as much as to say " he shall put thy thoughts into words " ; but he adds " he shall be thy mouth " ; for the stream of speech flowing over tongue and mouth carries forth the thoughts with it. But, whereas speech is understanding's interpreter manward, understanding occupies toward speech the position of its Godward things, namely thoughts and intents, which are in God's charge solely.[a]   It is a 82 vital matter, then, for one about to face a contest with sophists to have paid attention to words with such thoroughness as not only to elude the grips of his adversary but to take the offensive in his turn and prove himself superior both in skill and strength. You must have observed how the aim of those who 83 use charms and enchantments, when they bring their trickery into play against the Divine word and dare to attempt to do things like those which it does, is not so much to win honour for their own skill as to traduce and ridicule the miracles which are taking place. They transform the rods into real snakes, and turn the water to the colour of blood, and by incantations draw up on to land what frogs are still left[b] (Ex. vii. 12, 22, viii. 7), and, as they add one thing to another tending to their own destruction, they are cheated, miserable fools, while they think that they are cheating.   How would it have been possible for Moses to 84 encounter these men, had he not had in readiness speech the interpreter of thought, who is called Aaron ? In this place Aaron or speech is spoken of as a " mouth " ; further on he will also bear the

[b] *i.e.* after Aaron had called up frogs over the whole land of Egypt.

καὶ προφήτης κεκλήσεται, ὅταν καὶ ὁ νοῦς ἐπιθειά-
σας προσρηθῇ θεός· " δίδωμι γάρ σε " φησί " θεὸν
Φαραώ, καὶ ᾽Ααρὼν ὁ ἀδελφός σου ἔσται σου
προφήτης." ὦ ἀκολουθίας ἐναρμονίου· τὸ γὰρ
ἑρμηνεῦον τὰ θεοῦ προφητικόν ἐστι γένος ἐνθέῳ
85 κατοκωχῇ τε καὶ μανίᾳ χρώμενον.   τοιγαροῦν " ἡ ῥάβδος ἡ ᾽Ααρὼν κατέπιε τὰς ἐκείνων
ῥάβδους," ὡς δηλοῖ τὸ λόγιον· ἐγκαταπίνονται γὰρ
καὶ ἀφανίζονται πάντες οἱ σοφιστικοὶ λόγοι τῇ τῆς
φύσεως ἐντέχνῳ ποικιλίᾳ, ὡς ὁμολογεῖν ὅτι " δάκ-
τυλος θεοῦ " τὰ γινόμενά ἐστιν, ἴσον τῷ γράμμα
θεῖον διαγορεῦον ἀεὶ σοφιστείαν ὑπὸ σοφίας ἡττᾶ-
σθαι· δακτύλῳ γὰρ θεοῦ καὶ τὰς πλάκας, ἐν αἷς
ἐστηλιτεύθησαν οἱ χρησμοί, φησὶν ὁ ἱερὸς λόγος
γραφῆναι. διόπερ οὐκέτι δύνανται οἱ φαρμακευταὶ
στῆναι ἐναντίον Μωυσεῖ, πίπτουσι δ᾽ ὡς ἐν ἀγῶνι
ῥώμῃ τοῦ ἀντιπάλου νικηθέντες καρτερᾷ.[1]

86 XVI. Τίς οὖν ἡ τετάρτη δωρεά; τὸ μεγαλ-
ώνυμον· φησὶ γάρ· "μεγαλυνῶ τὸ ὄνομά σου." τὸ
δέ ἐστιν, ὥς γ᾽ ἐμοὶ φαίνεται, τοιόνδε· ὥσπερ τὸ
ἀγαθὸν εἶναι καὶ καλόν, οὕτω καὶ τὸ δοκεῖν εἶναι
λυσιτελές. καὶ ἀμείνων μὲν δόξης ἀλήθεια, εὔδαι-
μον δὲ τὸ ἐξ ἀμφοῖν· μυρίοι γὰρ ἀνόθως καὶ ἀκολα-
κεύτως προσελθόντες ἀρετῇ καὶ τὸ γνήσιον αὐτῆς
ἐναυγασάμενοι κάλλος, τῆς παρὰ τοῖς πολλοῖς
φήμης οὐ φροντίσαντες ἐπεβουλεύθησαν, κακοὶ
87 νομισθέντες οἱ πρὸς ἀλήθειαν ἀγαθοί. καὶ μὴν |
[450] οὐδὲ τοῦ δοκεῖν ὄφελος μὴ πολὺ πρότερον τοῦ εἶναι

───────
[1] Mangey suggests κραταιοτέρᾳ.

180

name of " prophet," when the mind too is inspired and entitled " God." For He says " I give thee as God to Pharaoh, and Aaron thy brother shall be thy prophet " (Ex. vii. 1). How perfect is the harmony shewn in the sequence of thought ! For it is the prophet kind, when under the influence of a Divine possession and ecstasy, that interprets the thoughts of God. Accordingly " Aaron's rod swallowed 85 up their rods " (Ex. vii. 12), as the oracle shews. For all the arguments of sophists are devoured and done away with by Nature's many-sided skill, and the acknowledgement is made that these events are the Finger of God (Ex. viii. 19), and the word " Finger " is equivalent to a divine rescript, declaring that sophistry is ever defeated by wisdom ; for holy writ, speaking of the tables on which the oracles were engraved, says that they were written by the Finger of God (Ex. xxxii. 16). Wherefore the sorcerers can no longer stand before Moses, but fall as in a wrestling-bout vanquished by the sturdy strength of the opponent (Ex. viii. 18).

XVI. What, then, is the fourth gift ? That of a 86 great name ; for He says " I will make thy name great " (Gen. xii. 2). The meaning of this appears to me to be as follows. As it is an advantage to be good and morally noble, so is it to be reputed such. And, while the reality is better than the reputation, happiness comes of having both. For very many, after coming to Virtue's feet with no counterfeit or unreal homage and with their eyes open to her genuine loveliness, through paying no regard to the general opinion have become the objects of hostility, just because they were held to be bad, when they were really good. It is true that there is no good in being 87

προσόντος, ὥσπερ ἐπὶ σωμάτων πέφυκεν ἔχειν· εἰ
γὰρ πάντες ἄνθρωποι τὸν νοσοῦντα ὑγιαίνειν ἢ τὸν
ὑγιαίνοντα νοσεῖν ὑπολάβοιεν, ἡ δόξα καθ' αὑτὴν
88 οὔτε νόσον οὔτε ὑγείαν ἐργάσεται. ᾧ δὲ ἀμφότερα
δεδώρηται ὁ θεός, καὶ τὸ εἶναι καλῷ καὶ ἀγαθῷ καὶ
τὸ δοκεῖν εἶναι, οὗτος πρὸς ἀλήθειαν εὐδαίμων καὶ
τῷ ὄντι μεγαλώνυμος. προνοητέον δ' ὡς μεγάλου
πράγματος καὶ πολλὰ τὸν μετὰ σώματος βίον
ὠφελοῦντος εὐφημίας. περιγίνεται δ' αὕτη σχεδὸν
ἅπασιν, ὅσοι χαίροντες σὺν ἀσμενισμῷ μηδὲν
κινοῦσι τῶν καθεστηκότων νομίμων, ἀλλὰ τὴν
πάτριον πολιτείαν οὐκ ἀμελῶς φυλάττουσιν.

89 Εἰσὶ γάρ τινες οἳ τοὺς ῥητοὺς νόμους σύμβολα
νοητῶν πραγμάτων ὑπολαμβάνοντες τὰ μὲν ἄγαν
ἠκρίβωσαν, τῶν δὲ ῥαθύμως ὠλιγώρησαν· οὓς
μεμψαίμην ἂν ἔγωγε τῆς εὐχερείας· ἔδει γὰρ
ἀμφοτέρων ἐπιμεληθῆναι, ζητήσεώς τε τῶν ἀφανῶν
ἀκριβεστέρας καὶ ταμείας τῶν φανερῶν ἀνεπι-
90 λήπτου. νυνὶ δ' ὥσπερ ἐν ἐρημίᾳ καθ' ἑαυτοὺς μόνοι
ζῶντες ἢ ἀσώματοι ψυχαὶ γεγονότες καὶ μήτε
πόλιν μήτε κώμην μήτ' οἰκίαν μήτε συνόλως
θίασον ἀνθρώπων εἰδότες, τὰ δοκοῦντα τοῖς πολλοῖς
ὑπερκύψαντες τὴν ἀλήθειαν γυμνὴν αὐτὴν ἐφ'
ἑαυτῆς ἐρευνῶσιν· οὓς ὁ ἱερὸς λόγος διδάσκει
χρηστῆς ὑπολήψεως πεφροντικέναι καὶ μηδὲν τῶν
ἐν τοῖς ἔθεσι λύειν, ἃ θεσπέσιοι καὶ μείζους ἄνδρες
91 ἢ καθ' ἡμᾶς ὥρισαν.   μὴ γὰρ ὅτι ἡ

thought to be this or that, unless you are so long before you are thought to be so. It is naturally so in the case of our bodies. Were all the world to suppose the sickly man to be healthy, or the healthy man to be sickly, the general opinion by itself will produce neither sickness nor health. But he on whom God 88 has bestowed both gifts, both to be morally noble and good and to have the reputation of being so, this man is really happy and his name is great in very deed. We should take thought for fair fame as a great matter and one of much advantage to the life which we live in the body. And this fair fame is won as a rule by all who cheerfully take things as they find them and interfere with no established customs, but maintain with care the constitution of their country.

There are some who, regarding laws in their literal 89 sense in the light of symbols of matters belonging to the intellect, are overpunctilious about the latter, while treating the former with easy-going neglect. Such men I for my part should blame for handling the matter in too easy and off-hand a manner : they ought to have given careful attention to both aims, to a more full and exact investigation of what is not seen and in what is seen to be stewards without reproach. As it is, as though they were living alone by them- 90 selves in a wilderness, or as though they had become disembodied souls, and knew neither city nor village nor household nor any company of human beings at all, overlooking all that the mass of men regard, they explore reality in its naked absoluteness. These men are taught by the sacred word to have thought for good repute, and to let go nothing that is part of the customs fixed by divinely empowered men greater than those of our time. It is quite true 91

183

ἑβδόμη δυνάμεως μὲν τῆς περὶ τὸ ἀγένητον, ἀ-
πραξίας δὲ τῆς περὶ τὸ γενητὸν δίδαγμά ἐστι, τὰ
ἐπ' αὐτῇ νομοθετηθέντα λύωμεν, ὡς πῦρ ἐναύειν
ἢ γεωπονεῖν ἢ ἀχθοφορεῖν ἢ ἐγκαλεῖν ἢ δικάζειν ἢ
παρακαταθήκας ἀπαιτεῖν ἢ δάνεια ἀναπράττειν ἢ
τὰ ἄλλα ποιεῖν, ὅσα κἂν τοῖς μὴ ἑορτώδεσι καιροῖς
92 ἐφεῖται· μηδ' ὅτι ἡ ἑορτὴ σύμβολον ψυχικῆς εὐφροσύνης ἐστὶ καὶ τῆς πρὸς θεὸν εὐχαριστίας,
ἀποταξώμεθα ταῖς κατὰ τὰς ἐτησίους ὥρας παν-
ηγύρεσι· μηδ' ὅτι τὸ περιτέμνεσθαι ἡδονῆς καὶ
παθῶν πάντων ἐκτομὴν καὶ δόξης ἀναίρεσιν ἀσε-
βοῦς ἐμφαίνει, καθ' ἣν ὑπέλαβεν ὁ νοῦς ἱκανὸς
εἶναι γεννᾶν δι' ἑαυτοῦ, ἀνέλωμεν τὸν ἐπὶ τῇ περι-
τομῇ τεθέντα νόμον· ἐπεὶ καὶ τῆς περὶ τὸ ἱερὸν
ἁγιστείας καὶ μυρίων ἄλλων ἀμελήσομεν, εἰ μόνοις
93 προσέξομεν τοῖς δι' ὑπονοιῶν δηλουμένοις. ἀλλὰ
χρὴ ταῦτα μὲν σώματι ἐοικέναι νομίζειν, ψυχῇ δὲ
[451] ἐκεῖνα· ὥσπερ οὖν σώματος, ἐπειδὴ | ψυχῆς ἐστιν
οἶκος, προνοητέον, οὕτω καὶ τῶν ῥητῶν νόμων
ἐπιμελητέον· φυλαττομένων γὰρ τούτων ἀριδηλό-
τερον κἀκεῖνα γνωρισθήσεται, ὧν εἰσιν οὗτοι
σύμβολα, πρὸς τῷ καὶ τὰς ἀπὸ τῶν πολλῶν μέμ-
94 ψεις καὶ κατηγορίας ἀποδιδράσκειν.   οὐχ
ὁρᾷς, ὅτι καὶ Ἀβραὰμ τῷ σοφῷ καὶ μεγάλα ἀγαθὰ
καὶ μικρὰ προσεῖναί φησι, καὶ καλεῖ τὰ μὲν μεγάλα

---

[a] The force of περί would perhaps be given better by
"inherent in." The thought is that the Sabbatical rest
reminds us that all our labouring is ineffectual compared
with the eternal activity of God. *Cf. Quis Rerum* 170, and
De Cher. 87 ff.

[b] Or "keeping of festivals (in general)." *Cf. De Spec.
Leg.* ii. 41.

that the Seventh Day is meant to teach the power of the Unoriginate and the non-action of created beings.[a] But let us not for this reason abrogate the laws laid down for its observance, and light fires or till the ground or carry loads or institute proceedings in court or act as jurors or demand the restoration of deposits or recover loans, or do all else that we are permitted to do as well on days that are not festival seasons. It is true also that the Feast[b] is a symbol of 92 gladness of soul and of thankfulness to God, but we should not for this reason turn our backs on the general gatherings of the year's seasons. It is true that receiving circumcision does indeed portray the excision of pleasure and all passions, and the putting away of the impious conceit, under which the mind supposed that it was capable of begetting by its own power : but let us not on this account repeal the law laid down for circumcising. Why, we shall be ignoring the sanctity of the Temple and a thousand other things, if we are going to pay heed to nothing except what is shewn us by the inner meaning of things. Nay, we should look on all these outward observances 93 as resembling the body, and their inner meanings as resembling the soul. It follows that, exactly as we have to take thought for the body, because it is the abode of the soul, so we must pay heed to the letter of the laws. If we keep and observe these, we shall gain a clearer conception of those things of which these are the symbols ; and besides that we shall not incur the censure of the many and the charges they are sure to bring against us. Notice that it 94 says that wise Abraham had good things both great and small, and it calls the great ones " property,"

ὑπάρχοντα καὶ ὑπαρκτά, ἃ τῷ γνησίῳ κληρονομεῖν
ἐφεῖται μόνῳ, τὰ δὲ μικρὰ δόματα, ὧν οἱ νόθοι καὶ
ἐκ παλλακῶν ἀξιοῦνται; ἐκεῖνα μὲν οὖν ἔοικε τοῖς
φύσει, ταῦτα δὲ τοῖς θέσει νομίμοις.

95 XVII. Ἄγαμαι καὶ τῆς παναρέτου Λείας, ἥτις
ἐπὶ τῆς Ἀσὴρ γενέσεως, ὅς ἐστι τοῦ αἰσθητοῦ καὶ
νόθου σύμβολον πλούτου, φησί· " μακαρία ἐγώ, ὅτι
μακαριοῦσί με αἱ γυναῖκες." στοχάζεται γὰρ
ὑπολήψεως ἐπιεικοῦς, δικαιοῦσα μὴ μόνον ὑπὸ
ἀρρένων καὶ ἀνδρείων ὡς ἀληθῶς λόγων ἐπαινεῖσθαι, παρ' οἷς ἡ ἀλώβητος φύσις καὶ τὸ ἀληθὲς
ἀδέκαστον τετίμηται, ἀλλὰ καὶ πρὸς τῶν θηλυ-
τέρων, οἳ τῶν φαινομένων πάντα τρόπον ἥττηνται
μηδὲν ἔξω τούτων θεωρητὸν νοῆσαι δυνάμενοι.
96 τελείας δὲ ψυχῆς ἐστι καὶ τοῦ εἶναι καὶ τοῦ δοκεῖν
εἶναι μεταποιεῖσθαι, καὶ σπουδάζειν μὴ μόνον παρὰ
97 τῇ ἀνδρωνίτιδι εὐδοκιμεῖν, ἀλλὰ καὶ πρὸς τῆς
γυναικωνίτιδος ἑστίας ἐπαινεῖσθαι.   διὸ
καὶ Μωυσῆς τὴν τῶν ἱερῶν ἔργων κατασκευὴν οὐ
μόνον ἀνδράσιν ἀλλὰ καὶ γυναιξὶν ἐπέτρεψε ποιεῖ-
σθαι· τά τε γὰρ νήματα πάντα τῆς ὑακίνθου καὶ πορφύρας καὶ κοκκίνου καὶ βύσσου καὶ τριχῶν αἰγείων
ἐπιτελοῦσι, καὶ τὸν ἑαυτῶν κόσμον ἀόκνως εἰσ-
φέρουσι, "σφραγῖδας, ἐνώτια, δακτυλίους, περιδέξια,
ἐμπλόκια," πάνθ' ὅσα χρυσὸν εἶχε τὴν ὕλην, τὸν
σώματος κόσμον ἀντικαταλλαττόμεναι τοῦ τῆς
98 εὐσεβείας· προσφιλοτιμούμεναι μέντοι καὶ τὰ
κάτοπτρα ἑαυτῶν συγκαθιεροῦσιν εἰς τὴν τοῦ
λουτῆρος κατασκευήν, ἵν' οἱ μέλλοντες ἱερουργεῖν

ᵃ Philo interprets the ὑπάρχοντα of the lxx (property), as
equivalent to the philosophical term ὑπαρκτά (really existing). See App. p. 563.

that is, realities,[a] which went by entail to his legitimate
son alone. The small ones it calls " gifts," and to
receive these the base-born sons of the concubines
are deemed worthy (Gen. xxv. 5, 6). The former
correspond to natural, the latter to positive laws.

XVII. I admire also all-virtuous Leah, because 95
when Asher was born, symbol of counterfeit wealth
the outward and visible, she cries " Happy am I, for
the women will call me happy " (Gen. xxx. 13). She
aims at being favourably regarded, thinking praise
due to her not only from thoughts[b] masculine and
truly manly, by which the nature that has no blemish
and truth impervious to bribes is held in honour, but
also from those which are more feminine, which are
wholly at the mercy of appearances and powerless
to understand anything presented to contemplation
outside them. It is characteristic of a perfect soul to 96
aspire both to be and to be thought to be, and to take
pains not only to have a good reputation in the men's
quarters, but to receive the praises of the women's as
well. It was for this reason that Moses 97
gave in charge not to men only but to women also to
provide the sacred appointments of the Tabernacle :
for it is the women who do all the weavings of blue
and scarlet and linen and goat's hair (Ex. xxxv. 22 f.),
and they contribute without hesitation their own
jewellery, " seals, ear-rings, rings, bracelets, hair-
clasps," all that was made of gold, exchanging the
adornment of their persons for the adornment of
piety. Nay, in their abounding enthusiasm, they 98
dedicate their mirrors for the making of the laver
(Ex. xxxviii. 26), to the end that those who are about

[b] Or " ways of thinking " " attitudes of mind " ; *cf. De
Plant.* 61.

ἀπονιπτόμενοι χεῖρας καὶ πόδας, τὰ ἐγχειρήματα
οἷς ἐφορμεῖ καὶ ἐνίδρυται[1] ὁ νοῦς, ἐνοπτρίζωνται
ἑαυτοὺς κατὰ μνήμην τῶν ἐσόπτρων, ἐξ ὧν ὁ
λουτὴρ δεδημιούργηται· οὕτω γὰρ οὐδὲν αἶσχος ἐν
τῷ τῆς ψυχῆς εἴδει περιόψονται γινόμενον, ἤδη δὲ
τὸ νηστείας καὶ καρτερίας ἀνάθημα ἀναθήσουσιν
ἱεροπρεπέστατον καὶ τελεώτατον ἀναθημάτων.

99 ἀλλ' αὗται μὲν ἀσταί τε καὶ ἀστεῖαι
γυναῖκες [αἰσθήσεις] ὡς ἀληθῶς, παρ' αἷς ἡ ἀρετὴ
Λεία τετιμῆσθαι βούλεται, αἱ δὲ προσαναφλέγουσαι
τὸ πῦρ ἐπὶ τὸν ἄθλιον νοῦν ἀπόλιδες· λέγεται γὰρ
ὅτι καὶ " γυναῖκες ἔτι προσεξέκαυσαν πῦρ ἐπὶ
100 Μωάβ." ἀλλ' οὐχ ἑκάστη | τῶν τοῦ ἄφρονος
[452] αἰσθήσεων ἐξαπτομένη πρὸς τῶν αἰσθητῶν ἐμπίπρησι τὸν νοῦν, πολλὴν καὶ ἀπέρατον φλόγα ἐπεισ-
χέουσα μετὰ ῥύμης ἀνηνύτου καὶ φορᾶς; ἄριστον
οὖν ἐξευμενίζεσθαι τὸ γυναικῶν τάγμα ἐν ψυχῇ,
τῶν αἰσθήσεων, καθάπερ καὶ τῶν ἀνδρῶν, τῶν
κατὰ μέρος λογισμῶν· οὕτως γὰρ ἀμείνονι βίου

---

[1] Perhaps ἐφίδρυται (G.H.W.); cf. ἐφιδρύσεις of feet, Leg.
All. iii. 138.

---

[a] This point, in which "hands" are clearly interpreted
by ἐγχειρήματα, and "feet" by ἐφορμεῖ καὶ ἐνίδρυται, follows
in the LXX after the statement that the laver was made out
of the mirrors of the women. In the Hebrew this does not
appear in this place, but the ordinance that the laver should
be so used comes in both Hebrew and LXX in Ex. xxx. 19 f.

[b] "Fasting," in the spiritual sense of course, is interpreted
by καρτερίας. The word is used because in the LXX the
women who offered the mirrors fasted on the day when the

to perform sacred rites, as they are washing hands and feet,[a] that is, the purposes which they take in hand and which form the base and support of the mind, may be helped to see themselves reflected by recollecting the mirrors out of which the laver was fashioned : for if they do this they will not overlook any ugly thing shewing itself in the appearance of the soul, and being thus purified will dedicate the most sacred and perfect of offerings, the offering of fasting[b] and perseverance.

These, in whose eyes Leah, that is 99 virtue, desires to be honoured are citizen women and worthy of their citizenship ; but there are others without citizenship who kindle a fire to add to the misery of the wretched mind ; for we read that " women further kindled in addition[c] a fire against Moab " (Num. xxi. 30). Is it not the case, that each 100 one of the fool's senses, kindled by the objects of sense, sets the mind on fire, pouring upon it a great and impassable flame, in violent and resistless current ? It is best, then, that the array of women, that is of the senses, in the soul, should be propitiated, as well as that of the men, that is of our several thoughts : for in this way shall we feel the journey of

base of the laver was made. The Hebrew word which seems to be obscure is given in A.V. as " assembled," in R.V. " serving." By ἤδη Philo seems to mean that only when the " mirror " has been used for self-examination, and the " feet and hands " of the soul cleansed, can the true offering of " fasting " be made.

[c] The προσ- in προσαναφλέγουσαι reproduces the προσεξέκαυσαν of the text. How Philo interprets the prefix appears in *Leg. All.* iii. 234. The fire kindled by the senses is an *addition* to purely mental troubles.

PHILO

101 διεξόδῳ χρησόμεθα. XVIII. παγκάλως[1]
διὰ τοῦτο καὶ ὁ αὐτομαθὴς Ἰσαὰκ εὔχεται τῷ
σοφίας ἐραστῇ καὶ τὰ νοητὰ καὶ τὰ αἰσθητὰ λαβεῖν
ἀγαθά· φησὶ γάρ· '' δώῃ σοι ὁ θεὸς ἀπὸ τῆς δρόσου
τοῦ οὐρανοῦ καὶ ἀπὸ τῆς πιότητος τῆς γῆς,'' ἴσον
τῷ πρότερον μὲν συνεχῆ σοι τὸν νοητὸν καὶ οὐράνιον ὑετὸν ἄρδοι, μὴ λάβρως ὡς ἐπικλύσαι, ἀλλ'
ἠρέμα καὶ πράως καθάπερ δρόσον ὡς ὀνῆσαι·
δεύτερον δὲ τὸν αἰσθητὸν καὶ γήινον πλοῦτον
χαρίσαιτο λιπαρὸν καὶ πίονα, τὴν ἐναντίαν πενίαν
ψυχῆς τε καὶ τῶν αὐτῆς μερῶν ἀφανάνας.

102 Ἐὰν μέντοι καὶ τὸν ἀρχιερέα λόγον ἐξετάζῃς,
εὑρήσεις συνῳδὰ φρονοῦντα καὶ τὴν ἱερὰν ἐσθῆτα
αὐτῷ πεποικιλμένην ἔκ τε νοητῶν καὶ αἰσθητῶν
δυνάμεων· ἧς τὰ μὲν ἄλλα μακροτέρων ἢ κατὰ τὸν
παρόντα καιρὸν δεῖται λόγων καὶ ὑπερθετέον, τὰ
δὲ πρὸς τοῖς πέρασιν ἐξετάσωμεν, κεφαλῇ τε καὶ
103 βάσεσιν. οὐκοῦν ἐπὶ μὲν τῆς κεφαλῆς ἐστι '' πέτα-
λον χρυσοῦν καθαρόν, ἔχον ἐκτύπωμα σφραγῖδος,
ἁγίασμα κυρίῳ,'' ἐπὶ δὲ τοῖς ποσὶν ἐπὶ τοῦ τέλους
τοῦ ὑποδύτου κώδωνες καὶ ἄνθινα. ἀλλ' ἐκείνη μὲν
ἡ σφραγὶς ἰδέα ἐστὶν ἰδεῶν, καθ' ἣν ὁ θεὸς ἐτύπωσε

---

[1] Previous editions print παγκάλως with the preceding
sentence as adverb to χρησόμεθα. But this seems a little
overdone as praise of the more or less compromising life here
described. An examination of the other 35 examples of παγκ.
in the index shows that Philo generally uses it near the
beginning of the sentence, in nearly all in praise of some
saying or incident in Scripture, and in all in connexion with
some verb, expressed or implied, of speaking. The form
παγκάλως διὰ τοῦτο καί is exceptional, but differs very slightly
from the common διὰ τοῦτο παγκάλως.

life better than it else would be.   XVIII.

Admirable therefore also is the prayer of Isaac the 101
self-taught for the lover of wisdom that he may receive
the good things both of mind and of sense : " May
God give thee," he says, " of the dew of heaven and
of the fatness of the earth " (Gen. xxvii. 28), which is
equivalent to saying in the first place " May He pour
down on thee perpetually the heavenly rain apprehended by mind alone, not violently so as to deluge
thee, but in gentle stillness like dew so as to do thee
good " ; and secondly " May He grant thee the
earthly, the outward and visible wealth ; may that
wealth abound in marrow and fatness and may its
opposite, the poverty of the soul and its parts, be
withered and dried up by His grace."

If again you examine the High Priest the Logos,[a] 102
you will find him to be in agreement with this, and
his holy vesture to have a variegated beauty derived
from powers belonging some to the realm of pure
intellect, some to that of sense-perception.   The
other parts of that vesture call for a longer treatment
than the present occasion allows, and must be de-
ferred.   Let us however examine the parts by the
extremities, head and feet.   On the head, then, there 103
is " a plate of pure gold, bearing as an engraving of
a signet, ' a holy thing to the Lord ' " (Ex. xxviii. 32) ;
and at the feet on the end of the skirt, bells and
flower patterns (Ex. xxviii. 29 f.).   The signet spoken
of is the original principle behind all principles, after
which God shaped or formed the universe, incorporeal,

[a] Or "the Logos as revealed in the High Priest."   The
thought that the High Priest (in general, not Aaron in
particular) represents the Divine Logos is worked out in
De Fug. 108 ff.   In *De Gig.* 52 the phrase is given a less
exalted meaning.

τὸν κόσμον, ἀσώματος δήπου καὶ νοητή, τὰ δ᾽
ἄνθινα καὶ οἱ κώδωνες αἰσθητῶν ποιοτήτων σύμβολα, ὧν ὅρασις καὶ ἀκοὴ τὰ κριτήρια.

104 ἄγαν δ᾽ ἐξητασμένως ἐπιφέρει ὅτι '' ἔσται ἀκουστὴ
φωνὴ αὐτοῦ εἰσιόντος εἰς τὰ ἅγια,'' ἵνα πρὸς τὰ
νοητὰ καὶ θεῖα καὶ ὄντως ἅγια εἰσιούσης τῆς ψυχῆς
καὶ αἱ αἰσθήσεις ὠφελούμεναι κατ᾽ ἀρετὴν συν-
ηχῶσι καὶ ὅλον τὸ σύστημα ἡμῶν, ὥσπερ ἐμμελὴς
καὶ πολυάνθρωπος χορός, ἐκ διαφερόντων φθόγγων
ἀνακεκραμένων ἓν μέλος ἐναρμόνιον συνᾴδῃ, τὰ μὲν
ἐνδόσιμα τῶν νοημάτων ἐμπνεόντων—ἡγεμόνες γὰρ
τοῦ χοροῦ τούτου τὰ νοητά—, τὰ δ᾽ ἑπόμενα τῶν
αἰσθητῶν συναναμελπόντων, ἃ τοῖς κατὰ μέρος
105 χορευταῖς ἀπεικάζεται. συνόλως γάρ, ᾗ φησιν ὁ
νόμος, '' τὰ δέοντα καὶ τὸν ἱματισμὸν καὶ τὴν
ὁμιλίαν,'' τὰ τρία ταῦτα, ἀφαιρεῖσθαι τὴν ψυχὴν οὐκ
ἔδει, ἀλλ᾽ ἕκαστον αὐτῶν βεβαίως προσνέμειν. τὰ
μὲν οὖν δέοντα ⟨τὰ⟩ νοητά ἐστιν ἀγαθά, ἃ δεῖ καὶ
ἃ χρὴ γενέσθαι λόγῳ φύσεως, ὁ δὲ ἱματισμὸς τὰ
περὶ τὸν φαινόμενον τοῦ βίου κόσμον, ἡ δ᾽ ὁμιλία ἡ
καθ᾽ ἑκάτερον τῶν εἰρημένων εἰδῶν συνέχεια καὶ
μελέτη, ἵν᾽ οἷα τὰ ἀφανῆ νοητὰ τοιαῦτα καὶ τὰ
106 αἰσθητὰ φαίνηται.

[453] XIX. | Πέμπτη τοίνυν ἐστὶ δωρεὰ ἡ κατὰ ψιλὸν
μόνον τὸ εἶναι[1] συνισταμένη· λέλεκται δὲ ἐπὶ ταῖς

---

[1] Mangey regarded this as corrupt and proposed κατὰ τὸ
εὐλογημένον αὐτὸν εἶναι. Possibly we might read τό ⟨τι⟩ εἶναι.

[a] In R.V. "Her food, her raiment, and her duty of
marriage." By "fellowship" or perhaps "intimacy" Philo
may mean either that the νοητά are brought into close association with the αἰσθητά, or that the soul is brought into
intimate touch with both.

we know, and discerned by the intellect alone ; whereas the flower patterns and bells are symbols of qualities recognized by the senses and tested by sight and hearing.   And he has well weighed 104 his words when he adds : " His sound shall be audible when he is about to enter into the Holy Place " (Ex. xxviii. 31), to the end that when the soul is about to enter the truly holy place, the divine place which only mind can apprehend, the senses also may be aided to join in the hymn with their best, and that our whole composite being, like a full choir all in tune, may chant together one harmonious strain rising from varied voices blending one with another; the thoughts of the mind inspiring the keynotes—for the leaders of this choir are the truths perceived by mind alone—while the objects of sense-perception, which resemble the individual members of the choir, chime in with their accordant tuneful notes. For, to say all in a word, 105 we must not, as the Law tells us, take away from the soul these three things, " the necessaries, the clothing, the fellowship " [a] (Ex. xxi. 10), but afford each of them steadily. Now, the " necessaries " are the good things of the mind, which are necessary, being demanded by the law of nature ; the " clothing," all that belongs to the phenomenal world of human life ; and the " fellowship," persistent study directed to each of these kinds, that so in the world of sense we may come to find the likeness of the invisible world of mind.

XIX. To proceed then ; the fifth gift is that which 106 consists in simple being only,[b] and it is mentioned

[b] *i.e.* in being (something) as opposed to "seeming," which was the keynote of the Fourth Gift. See critical note.

προτέραις, οὐχ ὡς εὐτελεστέρα ἐκείνων, ἀλλ᾽ ὡς
ὑπερκύπτουσα καὶ ὑπερβάλλουσα πάσας. τί γὰρ ἂν
εἴη τοῦ πεφυκέναι καὶ ἀψευδῶς καὶ ἀπλάστως
ἀγαθὸν εἶναι καὶ εὐλογίας ἐπάξιον τελεώτερον;
107 "ἔσῃ" γάρ φησιν "εὐλογητός," οὐ μόνον εὐλογη-
μένος· τὸ μὲν γὰρ ταῖς τῶν πολλῶν δόξαις τε καὶ
φήμαις παραριθμεῖται, τὸ δὲ τῷ πρὸς ἀλήθειαν
108 εὐλογητῷ. ὥσπερ γὰρ τὸ ἐπαινετὸν εἶναι τοῦ
ἐπαινεῖσθαι διαφέρει κατὰ τὸ κρεῖττον καὶ τὸ
ψεκτὸν εἶναι τοῦ ψέγεσθαι κατὰ τὸ χεῖρον—τὰ μὲν
γὰρ τῷ πεφυκέναι, τὰ δὲ τῷ νομίζεσθαι λέγεται
μόνον, φύσις δὲ ἡ ἀψευδὴς δοκήσεως ἐχυρώτερον—,
οὕτως καὶ τοῦ εὐλογεῖσθαι πρὸς ἀνθρώπων, ὅπερ
ἦν εἰς εὐλογίαν ἄγεσθαι δοξαζόμενον, τὸ πεφυκέναι[1]
εὐλογίας ἄξιον, κἂν πάντες ἡσυχάζωσι, κρεῖττον,
ὅπερ εὐλογητὸν ἐν τοῖς χρησμοῖς ᾄδεται.
109 XX. Ταῦτα μὲν τὰ ἆθλα[2] τῷ γενησομένῳ δωρεῖται σοφῷ· ἃ δὲ καὶ τοῖς ἄλλοις ἀπονέμει διὰ τὸν
σοφόν, ἑξῆς ἴδωμεν· "εὐλογήσω" φησί "τοὺς
εὐλογοῦντάς σε, καὶ τοὺς καταρωμένους σε κατ-
110 αράσομαι." τὸ μὲν οὖν ἐπὶ τιμῇ τοῦ σπουδαίου καὶ
ταῦτα γίνεσθαι παντί τῳ δῆλον, λέγεται δ᾽ οὐ δι᾽
ἐκεῖνο μόνον, ἀλλὰ καὶ διὰ τὴν ἐν τοῖς πράγμασιν
εὐάρμοστον ἀκολουθίαν· τὸν γὰρ ἀγαθὸν καὶ ὁ
ἐπαινῶν ἐγκωμιαστὸς καὶ ὁ ψέγων ἔμπαλιν ψεκτός.
ἔπαινον δὲ καὶ ψόγον οὐχ οὕτως ἡ τῶν λεγόντων
καὶ γραφόντων πιστοῦται δύναμις, ὡς ἡ τῶν γινομένων ἀλήθεια· ὥστ᾽ οὔτε ἐπαινεῖν οὔτε ψέγειν ἂν

---

[1] mss. τὸ εὐλογεῖσθαι . . . τῷ πεφυκέναι.   [2] mss. ἐσθλά.

194

after those which precede it not as being of less value
than they, but as outtopping and over-passing them
all. For what could be more perfect than to be by
nature good and free from all feigning and pretence,
and worthy of blessing? For he says "Thou shalt 107
be one to be blessed" (Gen. xii. 2), not only "one
who has been blessed," for the latter is reckoned by
the standard of the opinions and report of the many;
but the former by that of Him Who is in reality
"blessed." For as being praiseworthy differs for the 108
better from being praised, and being blameworthy
for the worse from being blamed, the one pair expressing an inherent character, and the other nothing
more than men's opinion of us; and nature that
cannot lie is a more sure foundation than opinion; so
being blessed by men, which we have found to be an
introduction into blessing by the avenue of repute, is
inferior to natural worthiness of blessing, even though
that finds no expression on human lips; and it is this
which is celebrated in the sacred oracles as "blessed."

XX. These are the prizes which He bestows upon 109
him who is to become wise. Let us see next those
which He accords to others too for the wise man's
sake. "I will bless," He says, "those that bless thee,
and those that curse thee I will curse" (Gen. xii. 3).
That these promises as well as the others are made to 110
shew honour to the righteous man is clear to every-
body, but they are set forth not on that account only,
but because they so admirably fit in with and follow
the truth of facts, for encomiums are due to him who
praises the good man and blame again to him who
blames him. Praise and blame are not accredited so
much by the ability of speakers and authors, as by the
truth of facts; so that we do not feel that either

δοκοῖεν, ὅσοι τι ψεῦδος ἐν ἑκατέρῳ παραλαμ-
111 βάνουσιν εἴδει.[1]   τοὺς κόλακας οὐχ ὁρᾷς,
οἳ μεθ' ἡμέραν καὶ νύκτωρ ἀποκναίουσι τῶν κολα-
κευομένων τὰ ὦτα θρύπτοντες, οὐκ ἐπινεύοντες ἐφ'
ἑκάστῳ τῶν λεγομένων αὐτὸ μόνον ἀλλὰ καὶ ῥήσεις
μακρὰς συνείροντες καὶ ῥαψῳδοῦντες καὶ εὐχόμενοι
μὲν τῇ φωνῇ πολλάκις, ἀεὶ δὲ τῇ διανοίᾳ κατ-
112 αρώμενοι; τί οὖν ἄν τις εὖ φρονῶν εἴποι; ἆρ' οὐχ
ὥσπερ ἐχθροὺς μᾶλλον ἢ φίλους τοὺς λέγοντας
οὕτως[2] καὶ ψέγειν μᾶλλον ἢ ἐπαινεῖν, κἂν δράματα
ὅλα συντιθέντες ἐγκωμίων ἐπάδωσι;
113 τοιγαροῦν ὁ μάταιος Βαλαὰμ ὕμνους μὲν εἰς τὸν
θεὸν ὑπερβάλλοντας ᾄδων, ἐν οἷς καὶ τὸ '' οὐχ ὡς
ἄνθρωπος ὁ θεός,'' ἀσμάτων τὸ ἱεροπρεπέστατον,
ἐγκώμια δ' εἰς τὸν ὁρῶντα, Ἰσραήλ, μυρία διεξ-
ερχόμενος ἀσεβὴς μὲν καὶ ἐπάρατος καὶ παρὰ τῷ
σοφῷ κέκριται νομοθέτῃ, καταρᾶσθαι δέ, οὐκ
114 εὐλογεῖν,[3] νενόμισται. τοῖς γὰρ πολεμίοις φησὶν
αὐτὸν ἐπὶ μισθῷ συνταχθέντα μάντιν[4] γενέσθαι
[454] κακὸν κακῶν, ἀρὰς | μὲν ἐν ψυχῇ θέμενον χαλεπω-
τάτας γένει τῷ θεοφιλεῖ, εὐχὰς δὲ ἀναγκασθέντα
διὰ στόματος καὶ γλώττης ὑπερφυεστάτας προφη-
τεῦσαι· τὰ μὲν γὰρ λεγόμενα καλὰ ὄντα ὁ φιλάρετος
ὑπήχει θεός, τὰ δ' ἐννοούμενα—φαυλότερα γὰρ ἦν—
115 ἔτικτεν ἡ μισάρετος διάνοια.   μαρτυρεῖ
δὲ ὁ περὶ τούτων χρησμός· '' οὐ γὰρ ἔδωκε '' φησίν
'' ὁ θεὸς τῷ Βαλαὰμ καταράσασθαί σοι, ἀλλ'
ἔστρεψε τὰς κατάρας εἰς εὐλογίαν,'' καίτοι πάντων

---

[1] mss. ἴδιον.
[2] So all mss. (except H[2]): Wend. ὄντας.
[3] mss. εὐλογῶν (-ον).
[4] mss. μάτην or μηνυτήν.

term is applicable to the words of those who give falsehood any place in either. Do you 111 not see the toadies who by day and night batter to pieces and wear out the ears of those on whom they fawn, not content with just assenting to everything they say, but spinning out long speeches and declaiming and many a time uttering prayers with their voice, but never ceasing to curse with their heart ? What then would a man of good sense say ? Would 112 he not say that those who talk in this way talk as though they were enemies rather than friends, and blame rather than praise, even though they compose and recite whole oratorios of panegyric to charm them ? Accordingly, that empty one, 113 Balaam, though he sang loftiest hymns to God, among which is that most Divine of canticles " God is not as man " (Num. xxiii. 19), and poured out a thousand eulogies on him whose eyes were open, even Israel, has been adjudged impious and accursed even by the wise lawgiver, and held to be an utterer not of blessings but of curses. For Moses says that as 114 the hired confederate of Israel's enemies he became an evil prophet of evil things, nursing in his soul direst curses on the race beloved of God, but forced with mouth and tongue to give prophetic utterance to most amazing benedictory prayers : for the words that were spoken were noble words, whose utterance was prompted by God the Lover of Virtue, but the intentions, in all their vileness, were the offspring of a mind that looked on virtue with loathing.

Evidence of this is afforded by the oracles relating to 115 the matter ; for it says " God did not give Balaam leave to curse thee, but turned his curses into blessing " (Deut. xxiii. 5), though indeed every word he

ὅσα εἶπε πολλῆς γεμόντων εὐφημίας. ἀλλ' ὁ τῶν
ἐν ψυχῇ ταμιευομένων ἐπίσκοπος ἰδών, ᾧ κατιδεῖν
ἔξεστι μόνῳ, τὰ ἀθέατα γενέσει, τὴν καταδικά-
ζουσαν ἀπὸ τούτων ψῆφον ἤνεγκε, μάρτυς ἀψευδέστατος ὁμοῦ καὶ κριτὴς ἀδέκαστος ὁ αὐτὸς ὤν·
ἐπεὶ καὶ τοὐναντίον ἐπαινετὸν βλασφημεῖν καὶ κατηγορεῖν δοκοῦντα τῇ φωνῇ κατὰ
116 διάνοιαν εὐλογεῖν τε καὶ εὐφημεῖν. σωφρονιστῶν
ὡς ἔοικε τοῦτό ἐστι τὸ ἔθος, παιδαγωγῶν, διδα-
σκάλων, γονέων, πρεσβυτέρων, ἀρχόντων, νόμων·
ὀνειδίζοντες γάρ, ἔστι δ' ὅπου καὶ κολάζοντες
ἕκαστοι τούτων ἀμείνους τὰς ψυχὰς ἀπεργάζονται
τῶν παιδευομένων. καὶ ἐχθρὸς μὲν οὐδεὶς οὐδενί,
φίλοι δὲ πᾶσι πάντες· φίλων δὲ ἀνόθῳ καὶ ἀκιβδήλῳ
χρωμένων εὐνοίᾳ τοῦτ' ἐστὶν ἔργον ἐλευθερο-
117 στομεῖν ἄνευ τοῦ κακονοεῖν. μηδὲν οὖν μήτε τῶν εἰς
εὐλογίας καὶ εὐχὰς μήτε τῶν εἰς βλασφημίας καὶ
κατάρας ἐπὶ τὰς ἐν προφορᾷ διεξόδους ἀναφερέσθω
μᾶλλον ἢ διάνοιαν, ἀφ' ἧς ὥσπερ ἀπὸ πηγῆς ἑκάτερον εἶδος τῶν λεχθέντων δοκιμάζεται.
118 XXI. Ταῦτα μὲν δὴ πρῶτον διὰ τὸν ἀστεῖον
ἑτέροις συντυγχάνειν φησίν, ὅταν ἢ ψόγον ἢ ἔπαινον
ἢ εὐχὰς ἢ κατάρας ἐθελήσωσιν αὐτῷ τίθεσθαι·
μέγιστον δ' ἑξῆς, ὅταν ἡσυχάζωσιν ἐκεῖνοι, τὸ
μηδὲν μέρος φύσεως λογικῆς ἀμέτοχον εὐεργεσίας
ἀπολείπεσθαι· λέγει γὰρ ὅτι " ἐνευλογηθήσονται ἐν

___
a i.e. the text speaks of his "curses," though actually
there was no cursing at all.
b The translation supposes that Philo is alluding to the
Athenian office of σωφρονισταί, officials appointed to look
after the morals of the Ephebi in general and particularly
in the gymnasia. Philo certainly often introduces special
Attic terms from his reading. But it is at least as probable

uttered was charged with fulness of benediction.[a]
But He Who looks upon what is stored up in the soul,
saw, with the Eye that alone has power to discern
them, the things that are out of sight of created beings, and on the ground of these passed the sentence
of condemnation, being at once an absolutely true
Witness, and an incorruptible Judge.   For
on the same principle praise is due to the converse of
this, namely, when one seems to revile and accuse
with the voice, and is in intent conveying blessing
and benediction. This is obviously the custom of 116
proctors,[b] of home tutors, schoolmasters, parents,
seniors, magistrates, laws : all of these, by reproaches,
and sometimes by punishments, effect improvement
in the souls of those whom they are educating.   And
not one of them is an enemy to a single person, but all
are friends of them all : and the business of friends
inspired by genuine and unfeigned goodwill is to use
plain language without any spite whatever. Let no 117
treatment, then, that is marked by prayers and
blessings on the one hand, or by abusing and cursing
on the other hand, be referred to the way it finds vent
in speech, but rather to the intention ; for from this,
as from a spring, is supplied the means of testing each
kind of spoken words.

XXI. This is Moses' first lesson ; he tells us what 118
befalls others for the virtuous man's sake, whenever
they consent to visit him with blame or praise, with
prayers or imprecations : but greatest of all is that
which follows ; he tells us that, when these hold their
peace, no portion of rational existence is left without
its share of benefit bestowed : for He says that " In

that the word here means " moral censors " in general, and
sums up the various forms of guardianship which follow.

119 σοὶ πᾶσαι αἱ φυλαὶ τῆς γῆς.'' ἔστι δὲ τοῦτο
δογματικώτατον· ἐὰν γὰρ ὁ νοῦς ἄνοσος καὶ ἀπήμων διατελῇ, ταῖς περὶ αὐτὸν ἁπάσαις φυλαῖς
τε καὶ δυνάμεσιν ὑγιαινούσαις χρῆται, ταῖς τε
καθ' ὅρασιν καὶ ἀκοὴν καὶ ὅσαι αἰσθητικαὶ καὶ
πάλιν ταῖς κατὰ τὰς ἡδονάς τε καὶ ἐπιθυμίας καὶ
ὅσαι ἀντὶ παθῶν εἰς εὐπάθειαν[1] μεταχαράττονται.
120   ἤδη μέντοι καὶ οἶκος καὶ πόλις καὶ
χώρα καὶ ἔθνη καὶ κλίματα γῆς ἑνὸς ἀνδρὸς καλοκἀγαθίας προμηθουμένου μεγάλης ἀπήλαυσαν εὐδαιμονίας, καὶ μάλισθ' ὅτῳ μετὰ γνώμης ἀγαθῆς
ὁ θεὸς καὶ δύναμιν ἔδωκεν ἀνανταγώνιστον, ὡς
μουσικῷ καὶ παντὶ τεχνίτῃ τὰ κατὰ μουσικὴν καὶ
121 πᾶσαν τέχνην ὄργανα ἢ ξύλων ὕλην πυρί. τῷ γὰρ
ὄντι ἔρεισμα τοῦ γένους τῶν ἀνθρώπων ἐστὶν ὁ
δίκαιος, καὶ ὅσα μὲν αὐτὸς ἔχει, προφέρων εἰς
[455] μέσον ἐπ' ὠφελείᾳ τῶν | χρησομένων ἄφθονα
δίδωσιν, ὅσα δ' ἂν μὴ εὑρίσκῃ παρ' ἑαυτῷ, τὸν
μόνον πάμπλουτον αἰτεῖται θεόν· ὁ δὲ τὸν οὐράνιον
ἀνοίξας θησαυρὸν ὀμβρεῖ καὶ ἐπινίφει τὰ ἀγαθὰ
ἀθρόα, ὡς τῶν περιγείων ἁπάντων τὰς δεξαμενὰς
122 πλημμυρούσας ἀναχυθῆναι. ταῦτα δὲ τὸν ἱκέτην
ἑαυτοῦ λόγον οὐκ ἀποστραφεὶς εἴωθε δωρεῖσθαι·
λέγεται γὰρ ἑτέρωθι Μωυσέως ἱκετεύσαντος·
''ἵλεως αὐτοῖς εἰμι κατὰ τὸ ῥῆμά σου''· τοῦτο δέ,
ὡς ἔοικεν, ἰσοδυναμεῖ τῷ '' ἐνευλογηθήσονται ἐν

[1] Perhaps read εὐπαθείας. Elsewhere the plural is used
when in contrast with πάθη.

[a] λόγος seems to anticipate ῥῆμα. Otherwise we might
translate '' His suppliant Word,'' as Moses is sometimes
identified with the Divine Logos.

thee shall all the tribes of the earth be blessed "
(Gen. xii. 3). This is a pregnant and significant 119
announcement ; for it implies that, if the mind continues free from harm and sickness, it has all its tribes
and powers in a healthy condition, those whose
province is sight and hearing and all others concerned
with sense-perception, and those again that have to
do with pleasures and desires, and all that are under-
going transformation from the lower to the higher
emotions.   Further there have been in- 120
stances of a household or a city or a country or nations
and regions of the earth enjoying great prosperity
through a single man giving his mind to nobility of
character. Most of all has this been so in the case of
one on whom God has bestowed, together with a good
purpose, irresistible power, just as He gives to the
musician and every artist the instruments which his
music or his art requires, or as He gives to fire logs as
its material. For in truth the righteous man is the 121
foundation on which mankind rests. All that he
himself has he brings into the common stock and
gives in abundance for the benefit of all who shall use
them. What he does not find in his own store, he asks
for at the hands of God, the only possessor of unlimited riches ; and He opens his heavenly treasury
and sends His good things, as He does the snow and
the rain, in ceaseless downpour, so that the channels
and cavities of earth's whole face overflow. And it 122
is His wont to bestow these gifts in answer to the
word[a] of supplication, from which He does not turn His
ear away ; for it is said in another place, when Moses
had made a petition, " I am gracious to them in
accordance with thy word " (Num. xiv. 20) ; and this
is evidently equivalent to " In thee shall all the tribes

σοὶ πᾶσαι αἱ φυλαὶ τῆς γῆς." οὗ χάριν
καὶ ὁ σοφὸς Ἀβραὰμ πεπειραμένος τῆς ἐν ἅπασι
τοῦ θεοῦ χρηστότητος πεπίστευκεν ὅτι, κἂν πάντα
τὰ ἄλλα ἀφανισθῇ, μικρὸν δέ τι λείψανον ἀρετῆς
ὥσπερ ἐμπύρευμα διασῴζηται, διὰ τὸ βραχὺ τοῦτο
κἀκεῖνα οἰκτείρει, ὡς πεπτωκότα ἐγείρειν καὶ
123 τεθνηκότα ζωπυρεῖν. σπινθὴρ γὰρ καὶ ὁ βραχύ-
τατος ἐντυφόμενος, ὅταν καταπνευσθεὶς ζωπυρηθῇ,
μεγάλην ἐξάπτει πυράν· καὶ τὸ βραχύτατον οὖν
ἀρετῆς, ὅταν ἐλπίσι χρησταῖς ὑποθαλπόμενον
ἀναλάμψῃ, καὶ τὰ τέως μεμυκότα καὶ τυφλὰ ἐξ-
ωμμάτωσε καὶ τὰ ἀφαυανθέντα ἀναβλαστεῖν ἐποίησε καὶ ὅσα ὑπὸ ἀγονίας[1] ἐστείρωτο εἰς εὐφορίαν εὐ-
τοκίας περιήγαγεν. οὕτω τὸ σπάνιον ἀγαθὸν ἐπι-
φροσύνη θεοῦ πολὺ γίνεται χεόμενον, ἐξομοιοῦν τὰ
124 ἄλλα ἑαυτῷ.   XXII. εὐχώμεθα οὖν τὸν
ὡς ἐν οἰκίᾳ στύλον νοῦν μὲν ἐν ψυχῇ, ἄνθρωπον δὲ
ἐν τῷ γένει τῶν ἀνθρώπων τὸν δίκαιον διαμένειν εἰς
τὴν τῶν νόσων ἄκεσιν· τούτου γὰρ ὑγιαίνοντος τὰς
εἰς παντελῆ σωτηρίαν οὐκ ἀπογνωστέον ἐλπίδας,
διότι[2] οἶμαι ὁ σωτὴρ θεὸς τὸ πανακέστατον φάρ-
μακον, τὴν ἵλεω δύναμιν, τῷ ἱκέτῃ καὶ θεραπευτῇ
προτείνας ἑαυτοῦ χρῆσθαι πρὸς τὴν τῶν καμνόντων
σωτηρίαν ἐπιτρέπει, καταπλάττοντι τῶν ψυχῆς
τραυμάτων, ἅπερ ἀφροσύναι καὶ ἀδικίαι καὶ ὁ
ἄλλος τῶν κακῶν ὅμιλος ἀκονηθεὶς διεῖλεν.
125   ἐναργέστατον δὲ παράδειγμα Νῶε ὁ
δίκαιος, ὃς τῷ μεγάλῳ κατακλυσμῷ τῶν τοσούτων
μερῶν τῆς ψυχῆς ἐγκαταποθέντων ἐρρωμένως

---

[1] MSS. ἀγνοίας.   [2] MSS. δι' οὗ ἔτι.

of the earth be blessed." And it is by reason of this that Abraham, the wise, when he had made trial of God's unvarying loving-kindness, believed that, even if all else be done away, but some small relic of virtue be preserved as a live coal to kindle with, for the sake of this little piece He looks with pity on the rest also, so as to raise up fallen things and to quicken dead things (Gen. xviii. 24 ff.). For a 123 smouldering spark, even the very smallest, when it is blown up and made to blaze, lights a great pile ; and so the least particle of virtue, when, warmed into life by bright hopes, it has shone out, gives sight to eyes that erst were closed and blind, and causes withered things to bloom again, and recovers to prolific fertility all that were barren by nature and therefore without offspring. Even so scanty goodness by God's favour expands and becomes abundant, assimilating all else to itself. XXII. Let us pray then that, like a 124 central pillar in a house, there may constantly remain for the healing of our maladies the righteous mind in the soul and in the human race the righteous man ; for while he is sound and well, there is no cause to despair of the prospect of complete salvation, for our Saviour God holds out, we may be sure, the most all-healing remedy, His gracious Power, and commits it to His suppliant and worshipper to use for the deliverance of those who are sickly, that he may apply it as an embrocation to those soul-wounds which were left gaping by the sword-edge of follies and injustices and all the rest of the horde of vices. The 125 most patent example is righteous Noah, who, when so many parts of the soul had been swallowed up by the

ἐπικυματίζων καὶ ἐπινηχόμενος ὑπεράνω μὲν ἔστη
τῶν δεινῶν ἁπάντων, διασωθεὶς δὲ μεγάλας καὶ
καλὰς ἀφ᾽ αὑτοῦ ῥίζας ἐβάλετο, ἐξ ὧν οἷα φυτὸν τὸ
σοφίας ἀνεβλάστησε γένος· ὅπερ ἡμεροτοκῆσαν τοὺς
τοῦ ὁρῶντος, Ἰσραήλ, τριττοὺς ἤνεγκε καρπούς,
αἰῶνος μέτρα, τὸν Ἀβραάμ, τὸν Ἰσαάκ, τὸν
126 Ἰακώβ· καὶ γὰρ ἔστι καὶ ἔσται καὶ γέγονεν ἐν τῷ
παντὶ ἀρετή, ἣν ἀκαιρίαι μὲν ἴσως ἀνθρώπων ἐπι-
σκιάζουσιν, ὁ δὲ ὀπαδὸς θεοῦ καιρὸς ἀποκαλύπτει
πάλιν, ἐν ᾧ καὶ ἡ φρόνησις ἀρρενογονεῖ Σάρρα,
οὐ κατὰ τὰς χρονικὰς τοῦ ἔτους ὥρας, ἀλλὰ κατὰ
τὰς ἀχρόνους ἀκμὰς καὶ εὐκαιρίας ἐπανθοῦσα·
[456] λέγεται γάρ· | " ἐπαναστρέφων ἥξω πρὸς σὲ κατὰ
τὸν καιρὸν τοῦτον εἰς ὥρας, καὶ ἕξει υἱὸν Σάρρα ἡ
γυνή σου."
127   XXIII. Περὶ μὲν οὖν τῶν δωρεῶν, ἃς καὶ τοῖς
γενησομένοις τελείοις καὶ δι᾽ αὐτοὺς ὁ θεὸς ἑτέροις
εἴωθε χαρίζεσθαι, δεδήλωται. λέγεται δὲ ἑξῆς ὅτι
" ἐπορεύθη Ἀβραὰμ καθάπερ ἐλάλησεν αὐτῷ κύ-
128 ριος." τοῦτο δέ ἐστι τὸ παρὰ τοῖς ἄριστα φιλο-
σοφήσασιν ᾀδόμενον τέλος, τὸ ἀκολούθως τῇ φύσει
ζῆν· γίνεται δέ, ὅταν ὁ νοῦς εἰς τὴν ἀρετῆς ἀτραπὸν
ἐλθὼν κατ᾽ ἴχνος ὀρθοῦ λόγου βαίνῃ καὶ ἕπηται
θεῷ, τῶν προστάξεων αὐτοῦ διαμεμνημένος καὶ
πάσας ἀεὶ καὶ πανταχοῦ ἔργοις τε καὶ λόγοις
129 βεβαιούμενος. " ἐπορεύθη γάρ, καθὰ ἐλάλησεν

---

^a Here for the moment Noah represents the righteous
mind in the soul, but in the rest of the section he is rather
the righteous man in the race.

^b Possibly, to judge from the similar passage in *De
Sobr.* 65, Shem, or perhaps more generally the ancestors of
Abraham.   ^c See App. p. 563.

great Flood,[a] valiantly riding upon the waves that buoyed him up, stood firm high above every peril, and, when he had come safe through all, put forth from himself fair roots and great,[b] out of which there grew up like a plant wisdom's breed and kind ; which, attaining goodly fertility, bore those threefold fruits of the seeing one, even of " Israel," that mark the threefold divisions of eternity,[c] Abraham, Isaac, Jacob; for in the All virtue is, shall be, has been : covered 126 with a dark shadow, it may be, by men's missings of the due season but revealed again by due season that ever follows in God's steps. In such due season does " Sarah " who is sound sense, give birth to a man-child, putting forth her fruit not according to the changes of the year measured by lapse of time, but in accordance with a fitness and fulness of season that time does not determine : for it is said " I will certainly return unto thee according to this season when the time comes round ; and Sarah thy wife shall have a son " (Gen. xviii. 10).

XXIII. We have now dealt with the subject of the 127 gifts which God is wont to bestow both on those who are to become wise and for their sake on others. We are told next that " Abraham journeyed even as the Lord spoke to him " (Gen. xii. 4). This is the aim extolled 128 by the best philosophers, to live agreeably to nature ;[d] and it is attained whenever the mind, having entered on virtue's path, walks in the track of right reason and follows God, mindful of His injunctions, and always and in all places recognizing them all as valid both in action and in speech. For " he journeyed just as the 129

---

[d] Cf. De Op. 3 and note. Philo here as elsewhere (e.g. Quis Rerum 214) is suggesting that Greek philosophy is derived from Moses.

αὐτῷ κύριος·" τοῦτο δέ ἐστι τοιοῦτον· ὡς λαλεῖ ὁ
θεός—λαλεῖ δὲ παγκάλως καὶ ἐπαινετῶς—, οὕτως ὁ
σπουδαῖος ἕκαστα δρᾷ τὴν ἀτραπὸν εὐθύνων ἀμέμ-
πτως τοῦ βίου, ὥστε τὰ ἔργα τοῦ σοφοῦ λόγων
130 ἀδιαφορεῖν θείων. ἑτέρωθι γοῦν φησιν ὅτι ἐποίησεν
Ἀβραὰμ " πάντα τὸν νόμον μου"· νόμος δὲ οὐδὲν
ἄρα ἢ λόγος θεῖος προστάττων ἃ δεῖ καὶ ἀπαγο-
ρεύων ἃ μὴ χρή, ὡς μαρτυρεῖ φάσκων ὅτι " ἐδέξατο
ἀπὸ τῶν λόγων αὐτοῦ νόμον." εἰ τοίνυν λόγος μέν
ἐστι θεῖος ὁ νόμος, ποιεῖ δ' ὁ ἀστεῖος τὸν νόμον,
ποιεῖ πάντως καὶ τὸν λόγον· ὥσθ', ὅπερ ἔφην, τοὺς
131 τοῦ θεοῦ λόγους πράξεις εἶναι τοῦ σοφοῦ. τέλος
οὖν ἐστι κατὰ τὸν ἱερώτατον Μωυσῆν τὸ ἕπεσθαι
θεῷ, ὡς καὶ ἐν ἑτέροις φησίν· " ὀπίσω κυρίου τοῦ
θεοῦ σου πορεύσῃ," κινήσει ⟨μὴ⟩[1] χρώμενον τῇ διὰ
σκελῶν—ἀνθρώπου μὲν γὰρ ὄχημα γῆ, θεοῦ δὲ εἰ
καὶ σύμπας ὁ κόσμος, οὐκ οἶδα—, ἀλλ' ἔοικεν
ἀλληγορεῖν τὴν τῆς ψυχῆς πρὸς τὰ θεῖα δόγματα
παριστὰς ἀκολουθίαν, ὧν ἡ ἀναφορὰ πρὸς τὴν τοῦ
132 πάντων αἰτίου γίνεται τιμή.   XXIV. ἐπι-
τείνων δὲ τὸν ἀκάθεκτον πόθον τοῦ καλοῦ παραινεῖ
καὶ κολλᾶσθαι αὐτῷ· " κύριον " γάρ φησι " τὸν
θεόν σου φοβηθήσῃ καὶ αὐτῷ λατρεύσεις καὶ πρὸς
αὐτὸν κολληθήσῃ." τίς οὖν ἡ κόλλα; τίς; εὐσέβεια δήπου καὶ πίστις· ἁρμόζουσι γὰρ καὶ ἑνοῦσιν
αἱ ἀρεταὶ ἀφθάρτῳ φύσει διάνοιαν· καὶ γὰρ Ἀβραὰμ

---

[1] Some mss. κινήσει μέν.

[a] In the LXX, however, the verb is ἐφύλαξε, and not ἐποίησε
which is demanded by the argument.

Lord spake to him " : the meaning of this is that as
God speaks—and He speaks with consummate beauty
and excellence—so the good man does everything,
blamelessly keeping straight the path of life, so that
the actions of the wise man are nothing else than the
words of God. So in another place He says, " Abraham 130
did *a* ' all My law ' " (Gen. xxvi. 5) : " Law " being
evidently nothing else than the Divine word enjoin-
ing what we ought to do and forbidding what we
should not do, as Moses testifies by saying " he
received a law from His words " (Deut. xxxiii. 3 f.).
If, then, the law is a Divine word, and the man of true
worth " does " the law, he assuredly " does " the
word : so that, as I said, God's words are the wise
man's " doings." To follow God is, then, according 131
to Moses, that most holy man, our aim and object, as
he says elsewhere too, " thou shalt go in the steps of
the Lord thy God " (Deut. xiii. 4). He is not speaking
of movement by the use of our legs, for, while earth
carries man, I do not know whether even the whole
universe carries God ; but is evidently employing
figurative language to bring out how the soul should
comply with those Divine ordinances, the guiding
principle of which is the honouring of Him to Whom
all things owe their being.   XXIV. Using 132
still loftier language to express the irrepressible
craving for moral excellence, he calls on them to
cleave to Him. His words are : " Thou shalt fear the
Lord thy God, and Him shalt thou serve, and to Him
shalt thou cleave " (Deut. x. 20). What then is the
cementing substance ? Do you ask, what ? Piety,
surely, and faith : for these virtues adjust and unite
the intent of the heart to the incorruptible Being :
as Abraham when he believed is said to " come near

133 πιστεύσας " ἐγγίζειν θεῷ " λέγεται.   ἐὰν
μέντοι πορευόμενος μήτε κάμῃ, ὡς ὑπενδοὺς
ὀκλάσαι, μήτε ῥᾳθυμήσῃ, ὡς παρ' ἑκάτερα ἐκ-
τραπόμενος πλανᾶσθαι τῆς μέσης καὶ εὐθυτενοῦς
διαμαρτὼν ὁδοῦ, μιμησάμενος δὲ τοὺς ἀγαθοὺς
δρομεῖς τὸ στάδιον ἀπταίστως ἀνύσῃ τοῦ βίου,
στεφάνων καὶ ἄθλων ἐπαξίων τεύξεται πρὸς τὸ
134 τέλος ἐλθών. ἢ οὐ τοῦτ' εἰσὶν οἱ στέφανοι καὶ τὰ
[457] ἆθλα, μὴ ἀτυχῆσαι τοῦ | τέλους τῶν πονηθέντων,
ἀλλ' ἐφικέσθαι τῶν δυσεφίκτων φρονήσεως περάτων;   τί οὖν τοῦ φρονεῖν ὀρθῶς ἐστι
τέλος; ἀφροσύνην ἑαυτοῦ καὶ παντὸς τοῦ γενητοῦ
καταψηφίσασθαι· τὸ γὰρ μηδὲν οἴεσθαι εἰδέναι
πέρας ἐπιστήμης, ἑνὸς ὄντος μόνου σοφοῦ τοῦ καὶ
135 μόνου θεοῦ.   διὸ καὶ παγκάλως Μωυσῆς καὶ
πατέρα τῶν ὅλων καὶ ἐπίσκοπον τῶν γενομένων
αὐτὸν εἰσήγαγεν εἰπών· " εἶδεν ὁ θεὸς τὰ πάντα
ὅσα ἐποίησε, καὶ ἰδοὺ καλὰ λίαν·" οὐδενὶ γὰρ ἐξῆν
τὰ συσταθέντα κατιδεῖν ἄκρως ὅτι μὴ τῷ πεποιη-
136 κότι.   πάριτε νῦν οἱ τύφου καὶ ἀπαιδευσίας καὶ πολλῆς ἀλαζονείας γέμοντες, οἱ δοκη-
σίσοφοι καὶ μὴ μόνον ὅ ἐστιν ἕκαστον εἰδέναι
σαφῶς ἐπιφάσκοντες,[1] ἀλλὰ καὶ τὰς αἰτίας προσ-
αποδιδόναι διὰ θρασύτητα τολμῶντες, ὥσπερ ἢ τῇ
τοῦ κόσμου γενέσει παρατυχόντες καὶ ὡς ἕκαστα
καὶ ἐξ ὧν ἀπετελεῖτο κατιδόντες ἢ σύμβουλοι περὶ
τῶν κατασκευαζομένων τῷ δημιουργῷ γενόμενοι.
137 εἶτα τῶν ἄλλων ἅπαξ ἁπάντων μεθέμενοι γνωρί-

----

[1] MSS. ἔτι φάσκοντες.

to God" (Gen. xviii. 23). If, however, as 133
he goes on his way, he neither becomes weary, so that
he gives in and collapses, nor grows remiss, so that he
turns aside, now in this direction, now in that, and
goes astray missing the central road that never
diverges; but, taking the good runners as his example,
finishes the race of life without stumbling, when he
has reached the end he shall obtain crowns and prizes
as a fitting guerdon. Are not the crowns and prizes 134
just this, not to have missed the end of his labours,
but to have obtained those final aims of good sense
that are so hard of attainment ? What,
then, is the end of right-mindedness ? To pronounce
on himself and all created being the verdict of folly ;
for the final aim of knowledge is to hold that we know
nothing, He alone being wise, who is also alone God.
Accordingly Moses does right well in representing 135
Him as both the Father of the universe and Overseer
of the things created, where he says : " God saw all
things which He had made, and lo ! they were fair
exceedingly " (Gen. i. 31) : for it was not possible for
anyone perfectly to see the things which had been
formed save their Maker. Come forward 136
now, you who are laden with vanity and gross stupidity
and vast pretence, you that are wise in your own
conceit and not only declare (in every case) that you
perfectly know what each object is, but go so far as to
venture in your audacity to add the reasons for its
being what it is, as though you had either been standing by at the creation of the world, and had observed
how and out of what materials its several parts were
fashioned, or had acted as advisers to the Creator
regarding the things He was forming—come, I say, 137
and then, letting go all other things whatever, take

σατε ἑαυτοὺς καὶ οἵτινές ἐστε σαφῶς εἴπατε, κατὰ
τὸ σῶμα, κατὰ τὴν ψυχήν, κατὰ τὴν αἴσθησιν, κατὰ
τὸν λόγον, καθ᾽ ἕν τι κἂν τὸ βραχύτατον τῶν εἰδῶν.
τί ἐστιν ὅρασις ἀποφήνασθε καὶ πῶς ὁρᾶτε, τί ἀκοὴ
καὶ πῶς ἀκούετε, τί γεῦσις, τί ἀφή, τί ὄσφρησις καὶ
πῶς καθ᾽ ἑκάστην ἐνεργεῖτε ἢ τίνες εἰσὶν αἱ τούτων
138 πηγαί, ἀφ᾽ ὧν καὶ τὸ εἶναι ταῦτα συμβέβηκε. μὴ
γάρ μοι περὶ σελήνης καὶ ἡλίου καὶ τῶν ἄλλων ὅσα
κατ᾽ οὐρανὸν καὶ κόσμον οὕτως μακρὰν διῳκισμένων καὶ τὰς φύσεις διαφερόντων ἀερομυθεῖτε, ὦ
κενοὶ φρενῶν, πρὶν ἑαυτοὺς ἐρευνῆσαι καὶ γνῶναι.
τηνικαῦτα γὰρ ἴσως καὶ περὶ ἑτέρων διεξιοῦσι
πιστευτέον· πρὶν δὲ οἵτινές ἐστε αὐτοὶ παραστῆσαι,
μὴ νομίζετε κριταὶ τῶν ἄλλων ἢ μάρτυρες ἀψευδέ-
στατοί ποτε γενήσεσθαι.

139   XXV. Τούτων δὴ τοῦτον ἐχόντων τὸν τρόπον
τελειωθεὶς ὁ νοῦς ἀποδώσει τὸ τέλος τῷ τελεσφόρῳ
θεῷ κατὰ τὸ ἱερώτατον γράμμα· νόμος γάρ ἐστι τὸ
τέλος εἶναι κυρίου. πότε οὖν ἀποδίδωσιν; ὅταν
"ἐπὶ τὸν τόπον ὃν εἶπεν αὐτῷ ὁ θεὸς τῇ ἡμέρᾳ
τῇ τρίτῃ" παραγένηται, παρελθὼν τὰς πλείους
μοίρας τῶν χρονικῶν διαστημάτων καὶ ἤδη πρὸς
140 τὴν ἄχρονον μεταβαίνων φύσιν· τότε γὰρ καὶ τὸν
ἀγαπητὸν υἱὸν ἱερουργήσει, οὐχὶ ἄνθρωπον—οὐ γὰρ
τεκνοκτόνος ὁ σοφός—, ἀλλὰ τὸ τῆς ἀρετώσης
ψυχῆς γέννημα ἄρρεν, τὸν ἐπανθήσαντα καρπὸν
αὐτῇ, ὃν πῶς ἤνεγκεν οὐκ ἔγνω, βλάστημα θεῖον,

---

[a] See App. p. 563.

[b] i.e. since God is all and self nothing. But perhaps
"when these things are so," "the mind being now perfected,"
i.e. when it has reached the τέλος described in § 133, after
which the argument was interrupted to explain what the
τέλος is.

knowledge of yourselves, and say clearly who you are,
in body, in soul, in sense-perception, in reason and
speech, in each single one, even the most minute, of
the subdivisions of your being. Declare what sight
is and how you see, what hearing is and how you hear,
what taste, touch, smelling are, and how you act in
accordance with each of them, or what are the springs
and sources of these, from which is derived their very
being. For pray do not, O ye senseless ones, spin 138
your airy fables *a* about moon or sun or the other objects
in the sky and in the universe so far removed from us
and so varied in their natures, until you have scrutin-
ized and come to know yourselves. After that, we
may perhaps believe you when you hold forth on
other subjects : but before you establish who you
yourselves are, do not think that you will ever become
capable of acting as judges or trustworthy witnesses
in the other matters.

XXV. This being the case,*b* the Mind, when he has 139
reached the summit, will render the sum of his tribute
to God the consummator, in accordance with the all-
holy writ, for there is a law that the sum *c* is the Lord's
(Num. xxxi. 28 ff.). When, then, does he render it ?
When he has arrived " on the third day at the place
which God had told him of " (Gen. xxii. 3), having
passed the greater number of the divisions of time,
and already quitting them for the existence that is
timeless : for then too he will sacrifice his only son, 140
no human being (for the wise man is not a slayer of his
offspring), but the male progeny of the rich and fertile
soul, the fruit that blossomed upon it. How the soul
bore it she does not know : it is a Divine growth ; and

c Or " due." Philo is playing on the double meaning of
τέλος.

οὗ φανέντος ἡ δόξασα κυοφορῆσαι τὴν ἄγνοιαν τοῦ
συμβάντος ἀγαθοῦ διηγεῖται φάσκουσα· "τίς
ἀναγγελεῖ 'Αβραὰμ" ὡς ἀπιστοῦντι[1] δήπου περὶ
τὴν τοῦ αὐτομαθοῦς γένους ἀνατολήν, ὅτι "θηλάζει
παιδίον Σάρρα," οὐχὶ πρὸς Σάρρας θηλάζεται; τὸ
γὰρ αὐτοδίδακτον τρέφεται μὲν ὑπ' οὐδενός, |
[458] τροφὴ δ' ἐστὶν ἄλλων, ἅτε ἱκανὸν διδάσκειν καὶ
141 μανθάνειν οὐ δεόμενον.   "ἔτεκον γὰρ
υἱόν," οὐχ ὡς γυναῖκες Αἰγύπτιαι κατὰ τὴν τοῦ
σώματος ἀκμήν, ἀλλ' ὡς αἱ Ἑβραῖαι ψυχαί, "ἐν
τῷ γήρᾳ μου," ὅτε τὰ μὲν ὅσα αἰσθητὰ καὶ θνητὰ
μεμάρανται, τὰ δὲ νοητὰ καὶ ἀθάνατα ἀνήβηκεν, ἃ
142 γέρως καὶ τιμῆς ἐστιν ἐπάξια.   καὶ
ἔτεκον μαιευτικῆς τέχνης οὐ προσδεηθεῖσα· τίκτο-
μεν γὰρ καὶ πρὶν εἰσελθεῖν τινας ἐπινοίας καὶ
ἐπιστήμας ἀνθρώπων πρὸς ἡμᾶς ἄνευ τῶν ἐξ ἔθους
συνεργούντων, σπείροντος καὶ γεννῶντος θεοῦ τὰ
ἀστεῖα γεννήματα, ἃ τῷ δόντι προσηκόντως κατὰ
τὸν ἐπ' εὐχαριστίᾳ τεθέντα νόμον ἀποδίδοται· "τὰ
γὰρ δῶρά μου, δόματά μου, καρπώματά μου" φησί
"διατηρήσατε προσφέρειν ἐμοί."

143   XXVI. Τοῦτ' ἐστὶ τὸ τέλος τῆς ὁδοῦ τῶν
ἑπομένων λόγοις καὶ προστάξεσι νομίμοις καὶ
ταύτῃ βαδιζόντων, ᾗ ἂν ὁ θεὸς ἀφηγῆται· ὁ δὲ

---

[1] MSS. ἀπειθοῦντι.

---

[a] See App. p. 563.
[b] "Midwife," in allusion to Ex. i. 19; "goodly," to
Ex. ii. 2 (LXX. ἀστεῖον: cf. Heb. xi. 23). The connexion of
thought in §§ 139-142 is as follows. The idea that Isaac's
sacrifice typifies the offering of the soul's consummation suggests other thoughts about this soul-birth: (1) that the soul
is unconscious of what it is bearing, (2) that it comes in the

when it appeared she that seemed to have given birth to it acknowledges her ignorance of the good thing that had occurred in the words " who shall announce to Abraham " (for she assumed that he did not believe in the rising up of the breed that learns without a teacher), " who shall tell Abraham that Sarah is suckling a child " (Gen. xxi. 7) ? It does not say " a child is being suckled by Sarah,"[a] for the kind that is taught without a teacher is nourished by no one, but is a source of nourishment to others, being capable of teaching and not needing to learn.   " For 141 I bare a son," she continues, not as Egyptian women do in their bodily prime (Ex. i. 19), but as the Hebrew souls do, " in my old age " (Gen. xxi. 7), at a time, that is, when all things that are mortal and objects of sense-perception have decayed, while things immortal and intellectually discerned have grown young again, meet recipients of honour and esteem.

Furthermore, " I gave birth " without requiring 142 extraneous aid from the midwife's skill : for we give birth even before there come in to us any imaginations of man's knowledge, without the co-operation that custom supplies, for God begets and sows the seed of those goodly births, which, as is meet and right, are rendered to Him Who gave them, in fulfilment of the law laid down for thanksgiving : " My gifts, My endowments, My fruits " He says, " be careful to offer unto Me " (Num. xxviii. 2).[b]

XXVI. This is the end of the way of those who 143 follow the words and injunctions of the law, and march in whatever direction God leads the way : but

ripeness of spiritual " old age "; and this contrast between Sarah and the Egyptians suggests a further contrast, namely that the Hebrew-soul needs no " midwife."

ὑπενδοὺς ὑπὸ τοῦ πεινῶντος ἡδονῆς καὶ λίχνου
παθῶν, ὄνομα Ἀμαλὴκ—ἑρμηνεύεται γὰρ λαὸς
144 ἐκλείχων—, ἐκτετμήσεται. μηνύουσι δὲ οἱ χρησμοὶ
ὅτι λοχῶν ὁ τρόπος οὗτος, ἐπειδὰν τὸ ἐρρωμενέ-
στερον τῆς ψυχικῆς δυνάμεως κατίδῃ περαιωθέν,
ὑπανιστάμενος τῆς ἐνέδρας τὸ κεκμηκὸς μέρος ὡς
" οὐραγίαν κόπτει." κάματος δ' ὁ μέν
ἐστιν εὐένδοτος ἀσθένεια λογισμοῦ μὴ δυναμένου
τοὺς ὑπὲρ¹ ἀρετῆς ἀχθοφορῆσαι πόνους, ἐν ἐσχατιαῖς
οὗτος εὑρισκόμενος εὐαλωτότατος, ὁ δέ ἐστιν
ὑπομονὴ τῶν καλῶν, τὰ μὲν καλὰ ἀθρόα ἐρρωμένως ἀναδεχόμενος, μηδὲν δὲ τῶν φαύλων, κἂν εἰ
κουφότατον εἴη, βαστάσαι δικαιῶν, ἀλλ' ὡς βαρύ-
145 τατον ἄχθος ἀπορρίπτων. διὸ καὶ τὴν
ἀρετὴν ὁ νόμος εὐθυβόλῳ προσεῖπεν ὀνόματι Λείαν,
ἥτις ἑρμηνευθεῖσα λέγεται κοπιῶσα· τὸν γὰρ τῶν
φαύλων βίον ἐπαχθῆ καὶ βαρὺν ὄντα φύσει κοπώδη
προσηκόντως αὕτη νενόμικε καὶ οὐδὲ προσιδεῖν
ἀξιοῖ, τὰς ὄψεις πρὸς μόνον τὸ καλὸν ἀποκλίνουσα.
146 σπουδαζέτω δ' ὁ νοῦς μὴ μόνον
ἀνενδότως καὶ εὐτόνως ἔπεσθαι θεῷ, ἀλλὰ καὶ τὴν
εὐθεῖαν ἀτραπὸν ἰέναι πρὸς μηδέτερα νεύων, μήτε
τὰ δεξιὰ μήτε τὰ εὐώνυμα, οἷς ὁ γήινος Ἐδὼμ
ἐμπεφώλευκε, τοτὲ μὲν ὑπερβολαῖς καὶ περιουσίαις,
τοτὲ δὲ ἐλλείψεσι καὶ ἐνδείαις χρώμενος. ἄμεινον

¹ MSS. ὑπ'.

---

[a] As Heinemann suggests, there may be a play on λείχων
and λοχῶν.
[b] For Philo's treatment of this interpretation of Leah's
name see note on *De Cher.* 41.

the man who gives in under the assaults of the foe, who hungers after pleasure and is lickerish for passion, whose name is " Amalek," which means " a people licking up "—this man shall find himself cut off. The oracles signify that the Amalek type of 144 character lies in ambush,[a] when it is aware that the more stalwart portion of the soul-army has gone by, rises up from its ambuscade and " smites or ' cuts ' the hindmost " (Deut. xxv. 17 f.) or the labouring rear.

  " Labouring " may be used of a readiness to give in, a feebleness of reason's functioning, an inability to bear the burdens needed to win virtue. This is a condition which, when found lagging at the extreme rear, falls an easy prey. Or the word may connote brave endurance in a noble cause, a sturdy readiness to undertake all noble tasks together, a refusal to support the weight of any base thing, though it be the very lightest, nay a rejection of it as though it were the heaviest burden.

Hence it comes that the Law gave Virtue the appro- 145 priate name " Leah," which when translated is " growing weary "[b] ; for Virtue has, as she well may do, made up her mind that the way of life of the wicked, so essentially burdensome and heavy, is full of weariness, and she refuses so much as to look at it, turning her gaze away from it and fixing it on the morally beautiful alone.   But let the mind be bent 146 not only on following God with alert and unfailing steps, but also on keeping the straight course. Let it not incline to either side, either to what is on the right hand or to what is on the left, where Edom, of the earth earthy, has his lurking holes, and thus be the victim now of excesses and extravagances, now of shortcomings and deficiencies. For better is it to

γὰρ ὁδῷ τῇ μέσῃ βαδίζειν ἐστὶ τῇ πρὸς ἀλήθειαν
βασιλικῇ, ἣν ὁ μέγας καὶ μόνος βασιλεὺς θεὸς ταῖς
φιλαρέτοις ψυχαῖς ηὔρυνεν ἐνδιαίτημα κάλλιστον.
147 διὸ καί τινες τῶν τὴν ἥμερον καὶ κοινωνικὴν
μετιόντων φιλοσοφίαν μεσότητας τὰς ἀρετὰς εἶπον
εἶναι, ἐν μεθορίῳ στήσαντες αὐτάς, ἐπειδὴ τό τε
[459] ὑπέραυχον ἀλαζονείας γέμον πολλῆς | κακὸν καὶ τὸ[1]
ταπεινοῦ καὶ ἀφανοῦς μεταποιεῖσθαι σχήματος
εὐεπίβατον, τὸ δὲ μεταξὺ ἀμφοῖν κεκραμένον
ἐπιεικῶς ὠφέλιμον.

148 XXVII. Τὸ δὲ " ᾤχετο μετ' αὐτοῦ Λώτ "
τίνα ἔχει λόγον σκεπτέον. ἔστι μὲν οὖν Λὼτ
ἑρμηνευθεὶς ἀπόκλισις· κλίνεται δὲ ὁ νοῦς τοτὲ μὲν
τἀγαθόν, τοτὲ δ' αὖ τὸ κακὸν ἀποστρεφόμενος.
ἄμφω δὲ ταῦτα πολλάκις περὶ ἕνα καὶ τὸν αὐτὸν
θεωρεῖται· εἰσὶ γάρ τινες ἐνδοιασταὶ καὶ ἐπαμφο-
τερισταί, πρὸς ἑκάτερον τοῖχον ὥσπερ σκάφος
ὑπ' ἐναντίων πνευμάτων διαφερόμενον ἀποκλίνον-
τες ἢ καθάπερ ἐπὶ πλάστιγγος ἀντιρρέποντες,
ἐφ' ἑνὸς στηριχθῆναι βεβαίως ἀδυνατοῦντες, ὧν
οὐδὲ τὴν ἐπὶ τὰ ἀμείνω τροπὴν ἐπαινετέον· φορᾷ
149 γάρ, ἀλλ' οὐ γνώμῃ γίνεται. τούτων καὶ ὁ Λὼτ
ἐστι θιασώτης,[2] ὅν φησιν οἴχεσθαι μετὰ τοῦ σοφίας
ἐραστοῦ. καλὸν δ' ἦν ἀρξάμενον ἐκείνῳ παρα-
κολουθεῖν ἀπομαθεῖν ἀμαθίαν καὶ μηκέτι παλιν-
δρομῆσαι πρὸς αὐτήν. ἀλλὰ γὰρ οὐχ ἕνεκα τοῦ
μιμησάμενον τὸν ἀμείνω βελτιωθῆναι συνέρχεται,
ἀλλ' ὑπὲρ τοῦ κἀκείνῳ παρασχεῖν ἀντισπάσματα

---

[1] mss. τοῦ.   [2] mss. θεατής.

---

[a] For the thought of this section see *Quod Deus* 162 ff.,
where the meaning of " excess " and " deficiency " is fully
explained.

walk on the central road, the road that is truly " the king's " (Num. xx. 17), seeing that God, the great and only King, laid it out a broad and goodly way for virtue-loving souls to keep to.[a] Hence it is that some 147 of those who followed the mild and social form of philosophy,[b] have said that the virtues are means, fixing them in a borderland, feeling that the over-weening boastfulness of a braggart is bad, and that to adopt a humble and obscure position is to expose yourself to attack and oppression, whereas a fair and reasonable mixture of the two is beneficial.

XXVII. We have to consider what is meant by 148 " Lot went with him " (Gen. xii. 4). " Lot " by inter-pretation is " turning aside " or " inclining away." The mind " inclines," sometimes turning away from what is good, sometimes from what is bad. Often-times both tendencies are observable in one and the same person : for some men are irresolute, facers both ways, inclining to either side like a boat tossed by winds from opposite quarters, or swaying up and down as though on a pair of scales, incapable of becoming firmly settled on one : with such there is nothing praiseworthy even in their taking a turn to the better course ; for it is the result not of judgement but of drift. Of this crew Lot is a member, who is 149 said to have left his home with the lover of wisdom. When he had set out to follow his steps, it would have been well for him to unlearn lack of learning and to have retraced his steps to it no more. The fact is, however, that he comes with him, not that he may imitate the man who is better than he and so gain improvement, but actually to create obstacles which pull him back, and drag him elsewhere and

[b] Probably a definite reference to the Peripatetic school.

καὶ μεθολκὰς καὶ κατὰ τὴν ἔνθεν ⟨καὶ ἔνθεν⟩[1]
150 ὀλίσθους. τεκμήριον δέ· ὁ μὲν ἐπὶ τὴν ἀρχαίαν
ὑποτροπιάσας νόσον οἰκήσεται ληφθεὶς αἰχμάλωτος
ὑπὸ τῶν ἐν ψυχῇ πολεμίων, ὁ δὲ τὰς ἐξ ἐνέδρας
ἐπιβουλὰς αὐτοῦ φυλαξάμενος πάσῃ μηχανῇ δι-
οικισθήσεται.   τὸν δὲ διοικισμὸν αὖθις
μέν, οὔπω δὲ ποιήσεται. νῦν μὲν γὰρ τὰ θεωρήματα αὐτῷ ὡς ἂν ἄρτι ἀρχομένῳ τῆς θείας θεωρίας
πλαδᾷ καὶ σαλεύει· ὅταν δ᾽ ἤδη παγέντα κραταιό-
τερον ἱδρυθῇ, δυνήσεται τὸ δελεάζον καὶ κολακεῦον
ὡς ἐχθρὸν ἀκατάλλακτον καὶ δυσθήρατον φύσει
151 διαζεῦξαι. τοῦτο γὰρ ἔσθ᾽ ὃ δυσαπότριπτον[2] ὂν
παρέπεται ψυχῇ κωλῦον αὐτὴν πρὸς ἀρετὴν ὠκυ-
δρομεῖν· τοῦθ᾽, ἡνίκα καὶ τὴν Αἴγυπτον ἀπελείπομεν,
τὴν σωματικὴν χώραν ἅπασαν, ἀπομαθεῖν τὰ πάθη
σπουδάσαντες κατὰ τὰς τοῦ προφήτου λόγους,
Μωυσέως,[3] ὑφηγήσεις, ἠκολούθησεν ἡμῖν, ἐλλαμ-
βανόμενον τῆς περὶ τὴν ἔξοδον σπουδῆς καὶ τῷ
τάχει τῆς ἀπολείψεως ὑπὸ φθόνου βραδυτῆτας
152 ἐμποιοῦν· λέγεται γὰρ ὅτι " καὶ ἐπίμικτος πολὺς
συνανέβη αὐτοῖς, καὶ πρόβατα καὶ βόες καὶ κτήνη
πολλὰ σφόδρα," ὁ δὲ ἐπίμικτος οὗτος ἦν τὰ κτη-
νώδη καὶ ἄλογα τῆς ψυχῆς, εἰ δεῖ τἀληθὲς εἰπεῖν,
δόγματα. XXVIII. παγκάλως δὲ καὶ εὐθυβόλως
τὴν τοῦ φαύλου ψυχὴν ἐπίμικτον καλεῖ· συνηρημένη
γὰρ καὶ συμπεφορημένη καὶ μιγὰς ὄντως ἐκ

---

[1] κατὰ τὴν ἔνθεν ⟨καὶ ἔνθεν⟩, sc. ὁδὸν G.H.W.: Wend. conjectures κατὰ τὴν ὁδὸν ἐμποιεῖν (or ἐνθεῖναι).
[2] Mangey δυσαπότρεπτον, which suits παρέπεται better.
[3] mss. κατὰ τοὺς τοῦ προφήτου λόγους (one ms. λόγον) Μω.]
so Mangey, who inserts (again with one ms.) καὶ after Μω.:
Wend.'s correction is certainly right, cf. De Cong. 170
ὁ προφήτης λόγος ὄνομα Μωυσῆς.

make him slip in this direction or that. Here 150
is a proof of it. We shall find Lot having a relapse,
suffering from the old complaint, carried off a pri-
soner of war by the enemies in the soul; and Abraham,
resorting to every device to guard against his ambus-
cades and attacks, setting up separate quarters.[a]

This separation he will effect later on,
but not as yet. For at present he is but a novice
in the contemplation and study of things Divine and
his principles are unformed and wavering. By and
by they will have gained consistency and rest on a
firmer foundation, and he will be able to dissociate
from himself the ensnaring and flattering element as
an irreconcilable and elusive foe. For it is this from 151
which the soul can so hardly disengage itself as it
clings to it and hinders it from making swift progress
in reaching virtue. This it was, when we were
abandoning Egypt, all the bodily region, and were
hastening to unlearn the passions in obedience to the
instructions of the word of prophecy,[b] even Moses,—
it was this, I say, that followed us, checking our zeal
to be gone, and moved by envy to retard the speed
of our departure : for we read " and a mixed multi- 152
tude went up with them, both[c] sheep and oxen and
beasts very many " (Ex. xii. 38), and this mixed
multitude was, in fact, the soul's herd of beast-like
doctrines. XXVIII. And very well and appropriately
does he call the soul of the bad man " mixed " : for
it is brought together and collected and a medley in

[a] See App. p. 564.
[b] A reference to Ex. xii. 11, quoted with the same interpretation above, § 25.
[c] " both " better than " and " as the next words show,
though later the thought is changed, and the ἐπίμικτος
becomes human.

πλειόνων καὶ μαχομένων δοξῶν, μία μὲν οὖσα
153 ἀριθμῷ, μυριὰς δὲ τῷ πολυτρόπῳ. διὸ καὶ τῷ
ἐπίμικτος πρόσκειται πολύς· ὁ μὲν γὰρ πρὸς ἓν
[460] μόνον ἀφορῶν ἁπλοῦς καὶ | ἀμιγὴς καὶ λεῖος ὄντως,
ὁ δὲ πολλὰ τέλη τοῦ βίου προτιθέμενος πολὺς καὶ
μιγὰς καὶ δασὺς ἀληθείᾳ. οὗ χάριν οἱ χρησμοὶ τὸν
μὲν ἀσκητὴν τῶν καλῶν Ἰακὼβ λεῖον, τὸν δὲ τῶν
154 αἰσχίστων Ἠσαῦ δασὺν εἰσάγουσι.   διὰ
τὸν ἐπίμικτον καὶ δασὺν τοῦτον ὄχλον ἐκ μιγάδων
καὶ συγκλύδων συμπεφυρμένον δοξῶν ὠκυδρομῆ-
σαι δυνάμενος ὁ νοῦς, ὅτε τὴν σωματικὴν χώραν
ἀπεδίδρασκεν Αἴγυπτον, καὶ τρισὶν ἡμέραις δια-
δέξασθαι τὸν ἀρετῆς κλῆρον φωτὶ τρισσῷ, μνήμῃ
τῶν παρεληλυθότων καὶ ἐναργείᾳ[1] τῶν παρόντων
καὶ τῇ τῶν μελλόντων ἐλπίδι, τεσσαράκοντα ἐτῶν
ἀριθμόν, μῆκος τοσούτου χρόνου, τρίβεται τὴν ἐν
κύκλῳ περιάγων καὶ ἀλώμενος ἕνεκα τοῦ πολυ-
τρόπου, τὴν ἐπ᾽ εὐθείας ἀνυσιμωτάτην οὖσαν δέον.
155   οὗτός ἐστιν ὁ μὴ μόνον ὀλίγοις εἴδεσιν
ἐπιθυμίας χαίρων, ἀλλὰ μηδὲν τὸ παράπαν ἀπολιπεῖν δικαίων, ἵνα ὅλον δι᾽ ὅλων τὸ γένος, ᾧ πᾶν
εἶδος ἐμφέρεται, μετέρχηται· λέγεται γὰρ ὅτι " ὁ
ἐπίμικτος ὁ ἐν αὐτοῖς ἐπεθύμησεν ἐπιθυμίαν "
αὐτοῦ τοῦ γένους, οὐχ ἑνός τινος τῶν εἰδῶν, " καὶ
καθίσαντες ἔκλαιον."   συνίησι γὰρ ὀλιγο-

---

[1] mss. ἐνεργείᾳ.

---

a Philo takes ἐπιθυμίαν, which in the lxx. is a cognate
accusative representing the familiar Hebrew way of intensify-
ing the verb (though that more often employs the dative;
cf. Leg. All. i. 90), as if it was the direct object of ἐπεθύμησεν.
The verb does occasionally take an accusative, though

very deed, consisting of many discordant opinions, one in number but myriad in its manifoldness. For 153 this reason it is called a " multitude " or " numerous " as well as " mixed " ; for he that has an eye to a single aim only is single and unmixed and truly smooth and level, but he that sets before himself many aims for his life is manifold and mixed and truly rough. It is for this reason that the oracles represent Jacob, the trainer of himself for nobility, as smooth, but Esau, who exercised himself in basest things, as rough with hair (Gen. xxvii. 11).

What befell the Mind, when it escaped from Egypt 154 the country of the body, was due to this mixed and rough multitude, a conglomeration of promiscuous and diverse opinions. It could have made rapid progress and in three days (Gen. xxii. 3) have entered upon the inheritance of virtue by a threefold light, memory of things gone by, clear sight of things present, and the expectation of things to come. Instead of this, for the space of forty years, for all that length of time, it wears itself out wandering and going round circle-wise, in obedience to the " manifold " element with its many twistings, when it behoved it to have taken the straight way which was the speediest. It is this mixed mul- 155 titude which takes delight not in a few species of lusting only, but claims to leave out nothing at all, that it may follow after lust's entire genus, including all its species. For we read " the mixed people that was among them ' craved after lust,' [a] after the genus itself, not some single species, ' and sat down and wept ' " (Num. xi. 4). For the understand-

commonly the genitive, on which he falls back in the next words.

δρανοῦσα ἡ διάνοια καί, ὁπότε μὴ δύναται τυχεῖν
ὧν ὀρέγεται, δακρύει καὶ στενάζει· καίτοι ὤφειλε
χαίρειν παθῶν καὶ νοσημάτων ἀτυχοῦσα καὶ μεγάλην εὐπραγίαν νομίζειν τὴν ἔνδειαν καὶ ἀπουσίαν
156 αὐτῶν. ἀλλὰ γὰρ καὶ τοῖς χορευταῖς ἀρετῆς
σφαδάζειν καὶ δακρύειν ἔθος, ἢ τὰς τῶν ἀφρόνων
ὀδυρομένοις συμφορὰς διὰ τὸ φύσει κοινωνικὸν καὶ
φιλάνθρωπον ἢ διὰ περιχάρειαν. γίνεται δὲ αὕτη,
ὅταν ἀθρόα ἀγαθὰ μηδὲ προσδοκηθέντα ποτὲ
αἰφνίδιον ὀμβρήσαντα πλημμυρῇ· ἀφ' οὗ καὶ τὸ
ποιητικὸν εἰρῆσθαί μοι δοκεῖ '' δακρυόεν γελά-
157 σασα''· προσπεσοῦσα γὰρ ἐκ τοῦ ἀνελπίστου ἡ
εὐπαθειῶν ἀρίστη χαρὰ ψυχῇ μείζονα αὐτὴν ἢ
πρότερον ἦν ἐποίησεν, ὡς διὰ τὸν ὄγκον μηκέτι
χωρεῖν τὸ σῶμα, θλιβόμενον δὲ καὶ πιεζόμενον
ἀποστάζειν λιβάδας, ἃς καλεῖν ἔθος δάκρυα, περὶ
ὧν ἐν ὕμνοις εἴρηται· '' ψωμιεῖς ἡμᾶς ἄρτον δα-
κρύων'' καὶ '' ἐγένετο τὰ δάκρυά μοι ἄρτος ἡμέρας
καὶ νυκτός.'' τροφὴ γάρ ἐστι διανοίας τὰ τοῦ
ἐνδιαθέτου καὶ σπουδαίου γέλωτος ἐμφανῆ δάκρυα,
ἐπειδὰν ὁ θεῖος ἐντακεὶς ἵμερος τὸν τοῦ γενητοῦ
θρῆνον ᾆσμα εἰς τὸν ἀγένητον ὕμνου ποιήσῃ.[1]

158 XXIX. Ἔνιοι μὲν οὖν τὸν μιγάδα καὶ δασὺν
τοῦτον ἀπορρίπτουσι καὶ διατειχίζουσιν ἀφ' ἑαυ-
[461] τῶν τῷ θεοφιλεῖ | μόνῳ γένει χαίροντες· ἔνιοι δὲ
καὶ πρὸς αὐτὸν ἑταιρίαν τίθενται, μεσιτεύειν τὸν

----

[1] MSS. ποιήσειεν.

----

[a] Hom. *Il.* vi. 484.
[b] E.V. "Thou hast fed us." The future perhaps makes
Philo's perversion of the meaning a little less unreasonable.

ing is conscious of its feebleness, and when it cannot obtain what it is longing for, it weeps and groans ; and yet it had cause to rejoice at missing passions and sicknesses, and to consider the dearth and absence of them great prosperity. And yet indeed it is 156 not unusual for the devotees of virtue themselves to be much moved and to shed tears, either when bemoaning the misfortunes of the unwise owing to their innate fellow-feeling and humaneness, or by reason of being overjoyed. This last occurs when, as is sometimes the case, a sudden shower of unexpected good things falls, and they come all at once like a flood. I fancy that it is to this that we must refer the expression of the poet,

> She laughed with glad tears in her eyes.[a]

For joy, that best of the good emotions, when it 157 has fallen upon the soul unexpectedly, makes it larger than it was before, so that owing to its size the body has no longer room for it, and as it is squeezed and compressed it distils moist drops, which we are in the habit of calling " tears." Of these it is said in the Psalms, " Thou shalt feed us[b] with the bread of tears " (Ps. lxxix. [lxxx.] 6), and " My tears have been my bread by day and by night " (Ps. xli. [xlii.] 4). For tears, that rise to the surface from the inward heart-felt laughter, are food to the understanding, coming when the love of God has sunk deep in and turned the dirge of created being into a canticle of praise to the Uncreate.

XXIX. While some regard this rough and motley 158 type as outcast, and keep it at a distance from themselves, having delight in the God-beloved kind only, others actually form ties of fellowship with it,

ἑαυτῶν βίον ἀξιοῦντες καὶ μεθόριον ἀνθρωπίνων
τε καὶ θείων ἀρετῶν τιθέντες, ἵν' ἑκατέρων ἐφάπ-
159 τωνται, καὶ τῶν ἀληθείᾳ καὶ τῶν δοκήσει. τούτου
τοῦ δόγματος ὁ πολιτευόμενός ἐστι τρόπος, ὃν
Ἰωσὴφ ὀνομάζειν ἔθος, ᾧ συναπέρχονται μέλλοντι
τὸν πατέρα κηδεύειν '' πάντες οἱ παῖδες Φαραὼ καὶ
οἱ πρεσβύτεροι τοῦ οἴκου αὐτοῦ καὶ πάντες οἱ
πρεσβύτεροι τῆς Αἰγύπτου καὶ πᾶσα ἡ πανοικία
αὐτοῦ, Ἰωσὴφ καὶ οἱ ἀδελφοὶ αὐτοῦ καὶ πᾶσα ἡ
160 οἰκία ἡ πατρικὴ αὐτοῦ.'' ὁρᾷς ὅτι μέσος τῆς
Φαραὼ καὶ τῆς πατρικῆς οἰκίας ὁ πολιτικὸς οὗτος
τάττεται, ἵνα καὶ τῶν κατὰ σῶμα, τὴν Αἴγυπτον,
καὶ τῶν κατὰ ψυχήν, ἅπερ ἐν τῷ πατρικῷ οἴκῳ
θησαυροφυλακεῖται, κατ' ἴσον ἐφάπτηται[1]; ὅταν
μὲν γὰρ λέγῃ '' τοῦ θεοῦ εἰμι '' καὶ τὰ ἄλλα ὅσα
συγγενῆ τούτῳ, τοῖς τῆς πατρῴας οἰκίας ἐμμένει
νομίμοις· ὅταν δὲ ἐπὶ '' τὸ δευτερεῖον ἅρμα '' τοῦ
βασιλεύειν νοῦ δοκοῦντος ἀνέρχηται, Φαραώ, τὸν
161 Αἰγυπτιακὸν πάλιν ἱδρύεται τῦφον. ἀθλιώτερος
δ' ὁ νομιζόμενος ἐνδοξότερος εἶναι βασιλεύς, ὃς τῷ
προηγουμένῳ τῶν ἁρμάτων ἐποχεῖται· τὸ γὰρ μὴ
ἐν καλοῖς διαπρέπειν ἐπιφανέστατον αἶσχος, ὡς τὸ
φέρεσθαι τὰ ἐν τούτοις δευτερεῖα κουφότερον κακόν.
162   τὸ μέντοι γε ἐπαμφοτερίζον αὐτοῦ
καταμάθοις ἂν κἀκ τῶν ὅρκων οὓς πεποίηται, τοτὲ
μὲν ὀμνὺς '' νὴ τὴν ὑγείαν Φαραώ,'' τοτὲ δ' ἔμπαλιν

---

[1] mss. ἐφῆται (ἐφεῖται).

holding that their own place in human life should be midway, set as a borderland between virtues human and Divine, and thus they aim at being in touch with both the real and the reputed virtues. To this school 159 belongs the politician's frame of mind, to which it is customary to give the name " Joseph." When he is about to bury his father there go off with him " all the servants of Pharaoh and the elders of his house and all the elders of Egypt and all his whole household,[a] Joseph and his brethren and all his father's house " (Gen. l. 7 f.). Do you notice that this 160 politician takes his position in the midst between the house of Pharaoh and his father's house ? that his object is to be equally in touch with the concerns of the body, which is Egypt, and those of the soul which are kept as in a treasury in his father's house ? For when he says " I belong to God " (Gen. l. 19) and other things of this kind, he is abiding by the customs of his father's house. But when he mounts " the second chariot " of the mind that fancies itself a king, even Pharaoh (Gen. xli. 43), he again sets up the idol of Egyptian vanity.[b] Though indeed more wretched 161 than he is the king who is thought to be more glorious, who rides in the principal chariot : for to win distinction in things that are without moral beauty is a most patent disgrace, just as to carry off the second prize in such things is a less weighty evil. Of his 162 proneness to face both ways you may get an idea from the oaths which he is represented as taking, at one moment swearing " yea by the health of Pharaoh " (Gen. xlii. 16) and then on the contrary, " no, by the

---

[a] The LXX has ἡ πανοικία Ἰωσήφ (evidently genitive), but Philo's comments shew that he took it as in the translation.
[b] See App. p. 564. πάλιν perhaps " on the other hand."

" οὐ τὴν ὑγείαν Φαραώ." ἀλλ' ὁ μὲν περιέχων τὴν
ἀπόφασιν ὅρκος τῆς πατρικῆς ἂν εἴη διάταγμα
οἰκίας ἀεὶ φονώσης κατὰ τοῦ πάθους καὶ βουλο-
μένης αὐτὸ τεθνάναι, ὁ δ' ἕτερος Αἰγύπτου, ᾗ
163 φίλον ἐστὶ τοῦτο σῴζεσθαι. διόπερ καίτοι τοσαύτης πληθύος συνανιούσης ἐπίμικτον ὄχλον οὐκ
εἶπεν, ἐπειδὴ τῷ μὲν ἄκρως ὁρατικῷ καὶ φιλαρέτῳ
πᾶν ὃ μὴ ἀρετὴ ἢ ἀρετῆς ἔργον ἀναμεμῖχθαι καὶ
συγκεχύσθαι δοκεῖ, τῷ δὲ ἔτι χαμαιζήλῳ καθ'
αὑτὰ τὰ γῆς ἆθλα ἀξιέραστα καὶ ἀξιοτίμητα
νενόμισται.

164 XXX. Τὸν μὲν οὖν ὡς κηφῆνα τοὺς μελιττῶν[1]
ὠφελίμους πόνους λυμαίνεσθαι διεγνωκότα καὶ διὰ
τοῦτο ἐπακολουθοῦντα διατειχιεῖ, καθάπερ ἔφην, ὁ
φρονήσεως ἐραστής, τοὺς δὲ ἕνεκα μιμήσεως
παρεπομένους κατὰ τὸν τῶν καλῶν ζῆλον ἀπο-
δέξεται μοίρας αὐτοῖς τὰς ἁρμοττούσας δασάμενος·
" τῶν " γάρ φησι " συμπορευθέντων ἀνδρῶν μετ'
ἐμοῦ Ἐσχώλ, Αὐνάν, Μαμβρῆ οὗτοι λήψονται
μερίδα"· λέγει δὲ τοὺς εὐφυεῖς τρόπους καὶ φιλο-
165 θεάμονας. ὁ μὲν γὰρ Ἐσχὼλ εὐφυΐας σύμβολον

───────

[1] μελιττῶν is my conjecture for the ms. μὲν αὐτῶν. See
App. p. 564.

───────

[a] The lxx has νὴ (some texts μὰ) τὴν ὑγίειαν Φαραώ, οὐ μὴ
ἐξέλθητε. Philo presumably found οὐ in his copy. It will
make the point a little more sensible, if we understand him
to take the words " I will not swear by the health of Pharaoh,
(but) you shall not go forth."

[b] The meaning of the section seems to be as follows. To
the Israel mind the mixed cavalcade of Ex. xli. is confusion;
that of Gen. l. is not so to the Joseph mind. Moses regulates
his language in speaking of each multitude by what the two
minds would think of them.

health of Pharaoh " [a] (Gen. xlii. 15). The oath containing the negative is one that his father's house would prescribe, being always a mortal foe to passion and wishing it dead ; the other oath is one that Egypt might prescribe, for passion's welfare is dear to it. It **163** is for all these reasons that, though so great a number went up with Joseph, Moses does not call them a mixed multitude ; for whereas in the view of the man whose vision is quite perfect and who is a lover of virtue, all that is not virtue and virtue's doing seems to be mixed up and to be in confusion, in the eyes of the man who still cherishes low aims earth's prizes are deemed to be in themselves worthy of love and worthy of honour.[b]

XXX. The lover of sound sense will, therefore, as I **164** said, set a barrier between him and the man who, like a drone, has set himself to make havoc of the useful labours of the bees, and who follows for the sake of doing this, while those who in their enthusiasm for all that is morally excellent accompany them on their journey from a wish to copy them, he will welcome and allot to them such portions as are suitable : for Abraham says " of the men that journeyed with me Eshcol and Aunan,[c] these shall receive Mamre as their portion " (Gen. xiv. 24) ; meaning characters well endowed by nature and lovers of the higher vision. For Eshcol is a symbol of good natural ability, his **165**

[c] Though Wend.'s punctuation evidently takes Mamre (as no doubt it is) as nom., Philo's language shews clearly that Mamre is, not has, the κλῆρος. That he should so take it, is not surprising. Except here and perhaps in Gen. xiv. 13, he would find no suggestion that Mamre was a man. It is either a town or occurs in the phrase ἡ δρῦς Μαμβρή. Even in Gen. xiv. 13 the words might without violation of grammar be so taken as to avoid such a suggestion.

[462] πυρὸς ἔχων ὄνομα, ἐπειδὴ καὶ τὸ | εὐφυὲς εὔτολμον
καὶ ἔνθερμον καὶ ἐχόμενον ὧν ἂν προσάψηται, ὁ
δὲ Αὐνὰν τοῦ φιλοθεάμενος—ὀφθαλμοὶ γὰρ ἑρμηνεύεται[1]—τῷ καὶ τὰ ψυχῆς ὑπ' εὐθυμίας[2] ὄμματα
διοίγνυσθαι. τούτων δ' ἀμφοτέρων ἐστὶν ὁ θεωρη-
τικὸς βίος κλῆρος, προσαγορευόμενος Μαμβρῆ, ὃ
μεταληφθὲν ἀπὸ ὁράσεως καλεῖται· τῷ δὲ θεωρητι-
κῷ τὸ ὁρᾶν συνῳδόν τε καὶ οἰκειότατον.

166 ἐπειδὰν δὲ τούτοις ἀλείπταις χρησάμενος ὁ νοῦς
μηδὲν ἐλλείπῃ τῶν πρὸς ἄσκησιν, συνομαρτεῖ καὶ
συντρέχει τελείᾳ φρονήσει, μήθ' ὑπερέχων μήθ'
ὑπερεχόμενος, ἀλλὰ ἰσαίτατα καὶ ἰσοστάσια βαίνων.
δηλοῖ δὲ τὸ λόγιον ἐν ᾧ σαφῶς εἴρηται, διότι
" πορευθέντες ἀμφότεροι ἅμ' ἦλθον[3] ἐπὶ τὸν τόπον
167 ὃν εἶπεν ὁ θεός." ὑπερβάλλουσά γε ἰσότης ἀρετῶν,
ἁμιλλησαμένων[4] πόνου μὲν πρὸς εὐεξίαν, τέχνης δὲ
πρὸς τὴν αὐτοδίδακτον φύσιν, καὶ δυνηθέντων ἴσα
τὰ ἆθλα τῆς ἀρετῆς ἐνέγκασθαι· ὥσπερ ἂν εἰ
ζωγραφία καὶ πλαστικὴ μὴ μόνον ὡς νῦν ἀκίνητα
καὶ ἄψυχα ἐδημιούργουν, ἴσχυον δὲ κινούμενά τε
καὶ ἔμψυχα τὰ γραφόμενα καὶ πλαττόμενα ποιεῖν·
ἐδόκουν γὰρ ἂν φύσεως ἔργων οὖσαι τὸ πάλαι
μιμητικαὶ τέχναι φύσεις αὐταὶ γεγενῆσθαι τὰ νῦν.

---

[1] Wend. prints ὀφθαλμοὶ γὰρ ἑρμηνεύεται τῷ κτλ. without
dashes. But clearly the opening of the soul's eye is not the
reason why the name Aunan means eyes.

[2] For ὑπ' εὐθυμίας (most mss. ὑπὲρ) see App. p. 565.

[3] mss. and Wend. ἀνῆλθον: the correction (Heinemann's)
is certain. The reference is to Gen. xxii. 8, not, as W. supposed, Gen. xxii. 3. That they came *together* is the point of
both this and the following section.

[4] mss. ἀμίλλης ἀμείνων.

---

[a] The gist of this and the preceding sections may be
summed up thus. When the Abraham soul of Gen. xiv. has

name meaning " fire," for natural ability like fire is
full of daring, and hot, and fastens on whatever it
touches. Aunan represents the vision-lover, for it
means " eyes," since the eyes of the soul also are
opened by cheerfulness. And of both of these the
contemplative life is the inheritance receiving the
name of Mamre, which in our language is " from
seeing " ; and there is an intimate connexion between seeing and contemplation. When 166
the mind, having such trainers as these, omits nothing
that will make for its training, it runs by the side of
perfect sound sense, neither getting in front nor
dropping behind, but taking strides of the same length
and strength. This is manifest from the plain statement of the oracle that they " both journeyed and
came together to the place of which God had told
him " (Gen. xxii. 8). There is indeed an extra- 167
ordinary equality in virtues, when labour has vied
with natural fitness, and acquired skill with self-
tutored nature, and the pair have proved capable of
carrying off virtue's prizes in equal measure. It is just
as though painting and sculpture were producing not
only as they do now creations destitute of movement
and life, but had the power to make the works of
brush and chisel living and moving things ; it would
then be felt, that whereas they were formerly arts
copying Nature's works, they had now become themselves embodiments of nature.[a] XXXI. One 168

been trained by journeyings with the εὐφυής and the φιλοθεάμων, it will rise to the stage of the Abraham of Gen. xxii.,
who went *together* with Isaac, that is διδακτικὴ ἀρετή side by
side with αὐτομαθὴς ἀρετή. When this higher stage is reached,
the old antithesis between labour and natural gifts, between
art the imitator and nature the creator, is wiped out. See
further App. p. 565.

168   XXXI. ὁ δὲ ἐπὶ τοσοῦτον ἄνω μετέωρος ἐξαρθεὶς οὐδὲν ἔτι τῶν τῆς ψυχῆς μερῶν κάτω
τοῖς θνητοῖς ἐνδιατρίβειν ἐάσει, πάντα δ' ὥσπερ
ἐκ σειρᾶς ἐκκρεμασθέντα συνεπισπάσεται. διὸ καὶ
λόγιον ἐχρήσθη τῷ σοφῷ τοιόνδε· " ἀνάβηθι πρὸς
κύριόν σου, σὺ καὶ 'Ααρὼν καὶ Ναδὰβ καὶ 'Αβιοὺδ
169 καὶ ἑβδομήκοντα τῆς γερουσίας 'Ισραήλ." τοῦτο
δέ ἐστι τοιοῦτον· ἀνάβηθι, ὦ ψυχή, πρὸς τὴν
τοῦ ὄντος θέαν εὐαρμόστως, λογικῶς, ἑκουσίως, ἀ-
φόβως, ἀγαπητικῶς, ἐν ἀριθμοῖς ἁγίοις καὶ τελείοις
ἑβδομάδος δεκαπλασιασθείσης. 'Ααρὼν μὲν γὰρ
προφήτης λέγεται Μωυσέως ἐν τοῖς νόμοις, ὁ
γεγωνὸς[1] λόγος προφητεύων διανοίᾳ, Ναδὰβ δὲ
ἑκούσιος ἑρμηνεύεται, ὁ μὴ ἀνάγκῃ τιμῶν τὸ θεῖον,
καὶ 'Αβιοὺδ πατήρ μου· οὗτος ὁ μὴ δι' ἀφροσύνην
δεσπότου μᾶλλον ἢ πατρὸς διὰ φρόνησιν ἄρχοντος
170 θεοῦ δεόμενος. αἵδ' εἰσὶν αἱ τοῦ βασιλεύειν ἀξίου
νοῦ δορυφόροι δυνάμεις, ἃς συνέρχεσθαι τῷ βασιλεῖ
παραπεμπούσας αὐτὸν θέμις.   ἀλλὰ γὰρ
δέος ἐστὶν ἀναβαίνειν πρὸς τὴν τοῦ ὄντος θέαν ψυχῇ
δι' ἑαυτῆς ἀγνοούσῃ τὴν ὁδόν, ὑπὸ ἀμαθίας ἅμα
καὶ τόλμης ἐπαρθείσῃ—μεγάλα δὲ τὰ ἐξ ἀνεπ-
ιστημοσύνης καὶ πολλοῦ θράσους παραπτώματα—·
171 διόπερ εὔχεται Μωυσῆς αὐτῷ τῷ θεῷ χρῆσθαι
[463] ἡγεμόνι πρὸς τὴν | πρὸς αὐτὸν ἄγουσαν ὁδόν· λέγει
γάρ· " εἰ μὴ αὐτὸς σὺ συμπορεύῃ, μή με ἀναγάγῃς
ἐντεῦθεν·" διότι πᾶσα κίνησις ἡ ἄνευ θείας ἐπι-
φροσύνης ἐπιζήμιον, καὶ ἄμεινον ἐνταυθοῖ κατα-

──────────
[1] mss. γεγονώς.

──────────
[a] Here Moses and Aaron represent λογικῶς (combining
understanding and speech), Nadab ἑκουσίως, Abihu ἀφόβως
καὶ ἀγαπητικῶς, while εὐαρμόστως embraces all four.
[b] See above, § 84.

that has been exalted so high above the earth will no longer suffer any parts of his soul to have their converse down below among things mortal, but will draw them all up with him, just like bodies hanging on a rope. So a divine intimation was given to the wise man to this effect : " Come up to thy Lord, thou and Aaron and Nadab and Abihu and seventy of the Senate of Israel " (Ex. xxiv. 1). This means : " Come 169 up, O soul, to behold the Existent One, come with thy being in harmony, that is, with thy speech and reason active, come willingly, fearlessly, affectionately,ᵃ come in the holy and perfect measures of seven multiplied tenfold." For " Aaron " is called in the Laws Moses' prophet (Ex. vii. 1),ᵇ speech acting as prophet to understanding, and " Nadab," meaning voluntary, is he that under no constraint does honour to the Deity, while " Abihu " means " my father," and represents the man who stands in need of God to govern him, not as a master owing to his folly, but much rather as a father owing to his good sense. These are the powers that form the bodyguard of the 170 mind that is worthy of sovereignty, and it is meet that they should accompany the King as His escort.

But the soul has reason to fear ascending in its own strength to the sight of Him that is, ignorant as it is of the way, lifted up as it is at once by ignorance and by daring, and grievous are the falls that have been occasioned by lack of knowledge and excess of boldness ; and therefore Moses prays that 171 he may have God Himself, to guide him to the way that leads to Him ; for he says : " If Thou Thyself goest not with me on my journey, lead me not up hence " (Ex. xxxiii. 15) : for loss is entailed by all movement that is not under Divine direction, and it

μένειν τὸν θνητὸν βίον ἀλητεύοντας, ὡς τὸ πλεῖστον
ἀνθρώπων γένος, ἢ πρὸς τὸν οὐρανὸν ἐξάραντας
ἑαυτοὺς ὑπὸ ἀλαζονείας ἀνατραπῆναι· καθάπερ
μυρίοις συνέβη τῶν σοφιστῶν, οἵτινες ᾠήθησαν
σοφίαν πιθανὴν εἶναι λόγων εὕρεσιν, ἀλλ' οὐ πραγ-
172 μάτων ἀληθεστάτην πίστιν.   ἴσως δὲ
καὶ τοιοῦτόν τι δηλοῦται· μή με ἄνω μετέωρον
ἐξάρῃς, πλοῦτον ἢ δόξαν ἢ τιμὰς ἢ ἀρχὰς ἢ ὅσα
ἄλλα τῶν ἐν ταῖς λεγομέναις εὐτυχίαις δωρησάμενος,
εἰ μὴ μέλλοις αὐτὸς συνέρχεσθαι. ταῦτα γὰρ καὶ
ζημίας καὶ ὠφελείας μεγίστας πολλάκις περιποιεῖται τοῖς ἔχουσιν, ὠφελείας μέν, ὅταν ἀφηγῆται
τῆς γνώμης ὁ θεός, βλάβας δέ, ὅταν τοὐναντίον·
μυρίοις γὰρ τὰ λεγόμενα ἀγαθὰ πρὸς ἀλήθειαν οὐκ
173 ὄντα κακῶν ἀνηκέστων γέγονεν αἴτια.   ὁ
δὲ ἑπόμενος θεῷ κατὰ τἀναγκαῖον συνοδοιπόροις
χρῆται τοῖς ἀκολούθοις αὐτοῦ λόγοις, οὓς ὀνομάζειν
ἔθος ἀγγέλους· λέγεται γοῦν ὅτι "'Αβραὰμ συν-
επορεύετο συμπροπέμπων αὐτούς." ὦ παγκάλης
ἐπανισώσεως, καθ' ἣν ὁ παραπέμπων παρεπέμ-
πετο, διδοὺς ὃ ἐλάμβανεν, οὐκ ἀνθ' ἑτέρου ἕτερον,
ἀλλὰ ἓν αὐτὸ μόνον ἐκεῖνο τὸ πρὸς τὰς ἀντιδόσεις
174 ἕτοιμον. ἕως μὲν γὰρ οὐ τετελείωται, ἡγεμόνι τῆς
ὁδοῦ χρῆται λόγῳ θείῳ· χρησμὸς γάρ ἐστιν· " ἰδοὺ
ἀποστέλλω τὸν ἄγγελόν μου πρὸ προσώπου σου,
ἵνα φυλάξῃ σε ἐν τῇ ὁδῷ, ὅπως εἰσαγάγῃ σε εἰς τὴν
γῆν ἣν ἡτοίμασά σοι. πρόσεχε αὐτῷ καὶ εἰσάκουε
αὐτοῦ, μὴ ἀπείθει αὐτῷ· οὐ γὰρ μὴ ὑποστείληται

───────────────
ª See on *De Conf.* 28.

is better to stay where we are, roaming, with the bulk of mankind, through this mortal life, rather than to lift ourselves heavenward and incur shipwreck as imposters. This has been the fate of multitudes of sophists, through their imagining that wisdom consists in finding specious arguments, and not in appealing to the solid evidence of facts. But 172 perhaps the force of the prayer may be such as this : " Raise me not up on high, endowing me with wealth or fame or honours or offices, or aught else that is called good fortune, unless Thou Thyself art about to come with me." For these things often bring upon those who have them very great losses as well as very great advantages, advantages, when the judgement is under God's guidance ; hurts, when this is not so : for to thousands the things I have named, not being really good things, have become the cause of incurable evils. Now he that follows 173 God has of necessity as his fellow-travellers the words and thoughts[a] that attend Him, angels as they are often called. What we read is that " Abraham travelled with them, joining with them in escorting them on their way " (Gen. xviii. 16). What a glorious privilege to be put on a level with them ! The escort is escorted ; he gives what he was receiving ; not one thing in return for another, but just one thing only that lies ready to be passed backwards and forwards from one to the other. For as long as he falls short of 174 perfection, he has the Divine Word as his leader : since there is an oracle which says, " Lo, I send My messenger before thy face, to guard thee in thy way, that he may bring thee in into the land which I have prepared for thee : give heed to him, and hearken to him, disobey him not ; for he will by no means with-

175 σε· τὸ γὰρ ὄνομά μού ἐστιν ἐπ' αὐτῷ." ἐπειδὰν δὲ
πρὸς ἄκραν ἐπιστήμην ἀφίκηται, συντόνως ἐπιδραμὼν ἰσοταχήσει τῷ πρόσθεν ἡγουμένῳ τῆς ὁδοῦ·
ἀμφότεροι γὰρ οὕτως ὀπαδοὶ γενήσονται τοῦ
πανηγεμόνος θεοῦ μηδενὸς ἔτι τῶν ἑτεροδόξων
παρακολουθοῦντος, ἀλλὰ καὶ τοῦ Λώτ, ὃς ἔκλινε
τὴν ψυχὴν ὀρθὴν καὶ ἀκαμπῆ φύεσθαι δυναμένην,
διοικισθέντος.

176 XXXII. "'Αβραὰμ δὲ ἦν" φησίν "ἐτῶν ἑβδομήκοντα πέντε, ὅτε ἐξῆλθεν ἐκ Χαρράν." περὶ μὲν
οὖν τοῦ τῶν πέντε καὶ ἑβδομήκοντα ἐτῶν ἀριθμοῦ
—λόγον γὰρ ἔχει συνῳδὸν τοῖς πρόσθεν εἰρημένοις
—αὖθις ἀκριβώσομεν. τίς δέ ἐστι Χαρρὰν καὶ τίς
ἡ ἐκ ταύτης ἀποικία τῆς χώρας, πρότερον ἐρευ-

177 νήσωμεν. οὐδένα τοίνυν τῶν ἐντετυχηκότων τοῖς
νόμοις ἀγνοεῖν εἰκός, ὅτι πρότερον μὲν ἐκ τῆς
Χαλδαϊκῆς ἀναστὰς γῆς 'Αβραὰμ ᾤκησεν εἰς
[464] Χαρράν, | τελευτήσαντος δὲ αὐτῷ τοῦ πατρὸς
ἐκεῖθι κἀκ ταύτης μετανίσταται, ὡς δυεῖν ἤδη

178 τόπων ἀπόλειψιν πεποιῆσθαι. τί οὖν
λεκτέον; Χαλδαῖοι τῶν ἄλλων ἀνθρώπων ἐκπεπο-
νηκέναι καὶ διαφερόντως δοκοῦσιν ἀστρονομίαν καὶ
γενεθλιαλογικήν, τὰ ἐπίγεια τοῖς μετεώροις καὶ τὰ
οὐράνια τοῖς ἐπὶ γῆς ἁρμοζόμενοι καὶ ὥσπερ διὰ
μουσικῆς λόγων τὴν ἐμμελεστάτην συμφωνίαν τοῦ
παντὸς ἐπιδεικνύμενοι τῇ τῶν μερῶν πρὸς ἄλληλα
κοινωνίᾳ καὶ συμπαθείᾳ, τόποις μὲν διεζευγμένων,

179 συγγενείᾳ δὲ οὐ διῳκισμένων. οὗτοι τὸν φαινό-

---

[a] See App. p. 565.
[b] That this is the meaning of διὰ μουσικῆς λόγων, rather
than " by a music of λόγοι," in which case λόγοι would be used
in the Stoic sense of " nature-forces," is shewn by *De Mut.*

draw from thee ;[a] for My name is on him " (Ex. xxiii.
20 f.).   But when he has arrived at full knowledge, he 175
will run with more vigorous effort, and his pace will
be as great as that of him who before led the way ;
for so they will both become attendants on the All-
leading God, and no holder of strange doctrines will
follow after them any more.   Nay, even Lot has been
severed from their company, for he bent aside his soul
which had the capacity to grow up straight and unswerving.

XXXII. " And Abraham was," he says " seventy 176
and five years old when he went out from Haran "
(Gen. xii. 4).   On the number of the five and seventy
years, whose import agrees with what has just been
said, we will dwell in detail at a later time.   Let us
first examine the significance of Haran and the
removal from this country.   No one versed in the 177
Laws is likely to be unaware that at an earlier date
Abraham migrated from Chaldea and dwelt in Haran,
and that after his father's death there, he removes
from that country also, so that he has at this point
already quitted two places.   What remark 178
does this call for ?   The Chaldeans have the reputation of having, in a degree quite beyond that of other
peoples, elaborated astronomy and the casting of
nativities.   They have set up a harmony between
things on earth and things on high, between heavenly
things and earthly.   Following as it were the laws of
musical proportion,[b] they have exhibited the universe
as a perfect concord or symphony produced by a
sympathetic affinity between its parts, separated
indeed in space, but housemates in kinship.   These 179

184 θείου καὶ θνητοῦ συγκερασθέντων καὶ κατὰ τοὺς τῆς τελείας
μουσικῆς λόγους ἁρμοσθέντων.

μενον τοῦτον κόσμον ἐν τοῖς οὖσιν ὑπετόπησαν εἶναι
μόνον, ἢ θεὸν ὄντα αὐτὸν ἢ ἐν αὐτῷ θεὸν περιέχοντα, τὴν τῶν ὅλων ψυχήν· εἱμαρμένην τε καὶ
ἀνάγκην θεοπλαστήσαντες ἀσεβείας πολλῆς κατ-
έπλησαν τὸν ἀνθρώπινον βίον, ἀναδιδάξαντες ὡς
δίχα τῶν φαινομένων οὐδενός ἐστιν οὐδὲν αἴτιον
τὸ παράπαν, ἀλλ' ἡλίου καὶ σελήνης καὶ τῶν
ἄλλων ἀστέρων αἱ περίοδοι τά τε ἀγαθὰ καὶ τὰ
ἐναντία ἑκάστῳ τῶν ὄντων ἀπονέμουσι.

180 Μωυσῆς μέντοι τῇ μὲν ἐν τοῖς μέρεσι κοινωνίᾳ
καὶ συμπαθείᾳ τοῦ παντὸς ἔοικε συνεπιγράφεσθαι,
ἕνα καὶ γενητὸν ἀποφηνάμενος τὸν κόσμον εἶναι—
γενομένου γὰρ καὶ ἑνὸς ὑπάρχοντος εὔλογον τάς
γε στοιχειώδεις οὐσίας ὑποβεβλῆσθαι τοῖς ἀποτελου-
μένοις τὰς αὐτὰς ἅπασι κατὰ μέρη, καθάπερ ἐπὶ
σωμάτων συμβέβηκε τῶν ἡνωμένων ἀλληλουχεῖν—,

181 τῇ δὲ περὶ θεοῦ δόξῃ διαφέρεσθαι· μήτε γὰρ τὸν
κόσμον μήτε τὴν τοῦ κόσμου ψυχὴν τὸν πρῶτον
εἶναι θεὸν μηδὲ τοὺς ἀστέρας ἢ τὰς χορείας αὐτῶν
τὰ πρεσβύτατα τῶν συμβαινόντων ἀνθρώποις αἴτια,
ἀλλὰ συνέχεσθαι μὲν τόδε τὸ πᾶν ἀοράτοις δυνάμεσιν, ἃς ἀπὸ γῆς ἐσχάτων ἄχρις οὐρανοῦ περάτων
ὁ δημιουργὸς ἀπέτεινε, τοῦ μὴ ἀνεθῆναι τὰ δεθέντα
καλῶς προμηθούμενος· δεσμοὶ γὰρ αἱ δυνάμεις τοῦ

182 παντὸς ἄρρηκτοι.   διό, κἄν που τῆς
νομοθεσίας λέγηται " ὁ θεὸς ἐν τῷ οὐρανῷ ἄνω καὶ
ἐπὶ τῆς γῆς κάτω," μηδεὶς ὑποτοπησάτω τὸν κατὰ

---

[a] Cf. Leg. All. i. 91 and note.   [b] See App. p. 565.
[c] Or perhaps " taking wise forethought that what was
bound," etc.   But I think the passage is probably reminiscent
of Timaeus 41A τὸ καλῶς ἁρμοσθὲν καὶ ἔχον εὖ λύειν ἐθέλειν
κακοῦ.   For the position of καλῶς cf. De Dec. 27 τὰ γεγονότα
καλῶς θεωρεῖν.

men imagined that this visible universe was the only thing in existence, either being itself God or containing God in itself as the soul of the whole.[a] And they made Fate and Necessity divine, thus filling human life with much impiety, by teaching that apart from phenomena there is no originating cause of anything whatever, but that the circuits of sun and moon and of the other heavenly bodies determine for every being in existence both good things and their opposites. Moses, however, while he seems 180 to confirm the sympathetic affinity of its parts displayed throughout the universe, is at variance with their opinion concerning God. He endorses the former doctrine by declaring the universe to be one and to have been made ; for if it came into being and is one, it stands to reason that all its completed several parts have the same elementary substances for their substratum, on the principle that interdependence of the parts is a characteristic of bodies which constitute a unity.[b] He differs from their opinion about 181 God, holding that neither the universe nor its soul is the primal God, and that the constellations or their revolutions are not the primary causes of the things that happen to men. Nay, he teaches that the complete whole around us is held together by invisible powers, which the Creator has made to reach from the ends of the earth to heaven's furthest bounds, taking forethought that what was well bound [c] should not be loosened : for the powers of the Universe are chains that cannot be broken. Wherefore, even 182 though it be said somewhere in the Law-book " God in heaven above and on the earth below " (Deut. iv. 39), let no one suppose that He that is is spoken of,

τὸ εἶναι λέγεσθαι—τὸ γὰρ ὂν περιέχειν ἀλλ' οὐ
περιέχεσθαι θέμις—, δύναμιν δ' αὐτοῦ, καθ' ἣν
183 ἔθηκε καὶ διετάξατο καὶ διεκόσμησε τὰ ὅλα. αὕτη
δὲ κυρίως ἐστὶν ἀγαθότης, φθόνον μὲν τὸν μισ-
άρετον καὶ μισόκαλον ἀπεληλακυῖα ἀφ' ἑαυτῆς,
χάριτας δὲ γεννῶσα αἷς τὰ μὴ ὄντα εἰς γένεσιν
ἄγουσα ἀνέφηνεν· ἐπεὶ τό γε ὂν φαντασιαζόμενον
δόξῃ πανταχοῦ πρὸς ἀλήθειαν οὐδαμοῦ φαίνεται, ὡς
ἀψευδέστατον ἐκεῖνο εἶναι τὸν χρησμόν, ἐν ᾧ
[465] λέλεκται· | " ὧδε ἐγώ," ἄδεικτος ὡς ἂν δεικνύ-
μενος, ἀόρατος ὡς ἂν ὁρατὸς ὤν, " πρὸ τοῦ σέ".
πρὸ γὰρ παντὸς τοῦ γενητοῦ, ἔξω βαίνων ἐκείνου
καὶ μηδενὶ τῶν μετ' αὐτὸν ἐμφερόμενος.

184 XXXIII. Τούτων λεγομένων ἐπὶ τῇ τῆς Χαλδαϊκῆς δόξης ἀνατροπῇ τοὺς ἔτι τὴν γνώμην
χαλδαΐζοντας μετακλίνειν καὶ μετακαλεῖν οἴεται
δεῖν ἐπὶ τὴν ἀλήθειαν, τῆς διδασκαλίας ἀρχόμενος
ὧδε· τί, φησίν, ὦ θαυμάσιοι, τοσοῦτον αἰφνίδιον
ἀρθέντες ἀπὸ γῆς εἰς ὕψος ἐπινήχεσθε καὶ τὸν ἀέρα
ὑπερκύψαντες αἰθεροβατεῖτε, ὡς ἡλίου κινήσεις καὶ
σελήνης περιόδους καὶ τῶν ἄλλων ἀστέρων τὰς
ἐμμελεῖς καὶ ἀοιδίμους ἀκριβοῦν χορείας; ταῦτα
γὰρ μείζονα ἢ κατὰ τὰς ὑμετέρας ἐστὶν ἐπινοίας
ἅτε εὐδαιμονεστέρας καὶ θειοτέρας μοίρας λαχόντα.

ᵃ Cf. De Conf. 138 and De Sac. 67 (with note).
ᵇ The meaning is that while the Pentateuch contains the
just-mentioned disproof of astrology, *at the same time* (note
the present λεγομένων) it gives practical advice to those
inclined that way. This advice is given in the statement
that " Abraham went from Chaldaea to Haran," it being
implied that these persons should do the same. What
" going to Haran " means is expanded into the discourse
of §§ 184 ff.

since the existent Being can contain, but cannot be contained. What is meant is that potency of His by which He established and ordered and marshalled the whole realm of being. This potency is nothing else 183 than loving-kindness ; it has driven away from itself envy with its hatred of virtue and of moral beauty ; it is the mother of gracious deeds by which, bringing into created existence things that were not, it displayed them to view ; for that which is, though in opinion it be imagined everywhere, in reality shews itself nowhere, so that that is a most true oracle in which the words " Here am I " which describe Him— Him that cannot be pointed out, as though He were being pointed out, Him that is invisible, as though He were visible—are followed by the words, " before that thou wert made " (Ex. xvii. 6)[a] : for He is before all creation ; His goings are outside it ; nor is He present in any of the things that come after Him.

XXXIII. All this is said to refute the Chaldean 184 opinion, but side by side[b] with this Moses deems it his duty to change the way of thinking of those whose judgement still inclines to Chaldeanism, and to recall them to the truth, and he begins his lesson in this way : " How strange it is, my friends, that you have been suddenly lifted to such a height above the earth and are floating there, and, leaving the lower air beneath you, are treading the ether above, thinking to master every detail respecting the movements of the sun, and of the circuits of the moon, and of the glorious rhythmical dances of the other constellations. These[c] are too high to be reached by your powers of thought, for a lot is theirs happy and divine beyond

[c] *i.e.*, the sun, etc., as usual in Philo regarded as divine beings.

185 κατάβητε οὖν ἀπ᾽ οὐρανοῦ καὶ καταβάντες μὴ
πάλιν γῆν καὶ θάλατταν καὶ ποταμοὺς καὶ φυτῶν
καὶ ζῴων ἰδέας ἐξετάζετε, μόνους δὲ ἑαυτοὺς καὶ
τὴν ἑαυτῶν φύσιν ἐρευνᾶτε, μὴ ἑτέρωθι μᾶλλον
οἰκήσαντες ἢ παρ᾽ ἑαυτοῖς· διαθεώμενοι γὰρ τὰ
κατὰ τὸν ἴδιον οἶκον, τὸ δεσπόζον ἐν αὐτῷ, τὸ
ὑπήκοον, τὸ ἔμψυχον, τὸ ἄψυχον, τὸ λογικόν, τὸ
ἄλογον, τὸ ἀθάνατον, τὸ θνητόν, τὸ ἄμεινον, τὸ
χεῖρον, εὐθὺς ἐπιστήμην θεοῦ καὶ τῶν ἔργων αὐτοῦ
186 σαφῆ λήψεσθε. λογιεῖσθε γὰρ ὅτι, ὡς ἐν ὑμῖν ἐστι
νοῦς, καὶ τῷ παντί ἐστι, καὶ ὡς ὁ ὑμέτερος ἀρχὴν
καὶ δεσποτείαν τῶν περὶ ὑμᾶς ἀναψάμενος ἕκαστον
τῶν μερῶν ὑπήκοον ἀπέφηνεν ἑαυτῷ, οὕτω καὶ ὁ
τοῦ παντὸς τὴν ἡγεμονίαν περιβεβλημένος αὐτοκράτορι νόμῳ καὶ δίκῃ τὸν κόσμον ἡνιοχεῖ προμη-
θούμενος οὐ τῶν ἀξιονικοτέρων αὐτὸ μόνον ἀλλὰ
καὶ τῶν ἀφανεστέρων εἶναι δοκούντων.

187 XXXIV. μεταναστάντες οὖν ἀπὸ τῆς κατ᾽ οὐρανὸν
περιεργίας ἑαυτούς, ὅπερ εἶπον, οἰκήσατε, τὴν μὲν
Χαλδαίων γῆν, δόξαν, καταλιπόντες, μετοικισά-
μενοι δὲ εἰς Χαρράν, τὸ τῆς αἰσθήσεως χωρίον,
188 ὃ δὴ σωματικός ἐστιν οἶκος διανοίας. Χαρρὰν γὰρ
ἑρμηνεύεται τρώγλη, τρῶγλαι δὲ σύμβολα αἰσθήσεως ὀπῶν[1] εἰσίν· ὀπὰς γὰρ καὶ φωλεοὺς τρόπον τινὰ
ὀφθαλμοὺς μὲν ὁράσεως, ἀκοῆς δὲ ὦτα, ῥῖνας δὲ
ὀσμῶν καὶ γεύσεως φάρυγγα καὶ πᾶσαν τὴν σώ-
189 ματος κατασκευὴν ἁφῆς εἶναι συμβέβηκε. τούτοις
οὖν ἔτι διατρίψαντες[2] ἐνηρεμήσατε καὶ σχολάσατε
καὶ τὴν ἑκάστου φύσιν ὡς ἔνι μάλιστα ἀκριβώσατε,

---

[1] mss. τόπων.　　　　　　　　　　　　[2] ἐπιδιατρίψαντες.

the common. Come down therefore from heaven, 185 and, when you have come down, do not begin in turn to pass in review earth and sea and rivers, and plants and animals in their various kinds ; but explore yourselves only and your own nature, and make your abode with yourselves and not elsewhere : for by observing the conditions prevailing in your own individual household, the element that is master in it, and that which is in subjection, the living and the lifeless element, the rational and the irrational, the immortal and the mortal, the better and the worse, you will gain forthwith a sure knowledge of God and of His works. Your reason will shew you that, as 186 there is mind in you, so is there in the universe, and that as your mind has taken upon itself sovereign control of all that is in you, and brought every part into subjection to itself, so too He, that is endued with lordship over all, guides and controls the universe by the law and right of an absolute sway, taking forethought not only for those which are of greater, but for those which are of less importance in our eyes.

XXXIV. Quit, then, your meddling with 187 heavenly concerns, and take up your abode, as I have said, in yourselves ; leave behind you opinion, the country of the Chaldeans, and migrate to Haran, the place of sense-perception, which is understanding's bodily tenement. For the translation of Haran is 188 " hole," and holes are figures of openings used by sense-perception : for eyes are, in a way, openings and lairs used by sight, ears by hearing, nostrils to receive scents, the throat for tasting, and the whole structure of the body for touch. Gain, therefore, by 189 a further sojourn, a peaceful and unhurried familiarity with these, and to the utmost of your power get an

καὶ τὸ ἐν ἑκάστοις εὖ τε καὶ χεῖρον καταμαθ
τὸ μὲν φύγετε, τὸ δ' ἔμπαλιν ἑλέσθε.
ἐπειδὰν μέντοι σφόδρα ἀκριβῶς πάντα τὸν ἴ

[466] διασκέψησθε οἶκον καὶ ὃν ἔχει λόγον ἕκαστον
τῶν μερῶν αὐγάσησθε, διακινήσαντες αὐτοὺ
ἐνθένδε μετανάστασιν ζητεῖτε, οὐ θάνατον

190 ἀθανασίαν καταγγέλλουσαν. ἧς δείγματα σαφ
ἐν τοῖς σωματικοῖς καὶ ἐν τοῖς αἰσθητοῖς ἐγκατε
μένοι φωλεοῖς κατόψεσθε, τοτὲ μὲν ἐν τοῖς βα
ὕπνοις—ἀναχωρήσας γὰρ ὁ νοῦς καὶ τῶν αἰσθή
καὶ τῶν ἄλλων ὅσα κατὰ τὸ σῶμα ὑπεξε
ἑαυτῷ προσομιλεῖν ἄρχεται ὡς πρὸς κάτο
ἀφορῶν ἀλήθειαν, καὶ ἀπορρυψάμενος πάνθ' ὅ
τῶν κατὰ τὰς αἰσθήσεις φαντασιῶν ἀπεμάξατ
περὶ τῶν μελλόντων ἀψευδεστάτας διὰ τῶν ὀν
μαντείας[1] ἐνθουσιᾷ—, τοτὲ δὲ κἂν ταῖς ἐγρηγόρ

191 ὅταν γὰρ ἔκ τινος τῶν κατὰ φιλοσοφίαν
σχεθεὶς θεωρημάτων ἀχθῇ πρὸς αὐτοῦ, τῷ
ἕπεται, τῶν δ' ἄλλων ὅσα κατὰ τὸν σωμα
ὄγκον ἀμνημονεῖ δήπου. κἂν ἐμποδίζωσ
αἰσθήσεις πρὸς τὴν ἀκριβῆ θέαν τοῦ νοητοῦ,
τοῖς φιλοθεάμοσι καθαιρεῖν αὐτῶν τὴν ἐπίθεσι
τε γὰρ ὄψεις καταμύουσι καὶ τὰ ὦτα ἐπιφράτ
καὶ τὰς τῶν ἄλλων ⟨αἰσθήσεων⟩ ἐπέχουσιν
καὶ ἐν ἐρημίᾳ καὶ σκότῳ διατρίβειν ἀξιοῦσι
μὴ πρός τινος αἰσθητοῦ τὸ ψυχῆς ὄμμα, ᾧ
βλέπειν ἔδωκεν ὁ θεός, ἐπισκιασθῇ.

192 XXXV. τοῦτον μέντοι τὸν τρόπον μαθόντες

---

[1] Mangey (and also H²) ταῖς . . ἀψευδεστάταις . . μα
which perhaps suits the construction better. No exam
given in the Lexica of an accusative in this sense
ἐνθουσιᾶν.

exact knowledge of the nature of each, and, when you have thoroughly learned what is good and bad in each, shun the one, and choose the other.

And when you have surveyed all your individual dwelling with absolute exactitude, and have acquired an insight into the true nature of each of its parts, bestir yourselves and seek for your departure hence, for it is a call not to death but to immortality. You will be able to descry sure indications of this, even while held fast in the dens and caves of the body and of the objects of sense. In deep sleep the mind quits its place, and, withdrawing from the perceptions and all other bodily faculties, begins to hold converse with itself, fixing its gaze on truth as on a mirror, and, having purged away as defilements all the impressions made upon it by the mental pictures presented by the senses, it is filled with Divine frenzy and discerns in dreams absolutely true prophecies concerning things to come. Thus is it at times. Or again it may be in waking hours. For when the mind, possessed by some philosophic principle, is drawn by it, it follows this, and needs must be oblivious of other things, of all the concerns of the cumbersome body. And if the senses are a hindrance to the exact sight of the spiritual object, those who find happiness in beholding are at pains to crush their attack ; they shut their eyes, and stop up their ears, and check the impulses bred by their other senses, and deem it well to spend their days in solitude and darkness, that no object of sense-perception may bedim the eye of the soul, to which God has given the power to see things spiritual. XXXV. If in this way you learn to effect a divorce ^a from what

---

^a For this legal phrase see note on *De Cher.* 115.

λεῖψιν τοῦ θνητοῦ χρηματίζειν καὶ τὰς περὶ τοῦ
ἀγενήτου παιδευθήσεσθε δόξας· εἰ μὴ νομίζετε τὸν
μὲν ὑμέτερον νοῦν ἀποδυσάμενον σῶμα, αἴσθησιν,
λόγον, δίχα τούτων γυμνὰ[1] δύνασθαι τὰ ὄντα ὁρᾶν,
τὸν δὲ τῶν ὅλων νοῦν, τὸν θεόν, οὐκ ἔξω τῆς ὑλικῆς
φύσεως πάσης ἑστάναι περιέχοντα, οὐ περιεχόμενον
καὶ οὐκ ἐπινοίᾳ μόνον ἐπεξεληλυθέναι ὥσπερ ἄνθρωπον, ἀλλὰ καὶ τῷ οὐσιώδει, οἷα ἁρμόττει θεόν.

193 ὁ μὲν γὰρ ἡμέτερος νοῦς οὐ δεδημιούργηκε τὸ
σῶμα, ἀλλ' ἔστιν ἔργον ἑτέρου· διὸ καὶ περιέχεται,
ὡς ἐν ἀγγείῳ τῷ σώματι. ὁ δὲ τῶν ὅλων νοῦς τὸ
πᾶν γεγέννηκε, τὸ πεποιηκὸς δὲ τοῦ γενομένοι
κρεῖττον· ὥστ' οὐκ ἂν ἐμφέροιτο τῷ χείρονι, δίχα
τοῦ μηδὲ ἁρμόττειν πατέρα ἐν υἱῷ περιέχεσθαι
υἱὸν δὲ ταῖς τοῦ πατρὸς ἐπιμελείαις συναύξεσθαι

194   οὕτω κατὰ βραχὺ μεταβαίνων ὁ νοῦς
ἐπὶ τὸν εὐσεβείας καὶ ὁσιότητος ἀφίξεται πατέρα
γενεθλιαλογικῆς ἀποστὰς τὸ πρῶτον, ἥτις παρ-
έπεισεν αὐτὸν ὑπολαβεῖν τὸν κόσμον θεὸν τὸν
πρῶτον εἶναι, ἀλλὰ μὴ τοῦ πρώτου θεοῦ δημιούρ-
γημα, καὶ τὰς τῶν ἀστέρων φοράς τε καὶ κινήσεις αἰτίας ἀνθρώποις κακοπραγίας καὶ τοὐναντίον

195 εὐδαιμονίας.   ἔπειτ' εἰς τὴν ἐπίσκεψιν
ἐλθὼν τὴν αὐτὸς ἑαυτοῦ, φιλοσοφήσας τὰ κατὰ τὸν
ἴδιον οἶκον, τὰ περὶ σώματος, τὰ περὶ αἰσθήσεως,
τὰ περὶ λόγου, καὶ γνοὺς κατὰ τὸ ποιητικὸν γράμμα

[467] ὅττι τοι ἐν μεγάροισι κακόν τ' ἀγαθόν τε
       τέτυκται,

---

[1] mss. γυμνὸν. this correction of Wendland's, though sup
ported by the run of the sentence, and perhaps by § 90
seems to me doubtful.

is mortal, you will go on to receive an education in your conceptions regarding the Uncreate. For you surely do not imagine that, while your mind, having divested itself of body, sense-perception, speech, can, apart from these, see in their nakedness[a] the things that are, the Mind of the universe, God, has not His abiding-place outside all material nature, containing, not contained, or doubt that He has gone forth beyond its confines not in thought alone, as man does, but in essential being also, as befits God. For our mind 193 has not created the body, but is the workmanship of Another ; and it is therefore contained in the body as in a vessel. But the Mind of all things has brought the universe into existence ; and that which has made is superior to the thing made, so that it could not be included in its inferior ; nor indeed would it be fitting that a father should be contained in a son, but rather that a son should attain full growth under his father's care.   In this way the mind 194 gradually changing its place will arrive at the Father of piety and holiness. Its first step is to relinquish astrology, which betrayed it into the belief that the universe is the primal God, instead of being the handywork of the primal God, and that the courses and movements of the constellations are the causes of bad and good fortune to mankind.

Next it enters upon the consideration of itself, makes 195 a study of the features of its own abode, those that concern the body and sense-perception, and speech, and comes to know, as the phrase of the poet puts it,

> All that existeth of good and of ill in the halls of thy homestead.[b]

[a] Or " when thus naked " ; see critical note.
[b] Hom. Od. iv. 392.

ἔπειτ' ἀνατεμὼν ὁδὸν τὴν ἀφ' αὑτοῦ
καὶ διὰ ταύτης ἐλπίσας τὸν δυστόπαστον καὶ
δυστέκμαρτον πατέρα τῶν ὅλων κατανοῆσαι, μαθὼν
ἀκριβῶς ἑαυτὸν εἴσεται τάχα που καὶ θεόν, οὐκέτι
μένων ἐν Χαρράν, τοῖς αἰσθήσεως ὀργάνοις, ἀλλ' εἰς
ἑαυτὸν ἐπιστραφείς· ἀμήχανον γὰρ ἔτι κινούμενον
αἰσθητῶς μᾶλλον ἢ νοητῶς πρὸς τὴν τοῦ ὄντος
196 ἐλθεῖν ἐπίσκεψιν. XXXVI. οὗ χάριν καὶ
ὁ ταχθεὶς τὴν ἀρίστην τάξιν παρὰ θεῷ τρόπος,
ὄνομα Σαμουήλ, οὐχ ὑφηγεῖται τὰ τῆς βασιλείας
δίκαια τῷ Σαοὺλ [οὐδ'] ἔτι διατρίβοντι ἐν τοῖς
σκεύεσιν, ἀλλ' ἐπειδὰν ἐκεῖθεν αὐτὸν ἐξελκύσῃ.
πυνθάνεται μὲν γάρ, εἰ ἔτι ἔρχεται ἐνθάδε ὁ ἀνήρ,
ἀποκρίνεται δὲ τὸ λόγιον· " ἰδοὺ αὐτὸς κέκρυπται
197 ἐν τοῖς σκεύεσι." τί οὖν προσήκει τὸν ἀκούσαντα,
φύσει παιδευτικὸν ὄντα, ποιῆσαι, ὅτι μὴ μετὰ
σπουδῆς αὐτὸν ἐξελκύσαι; " ἐπιδραμὼν " γάρ
φησι " λαμβάνει αὐτὸν ἐκεῖθεν," διότι τοῖς ἀγγείοις
τῆς ψυχῆς, σώματι καὶ αἰσθήσει, ⟨ἐν⟩διατρίβων
οὐκ ἦν ἀξιόχρεως ἀκοῦσαι τῶν τῆς βασιλείας
δογμάτων καὶ νόμων—βασιλείαν δὲ σοφίαν εἶναι
λέγομεν, ἐπεὶ καὶ τὸν σοφὸν βασιλέα—, μεταστὰς
δέ, ἡνίκα τῆς ἀχλύος σκεδασθείσης ὀξυδορκήσειν
ἔμελλεν. εἰκότως οὖν καὶ τὴν αἰσθήσεως χώραν,
ὄνομα Χαρράν, ἀπολιπεῖν οἴεται δεῖν ὁ ἐπιστήμης
ἑταῖρος.
198 Ἀπολείπει δὲ ἐτῶν γεγονὼς πέντε καὶ ἑβδομή-
κοντα· ὁ δὲ ἀριθμὸς οὗτος αἰσθητῆς καὶ νοητῆς.

---

[a] Not so much to examine its own nature, which is not
ruled out in Haran, cf. § 185, but to attain the detached and
mystical condition described in § 190.

The third stage is when, having opened up the road that leads from self, in hope thereby to come to discern the Universal Father, so hard to trace and unriddle, it will crown maybe the accurate self-knowledge it has gained with the knowledge of God Himself. It will stay no longer in Haran, the organs of sense, but withdraw into itself.[a] For it is impossible that the mind whose course still lies in the sensible rather than the mental should arrive at the contemplation of Him that is. XXXVI. This 196 is why the character appointed to the highest post in God's service, who is called " Samuel," does not set forth the duties of kingship to Saul, while still lingering amid the baggage, but when he has drawn him out thence. For he inquires of the Lord whether the man is still on his way hither, and the divine reply is, " Lo, he hath hidden himself among the baggage." What, then, does it become the recipient of this 197 answer to do, endowed as he is by nature with power to exercise discipline, save to draw him forth with all haste ? So we read, " he ran thither and taketh him thence " (1 Sam. x. 22 f.), because, while lingering amid such vessels of the soul as body and sense-perception, he was not competent to listen to the principles and rules of kingship—and we pronounce wisdom to be kingship, for we pronounce the wise man to be a king. These principles could only be learnt through his changing his place, when the dark mist would disperse and he would have keen vision. No wonder, then, that the associate of knowledge deems it necessary to quit also the country of sense-perception, called Haran.

When he quits the country he is five and seventy 198 years old ; and this number represents the border-

πρεσβυτέρας τε καὶ νεωτέρας, ἔτι δὲ φθαρτῆς καὶ
199 ἀφθάρτου μεθόριος φύσεώς ἐστι. νοητὸς μὲν γὰρ
καὶ πρεσβύτερος καὶ ἄφθαρτος λόγος ὁ τῶν ἑβδομήκοντα, αἰσθητὸς δὲ καὶ νεώτερος ὁ ταῖς πέντε
ἰσάριθμος ὢν αἰσθήσεσι. τούτῳ καὶ ὁ ἔτι γυμνα-
ζόμενος[1] ἀσκητὴς ἐξετάζεται, μηδέπω δεδυνημένος
ἐνέγκασθαι τὰ τέλεια νικητήρια· λέγεται γὰρ ὅτι
" ἦσαν αἱ πᾶσαι ψυχαὶ ἐξ Ἰακὼβ πέντε καὶ ἑβδο-
200 μήκοντα". τοῦ[2] γὰρ ἀθλοῦντος καὶ τὸν ὑπὲρ κτή-
σεως ἀρετῆς ἱερὸν ὄντως ἀγῶνα μὴ διαφθείροντος
ψυχαὶ μὲν πρὸ σωμάτων γεννήματα, οὔπω δ'
ἐκτετμημέναι[3] τὸ ἄλογον, ἀλλ' ἔτι τὸν αἰσθήσεως
ὄχλον ἐφελκόμεναι. παλαίοντος γὰρ καὶ κονιομένου
καὶ πτερνίζοντος Ἰακὼβ ἐστιν ὄνομα, οὐ νενικη-
201 κότος· ὅταν δὲ τὸν θεὸν ὁρᾶν ἱκανὸς εἶναι δόξας
Ἰσραὴλ μετονομασθῇ, μόνῳ χρήσεται τῷ ἑβδομη-
[468] κοστῷ λόγῳ, | τὴν πεντάδα τῶν αἰσθήσεων ἐκ-
τεμών· λέγεται γὰρ ὅτι " ἐν ἑβδομήκοντα ψυχαῖς
κατέβησαν οἱ πατέρες σου εἰς Αἴγυπτον."
οὗτός ἐστιν ὁ ἀριθμὸς Μωυσέως τοῦ σοφοῦ γνώρι-
μος· τοὺς γὰρ ἀριστίνδην ἐκ παντὸς τοῦ πλήθους
ἐπιλελεγμένους ἑβδομήκοντα εἶναι συμβέβηκε καὶ
πρεσβυτέρους ἅπαντας, οὐχ ἡλικίαις ἀλλὰ φρονήσει
καὶ βουλαῖς, γνώμαις τε καὶ ἀρχαιοτρόποις ζηλώ-
202 σεσιν.   οὗτος ὁ ἀριθμὸς ἱερουργεῖταί τε
καὶ ἀποδίδοται θεῷ, ὅταν οἱ τέλειοι τῆς ψυχῆς

---

[1] mss. ἐπιγυμναζόμενος.   [2] mss. τούτου.
[3] mss. δὲ κεκτημέναι, which Mangey follows, reading τὸν
λόγον with H² for τὸ ἄλογον.

---

[a] Or "fail in," "spoil." For this rather curious use of
διαφθείρω cf. De Cong. 165 τὸν ἀγῶνα τοῦ βίου διήθλησαν
ἀδιάφθορον καὶ ἀήττητον φυλάξαντες.

land between perceptible and intelligible being, between older and younger, between corruptible and incorruptible. For seventy represents the principle 199 of intellectual apprehension, of seniority and of incorruption, while the principle that corresponds numerically to the five senses is that of juniority and sense-perception. Under the head of this principle is classed the Trainer of self still at his exercises, not yet qualified to carry off the prize of complete victory; for we read, " the full number of souls sprung from Jacob was five and seventy " (Ex. i. 5) : for the 200 offspring of the champion who does not make havoc[a] of the truly holy contest for the winning of virtue, are not bodies but souls, souls from which the irrational element has not yet been eliminated, and which still have sense-perception's gang hanging on to them. For " Jacob " is a name belonging to one wrestling, and preparing for the arena, and tripping up his adversary, not of one who has won the victory. But when, now deemed capable of seeing God, he 201 shall have received the new name of " Israel," he will have resort only to the principle of seventy, having cut out the five which pertains to the senses ; for it is written " amounting to seventy souls thy fathers went down into Egypt " (Deut. x. 22).

This is the number intimately associated with the wise Moses ; for the men picked out for their excellence from all the host were seventy, and all of them elders, not in age but in good sense and counsel and judgement and ways of thinking worthy of men of old. Sacrifices and dues paid 202 to God are determined by this number, whenever

συναχθῶσι καὶ συγκομισθῶσι καρποί· τῇ γὰρ τῶν
σκηνῶν ἑορτῇ χωρὶς τῶν ἄλλων θυμάτων ἑβδομήκοντα μόσχους ἀνάγειν θυσίαν ὁλόκαυστον διείρηται. κατὰ τὸν ἑβδομηκοστὸν λόγον καὶ αἱ τῶν
ἀρχόντων φιάλαι κατασκευάζονται—ἑκάστη γὰρ
ἑβδομήκοντα σίκλων ἐστιν ὁλκῆς—, ἐπειδὴ τὰ
ἔνσπονδα καὶ συμβατήρια καὶ φίλα τῆς ψυχῆς ὡς
ἀληθῶς ὁλκὸν ἔχει δύναμιν, τὸν ἑβδομηκοστὸν καὶ
ἅγιον λόγον, ὃν Αἴγυπτος, ἡ μισάρετος καὶ φιλο-
παθὴς φύσις, πενθοῦσα εἰσάγεται· ἑβδομήκοντα γὰρ
ἡμέραις καταριθμεῖται παρ' αὐτοῖς τὸ πένθος.

203 XXXVII. Οὗτος μὲν οὖν ὁ ἀριθμός, ὡς ἔφην,
Μωυσέως γνώριμος, ὁ δὲ τῶν πέντε αἰσθήσεων τοῦ
καὶ τὸ σῶμα καὶ τὰ ἐκτὸς ἀσπαζομένου, ὃν ἔθος
καλεῖν Ἰωσήφ. τοσαύτην γὰρ αὐτῶν ἐπιμέλειαν
πεποίηται, ὥστε τὸν μὲν ὁμογάστριον ἀδελφόν, τὸν
αἰσθήσεως ἔκγονον ὄντα—ἥκιστα γὰρ ὁμοπατρίους
οἶδε—, πέντε ἐξάλλοις δωρεῖται στολαῖς, διαπρεπεῖς
ἡγούμενος τὰς αἰσθήσεις καὶ κόσμου καὶ τιμῆς
204 ἀξίας. ὅλῃ δὲ Αἰγύπτῳ καὶ νόμους ἀναγράφει,
ὅπως τιμῶσιν αὐτὰς καὶ φόρους καὶ δασμοὺς ὡς
βασιλεῦσιν ἀνὰ πᾶν ἔτος κομίζωσι· τὸν γὰρ σῖτον
ἀποπεμπτοῦν κελεύει, τὸ δέ ἐστιν ὕλας καὶ τροφὰς
ἀφθόνους θησαυροφυλακεῖν ταῖς πέντε αἰσθήσεσιν,
ὅπως ἑκάστη τῶν οἰκείων ἀνεπισχέτως ἐμπιπλα-
μένη τρυφᾷ καὶ τὸν νοῦν τοῖς ἐπεισφορουμένοις
βαρύνουσα βαπτίζῃ· ταῖς γὰρ τῶν αἰσθήσεων

---

[a] The translation is an attempt to preserve something of
the play on words, ὁλκή weight (lit. "drawing down of the
scale ") suggesting ὁλκός "attracting."

the ripe fruits of the soul are gathered in and collected; for it is prescribed at the Feast of Tabernacles, over and above the other sacrifices, to offer seventy young bullocks as a burnt offering (Num. xxix. 13-36). The bowls of the princes are fashioned in keeping with the principle of seventy—for each of them is of the weight of seventy shekels (Num. vii. 13 ff.)—since everything in the soul that tends to peace and friendship and agreement has a truly weighty power[a] of attraction, that sacred principle set forth by seventy, which Egypt, the virtue-hating and passion-loving nature, is represented as mourning over; for among them mourning is reckoned as lasting seventy days (Gen. l. 3).

XXXVII. This number, then, is, as I have said, 203 intimately associated with Moses; but the number belonging to the five senses with him who hails as friends the body and the things outside the body, him who is usually called "Joseph." So great is his devotion to these, that, while hardly owning the tie of a common fatherhood, he bestows upon his uterine brother, the offspring of sense-perception, five changes of raiment (Gen. xlv. 22), deeming the senses pre-eminent and deserving of adornment and honour. He sets up laws moreover for all Egypt, 204 that honour may be paid to the senses and tribute and contributions rendered to them as sovereigns every year: for he commands the Egyptians to pay a fifth part of the corn, which means that they are to store in treasuries materials and food in abundance for the five senses, that so each of them incessantly glutting itself with its own objects may wanton and drown the mind under the weight of all that it devours. For understanding is starved when the senses feast,

εὐωχίαις λιμὸν ἄγει διάνοια, ὡς ἔμπαλιν ταῖς
205 νηστείαις εὐφροσύνας.　　　　οὐχ ὁρᾷς ὅτι
καὶ πέντε Σαλπαὰδ θυγατέρες, ἃς ἀλληγοροῦντες
αἰσθήσεις εἶναί φαμεν, ἐκ τοῦ δήμου Μανασσῆ
γεγόνασιν, ὃς υἱὸς Ἰωσήφ ἐστι, χρόνῳ μὲν πρεσβύτερος ὤν, δυνάμει δὲ νεώτερος; εἰκότως· καλεῖται
γὰρ ἐκ λήθης, τὸ δὲ ἰσοδυναμοῦν ἐστι πρᾶγμα
ἀναμνήσει.[1] ἀνάμνησις δὲ τὰ δευτερεῖα φέρεται
μνήμης, ἧς Ἐφραῒμ ἐπώνυμος γέγονεν, ὃς καρπο-
φορία μεταληφθεὶς προσαγορεύεται· καρπὸς δὲ κάλ-
λιστος καὶ τροφιμώτατος ψυχῆς τὸ ἄληστον ἐν
206 μνήμαις. λέγουσι γοῦν τὰ ἐναρμόνια ἑαυταῖς αἱ
παρθένοι· " ὁ πατὴρ ἡμῶν ἀπέθανεν "—ἀλλ' ὁ
θάνατος ἀναμνήσεώς ἐστι λήθη—" καὶ ἀπέθανεν οὐ
δι' ἁμαρτίαν ἑαυτοῦ "—παγκάλως· οὐ γὰρ ἑκούσιον
[469] ἡ λήθη | πάθος, ἀλλ' ἔν τι τῶν οὐ παρ' ἡμῖν, ἐπι-
γινόμενον ἔξωθεν— " υἱοὶ δὲ οὐκ ἐγένοντο αὐτῷ,"
ἀλλὰ θυγατέρες, ἐπειδὴ τὸ μὲν μνημονικὸν ἅτε φύσει
δ ιανιστάμενον[2] ἀρρενογονεῖ, τὸ δὲ ἐπιλανθανόμενον
ὕπνῳ λογισμοῦ χρώμενον θηλυτοκεῖ· ἄλογον γάρ,
ἀλόγου δὲ μέρους ψυχῆς αἰσθήσεις θυγατέρες.

207　　Εἰ δέ τις τὸν μὲν τάχει παρέδραμε, Μωυσῆ δὲ
ἠκολούθησε, μήπω δυνηθεὶς ἰσόδρομος αὐτῷ
γενέσθαι κεκραμένῳ καὶ μιγάδι ἀριθμῷ χρήσεται,
τῷ πέμπτῳ καὶ ἑβδομηκοστῷ, ὅς ἐστι σύμβολον
αἰσθητῆς καὶ νοητῆς φύσεως, συγκεκραμένων[3]
ἀμφοῖν εἰς εἴδους ἑνὸς ἀνεπιλήπτου[4] γένεσιν.
208　　XXXVIII. ἄγαμαι σφόδρα καὶ τὴν

---

[1] MSS. αἰσθήσει(ς).
[2] The present can hardly give the required meaning
"awake." I suggest διανεσταμένον. See App. p. 565.
[3] MSS. συναραμένων, συναρομένων.
[4] Mangey ⟨οὐκ⟩ ἀνεπιλήπτου. See App. p. 565.

as on the other hand it makes merry when they are fasting. Do you not notice, that the five 205 daughters of Zelophehad, whom we take to be a figure of the senses, are of the tribe of Manasseh, who is Joseph's son, elder in age, younger in efficiency? Fitly is he younger, for his name means " from forgetfulness," and that is a thing equivalent to " recalling to mind." But the first prize goes to Memory, the second to Recollection, and Ephraim is named after Memory, for his name when translated is " Fruit-bearing," and the fairest and most nourishing fruit of the soul is remembering with no forgetfulness. And so the maidens say what perfectly fits in with 206 what they really are. " Our father died "—yes, the death of recollection is forgetfulness—" and he died by reason of no sin of his own "—quite rightly said, for forgetfulness is no voluntary experience, but one of those things that are not in our power, coming upon us from outside—" and he had no sons " (Num. xxvii. 3), but only daughters, for whereas the faculty of memory, being naturally wide awake, has male progeny, forgetfulness, wrapt in a slumber of reasoning power, has female offspring ; for it is irrational, and the senses are daughters of the irrational portion of the soul.

But if anyone has outstripped Joseph in speed and 207 followed Moses, while he still lacks power to keep pace with him, he will live under a mixed and hybrid number, namely seventy-five, which denotes the nature alike of mind and sense-perception, which are both mingled together to produce a single kind, that does not call for our censure.[a]   XXXVIII.

[a] See App. p. 565.

ὑπομονὴν Ῥεβέκκαν, ἐπειδὰν τῷ τελείῳ τὴν ψυχὴν
καὶ τὰς τῶν παθῶν καὶ κακιῶν τραχύτητας καθ-
ῃρηκότι παραινῇ τότε εἰς Χαρρὰν ἀποδρᾶναι· λέγει
γάρ· "νῦν οὖν, τέκνον, ἄκουσον τῆς φωνῆς μου καὶ
ἀναστὰς ἀπόδραθι πρὸς Λάβαν τὸν ἀδελφόν μου εἰς
Χαρρὰν καὶ οἴκησον μετ' αὐτοῦ ἡμέρας τινάς, ἕως
τοῦ ἀποστρέψαι τὸν θυμὸν καὶ τὴν ὀργὴν τοῦ
ἀδελφοῦ σου ἀπὸ σοῦ, καὶ ἐπιλάθηται ἃ πεποίηκας
209 αὐτῷ." παγκάλως δὲ τὴν ἐπὶ τὰς αἰσθήσεις ὁδὸν
δρασμὸν εἴρηκεν· ὄντως γὰρ δραπέτης ὁ νοῦς τότε
γίνεται, ὅταν καταλιπὼν τὰ οἰκεῖα ἑαυτῷ νοητὰ
τράπηται πρὸς τὸ ἐναντίον τάγμα τῶν αἰσθητῶν.
ἔστι δὲ ὅπου καὶ τὸ δραπετεύειν χρήσιμον, ἐπειδάν
τις αὐτὸ ποιῇ μὴ ἕνεκα ἔχθους τοῦ πρὸς τὸν κρείτ-
τονα, ἀλλὰ τοῦ μὴ ἐπιβουλευθῆναι χάριν πρὸς τοῦ
210 χείρονος. τίς οὖν ἡ παραίνεσις τῆς
ὑπομονῆς; θαυμασιωτάτη καὶ περιμάχητος· ἐὰν
ποτε, φησίν, ὁρᾷς ἀνηρεθισμένον καὶ ἐξηγριωμένον
τὸ θυμοῦ καὶ ὀργῆς πάθος ἐν σαυτῷ ἤ τινι ἑτέρῳ,
ὃ ἡ ἄλογος καὶ ἀτίθασος ζῳοτροφεῖ[1] φύσις, μὴ
μᾶλλον αὐτὸ ἀκονήσας ἐκθηριώσῃς—δήξεται γὰρ
ἴσως ἀνίατα—, καταψύχων δὲ τὸ ζέον αὐτοῦ καὶ
πεπυρωμένον ἄγαν ἡμέρωσον· τιθασὸν γὰρ καὶ
211 χειρόηθες εἰ γένοιτο, ἥκιστα ἂν βλάψαι. τίς οὖν ὁ
τρόπος τῆς τιθασείας καὶ ἡμερώσεως αὐτοῦ; μεθ-
αρμοσάμενος καὶ μετασκευασάμενος, ὅσα τῷ δοκεῖν,
ἀκολούθησον τὸ πρῶτον οἷς ἂν ἐθέλῃ καὶ πρὸς

[1] Mangey ζωπυρεῖ. See App. p. 566.

I profoundly admire also Patience or Rebecca, when 208
she exhorts him who is full-grown in soul and has
overthrown the harsh tyranny of vice and passion,
even then[a] to flee away to Haran. She says, " Now
therefore, my child, hearken to my voice, and arise
and flee away to Laban my brother in Haran, and
abide with him some days, until the wrath and anger
of thy brother turn away from thee, and he forget
what thou hast done to him " (Gen. xxvii. 43-45).
Excellently well does she call the journey to the 209
senses a flight or running away ; for the mind proves
itself indeed a runaway, whenever it forsakes the
objects of intellectual apprehension which are proper
to it, and turns to the opposite array of the objects of
sense-perception. Yet sometimes even running away
is serviceable, when a man does it not out of hatred
for the better, but that he may not be exposed to the
designs of the worse. What, then, is the 210
advice of Patience ? A most marvellous and valuable
one ! If ever, she says, thou seest stirred up to
savagery in thyself or some other person the passion
of wrath and anger, one of the stock bred and reared
by our irrational and untamed nature, beware of
whetting its fierceness and yet more rousing the beast
in it, when its bites may be incurable, but cool down
its excessive heat and perfervid temper and quiet it,
for should it become tame and manageable it will
inflict but little hurt. What, then, is the method of 211
bringing it to a quiet and subdued state ? Adapt and
transform yourself in outward appearance and follow
for the moment whatever it pleases, and opposing

[a] *i.e.* even in the hour of victory over Esau. The " tides
of the spirit," he means, often demand a return to common
things, after the spirituality has been at its highest.—Wend.
who wished to read either τὴν or ποτε, did not grasp this.

μηδὲν ἐναντιωθεὶς ὁμολόγησον τὰ αὐτὰ φιλεῖν τε
καὶ μισεῖν· οὕτω γὰρ ἐξευμενισθήσεται. πρα-
ϋνθέντος δὲ ἀποθήσῃ τὴν ὑπόκρισιν, καὶ μηδὲν
ἔτι προσδοκῶν ἐξ ἐκείνου κακὸν πείσεσθαι μετὰ
ῥᾳστώνης ἐπανελεύσῃ πρὸς τὴν τῶν ἰδίων ἐπι-
212 μέλειαν.   εἰσάγεται γὰρ διὰ τοῦτο Χαρρὰν θρεμμάτων μὲν ἀνάπλεως, οἰκήτορσι δὲ κεχρη-
μένη κτηνοτρόφοις· τί γὰρ ἂν εἴη χωρίον ἀλόγῳ
φύσει καὶ τοῖς τὴν ἐπιμέλειαν καὶ προστασίαν
αὐτῆς ἀνειληφόσιν ἐπιτηδειότερον τῶν ἐν ἡμῖν
213 αἰσθήσεων;   πυθομένου γοῦν τοῦ ἀσκητοῦ " πόθεν
[470] | ἐστέ " ἀποκρίνονται τἀληθὲς οἱ ποιμένες ὅτι " ἐκ
Χαρράν·" ἐκ γὰρ αἰσθήσεως αἱ ἄλογοι ὡς ἐκ
διανοίας αἱ λογικαὶ δυνάμεις εἰσί. προσπυθομένου
δέ, εἰ γινώσκουσι Λάβαν, φασὶν εἰκότως εἰδέναι·
γνωρίζει γὰρ τὸ χρῶμα καὶ πᾶσαν ποιότητα αἴσθησις, ὡς οἴεται, χρωμάτων δὲ καὶ ποιοτήτων ὁ
214 Λάβαν σύμβολον.   καὶ αὐτὸς δὲ ἐπειδὰν
ἤδη τελειωθῇ, τὸν μὲν τῶν αἰσθήσεων οἶκον ἀπο-
λείψει, τὸν δὲ τῆς ψυχῆς ὡς ψυχῆς ἱδρύεται, ὃν ἔτι
ὢν ἐν τοῖς πόνοις καὶ ταῖς ἀσκήσεσιν[1] ἀναζωγραφεῖ·
λέγει γάρ· " πότε ποιήσω κἀγὼ ἐμαυτῷ οἶκον; "
πότε τῶν αἰσθητῶν καὶ αἰσθήσεων ὑπεριδὼν νοῦν
καὶ διάνοιαν οἰκήσω, λόγῳ θεωρητοῖς πράγμασι

_____

[1] mss. αἰσθήσεσι.

_____

[a] I understand these two sections to contain, not so much
advice to soothe an angry man by pretending to conform to
his views and wishes, as a description of the right attitude
of the mind to αἴσθησις and πάθος. It is well, when we feel
or see the ebullience of passion in ourselves or others to come
down from the contemplation of νοητά and accommodate
ourselves to outward things. Afterwards the mind may
return to the care of its proper charges (τῶν ἰδίων), the mind

256

no single suggestion of its, profess to share its likes and dislikes. In this way it will be made quite friendly. And when it has been softened, you will drop your feigning, and, free now from the expectation of suffering any evil at its hands, you will comfortably return to the care of your own charges.[a]

For this is the reason[b] why Haran is represented as full of beasts, and having cattle-rearers as its inhabitants; for what place could be more suitable for irrational nature and those who have taken upon them the charge and patronage of it, than our senses? For instance, when the trainer of self inquires " Whence are ye ? " the shepherds answer truly " from Haran " (Gen. xxix. 4); for the irrational faculties come from sense-perception, as do the rational from understanding. When he further inquires whether they know Laban, they naturally say that they know him (Gen. xxix. 5): for sense-perception is familiar, so it imagines, with every colour and every quality, and Laban is the symbol of colours and varieties of quality. But as for Jacob himself, when at last he has been perfected, he quits, as we shall find, the dwelling-place of the senses, and founds that of the soul in the true sense[c] of the word, the dwelling-place which he pictures to himself while still immersed in his toils and exercises; for he says, " When shall I also make for myself a dwelling-place ? " (Gen. xxx. 30). When shall I, looking beyond things perceived and the senses which perceive them, inhabit mind and understanding, educated in and associating with matters

being thought of as the shepherd of the herd of νοητά; *cf. De Mut.* 114. But see App. p. 566.
[b] *i.e.* because Haran is the place of αἴσθησις.
[c] See on § 5 above.

PHILO

συντρεφόμενος[1] καὶ συνδιαιτώμενος, καθάπερ αἱ
ζητητικαὶ τῶν ἀφανῶν ψυχαί—μαίας αὐτὰς ἔθος
215 ὀνομάζειν—· καὶ γὰρ αὗται ποιοῦσι σκεπάσματα
οἰκεῖα καὶ φυλακτήρια φιλαρέτοις ψυχαῖς· τὸ δὲ
εὐερκέστατον οἰκοδόμημα ἦν ὁ θεοῦ φόβος τοῖς
φρουρὰν καὶ τεῖχος αὐτὸν ἀκαθαίρετον πεποιη-
μένοις. " ἐπειδὴ " γάρ φησιν " ἐφοβοῦντο αἱ μαῖαι
τὸν θεόν, ἐποίησαν ἑαυταῖς οἰκίας."

216 XXXIX. Ἐξελθὼν οὖν ἐκ τῶν κατὰ τὴν Χαρρὰν
τόπων ὁ νοῦς λέγεται " διοδεῦσαι τὴν γῆν ἕως τοῦ
τόπου Συχὲμ ἐπὶ τὴν δρῦν τὴν ὑψηλήν." τί δέ
ἐστι τὸ διοδεῦσαι, σκεψώμεθα· τὸ φιλομαθὲς ζητη-
τικὸν καὶ περίεργόν ἐστι φύσει, πανταχῇ βαδίζον
ἀόκνως καὶ πανταχόσε διακῦπτον καὶ μηδὲν ἀδιερεύνητον τῶν ὄντων μήτε σωμάτων μήτε πραγμάτων ἀπολιπεῖν δικαιοῦν. λίχνον γὰρ ἐκτόπως
θεαμάτων καὶ ἀκουσμάτων εἶναι πέφυκεν, ὡς μὴ
μόνον τοῖς ἐπιχωρίοις ἀρκεῖσθαι, ἀλλὰ καὶ τῶν
ξενικῶν καὶ πορρωτάτω διῳκισμένων ἐφίεσθαι.

217 λέγουσι γοῦν, ὡς ἔστιν ἄτοπον ἐμ-
πόρους μὲν καὶ καπήλους γλίσχρων ἕνεκα κερδῶν
διαβαίνειν τὰ πελάγη καὶ τὴν οἰκουμένην ἐν κύκλῳ
περιέναι ἅπασαν, μὴ θέρος, μὴ χειμῶνα, μὴ πνεύ-
ματα βίαια, μὴ ἐναντία, μὴ νεότητα, μὴ γῆρας, μὴ
νόσον σώματος, μὴ φίλων συνήθειαν, μὴ τὰς ἐπὶ
γυναικὶ καὶ τέκνοις καὶ τοῖς ἄλλοις οἰκείοις ἀλέκ-
τους ἡδονάς, μὴ πατρίδος καὶ πολιτικῶν φιλανθρω-
πιῶν ἀπόλαυσιν, μὴ χρημάτων καὶ κτημάτων καὶ

---

[1] MSS. συστρεφόμενος.

[a] Hebrew " He made them houses," *i.e.* gave them families,
to perpetuate their names.—Driver.

which form reason's contemplation, even as souls do
that are in quest of things out of sight ? To such 215
souls it is customary to give the name of " midwives,"
for, like the midwives in Egypt, these make places
of shelter and security fit for virtue-loving souls : and
the fear of God is as of old the most sure dwelling-
place for those who have made Him their guard and
impregnable fastness. For it says, " Since the midwives feared God, they made for themselves houses "[a]
(Ex. i. 21).

XXXIX. To resume. The mind, when it has gone 216
forth from the places about Haran, is said to have
travelled through the country as far as the place of
Shechem, to the lofty oak-tree (Gen. xii. 6). Let us
consider what is meant by " travelled through."
Love of learning is by nature curious and inquisitive,
not hesitating to bend its steps in all directions,
prying into everything, reluctant to leave anything
that exists unexplored, whether material or immaterial. It has an extraordinary appetite for all
that there is to be seen and heard, and, not content
with what it finds in its own country, it is bent on
seeking what is in foreign parts and separated by
great distances. We are reminded that 217
merchants and traders for the sake of trifling profits
cross the seas, and compass the wide world, letting
stand in their way no summer heat nor winter cold,
no tempestuous or contrary winds, neither youth nor
age, no sickness of body, neither the daily intercourse
with friends nor the pleasure too great for words
which we take in wife and children and in all else that
is our own, nor the enjoyment of our fatherland and
of all the gracious amenities of civic life, nor the safe
use of money and property and abundance of other

PHILO

τῆς ἄλλης περιουσίας ἀσφαλῆ χρῆσιν, μὴ τῶν
ἄλλων ὁτιοῦν συνόλως μέγα ἢ μικρὸν ἐμποδὼν
218 τιθεμένους, τοῦ δὲ καλλίστου καὶ περιμαχήτου καὶ
μόνῳ τῷ γένει τῶν ἀνθρώπων οἰκειοτάτου χάριν,
σοφίας, μὴ οὐχὶ θάλατταν μὲν ἅπασαν περαιοῦ-
σθαι, πάντα δὲ γῆς μυχὸν ἐπέρχεσθαι, φιλοπευστοῦν-
τας εἴ πού τι καλὸν ἔστιν ἰδεῖν ἢ ἀκοῦσαι, καὶ μετὰ
[471] σπουδῆς καὶ προθυμίας τῆς | πάσης ἰχνηλατεῖν,
ἄχρις ἂν ἐγγένηται τῶν ζητουμένων καὶ ποθου-
219 μένων εἰς ἀπόλαυσιν ἐλθεῖν.   διόδευσον
μέντοι, ψυχή, καὶ τὸν ἄνθρωπον, εἰ θέλεις, ἕκαστον
τῶν περὶ αὐτὸν ἀγαγοῦσα εἰς ἐπίκρισιν, οἷον
εὐθέως τί τὸ σῶμα καὶ τί ποιοῦν ἢ πάσχον διανοίᾳ
συνεργεῖ, τί ἡ αἴσθησις καὶ τίνα τρόπον τὸν ἡγεμόνα
νοῦν ὠφελεῖ, τί λόγος καὶ τίνων γινόμενος ἑρμηνεὺς
πρὸς καλοκἀγαθίαν συμβάλλεται, τί ἡδονὴ καὶ τί
ἐπιθυμία, τί λύπη καὶ φόβος καὶ τίς ἡ πρὸς ταῦτα
ἰατρική, δι' ἧς ἢ ληφθείς τις εὐμαρῶς διεκδύσεται
ἢ οὐχ ἁλώσεται πρὸς αὐτῶν τὸ παράπαν, τί τὸ
ἀφραίνειν, τί τὸ ἀκολασταίνειν, τί τὸ ἀδικεῖν, τίς ἡ
τῶν ἄλλων πληθὺς νοσημάτων, ὅσα ἡ φθοροποιὸς
ἀποτίκτειν πέφυκε κακία, καὶ τίς ἡ τούτων ἀπο-
στροφή, καὶ κατὰ τὰ ἐναντία τί τὸ δίκαιον ἢ τὸ
φρόνιμον ἢ τὸ σῶφρον, τὸ ἀνδρεῖον, τὸ εὔβουλον,
ἀρετὴ συνόλως ἅπασα καὶ εὐπάθεια. καὶ ὃν τρόπον
220 ἕκαστον αὐτῶν εἴωθε περιγίνεσθαι   διόδευσον μέντοι καὶ τὸν μέγιστον καὶ τελεώτατον

---

a Philo here seems, as not unfrequently, to use εὐπάθεια in a
more general sense, not as in §§ 119 and 157 in the strict
Stoic sense of justifiable emotions.

good things, nor in a word anything else either great or small. If so, it is monstrous, such speakers urge, 218 when we stand to gain a thing most fair, worth all men's striving for, the special prerogative of the human race, namely wisdom, to refrain from crossing every sea, from exploring earth's every recess, in the joy of finding out whether there is in any place aught that is fair to see or hear, and from following the quest of it with utmost zest and keenness, until we can come to the enjoyment of the things that we are seeking and longing for. Travel through 219 man also, if thou wilt, O my soul, bringing to examination each component part of him. For instance, to take the first examples that occur, find out what the body is and what it must do or undergo to co-operate with the understanding ; what sense-perception is and in what way it is of service to its ruler, mind ; what speech is, and what thoughts it must express if it would contribute to nobility of character ; what pleasure is, and what desire is ; what pain and fear are, and what the healing art is that can counteract them, by means of which a man shall either, if he falls into their hand, without difficulty make his escape, or avoid capture altogether ; what it is to play the fool, what to be licentious, what to be unjust, what the multitude of other sicknesses to which it is the nature of pestilential wickedness to give birth, and what the preventive of these ; and on the other hand, what righteousness is, or good sense, or self-mastery, courage, discretion, in a word virtue gener-ally and moral welfare,[a] and in what way each of them is wont to be won. Travel again through 220 the greatest and most perfect man, this universe, and

ἄνθρωπον, τόνδε τὸν κόσμον, καὶ διάσκεψαι τὰ
μέρη, ὡς τόποις μὲν διέζευκται, δυνάμεσι δὲ
ἥνωται, καὶ τίς ὁ ἀόρατος οὗτος τῆς ἁρμονίας καὶ
ἐνώσεως πᾶσι δεσμός. ἐὰν μέντοι σκοπούμενος μὴ
ῥᾳδίως καταλαμβάνῃς ἃ ζητεῖς, ἐπίμενε μὴ κάμ-
νων· οὐ γὰρ τῇ ἑτέρᾳ[1] ληπτὰ ταῦτ' ἐστίν, ἀλλὰ
μόλις πολλοῖς καὶ μεγάλοις πόνοις ἀνευρισκόμενα.
221 οὗ χάριν ὁ φιλομαθὴς τοῦ τόπου Συχὲμ ἐνείληπται,
μεταληφθὲν δὲ τοὔνομα Συχὲμ ὠμίασις καλεῖται,
πόνου σύμβολον, ἐπειδὴ τοῖς μέρεσι τούτοις ἀχθοφορεῖν ἔθος, ὡς καὶ αὐτὸς ἑτέρωθι μέμνηται λέγων
ἐπί τινος ἀθλητοῦ τοῦτον τὸν τρόπον· " ὑπέθηκε
τὸν ὦμον εἰς τὸ πονεῖν, καὶ ἐγένετο ἀνὴρ γεωργός."
222   ὥστε μηδέποτε, ὦ διάνοια, μαλα-
κισθεῖσα ὀκλάσῃς, ἀλλά, κἂν τι δοκῇ δυσθεώρητον
εἶναι, τὸ ἐν σαυτῇ βλέπον διανοίξασα διάκυψον
εἴσω καὶ ἀκριβέστερον τὰ ὄντα ἐναύγασαι καὶ μήτε
ἑκοῦσα μήτε ἄκουσά ποτε μύσῃς· τυφλὸν γὰρ
ὕπνος, ὡς ὀξυωπὲς ἐγρήγορσις. ἀγαπητὸν δὲ τῷ
συνεχεῖ τῆς προσβολῆς[2] εἰλικρινῆ τῶν ζητουμένων
223 λαβεῖν φαντασίαν.   οὐχ ὁρᾷς ὅτι καὶ δρῦν
ὑψηλὴν ἐν Συχὲμ πεφυτεῦσθαί φησιν αἰνιττόμενος
τὸν ἀνένδοτον καὶ ἀκαμπῆ, στερρόν τε καὶ ἀρρα-
γέστατον παιδείας πόνον; ᾧ τὸν μέλλοντα ἔσεσθαι

---

[1] Wendland and Mangey τῇ ἐκεχειρίᾳ. The reading here
printed is, according to Wend., that of all mss. except H[2].
Wend. later (*Rhein. Mus.* liii. p. 34) repudiated ἐκεχ. and was
inclined instead to adopt a suggestion of Cohn, ῥαστώνῃ, based
on *De Sacr.* 37. But the phrase οὐ τῇ ἑτέρᾳ ληπτόν (not to
be caught with one hand) is a quotation from Plato, *Soph.*
226 A, where it is said to be a proverbial phrase (τὸ λεγόμενον)
and there is no reason to doubt its genuineness here. See
further App. p. 566.

[2] mss. προβολῆς.

scan narrowly its parts, how far asunder they are in the positions which they occupy, how wholly made one by the powers which govern them, and what constitutes for them all this invisible bond of harmony and unity. If, however, in your investigation, you do not easily attain the objects of your quest, keep on without giving in, for these " need both hands to catch them," and only by manifold and painful toil can they be discovered. That is why the lover of 221 learning took possession of the place called Shechem, a name which when translated is " shouldering," a figure of toil, since it is with these parts of the body that we are accustomed to carry loads, as Moses himself calls to mind elsewhere speaking in this wise of one who worked and strove, " he submitted his shoulder to labour, and became a tiller of the soil " (Gen. xlix. 15). Never, then, O my 222 understanding, do thou shew weakness and slacken, but even if aught seem to be hard to discern, open wide the organ in thyself that sees, and stoop to get a view of the inside, and behold with more accurate gaze the things that *are*, and never either willingly or unwillingly close thine eyes ; for sleep is a blind thing, as wakefulness is a thing of keen sight. And it is a sufficient [a] reward to obtain by unremitting inspection a clear impression of the things thou art in search of. Do you not see that he says 223 further that a tall oak had been planted in Shechem, thus shewing in a figure the toil of education as a hard and unbreakable substance that never yields or bends ?

[a] Or " one with which we must be content." The word is generally used of something we accept in default of something better. What that is in this case has been shewn in § 46. There is a higher realization than seeing, viz. possessing, but that is not given to men.

τέλειον καὶ ἀναγκαῖον κεχρῆσθαι, ἵνα μὴ¹ τὸ ψυχῆς
δικαστήριον, ὄνομα Δεῖνα—κρίσις γὰρ ἑρμηνεύεται—, συλληφθῇ πρὸς τοῦ τὸν ἐναντίον μοχθοῦντος
πόνον, τὸν φρονήσεως ἐπίβουλον.²   ὁ γὰρ
ἐπώνυμος τοῦ τόπου τούτου Συχέμ, Ἐμὼρ υἱὸς
ὤν, ἀλόγου φύσεως—καλεῖται γὰρ Ἐμὼρ ὄνος—,
ἀφροσύνην ἐπιτηδεύων καὶ συντραφεὶς ἀναισχυντίᾳ
καὶ θράσει τὰ κριτήρια τῆς διανοίας μιαίνειν ὁ
παμμίαρος καὶ φθείρειν ἐπεχείρησεν, εἰ μὴ θᾶττον
οἱ φρονήσεως ἀκουσταὶ³ καὶ γνώριμοι, Συμεών τε
καὶ Λευί, φραξάμενοι τὰ οἰκεῖα ἀσφαλῶς ἐπεξ-
ῆλθον, ἔτι ὄντας ἐν τῷ φιληδόνῳ καὶ φιλοπαθεῖ καὶ
ἀπεριμήτῳ πόνῳ καθελόντες· χρησμοῦ γὰρ ὄντος,
ὡς " οὐκ ἂν γένοιτό ποτε πόρνη τῶν τοῦ βλέποντος,
Ἰσραήλ, θυγατέρων," οὗτοι τὴν παρθένον ψυχὴν
ἐξαρπάσαντες λαθεῖν ἤλπισαν.   οὐ γὰρ
ἐρημία γε τῶν βοηθησόντων τοῖς παρασπονδου-
μένοις ἐστίν, ἀλλὰ κἂν οἴωνταί τινες, οἰήσονται
μόνον, ἀπελεγχθήσονται δὲ τῷ ἔργῳ ψευδοδοξοῦν-

¹ mss. μὴ δέ.
² So all mss. except H²; this has τοῦ . . . ἐπιβούλου, which
Wend. adopts.
³ Wend. suggested and later (Rhein. Mus. lviii. 34)
accepted ἐρασταί. But see De Ebr. 94, where Simeon is
φιλήκοος, " for his name means ἀκοή."

ᵃ Or "tribunals."
ᵇ The phrase is apparently an interpretation of the next
word, ἀσφαλῶς, which itself is taken from the lxx εἰσῆλθον
εἰς τὴν πόλιν ἀσφαλῶς. This word, which in the E.V. is
translated "unawares" (margin, "boldly"), was presumably
understood by the lxx translators as "running no risks
because the Shechemites were disabled." Philo reads into
it the thought that Virtue must fortify itself against Vice
before it can take the offensive.

It is a vital matter that he who would be perfect should ply this toil, to the end that the soul's court of justice, called " Dinah," which means " judgement," may not be ravished by him who sinks under the opposite kind of toil, which is the insidious foe of sound sense.　　　For the man who bears the 224 name of this place, Shechem, being son of Hamor, that is of an irrational being—for " Hamor " means " ass "—practising folly and nursed in shamelessness and effrontery, essayed—foul wretch that he was—to corrupt and defile the judgement faculties[a] of the understanding. But the hearers and pupils of sound sense, Symeon and Levi, were too quick for him. They made secure their own quarters[b] and went forth against them in safety, and overthrew them when still occupied in the pleasure-loving, passion-loving, toil[c] of the uncircumcised : for albeit there was a Divine decree that " of the daughters of Israel, the seeing one, none might ever become a harlot " (Deut. xxiii. 17), these men hoped to carry off unobserved the virgin soul (Gen. xxxiv.).[d]　　　Vain hope, for 225 there is no lack of succourers to victims of a breach of faith ; but even if some imagine that there is, they will only imagine, but will be convicted by events of

[c] A reference to LXX Gen. xxiv. 25 ὅτε ἦσαν ἐν τῷ πόνῳ. where πόνος refers to their disablement from circumcision (E.V. " when they were sore "). This strangely-used word comes in happily for Philo's allegory of Shechem as the false πόνος.

[d] Philo takes great liberties with the story, ignoring the actual seduction of Dinah (μιαίνειν ἐπεχείρησεν) and the circumcision of Hamor and Shechem (ἀπεριτμήτῳ πόνῳ). He gives, however, a sort of apology for this in § 225 by suggesting that in the spiritual sphere the defilement of the truly virtuous soul, and the " circumcision " of the truly wicked, are only illusory.

τες. ἔστι γάρ, ἔστιν ἡ μισοπόνηρος καὶ ἀμείλικτος
καὶ ἀδικουμένων ἀρωγὸς ἀπαραίτητος δίκη, σφάλ-
λουσα τὰ τέλη τῶν αἰσχυνόντων ἀρετήν, ὧν πεσόν-
των εἰς παρθένον πάλιν ἡ δόξασα αἰσχυνθῆναι
μεταβάλλει ψυχή· δόξασα δ' εἶπον, ὅτι οὐδέποτε
ἐφθείρετο· τῶν γὰρ ἀκουσίων οὐδὲν τοῦ πάσχοντος
πρὸς ἀλήθειαν πάθος, ὡς οὐδὲ τοῦ μὴ ἀπὸ γνώμης
ἀδικοῦντος τὸ πραττόμενον ἔργον.

holding a false opinion. For Justice has indeed existence, Justice the abhorrer of wickedness, the relentless one, the inexorable, the befriender of those who are wronged, bringing failure upon the aims of those who shame virtue, upon whose fall the soul, that had seemed to have been shamed, becomes again a virgin. Seemed, I said, because it never was defiled. It is with sufferings which we have not willed, as it is with wrongdoings which we have not intended. As there is no real doing in the second case, so there is no real suffering in the first.

WHO IS THE HEIR OF DIVINE THINGS
THINGS
(QUIS RERUM DIVINARUM HERES)

ANALYTICAL INTRODUCTION

THIS treatise, the longest of the whole series and containing many fine passages, is a straightforward commentary with comparatively few digressions on Gen. xv. 2-18.

2. And Abram says, Master, what wilt Thou give me? I depart childless. But the son of Masek, the woman born in my household, is this Damascus Eliezer.

3. And Abram said, Since Thou hast given me no seed, the son of my household shall be my heir.

4. And immediately the voice of the Lord came to him, saying, He shall not be thy heir, but he who shall come forth from thee, he shall be thy heir.

5. And He led him forth outside and said to him, Look up indeed into heaven, and count the stars if thou shalt be able to number them, and He said, So shall be thy seed.

6. And Abram believed on God, and it was counted to him for righteousness.

7. And He said to him, I am the God who brought thee from the land of the Chaldeans to give thee this land to inherit.

8. And he said, Master, by what shall I know that I shall inherit it?

9. And He said to him, Take Me a heifer of three years old, and a goat of three years old, and a
270

am of three years old, and a turtledove and a
pigeon.

10. And he took for Him all these, and divided
hem in the middle, and placed them facing each
other ; but the birds he did not divide.

11. And the birds came down to the bodies their
half pieces, and Abram sat with them.

12. And about sunset a trance (ecstasy) fell upon
Abram, and lo, a great dark terror falls upon him.

13. And it was said to Abram, Knowing thou
shalt know that thy seed shall be a sojourner in a
and not their own, and they shall enslave them and
ill-treat them and humble them four hundred years.

14. And the nation which they shall be slaves to
I will judge, and after this they shall come forth
hither with much substance (stock) .

15. But thou shalt depart to thy fathers in peace,
nourished in a good old age (or, as Philo, "nourished
with peace ").

16. And in the fourth generation they shall turn
away hither, for the iniquities of the Amorites are
not yet fulfilled until now.

17. And when the sun was at its setting, a flame
arose, and lo, a furnace (oven) smoking, and torches of
fire, which went in the midst of these half pieces.

18. In that day the Lord made a covenant with
Abram saying, To thy seed will I give this land
from the river of Egypt to the great river Euphrates.

The first point to which Philo calls attention is
Abraham's boldness of speech, the proper attitude
of the faithful servant (1-9). Silence indeed is more
fitting in the ignorant, as is expressed in the text,
" Be silent and listen " (10), and we should remember

that this includes the silence of the soul, which is the
opposite of that wandering mind, which so often
accompanies mere silence of speech (11-13). But
that the wise have a right to boldness of speech is
shewn emphatically in the story of Moses, and here
Philo quotes several of his pathetic appeals to God
and concludes that such appeals are the mark of the
" friend of God " (14-21). Yet in Abraham's words
there is a sense of pious awe or caution (εὐλάβεια) as
well as boldness. Philo notes the term " Master "
connoting a greater degree of fear than " Lord,"
and thence passes on into an impassioned meditation
expressing the combination of awe and gratitude
which the words " Master what wilt thou give me ? "
(which he takes in the sense of " what more canst
thou give, who hast given all?") call up in the mind
of the devout worshipper (15-22). And in the same
way he treats the verse, "Shall I depart childless?"
Shall I, that is, be denied the spiritual offspring or
higher thought ? Shall I have no heir but the son
of Masek (34-39).

Thus we are necessarily led to the interpretation
of Masek the " homeborn " and her son. The name
means " from a kiss " and kiss (φίλημα) differs from
love (φιλεῖν) as marking a lower and less genuine
kind of affection (40-41). Thus it may stand for
the life of sense, which the wise will regard as a
servant, but not love (42). Philo then gives two
examples where " kiss " (καταφιλεῖν) signifies the
kiss of insincerity, while φιλεῖν shews true affection,
and then introduces somewhat inappropriately his
favourite parable of the Hated and the Beloved Wife
(Deut. xxi. 15-17), the latter of whom he identifies
with Masek (45-49) and touches on the analogy

between the two wives and Leah and Rachel (50). Masek's son Damascus represents all of us who honour Sense. The name means "Blood of sackcloth" and thus symbolizes the animal or "blood"-life as opposed to the life of mind and reason (52-57). Damascus is also called Eliezer (God is my help) which signifies the inability of the blood-life to maintain itself without God's help. And again his inferiority is marked by the absence of any named father (58-62).

Abraham's question then means " can this blood-life be the heir of higher things ? " and the profound inward conviction symbolized by the voice of God answers—No, not that, but he that shall come out of thee shall be thy heir (63-68). These words Philo audaciously understands to mean that the " heir " must come out of, or leave, that is surrender and dedicate to God, not only body, sense and speech,[a] but his whole self (69-74). What the inheritance is is shewn by the next words, "He led him forth outside and said, 'Look (or 'See') up into heaven,'" for heaven is another name for the treasure-house of divine blessings, as it is called in Deuteronomy (75-76), and to be able to " see " up to this is the privilege of the true Israel which does not like its unworthy representatives in the wilderness refuse to " look to the Manna," preferring the onions and fishes of Egypt (76-80). As for the phrase " He led him up out outside," there is no tautology, for since we may well be called both outside and inside, if our inward feelings are not in accord with our outward actions, so the phrase shews that the Abraham-mind

---

[a] Which, on Philo's interpretation of Gen. xii. 1, were symbolized by the " land," " kinsfolk " and " father's house," which Abraham was commanded to leave.

is altogether outside, outside that is of the trammels of
sense, speech and body and above all of SELF (81-85)

The next words " count the stars " do not refer to
mere number, as is shewn by " so (not " so many ")
shall be thy seed," but to the " star-like " nature of
the soul-children, and the stars themselves are not
those which we see, but the vastly greater glories
of the Ideal Universe, of which these are but the
copies (86-89).

The next verse raises the question why Abraham's
believing God should be counted to him for righteousness. How can anyone disbelieve God? Philo replies
that while in itself there is nothing marvellous in
this belief, yet in view of the proneness of human
nature to trust in lower things, it may well be
described as a "just" or "righteous" action (90-95).

In verse 7, the words " I am the God who brought
thee from the land of the Chaldeans to give thee this
land to inherit," send our thoughts to a fulfilled
boon, as well as that which is to come. God had
brought the soul out of the land of star-lore, where
heaven itself is God, and has led him to the land of
" wisdom," that is of acknowledging the Creator
instead of the creature (96-99).

Abraham's question in verse 8 " How shall I
know ? " does not imply doubt of the promise, but
only the natural desire to know how it will come
about, and the immediate answer of God shews that
the question is accepted as right (100-102). In the
answer (verse 9), we first note the words " take for
me," which indicate first that all we have we do but
receive (103), and secondly that we should receive or
" take " them for God and not for ourselves. Philo
develops this theme in his familiar manner in appli-

cation to our senses, mind and all other gifts (104-111).
An illustration of this from the phrase *My* first-
fruits or " beginnings " leads to some thoughts on
the divine origin of the fruits of the earth, as well as
of human parentage (112-119). And again if the
beginnings are God's so also are the ends (120-121),
and finally we have to remember that God deigns to
" take " from us, as He shewed, when He took the
Levites as a ransom for the others (123-124).

Proceeding with the same verse, the heifer signifies the soul, the ram speech, and the goat sense-
perception. They are all " three years old," the
perfect number signifying beginning, middle and
end, while the solitary turtle-dove and the sociable
pigeon are respectively divine and human wisdom.
The first three are divided, soul into reasoning and
unreasoning, speech into true and false, sense-
perception into real and illusory, while the two
" wisdoms " are incapable of division (125-132).
This work of division is one of the functions of the
creative Logos and is illustrated from various aspects
of creation (133-140). But we must note also that
the three creatures divided in the story are divided
in the middle, that is equally, and this brings us to
the disquisition " about the division into equals and
opposites," which supplies the second half of the
traditional title of the treatise and occupies the next
sixty-five sections.

Equality which in actual practice cannot be
obtained exactly and is therefore an attribute of
the divine Division by the Logos (141-143) may be
equality in number or magnitude or capacity, and
again it may be numerical or proportional (144-145).
Philo illustrates all these at somewhat wearisome

length. He first gives a catalogue of natural phenomena where we find the numerical balance (146-151),
and then examples of proportional equality, concluding with the thought of man as the Micro-
cosm and the Cosmos (152-155), and this leads him
on to shew how God deals with small and great on
the same principle (156-160). Moses too shews his
reverence for equality partly by his praises of justice,
the very essence of which is equality, and also in the
examples of it scattered throughout the Law. Such
are the divisions of day and night, of man and woman,
and others mentioned in the early chapters of
Genesis (161-165), and in the body of the Law itself,
the Divine Presence dividing the Cherubim, that is
the two Potencies, on the ark, and the division of the
Ten Commandments into two tables of five each
(166-169), which gives occasion for stating shortly
the meaning of each commandment (169-173).
Other examples are the permanent sacrifices (174),
the two sets of the shewbread (175), the two jewels
on the High Priest's robe (176), the two mountains
of blessing and cursing, and the two goats of Lev. xvi.
with a short digression on the meaning of the rite
(177-181). Two other examples which follow give
occasion for longer mystical meditation. The blood
which was poured partly on the altar and partly into
the mixing-bowls shews how divine wisdom, that is
mind in its pure form, is an offering to God, and
human wisdom, set by God in the mixing-bowls of the
senses, may be purified by the cleansing blood
(182-185). So too the offering of the half-shekel
indicates the ransoming of the suppliant soul, while
the un-offered half stands for the mind which is
content with its slavery (186-190). Again we have

examples of equal division in the Manna, where he that had much had not too much, and he that had little did not lack (191), and the Passover, where the lamb is to be distributed, so that each may have sufficient (192-193). And after two other briefly mentioned examples there follows a longer allegorical treatment of the ingredients of the incense-offering interpreted as the thanksgiving of the four elements and therefore of the World (194-200), and finally a fine passage in which citing the story of Aaron standing between the living and the dead, and the cloud which divided the host of Egypt from Israel, he describes the work of the Logos as mediating between the creature and the Creator, on the one hand proclaiming the divine mercy, on the other hand standing surety for the ultimate obedience of mankind—a passage which must surely have deeply impressed his Christian readers (201-206).

The words " facing each other " suggest that these divisions are into opposites, and so we find this phenomenon of oppositeness running throughout creation. In a long catalogue which begins with such physical examples as hot and cold and ends with human qualities, Philo brings this out and finally points out in triumph that it is in vain for the Greeks to boast of this philosophy of opposites as due to Heracleitus, since Moses knew and shewed it long before (207-214).

We might now pass on, but there is one example of division which Philo feels needs special attention. As in the story of Genesis three creatures were divided, there were six halves, and therefore the dividing Logos stands in the sacred position of seventh. We have a parallel to this in the great chandelier of the

Tabernacle and Philo deals with this in considerable detail, shewing that its general structure is seven-fold, *i.e.* three of each kind on each side of the main stalk (215-220). He goes on to suggest that it represents the seven planets with the sun in the centre, as well as the three pairs of soul division mentioned above with the Logos as the seventh (221-225). And this gives him opportunity for two other remarks on the chandelier. He notes that while the incense-altar (as mentioned before) represents thanksgiving of the elements, and the table with its loaves thanksgiving of the creatures formed of these elements, the chandelier signifies the thanksgiving of the heavens (226). And so while we are told the dimensions of the first two we hear nothing of the dimensions of the chandelier, in accordance with the truth that heaven has no bounds of which the human mind has ken (227-229).

" The birds he did not divide." We have already had a brief explanation of this, but it needs filling out. While the unreasoning part of the soul has its seven divisions, the mind (the pigeon of the story) like the sphere of the fixed stars, which is its heavenly analogy, has no divisions, and so too the turtle-dove, the Logos, is indivisible : and yet both though un-divided themselves are perpetually dividing and distinguishing everything that comes before them (230-236).

" The birds came down to the bodies, the half pieces." Here of course " birds " is used in a different sense, as is shewn by their " coming down," for it is the nature of birds to fly up (237-238). Rather these birds are like the reptiles banned in Leviticus, and have left their natural home of heaven for earth. They are the numberless thoughts which beset the mind and drag it " down " and feast upon the bodily element in us (239-243). And when we read that " Abraham sat down with them " it signifies the wise man's attitude to these thoughts. He is like the statesman who puts an end to foreign wars, that is to wicked thoughts which attack the soul, and to civil faction, that is to the contention of opposing doctrines (243-246). And here once again Philo catalogues the different theories of the schools on physical and theological problems, and pictures the Sage, who sits down with them, as half-midwife, half-judge, discarding the evil offspring of the soul and saving the good (246-248).

And about sunset an " ecstasy " fell upon Abraham. Philo enumerates four meanings of this word—madness, astonishment, mental tranquillity (or vacancy) and prophetic inspiration (249). He proceeds to give examples of each (250-252), but two examples of the second, viz. that Isaac was in an " ecstasy," *i.e.* astonished, when Jacob brought him the savoury meats, and Jacob was in an " ecstasy " *i.e.* astonished, that Joseph still lived and ruled over Egypt, cause him to break off strangely into the lessons which may be drawn from these two passages (252-256).[a] When he resumes he gives an example of the third meaning, viz. the ecstasy (trance) " which fell upon Adam and he slept " (267), and proceeds to the fourth, which he holds to be the meaning of the word in our text. He shews that either in the sense of predicter or of spokesman Noah, Abraham, Isaac, Jacob and above all Moses are prophets (258-262). And the phrase " about sunset," he

[a] See notes on these sections.

thinks, well suits this meaning. For when the
" sun " of the mind is in action, we cannot be god-
possessed. It is when something higher takes
possession of him and plays upon him like the
musician on the chords that the prophet becomes the
voice of God (263-266).

We turn to the promises given to Abraham in
verses 13-16. "Thy seed shall be a sojourner in a
land not their own." The soul-children must dwell a
while in that " earth " which stands for bodily things
(262-268). They will serve for four hundred years, and
with Philo's usual recklessness about numbers the four
hundred years stand for the four passions (who are
also the people whom they serve and whom God will
judge), and what slavery to the passions means is
described briefly (269-271). But when the redemption comes, we shall depart with much substance or
stock, to be our supply for the journey. This supply
is the fruits of education, beginning with the school
learning, which creates the desire for the higher
philosophy (272-274).

" But thou shalt depart to thy fathers, nourished
with peace, in a good old age." First we note the
contrast here implied between the peace of the Sage
and the war and slavery described above (275).
Secondly, that he " departs," not " dies " (276). But
who are the " fathers " ? Not those whom he left
behind in Chaldea, from whom God had called him
away (277-279). Some think the heavenly bodies
are meant, some the " ideas," others again the four
elements to which our bodies return. And Philo
seems ready to accept this, if we add also the " fifth
element," to which the soul returns—at any rate he
gives no other (279-283). When the promise adds

' nourished with peace," it contrasts the wise man's lot with the spiritual welfare of ordinary men. In that war our enemies may be the " external things " or the passions and vices within us. And then Philo repeats in a slightly different form the parable of the guards of the soul and body which he has already used in *De Ebr.* 201 and *De Conf.* 18 (284-286). That the peace cannot be literally meant is clear when we remember that Abraham's life was beset by war, exile and even want (286-288). Yet all these, allegorically considered, are blessings—war against wrongdoing, exile from the false star-lore, want of passion (289). And the " good old age " must mean the life of wisdom, for a day well-spent is more than years of folly (290-292).

" And in the fourth generation they shall return here." The " fourth generation " is interpreted to mean the fourth of the seven-year periods of life. In the first the child knows nothing of good or evil. The second is the time when vice shews itself, partly owing to the natural disposition, partly to mishandled education. In the third comes the healing influence of philosophy, and thus in the fourth the man is in his strength ready to travel to the land of wisdom (293-299).

" For the sins of the Amorites are not yet filled up." Some read a fatalistic meaning into these words, but Moses is no fatalist (300-301). The name " Amorites " means " talkers " and here they are the deceivers who misuse the gift of speech. It is not till sophistry is convicted, and thus " filled," that we can fly from the land of lies and seek the wisdom indicated by " here " (302-306).

" When the sun was at its setting a flame arose

and behold a smoking furnace." The flame of virtue often appears late and at the close of life (307), and while we are still in the land of the Amorites it is like the smoke of a furnace. Smoke brings tears to the eyes and so when we see virtue in this obscured form, we weep for its perfected form (308-310). In another way this furnace or oven may be the type of the earnest soul, which contains and " cooks " the nourishment supplied by the virtues (311). As for " the torches of fire which went in the midst of the half-pieces," they are the judgements of God, passing through and dividing all things (312).

Finally we have the summing up. In that day the Lord made a covenant with Abraham saying, " to thy seed will I give this land from the river of Egypt to the great river, the river Euphrates." Here then we have the wise man declared the heir. For we have already seen that the land is wisdom (313-315), and when he adds the words about the rivers we must note that Egypt is put first and Euphrates last. For the process of perfecting begins with Egypt, the body, and the bodily things which are necessary to our existence, and ends with the great river of God's wisdom with all its joys and blessings (315-316).

In this treatise we once more have, as in the *De Sacrificiis*,[a] the help of the Papyrus discovered in Upper Egypt in 1889 and stated to be as early as, and probably earlier than, the 6th century, A very cursory examination of Wendland's *Apparatus Criticus*, will shew how valuable is this addition to our textual authorities. Particularly interesting is the frequent

[a] See Introduction to that treatise, vol. ii. p. 93.

note "Pap. (Mangey)," shewing how often the acumen of Mangey anticipated the discovery. But like all documents it is not infallible, and while in most cases I thoroughly endorse Wendland's preference for the readings of the Papyrus against those of the MSS.,[a] there are a few in which I think he has been too subservient to it; and there are also many places in which though it supports the MSS. there is evidently or probably some corruption, on which conjecture may exercise its ingenuity.

[a] As the object of the critical notes is chiefly to indicate to the reader where the text adopted has no MS. authority (see Preface, pp.v–vi), I have not, except in a very few special instances, recorded the cases in which the Papyrus's readings are accepted by Wendland in preference to those of the Codices.

ΠΕΡΙ ΤΟΥ ΤΙΣ Ο ΤΩΝ ΘΕΙΩΝ ΕΣΤΙΝ
ΚΛΗΡΟΝΟΜΟΣ ΚΑΙ ΠΕΡΙ ΤΗΣ ΕΙΣ
ΤΑ ΙΣΑ ΚΑΙ ΕΝΑΝΤΙΑ ΤΟΜΗΣ

1 I. Ἐν μὲν τῇ πρὸ ταύτης συντάξει τὰ περὶ
μισθῶν ὡς ἐνῆν ἐπ' ἀκριβείας διεξήλθομεν· νυνὶ δὲ
πρόκειται ζητεῖν, τίς ὁ τῶν θείων πραγμάτων
κληρονόμος ἐστίν. ἐπειδὴ γὰρ θεσπισθέντος ὁ
2 σοφὸς ἤκουσε λογίου τοιούτου· '' ὁ μισθός σου
πολὺς ἔσται σφόδρα,'' πυνθάνεται φάσκων· '' δέσποτα, τί μοι δώσεις; ἐγὼ δὲ ἀπολύομαι ἄτεκνος.
ὁ δὲ υἱὸς Μασὲκ[1] τῆς οἰκογενοῦς μου οὗτος Δαμασκὸς Ἐλιέζερ,'' καὶ πάλιν '' ἐπειδὴ ἐμοὶ οὐκ
ἔδωκας σπέρμα, ὁ δὲ οἰκογενής μου κληρο-
3 νομήσει με.''   καίτοι τίς οὐκ ἂν τὸ τοῦ
χρησμῳδοῦντος ἀξίωμα καὶ μέγεθος καταπλαγεὶς
ἄφωνος καὶ ἀχανὴς ἐγένετο, καὶ εἰ μὴ διὰ δέος,
ἀλλά τοι τῷ περιχαρεῖ; ἐπιστομίζουσι γὰρ ὡς
αἱ σφοδραὶ λῦπαι καὶ αἱ ὑπερβάλλουσαι χαραί.
4 διὸ καὶ Μωυσῆς ἰσχνόφωνος ὁμολογεῖ καὶ βραδύγλωσσος γενέσθαι, ἀφ' οὗ ἤρξατο ὁ θεὸς αὐτῷ
διαλέγεσθαι. καὶ ἀψευδής ἐστιν ἡ τοῦ προφήτου
μαρτυρία· τότε γὰρ εἰκὸς τὸ μὲν φωνητήριον

____
[1] So Pap.: mss. μου ὁ ἐκ.

____
[a] Not the *De Migratione*, in which δωρεά not μισθός is
284

WHO IS THE HEIR OF DIVINE THINGS

AND ON THE DIVISION INTO EQUALS AND OPPOSITES

I. In the preceding treatise[a] we have discussed as 1
carefully as was possible the question of rewards.
Now our task is to inquire who is the heir of divine
things. When the Sage heard the oracular promise to
this purport, "Thy reward shall be exceeding great," 2
he answers with the question, "Master, what wilt
thou give me? I go hence childless. The son of
Masek, she who was born in my house, is this Damascus Eliezer."[b] And again he says "Since thou hast
given me no seed, he that was born in my house shall
be my heir" (Gen. xv. 1-3). Yet we 3
should have expected that he (for who would not?)
would have been struck mute and speechless in
amazement at the majesty and greatness of the Giver
of the oracle, if not for fear, at any rate for exceeding
joy. For men are tongue-tied by overwhelming joy,
as well as by violent grief. This it is that led Moses 4
to confess that he has become feeble of voice and slow
of tongue, ever since God began to hold converse with
him (Ex. iv. 10). And the testimony of the prophet
is true indeed. For at such times it is natural that

always used, but a lost treatise on Gen. xv. 1, part of which
verse is quoted in the second section.
  [b] R.V. "He that shall be the possessor of my house is
Dammesek Eliezer." (A.V. "The steward of my house is
this Eliezer of Damascus.")

ὄργανον ἐπέχεσθαι, τὸν δὲ κατὰ διάνοιαν λόγον
ἀρθρούμενον ἀνυποτάκτῳ φορᾷ χρῆσθαι, νοημάτων οὐ ῥημάτων ἐπάλληλα κάλλη μετ' εὐτρόχου
5 καὶ ὑψηγόρου δυνάμεως φιλοσοφοῦντα. θαυμάσιοι
δὲ ἀρεταὶ ἥ τε εὐτολμία καὶ ἡ ἐν τῷ δέοντι
παρρησία πρὸς τοὺς ἀμείνους, ὡς καὶ τὸ κωμικὸν
ἀψευδῶς μᾶλλον ἢ κωμικῶς εἰρῆσθαι δοκεῖν

ἂν πάνθ' ὁ δοῦλος ἡσυχάζειν μανθάνῃ,
πονηρὸς ἔσται· μεταδίδου παρρησίας.

6 II. πότε οὖν ἄγει παρρησίαν οἰκέτης
πρὸς δεσπότην; ἆρ' οὐχ ὅταν ἠδικηκότι μὲν
[474] ἑαυτῷ μηδὲν | συνειδῇ, πάντα δ' ὑπὲρ τοῦ κεκτη-
7 μένου καὶ λέγοντι καὶ πράττοντι; πότε οὖν
ἄξιον καὶ τὸν τοῦ θεοῦ δοῦλον ἐλευθεροστομεῖν
πρὸς τὸν ἑαυτοῦ τε καὶ τοῦ παντὸς ἡγεμόνα καὶ
δεσπότην ἢ ὅταν ἁμαρτημάτων καθαρεύῃ καὶ τὸ
φιλοδέσποτον ἐκ τοῦ συνειδότος κρίνῃ, πλείονι
χαρᾷ χρώμενος ἐπὶ τῷ θεράπων θεοῦ γενέσθαι, ἢ
εἰ τοῦ παντὸς ἀνθρώπων γένους ἐβασίλευσε τὸ
γῆς ὁμοῦ καὶ θαλάττης ἀναψάμενος ἀκονιτὶ
8 κράτος; τὰς δὲ φιλοδεσπότους θεραπείας καὶ
λειτουργίας τοῦ Ἀβραὰμ διασυνίστησιν ἀκρο-
τελεύτιον λογίου τοῦ χρησθέντος αὐτοῦ τῷ υἱεῖ·
" δώσω σοι καὶ τῷ σπέρματί σου πᾶσαν τὴν
γῆν ταύτην, καὶ ἐνευλογηθήσονται ἐν τῷ σπέρματί
σου πάντα τὰ ἔθνη τῆς γῆς, ἀνθ' ὧν ὑπήκουσεν
Ἀβραὰμ ὁ πατήρ σου τῆς ἐμῆς φωνῆς, καὶ
ἐφύλαξε τὰ προστάγματά μου καὶ τὰς ἐντολάς
μου καὶ τὰ δικαιώματά μου καὶ τὰ νόμιμά μου."
9 μέγιστον δ' ἐγκώμιον οἰκέτου μηδενὸς ὧν ἂν

the organ of speech should be held in check, while the language of the understanding becomes articulate and flows in resistless stream, as its wisdom pours forth beauty after beauty, not of words but of thoughts, with a power as easy as it is sublime. Yet courage 5 and well-timed frankness before our superiors are admirable virtues also, so that there seems to be more truth than comedy in the words of the comic poet,[a]

> The servant, trained to keep a quiet tongue
> Whate'er befalls, is sure to prove a knave.
> Grant to thy man some measure of free speech.

II. When, then, is it that the servant 6 speaks frankly to his master ? Surely it is when his heart tells him that he has not wronged his owner, but that his words and deeds are all for that owner's benefit. And so when else should the slave of God 7 open his mouth freely to Him Who is the ruler and master both of himself and of the All, save when he is pure from sin and the judgements of his conscience are loyal to his master, when he feels more joy at being the servant of God than if he had been king of all the human race and assumed an uncontested sovereignty over land and sea alike ? The loyalty of 8 Abraham's service and ministry is shewn by the concluding words of the oracle addressed to Abraham's son, "I will give to thee and thy seed all this land, and all the nations of the earth shall be blessed in thy seed, because Abraham thy father hearkened to My voice and kept My injunctions, My commands, My ordinances and My statutes" (Gen. xxvi. 3-5). It is 9 the highest praise which can be given to a servant, that he neglects none of his master's commands, that never hesitating in his labour of love he employs all

[a] Menander.

PHILO

προστάξῃ ὁ δεσπότης ὀλιγωρεῖν, ἀόκνως δὲ καὶ
φιλοπόνως ὑπὲρ δύναμιν πάντα σπουδάζειν αἰσίῳ
10 γνώμῃ κατορθοῦν.   III. εἰσὶ μὲν
οὖν, οἷς ἀκούειν ἀλλ᾽ οὐ λέγειν ἐμπρεπές, ἐφ᾽
ὧν λέγεται " σιώπα καὶ ἄκουε," πάγκαλον παρ-
άγγελμα. θρασύτατον γὰρ καὶ λαλίστατον ἀμαθία,
ἧς πρῶτον μέν ἐστιν ἄκος ἡσυχία, δεύτερον δὲ
προσοχὴ τῶν ἄξιόν τι προφερομένων ἀκοῆς.
11 μηδεὶς μέντοι νομισάτω τοῦτ᾽ αὐτὸ μόνον ἐμφαίνεσθαι διὰ τοῦ " σιώπα καὶ ἄκουε," ἀλλὰ καὶ
προτρέψασθαι δυνατώτερον ἕτερον· οὐ γὰρ παραινεῖ
μόνον γλώττῃ σιωπᾶν καὶ ὠσὶν ἀκούειν, ἀλλὰ
12 καὶ ψυχῇ ταῦτα παθεῖν ἀμφότερα.   πολλοὶ γὰρ
ἐπ᾽ ἀκρόασιν ἥκοντές τινος οὐκ ἐληλύθασι ταῖς
διανοίαις, ἀλλ᾽ ἔξω πλανῶνται καὶ μυρία περὶ
μυρίων ἑαυτοῖς διεξέρχονται, τὰ συγγενικά, τὰ
ὀθνεῖα, τὰ ἴδια, τὰ κοινά,¹ ὧν εἰκὸς ἦν ἐν τῷ
παρόντι μὴ μεμνῆσθαι, πάνθ᾽ ὡς ἔπος εἰπεῖν
ἑξῆς συναριθμούμενοι, καὶ διὰ τὸν ἐν ἑαυτοῖς
πολὺν θροῦν ἀδυνατοῦσι τοῦ λέγοντος ἀκροᾶσθαι·
λέγει γὰρ ἐκεῖνος ὥσπερ οὐκ ἐν ἀνθρώποις, ἀλλ᾽
ἐν ἀψύχοις ἀνδριᾶσιν, οἷς ὦτα μέν ἐστιν, ἀκοαὶ
13 δ᾽ οὐκ ἔνεισιν.   ἐὰν οὖν μηδενὶ τῶν
ἔξωθεν ἐπιφοιτώντων ἢ ἔνδον ταμιευομένων πραγμάτων ὁ νοῦς ἀξιώσῃ προσομιλεῖν, ἀλλ᾽ ἠρεμίαν
ἀγαγὼν καὶ ἡσυχάσας πρὸς τὸν λέγοντα ἑαυτὸν
ἀποτείνῃ, σιωπήσας κατὰ τὸ Μωυσέως παρ-
άγγελμα δυνήσεται μετὰ τῆς πάσης προσοχῆς
ἀκροάσασθαι, ἑτέρως δ᾽ οὐκ ἂν ἰσχύσαι.

---

¹ Wend. δημόσια: Cohn κοινά: the Papyrus according to
Wend. has *sex litteras evanidas*: the mss. omit altogether.
I prefer κοινά as the regular antithesis to ἴδια in Philo.

288

and more than all his powers as he strives by sound judgement to bring all his business to a successful issue.   III. There are indeed some whom it 10 befits to hear but not to speak, those to whom the words apply, " Be silent and hear " (Deut. xxvii. 9). An excellent injunction ! For ignorance is exceeding bold and glib of tongue ; and the first remedy for it is to hold its peace, the second to give ear to those who advance something worth hearing. Yet let no one 11 suppose that this exhausts the significance of the words " be silent and hear." No, they enjoin something else of greater weight. They bid us not only be silent with the tongue and hear with the ears, but be silent and hear with the soul also. For many 12 who come to hear a discourse have not come with their minds, but wander abroad rehearsing inwardly numberless thoughts on numberless subjects, thoughts on their families, on outsiders, on things private and things public, which properly should be forgotten for the moment. All these, we may say,[a] form a series of successions in the mind, and the inward uproar makes it impossible for them to listen to the speaker, who discourses as in an audience not of human beings, but of lifeless statues who have ears, but no hearing is in those ears.   If then the mind deter- 13 mines to have no dealing with any of the matters which visit it from abroad or are stored within it, but maintaining peace and tranquillity addresses itself to hear the speaker, it will be " silent," as Moses commands, and thus be able to listen with complete attention. Otherwise it will have no such power.   IV. For the ignorant then it is well to 14

---

[a] Or " All or practically all," ὡς ἔπος εἰπεῖν serving, as usual, to qualify a round statement.

IV. τοῖς μὲν οὖν ἀμαθέσι συμφέρον ἡσυχία, τοῖς δὲ ἐπιστήμης ἐφιεμένοις καὶ ἅμα φιλοδεσπότοις ἀναγκαιότατον ἡ παρρησία κτῆμα. λέγεται γοῦν ἐν Ἐξαγωγῇ· '' κύριος πολεμήσει ὑπὲρ ὑμῶν, καὶ ὑμεῖς σιγήσετε,'' καὶ χρησμὸς εὐθὺς ὑπόκειται [475] τοιόσδε· '' καὶ εἶπε | κύριος πρὸς Μωυσῆν· τί βοᾷς πρὸς μέ;'' ὡς δέον καὶ σιωπᾶν τοὺς μηδὲν ἄξιον ἀκοῆς ἐροῦντας καὶ λέγειν τοὺς ἔρωτι σοφίας θείῳ πεπιστευκότας καὶ μὴ μόνον λέγειν σὺν ἠρεμίᾳ, ἀλλὰ καὶ μετὰ κραυγῆς μείζονος ἐκβοᾶν, οὐ στόματι καὶ γλώττῃ, δι' ὧν ἀέρα λόγος ἔχει σφαιρούμενον αἰσθητὸν ἀκοῇ γίνεσθαι, ἀλλὰ τῷ παμμούσῳ καὶ μεγαλοφωνοτάτῳ ψυχῆς ὀργάνῳ, οὗ θνητὸς μὲν ἀκροατὴς οὐδὲ εἷς, ὁ δὲ
15 ἀγένητος καὶ ἄφθαρτος μόνος. τὸ γὰρ νοητῆς ἁρμονίας εὐάρμοστον καὶ σύμφωνον μέλος ὁ νοητὸς μουσικὸς μόνος καταλαβεῖν ἱκανός, τῶν δὲ ἐν αἰσθήσει φυρομένων οὐδὲ εἷς. ὅλου δὴ τοῦ διανοίας ὀργάνου κατὰ τὴν διὰ πασῶν ἢ δὶς διὰ πασῶν συμφωνίαν ἐξηχοῦντος ὁ ἀκροατὴς ὡσανεὶ πυνθάνεται πρὸς ἀλήθειαν οὐ πυνθανόμενος— πάντα γὰρ γνώριμα θεῷ— '' τί βοᾷς πρὸς μέ;'' καθ' ἱκεσίαν κακῶν ἀποτροπῆς ἢ κατ' εὐχαριστίαν
16 μετουσίας ἀγαθῶν ἢ κατὰ ἀμφότερα; V. λάλος δὲ οὕτως ὁ ἰσχνόφωνος καὶ βραδύγλωσσος καὶ ἄλογος εἶναι δοκῶν ἀνευρίσκεται, ὥστε πῇ μὲν οὐ μόνον λέγων ἀλλὰ καὶ βοῶν εἰσάγεται, ἑτέρωθι δὲ ἀπαύστῳ καὶ ἀδιαστάτῳ χρώμενος λόγων
17 ῥύμῃ. '' Μωυσῆς '' γάρ φησιν '' ἐλάλει, καὶ ὁ

ᵃ Or '' Why dost thou shout? '' But the other is more probably Philo's interpretation, since he implies that God does not disapprove of Moses' speaking.
290

keep silence, but for those who desire knowledge and also love their master, frank speech is a most essential possession. Thus we read in Exodus, " The Lord will war for you and ye shall be silent," and at once there follows a divine oracle in these words, " What is it that thou shoutest to me ? " [a] (Ex. xiv. 14, 15). The meaning is that those should keep silent who have nothing worth hearing to say, and those should speak who have put their faith in the God-sent love of wisdom, and not only speak with ordinary gentleness but shout with a louder cry. That cry is not made with mouth and tongue, through which, as we are told, the air assumes a spherical [b] shape and thus is rendered perceptible by the sense of hearing, but by the organ of the soul, uniting all music in its mighty tones, heard by no mortal whatsoever, but only by Him Who is uncreated and imperishable. For the 15 sweet and harmonious melody of the mind's music can only be apprehended by the mind's musician, not by any of those who are entangled in sense. But when the full organ of the understanding sounds forth its symphony of the single or double octave, the Hearer asks—asks we may call it, though He does not really ask, since all things are known to God—" What is it that thou criest so loud to me ? " Is it in supplication for ills to be averted, or is in thanksgiving for blessings imparted, or in both ? V. And he that 16 seemed to be feeble of speech and slow of tongue and wordless is found to be so loquacious, that in one place he is represented as not only speaking, but shouting, and in another as pouring forth a stream of words without cessation or pause. For " Moses," we read, 17 " was talking to God, and God was answering him

[b] See App. p. 567.

θεὸς ἀπεκρίνετο αὐτῷ φωνῇ," οὐ κατὰ συντέλειαν ἐλάλησεν, ἀλλὰ κατὰ μηκυνομένην παρά-
τασιν ἐλάλει, καὶ ὁ θεὸς οὐ κατὰ συντέλειαν
18 ἐδίδαξεν, ἀλλ' αἰεὶ καὶ συνεχῶς ἀπεκρίνετο. ὅπου
δὲ ἀπόκρισις, ἐκεῖ πάντως ἐρώτησις. ἐρωτᾷ δὲ
ἕκαστος ὃ μὴ ἐπίσταται, μαθεῖν ἀξιῶν γνούς τε
τῶν εἰς ἐπιστήμην ὠφελιμώτατον ἔργον εἶναι
ζητεῖν, ἐρωτᾶν, πυνθάνεσθαι, μηδὲν δοκεῖν εἰδέναι
19 μηδέ τι οἴεσθαι παγίως κατειληφέναι. σοφοὶ μὲν
οὖν ὑφηγητῇ καὶ διδασκάλῳ χρῶνται θεῷ, οἱ δ'
ἀτελέστεροι τῷ σοφῷ. διὸ καὶ λέγουσι· " λάλησον
σὺ ἡμῖν, καὶ μὴ λαλείτω πρὸς ἡμᾶς ὁ θεός, μή
ποτε ἀποθάνωμεν." τοσαύτη δ' ἄρα χρῆται
παρρησίᾳ ὁ ἀστεῖος, ὥστε οὐ μόνον λέγειν καὶ
βοᾶν, ἀλλ' ἤδη καὶ καταβοᾶν ἐξ ἀληθοῦς πίστεως
20 καὶ ἀπὸ γνησίου τοῦ πάθους θαρρεῖ. τὸ γὰρ
" εἰ μὲν ἀφεῖς αὐτοῖς τὴν ἁμαρτίαν, ἄφες· εἰ δὲ
μή, ἐξάλειψόν με ἐκ τῆς βίβλου σου ἧς ἔγραψας "
καὶ τὸ " μὴ ἐγὼ ἐν γαστρὶ ἔλαβον πάντα τὸν λαὸν
τοῦτον, ἢ ἐγὼ ἔτεκον αὐτόν, ὅτι λέγεις μοι· λάβε
αὐτὸν εἰς τὸν κόλπον σου, ὡσεὶ ἄραι τιθηνὸς τὸν
θηλάζοντα; " καὶ τὸ " πόθεν μοι κρέα δοῦναι
παντὶ τῷ λαῷ τούτῳ, ὅτι κλαίουσιν ἐπ' ἐμοί; μὴ
πρόβατα καὶ βόες σφαγήσονται ἢ πᾶν τὸ ὄψος
τῆς θαλάσσης συναχθήσεται καὶ ἀρκέσει; " καὶ
[476] τὸ " κύριε, διὰ τί | ἐκάκωσας τὸν λαὸν τοῦτον;
καὶ ἵνα τί ἀπέσταλκάς με; καὶ ἀφ' οὗ πεπόρευμαι
πρὸς Φαραὼ λαλῆσαι ἐπὶ τῷ σῷ ὀνόματι, ἐκάκωσε

---

^a παρατατικός is the technical term in the Greek gram-
marians for the imperfect tense. On κατὰ συντέλειαν or
συντελικός see App. p. 567.

292

with a voice " (Ex. xix. 19). We do not have the tense of completed action " he talked," but the tense of prolonged and continuous action *a* " he was talking " ; and similarly God did not teach him (as a complete action) but was answering him always and uninterruptedly. Now an answer always pre- 18 supposes a question ; and everyone asks what he does not know, because he thinks it good to learn and is aware that of all the steps which he can take to get knowledge, the most profitable is to seek, to ask questions, to think that he has no knowledge, and not to imagine that he has a firm apprehension of anything. Now wise men take God for their guide and 19 teacher, but the less perfect take the wise man ; and therefore the Children of Israel say " Talk thou to us, and let not God talk to us lest we die " (Ex. xx. 19).

But the man of worth has such courage of speech, that he is bold not only to speak and cry aloud, but actually to make an outcry of reproach, wrung from him by real conviction, and expressing true emotion. Take the words " if Thou wilt forgive them their sin, 20 forgive them ; but if not, blot me out of the book which Thou hast written " (Ex. xxxii. 32) ; and " Did I conceive all this people in the womb, or did I bring them forth, because Thou sayest unto me, ' take them to thy bosom, as a nurse lifts the suckling ' ? " (Num. xi. 12) ; or again " Whence shall I get flesh to give to this people, because they weep against me ? Shall sheep and oxen be slaughtered, or all the meat that is in the sea be collected and suffice ? " (Num. xi. 13, 22). Or " Lord, why hast Thou afflicted this people and why hast Thou sent me ? And ever since I went to Pharoah to speak in Thy name, he has afflicted the people, and Thou hast not saved

293

τὸν λαόν, καὶ οὐκ ἐρρύσω τὸν λαόν σου," ταῦτα
γὰρ καὶ τὰ τοιαῦτα ἔδεισεν ἄν τις καὶ πρὸς ἕνα
τῶν ἐν μέρει βασιλέων εἰπεῖν· ὁ δ' ἀποφαίνεσθαι
21 καὶ πρὸς θεὸν ἐθάρρησεν.   τοῦτο δ' ἄρα πέρας
ἦν οὐ τόλμης ἁπλῶς, ἀλλ' εὐτολμίας αὐτῷ, διότι
οἱ σοφοὶ πάντες φίλοι θεοῦ, καὶ μάλιστα κατὰ
τὸν ἱερώτατον νομοθέτην.   παρρησία δὲ φιλίας
συγγενές· ἐπεὶ πρὸς τίνα ἄν τις ἢ πρὸς τὸν ἑαυτοῦ
φίλον παρρησιάσαιτο;   παγκάλως οὖν ἐν τοῖς
χρησμοῖς φίλος ᾄδεται Μωυσῆς, ἵν' ὅσα ἐπὶ
θάρσει παρακεκινδυνευμένα διεξέρχεται φιλίᾳ μᾶλλον ἢ αὐθαδείᾳ προφέρεσθαι δοκῇ. θρασύτης μὲν
γὰρ αὐθάδους, φίλου δὲ θαρραλεότης οἰκεῖον.

22   VI. Ἀλλὰ σκόπει πάλιν, ὅτι εὐλαβείᾳ τὸ θαρρεῖν ἀνακέκραται.   τὸ μὲν γὰρ " τί μοι δώσεις; "
θάρσος ἐμφαίνει, τὸ δὲ " δέσποτα " εὐλάβειαν.
εἰωθὼς δὲ χρῆσθαι μάλιστα διτταῖς ἐπὶ τοῦ αἰτίου
προσρήσεσι, τῇ θεὸς καὶ τῇ κύριος, οὐδετέραν νῦν
παρείληφεν, ἀλλὰ τὴν δεσπότου, λίαν εὐλαβῶς καὶ
σφόδρα κυρίως· καίτοι συνώνυμα ταῦτ' εἶναι
23 λέγεται, κύριος καὶ δεσπότης.   ἀλλ' εἰ καὶ τὸ
ὑποκείμενον ἓν καὶ ταὐτόν ἐστιν, ἐπινοίαις αἱ
κλήσεις διαφέρουσι· κύριος μὲν γὰρ παρὰ τὸ
κῦρος, ὃ δὴ βέβαιόν ἐστιν, εἴρηται, κατ' ἐναντιότητα ἀβεβαίου καὶ ἀκύρου, δεσπότης δὲ παρὰ τὸν
δεσμόν, ἀφ' οὗ τὸ δέος οἶμαι—ὥστε τὸν δεσπότην
κύριον εἶναι καὶ ἔτι ὡσανεὶ φοβερὸν κύριον, οὐ
μόνον τὸ κῦρος καὶ τὸ κράτος ἀνημμένον ἁπάντων,
ἀλλὰ καὶ δέος καὶ φόβον ἱκανὸν ἐμποιῆσαι—,

Thy people " (Ex. v. 22, 23). Anyone would have feared to say these or like words, even to one of the kings of particular kingdoms ; yet he had the courage to utter these thoughts to God. He reached this 21 limit, I will not say of daring in general but of good daring, because all the wise are friends of God, and particularly so in the judgement of the most holy law-giver. Frankness of speech is akin to friendship. For to whom should a man speak with frankness but to his friend? And so most excellent is it, that in the oracles Moses is proclaimed the friend of God (Ex. xxxiii. 11), to shew that all the audacities of his bold discourse were uttered in friendship, rather than in presumption. For the audacity of rashness belongs to the presumptuous, the audacity of courage or confidence to a friend.

VI. But observe on the other hand that confidence 22 is blended with caution. For while the words " What wilt thou give me " (Gen. xv. 2) shew confidence, " Master," shews caution. While Moses usually employs two titles in speaking of the Cause, namely God and Lord, here he uses neither, but substitutes " Master." In this he shews great caution and exactness in the use of terms. It is true that " Lord " and " Master " are said to be synonyms. But though one and the same thing is 23 denoted by both, the connotations of the two titles are different. Κύριος (Lord) is derived from κῦρος (power) which is a thing secure and is the opposite of insecure and invalid (ἄκυρος), while δεσπότης (master) is from δεσμός (bond) from which I believe comes δέος (fear). Thus δεσπότης is a lord and some-thing more, a terrible lord so to speak, one who is not only invested with the lordship and sovereignty of all things, but is also capable of inspiring fear and

τάχα μέντοι καὶ ἐπειδὴ τῶν ὅλων δεσμός[1] ἐστι
συνέχων αὐτὰ ἄλυτα καὶ σφίγγων διαλυτὰ ὄντα[2]
24 ἐξ ἑαυτῶν.   ὁ δὴ φάσκων '' δέσποτα,
τί μοι δώσεις '' δυνάμει ταῦτα διεξέρχεται· οὐκ
ἀγνοῶ σου τὸ ὑπερβάλλον κράτος, ἐπίσταμαι τὸ
φοβερὸν τῆς δυναστείας, δεδιὼς καὶ τρέμων
25 ἐντυγχάνω καὶ πάλιν θαρρῶ· σὺ γὰρ ἐθέσπισάς
μοι μὴ φοβεῖσθαι, σύ μοι γλῶσσαν παιδείας
ἔδωκας τοῦ γνῶναι ἡνίκα δεῖ φθέγξασθαι, σὺ τὸ
στόμα ἀπερραμμένον ἐξέλυσας, σὺ διοίξας ἐπὶ
πλέον ἤρθρωσας, σὺ τὰ λεκτέα συνεβίβασας
εἰπεῖν τὸν χρησμὸν βεβαιούμενος ἐκεῖνον· '' ἐγὼ
ἀνοίξω τὸ στόμα σου, καὶ συμβιβάσω σε ἃ μέλλεις
[477] | λαλήσειν.'' τίς γὰρ ἐγενόμην, ἵνα σύ μοι
26 λόγου μεταδῷς, ἵνα μισθὸν ὁμολογῇς, χάριτος καὶ
δωρεᾶς ἀγαθὸν τελεώτερον;   οὐ τῆς πατρίδος
εἰμὶ μετανάστης; οὐ τῆς συγγενείας ἀπελήλαμαι;
οὐ τῆς πατρῴας οἰκίας ἠλλοτρίωμαι; οὐκ ἀπο-
κήρυκτον καὶ φυγάδα πάντες ἔρημον καὶ ἄτιμον
27 ὀνομάζουσιν; ἀλλὰ σύ μοι, δέσποτα, ἡ πατρίς,
σὺ ἡ συγγένεια, σὺ ἡ πατρῴα ἑστία, σὺ ἡ ἐπιτιμία,
ἡ παρρησία, ὁ μέγας καὶ ἀοίδιμος καὶ ἀναφ-
28 αίρετος πλοῦτος. διὰ τί οὖν οὐχὶ θαρρήσω λέγειν
φρονῶ; διὰ τί δ' οὐ πεύσομαι μαθεῖν τι πλέον
ἃ ἀξιῶν; ἀλλ' ὁ λέγων ἐγὼ θαρρεῖν πάλιν ὁμο-
λογῶ δεδιέναι καὶ καταπεπλῆχθαι, καὶ οὐκ ἔχει
τὴν ἄμικτον ἐν ἐμοὶ μάχην φόβος τε καὶ θάρσος,
ὡς ἴσως ὑπολήψεταί τις, ἀλλὰ τὴν ἀνακεκρα-
29 μένην συμφωνίαν. ἀπλήστως οὖν εὐωχοῦμαι τοῦ

---

[1] mss. δεσπότης: Pap. δεσμῶν.
[2] mss. (and Pap.) διαλύοντα.

---

[a] See App. p. 567.

terror ; perhaps too, since he is the bond of all things, one who holds them together indissolubly and binds them fast, when in themselves they are dissoluble.

He who says, " Master, what wilt thou 24 give me ? " virtually says no less than this, " I am not ignorant of Thy transcendent sovereignty ; I know the terrors of Thy power ; I come before Thee in fear and trembling, and yet again I am confident. For Thou hast vouchsafed to bid me fear not ; Thou 25 hast given me a tongue of instruction that I should know when I should speak (Isaiah l. 4),[a] my mouth that was knitted up Thou hast unsewn, and when Thou hadst opened it, Thou didst strengthen its nerves for speech ; Thou hast taught me to say what should be said, confirming the oracle ' I will open thy mouth and teach thee what thou shalt speak ' (Ex. iv. 12). For who was I, that Thou shouldst impart speech to 26 me, that Thou shouldst promise me something which stood higher in the scale of goods than ' gift ' or grace, even a ' reward '. Am I not a wanderer from my country, an outcast from my kinsfolk, an alien from my father's house ? Do not all men call me excommunicate, exile, desolate, disfranchised ? But 27 Thou, Master, art my country, my kinsfolk, my paternal hearth, my franchise, my free speech, my great and glorious and inalienable wealth. Why 28 then shall I not take courage to say what I feel ? Why shall I not inquire of Thee and claim to learn something more ? Yet I, who proclaim my confidence, confess in turn my fear and consternation, and still the fear and the confidence are not at war within me in separate camps, as one might suppose, but are blended in a harmony. I find then a feast 29 which does not cloy in this blending, which has

κράματος, ὅ με ἀναπέπεικε μήτε ἄνευ εὐλαβείας
παρρησιάζεσθαι μήτε ἀπαρρησιάστως εὐλαβεῖσθαι.
τὴν γὰρ οὐδένειαν τὴν ἐμαυτοῦ μετρεῖν ἔμαθον
καὶ τὰς ἐν ὑπερβολαῖς ἀκρότητας τῶν σῶν εὐεργεσιῶν περιβλέπεσθαι· καὶ ἐπειδὰν " γῆν καὶ τέ-
φραν " καὶ εἴ τι ἐκβλητότερον ἐμαυτὸν αἴσθωμαι,
τηνικαῦτα ἐντυγχάνειν σοι θαρρῶ, ταπεινὸς γεγονώς,
καταβεβλημένος εἰς χοῦν, ὅσα εἴς γε τὸ μηδ᾽
ὑφεστάναι δοκεῖν ἀνεστοιχειωμένος.

30 VII. καὶ τοῦτό μου τὸ πάθος τῆς ψυχῆς ἐστηλο-
γράφησεν ἐν τῷ ἐμῷ μνημείῳ ὁ ἐπίσκοπος
Μωυσῆς. " ἐγγίσας " γάρ φησιν " Ἀβραὰμ εἶπε·
νῦν ἠρξάμην λαλῆσαι πρὸς τὸν κύριον, ἐγὼ δέ
εἰμι γῆ καὶ σποδός," ἐπειδὴ τότε καιρὸς ἐντυγχάνειν γένεσιν τῷ πεποιηκότι, ὅτε τὴν ἑαυτῆς
31 οὐδένειαν ἔγνωκεν. τὸ δὲ " τί μοι δώσεις; "
οὐκ ἀποροῦντός ἐστι φωνὴ μᾶλλον ἢ ἐπὶ τῷ
πλήθει καὶ μεγέθει ὧν ἀπήλαυκεν ἀγαθῶν εὐ-
χαριστοῦντος. " τί μοι δώσεις; " ἔτι γὰρ ἀπο-
λείπεταί τι πλέον προσδοκῆσαι; ἄφθονοι μέν, ὦ
φιλόδωρε, αἱ σαὶ χάριτες καὶ ἀπερίγραφοι καὶ
ὅρον ἢ τελευτὴν οὐκ ἔχουσαι, πηγῶν τρόπον πλείω[1]
32 τῶν ἀπαντλουμένων ἀνομβροῦσαι. σκοπεῖν δὲ
ἄξιον οὐ μόνον τὸν αἰεὶ πλημμυροῦντα χείμαρρουν
τῶν σῶν εὐεργεσιῶν, ἀλλὰ καὶ τὰς ἀρδομένας
ἡμῶν ἀρούρας· εἰ γὰρ περιττὸν ἀναχυθείη τὸ
ῥεῦμα, λιμνῶδες καὶ τελματῶδες ἀντὶ καρπο-
φόρου γῆς ἔσται τὸ πεδίον. πρὸς εὐφορίαν οὖν[2]
μεμετρημένης, ἀλλ᾽ οὐκ ἀμέτρου δεῖ τῆς ἐπιρ-

---

[1] mss. τελείων (Pap. ?).
[2] mss. γὰρ (some with Pap. οὐ).

schooled my speech to be neither bold without caution, nor cautious without boldness. For I have learnt to measure my own nothingness, and to gaze with wonder on the transcendent heights of Thy loving-kindnesses. And when I perceive that I am earth and cinders or whatever is still more worthless, it is just then that I have confidence to come before Thee, when I am humbled, cast down to the clay, reduced to such an elemental state,[a] as seems not even to exist. VII. And the watchful 30 pen of Moses has recorded this my soul's condition in his memorial of me. For Abraham, he says, drew near and said, ' Now I have begun to speak to the Lord, and I am earth and ashes ' (Gen. xviii. 27), since it is just when he knows his own nothingness that the creature should come into the presence of his Maker. The words ' What wilt Thou give me ? ' 31 are the cry not so much of uncertainty as of thankfulness for the multitude and greatness of the blessings which one has enjoyed. ' What wilt Thou give me ? ' he says. Is there aught still left for me to expect ? Lavish indeed, Thou bounteous God, are Thy gifts of grace, illimitable without boundary or end, welling up like fountains to replace and more than replace what we draw. But we should look not only 32 to the ever-flowing torrent of Thy loving-kindnesses but also to the fields—they are ourselves—which are watered by them. For if the stream pour forth in over-abundance, the plain will be marshy and fenny, instead of fruitful soil. I need then that the inflow on me should be in due measure for fertility, not un-

[a] See App. p. 567.

33 ροῆς ἐμοί. διὸ πεύσομαι " τί μοι δώσεις " ἀ-
μύθητα δοὺς καὶ σχεδὸν πάντα ὅσα θνητὴν φύσιν
[478] χωρῆσαι | δυνατὸν ἦν; ὃ γὰρ λοιπὸν ἐπιζητῶ
μαθεῖν τε καὶ κτήσασθαι,[1] τοῦτ' ἐστίν, τίς ἂν
γένοιτο ἄξιος τῶν σῶν εὐεργεσιῶν [καὶ] κληρο-
34 νόμος.   ἢ " ἐγὼ ἀπολυθήσομαι ἄτεκνος,"
ὀλιγοχρόνιον καὶ ἐφήμερον καὶ ὠκύμορον λαβὼν
ἀγαθόν, εὐχόμενος τοὐναντίον, πολυήμερον καὶ
μακροχρόνιον καὶ ἀκήρατον καὶ ἀθάνατον, ὡς
δυνηθῆναι καὶ σπέρματα βαλέσθαι καὶ ῥίζας
ἐχυρότητος ἕνεκα ἀποτεῖναι καὶ ἄνω πρὸς οὐρανὸν
35 τὸ στέλεχος ἀνεγεῖρον μετεωρίσαι;   τὴν γὰρ
ἀνθρωπίνην ἀρετὴν βαίνειν μὲν ἐπὶ γῆς, φθάνειν
δὲ πρὸς οὐρανὸν ἀναγκαῖον, ἵν' ἐκεῖ τῆς ἀφθαρσίας
36 ἑστιαθεῖσα τὸν ἀεὶ χρόνον ἀπήμων διαμένῃ.   ἄ-
τεκνον γὰρ καὶ στεῖραν οἶδ' ὅτι ψυχὴν ὁ τὰ μὴ
ὄντα φέρων καὶ τὰ πάντα γεννῶν μεμίσηκας, ἐπεὶ
καὶ χάριν ἔδωκας ἐξαίρετον τῷ διορατικῷ γένει τὸ
μηδέποτε στειρωθῆναι καὶ ἀτοκῆσαι, ᾧ καὶ αὐτὸς
προσνεμηθεὶς ἐφίεμαι κληρονόμου δικαίως.   ἄ-
σβεστον γὰρ αὐτὸ καταθεώμενος αἴσχιστον εἶναι
νομίζω τὴν ἐμαυτοῦ ἔφεσιν[2] τοῦ καλοῦ περιιδεῖν
37 καταλυθεῖσαν.   ἱκέτης οὖν γίνομαι καὶ ποτνιῶμαι,
ἵνα σπερμάτων καὶ ἐμπυρευμάτων ὑποτυφομένων
τὸ ἀρετῆς ἀνακαίηται καὶ ἀναφλέγηται σωτήριον
φέγγος, ὃ λαμπαδευόμενον ἐπαλλήλοις διαδοχαῖς
38 ἰσοχρόνιον γενήσεται κόσμῳ.   ζῆλον καὶ τοῖς
ἀσκητικοῖς ἔδωκας τέκνων τῶν ψυχῆς σπορᾶς

---

[1] mss. ἐπιζητῶ τέκνον κτήσασθαι (Pap. μανειν τε και?).
[2] My correction for mss. and Pap. φύσιν; see App. p. 567.
But another, and possibly preferable, solution would be τοῦ
⟨φιλο⟩κάλου agreeing with ἐμαυτοῦ.

measured. Therefore I will ask ' What wilt Thou 33
give me ? ' Thou whose gifts have been countless,
almost to the very sum of what human nature can
contain. For all that I still seek to learn and to
gain is but this ' Who should be a worthy heir of
thy benefits ? ' Or shall I go hence child- 34
less (Gen. xv. 2), the recipient of a boon shortlived,
dying with the day, passing swiftly to its doom ; I,
who pray for the opposite, a boon of many days and
years, proof against decay or death, so that it can lay
the seed and extend the roots, which shall make the
growth secure, and raise and uplift the stalk heaven-
wards. For man's excellence must not tread the 35
earth, but press upwards to heaven, that it may
banquet there on incorruption and remain unscathed
for ever. For I know that Thou, who givest [a] being 36
to what is not and generatest all things, hast hated
the childless and barren soul, since Thou hast given
as a special grace to the race of them that see that
they should never be without children or sterile.
And I myself having been made a member of that
race justly desire an heir. For when I contemplate
the race's security from extinction, I hold it a deep
disgrace to leave my own desire of excellence to
come to naught. Therefore I beseech and suppli- 37
cate that out of the smouldering tinder and embers
the saving light of virtue may burn up with full flame
and carried on as in the torch-race by unfailing succession may be coeval with the world. Also in the 38
votaries of practice Thou hast implanted a zeal to sow
and beget the children of the soul, and when they

---

[a] A curious use of φέρω, but paralleled by *De Mut.* 192
τῷ τῆς ψυχῆς φέροντι καὶ αὔξοντι καὶ πληροῦντι καρποὺς θεῷ;
cf. ibid. 256.

καὶ γενέσεως, καὶ μοιραθέντες ὑφ᾽ ἡδονῆς ἐξελάλη-
σαν εἰπόντες· " τὰ παιδία οἷς ἠλέησεν ὁ θεὸς τὸν
παῖδά σου," ὧν ἀκακία καὶ τροφὸς καὶ τιθήνη,
ὧν ἄβατοι καὶ ἁπαλαὶ καὶ εὐφυεῖς ψυχαί, τῶν
ἀρετῆς παγκάλων καὶ θεοειδεστάτων εὐπαρά-
39 δεκτοι χαρακτήρων. δίδαξον δέ με κἀκεῖνο, εἰ
" ὁ υἱὸς Μασὲκ τῆς οἰκογενοῦς μου " τῶν σῶν
χαρίτων ἱκανὸς γενέσθαι κληρονόμος ἐστίν. ἐγὼ
γὰρ ἄχρι νῦν τὸν μὲν ἐλπιζόμενον οὐκ ἔλαβον, ὃν
δ᾽ ἔλαβον, οὐκ ἐλπίζω.

40 VIII. Τίς δὲ ἡ Μασὲκ καὶ τίς αὐτῆς ὁ υἱός, οὐ
παρέργως ἐπισκεπτέον. ἑρμηνεύεται τοίνυν Μασὲκ
ἐκ φιλήματος. φίλημα δὲ διαφέρει τοῦ φιλεῖν· τὸ
μὲν γὰρ ψυχῶν ἕνωσιν ἁρμοζομένων εὐνοίᾳ, τὸ δὲ
ἐπιπόλαιον καὶ ψιλὴν δεξίωσιν χρείας τινὸς εἰς
41 ταὐτὸ συναγαγούσης ἔοικεν ἐμφαίνειν. ὥσπερ γὰρ
ἐν τῷ ἀνακύπτειν οὐκ ἔστι τὸ κύπτειν οὐδ᾽ ἐν τῷ
καταπίνειν ἦν πάντως τὸ πίνειν οὐδ᾽ ἐν μαρσίππῳ
ὁ ἵππος, οὕτως οὐδ᾽ ἐν τῷ καταφιλεῖν τὸ φιλεῖν,
ἐπεὶ καὶ τῶν ἐχθρῶν μυρίους εἴκοντές τινες ταῖς
42 τοῦ βίου χαλεπαῖς ἀνάγκαις δεξιοῦνται. τίς οὖν
ἐστιν ἡ ἐκ φιλήματος ἀλλὰ μὴ ἐξ ἀψευδοῦς φιλίας
ἡμῖν συσταθεῖσα, φράσω μηδὲν ὑποστειλάμενος· ἡ
[479] ζωὴ ἡ σὺν αἰσθήσει, ἡ πᾶσιν ὠχυρωμένη, | ἧς
ἀνέραστος οὐδείς, ἣν δέσποιναν μὲν οἱ πολλοί,
θεράπαιναν δὲ οἱ ἀστεῖοι νομίζουσιν, οὐκ ἀλλό-
φυλον ἢ ἀργυρώνητον, ἀλλ᾽ οἰκογενῆ καὶ τρόπον

---

[a] A reminiscence of Plato, *Phaedrus* 245 A. See note
on 249.

[b] Philo curiously ignores the quite common use of φιλεῖν
= to kiss. Possibly it may have carried with it the idea of
a kiss given in true affection, which was absent in the
compound.

are thus endowed they have cried out in their pleasure, ' The children, wherewith Thou hast shewn mercy to Thy servant' (Gen. xxxiii. 5). Of such children innocence is the nurse and fostermother ; their souls are virgin and tender and rich in nature's gifts,[a] ready to receive the glorious and divine impressions of virtue's graving. Tell me this too, 39 whether the son of Masek, she who was born in my house, is fit to become the heir of thy gifts of grace. For till now I have not received him whom I hope for, and he, whom I have received, is not the heir of my hopes."

VIII. Who Masek and her son are is a matter for 40 careful consideration. Well, the name Masek is interpreted " From a kiss." Now " kiss " is not the same as " loving." The latter appears to signify the uniting of souls which goodwill joins together, the former merely the bare superficial salutation, which passes when some occasion has caused a meeting. For just as in ἀνακύπτειν (rising up) there 41 is no idea of κύπτειν (stooping) nor in καταπίνειν (swallowing) the whole idea of πίνειν (drinking), nor in μάρσιππος (pouch) that of ἵππος (horse), so neither in καταφιλεῖν (kissing) do we have φιλεῖν (loving).[b] For people bowing to the hard necessities of life in hundreds of cases greet their enemies thus. Who then she is, with whom we are brought into 42 contact " from " or " in consequence of a kiss," and not from true friendship, I will shew without disguise. It is the life of the senses, the assured possession of us all, for which all have a feeling of affection. The multitude regard her as a mistress, the good as their servant, not a servant of alien race or purchased with money, but homeborn and in a

τινὰ ὁμόφυλον. οὗτοι καὶ πεπαίδευνται καταφιλεῖν αὐτήν, οὐ φιλεῖν, ἐκεῖνοι δὲ ὑπερφυῶς ἀγαπᾶν
43 καὶ τριπόθητον ἡγεῖσθαι.   Λάβαν δ' ὁ
μισάρετος οὐδὲ καταφιλῆσαι δυνήσεται τὰς προσκεκληρωμένας τῷ ἀσκητικῷ δυνάμεις, ἀλλ' ὑποκρίσεως καὶ ψευδῶν πλασμάτων ἀνηρτηκὼς τὸν
ἑαυτοῦ βίον, ὡσανεὶ δυσχεραίνων, οὐ πρὸς ἀλήθειαν
ἀλγῶν, φησίν· " οὐκ ἠξιώθην καταφιλῆσαι τὰ
παιδία μου καὶ τὰς θυγατέρας ·" εἰκότως γε καὶ
προσηκόντως· εἰρωνείαν γὰρ μισεῖν ἀκαταλλάκτως
44 ἐπαιδεύθημεν. ἀγάπησον οὖν ἀρετὰς καὶ ἄσπασαι
ψυχῇ τῇ σεαυτοῦ καὶ φίλησον ὄντως, καὶ ἥκιστα
βουλήσῃ τὸ φιλίας παράκομμα ποιεῖν, καταφιλεῖν.
" μὴ γάρ ἐστιν αὐταῖς ἔτι μερὶς ἢ κληρονομία ἐν
τῷ σῷ οἴκῳ; οὐχ ὡς αἱ ἀλλότριαι ἐλογίσθησαν
παρὰ σοί; ἢ οὐ πέπρακας αὐτάς, καὶ κατέφαγες
τὸ ἀργύριον," ἵνα μηδὲ εἰσαῦθις ἀνακομίσασθαι
δυνηθῇς τὰ σῶστρα καὶ τὰ λύτρα κατεδηδοκώς;
προσποιοῦ νῦν βούλεσθαι καταφιλεῖν ὁ πᾶσι τοῖς
κριταῖς ἄσπονδος.   ἀλλ' οὐ γαμβρὸν[1]
καταφιλήσει Μωυσῆς, ἀλλ' ἀπὸ γνησίου τοῦ
ψυχῆς πάθους φιλήσει· " ἐφίλησε " γάρ φησιν
" αὐτόν, καὶ ἠσπάσαντο ἀλλήλους."
45 IX. ζωῆς δὲ τριττὸν γένος, τὸ μὲν πρὸς θεόν, τὸ
δὲ πρὸς γένεσιν, τὸ δὲ μεθόριον, μικτὸν ἀμφοῖν.
τὸ μὲν οὖν πρὸς θεὸν οὐ κατέβη πρὸς ἡμᾶς οὐδὲ
ἦλθεν εἰς τὰς σώματος ἀνάγκας. τὸ δὲ πρὸς

---

[1] So Mangey and Wend.: mss. and Pap. Ἀαρών. It may
be questioned whether this is not what Philo wrote, by confusing Ex. xviii. 7 with iv. 27, where Moses meets Aaron
(συνήντησεν αὐτῷ . . . καὶ κατεφίλησαν ἀλλήλους).

sense a kinswoman. The wise have been trained to greet her with a kiss, but not to love her, the others to love her deeply and regard her worthy of a triple measure of their affection.   Now 43 Laban the virtue-hater will not be able even to kiss the qualities which are allotted to the Man of Practice. Still since he has made hypocrisy and false inventions the cardinal principle of his life, he says, as though in dudgeon, though he has no real grief, " I was not held worthy to kiss my children and my daughters " (Gen. xxxi. 28). The refusal of the kiss is natural and proper. For we the children have been trained to hate dissimulation, with a hatred that refuses all dealing. Hold then the virtues dear, 44 embrace them with thy soul and love them truly, and thou wilt never desire to be the maker of that travesty of friendship, the kiss. " Have they, we shall say, any part or inheritance in your home ? Were they not counted as aliens in your sight, or have you not sold them and devoured the money ? " (Gen. xxxi. 14, 15). You devoured the price of their redemption, lest you should ever again be able to buy them back. And now you pretend to wish to kiss them, you in the judgement of all their deadly foe.   Moses on the other hand will not kiss his father-in-law, but loves him with genuine heart-felt affection. For " he loved him " we read " and they greeted each other " (Ex. xviii. 7).

IX. Now there are three kinds of life, 45 one looking Godwards, another looking to created things, another on the border-line, a mixture of the other two. The God-regarding life has never come down to us, nor submitted to the constraints of the body. The life that looks to creation has never risen

γένεσιν οὐδ' ὅλως ἀνέβη οὐδ' ἐζήτησεν ἀναβῆναι,
φωλεῦον δὲ ἐν μυχοῖς Ἅιδου τῷ ἀβιώτῳ βίῳ
46 χαίρει. τὸ δὲ μικτόν ἐστιν, ὃ πολλάκις μὲν ὑπὸ
τῆς ἀμείνονος ἀγόμενον τάξεως θειάζει καὶ θεο-
φορεῖται, πολλάκις δ' ὑπὸ τῆς χείρονος ἀντι-
σπώμενον ἐπιστρέφει. τοῦθ', ὅταν ὥσπερ ἐπὶ πλάστιγγος ἡ τῆς κρείττονος ζωῆς μοῖρα τοῖς ὅλοις
βρίσῃ, συνεπισπασθὲν τὸ τῆς ἐναντίας ζωῆς[1] βάρος
47 κουφότατον ἄχθος ἀπέφηνε. Μωυσῆς δὲ τὸ τῆς
πρὸς θεὸν ζωῆς γένος ἀκονιτὶ στεφανώσας εἰς
ἐπίκρισιν τὰ λοιπὰ ἄγει δυσὶν ἀπεικάζων γυναιξίν,
ὧν τὴν μὲν ἀγαπωμένην, τὴν δὲ μισουμένην καλεῖ
48 προσφυέστατα θεὶς ὀνόματα. τίς γὰρ οὐ τὰς δι'
ὀφθαλμῶν, τίς δ' οὐ τὰς δι' ὤτων, τίς δ' οὐ τὰς
διὰ γεύσεως ὀσφρήσεώς τε καὶ ἁφῆς ἡδονὰς καὶ
τέρψεις ἀποδέχεται; τίς δ' οὐ τὰ ἐναντία με-
μίσηκεν, ὀλιγοδεΐαν, ἐγκράτειαν, αὐστηρὸν καὶ ἐπι-
στημονικὸν βίον, γέλωτος καὶ παιδιᾶς ἀμέτοχον,
[480] συννοίας καὶ | φροντίδων καὶ πόνων μεστόν, φίλον
τοῦ θεωρεῖν, ἀμαθίας ἐχθρόν, χρημάτων μὲν καὶ
δόξης καὶ ἡδονῶν κρείττω, ἥττω δὲ σωφροσύνης
καὶ εὐκλείας καὶ βλέποντος οὐ τυφλοῦ πλούτου;
πρεσβύτερα μὲν οὖν ἀεὶ τὰ γεννήματα
49 τῆς μισουμένης ἀρετῆς. Χ. ὁ δὲ Μωυσῆς, εἰ καὶ
νεώτερα χρόνῳ, [καὶ] ταῦτα φύσει πρεσβείων ἀξιοῖ

---

[1] Pap. between ζωῆς and βάρος inserts αντηεν. May this
perhaps stand for Ἀνταίειον? The myth of Antaeus, who
became helpless when lifted by Heracles from the ground,
would suit the parable well. Cf. Σισύφειος De Cher. 78,
Ταντάλειος below, § 269. It is true of course that these stories
were far better known than that of Antaeus.

---

[a] This description of the "mixed life" closely resembles

at all nor sought to rise, but makes its lair in the recesses of Hades and rejoices in a form of living, which is not worth the pains. It is the mixed life,[a] which 46 often drawn on by those of the higher line is possessed and inspired by God, though often pulled back by the worse it reverses its course. And when the better life placed as a weight on the scales completely preponderates, the mixed life carried with it makes the opposite life seem light as air in the balance. Now 47 Moses while he gives the crown of undisputed victory to the Godward kind of life, brings the other two into comparison by likening them to two women, one of whom he calls the beloved and the other the hated. These names are very suitable, for who does not look 48 with favour on the pleasures and delights that come through the eyes, or the ears, or through taste and smell and touch ? Who has not hated the opposites of these ?—frugality, temperance, the life of austerity and knowledge, which has no part in laughter and sport, which is full of anxiety and cares and toils, the friend of contemplation, the enemy of ignorance, which puts under its feet money and mere reputation and pleasure, but is mastered by self-restraint and true glory and the wealth which is not blind but sees.

Now the children of virtue, the hated one, are always the senior. X. And Moses holds them 49 to be by their nature worthy of the rights of the senior, even though they be younger in point of

that of the ἀσκητής in *De Som.* i. **151**, who is midway between the wise who live in the Olympian region and the bad who live in the recesses of Hades. In fact the " mixed " seems to represent the ordinary virtuous man (ὁ προκόπτων), and in the sequel is equated to the Hated Wife and to Leah, both of whom regularly represent Virtue. For the last part of the sentence see App. p. 568.

τὰ διπλᾶ διδούς, τῶν δὲ ἀφαιρῶν τὴν ἡμίσειαν.
ἐὰν γὰρ γένωνται, φησίν, ἀνθρώπῳ δύο γυναῖκες,
ἠγαπημένη καὶ μισουμένη, καὶ τέκωσιν ἀμφότεραι,
μέλλων τὰ ἑαυτοῦ διανέμειν οὐ δυνήσεται πρεσβείων ἀξιῶσαι τὸν υἱὸν τῆς ἠγαπημένης, ἡδονῆς,
—νέος γὰρ οὗτος, εἰ καὶ χρόνῳ πολιὸς[1] γένοιτο,—
ἀλλὰ τὸν τῆς μισουμένης, φρονήσεως, πρεσβύτερον
ἐκ παίδων εὐθὺς ὄντα, ὡς διμοιρίαν ἀπονεῖμαι.
50 τὴν δὲ τροπικωτέραν τούτων ἀπόδοσιν ἐν ἑτέροις
εἰρηκότες ἐπὶ τὰ ἀκόλουθα τῶν ἐν χερσὶ τρεψώ-
μεθα ἐκεῖνο προϋποδείξαντες, ὅτι τῆς μισουμένης ὁ
θεὸς λέγεται τὴν μήτραν διοίξας γένεσιν ἀστείων ἐπιτηδευμάτων καὶ καλῶν ἔργων ἀνατεῖλαι, τῆς φιλεῖ-
51 σθαι νομιζομένης αὐτίκα στειρουμένης. "ἰδὼν"
γάρ φησι "κύριος ὅτι μισεῖται Λεία, ἤνοιξε
τὴν μήτραν αὐτῆς· Ῥαχὴλ δὲ ἦν στεῖρα." ἆρ'
οὐχ ὅταν ἡ ψυχὴ κυοφορῇ καὶ τίκτειν ἄρχηται
τὰ ψυχῇ πρέποντα, τηνικαῦτα ὅσα αἰσθητὰ στει-
ρούμενα ἀτοκεῖ, οἷς πρόσεστιν ἡ ἐκ φιλήματος
ἀλλ' οὐχ ἡ διὰ γνησίου φιλίας ἀποδοχή; XI.
52 ταύτης οὖν τῆς κατ' αἴσθησιν ζωῆς, ἣν καλεῖ
Μασέκ, υἱὸς ἕκαστος ἡμῶν ἐστι τιμῶν καὶ θαυμάζων τὴν τροφὸν καὶ τιθήνην τοῦ θνητοῦ
γένους, αἴσθησιν, ἣν καὶ ὁ γήινος νοῦς, ὄνομα
Ἀδάμ, ἰδὼν διαπλασθεῖσαν τὸν ἑαυτοῦ θάνατον

[1] MSS. παλαιὸς (Pap. παλιος).

---

[a] Or, if the καί, is retained, "And if any be younger in
point of years, even them too in virtue of their nature does
Moses hold worthy," etc. In this case ταῦτα, and consequently the text quoted from Deuteronomy, is restricted to
the νεώτερα χρόνῳ. Philo implies, what he actually argues

years,[a] for he gives them the double portion, and takes from the others their half-share. " For if a man," he says, " has two wives, one beloved and one hated, and both bear him children, when he purposes to divide his possessions, he shall not be able to adjudge the elder's rights to the son of the beloved (that is, of Pleasure) for he is but ' young,' even if years have made him grey-headed, but to the son of Prudence, the hated wife, the son who from earliest childhood is an ' elder,' he must give these rights and thus assign to him a double portion " (Deut. xxi. 15-17). Now we have given the allegorical inter- 50 pretation of this more closely elsewhere [b] and therefore let us turn to the next part of our theme. One thing however we must first point out, namely that we are told that God by opening the womb of the hated wife brought to its rising the birth of worthy practices and excellent deeds, while she, who was thought to be beloved, immediately became barren. For " the Lord " it runs " seeing that Leah is hated 51 opened her womb, but Rachel was barren "(Gen. xxix. 31). Is it not just then, when the soul is pregnant and begins to bear what befits a soul, that all objects of sense become barren and incapable of child-bearing, those objects which find acceptance with us " from the kiss " and not through genuine friendship. XI. This life of the senses, then, which he calls 52 Masek, has for her son each one among us who honours and admires the nurse and foster-mother of our mortal race, that is Sense, on whose just-fashioned form the earthly mind, called Adam, looked and gave

---

in *De Sobr.* 22, that the words of Deut. make the son of the Beloved to be, in the literal sense, the elder.
[b] In *Leg. All.* ii. 48, *De Sac.* 19 ff., *De Sobr.* 21 ff.

53 ζωὴν ἐκείης[1] ὠνόμασεν. "ἐκάλεσε" γάρ φησιν
"Ἀδὰμ τὸ ὄνομα τῆς γυναικὸς αὐτοῦ ζωή, ὅτι
αὕτη μήτηρ πάντων τῶν ζώντων," τῶν πρὸς
ἀλήθειαν τὸν ψυχῆς τεθνηκότων δήπου βίον. οἱ
δὲ ζῶντες ὄντως μητέρα μὲν ἔχουσι σοφίαν,
αἴσθησιν δὲ δούλην πρὸς ὑπηρεσίαν ἐπιστήμης ὑπὸ
φύσεως δημιουργηθεῖσαν.

54 Ὄνομα δὲ τοῦ γεννηθέντος ἐκ ζωῆς, ἣν ἐκ φιλήματος ἐγνωρίσαμεν, διασυνίστησι Δαμασκόν[2]—τὸ δὲ
μεταληφθέν ἐστιν αἷμα σάκκου,—σφόδρα δυνατῶς
καὶ εὐθυβόλως σάκκον μὲν τὸ σῶμα αἰνιξάμενος,

55 αἷμα δὲ ζωὴν τὴν ἔναιμον. ἐπειδὴ γὰρ ψυχὴ διχῶς
λέγεται, ἥ τε ὅλη καὶ τὸ ἡγεμονικὸν αὐτῆς μέρος, ὃ
κυρίως εἰπεῖν ψυχὴ ψυχῆς ἐστι, καθάπερ ὀφθαλμὸς
ὅ τε κύκλος σύμπας καὶ τὸ κυριώτατον μέρος τὸ
ᾧ βλέπομεν, ἔδοξε τῷ νομοθέτῃ διττὴν καὶ τὴν
[481] οὐσίαν εἶναι ψυχῆς, αἷμα μὲν τῆς ὅλης, τοῦ | δ'
ἡγεμονικωτάτου πνεῦμα θεῖον. φησὶ γοῦν ἄντι-

56 κρυς· "ψυχὴ πάσης σαρκὸς αἷμά ἐστιν." εὖ
γε τὸ προσνεῖμαι τῷ σαρκῶν ὄχλῳ τὴν αἵματος
ἐπιρροήν, οἰκεῖον οἰκείῳ· τοῦ δὲ νοῦ τὴν οὐσίαν
ἐξ οὐδενὸς ἤρτησε γενητοῦ, ἀλλ' ὑπὸ θεοῦ κατα-
πνευσθεῖσαν εἰσήγαγεν· "ἐνεφύσησε" γάρ φησιν "ὁ
ποιητὴς τῶν ὅλων εἰς τὸ πρόσωπον αὐτοῦ πνοὴν
ζωῆς, καὶ ἐγένετο ὁ ἄνθρωπος εἰς ψυχὴν ζῶσαν,"
ᾗ καὶ κατὰ τὴν εἰκόνα τοῦ ποιητοῦ λόγος ἔχει

57 τυπωθῆναι. XII. ὥστε διττὸν εἶδος ἀνθρώπων,

---

[1] ? ἐκείνην with Pap. and some mss. See App. p. 568.
[2] So mss.: Wend. from Pap. Δαμασκός. But would not
Philo have written τὸ Δαμασκός if he used the nominative?

---

[a] See note on the phrase "soul as soul," *De Mig.* 5.

the name of what was his own death to her life. "For Adam," it says, "called the name of his wife 53 'Life,' because she is the mother of all things living" (Gen. iii. 20), that is doubtless of those who are in truth dead to the life of the soul. But those who are really living have Wisdom for their mother, but Sense they take for a bond-woman, the handiwork of nature made to minister to knowledge.

The name of the child born of the life which we 54 have explained as the "life from a kiss" he puts before us as Damascus, which is interpreted as "the blood of a sackcloth robe." By sackcloth robe he intimates the body, and by blood the "blood-life," and the symbolism is very powerful and apt. We use "soul" in two senses, both for the whole 55 soul and also for its dominant part, which properly speaking is the soul's soul,[a] just as the eye can mean either the whole orb, or the most important part, by which we see. And therefore the lawgiver held that the substance of the soul is twofold, blood being that of the soul as a whole, and the divine breath or spirit that of its most dominant part. Thus he says plainly "the soul of every flesh is the blood" (Lev. xvii. 11). He does well in assigning the blood with its 56 flowing stream to the riot[b] of the manifold flesh, for each is akin to the other. On the other hand he did not make the substance of the mind depend on anything created, but represented it as breathed upon by God. For the Maker of all, he says, "blew into his face the breath of life, and man became a living soul" (Gen. ii. 7); just as we are also told that he was fashioned after the image of his Maker (Gen. i. 27). XII. So we have two kinds of men, one 57

<hr/>

[b] Or "horde." See note on *Quod Deus* 2.

τὸ μὲν θείῳ πνεύματι λογισμῷ βιούντων, τὸ δὲ
αἵματι καὶ σαρκὸς ἡδονῇ ζώντων. τοῦτο τὸ εἶδός
ἐστι πλάσμα γῆς, ἐκεῖνο δὲ θείας εἰκόνος ἐμφερὲς
58 ἐκμαγεῖον.   χρεῖος δ' ἐστὶν οὐ μετρίως
ὁ πεπλασμένος ἡμῶν χοῦς καὶ ἀναδεδευμένος
αἵματι βοηθείας τῆς ἐκ θεοῦ· διὸ λέγεται " οὗτος
Δαμασκὸς Ἐλιέζερ"—ἑρμηνευθεὶς δέ ἐστιν Ἐλιέζερ
θεός μου βοηθός,—ἐπειδὴ ὁ ἔναιμος ὄγκος ἐξ
ἑαυτοῦ διαλυτὸς ὢν καὶ νεκρὸς συνέστηκε καὶ
ζωπυρεῖται προνοίᾳ θεοῦ τοῦ τὴν χεῖρα ὑπερέχοντος
καὶ ὑπερασπίζοντος, μηδεμίαν ἡμέραν ἱδρυθῆναι
παγίως δυνηθέντος ἐξ ἑαυτοῦ τοῦ γένους ἡμῶν.
59 οὐχ ὁρᾷς ὅτι καὶ Μωυσέως ὁ δεύτερος τῶν υἱῶν
ὁμωνυμεῖ τούτῳ; " τὸ γὰρ ὄνομα" φησί " τοῦ
δευτέρου Ἐλιέζερ," καὶ τὴν αἰτίαν ἐπιφέρει· " ὁ
γὰρ θεὸς τοῦ πατρός μου βοηθός μου, καὶ ἐξείλατό
60 με ἐκ χειρὸς Φαραώ." τοῖς δ' ἔτι τῆς ἐναίμου καὶ
αἰσθητῆς ζωῆς ἑταίροις ἐπιτίθεται ὁ σκεδάσαι τὰς
θεοσεβείας δεινὸς τρόπος, ὄνομα Φαραώ, οὗ τὴν
παρανομίας καὶ ὠμότητος μεστὴν δυναστείαν
ἀμήχανον ἐκφυγεῖν ἄνευ τοῦ γεννηθῆναι τὸν
Ἐλιέζερ ἐν ψυχῇ καὶ ἐπελπίσαι τὴν παρὰ τοῦ
61 μόνου σωτῆρος θεοῦ βοήθειαν.   παγκάλως δὲ τὸν Δαμασκὸν οὐκ ἀπὸ πατρός, ἀλλ'
ἀπὸ μητρὸς τῆς Μασὲκ διασυνέστησεν, ἵνα διδάξῃ
ὅτι ἡ ἔναιμος ψυχή, καθ' ἣν ζῇ καὶ τὰ ἄλογα, τοῦ
πρὸς γυναικῶν μητρῴου γένους οἰκεῖόν ἐστιν,
62 ἄρρενος γενεᾶς ἀμέτοχον. ἀλλ' οὐχ ἡ ἀρετὴ
Σάρρα· μόνου γὰρ τοῦ πρὸς ἀνδρῶν μεταποιεῖται,

that of those who live by reason, the divine inbreathing, the other of those who live by blood and the pleasure of the flesh. This last is a moulded clod of earth, the other is the faithful impress of the divine image.

Yet this our piece of moulded clay, 58 tempered with blood for water, has imperative need of God's help, and thus we read "this Damascus Eliezer." Now Eliezer interpreted is "God is my helper," for this mass of clay and blood, which in itself is dissoluble and dead, holds together and is quickened as into flame by the providence of God, who is its protecting arm and shield, since our race cannot of itself stand firmly established for a single day. Observe, too, that the second son of Moses 59 bears the same name. "The name of the second," he says, "was Eliezer," and then he adds the reason: "for the God of my father is my helper and delivered me from the hand of Pharoah" (Ex. xviii. 4). But those who still consort with the life of sense and 60 blood suffer the attacks of the spirit so expert in scattering[a] pious thoughts and deeds, the spirit called Pharoah, whose tyranny rife with lawlessness and cruelty it is impossible to escape, unless Eliezer be born in the soul and looks with hope to the help which God the only Saviour can give.

Right well, too, does Moses describe Damascus as the 61 son not of his father but of his mother, Masek, to shew us that the blood-soul, by which irrational animals also live, has kinship with the maternal and female line, but has no part in male descent. Not 62 so was it with Virtue or Sarah, for male descent is the sole claim of her, who is the motherless ruling

---

[a] Cf. the regular epithet of Pharoah, ὁ σκεδαστὴς τῶν καλῶν, e.g. De Sac. 48.

ἐκ πατρὸς τοῦ πάντων θεοῦ μόνου γεννηθεῖσα ἡ ἀμήτωρ ἀρχή· " ἀληθῶς " γάρ φησιν " ἀδελφή μού ἐστιν ἐκ πατρός, ἀλλ᾽ οὐκ ἐκ μητρός."

63 XIII. Ἃ μὲν οὖν ἦν ἀναγκαῖον προακοῦσαι, διεπτύξαμεν· καὶ γὰρ εἶχεν ἀσάφειαν ἡ πρότασις αἰνιγματώδη. τί δὲ ὁ φιλομαθὴς ζητεῖ, διερμηνευτέον ἀκριβέστερον· μήποτ᾽ οὖν ἐστι τοιοῦτον, [482] εἰ δύναταί | τις ἐφιέμενος τῆς ἐναίμου ζωῆς καὶ μεταποιούμενος ἔτι τῶν κατ᾽ αἴσθησιν γενέσθαι τῶν ἀσωμάτων καὶ θείων πραγμάτων κληρονόμος.

64 τούτων μόνος ἀξιοῦται ὁ καταπνευσθεὶς ἄνωθεν, οὐρανίου τε καὶ θείας μοίρας ἐπιλαχών, ὁ καθαρώτατος νοῦς, ἀλογῶν οὐ μόνον σώματος ἀλλὰ καὶ τοῦ ἑτέρου ψυχῆς τμήματος, ὅπερ ἄλογον ὑπάρχον αἵματι πέφυρται, θυμοὺς ζέοντας καὶ πεπυρω-

65 μένας ἐπιθυμίας ἀναφλέγον. πυνθάνεται γοῦν τὸν τρόπον τοῦτον· ἐπειδὴ ἐμοὶ οὐκ ἔδωκας σπέρμα τὸ νοητὸν ἐκεῖνο, τὸ αὐτοδίδακτον, τὸ θεοειδές, ἆρά γε " ὁ οἰκογενής μου κληρονομήσει με," ὁ

66 τῆς ἐναίμου ζωῆς ἔγγονος;   τότε καὶ ἐπισπεύσας ὁ θεὸς ἔφθασε τὸν λαλοῦντα, τῆς ῥήσεως προαποστείλας ὡς ἔπος εἰπεῖν διδασκαλίαν. " εὐθὺς " γάρ φησι " φωνὴ θεοῦ ἐγένετο πρὸς αὐτὸν τῷ λέγειν· οὐ κληρονομήσει σε οὗτος," τῶν εἰς τὴν δι᾽ αἰσθήσεως δεῖξιν ἐρχομένων οὐδὲ εἷς· ἀσώματοι γὰρ φύσεις νοητῶν πραγμάτων εἰσὶ

67 κληρονόμοι. παρατετήρηται δὲ ἄκρως τὸ μὴ

─────

^a ἀρχή no doubt carries with it, in addition to the sense of " beginning " or " first principle," the thought of sovereignty

principle[a] of things, begotten of her father alone, even God the Father of all. For "indeed," it runs, "she is my sister from the father, not from the mother" (Gen. xx. 12).

XIII. So much for the elucidation needed as a pre- 63 liminary; for the problem was seen to involve obscurities and difficulties. We must now explain more exactly what it is that the lover of learning seeks to know. Surely it is something of this kind: "Can he who desires the life of the blood and still claims for his own the things of the senses become the heir of divine and incorporeal things?" No; one 64 alone is held worthy of these, the recipient of inspiration from above, of a portion heavenly and divine, the wholly purified mind which disregards not only the body, but that other section of the soul which is devoid of reason and steeped in blood, aflame with seething passions and burning lusts. His question, we see, takes this form: "Since thou 65 hast not given me that other seed, the mentally perceived, the self-taught, the divine of form, shall the child of my household be my heir, he who is the offspring of the blood-life?"   At that point 66 God in His turn hastens to forestall the questioner, with a message of instruction, which we may almost say anticipates his speaking. For "straightway," we are told, "a voice of God came to him with the words ' He shall not be thy heir ' " (Gen. xv. 4). No, none of those who fall under the evidence which the senses give. For it is incorporeal natures that inherit intellectual things. The wording is chosen 67 very carefully. Moses does not say "God said"

which Philo regularly connects with the name of Sarah, *e.g. De Cher.* 7.

" εἶπεν" ἢ " ἐλάλησεν" φάναι, ἀλλὰ τὸ " φωνὴ
θεοῦ ἐγένετο πρὸς αὐτὸν" ὥσπερ εὐτόνως ἐμβοή-
σαντος καὶ ἀρρήκτως ἐνηχήσαντος, ἵν᾽ εἰς πᾶσαν
τὴν ψυχὴν διαδοθεῖσα ἡ φωνὴ μηδὲν ἔρημον ἐάσῃ
καὶ κενὸν ὑφηγήσεως ὀρθῆς μέρος, ἀλλὰ πάντα
διὰ πάντων ὑγιαινούσης μαθήσεως ἀναπλησθῇ.

68　　　　　XIV. τίς οὖν γενήσεται κληρονόμος;
οὐχ ὁ μένων ἐν τῇ τοῦ σώματος εἱρκτῇ λογισμὸς
καθ᾽ ἑκούσιον γνώμην, ἀλλ᾽ ὁ λυθεὶς τῶν δεσμῶν
καὶ ἐλευθερωθεὶς καὶ ἔξω τειχῶν προεληλυθὼς καὶ
καταλελοιπώς, εἰ οἷόν τε τοῦτο εἰπεῖν, αὐτὸς
ἑαυτόν. " ὃς γὰρ ἐξελεύσεται ἐκ σοῦ" φησίν,
69 " οὗτος κληρονομήσει σε."　　　　　πόθος οὖν
εἴ τις εἰσέρχεταί σε, ψυχή, τῶν θείων ἀγαθῶν
κληρονομῆσαι, μὴ μόνον " γῆν," τὸ σῶμα, καὶ
" συγγένειαν," ⟨τὴν⟩ αἴσθησιν, καὶ " οἶκον πατρός," τὸν λόγον, καταλίπῃς, ἀλλὰ καὶ σαυτὴν
ἀπόδραθι καὶ ἔκστηθι σεαυτῆς, ὥσπερ οἱ κατ-
εχόμενοι καὶ κορυβαντιῶντες βακχευθεῖσα καὶ
θεοφορηθεῖσα κατά τινα προφητικὸν ἐπιθειασμόν·
70 ἐνθουσιώσης γὰρ καὶ οὐκέτ᾽ οὔσης ἐν ἑαυτῇ
διανοίας, ἀλλ᾽ ἔρωτι οὐρανίῳ σεσοβημένης κἀκμε-
μηνυίας καὶ ὑπὸ τοῦ ὄντως ὄντος ἠγμένης καὶ
ἄνω πρὸς αὐτὸ[1] εἱλκυσμένης, προϊούσης ἀληθείας
καὶ τὰν ποσὶν ἀναστελλούσης, ἵνα κατὰ λεωφόρου
71 βαίνοι τῆς ὁδοῦ, κλῆρος οὗτος.　　　　　πῶς
οὖν μετανίστασο τῶν προτέρων ἐκείνων, λέγε
θαρροῦσα ἡμῖν, ὦ διάνοια, ἢ τοῖς ἀκούειν τὰ
νοητὰ δεδιδαγμένοις ἐνηχεῖς, ἀεὶ φάσκουσα ὅτι
μετῳκισάμην τοῦ σώματος, ἡνίκα τῆς σαρκὸς
ἠλόγουν ἤδη, καὶ τῆς αἰσθήσεως, ὁπότε τὰ αἰσθητὰ

　　　　　[1] Or αὐτὸν as some mss.

316

or " God spake," but " a voice of God came to him."
It suggests a loud, sonorous, continuous appeal,
pitched so as to spread abroad throughout the soul,
whereby no part shall be left to which its right
instruction has not penetrated, but all are filled from
end to end with sound learning. XIV.
Who then shall be the heir ? Not that way of think- 68
ing which abides in the prison of the body of its own
free will, but that which released from its fetters into
liberty has come forth outside the prison walls, and
if we may so say, left behind its own self. For " he
who shall come out of thee," it says, " shall be thy
heir " (Gen. xv. 4). Therefore, my soul, 69
if thou feelest any yearning to inherit the good things
of God, leave not only thy land, that is the body, thy
kinsfolk, that is the senses, thy father's house
(Gen. xii. 1), that is speech, but be a fugitive from
thyself also and issue forth from thyself. Like
persons possessed and corybants, be filled with inspired frenzy, even as the prophets are inspired.
For it is the mind which is under the divine afflatus, 70
and no longer in its own keeping, but is stirred to its
depths and maddened by heavenward yearning,
drawn by the truly existent and pulled upward
thereto, with truth to lead the way and remove all
obstacles before its feet, that its path may be smooth
to tread—such is the mind, which has this inheritance. To that mind I say, " Fear not to 71
tell us the story of thy departure from the first
three. For to those who have been taught to give
ear to the things of the mind, thou ever repeatest
the tale." " I migrated from the body," she answers,
" when I had ceased to regard the flesh ; from sense,
when I came to view all the objects of sense as having

πάντα ὡς μὴ πρὸς ἀλήθειαν ὄντα ἐφαντασιώθην
[483] καταγνοῦσα μὲν αὐτῆς τῶν | κριτηρίων ὡς νενοθευ-
μένων καὶ δεδεκασμένων καὶ ψευδοῦς ὑποπεπλη-
σμένων δόξης, καταγνοῦσα δὲ καὶ τῶν κρινομένων,
ὡς δελεάσαι καὶ ἀπατῆσαι καὶ ἐκ μέσης τῆς
φύσεως ἁρπάσαι τὴν ἀλήθειαν εὐτρεπισμένων·
μετανέστην καὶ τοῦ λόγου, ἡνίκα πολλὴν ἀλογίαν
αὐτοῦ κατέγνων καίτοι μετεωρίζοντος καὶ φυσῶν-
72 τος ἑαυτόν. ἐτόλμα γὰρ τόλμημα οὐ μικρόν, διὰ
σκιῶν μοι σώματα, διὰ ῥημάτων πράγματα, ἅπερ
ἀμήχανον ἦν, δεικνύναι· καίτοι σφαλλόμενος περι-
ελάλει καὶ περιέρρει κοινότητι τῶν ὀνομάτων τὰς
ἰδιότητας τῶν ὑποκειμένων ἀδυνατῶν ἐμφάσει
73 τρανῇ παραστῆσαι. παθοῦσα δ᾽ ὡς ἄφρων καὶ
νήπιος παῖς ἔμαθον, ὡς ἄμεινον ἦν ἄρα πάντων
μὲν τούτων ὑπεξελθεῖν, ἑκάστου δὲ τὰς δυνάμεις
ἀναθεῖναι θεῷ τῷ καὶ τὸ σῶμα σωματοῦντι καὶ
πηγνύντι καὶ τὴν αἴσθησιν αἰσθάνεσθαι παρα-
σκευάζοντι καὶ τῷ λόγῳ τὸ λέγειν ὀρέγοντι.
74   τὸν αὐτὸν δὴ τρόπον ὅνπερ τῶν ἄλλων
ὑπεξελήλυθας, ὑπέξελθε καὶ μετανάστηθι σεαυτῆς.
τί δὲ τοῦτό ἐστιν; μὴ ταμιεύσῃ τὸ νοεῖν καὶ
διανοεῖσθαι καὶ καταλαμβάνειν σεαυτῇ, φέρουσα
δὲ καὶ ταῦτα ἀνάθες τῷ τοῦ νοεῖν ἀκριβῶς καὶ
καταλαμβάνειν ἀνεξαπατήτως αἰτίῳ.
75   XV. Τὴν δὲ ἀνάθεσιν δέξεται τῶν πανιέρων
τεμενῶν τὸ ἁγιώτερον· δύο γὰρ ἔοικε συστῆναι, τὸ
μὲν νοητόν, τὸ δ᾽ αἰσθητόν. αἰσθητῶν μὲν οὖν
φύσεων ὁ κόσμος οὗτος, ἀοράτων δ᾽ ὡς ἀληθῶς ὁ
76 νοητὸς τὸ πάνθειόν ἐστιν.   ὅτι δ᾽ ὁ

─────────────

ᵃ The translation takes κοινότητι as dative of cause after

no true existence, when I denounced its standards of
judgement as spurious and corrupt and steeped in
false opinion, and its judgements as equipped to
ensnare and deceive and ravish truth away from its
place in the heart of nature ; from speech, when I
sentenced it to long speechlessness, in spite of all its
self-exaltation and self-pride. Great indeed was its 72
audacity, that it should attempt the impossible task
to use shadows to point me to substances, words
to point me to facts. And, amid all its blunders,
it chattered and gushed about, unable to present
with clear expression those distinctions in things
which baffled its vague and general vocabulary.[a] Thus 73
through experience, as a foolish child learns, I learnt
that the better course was to quit all these three, yet
dedicate and attribute the faculties of each to God,
who compacts the body in its bodily form, who equips
the senses to perceive, and extends to speech the
power of speaking."   Such is the mind's 74
confession, and to it I reply, " even as thou hast
quitted the others, quit thyself, depart from thyself."
And what does this " departing " mean ? It means
" do not lay up as treasure for thyself, thy gifts of
thinking, purposing, apprehending, but bring them
and dedicate them to Him Who is the source of
accurate thinking and unerring apprehension."

XV. This dedication will be enshrined in the holier 75
of the great sanctuaries. For two such sanctuaries,
we feel, exist, one sensible, one mental. This world
is the cathedral[b] of the sense-perceived order, the
world which the mind discovers of the truly invisible
order.   Now that he who has gone forth 76

ἀδυνατῶν. It may be, however, dative of means after
παραστῆσαι.   [b] See App. p. 568.

ὑπεξελθὼν ἐξ ἡμῶν[1] καὶ γλιχόμενος ὀπαδὸς εἶναι
θεοῦ τοῦ φύσεως ἀοιδίμου πλούτου κληρονόμος
ἐστί, μαρτυρεῖ λέγων· '' ἐξήγαγεν δὲ αὐτὸν ἔξω
καὶ εἶπεν· ἀνάβλεψον εἰς τὸν οὐρανόν,'' ἐπειδήπερ
οὗτος ὁ τῶν θείων θησαυρὸς ἀγαθῶν—'' ἀνοίξαι
γάρ σοι '' φησί '' κύριος τὸν θησαυρὸν αὐτοῦ τὸν
ἀγαθόν, τὸν οὐρανόν,'' ἐξ οὗ δὴ τὰς τελεωτάτας
εὐφροσύνας ὁ χορηγὸς ἀδιαστάτως ὕει— '' ἀνά-
βλεψον '' δὲ εἰς ἔλεγχον τοῦ τυφλοῦ τῶν ἀγελαίων
ἀνθρώπων γένους, ὃ βλέπειν δοκοῦν πεπήρωται·
77 πῶς γὰρ οὐ πεπήρωται, ὅτε κακὰ μὲν ἀντ' ἀγαθῶν
αἰσχρὰ ἀντὶ καλῶν, ἄδικα ἀντὶ δικαίων καὶ πάθη
μὲν ἀντ' εὐπαθειῶν, θνητὰ δὲ ἀντ' ἀθανάτων
ᾕρηται, καὶ νουθετητὰς μὲν καὶ σωφρονιστάς, ἔτι
δὲ ἔλεγχον καὶ παιδείαν ἀποδιδράσκει, κόλακας δὲ
καὶ τοὺς πρὸς ἡδονὴν λόγους ἀργίας καὶ ἀμαθίας
78 καὶ θρύψεως δημιουργοὺς ἀποδέχεται; μόνος οὖν
βλέπει ὁ ἀστεῖος, οὗ χάριν καὶ τοὺς προφήτας
ὠνόμασαν οἱ παλαιοὶ ὁρῶντας. ὁ δὲ ἔξω προεληλυθὼς οὐ μόνον ὁρῶν, ἀλλὰ καὶ θεὸν ὁρῶν προσ-
ερρήθη, Ἰσραήλ [ὅς ἐστι θεὸν ὁρῶν].
[484] οἱ δέ, κἄν ποτε | τοὺς ὀφθαλμοὺς διοίξωσι, πρὸς
γῆν ἀπονενεύκασι τὰ γήινα μετιόντες καὶ τοῖς ἐν
79 Ἅιδῃ συντρεφόμενοι. ὁ μὲν γὰρ ἀνατείνει τὰς
ὄψεις πρὸς αἰθέρα καὶ τὰς οὐρανοῦ περιόδους
πεπαίδευται δὲ καὶ εἰς τὸ μάννα ἀφορᾶν, τὸν
θεῖον λόγον, τὴν οὐράνιον ψυχῆς φιλοθεάμονος
ἄφθαρτον τροφήν, οἱ δὲ πρὸς τὰ κρόμμυα καὶ τὰ
σκόρδα, τὰ περιοδυνῶντα τὰς κόρας καὶ κακοῦντα

---

[1] Wend. from Pap. ἐξ ἡμῶν νοητῶν καὶ κτλ. See App.
p. 568.　　　　　　　　　　　　　　[2] MSS. κυκῶντα.

from us and desires to be God's attendant is the
heir of the glorious wealth that nature has to give is
testified by Moses in the words " He led him out outside and said ' Look up into heaven ' " (Gen. xv. 5).
For heaven is the treasury of divine blessings.
" May the Lord," he says, " open to thee His good
treasure, the heaven " (Deut. xxviii. 12)—that heaven
from which the bountiful Giver rains down continually His most perfect joys. Yes, look up, and thus
convict of their errors the multitude of common
men, the blind race, which has lost the sight which
it thinks it possesses. How could it be other than 77
blind, when it prefers bad to good, base to honourable, unjust to just, and again lower passions to
higher emotions, the mortal to the immortal ; when
once more it shuns the voice of the warner and the
censor, and with them conviction and instruction,
while it welcomes flatterers and the words that lead
to pleasure, the makers of idleness and ignorance
and luxury ? And so it is only the man of worth 78
who sees, and therefore they of old called prophets
" seers " (1 Sam. ix. 9). He who advances " outside " is called not only the seer, but the seer of God,
that is Israel.   But the others even if they
do ever open their eyes have bent them earthwards ;
they pursue the things of earth and their conversa-
tion is with the dwellers in Hades. The one ex- 79
tends his vision to the ether and the revolutions of
the heaven ; he has been trained also to look sted-
fastly for the manna, which is the word of God,
the heavenly incorruptible food of the soul which
delights in the vision. But the others see but the
onions and the garlic, which give great pain and
trouble to their eyes and make them close, or the

καὶ καταμύειν ποιοῦντα, καὶ τὰς ἄλλας πράσων
καὶ νεκρῶν ἰχθύων δυσοδμίας, οἰκείας Αἰγύπτου
80 τροφάς. "ἐμνήσθημεν" γάρ φασι "τοὺς ἰχθύας,
οὓς ἠσθίομεν ἐν Αἰγύπτῳ δωρεάν, καὶ σικύας,
πέπονας, πράσα, κρόμμυα, σκόρδα· νυνὶ δὲ ἡ
ψυχὴ ἡμῶν κατάξηρος, οὐδὲν πλὴν εἰς τὸ μάννα
οἱ ὀφθαλμοὶ ἡμῶν."

81 XVI. Συντείνει δὲ πρὸς ἠθοποιίαν καὶ τὸ
"ἐξήγαγεν αὐτὸν ἔξω," ὅ τινες εἰώθασιν ὑπ'
ἀμουσίας ἤθους γελᾶν φάσκοντες· εἴσω γάρ τις
ἐξάγεται, ἢ ἔμπαλιν εἰσέρχεται ἔξω; ναί, φαίη
ἄν, ὦ καταγέλαστοι καὶ λίαν εὐχερεῖς· ψυχῆς γὰρ
τρόπους ἰχνηλατεῖν οὐκ ἐμάθετε ἀλλὰ σωμάτων,
⟨καὶ⟩[1] τὰς ἐν τούτοις μεταβατικὰς κινήσεις μόνας
ἐρευνᾶτε. διὸ καὶ παράδοξον ὑμῖν φαίνεται εἴ τις
ἐξέρχεται εἴσω ἢ εἰσέρχεται ἔξω· τοῖς δὲ Μωυσέως γνωρίμοις ἡμῖν οὐδὲν τῶν τοιούτων ἀπῳδόν
82 ἐστιν. ἢ οὐκ ἂν εἴποιτε, τὸν μὴ τέλειον ἀρχιερέα,
ὁπότε ἐν τοῖς ἀδύτοις τὰς πατρῴους ἁγιστείας
ἐπιτελεῖ, ἔνδον εἶναί τε καὶ ἔξω, ἔνδον μὲν τῷ
φανερῷ σώματι, ἔξω δὲ ψυχῇ τῇ περιφοίτῳ καὶ
πεπλανημένῃ, καὶ ἔμπαλίν τινα μηδὲ γένους ὄντα
τοῦ ἱερωμένου θεοφιλῆ καὶ φιλόθεον ἔξω τῶν
περιρραντηρίων ἑστῶτα ἐσωτάτω διατρίβειν, ἀποδημίαν ἡγούμενον ὅλον τὸν μετὰ σώματος βίον,
ὁπότε δὲ δύναιτο τῇ ψυχῇ μόνῃ ζῆν, ἐν πατρίδι
83 καταμένειν ὑπολαμβάνοντα[2]; καὶ γὰρ φλιᾶς μέν
ἐστιν ἔξω πᾶς ἄφρων, κἂν συνημερεύων μηδ'
ἀκαρὲς ἀπολείπηται, εἴσω δὲ πᾶς σοφός, κἂν μὴ

---

[1] ⟨καὶ⟩ ins. W.H.D.R.: Wend. places the comma after
ἐμάθετε. See App. p. 568.
[2] mss. and Pap. ὑπολαμβάνει(ν).

other ill-smelling things, the leeks and dead fishes, which are food proper to Egypt ; " we remember," 80 they say, " the fishes which we used to eat in Egypt freely, the cucumbers and the gourds, the leeks, the onions, the garlic. But now our soul is dried up, our eyes have nothing to look to, save the manna " (Num. xi. 5, 6).

XVI. There is a moral bearing too in the phrase 81 " He led him out outside," which some, because of the grossness of their moral sense, are in the habit of holding up to ridicule. " Can any be led out inside," they ask, " or conversely go in outside ? " " Indeed they can," I would reply. In your ludicrous, thoughtless folly you have never learnt to trace the ways of the soul, but only of bodies, and all you look for is their movements from place to place. Therefore it seems to you a contradiction in terms that one should go out inside or go in outside. But we the disciples of Moses find nothing conflicting in such phrases. Would you not agree that the 82 high priest whose heart is not perfect is both inside and outside, when he is performing the ancestral rites in the inmost shrine ; inside in his visible body, outside in his wandering vagrant, soul ; and on the contrary that one who loves and is loved by God, even if he is not of the consecrated line, though he stands outside the sacred limits[a] abides right inside them ? For he holds all his life in the body to be a sojourning in a foreign land, but when he can live in the soul alone, he feels that he is a dweller in his fatherland. Every fool is outside the threshold, 83 even if he spend the livelong day within, nor leave it for a moment ; and every wise man is inside it

[a] Cf. Quod Deus 2.

μόνον χώραις ἀλλὰ καὶ μεγάλοις κλίμασι γῆς διωκισμένος τυγχάνῃ· κατὰ δὲ Μωυσῆν οὕτως ὁ φίλος ἐγγύς ἐστιν, ὥστε ἀδιαφορεῖ ψυχῆς· λέγει γάρ· '' ὁ φίλος, ὁ ἴσος τῇ ψυχῇ σου.''

84 καὶ ὁ ἱερεὺς μέντοι '' ἄνθρωπος οὐκ ἔσται '' κατ' αὐτὸν ὅταν εἰσίῃ εἰς τὰ ἅγια τῶν ἁγίων, '' ἕως ἂν ἐξέλθῃ,'' οὐ σωματικῶς, ἀλλὰ ταῖς κατὰ ψυχὴν κινήσεσιν. ὁ γὰρ νοῦς, ὅτε μὲν καθαρῶς λειτουργεῖ θεῷ, οὐκ ἔστιν ἀνθρώπινος, ἀλλὰ θεῖος· ὅτε δὲ ἀνθρωπίνῳ τινί, τέτραπται καταβὰς ἀπ' οὐρα-
[485] νοῦ, μᾶλλον δὲ πεσὼν ἐπὶ γῆν ἐξέρχεται, | κἂν
85 ἔτι μένῃ τὸ σῶμα ἔνδον αὐτῷ. ὀρθότατα οὖν εἴρηται· '' ἐξήγαγεν αὐτὸν ἔξω '' τῶν κατὰ τὸ σῶμα δεσμωτηρίων, τῶν κατὰ τὰς αἰσθήσεις φωλεῶν, τῶν κατὰ τὸν ἀπατεῶνα λόγον σοφιστειῶν, ἐπὶ πᾶσιν αὐτὸν ἐξ ἑαυτοῦ καὶ τοῦ δοκεῖν αὐτ-εξουσίῳ καὶ αὐτοκράτορι γνώμῃ νοεῖν τε καὶ κατα-λαμβάνειν.

86 XVII. Προαγαγὼν δὲ αὐτὸν ἔξω φησίν· '' ἀνά-βλεψον εἰς τὸν οὐρανὸν καὶ ἀρίθμησον τοὺς ἀστέρας, ἐὰν δυνηθῇς ἐξαριθμῆσαι αὐτούς. οὕτως ἔσται τὸ σπέρμα σου.'' παγκάλως εἶπεν '' οὕτως ἔσται,'' ἀλλ' οὐ τοσοῦτον, τοῖς ἄστροις ἰσάριθμον. οὐ γὰρ τὸ πλῆθος αὐτὸ μόνον, ἀλλὰ καὶ μυρία ἄλλα τῶν εἰς εὐδαιμονίαν ὁλόκληρον καὶ παντελῆ
87 βούλεται παρεμφῆναι. οὕτως οὖν ἔσται, φησίν, ὡς ἔχει τὸ ὁρώμενον αἰθέριον, οὕτως οὐράνιον, οὕτως αὐγῆς γέμον ἀσκίου καὶ καθαρᾶς—οὐρανοῦ γὰρ ἀπελήλαταί νὺξ καὶ αἰθέρος τὸ σκότος,—ἀστερο-

---

though he be separated from it not merely by countries but even by vast latitudes. And in Moses' view a friend is so near that he differs not a whit from one's own soul, for he says, " the friend, who is equal to thy soul " (Deut. xiii. 6). Again, ac- 84 cording to Moses, the priest when he goes into the holy of holies "will not be a man until he comes out"[a] (Lev. xvi. 17); no man, that is, in the movements of his soul though in the bodily sense he is still a man. For when the mind is ministering to God in purity, it is not human, but divine. But when it ministers to aught that is human, it turns its course and descending from heaven, or rather falling to earth, comes forth, even though his body still remains within. Most rightly, then, is it said, " He led him out outside," 85 outside of the prison-houses of the body, of the lairs where the senses lurk, of the sophistries of deceitful word and thought; above all He led him out of himself, out of the belief that he thought and apprehended through an intelligence which acknowledged no other authority and owed no allegiance to any other than itself.

XVII. When the Lord led him outside He said 86 " Look up into heaven and count the stars, if thou canst count their sum. So shall be thy seed" (Gen. xv. 5). Well does the text say " so " not " so many," that is, " of equal number to the stars." For He wishes to suggest not number merely, but a multitude of other things, such as tend to happiness perfect and complete. The seed shall be, He says, as 87 the ethereal sight spread out before him, celestial as that is, full of light unshadowed and pure as that is, for night is banished from heaven and darkness from ether. It shall be the very likeness of the stars,

εἰδέστατον, εὖ διακεκοσμημένον, τάξει χρώμενον
ἀκλινεῖ τῇ κατὰ ταὐτὰ καὶ ὡσαύτως ἐχούσῃ.
88 βούλεται γὰρ ἀντίμιμον οὐρανοῦ, εἰ δὲ χρὴ καὶ
προσυπερβάλλοντα εἰπεῖν, οὐρανὸν ἐπίγειον ἀποφῆναι τὴν τοῦ σοφοῦ ψυχὴν ἔχουσαν ⟨ἐν ἑαυτῇ
καθάπερ⟩[1] ἐν αἰθέρι καθαρὰς φύσεις, τεταγμένας
κινήσεις, χορείας ἐμμελεῖς, θείας περιόδους, ἀρετῶν
ἀστεροειδεστάτας καὶ περιλαμπεστάτας αὐγάς. εἰ
δ᾽ ἀμήχανον αἰσθητῶν ἀστέρων ἀριθμὸν εὑρεῖν,
89 πῶς οὐχὶ μᾶλλον νοητῶν; ἐφ᾽ ὅσον γὰρ οἶμαι τὸ
κρῖνον τοῦ κρίνοντος[2] ἄμεινον ἢ χεῖρον—νοῦς μὲν
γὰρ ἄμεινον αἰσθήσεως, διανοίας δὲ ἀμβλύτερον
αἴσθησις,—ἐπὶ τοσοῦτον καὶ τὰ κρινόμενα δι-
ενήνοχεν· ὥστε μυρίῳ πλήθει τὰ νοητὰ τῶν αἰσθητῶν ὑπερβάλλειν. τοῦ γὰρ ψυχῆς ὄμματος βραχυτάτη μοῖρα οἱ κατὰ τὸ σῶμα ὀφθαλμοί· τὸ μὲν
γὰρ ἔοικεν ἡλίῳ, λυχνούχοις δὲ οὗτοι μελετῶσιν[3]
ἐξάπτεσθαί τε καὶ σβέννυσθαι.
90 XVIII. Ἀναγκαίως οὖν ἐπιλέγεται " ἐπίστευσεν
Ἀβραὰμ τῷ θεῷ " πρὸς ἔπαινον τοῦ πεπιστευκότος. καίτοι, τάχα ἄν τις εἴποι, τοῦτ᾽ ἄξιον
ἐπαίνου κρίνετε; τίς δὲ οὐκ ἄν τι λέγοντι καὶ
ὑπισχνουμένῳ θεῷ προσέχοι τὸν νοῦν, κἂν εἰ
πάντων ἀδικώτατος καὶ ἀσεβέστατος ὢν τυγ-
91 χάνοι; πρὸς ὃν ἐροῦμεν· ὦ γενναῖε, μὴ ἀνεξετάστως
ἢ τὸν σοφὸν ἀφέλῃ τὰ πρέποντα ἐγκώμια ἢ τοῖς
ἀναξίοις τὴν τελειοτάτην ἀρετῶν, πίστιν, μαρ-

---

[1] The insertion by Wend. corresponds in length nearly
with some illegible words in Pap. It is omitted altogether
in mss.   [2] mss. and Pap. κρινομένου.
[3] Perhaps, as Wend. conjectures, μέλλουσι.

marshalled in goodly array, following an unswerving order which never varies or changes. For He wished to picture the soul of the Sage as the counterpart of heaven, or rather, if we may so say, transcending it, a heaven on earth having within it, as the ether has, pure forms of being, movements ordered, rhythmic, harmonious, revolving as God directs, rays of virtues, supremely starlike and dazzling.[a] And if it be beyond our powers to count the stars which are visible to the senses, how much more truly can that be said of those which are visible to the mind. For I hold that even as of the two faculties of judgement one is better and one worse, since mind is better than sense and sense duller than understanding, even so do the objects which these two faculties judge differ ; and thus things intelligible vastly exceed in number the things perceptible by sense. The eyes of the body are but the tiniest part of the eye of the soul. That is like the sun ; the others are like candles, whose business is to be lighted and extinguished.

XVIII. The words "Abraham believed God" (Gen. xv. 6) are a necessary addition to speak the praise due to him who has believed. Yet, perhaps it may be asked, do you consider this worthy of praise ? When it is God who speaks and promises, who would not pay heed, even though he were the most unjust and impious of mankind ? To such a questioner we will answer, " Good sir, do not without due scrutiny rob the Sage of his fitting tribute, or aver that the unworthy possess the most perfect of virtues, faith,

88

89

90

91

---

[a] For the general sense of this section *cf. Timaeus* 47 B-E, though there is not much likeness of phraseology, except in περιόδους, on which see note on § 185

τυρήσῃς ἢ τὴν ἡμετέραν περὶ τούτω- γνῶσιν
92 αἰτιάσῃ. βαθυτέραν γὰρ εἰ βουληθείης ἔρευναν καὶ
μὴ σφόδρ᾽ ἐπιπόλαιον ποιήσασθαι, σαφῶς γνώσῃ,
ὅτι μόνῳ θεῷ χωρὶς ἑτέρου προσπαραλήψεως
οὐ ῥᾴδιον πιστεῦσαι διὰ τὴν πρὸς τὸ θνητὸν ᾧ
συνεζεύγμεθα συγγένειαν· ὅπερ ἡμᾶς καὶ χρήμασι
καὶ δόξῃ καὶ ἀρχῇ καὶ φίλοις ὑγείᾳ τε καὶ ῥώμῃ
σώματος καὶ ἄλλοις πολλοῖς ἀναπείθει πεπι-
93 στευκέναι. τὸ δὲ | ἐκνίψασθαι τούτων ἕκαστον
[486] καὶ ἀπιστῆσαι γενέσει τῇ πάντα ἐξ ἑαυτῆς ἀπίστῳ,
μόνῳ δὲ πιστεῦσαι θεῷ τῷ καὶ πρὸς ἀλήθειαν μόνῳ
πιστῷ μεγάλης καὶ ὀλυμπίου ἔργον διανοίας ἐστί,
οὐκέτι πρὸς οὐδενὸς δελεαζομένης τῶν παρ᾽ ἡμῖν.
94   XIX. εὖ δὲ τὸ φάναι "λογισθῆναι τὴν
πίστιν εἰς δικαιοσύνην αὐτῷ"· δίκαιον γὰρ οὐδὲν
οὕτως, ὡς ἀκράτῳ καὶ ἀμιγεῖ τῇ πρὸς θεὸν μόνον
95 πίστει κεχρῆσθαι. τὸ δὲ δίκαιον καὶ ἀκόλουθον
τοῦτο τῇ φύσει παράδοξον ἐνομίσθη διὰ τὴν τῶν
πολλῶν ἀπιστίαν ἡμῶν, οὓς ἐλέγχων ὁ ἱερὸς λόγος
φησίν, ὅτι τὸ ἐπὶ μόνῳ τῷ ὄντι βεβαίως καὶ ἀκλινῶς
ὁρμεῖν θαυμαστὸν μὲν παρ᾽ ἀνθρώποις, οἷς ἀγαθῶν
ἀδόλων κτῆσις οὐκ ἔστιν, οὐ θαυμαστὸν δὲ παρ᾽
ἀληθείᾳ βραβευούσῃ, δικαιοσύνης δ᾽ αὐτὸ μόνον
ἔργον.
96   XX. "Εἶπε δὲ" φησί "πρὸς αὐτόν· ἐγὼ ὁ
θεὸς ὁ ἐξαγαγών σε ἐκ χώρας Χαλδαίων, ὥστε
δοῦναί σοι τὴν γῆν ταύτην κληρονομῆσαι." τοῦτ᾽
οὐχ ὑπόσχεσιν μόνον, ἀλλὰ καὶ παλαιᾶς ὑποσχέσεως
97 βεβαίωσιν ἐμφαίνει. τὸ μὲν οὖν πάλαι δωρηθὲν
ἀγαθὸν ἔξοδος ἦν ἀπὸ τῆς Χαλδαϊκῆς μετεωρο-

or censure our claim to knowledge of this matter.
For if you should be willing to search more deeply 92
and not confine yourself to the mere surface, you
will clearly understand that to trust in God alone and
join no other with Him is no easy matter, by reason
of our kinship with our yokefellow, mortality, which
works upon us to keep our trust placed in riches and
repute and office and friends and health and strength
and many other things. To purge away each of 93
these, to distrust created being, which in itself is
wholly unworthy of trust, to trust in God, and in Him
alone, even as He alone is truly worthy of trust—
this is a task for a great and celestial understanding
which has ceased to be ensnared by aught of the
things that surround us." XIX. And it is 94
well said " his faith was counted to him for justice "
(Gen. xv. 6), for nothing is so just or righteous as
to put in God alone a trust which is pure and unalloyed. Yet this act of justice and conformity with 95
nature has been held to be a marvel because of the
untrustfulness of most of us. And it is in reproof of
us that the holy text tells us, that to rest on the
Existent only, firmly and without wavering, though
it is a marvel in the sight of men who have no hold
of good things unsullied, is deemed no marvel at the
judgement-bar of truth, but just an act of justice and
nothing more.

XX. The text continues " He said to him, I am 96
the God who brought thee out of the land of the
Chaldaeans, to give thee this land to inherit "
(Gen. xv. 7). These words indicate not only a
promise, but also the confirmation of an old promise.
The good bestowed in the past was his departure 97
from Chaldaean sky-lore, which taught the creed

λογίας, ἥτις ἀνεδίδασκεν οὐ θεοῦ ἔργον, ἀλλὰ θεὸν
ὑπολαμβάνειν τὸν κόσμον εἶναι καὶ τό τε εὖ καὶ
τὸ χεῖρον ἅπασι τοῖς οὖσι φοραῖς καὶ τεταγμέναις
περιόδοις ἀστέρων ἀριθμεῖσθαι καὶ ἐνθένδε τὴν
ἀγαθοῦ καὶ κακοῦ γένεσιν ἠρτῆσθαι—ταῦτα δ' ἡ
τῶν κατ' οὐρανὸν ὁμαλὴ καὶ τεταγμένη κίνησις
τοὺς εὐχερεστέρους ἀνέπεισε τερατεύεσθαι· καὶ
γὰρ τὸ Χαλδαίων ὄνομα μεταληφθὲν ὁμαλότητι
98 παρωνυμεῖ,—τὸ δὲ νέον ἀγαθὸν κληρονομῆσαι
σοφίαν τὴν ἄδεκτον μὲν αἰσθήσει, νῷ δ' εἰλι-
κρινεστάτῳ καταλαμβανομένην, δι' ἧς ἀποικιῶν
ἡ ἀρίστη βεβαιοῦται μετανισταμένης τῆς ψυχῆς
ἀπὸ ἀστρονομίας ἐπὶ φυσιολογίαν καὶ ἀπὸ ἀβεβαίου
εἰκασίας ἐπὶ πάγιον κατάληψιν καὶ κυρίως εἰπεῖν
ἀπὸ τοῦ γεγονότος πρὸς τὸ ἀγένητον, ἀπὸ τοῦ
99 κόσμου πρὸς τὸν ποιητὴν καὶ πατέρα αὐτοῦ. τοὺς
μὲν γὰρ τὰς γνώμας χαλδαΐζοντας οὐρανῷ πεπι-
στευκέναι, τὸν δ' ἐνθένδε μεταναστάντα τῷ ἐπόχῳ
τοῦ οὐρανοῦ καὶ ἡνιόχῳ τοῦ παντὸς κόσμου, θεῷ,
φασὶν οἱ χρησμοί. καλός γε ὁ κλῆρος, μείζων
ἴσως τῆς δυνάμεως τοῦ λαμβάνοντος, ἐπάξιος δὲ
τοῦ μεγέθους τοῦ διδόντος.
100 XXI. Ἀλλ' οὐκ ἐξαρκεῖ χρηστὰ ἐλπίσαι καὶ
θαυμάσια ἡλίκα προσδοκῆσαι τῷ σοφίας ἐραστῇ
διὰ τῶν θεσπισθέντων· ἀλλ' εἰ μὴ καὶ τρόπον
γνώσεται καθ' ὃν ἐφίξεται τῆς τοῦ κλήρου διαδοχῆς,
[487] παγχάλεπον | ἡγεῖται, ἅτε διψῶν ἐπιστήμης καὶ
ἀπλήστως ἔχων αὐτῆς· διὸ πυνθάνεται φάσκων·
" δέσποτα, κατὰ τί γνώσομαι, ὅτι κληρονομήσω
101 αὐτήν;" ἴσως ἄν τις εἴποι μάχεσθαι τοῦτο τῷ

that the world was not God's work, but itself God, and that to all existing things the vicissitudes of better and worse are reckoned by the courses and ordered revolutions of the stars, and that on these depends the birth of good and ill. The even tenour, the uniformly ordered motion of the heavenly bodies have induced weak-minded people to adopt this fantastic creed. Indeed, the name Chaldaean when interpreted corresponds to even tenour or levelness. The new good gift is inheritance of the 98 wisdom which cannot be received by sense, but is apprehended by a wholly pure and clear mind. Through this wisdom the best of all migrations becomes an established fact, the migration of the soul which passes from astrology to real nature study, from insecure conjecture to firm apprehension, and to give it its truest expression, from the created to the uncreated, from the world to its Maker and Father. Thus the oracles tell us that 99 those whose views are of the Chaldaean type have put their trust in heaven, while he who has migrated from this home has given his trust to Him who rides on the heaven and guides the chariot of the whole world, even God. Excellent indeed is this heritage, too great it may be for the powers of the recipient, but worthy of the greatness of the Giver.

XXI. But it is not enough for the lover of wisdom 100 to have high hopes and vast expectations through the oracular promises. If he does not know in what way he will attain the succession of the heritage, it irks him greatly ; so thirsty is he for knowledge and insatiate of it. And therefore he asks, " Master, by what shall I know that I shall inherit it ? " (Gen. xv. 8). Now perhaps it may be said that this ques- 101

πεπιστευκέναι· τὸ μὲν γὰρ ἀπορεῖν ἐνδοιάζοντος,
τὸ δὲ μηκέτι ζητεῖν ἔργον εἶναι πεπιστευκότος.
λεκτέον οὖν, ὅτι καὶ ἀπορεῖ καὶ πεπίστευκεν, οὐ
μὴν περὶ τοῦ αὐτοῦ, πολλοῦ γε καὶ δεῖ. πεπί-
στευκε μὲν γὰρ ὅτι κληρονόμος ἔσται σοφίας, τὸν
δὲ τρόπον αὐτὸ μόνον ζητεῖ καθ' ὃν ἂν γένοιτο·
τὸ δ' ὅτι γενήσεται, πάντως κατὰ τὰς θείας
102 ὑποσχέσεις βεβαίως κατείληφεν. τὸν πόθον οὖν,
ᾧ κέχρηται πρὸς τὸ μαθεῖν, ἐπαινέσας ὁ διδάσκαλος
ἄρχεται τῆς ὑφηγήσεως ἀπὸ στοιχειώδους εἰσ-
αγωγῆς, ἐν ᾗ πρῶτον καὶ ἀναγκαιότατον γέγραπται
'' λάβε μοι ''· βραχεῖα μὲν ἡ λέξις, πολλὴ δὲ ἡ
δύναμις· ἐμφαίνει γὰρ οὐκ ὀλίγα.
103 πρῶτον μέν, ἴδιον, φησίν, οὐδὲν ἔχεις ἀγαθόν, ἀλλ'
ὅ τι ἂν νομίσῃς ἔχειν, ἕτερος παρέσχηκεν. ἐξ οὗ
συνάγεται ὅτι θεοῦ τοῦ διδόντος κτήματα πάντα,
ἀλλ' οὐ τῆς μεταίτου[1] καὶ τὰς χεῖρας εἰς τὸ λαβεῖν
104 προτεινούσης γενέσεως.   δεύτερον δέ,
κἂν λάβῃς, λάβε μὴ σεαυτῷ, δάνειον δὲ ἢ παρα-
καταθήκην νομίσας τὸ δοθὲν τῷ παρακαταθεμένῳ
καὶ συμβαλόντι ἀπόδος, πρεσβυτέραν χάριν χάριτι
νεωτέρᾳ, προκατάρχουσαν ἀντεκτινούσῃ δικαίως
105 καὶ προσηκόντως ἀμειψάμενος.   XXII. μυρίοι γὰρ
ἔξαρνοι παρακαταθηκῶν ἐγένοντο ἱερῶν, τοῖς
ἀλλοτρίοις ὡς ἰδίοις ὑπ' ἀμέτρου τῆς πλεονεξίας
καταχρησάμενοι. σὺ δέ, ὦ γενναῖε, παντὶ σθένει
πειρῶ μὴ μόνον ἀσινῆ καὶ ἀκιβδήλευτα φυλάττειν
ἃ ἔλαβες, ἀλλὰ καὶ πάσης ἐπιμελείας ἀξιοῦν, ἵν'
ὁ παρακαταθέμενος μηδὲν ἔχῃ τῆς παρὰ σοῦ

---

[1] So Pap., evidently rightly: the mss. have μετ' αὐτὸν or
μετ' αὐτοῦ.

tion is inconsistent with the belief ascribed to him. It is the doubter, we may be told, who feels difficulties; what the believer does is to cease from further questioning. We must say, then, that the difficulties and the fact of belief are both there, but do not apply to the same subject. Far from it! He has believed that he will be the inheritor of wisdom; he merely asks how this shall come to pass. That it will come to pass is a fact that he has completely and firmly grasped in virtue of the divine promises. And so his Teacher praising the desire 102 for learning which he shews, begins His instruction with a rudimentary lesson, in which the first and most vital words are " take for me " (Gen. xv. 9). A short phrase, but with a wide meaning, for it suggests not a few thoughts. First it says to us 103 " you have no good thing of your own, but whatever you think you have, Another has provided." Hence we infer that all things are the possession of Him who gives, not of creation the beggar, who ever holds out her hands to take. The second is " even 104 if you take, take not for yourself, but count that which is given a loan or trust and render it back to Him who entrusted and leased it to you, thus as is fit and just requiting goodwill with goodwill." His was the earlier, yours is the later; His made the advance, yours shall repay. XXII. For vast is 105 the number of those who repudiate the sacred trusts and in their unmeasured greed use up what belongs to Another as though it was their own. But thou, my friend, try with all thy might, not merely to keep unharmed and unalloyed what thou hast taken, but also deem it worthy of all carefulness, that He who entrusted it to thee may find nothing to blame

106 φυλακῆς αἰτιάσασθαι. παρακατέθετο δέ σοι αὐτῷ
ψυχήν, λόγον, αἴσθησιν ὁ ζωοπλάστης, ἃ συμβολικῶς δάμαλις, κριός, αἴξ ἐν ἱεραῖς γραφαῖς
ὠνομάσθησαν. ταῦτα δ' οἱ μὲν εὐθὺς ὑπὸ
φιλαυτίας ἐνοσφίσαντο, οἱ δὲ ἐταμιεύσαντο πρὸς
107 καιριωτάτην ἀπόδοσιν. τῶν μὲν οὖν νοσφιζο-
μένων οὐκ ἔστιν ἀριθμὸν εὑρεῖν· τίς γὰρ ἡμῶν
ψυχὴν καὶ αἴσθησιν καὶ λόγον, πάνθ' ὁμοῦ ταῦτ'
οὔ φησιν ἑαυτοῦ κτήματ' εἶναι, τὸ αἰσθάνεσθαι,
τὸ λέγειν, τὸ καταλαμβάνειν οἰόμενος ἐφ' ἑαυτῷ
108 μόνῳ κεῖσθαι; τῶν δὲ τὴν πίστιν ἱερὰν καὶ ἄσυλον
ὄντως διαφυλαττόντων ὀλίγος ἐστὶν ἀριθμός.
οὗτοι ταῦτα τὰ τρία ἀνατεθείκασι θεῷ, ψυχήν,
αἴσθησιν, λόγον· ἔλαβον γὰρ οὐχ ἑαυτοῖς, ἀλλ'
ἐκείνῳ πάντα ταῦτα, ὥστε εἰκότως ὡμολόγησαν
κατ' αὐτὸν εἶναι τὰς ἑκάστων ἐνεργείας, τοῦ νοῦ
τὰς διανοήσεις, τοῦ λόγου τὰς ἑρμηνείας, τῆς
109 αἰσθήσεως τὰς φαντασίας.   οἱ μὲν οὖν
ἑαυτοῖς ταῦτα ἐπιγράφοντες ἄξια τῆς ἑαυτῶν
[488] βαρυδαιμονίας | ἐκληρώσαντο, ψυχὴν μὲν ἐπί-
βουλον, ἀλόγοις πάθεσι πεφυρμένην καὶ πλήθει
κακιῶν κατειλημμένην, τοτὲ μὲν ὑπὸ λαιμαργίας
καὶ λαγνείας ὥσπερ ἐν χαμαιτυπείῳ περιυβρι-
ζομένην, τοτὲ δὲ ὑπὸ πλήθους ἀδικημάτων ὥσπερ
ἐν δεσμωτηρίῳ καθειργμένην μετὰ κακούργων,
οὐκ ἀνθρώπων, ἀλλ' ἐπιτηδευμάτων, ἃ πᾶσι τοῖς
κριταῖς [ἢ τιμωρηταῖς] ἀγώγιμα γέγονε, λόγον δὲ
στόμαργον, ἠκονημένον κατὰ τῆς ἀληθείας, βλαβερὸν μὲν τοῖς ἐντυγχάνουσιν, αἰσχύνην δὲ τοῖς
κεκτημένοις ἐπιφέροντα, αἴσθησιν δὲ ἀκόρεστον,
ἐμφορουμένην μὲν ἀεὶ τῶν αἰσθητῶν, ὑπὸ δὲ
ἀκράτορος τῆς ἐπιθυμίας μηδέποτε ἐμπλησθῆναι
334

in thy guardianship of it. Now the Maker of all that 106
lives has given into thy trust soul, speech, and sense,
which the sacred scripture calls in its parable heifer,
ram, and goat (Gen. xv. 9). Some in their selfishness
at once annex these, others store them up, to repay
when the moment for repayment has come. Those 107
who appropriate the trust are countless in number.
For which of us does not assert that soul and sense
and speech, each and all are his own possession,
thinking that to perceive, to speak, to apprehend,
rest with himself alone. But small is the number of 108
those who guard the trust as something holy and
inviolable. These have dedicated these three, soul,
sense, and speech, to God, for they " took " them all
for God, not for themselves ; so that they naturally
acknowledge that through Him come the activities
of each, the reflections of the mind, the language in
which speech expresses itself, the pictures presented to sense. Those, then, who assert 109
their ownership of the three, receive the heritage
which their miserable state deserves ; a soul male-
volent, a chaos of unreasoning passions, held down
by a multitude of vices ; sometimes mauled by greed
and lust, like a strumpet in the stews, sometimes fast
bound as in a prison by a multitude of ill deeds,
herded with malefactors, not of human kind, but
habits which an unanimous judgement has declared
worthy of arrest ; speech brow-beating, keen-
edged against truth, working harm to its victims and
shame to its employers ; sense insatiable, ever
imbibing the objects of sense, yet through its un-

δυναμένην, ἀλογοῦσαν τῶν σωφρονιστῶν, ὡς
παρορᾶν καὶ παρακούειν καὶ ὅσα ἂν ἐπ᾽ ὠφελείᾳ
110 διεξέρχωνται παραπτύειν.   οἱ δὲ λαβόντες
μὴ ἑαυτοῖς, ἀλλὰ θεῷ τούτων ἕκαστον αὐτῷ
ἀνέθεσαν, ἱεροπρεπὲς καὶ ἅγιον ὄντως φυλάξαντες
τῷ κτησαμένῳ, τὴν μὲν διάνοιαν, ἵνα μηδὲν ἄλλο
ἢ περὶ θεοῦ καὶ τῶν ἀρετῶν αὐτοῦ διανοῆται, τὸν
δὲ λόγον, ἵν᾽ ἀχαλίνῳ στόματι ἐγκωμίοις καὶ
ὕμνοις καὶ εὐδαιμονισμοῖς γεραίρῃ τὸν τῶν ὅλων
πατέρα, τὰς πρὸς ἑρμηνείαν ἁπάσας ἀρετὰς εἰς
ἓν τοῦτο μόνον ἔργον συγκροτῶν καὶ ἐπιδεικνύμενος, τὴν δὲ αἴσθησιν, ἵνα φαντασιουμένη τὸν
αἰσθητὸν ἅπαντα κόσμον οὐρανὸν καὶ γῆν καὶ τὰς
μεταξὺ φύσεις, ζῷά τε καὶ φυτά, ἐνεργείας τε καὶ
δυνάμεις αὐτῶν καὶ ὅσαι κινήσεις καὶ σχέσεις,
111 ἀδόλως καὶ καθαρῶς ψυχῇ διαγγέλλῃ.   νῷ γὰρ
ὁ θεὸς καταλαμβάνειν τὸν μὲν νοητὸν κόσμον δι᾽
ἑαυτοῦ, τὸν δὲ ὁρατὸν δι᾽ αἰσθήσεως ἐφῆκεν. εἰ
δὴ δύναιτό τις πᾶσι τοῖς μέρεσι ζῆσαι θεῷ μᾶλλον
ἢ ἑαυτῷ, διὰ μὲν τῶν αἰσθήσεων εἰς τὰ αἰσθητὰ
διακύψας ἕνεκα τοῦ τἀληθὲς εὑρεῖν, διὰ δὲ τῆς
ψυχῆς τὰ νοητὰ καὶ ὄντα ὄντως φιλοσοφήσας, διὰ
δὲ τοῦ κατὰ τὴν φωνὴν ὀργάνου καὶ τὸν κόσμον
καὶ τὸν δημιουργὸν ὑμνήσας, εὐδαίμονι καὶ μακαρίῳ
βίῳ χρήσεται.
112   XXIII. Ταῦτα ἐκ τοῦ " λάβε μοι " παρεμφαί-
νεσθαι νομίζω. βουληθεὶς μέντοι καὶ τῆς θείας
ἀρετῆς ἀπ᾽ οὐρανοῦ τὴν εἰκόνα ἐπὶ γῆν κατα-
πέμψαι δι᾽ ἔλεον τοῦ γένους ἡμῶν, ἵνα μὴ ἀτυχήσῃ
τῆς ἀμείνονος μοίρας, συμβολικῶς τὴν ἱερὰν
σκηνὴν καὶ τὰ ἐν αὐτῇ κατασκευάζει, σοφίας

controlled avidity incapable of reaching satisfaction, regardless of its monitors, blind, deaf and derisive to all that they preach for its benefit.   But 110 those who have " taken," not for themselves but for God, have dedicated each of the three to Him, guarding them for the Owner, as in truth sancti- fied and holy : the thinking faculty, that it should think of nothing else but God and His excellences ; speech, that with unbridled mouth it should honour the Father of all with laud and hymn and bene- diction, that it should concentrate all the graces of expression to be exhibited in this task only ; sense, that it should report faithfully and honestly to the soul the pictures presented to it by the whole world within its ken, heaven and earth and the inter- mediate forms of nature, both living creatures and plants, their activities, their faculties, their con- ditions whether in motion or rest.   For God has per- 111 mitted the mind to comprehend of itself the world of the mind, but the visible world only through sense. Oh ! if one can live with all the parts of his being to God rather than to himself, using the eye of sense to penetrate into the objects of sense and thus dis- cover the truth, using the soul to study the higher verities of mental things and real existences, using the organ of his voice to laud both the world and its Maker, he will live a happy and blessed life.

XXIII. This is what I hold the words " take for 112 me " to suggest. Here is another illustration. When God willed to send down the image of divine excellence from heaven to earth in pity for our race, that it should not lose its share in the better lot, he constructs as a symbol of the truth the holy tabernacle and its contents to be a representation

113 ἀπεικόνισμα καὶ μίμημα. τῆς γὰρ ἀκαθαρσίας
ἡμῶν ἐν μέσῳ φησὶ τὴν σκηνὴν ἱδρῦσθαι τὸ λόγιον,
ἵν᾽ ἔχωμεν ᾧ καθαρθησόμεθα ἐκνιψάμενοι καὶ
ἀπολουσάμενοι τὰ καταρρυπαίνοντα ἡμῶν τὸν
[489] ἄθλιον καὶ | δυσκλείας γέμοντα βίον.   τὰ
συντείνοντα οὖν πρὸς τὴν κατασκευὴν ἴδωμεν ὃν
τρόπον εἰσφέρειν προσέταξεν. " ἐλάλησε " φησί
" κύριος πρὸς Μωυσῆν λέγων· εἰπὸν τοῖς υἱοῖς
Ἰσραήλ, καὶ λάβετέ μοι ἀπαρχάς, παρὰ πάντων
οἷς ἂν δόξῃ τῇ καρδίᾳ, λήψεσθε τὰς ἀπαρχάς μου."
114 οὐκοῦν κἀνταῦθα παραίνεσις μὴ ἑαυτοῖς ἀλλὰ θεῷ
λαβεῖν, τίς τε ὁ διδούς ἐστιν ἐξετάζοντας καὶ τὰ
δοθέντα μὴ σινομένους, ἀσινῆ δὲ καὶ ἄμωμα τέλειά
τε αὖ καὶ ὁλόκληρα διαφυλάττοντας. τὰς δ᾽ ἀρχὰς
δογματικώτατα ἀνέθηκεν αὐτῷ· τῷ γὰρ ὄντι καὶ
σωμάτων καὶ πραγμάτων αἱ ἀρχαὶ κατὰ θεὸν
115 ἐξετάζονται μόνον. ἐρεύνησον δέ, εἰ θέλεις γνῶναι,
ἕκαστα, φυτά, ζῷα, τέχνας, ἐπιστήμας. ἆρ᾽ οὖν
αἱ πρῶται τῶν φυτῶν ἀρχαὶ σπέρματα καὶ κατα-
βολαὶ[1] γεωργίας ἢ τῆς ἀοράτου φύσεώς εἰσιν
ἀόρατα ἔργα; τί δ᾽ αἱ ἀνθρώπων καὶ τῶν ἄλλων
ζῴων γενέσεις; οὐχ ὡσανεὶ μὲν συναιτίους ἔχουσι
τοὺς τοκέας, τὴν δ᾽ ἀνωτάτω καὶ πρεσβυτάτην
116 καὶ ὡς ἀληθῶς αἰτίαν τὴν φύσιν; τέχναις δὲ καὶ
ἐπιστήμαις οὐ πηγὴ καὶ ῥίζα καὶ θεμέλιος[2] καὶ εἴ

---

[1] So some mss.: Mangey and Wend. adopt the reading
of others (and Pap.?), τῶν φυτῶν σπερματικαὶ καταβολαί.
See App. p. 569.

[2] So mss.; Wend. (from Pap.) θεμέλιοι; but the evidence
of the index shows that Philo regularly uses the singular

and copy of wisdom. For the oracle tells us that the 113 tabernacle " was set up in the midst of our unclean-ness " (Lev. xvi. 16) that we may have wherewith to scour and wash away all that defiles our life, miserable and laden with ill fame as it is. Let us consider, then, how he bade them contribute the ways and means needed for the building of the tabernacle. " The Lord spake unto Moses," it says, saying : ' Speak to the sons of Israel and take ye for me first beginnings ; from all who are so minded in their heart, ye shall take my first beginnings " (Ex. xxv. 1, 2). Here then also we have an exhortation not to 114 take for ourselves but for God, closely considering who the Giver is and doing no damage to the gifts, but preserving them undamaged and faultless, aye perfect and complete. In this dedication of the beginnings to God Moses teaches us a high truth. For indeed the beginnings of things both material and immaterial are found to be by God only. Look 115 well, if you would have knowledge, at each several kind, plants, living creatures, arts, sciences. What of the first beginnings of plants ? Do they consist in the dropping of the seed by the farmer, or are they the invisible works of invisible nature ?[a] What of the generation of men and the other animals ? Are not the parents as it were the accessories, while nature is the original, the earliest and the real cause ? So again with the arts and sciences. Is not nature 116 the underlying fact, the fountain or root or founda-tion, or whatever name you give to the beginning

[a] For the identification of Nature with the Divine Agency in things cf. De Sac. 98 and note.

---

when speaking of a single thing, e.g. Leg. All. iii. 138 ὥσπερ τις ἀρχὴ καὶ θεμέλιος.

τι ἄλλο πρεσβυτέρας ὄνομα ἀρχῆς ὑπόκειται ἡ
φύσις, ᾗ πάντ' ἐποικοδομεῖται τὰ καθ' ἑκάστην
θεωρήματα; φύσεως δὲ μὴ προϋποκειμένης ἀτελῆ
τὰ πάντα. ἐνθένδε μοι δοκεῖ τις ὁρμηθεὶς
εὐστόχως εἰπεῖν

ἀρχὴ δέ τοι ἥμισυ παντός,

ἀρχὴν αἰνιξάμενος τὴν φύσιν, ἥτις ὡσανεὶ ῥίζα
καταβέβληται πρὸς τὴν ἑκάστου συναύξησιν, ᾗ
καὶ τὸ ἥμισυ τοῦ παντὸς ἀπένειμεν. XXIV.
117 εἰκότως οὖν τὸ λόγιον ἀνέθηκε τὰς ἀρχὰς τῷ
ἡγεμόνι θεῷ. καὶ ἐν ἑτέροις " εἶπεν " φησὶν
" κύριος πρὸς Μωυσῆν λέγων· ἁγίασόν μοι πᾶν
πρωτότοκον, πρωτογενές, διανοῖγον πᾶσαν μήτραν
ἐν υἱοῖς Ἰσραὴλ ἀπὸ ἀνθρώπου ἕως κτήνους· ἐμοί
118 ἐστιν"· ὥστε ἀνωμολογῆσθαι καὶ διὰ τούτων,
ὅτι τὰ πρῶτα καὶ χρόνῳ καὶ δυνάμει κτήματα
θεοῦ, καὶ διαφερόντως τὰ πρωτογενῆ. ἐπειδὴ γὰρ
πᾶν γένος ἄφθαρτον, δικαίως τῷ ἀφθάρτῳ προσ-
νεμηθήσεται, καὶ εἴ τι καὶ συνόλως μήτραν δι-
οιγνύει[1] ἀπὸ ἀνθρώπου, τοῦ λογισμοῦ καὶ λόγου,
119 ἕως κτήνους, αἰσθήσεώς τε καὶ σώματος. ὁ γὰρ
διοιγνὺς τὴν μήτραν ἑκάστων, τοῦ μὲν νοῦ πρὸς
τὰς νοητὰς καταλήψεις, τοῦ δὲ λόγου πρὸς τὰς διὰ
φωνῆς ἐνεργείας, τῶν δὲ αἰσθήσεων πρὸς τὰς ἀπὸ
τῶν ὑποκειμένων ἐγγινομένας φαντασίας, τοῦ δὲ
σώματος πρὸς τὰς οἰκείους αὐτῷ σχέσεις τε καὶ
κινήσεις ἀόρατος καὶ σπερματικὸς καὶ τεχνικὸς

---

[1] Wend. prints εἴ τις (Pap.) διοιγνύειν (Pap. and some
mss.). He suggests ὃς οἷός τε καὶ for εἴ τις καὶ to preserve
the infinitive.

---

[a] Apparently a proverbial saying already quoted in *Quod*

which precedes all else, and is not the lore of each
science a superstructure built on nature, whereas if
we do not start with this as a groundwork, all that
lore is imperfect? It was this, I take it, which led
someone to say so aptly

> The beginning is half the whole.[a]

In these words the hidden meaning of " beginning "
is nature, the underlying root as it were, the setting
needed for growth in each case, to whose credit the
writer assigned half the whole. XXIV. Not without 117
reason then did the oracle dedicate " beginnings " to
the great Leader, God. And elsewhere he says " The
Lord spake unto Moses saying ' sanctify to me every
first born, first in generation, which openeth every
womb among the sons of Israel from man to beast.
It is to Me ' " (Ex. xiii. 1, 2). Thus it is admitted 118
here also that the first in time and value are God's
possessions and especially the first in generation.[b]
For since genus in every case is indestructible,
to the indestructible God will it be justly assigned.
And that is true too of one who opens the womb of
all from man, that is reason and speech, to beast,
that is sense and body. For he that opens the womb 119
of each of these, of mind, to mental apprehensions,
of speech, to the activities of the voice, of the senses,
to receive the pictures presented to it by objects, of
the body, to the movements and postures proper to
it, is the invisible, seminal artificer, the divine Word,

Det. 64. *Cf.* Plato, *Leg.* vi. 753 ε, and the ὅσῳ πλέον ἥμισυ
παντός of Hesiod, *Op.* 40.

[b] The -γενῆ in πρωτογενῆ is equated by Philo with γένος in
its philosophical sense. The play cannot be well brought
out in translation.

θεῖός ἐστι λόγος, ὃς προσηκόντως ἀνακείσεται τῷ
120 πατρί.   καὶ μὴν ὥσπερ αἱ ἀρχαὶ θεοῦ,
οὕτως καὶ τὰ τέλη θεοῦ. μάρτυς δὲ Μωυσῆς
προστάττων ἀφαιρεῖν καὶ ὁμολογεῖν τὸ τέλος τῷ
121 κυρίῳ. μαρτυρεῖ δὲ καὶ τὰ ἐν κόσμῳ. πῶς; φυτοῦ
μὲν ἀρχὴ σπέρμα, τέλος δ' ὁ καρπός, ἑκάτερον οὐ
γεωργίας, ἀλλὰ φύσεως ἔργον. πάλιν ἐπιστήμης
[490] ἀρχὴ μὲν ἡ φύσις, | ὡς ἐδείχθη, πέρας δ' οὐδ'
ἦλθεν εἰς ἀνθρώπους. τέλειος γὰρ οὐδεὶς ἐν οὐδενὶ
τῶν ἐπιτηδευμάτων, ἀλλ' ἀψευδῶς αἱ τελειότητες
καὶ ἀκρότητες ἑνός εἰσι μόνου. φορούμεθ' οὖν
λοιπὸν ἡμεῖς ἐν τῷ τέλους καὶ ἀρχῆς μεθορίῳ,
μανθάνοντες, διδάσκοντες, γεωπονοῦντες, ἐργαζό-
μενοι τῶν ἄλλων ἔκαστον ὡς ἂν ἱδρῶντες,[1] ἵνα τι
122 καὶ γένεσις πράττειν δοκῇ. γνωριμώτερον μέντοι
τὰς ἀρχὰς καὶ τὰ τέλη κατὰ θεὸν ὡμολόγησεν ἐπὶ
τῆς τοῦ κόσμου γενέσεως εἰπών· '' ἐν ἀρχῇ
ἐποίησε '' καὶ πάλιν '' συνετέλεσεν ὁ θεὸς τὸν
123 οὐρανὸν καὶ τὴν γῆν.''   νυνὶ μὲν οὖν
'' λάβετέ μοι '' φησὶ διδοὺς τὰ πρέπονθ' ἑαυτῷ
καὶ προτρέπων τὰ δοθέντα μὴ κιβδηλεύειν, ἀλλ'
ἀξίως τοῦ δόντος φυλάττειν, αὖθις δ' ἐν ἑτέροις ὁ
μηδενὸς χρεῖος ὢν καὶ διὰ τοῦτο λαμβάνων μηδὲν
ὁμολογήσει λαμβάνειν, ἕνεκα τοῦ πρὸς εὐσέβειαν
ἀλεῖψαι καὶ προθυμίαν ὁσιότητος ἐμποιῆσαι καὶ
πρὸς θεραπείαν ἀκονῆσαι τὴν ἑαυτοῦ, ὡς ἀπο-
δεχομένου καὶ δεχομένου τὰς ψυχῆς ἑκουσίους
124 ἀρεσκείας καὶ γνησίους θεραπείας. '' ἰδοὺ '' γάρ

---

[1] mss. ὡσανεὶ δρῶντες (but Pap. ωσαν ιδρουντες).

which will be fitly dedicated to its Father.

And as the beginnings are God's, so also are the ends. 120 Moses testifies to this when he bids set apart and accord the end to the Lord (Num. xxxi. 28 ff.). And what happens in the world testifies to it also. How 121 so ? you ask. In the plant the seed is the beginning and the fruit the end, and both are the work of nature, not of husbandry. Again in science, the beginning, as has been shewn, is nature, but its limit is actually outside the range of human possibilities. For no one reaches perfection in any of his pursuits, but undoubtedly all perfection and finality belong to One alone. And so we are fain *a* to range in the border-land between beginning and end, learning, teaching, tilling, and whatever work we carry on, labouring with the sweat of our brow, as it were, that the mere creature may seem to accomplish something. Still 122 more clearly indeed does Moses acknowledge that beginnings and ends are willed by God, when he says in the creation-story, " In the beginning He made " (Gen. i. 1), and afterwards, " God finished the heavens and the earth " (Gen. ii. 1, 2).

And so in the text we are treating, He says " take 123 ye for Me," thus giving to Himself what is His due and bidding us not to adulterate the gifts, but guard them in a way worthy of the Giver. And again elsewhere, He that has no need of aught and therefore takes nothing will acknowledge that He " takes," in order to train us to piety, and to implant a zeal for holiness, and to spur us to His service, as one who welcomes and accepts the free-will homage and genuine service of the soul. For He says " be- 124

---

a This is an idiomatic use of λοιπόν, " it is left to us," " we have to." Thus it almost = " therefore."

φησιν " εἴληφα τοὺς Λευίτας ἀντὶ παντὸς πρωτο-
τόκου διανοίγοντος μήτραν παρὰ τῶν υἱῶν Ἰσραήλ·
λύτρα αὐτῶν ἔσονται." οὐκοῦν λαμβάνομεν καὶ
δίδομεν, ἀλλὰ κυρίως μὲν λαμβάνομεν, κατα-
χρηστικῶς δὲ διδόναι λεγόμεθα δι' ἃς αἰτίας εἶπον.
εὐθυβόλως δὲ λύτρα ὠνόμασε τοὺς Λευίτας· εἰς
ἐλευθερίαν γὰρ οὐδὲν οὕτως ἐξαιρεῖται τὴν διάνοιαν
ὡς τὸ πρόσφυγα καὶ ἱκέτην γενέσθαι θεοῦ. τοῦτο
δ' ἡ ἱερωμένη φυλὴ Λευιτῶν ἐπαγγέλλεται.

125 XXV. Λελαληκότες οὖν τὰ πρέποντα περὶ
τούτων ἀναδράμωμεν ἐπὶ τὰ ἐξ ἀρχῆς· ὑπερεθέμεθα
γὰρ πολλὰ τῶν ὀφειλόντων ἀκριβωθῆναι. " λάβε
μοι " φησί " δάμαλιν " ἄζυγα καὶ ἀκάκωτον,
ἁπαλὴν ἔτι καὶ νέαν καὶ σφριγῶσαν, ἡνιόχησιν
καὶ παιδείαν καὶ ἐπιστασίαν εὐμαρῶς δέξασθαι
δυναμένην ψυχήν· " λάβε μοι κριόν," λόγον
ἀγωνιστὴν καὶ τέλειον, ἱκανὸν μὲν τὰ σοφίσματα
τῶν ἀντιδοξούντων ἀνατεμεῖν τε καὶ λῦσαι, ἱκανὸν
δὲ καὶ ἀσφάλειαν ὁμοῦ καὶ εὐκοσμίαν τῷ χρωμένῳ
126 περιποιῆσαι. " λάβε μοι " καὶ τὴν ᾄττουσαν[1]
αἴσθησιν ἐπὶ τὸν αἰσθητὸν κόσμον, " αἶγα," πάντα
" τριετίζοντα," κατ' ἀριθμὸν τέλειον παγέντα,
ἀρχὴν μεσότητα τελευτὴν ἔχοντα·   πρὸς

---

[1] mss. διάγουσαν (but Pap. διττουσαν). Why not διάττουσαν,
as Mangey before the discovery of Pap. suggested? This
would still preserve the derivation of αἴξ from ᾄττ- which
Philo obviously intends.

---

[a] " Ransom " (*cf. De Sac.* 118) does not appear in the
Hebrew (E.V. " The Levites shall be mine ").

[b] Clearly, to suit the heifer, ψυχή must here be used in the
limited sense of the mind or reasonable soul ; yet in § 122 it
is divided into reasonable and unreasonable. So, too, with

344

hold, I have taken the Levites in place of everyone
who opens the womb from among the sons of Israel ;
they shall be their ransom " (Num. iii. 12). So then ·
we take and give, but in the full sense of the word
we take only ; it is by a license of language that we
are said to give, for the reasons which I have mentioned. Note that He gives the Levites a correct
name in calling them " ransom." [a] For nothing so
well redeems the mind to freedom, as to take refuge
with God and become His suppliant. And such is
the profession of the consecrated tribe of Levi.

XXV. We have said what was fitting on these points. 125
Let us now return to the original subject, for we
postponed much of what requires precise discussion.
Take for me, it says, a " heifer " unyoked, undamaged,
tender, young and fresh in spirit, a soul,[b] that is, which
can easily receive guidance and instruction and ruling ;
" take for me a ram," that is speech active in argument and fully developed, competent to analyse and
refute the sophisms of controversialists and to provide its possessor with a safe and well-ordered life ;[c]
take for me also the sense that dashes and darts on 126
to the sensible world, the she-goat that is ; and
take them all three years old, that is, formed
according to the perfect number with beginning,
middle and end.   And further take for

the ram and the goat. By definition they correspond to the
good side of λόγος and αἴσθησις, but in § 132 are divided into
good and bad. See also on § 225.
[c] Rhetoric is here conceived of as a means of defending
the innocent, and therefore a safeguard against injustice.
But there is also an allusion to the thought developed in
De Mut. 246, that the sheep is the best of animals because
its wool provides man with protection from the weather and
decent covering (ἀσφάλειαν καὶ κόσμον).

δὲ τούτοις " τρυγόνα καὶ περιστεράν," τήν τε
θείαν καὶ τὴν ἀνθρωπίνην σοφίαν, πτηνὰς μὲν
ἀμφοτέρας καὶ ἄνω πηδᾶν μεμελετηκυίας, δια-
φερούσας δ' ἀλλήλων, ᾗ διαφέρει γένος εἴδους ἢ
127 μίμημα ἀρχετύπου. φιλέρημος μὲν γὰρ ἡ θεία
[491] σοφία, διὰ τὸν μόνον θεόν, | οὗ κτῆμά ἐστι, τὴν
μόνωσιν ἀγαπῶσα—συμβολικῶς αὕτη τρυγὼν
καλεῖται—, ἥμερος δὲ καὶ τιθασὸς καὶ ἀγελαῖος ἡ
ἑτέρα, τὰ ἀνθρώπων ἄστη περιπολοῦσα καὶ διαίτῃ
τῇ μετὰ θνητῶν ἀσμενίζουσα· περιστερᾷ ταύτην
128 ἀπεικάζουσιν. XXVI. ταύτας μοι δοκεῖ τὰς
ἀρετὰς Μωυσῆς αἰνιξάμενος μαίας Ἑβραίων
ὀνομάσαι Σεπφώραν τε καὶ Φουάν· ἡ μὲν γὰρ
ὀρνίθιον, Φουὰ δὲ ἐρυθρὸν ἑρμηνεύεται. τῆς μὲν
οὖν θείας ἐπιστήμης ὄρνιθος τρόπον τὸ ἀεὶ μετεωροπολεῖν ἴδιον, τῆς δὲ ἀνθρωπίνης αἰδῶ καὶ
σωφροσύνην ἐμποιεῖν, ὧν τὸ ἐρυθριᾶν ἐφ' οἷς ἄξιον
129 δεῖγμα ἐναργέστατον.   " ἔλαβεν δὲ "
φησίν " αὐτῷ πάντα ταῦτα." τοῦτ' ἔπαινός ἐστι
τοῦ σπουδαίου, τὴν ἱερὰν ὧν ἔλαβε παρακατα-
θήκην, ψυχῆς, αἰσθήσεως, λόγου, θείας σοφίας,
ἀνθρωπίνης ἐπιστήμης, καθαρῶς καὶ ἀδόλως μὴ
ἑαυτῷ, μόνῳ δὲ τῷ πεπιστευκότι φυλάξαντος.
130   εἶτ' ἐπιλέγει· " διεῖλεν αὐτὰ μέσα,"
τὸ τίς μὴ προστιθείς, ἵνα τὸν ἄδεικτον ἐννοῇς θεὸν
τέμνοντα τὰς τῶν σωμάτων καὶ τὰς τῶν πραγμάτων ἑξῆς ἁπάσας ἡρμόσθαι καὶ ἡνῶσθαι δο
κούσας φύσεις τῷ τομεῖ τῶν συμπάντων ἑαυτοῦ
λόγῳ, ὃς εἰς τὴν ὀξυτάτην ἀκονηθεὶς ἀκμὴν διαιρῶν

me a turtle-dove and a pigeon, that is divine and human reason, both of them winged creatures, skilled by practice to speed upwards, yet differing from each other, as the genus differs from the species, or the copy from the archetype. For Divine wisdom 127 is a lover of solitudes, since loneliness is dear to her because of the solitary God who is her owner, and thus in parable she is called the turtle-dove. The other is gentle and tame and sociable, frequenting the cities of men and pleased to dwell with mortals. Men liken her to a pigeon. XXVI. These virtues 128 Moses, I think, spoke of in allegory when he named the midwives of the Hebrews, Zipporah and Phuah (Ex. i. 15), for Zipporah is by interpretation " bird " and Phuah " ruddy." It is a special property of divine wisdom that it ever soars aloft like a bird, of human wisdom that it implants modesty and discretion ; and a blush, where the matter calls for blushing, is the clearest proof of the presence of these qualities. " Abraham took all 129 these for Him " (Gen. xv. 10) says the text. These words speak the praise of the man of worth who faithfully and honestly guards the sacred trust, which he has received of soul, sense, and speech, of divine wisdom and human knowledge, but guards it not for himself, but solely for Him who gave the trust. Then he continues, " he divided 130 them in the middle," but he does not add who this " he " is. He wishes you to think of God who cannot be shewn, as severing through the Severer of all things, that is his Word, the whole succession of things material and immaterial whose natures appear to us to be knitted together and united. That severing Word whetted to an edge of utmost

131 οὐδέποτε λήγει. τὰ γὰρ αἰσθητὰ πάντα ἐπειδὰν
μέχρι τῶν ἀτόμων καὶ λεγομένων ἀμερῶν διεξέλθῃ,
πάλιν ἀπὸ τούτων τὰ λόγῳ θεωρητὰ εἰς ἀμυθήτους
καὶ ἀπεριγράφους μοίρας ἄρχεται διαιρεῖν οὗτος ὁ
τομεύς, καὶ " τὰ πέταλα τοῦ χρυσίου τέμνει
τρίχας," ὥς φησι Μωυσῆς, εἰς μῆκος ἁπλατὲς
132 ἀσωμάτοις γραμμαῖς ἐμφερές.   ἕκαστον
οὖν τῶν τριῶν διεῖλε μέσον, τὴν μὲν ψυχὴν εἰς
λογικὸν καὶ ἄλογον, τὸν δὲ λόγον εἰς ἀληθές τε
καὶ ψεῦδος, τὴν δὲ αἴσθησιν εἰς καταληπτικὴν
φαντασίαν καὶ ἀκατάληπτον· ἅπερ εὐθὺς τμήματα
" ἀντιπρόσωπα τίθησιν ἀλλήλοις," λογικὸν ἄλογον,
ἀληθὲς ψεῦδος, καταληπτὸν ἀκατάληπτον, ἀπο-
λιπὼν τὰ πτηνὰ ἀδιαίρετα· τὰς γὰρ ἀσωμάτους
καὶ θείας ἐπιστήμας εἰς μαχομένας ἐναντιότητας
ἀδύνατον τέμνεσθαι.

133 XXVII. Πολὺν δὲ καὶ ἀναγκαῖον ὄντα λόγον
τὸν περὶ τῆς εἰς ἴσα τομῆς καὶ περὶ ἐναντιοτήτων
οὔτε παρήσομεν οὔτε μηκυνοῦμεν, ἀλλ' ὡς ἔστιν
ἐπιτέμνοντες ἀρκεσθησόμεθα μόνοις τοῖς καιρίοις.

[492] καθάπερ | γὰρ ἡμῶν τὴν ψυχὴν καὶ τὰ μέλη μέσα
διεῖλεν ὁ τεχνίτης, οὕτως καὶ τὴν τοῦ παντὸς
134 οὐσίαν, ἡνίκα τὸν κόσμον ἐδημιούργει. λαβὼν
γὰρ αὐτὴν ἤρξατο διαιρεῖν ὧδε· δύο τὸ πρῶτον
ἐποίει τμήματα, τό τε βαρὺ καὶ κοῦφον, τὸ παχυμερὲς ἀπὸ τοῦ λεπτομεροῦς διακρίνων· εἶθ'
ἑκάτερον πάλιν διαιρεῖ, τὸ μὲν λεπτομερὲς εἰς
ἀέρα καὶ πῦρ, τὸ δὲ παχυμερὲς εἰς ὕδωρ καὶ γῆν,
ἃ καὶ στοιχεῖα αἰσθητὰ αἰσθητοῦ κόσμου, ὡσανεὶ
135 θεμελίους, προκατεβάλετο. πάλιν δὲ τὸ βαρὺ καὶ

ᵃ καταληπτικός and καταληπτός seem to be convertible

sharpness never ceases to divide. For when it has 131
dealt with all sensible objects down to the atoms and
what we call " indivisibles," it passes on from them
to the realm of reason's observation and proceeds
to divide it into a vast and infinite number of parts.
It divides the " plates of gold," as Moses tells us,
" into hairs " (Ex. xxxvii. 10), that is into length without breadth, like immaterial lines.   So it 132
divided each of the three in the middle, the soul into
rational and irrational, speech into true and false,
sense into presentations, where the object is real and
apprehended, and presentations where it is not.[a]
These sections He at once placed " opposite to each
other," rational to irrational, true to false, apprehending to non-apprehending. The birds He left
undivided, for incorporeal and divine forms of knowledge cannot be divided into conflicting opposites.

XXVII. The subject of division into equal parts 133
and of opposites is a wide one, and discussion of it
essential. We will neither omit nor protract it,
but abridge it as far as possible and content ourselves
with the vital points only. Just as the great Artificer
divided our soul and limbs in the middle, so too,
when He wrought the world, did He deal with the
being of all that is. This He took and began to 134
divide as follows. First He made two sections,
heavy and light, thus distinguishing the element of
dense from that of rare particles. Then again He
divided each of these two, the rare into air and fire,
the dense into water and land, and these four He
laid down as first foundations, to be the sensible
elements of the sensible world. Again He made 135

terms, since the mind may be conceived of as grasping the
φαντασία or *vice versa*. See further App. p. 569.

κοῦφον καθ' ἑτέρας ἔτεμνεν ἰδέας, τὸ μὲν κοῦφον
εἰς ψυχρόν τε καὶ θερμόν—ἐπεφήμισε δὲ τὸ μὲν
ψυχρὸν ἀέρα, τὸ δὲ θερμὸν φύσει πῦρ—, τὸ δὲ βαρὺ
εἰς ὑγρόν τε αὖ καὶ ξηρόν· ἐκάλεσε δὲ τὸ μὲν ξηρὸν
136 γῆν, τὸ δὲ ὑγρὸν ὕδωρ. ἕκαστον δὲ τούτων ἄλλας
τομὰς ἐδέχετο· γῆ μὲν γὰρ εἰς ἠπείρους καὶ νήσους
διῃρεῖτο, ὕδωρ δὲ εἰς θάλασσαν καὶ ποταμοὺς καὶ
ὅσον πότιμον ⟨καὶ οὐ πότιμον⟩[1], ἀὴρ δὲ εἰς τὰς
θέρους καὶ χειμῶνος τροπάς, πῦρ δὲ εἰς τὸ χρειῶδες
—ἄπληστον δ' ἐστὶ καὶ φθαρτικὸν τοῦτο—καὶ κατὰ
τοὐναντίον εἰς τὸ σωτήριον, ὅπερ εἰς τὴν οὐρανοῦ
137 σύστασιν ἀπεκληροῦτο.   ὥσπερ δὲ τὰ
ὁλοσχερῆ, οὕτω καὶ τὰ κατὰ μέρος ἔτεμνεν, ὧν τὰ
μὲν ἄψυχα, τὰ δ' ἔμψυχα ἦν· καὶ τῶν ἀψύχων τὰ
μὲν ἐν ταὐτῷ μένοντα, ὧν δεσμὸς ἕξις, τὰ δ' οὐ
μεταβατικῶς, ἀλλ' αὐξητικῶς κινούμενα, ἃ φύσις
ἡ ἀφάντασστος ἐζώου· καὶ τούτων τὰ μὲν τῆς ἀγρίας
ὕλης οἰστικὰ ἀγρίων καρπῶν, οἳ τροφὴ θηρίοις
εἰσίν, τὰ δὲ τῆς ἡμέρου, ὧν γεωργία τὴν προστασίαν καὶ ἐπιμέλειαν ἔλαχε· τίκτει δὲ καρποὺς
τῷ πάντων ἡμερωτάτῳ ζώῳ πρὸς ἀπόλαυσιν,
138 ἀνθρώπῳ. καὶ μὴν ὃν τρόπον τὰ ἄψυχα, καὶ τὰ
ψυχῆς μεμοιραμένα διῄρει—τούτων γὰρ ἓν μὲν
ἀλόγων, ἓν δὲ λογικῶν ἀπέκρινεν εἶδος—καὶ λαβὼν
ἑκάτερον πάλιν ἔτεμνεν τὸ μὲν ἄλογον εἰς ἀτίθασόν

---

[1] ⟨καὶ οὐ πότιμον⟩ is my insertion. *Cf. De Som.* i. 18 in a
similar discussion, καὶ τὸ μὲν πότιμον, τὸ δ' οὐ πότιμον. A
triple division into sea, rivers, and drinkable is not very
reasonable.

---

[a] See App. p. 569.

a second division of heavy and light on different principles. He divided the light into cold and hot, giving to the cold the name of air and to the naturally hot the name of fire. The heavy He divided into wet and dry, and He called the dry " land " and the wet " water." Each of these was subjected to 136 further dissections. Land was divided into continents and islands, water into sea and rivers and into drinkable and undrinkable, air into the changes which mark summer and winter, and fire into the merely useful variety, which is also voracious and destructive, and on the other hand the preservative variety which was set apart to form the heaven.[a]

Just as He divided the main con- 137 stituents of the universe, so did He also with their subdivisions. These are partly living and partly lifeless. Among the lifeless some remain in the same place, held together by the tie of " cohesion "[b]; others move by expansion, without changing their position, vitalized by a natural and unconscious[c] growth, and among them, those which are of wild stuff produce wild fruits, which serve for food to the beasts of the field. Others are of a stuff which admits of cultivation, the management of which is a charge allotted to husbandry, and these produce fruits for the enjoyment of the animal most removed from the wild, that is man. Further, as He had divided the 138 lifeless, so did He with those which participate in life, distinguishing one species as rational, the other as irrational. Then again He split up each of these. The irrational He divided into the domesticated

[b] See note on *Leg. All.* ii. 22, and the fuller explanation both of ἕξις and φύσις in this sense in *Quod Deus* 35 ff.

[c] Or " incapable of receiving impressions "; *cf. De Op.* 13, *De Plant.* 13.

τε καὶ χειρόηθες εἶδος, τὸ δὲ λογικὸν εἰς ἄφθαρτόν
139 τε καὶ θνητόν. καὶ τοῦ θνητοῦ δύο μοίρας εἰργάζετο, ὧν τὴν μὲν ἀνδρῶν, τὴν δὲ γυναικῶν ἐπεφήμισε. καὶ κατ' ἄλλον μὲν[τοι]¹ τρόπον τὸ ζῷον
εἰς ἄρρεν ἔτεμνε καὶ θῆλυ, ἐδέχετο δὲ καὶ ἄλλας
ἀναγκαίας τομάς, αἳ διέστελλον πτηνὰ μὲν χερσαίων, χερσαῖα δὲ ἐνύδρων, ἔνυδρα δὲ ἀμφοῖν τῶν
140 ἄκρων. οὕτως ὁ θεὸς ἀκονησάμενος τὸν τομέα
τῶν συμπάντων αὑτοῦ λόγον διῄρει τήν τε ἄμορφον
καὶ ἄποιον τῶν ὅλων οὐσίαν καὶ τὰ ἐξ αὐτῆς ἀπο-
κριθέντα τέτταρα τοῦ κόσμου στοιχεῖα καὶ τὰ διὰ
τούτων παγέντα ζῷά τε αὖ καὶ φυτά.
141 XXVIII. Ἐπεὶ δ' οὐ μόνον φησὶ " διεῖλεν,"
ἀλλὰ καὶ " μέσα διεῖλεν," ἀναγκαῖον κἂν ὀλίγα
περὶ τῶν ἴσων τμημάτων ὑπομνῆσαι. τὸ μὲν
[493] γὰρ ἄκρως κατὰ μέσον | διαιρεθὲν ἴσα ἀποτελεῖ
142 τμήματα. ἄνθρωπος μὲν οὖν οὐδεὶς δύναιτ'
ἀκριβῶς ἄν ποτε εἰς ἴσα διελεῖν οὐδέν, ἀλλ' ἀνάγκη
τῶν τμημάτων τὸ ἕτερον ἐνδεῖν ἢ περιττεύειν, καὶ
εἰ μὴ μείζονι, ἀλλά τοι βραχεῖ μέρει πάντως, ὃ
τάχα τὴν αἴσθησιν ἐκφεύγει τοῖς ἀδρομερεστέροις
ἐκ φύσεως καὶ ἔθους προσβάλλουσαν ὄγκοις, τοὺς
δὲ ἀτόμους καὶ ἀμερεῖς καταλαβεῖν ἀδυνατοῦσαν.
143 ἰσότητος δὲ οὐδὲν γενητὸν² αἴτιον ἀδεκάστῳ λόγῳ
τῆς ἀληθείας εὑρίσκεται. ἔοικεν οὖν ὁ θεὸς μόνος
ἀκριβοδίκαιος εἶναι καὶ μέσα μόνος δύνασθαι
διαιρεῖν τά τε σώματα καὶ πράγματα, ὡς μηδὲν

---

¹ Wend.'s text retains μέντοι and places a colon after θῆλυ,
thus making an antithesis between the sex-division of mankind and that of animals as a whole, which seems not very
reasonable. Possibly also ἐτέμνε⟨το⟩.
² mss. ἴσον (Pap. ἧττον).

and undomesticated, and the rational into immortal and mortal. Of the mortal He made two portions, 139 one of which He named men, the other women. And while following one principle[a] He split up the animal kingdom as a whole into male and female, it was also subjected to other necessary partitions, which distinguished the winged from land animals, these from the aquatic, the last named being intermediate to the other two. Thus God sharpened the 140 edge of his all-cutting Word, and divided universal being, which before was without form or quality, and the four elements of the world which were formed by segregation from it, and the animals and plants which were framed with them as materials.

XXVIII. But the text not only says " He divided " 141 but also " He divided them in the middle "; and it is therefore necessary to make a few remarks on the subject of equal sections, for when anything is divided exactly in the middle it produces equal sections. Now no man can divide anything into 142 equal sections with exactitude, but one of the sections is sure to be either less or greater than the other. Even if there is no great difference, there must always be a small one which easily eludes our perception, which by nature and habit establishes contact with masses of greater volume, but is unable to grasp those which do not admit of partition or division. No created thing is found to produce equality 143 if tested by the unprejudiced standard of truth. It seems, then, that God alone is exact in judgement and alone is able to " divide in the middle " things material and immaterial, in such a way that no

---

[a] Or " on another principle," if Wend.'s text and punctuation is followed. See critical note.

τῶν τμημάτων μηδ' ἀκαρεῖ καὶ ἀμερεῖ τινι πλέον
ἢ ἔλαττον γενέσθαι, τῆς δ' ἀνωτάτω καὶ ἄκρας
144 ἰσότητος μεταλαχεῖν ἰσχῦσαι. εἰ μὲν οὖν τὸ ἴσον
μίαν εἶχεν ἰδέαν, ἱκανῶς ἂν τὰ λεχθέντα εἴρητο,
πλειόνων δ' οὐσῶν οὐκ ἀποκνητέον τὰ ἁρμόττοντα
προσθεῖναι.   λέγεται γὰρ ἴσον καθ' ἕνα
μὲν τρόπον ἐν ἀριθμοῖς, ὡς δύο δυσὶ καὶ τρία τρισὶ
καὶ τὰ ἄλλα ταύτῃ, καθ' ἕτερον δὲ ἐν μεγέθεσιν,
ὧν μήκη, πλάτη, βάθη, διαστάσεις εἰσίν, παλαιστὴς
γὰρ παλαιστῇ καὶ πήχει πῆχυς ἴσα μεγέθει·
δυνάμει δέ ἐστιν ἄλλα, ὡς τὰ ἐν σταθμοῖς καὶ
145 μέτροις.   ἀναγκαία δέ ἐστιν ἰσότητος
ἰδέα καὶ ἡ διὰ ἀναλογίας, καθ' ἣν καὶ τὰ ὀλίγα
τοῖς πολλοῖς καὶ τὰ βραχέα τοῖς μείζοσιν ἴσα
νενόμισται· ᾗ καὶ πόλεις ἐπὶ καιρῶν εἰώθασι
χρῆσθαι κελεύουσαι τὸ ἴσον ἕκαστον τῶν πολιτῶν
ἀπὸ τῆς οὐσίας εἰσφέρειν, οὐ δήπου ἐν ἀριθμῷ,
ἀλλ' ἀναλογίᾳ τοῦ περὶ τὸν κλῆρον[1] τιμήματος,
ὥστ' ὁ δραχμὰς ἑκατὸν εἰσενεγκὼν τῷ τὸ τάλαντον
εἰσενεγκόντι δόξαι ἂν ἐπιδεδωκέναι τὸ ἴσον.
146   XXIX. τούτων προϋποτυπωθέντων
ἴδε πῶς μέσα διελὼν ἴσα διεῖλε κατὰ πάσας τὰς
ἰσότητος ἰδέας ἐν τῇ τοῦ παντὸς οὐρανοῦ γενέσει.
ἀριθμῷ μὲν οὖν ἴσα τὰ βαρέα τοῖς κούφοις ἔτεμνε,
δύο δυσί, γῆν καὶ ὕδωρ, τὰ βάρος ἔχοντα, τοῖς
φύσει κούφοις, ἀέρι καὶ πυρί, καὶ πάλιν ἐν ἑνί, τὸ
μὲν ξηρότατον τῷ ὑγροτάτῳ, γῆν ὕδατι, τὸ δὲ

[1] mss. and Pap. καιρὸν.

---

[a] See App. p. 569.   [b] See App. p. 570.

section is greater or less than another by even an
infinitesimal difference, and each can partake of the
equality which is absolute and plenary. Now if 144
equality had only one form, what has been said
would be enough ; but as it has several forms we
must not shrink from adding what is fitting.
The term " equal " is applied in one way to numbers,
as when we say that two is equal to two, and three
to three, and the same with other numbers. It is
applied in another way to magnitudes, the dimensions
of which are lengths, breadths and depths. For one
handbreadth is equal to another handbreadth and
one cubit to another cubit in magnitude. Other
things again are equal in capacity or force, as is the
case with weights and measures of content.[a]
One essential form of equality is the proportional, in 145
which the few are regarded as equal to the many, and
the small to the greater.[b] This is often employed by
states on special occasions when they order each
citizen to make an equal contribution from his
property, not of course numerically equal, but equal
in the sense that it is proportionate to the valuation
of his estate, so that one who had paid 100 drachmas
might be considered to have given a sum equal
to one who paid a talent.   XXIX. In 146
the light of this preliminary sketch, observe how
God in " dividing in the middle," actually did
divide equally according to all the forms of equality,
when he created the universe. First, as to equality
of number he made the light parts equal in number
to the heavy parts, earth and water which are heavy
being two, and fire and air which are naturally light
being two also. Again by this division we have one
and one in the driest and the wettest, that is earth

ψυχρότατον τῷ θερμοτάτῳ, πυρὶ ἀέρα, τὸν αὐτὸν
δὲ τρόπον καὶ σκότος φωτὶ καὶ ἡμέραν νυκτὶ καὶ
χειμῶνι θέρος καὶ ἔαρι μετόπωρον καὶ ὅσα τούτων
147 συγγενῆ· μεγέθει δ' ἴσα ἐν οὐρανῷ μὲν τοὺς
παραλλήλους κύκλους, τούς τε ἰσημερινούς, ἐαρινὸν
καὶ μετοπωρινόν, καὶ τοὺς τροπικούς, θερινόν τε
καὶ χειμερινόν, ἐπὶ γῆς δὲ ζώνας, δύο μὲν ἴσας
ἀλλήλαις, αἳ πρὸς τοῖς πόλοις εἰσὶ κατεψυγμέναι
καὶ διὰ τοῦτ' ἀοίκητοι, δύο δὲ τὰς μεθορίους
τούτων τε καὶ τῆς διακεκαυμένης, ἃς δι' εὐκρασίαν
φασὶν οἰκεῖσθαι, τὴν μὲν πρὸς τοῖς νοτίοις, τὴν
148 δὲ πρὸς τοῖς βορείοις κειμένην.   μήκει
δ' ἴσα ἐστὶ καὶ τὰ χρόνου διαστήματα, ἡ μεγίστη
[494] ἡμέρα τῇ μεγίστῃ νυκτὶ καὶ πάλιν ἡ | βραχυτάτη
τῇ βραχυτάτῃ καὶ ἡ μέση τῇ μέσῃ. τὰ δὲ τῶν
ἄλλων ἡμερῶν τε καὶ νυκτῶν ἴσα μεγέθη μάλιστα
149 μηνύειν αἱ ἰσημερίαι δοκοῦσιν. ἀπὸ μὲν γὰρ τῆς
ἐαρινῆς ἄχρι θερινῶν τροπῶν ἡ μὲν ἡμέρα πρόσθεσιν,
ἡ δὲ νὺξ ἀφαίρεσιν δέχεται, ἕως ἂν ἥ τε μεγίστη
ἡμέρα καὶ βραχυτάτη νὺξ ἀποτελεσθῶσιν· ἀπὸ δὲ
θερινῶν τροπῶν ἀνακάμπτων ὁ ἥλιος τὴν αὐτὴν
ὁδὸν οὔτε θᾶττον οὔτε βραδύτερον, ἀλλὰ κατὰ τὰ
αὐτὰ καὶ ὡσαύτως ἔχοντα διαστήματα, τάχεσιν
ἴσοις χρώμενος μέχρι τῆς μετοπωρινῆς ἰσημερίας
ἔρχεται, καὶ ἴσην ἀποτελέσας ἡμέραν νυκτὶ παρ-
αύξειν ἄρχεται τὴν νύκτα μειῶν τὴν ἡμέραν ἄχρι
150 χειμερινῆς τροπῆς· καὶ ὅταν ἀποτελέσῃ νύκτα μὲν
μεγίστην, ἡμέραν δὲ βραχυτάτην, κατὰ τὰ αὐτὰ
πάλιν διαστήματα ἀνακάμπτων ἐπὶ τὴν ἐαρινὴν
ἰσημερίαν ἀφικνεῖται. οὕτως τὰ χρόνων διαστή-

and water, and in the coldest and the hottest, that is air and fire. In the same way we have one and one in darkness and light, in day and night, in winter and summer, in spring and autumn, and in the other examples of the same nature. For equality of 147 magnitude, He gave us the parallel circles in heaven, those of the equinox in spring and autumn, and those of the solstice in summer and winter, while on earth there are the zones, two of which are equal to each other, namely those which adjoin the poles, frigid and therefore uninhabited, and two which are bordered by the last named and the torrid zone, these two habitable, as we are told, because of their temperate climate, one of them on the south side and the other on the north. The time intervals, 148 too, are equal in length, the longest day to the longest day and the shortest to the shortest and the two which come half-way to each other. And equality in magnitude in the other days and nights is shewn particularly well in the equinoxes. For from the 149 spring equinox to the summer solstice something is continually taken from the night and added to the day, until the longest day and shortest night are finally reached. And after the summer solstice the sun turns back along the same course, moving neither quicker nor slower, but with the same unchanging intervals, and thus maintaining equal speed it reaches the autumn equinox, and after completing the equality of day and night begins to increase the night and diminish the day until the winter solstice. And when it has brought the night to its longest and 150 the day to its shortest, it turns back again observing the same intervals and arrives at the spring equinox. In this way the time intervals, though they seem to

ματα ἄνισα εἶναι δοκοῦντα ἰσότητος τῆς κατὰ τὸ
μέγεθος ἐν οὐχὶ ταῖς αὐταῖς ἀλλ' ἐν διαφερούσαις
τοῦ ἔτους ὥραις μεταποιεῖται.   XXX.
151 τὸ παραπλήσιον μέντοι καὶ ἐν τοῖς μέρεσι τῶν
ζῴων καὶ μάλιστα ἀνθρώπων θεωρεῖται. ποὺς
γὰρ ποδὶ καὶ χεὶρ χειρὶ καὶ τὰ ἄλλα σχεδὸν ἅπαντα
ἴσα μεγέθει, τὰ ἐπὶ δεξιὰ τοῖς κατ' εὐώνυμα.
      τὰ δ' ἴσα δυνάμει πάμπολλά ἐστιν
ἔν τε ξηροῖς καὶ ὑγροῖς, ὧν ἡ ἐπίκρισις ἐν μέτροις
καὶ πλάστιγξι καὶ τοῖς παραπλησίοις θεωρεῖται.
152 Ἀναλογίᾳ δὲ σχεδὸν τὰ πάντα ἐστὶν ἴσα, μικρά
τε αὖ καὶ μεγάλα ὅσα ἐν τῷ παντὶ κόσμῳ. λέγουσι
γὰρ οἱ ἀκριβέστατα περὶ τῶν τῆς φύσεως ἐξητα-
κότες, ὅτι ἀναλογίᾳ μὲν ἴσα τὰ τέτταρα στοιχεῖά
ἐστιν, ἀναλογίᾳ δὲ καὶ ὁ κόσμος ἅπας κραθεὶς τὸ
ἴσον ἑκάστῳ τῶν μερῶν ἀπονεμούσῃ συνέστη τε
153 καὶ συσταθεὶς εἰς ἅπαν διαμένει· καὶ τὰ περὶ ἡμᾶς
μέντοι τέτταρα, ξηρόν, ὑγρόν, ψυχρόν τε αὖ καὶ
θερμόν, τὴν δι' ἀναλογίας ἰσότητα κερασαμένην
ἁρμόσασθαι, καὶ μηδὲν ἄλλο ⟨ἡμᾶς⟩[1] ἢ κρᾶσιν εἶναι
τῶν τεσσάρων δυνάμεων ἀναλογίας ἰσότητι κρα-
154 θεισῶν. XXXI. ἐπιὼν δέ τις ἕκαστα μῆκος ἂν
ἄπειρον τῷ λόγῳ δύναιτ' ἂν περιθεῖναι. τὰ ⟨γὰρ⟩
βραχύτατα ζῷα τοῖς μεγίστοις ἀναλογίᾳ σκοπῶν
ἴσα ἂν εὕροι, ὡς χελιδόνα ἀετῷ καὶ τρίγλαν
κήτει καὶ μύρμηκα ἐλέφαντι. καὶ γὰρ σῶμα καὶ
ψυχὴ καὶ πάθη, ἀλγηδόνες τε καὶ ἡδοναί, πρὸς δὲ
καὶ οἰκειώσεις καὶ ἀλλοτριώσεις καὶ ὅσα ζῴων

---

[1] ἡμᾶς is absent from the mss., but Pap. has ητιειαν.

be unequal, may lay claim to equality of magnitude, not indeed at the same, but at different seasons of the year. XXX. Much the same may **151** be observed in the parts of living animals, particularly of men. For one foot or one hand is equal in magnitude to the other and in almost all cases the same holds that the right side is equal to the left.

As for equality in force or capacity there is a host of examples in both wet and dry substances, of which we form our estimate by means of measures of content, balances and the like.

As for proportional equality, we find it practically **152** in everything great or small, throughout the whole world. Those who have most carefully examined the facts of nature say that the four elements are proportionally equal, and that the whole world received and retains for ever its frame, through being compounded according to this same proportion, which assigned an equal measure to each of the parts. They tell us, too, that our four constituents, dry, wet, **153** cold and hot, have been mixed and harmonized by proportional equality and that we are nothing more than a compound of the four factors mixed on this principle. XXXI. If we went into each case, we **154** could prolong the consideration of the subject to infinity. For we should find on observation that the smallest animals are proportionally equal to the largest, as the swallow to the eagle, the mullet to the whale, and the ant to the elephant. For their body, soul[a] and feelings, whether of pain or pleasure, and also their affinities and their aversions and every other sensation of which animal nature is capable,

---

[a] *i.e.* their φαντασίαι and ὁρμαί; see *Leg. All.* ii. 23. Perhaps " consciousness " or " animal nature."

φύσις χωρεῖ, πάντα σχεδόν ἐστιν ὁμοιότροπα τῷ
155 τῆς ἀναλογίας ἰσούμενα κανόνι. οὕτως ἐθάρρησαν
ἔνιοι καὶ τῷ παντὶ κόσμῳ τὸ βραχύτατον ζῷον,
ἄνθρωπον, ἴσον ἀποφῆναι κατιδόντες ὅτι ἑκάτερον
ἐκ σώματος καὶ ψυχῆς καθέστηκε λογικῆς, ὥστε
καὶ ἐναλλάττοντες βραχὺν μὲν κόσμον τὸν ἄνθρωπον, μέγαν δὲ ἄνθρωπον ἔφασαν τὸν κόσμον
156 εἶναι.   ταῦτα δ' οὐκ ἀπὸ σκοποῦ δι-
δάσκουσιν, ἀλλ' ἔγνωσαν ὅτι ἡ τοῦ θεοῦ τέχνη,
[495] καθ' ἣν | ἐδημιούργει τὰ σύμπαντα, οὔτε ἐπίτασιν
οὔτε ἄνεσιν δεχομένη, μένουσα δὲ ἡ αὐτὴ κατὰ
τὴν ἐν ὑπερβολαῖς ἀκρότητα τελείως ἕκαστον τῶν
ὄντων δεδημιούργηκε, πᾶσιν ἀριθμοῖς καὶ πάσαις
ταῖς πρὸς τελειότητα ἰδέαις καταχρησαμένου τοῦ
157 πεποιηκότος. XXXII. '' κατὰ γὰρ τὸν μικρὸν
καὶ κατὰ τὸν μέγαν,'' ὥς φησι Μωυσῆς, ἔκρινε
γεννῶν καὶ σχηματίζων ἕκαστα, μήτε δι' ἀφάνειαν
ὕλης ὑφελών τι τοῦ τεχνικοῦ μήτε διὰ λαμπρότητα
158 προσθείς· ἐπεὶ καὶ ὅσοι τῶν τεχνιτῶν εἰσι δόκιμοι,
ἃς ἂν παραλάβωσιν ὕλας, εἴτε πολυτελεῖς εἶεν
εἴτε καὶ εὐτελέσταται, δημιουργεῖν ἐθέλουσιν
ἐπαινετῶς. ἤδη δέ τινες καὶ προσφιλοκαλοῦντες
τὰ ἐν ταῖς εὐτελεστέραις οὐσίαις τεχνικώτερα τῶν
ἐν ταῖς πολυτελέσιν εἰργάσαντο βουληθέντες προσ-
θήκῃ τοῦ ἐπιστημονικοῦ τὸ κατὰ τὴν ὕλην ἐνδέον
159 ἐπανισῶσαι. τίμιον δ' οὐδὲν τῶν ἐν ὕλαις παρὰ θεῷ·
διὸ τῆς αὐτῆς μετέδωκε πᾶσι τέχνης ἐξ ἴσου. παρὸ
καὶ ἐν ἱεραῖς γραφαῖς λέγεται· '' εἶδεν ὁ θεὸς τὰ
πάντα ὅσα ἐποίησεν, καὶ ἰδοὺ καλὰ λίαν,'' τὰ δὲ τοῦ

ᵃ See App. p. 570.

are with hardly an exception alike when equalized by the rule of proportion. On this principle some 155 have ventured to affirm that the tiny animal man is equal to the whole world, because each consists of body and reasonable soul, and thus they declare that man is a small world and alternatively the world a great man. This pronouncement of theirs 156 is not wide of the mark. They judge that the master art of God by which He wrought all things is one that admits of no heightening or lowering of intensity [a] but always remains the same and that through its transcendent excellence it has wrought in perfection each thing that is, every number and every form that tends to perfectness being used to the full by the Maker. XXXII. For He judged equally about the 157 little and the great, to use Moses' words (Deut. i. 17), when He generated and shaped each thing, nor was He led by the insignificance of the material to diminish, or by its splendour to increase, the art which He applied. For all craftsmen of repute, whatever 158 materials they use, whether they be costly or of the cheapest, wish so to use them, that their work shall be worthy of praise. In fact people have been known to produce a higher class of work with the cheaper than with the more costly substances ; their feeling for beauty was enhanced [b] and by additional science they wished to compensate for inferiority of material. But with God no kind of material is held in honour, 159 and therefore He bestowed upon them all the same art, and in equal measure. And so in the holy Scriptures we read, " God saw all things which He had made and behold, they were very good " (Gen. i.

---

[b] Probably a reminiscence of the φιλοκαλοῦμεν μετ' εὐτελείας of Thuc. ii. 40.

αὐτοῦ τυγχάνοντα ἐπαίνου παρὰ τῷ ἐπαινοῦντι
160 πάντως ἐστὶν ἰσότιμα. ἐπῄνεσε δὲ ὁ θεὸς οὐ τὴν
δημιουργηθεῖσαν ὕλην, τὴν ἄψυχον καὶ πλημμελῆ
καὶ διαλυτήν, ἔτι δὲ φθαρτὴν ἐξ ἑαυτῆς ἀνώμαλόν
τε καὶ ἄνισον, ἀλλὰ τὰ ἑαυτοῦ τεχνικὰ ἔργα κατὰ
μίαν ἴσην καὶ ὁμαλὴν δύναμιν καὶ ἐπιστήμην
ὁμοίαν καὶ τὴν αὐτὴν ἀποτελεσθέντα. παρὸ καὶ
τοῖς τῆς ἀναλογίας κανόσιν ἴσα καὶ ὅμοια πάντα
πᾶσιν ἐνομίσθη κατὰ τὸν τῆς τέχνης καὶ ἐπιστήμης
λόγον.

161 XXXIII. Ἰσότητος δὲ εἰ καί τις ἄλλος ἐπαινέτης
γέγονε Μωυσῆς, πρῶτον μὲν ὑμνῶν ἀεὶ καὶ πανταχοῦ καὶ δικαιοσύνην, ἧς ἴδιον, ὡς καὶ αὐτό που
δηλοῖ τοὔνομα, τὸ δίχα τέμνειν εἰς μοίρας τά τε
σώματα καὶ τὰ πράγματα ἴσας, εἶτα ψέγων
ἀδικίαν, τὴν ἀνισότητος τῆς ἐχθίστης δημιουργόν.

162 ἀνισότης δὲ τοὺς διδύμους πολέμους ἔτεκε, τόν
τε ξενικὸν καὶ τὸν ἐμφύλιον, ὡς ἔμπαλιν εἰρήνην
ἰσότης. τὰ δ' ἐγκώμια δικαιοσύνης καὶ τοὺς
ψόγους ἀδικίας ἐναργέστατα διασυνίστησιν, ὅταν
λέγῃ· '' οὐ ποιήσετε ἄδικον ἐν κρίσει, ἐν μέτροις,
ἐν σταθμοῖς, ἐν ζυγοῖς· ζυγὰ δίκαια καὶ στάθμια
δίκαια καὶ μέτρα δίκαια καὶ χοῦς δίκαιος ἔσται
ὑμῖν,'' καὶ ἐν Ἐπινομίδι '' οὐκ ἔσται ἐν μαρσίππῳ
σου στάθμιον καὶ στάθμιον, μέγα ἢ μικρόν· οὐκ
ἔσται ἐν τῇ οἰκίᾳ σου μέτρον καὶ μέτρον, μέγα
ἢ μικρόν· στάθμιον ἀληθινὸν καὶ δίκαιον ἔσται σοι,
ἵνα πολυήμερος γένῃ ἐπὶ τῆς γῆς, ἧς κύριος ὁ
θεός σου δίδωσί σοι ἐν κλήρῳ, ὅτι βδέλυγμα κυρίῳ

---

^a δίκη being supposed to be derived from δίχα.

31), and things which receive the same praise must be of equal honour in the eyes of the praiser. Now **160** God praised not the material which He had used for His work, material soul-less, discordant and dissoluble, and indeed in itself perishable, irregular, unequal, but He praised the works of His own art, which were consummated through a single exercise of power equal and uniform, and through knowledge ever one and the same. And thus by the rules of proportion everything was accounted similar and equal to everything else, according to the principle which His art and His knowledge followed.

XXXIII. Moses too above all others shews him- **161** self a eulogist of equality; first by always and every-where lauding justice too whose special property it is, as the name itself seems to shew,[a] to divide into two equal parts things material and immaterial; secondly by censuring injustice, the creator of inequality in its most hateful form. Inequality is the mother **162** of the twins, foreign war and civil war, just as its opposite, equality, is the mother of peace. Moses presents most clearly his glorification of justice and his censure of injustice, when he says " ye shall do nothing unjust in judgement, in measures, in weights, in balances; your balances shall be just, your weights just and your measures just and your quart just " (Lev. xix. 35, 36) and in Deuteronomy, " There shall not be in thy bag divers weights, great and small : there shall not be in thy house divers measures, great and small. A true and a just weight thou shalt have, that thy days may be long in the land, which the Lord thy God gives thee in inherit-ance, because every one who doeth these things is an abomination to the Lord, every one who doeth injustice

163 πᾶς ποιῶν ταῦτα, πᾶς ποιῶν ἄδικα." οὐκοῦν ὁ
φιλοδίκαιος θεὸς ἀδικίαν βδελύττεται καὶ μεμίσηκε,
στάσεως καὶ κακῶν ἀρχήν.   ποῦ δ'
ἰσότητα τὴν δικαιοσύνης τροφὸν ὁ νομοθέτης οὐκ
[496] ἀποδέχεται ἀρξάμενος | ἀπὸ τῆς τοῦ παντὸς
οὐρανοῦ γενέσεως; " διεχώρισε " γάρ φησιν " ὁ
θεὸς ἀνὰ μέσον τοῦ φωτὸς καὶ ἀνὰ μέσον τοῦ
σκότους· καὶ ἐκάλεσεν ὁ θεὸς τὸ φῶς ἡμέραν καὶ
τὸ σκότος νύκτα." ἡμέραν γὰρ καὶ νύκτα καὶ
164 φῶς καὶ σκότος ἰσότης ἔταξε[1] τοῖς οὖσι. διεῖλεν
ἰσότης καὶ τὸν ἄνθρωπον εἰς ἄνδρα καὶ γυναῖκα, δύο
τμήματα, ἄνισα μὲν ταῖς ῥώμαις, πρὸς ὃ δὲ
ἔσπευσεν ἡ φύσις, τρίτου τινὸς ὁμοίου γένεσιν,
ἰσαίτατα. " ἐποίησε " γάρ φησιν " ὁ θεὸς τὸν
ἄνθρωπον, κατ᾽ εἰκόνα θεοῦ ἐποίησεν αὐτόν, ἄρσεν
καὶ θῆλυ ἐποίησεν " οὐκέτ᾽ αὐτόν, ἀλλ᾽ " αὐτοὺς "
ἐπιφέρει πληθυντικῶς, ἐφαρμόττων τὰ εἴδη τῷ
γένει διαιρεθέντα, ὡς εἶπον, ἰσότητι. XXXIV.
165 ψῦχός γε μὴν καὶ καῦμα καὶ θέρος καὶ ἔαρ ἀνέγραψε,
τὰς ἐτησίους ὥρας πάλιν τῷ αὐτῷ τομεῖ διαιρου-
μένας. αἵ γε μὴν πρὸ ἡλίου τρεῖς ἡμέραι ταῖς
μεθ᾽ ἥλιον ἰσάριθμοι γεγόνασιν, ἑξάδος τμηθείσης
ἰσότητι πρὸς αἰῶνος καὶ χρόνου δήλωσιν· αἰῶνι
μὲν γὰρ τὰς πρὸ ἡλίου τρεῖς ἀνατέθεικε, χρόνῳ
δὲ τὰς μεθ᾽ ἥλιον, ὅς ἐστι μίμημα αἰῶνος.

---

[1] Perhaps, as Wend. suggests, ἔταξεν (so Pap.) ⟨ἐν⟩ τοῖς οὖσι.

---

[a] The point of the sentence is not clear. Perhaps he
means that, as we have already shewn (§ 99) that day and
night are essentially equal, Moses, by putting them at the
outset of the creation story, praises equality. Or the stress
may lie on ἀνὰ μέσον as in itself indicating equality (so
in § 166). But in this case γάρ is unintelligible. Perhaps
correct to ἄρα.

(Deut. xxv. 13-16). So then the God who loves **163**
justice hates and abominates injustice, the source
of faction and evil.   As for equality, the
nurse of justice, where does the Lawgiver fail to
shew his approval ? We find it first in the story of
the creation of the whole heaven. " God separated,"
he says, " between the light and between the darkness, and God called the light day and the darkness
night " (Gen. i. 4, 5). For equality gave day and **164**
night, light and darkness, their place among the
things which are.[a] Equality too divided the human
being into man and woman, two sections unequal
indeed in strength, but quite equal as regards what
was nature's urgent purpose, the reproduction of
themselves in a third person. " God made man,"
he says, " made him after the image of God. Male
and female He made "—not now " him " but " them "
(Gen. i. 27). He concludes with the plural, thus
connecting with the genus mankind the species
which had been divided, as I said, by equality.
XXXIV. Then he mentions cold and heat, summer **165**
and spring, the seasons of the year, as being separated
by the same divider, equality (Gen. viii. 22). Again
the three days before the sun's creation are equal
in number to the three which followed it (Gen. i. 5 ff.),
the whole six being divided by equality to express
time and eternity.[b] For God dedicated the three
before the sun to eternity, and the three after it to
time, which is a copy of eternity.[c]   And the **166**

---

[b] See App. p. 570.
[c] A reminiscence of *Timaeus* 37 D. See *Quod Deus* 32
and note. The analogy to the *Timaeus* shews that χρόνῳ
and not ἥλιον is the antecedent of ὅς, as otherwise it
might have been thought to be by comparison with *De
Mig.* 40.

166 τὰς δὲ τοῦ ὄντος πρώτας δυνάμεις, τήν τε χαρι-
στικήν, καθ' ἣν ἐκοσμοπλάστει, ἢ προσαγορεύεται
θεός, καὶ τὴν κολαστικήν, καθ' ἣν ἄρχει καὶ
ἐπιστατεῖ τοῦ γενομένου, ἢ προσονομάζεται κύριος,
ὑπ' αὐτοῦ φησιν ἑστῶτος ἐπάνω μέσου δια-
στέλλεσθαι· "λαλήσω γάρ σοι" φησίν "ἄνωθεν
τοῦ ἱλαστηρίου ἀνὰ μέσον τῶν δυεῖν Χερουβίμ,"
ἵν' ἐπιδείξῃ ὅτι αἱ πρεσβύταται τοῦ ὄντος δυνάμεις
ἰσάζουσιν, ἥ τε δωρητικὴ καὶ κολαστήριος, αὐτῷ
167 τομεῖ χρώμεναι.   XXXV. τί δ'; αἱ
στῆλαι τῶν γενικῶν δέκα νόμων, ἃς ὀνομάζει
πλάκας, οὐ δύο εἰσὶν ἰσάριθμοι τοῖς τῆς ψυχῆς
μέρεσι, λογικῷ καὶ ἀλόγῳ, ἃ παιδευθῆναί τε καὶ
σωφρονισθῆναι χρή, τεμνόμεναι πάλιν ὑπὸ τοῦ
θεσμοθέτου[1] μόνου; "αἱ γὰρ πλάκες ἔργον θεοῦ
ἦσαν, καὶ ἡ γραφὴ γραφὴ θεοῦ κεκολαμμένη ἐν
168 ταῖς πλαξί." καὶ μὴν τῶν ἐν αὐταῖς δέκα λόγων,
οἳ κυρίως εἰσὶ θεσμοί, διαίρεσις ἴση γέγονεν εἰς
πεντάδας, ὧν ἡ μὲν προτέρα τὰ πρὸς θεὸν δίκαια,
169 ἡ δὲ ἑτέρα τὰ πρὸς ἀνθρώπους περιέχει. τῶν μὲν
οὖν πρὸς θεὸν δικαίων πρῶτός ἐστι θεσμὸς ὁ
ἐναντιούμενος τῇ πολυθέῳ δόξῃ, διδάσκων ὅτι
μοναρχεῖται ὁ κόσμος· δεύτερος δὲ ὁ περὶ τοῦ μὴ
θεοπλαστεῖν τὰ μὴ αἴτια γραφέων καὶ πλαστῶν
ἐπιβούλοις τέχναις, ἃς[2] Μωυσῆς ἐξήλασε τῆς καθ'

---

[1] Perhaps read θεσμοθέτου ⟨θεοῦ⟩. The absolute use of
θεσμοθέτης for God as legislator does not seem to have a
parallel.

[2] Wend. αἷς from Pap. This is undue subservience to the
Papyrus. The relative attraction is confined in Greek to
defining relative clauses, *i.e.* those without which the antecedent is unintelligible. See Madvig, *Greek Syntax*, 103
R. 1.

primary Potencies of the Existent, namely that through which He wrought the world, the beneficent, which is called God, and that by which He rules and commands what He made, that is the punitive, which bears the name of Lord, are as Moses tells us, separated by God Himself standing above and in the midst of them. " I will speak to thee," it says, " above the mercy-seat in the midst of the two Cherubim " (Ex. xxv. 21).[a] He means to shew that the primal and highest Potencies of the Existent, the beneficent and the punitive, are equal, having Him to divide them.   XXXV. Again, 167 are not the slabs of the ten general laws, which he calls tables, two, thus equal in number to the parts of the soul, the rational and irrational, which must be trained and chastened ? These tables too were cut [b] by the Divine Legislator and by Him only. For " the tables were the work of God and the writing on them was the writing of God, graven on the tables " (Ex. xxxii. 16). Further, the ten words 168 on them, divine ordinances in the proper sense of the word, are divided equally into two sets of five, the former comprising duties to God, and the other duties to men. The first commandment among the duties 169 to God, is that which opposes the creed of polytheism, and its lesson is that the world has one sole ruler. The second forbids us to make gods of things which are not the causes of existence, employing for that purpose the mischievous arts of the painter and sculptor which Moses expelled from his common-

---

[a] The same interpretation of the Cherubim is given in *De Fuga* 100, and (of the Cherubim in Gen. iii.) *De Cher.* 27 ff.
[b] " Cut " covers both the cutting out and the graving of the tables, but also suggests the thought of God as the τομεύς.

αὐτὸν πολιτείας ἀίδιον φυγὴν ἐπ' αὐταῖς ψηφισάμενος, ἵν' ὁ μόνος καὶ | πρὸς ἀλήθειαν τιμᾶται [497]
170 θεός· τρίτος δὲ ὁ περὶ ὀνόματος κυρίου,[1] ⟨οὐ τοῦ⟩
ὃ οὐδ' ἦλθεν εἰς γένεσιν—ἄρρητον γὰρ τὸ ὄν—,
ἀλλὰ τοῦ ταῖς δυνάμεσιν ἐπιφημισθέντος, διείρηται
γὰρ αὐτὸ μὴ λαμβάνειν ἐπὶ ματαίῳ· τέταρτος δὲ
ὁ περὶ τῆς ἀειπαρθένου καὶ ἀμήτορος ἑβδομάδος,
ἵνα τὴν ἀπραξίαν αὐτῆς μελετῶσα γένεσις εἰς
μνήμην τοῦ ἀοράτως πάντα δρῶντος ἔρχηται·
171 πέμπτος δὲ ὁ περὶ γονέων τιμῆς· καὶ γὰρ οὗτος
ἱερὸς ἔχων τὴν ἀναφορὰν οὐκ ἐπ' ἀνθρώπους, ἀλλ'
ἐπὶ τὸν σπορᾶς καὶ γενέσεως τοῖς ὅλοις αἴτιον,
παρ' ὃν μήτηρ τε καὶ πατὴρ γεννᾶν ἔδοξαν, οὐ
172 γεννῶντες, ἀλλ' ὄργανα γενέσεως ὄντες. μεθόριος
δ' ὁ θεσμὸς οὗτος ἐγράφη[2] τῆς τε πρὸς εὐσέβειαν
τεινούσης πεντάδος καὶ τῆς ἀποτροπᾶς τῶν πρὸς
τοὺς ὁμοίους ἀδικημάτων περιεχούσης, ἐπειδήπερ
οἱ θνητοὶ γονεῖς τέλος εἰσὶν ἀθανάτων δυνάμεων,
αἳ πάντα γεννῶσαι κατὰ φύσιν ἐπέτρεψαν ὑστάτῳ
καὶ τῷ θνητῷ γένει μιμησαμένῳ τὴν περὶ τὸ
γεννᾶν τέχνην σπείρειν· ἀρχὴ μὲν γὰρ γενέσεως
ὁ θεός, τὸ δ' ἔσχατον καὶ ἀτιμότατον, τὸ θνητὸν
173 εἶδος, τέλος. ἡ δ' ἑτέρα πεντάς ἐστιν ἀπαγόρευσις μοιχείας, ἀνδροφονίας, κλοπῆς, ψευδομαρτυρίας, ἐπιθυμίας. οὗτοι γενικοὶ σχεδὸν πάντων
ἁμαρτημάτων εἰσὶ κανόνες, ἐφ' οὓς ἕκαστον

---

[1] I suggest κυρίου ⟨τοῦ θεοῦ⟩ in accordance with the LXX.;
κύριος alone is not the name given to *both* Potencies, as the
sequel implies. See App. p. 570.
[2] So Wend. from Pap.: MSS. ἐτάγη.

---

[a] See App. p. 570.
[b] Or "seventh day." See App. p. 570.

wealth[a] and sentenced to perpetual banishment. The purpose of this law is that the sole and true god may be duly honoured. The third is concerned with the name of the Lord, not that name the knowledge of which has never even reached the world of mere becoming—He that is cannot be named in words—but the name which is given to His Potencies. We are commanded not to take this name in vain. The fourth is concerned with the number Seven,[b] the ever-virgin, the motherless. Its purpose is that creation, observing the inaction which it brings, should call to mind Him who does all things invisibly.[c] The fifth is about honouring parents. This is of the sacred kind, since its reference is not to men, but to Him who causes all things to be sown and come into being, through whom it is that the father and mother appear to generate, though they do not really do so, but are the instruments of generation. This commandment was graven on the borderline between the set of five which makes for piety to God and the set which comprises the prohibitions against acts of injustice to our fellows. The mortal parentage is but the final form which immortal powers take. They in virtue of their nature generate all things, but have permitted mortality also at the final stage to copy their creative art and to beget. For God is the primary cause of generation, but the nethermost and least honoured kind, the mortal-kind, is the ultimate. The other set of five forbids adultery, murder, theft, false witness, covetousness. These are general rules forbidding practically all sins,

---

[c] See note on *De Mig.* 91. The sense needed here is rather " who *ever* works." Perhaps ἀεί has fallen out before ἀοράτως.

ἀναφέρεσθαι τῶν ἐν εἴδει συμβέβηκεν.

174 XXXVI. ἀλλὰ καὶ τὰς ἐνδελεχεῖς θυσίας ὁρᾷς
εἰς ἴσα διῃρημένας, ἥν τε ὑπὲρ ἑαυτῶν οἱ ἱερεῖς
προσφέρουσι τῆς σεμιδάλεως καὶ τὴν ὑπὲρ τοῦ
ἔθνους τῶν δυεῖν ἀμνῶν, οὓς ἀναφέρειν διείρηται.
πρωὶ γὰρ τὰ ἡμίση τῶν λεχθέντων καὶ τὰ ἕτερα
δειλινῆς ἐκέλευσεν ἱερουργεῖν ὁ νόμος, ἵνα καὶ
ὑπὲρ τῶν μεθ' ἡμέραν καὶ ὑπὲρ τῶν νύκτωρ
ἀρδομένων ἅπασιν ἀγαθῶν ὁ θεὸς εὐχαριστῆται.

175 ὁρᾷς καὶ τοὺς προτιθεμένους ἄρτους
ἐπὶ τῆς ἱερᾶς τραπέζης, ὡς ⟨εἰς⟩ ἴσα μέρη
διανεμηθέντες οἱ δώδεκα ἀριθμῷ καθ' ἑξάδα
τίθενται μνημεῖα τῶν ἰσαρίθμων φυλῶν, ὧν τὴν
ἡμίσειαν ἡ ἀρετὴ Λεία κεκλήρωται ἐξ τεκοῦσα
φυλάρχας, τὴν δ' ἑτέραν ἡμίσειαν οἵ τε Ῥαχὴλ
176 καὶ οἱ τῶν παλλακῶν νόθοι. ὁρᾷς καὶ τοὺς ἐπὶ
τοῦ ποδήρους δύο λίθους τῆς σμαράγδου πρός τε
τοῖς δεξιοῖς καὶ πρὸς τοῖς εὐωνύμοις ἰσότητι δι-
ῃρημένους, οἷς καθ' ἑξάδα ἐγγέγλυπται τὰ τῶν
δώδεκα φυλάρχων ὀνόματα, θεῖα γράμματα ἐστηλιτευμένα, θείων φύσεων ὑπομνήματα.

177 τί δ'; οὐχὶ δύο ὄρη συμβολικῶς δύο γένη λαβὼν
καὶ πάλιν ἰσότητι διακρίνας ἀναλογούσῃ τὸ μὲν
ἀπένειμε τοῖς εὐλογοῦσι, τὸ δ' αὖ τοῖς κατ-
[498] αρωμένοις ἐξ ἐφ' ἑκατέρου | στήσας φυλάρχας,
ἵνα τοῖς χρείοις νουθεσίας οὖσιν ἐπιδείξῃ, ὅτι καὶ
ἰσάριθμοι ⟨ταῖς⟩ εὐλογίαις αἱ ἀραὶ καὶ σχεδόν, εἰ

---

a *i.e.* the twelve signs of the Zodiac. See *Quaest. in Ex.* ii.
109, where this is definitely stated, the two emeralds being
supposed to represent the two hemispheres, to each of which
six of the twelve signs at different parts of the year belong.

and to them the specific sins may in each case be referred. XXXVI. To pass to a different matter, you find the same division into equal parts in the permanent sacrifices, both in the oblation of fine flour, which the priests offer for themselves, and in that offered on behalf of the nation, consisting of the two lambs which they are ordered to bring. In both these the law prescribes that half of the offerings named shall be sacrificed in the morning and half in the evening (Lev. vi. 20 ; Ex. xxix. 38, 39), that God may be thanked both for the day-time and the night-time blessings which He showers upon all. 174

Observe also the loaves set forth upon the holy table, how the twelve are divided into equal parts and placed in sets of six each, as memorials of the twelve tribes, half of them belonging to Leah or Virtue the mother of six patriarchs, and half to the children of Rachel and the base-born sons of the concubines. You see, too, how the two emeralds on the long robe, one on the right and one on the left, are divided equally, on which are cut the names of the twelve patriarchs, six on each, inscribed by divine graving, to remind us of divine beings (Ex. xxviii. 9-12).[a] Once more, does not Moses take two mountains, that is symbolically two kinds, and again distinguishes between them according to proportional equality, assign one to those who bless, the other to those who curse ? Then he places upon them the twelve patriarchs (Deut. xxvii. 11-13) to shew to those who need warning, that curses are equal in number to blessings and (if we may say so 175 176 177

---

[a] So also *De Spec. Leg.* i. 87, though there it is said of the twelve stones on the breastplate in Ex. xxviii. 21. For divine natures = heavenly bodies *cf. De Conf.* 133.

178 θέμις εἰπεῖν, ἰσότιμοι; ὁμοίως γὰρ οἵ τε ἔπαινοι
τῶν ἀγαθῶν καὶ οἱ ψόγοι τῶν μοχθηρῶν ὠφελοῦσιν,
ἐπεὶ καὶ τὸ φυγεῖν τὸ κακὸν τῷ τἀγαθὸν ἑλέσθαι
παρὰ τοῖς εὖ φρονοῦσιν ὅμοιον καὶ ταὐτὸν ἐνομίσθη.

179 XXXVII. καταπλήττει με καὶ ἡ τῶν
προσαγομένων τῷ ἱλασμῷ δυεῖν τράγων ἐπίκρισις
ὁμοῦ καὶ διανομὴ τεμνομένων ἀδήλῳ καὶ ἀτεκμάρτῳ
τομεῖ, κλήρῳ· λόγων γὰρ δυεῖν ὁ μὲν τὰ τῆς θείας
ἀρετῆς πραγματευόμενος ἀνιεροῦται καὶ ἀνατίθεται θεῷ, ὁ δὲ τὰ τῆς ἀνθρωπίνης κακοδαιμονίας
ἐζηλωκὼς γενέσει τῇ φυγάδι· καὶ γὰρ ὃν ἔλαχεν
αὕτη κλῆρον, ἀποπομπαῖον καλοῦσιν οἱ χρησμοί,
ἐπειδὴ μετανίσταται καὶ διῴκισται καὶ μακρὰν

180 ἀπελήλαται σοφίας. ἐπισήμων γε μὴν καὶ ἀσήμων
ὥσπερ νομισμάτων, οὕτως καὶ πραγμάτων ὄντων ἐν
τῇ φύσει πολλῶν ὁ ἀόρατος τομεὺς οὐ δοκεῖ σοι
διελεῖν πάντ᾽ εἰς μοίρας ἴσας καὶ τὰ μὲν ἐπίσημα
καὶ δόκιμα τῷ παιδείας ἐραστῇ, τῷ δὲ ἀμαθαίνοντι
τὰ ἀτύπωτα καὶ ἄσημα προσνεῖμαι; " ἐγένετο "
γάρ φησι " τὰ μὲν ἄσημα τοῦ Λάβαν, τὰ δὲ

181 ἐπίσημα τοῦ Ἰακώβ." καὶ γὰρ ἡ ψυχή, τὸ
κήρινον, ὡς εἶπέ τις τῶν ἀρχαίων, ἐκμαγεῖον,
σκληρὰ μὲν οὖσα καὶ ἀντίτυπος ἀπωθεῖ καὶ
ἀποσείεται τοὺς ἐπιφερομένους χαρακτῆρας καὶ
ἀσχημάτιστος ἐξ ἀνάγκης διαμένει, πειθήνιος δ᾽
ὑπάρχουσα καὶ μετρίως ὑπείκουσα βαθεῖς τοὺς
τύπους δέχεται καὶ ἀναμαξαμένη τὰς σφραγῖδας
ἄκρως διαφυλάττει τὰ ἐνσημανθέντα ἀνεξάλειπτα

182 εἴδη. XXXVIII. θαυμαστὴ μέντοι καὶ

---

a Cf. De Plant. 61 and note.

without offence) of equal value. For praises given 178
to the good and censure given to the bad are equally
beneficial, since, in the judgement of men of sense,
avoiding evil and choosing good are one and the
same. XXXVII. I am deeply impressed, 179
too, by the contrast made between the two he-goats
offered for atonement, and the difference of fate
assigned to them even when the division is effected
by that uncertain and fortuitous divider, the lot.
We see two ways of thinking ; one whose concern is
with things of divine virtue is consecrated and dedicated to God ; the other whose aspirations turn to
poor miserable humanity is assigned to creation the
exile. For the lot which fell to creation is called by
the oracles the lot of dismissal[a] (Lev. xvi. 8), because
creation is a homeless wanderer, banished far away
from wisdom. Further, nature abounds in things 180
which bear some shape or stamp and others which
do not, even as it is with coins, and you may note
how the invisible Severer divides them all into equal
parts and awards those that are approved by their
stamp to the lover of instruction, but those that have
no stamp or mark to the man of ignorance. For we
are told " the unmarked fell to Laban, but the
marked to Jacob " (Gen. xxx. 42). For the soul is a 181
block of wax, as one of the ancients said,[b] and if it is
hard and resistent it rejects and shakes off the
attempted impressions and inevitably remains an
unformed mass, whereas if it is docile and reasonably
submissive it allows the imprints to sink deep into it,
and thus reproducing the shape of the seal preserves
the forms stamped upon it, beyond any possibility
of effacement. XXXVIII. Marvellous too 182

[b] *Theaetetus* 191 c ; *cf. Quod Deus* 43.

ἡ τοῦ τῶν θυσιῶν αἵματος ἴση διανομή, ἣν ὁ
ἀρχιερεὺς Μωυσῆς φύσει διδασκάλῳ χρησάμενος
διένειμε. "λαβὼν" γάρ φησι "τὸ ἥμισυ τοῦ αἵματος
ἐνέχεεν εἰς κρατῆρας· τὸ δὲ ἥμισυ προσέχεε πρὸς
τὸ θυσιαστήριον," ὅπως ἀναδιδάξῃ, ὅτι τὸ σοφίας
ἱερὸν γένος διττόν ἐστι, τὸ μὲν θεῖον, τὸ δὲ ἀν-
183 θρώπινον· καὶ τὸ μὲν θεῖον ἀμιγὲς καὶ ἄκρατον,
οὗ ἕνεκα τῷ ἀμιγεῖ καὶ ἀκράτῳ καὶ κατὰ τὴν
μόνωσιν μονάδι ὄντι σπένδεται θεῷ, τὸ δὲ ἀνθρώπινον μικτὸν καὶ κεκραμένον, ὃ τοῦ μικτοῦ
καὶ συνθέτου καὶ κεκραμένου γένους κατασκεδάν-
νυται ἡμῶν, ὁμόνοιαν καὶ κοινωνίαν καὶ τί γὰρ
ἄλλο ἢ κρᾶσιν μερῶν τε καὶ ἠθῶν ἐργασόμενον.
184 ἀλλὰ γὰρ καὶ τῆς ψυχῆς τὸ μὲν ἀμιγὲς καὶ ἄκρατον
μέρος ὁ ἀκραιφνέστατος νοῦς ἐστιν, ὃς ἀπ' οὐρανοῦ
καταπνευσθεὶς ἄνωθεν ὅταν ἄνοσος καὶ ἀπήμων
διαφυλαχθῇ, τῷ καταπνεύσαντι καὶ ἀπαθῆ παντὸς
κακοῦ διαφυλάξαντι προσηκόντως ὅλος εἰς ἱερὰν
[499] σπονδὴν ἀναστοιχειωθεὶς ἀνταποδίδοται | τὸ δ'
αὖ μικτὸν γένος τὸ αἰσθήσεών ἐστιν, ᾧ κρατῆρας
185 οἰκείους ἡ φύσις ἐδημιούργησε. κρατῆρες δὲ ὁράσεως μὲν ὀφθαλμοί, ἀκοῆς δὲ ὦτα καὶ μυκτῆρες
ὀσφρήσεως καὶ τῶν ἄλλων αἱ ἁρμόττουσαι δεξαμεναί.
τούτοις ἐπιχεῖ τοῖς κρατῆρσιν ὁ ἱερὸς λόγος τοῦ
αἵματος ἀξιῶν τὸ ἄλογον ἡμῶν μέρος ψυχωθῆναι
καὶ τρόπον τινὰ λογικὸν γενέσθαι, ταῖς μὲν νοῦ
θείαις περιόδοις[1] ἀκολουθῆσαν, ἀγνεῦσαν δὲ τῶν
ὁλκὸν ἀπατεῶνα προτεινόντων δύναμιν αἰσθητῶν.

---

[1] mss. and Pap. νουθεσίαις (-ας). The text here printed is
according to Wend.'s conjecture, though he does not actually
adopt it. See App. p. 571.

---

[a] See App. p. 571.

is the equal distribution of the sacrificial blood which the high priest Moses,[a] following Nature's guidance, made. He took, we read, the half of the blood and poured it into mixing-bowls and the half he poured upon the altar (Ex. xxiv. 6), to shew us that sacred wisdom is of a twofold kind, divine and human. The divine kind is without mixture or 183 infusion and therefore is poured as an offering to God, who knows no mixture or infusion and is in His isolation a unity. But the human is mixed with infusion and thus is scattered abroad upon us, who are a mixed compounded product of infusion, to create in us oneness of mind and fellowship, and in fact a " mixing " of our various parts and ways of conduct. But the part of the soul which is free from mixture and infusion is the mind in its perfect purity. This mind filled with the breath of inspira- 184 tion from heaven above is guarded from malady and injury, and then reduced to a single element is fitly rendered in its entirety as a holy libation to Him who inspired it and guarded it from all evil that could harm it. The mixed kind is the senses, and for this nature has created the proper mixing-bowls. The eyes are the " bowls " of sight, the 185 ears of hearing, the nostrils of the sense of smell, and each of the others has its fitting vessel. On these bowls the holy Word[b] pours of the blood, desiring that our irrational part should be quickened and become in some sense rational, following the divine courses of the mind, and purified from the objects of sense, which lure it with all their deceitful and seductive force. And was 186

[b] The High Priest as often is identified with the Logos. *Cf. De Mig.* 102.

186   ἆρά γε οὐχὶ τοῦτον τὸν τρόπον καὶ τὸ
δίδραχμον διενεμήθη τὸ ἅγιον, ἵνα τὸ μὲν ἥμισυ
αὐτοῦ, τὴν δραχμήν, καθιερῶμεν λύτρα τῆς ἑαυτῶν
ψυχῆς κατατιθέντες, ἣν ὁ μόνος ἀψευδῶς ἐλεύθερος
καὶ ἐλευθεροποιὸς θεὸς ὠμῆς καὶ πικρᾶς παθῶν
καὶ ἀδικημάτων δεσποτείας ἱκετευθείς, ἔστι δ᾽
ὅτε καὶ χωρὶς ἱκεσίας, ἀνὰ κράτος ἐκλύει, τὸ δ᾽
ἕτερον μέρος τῷ ἀνελευθέρῳ καὶ δουλοπρεπεῖ γένει
καταλίπωμεν, οὗ κεκοινώνηκεν ὁ λέγων· " ἠγάπηκα
τὸν κύριόν μου," τὸν ἡγεμόνα ἐν ἐμοὶ νοῦν, " καὶ
τὴν γυναῖκά μου," τὴν φίλην καὶ οἰκουρὸν παθῶν
αἴσθησιν, " καὶ τὰ παιδία," τὰ κακὰ τούτων
187 ἔγγονα, " οὐκ ἄπειμι ἐλεύθερος." ἀνάγκη γὰρ καὶ
τῷ τοιούτῳ γένει κλῆρον ἄκληρον καὶ ἀποπομπαῖον
ἐκ τοῦ διδράχμου δοθῆναι, ἐναντίον τῇ ἀνατεθειμένῃ
δραχμῇ τε καὶ μονάδι· μονὰς δὲ οὔτε προσθήκην
οὔτε ἀφαίρεσιν δέχεσθαι πέφυκε, εἰκὼν οὖσα τοῦ
188 μόνου πλήρους θεοῦ. χαῦνα γὰρ τά γε[1] ἄλλα ἐξ
ἑαυτῶν, εἰ δέ που καὶ πυκνωθείη, λόγῳ σφίγγεται
θείῳ. κόλλα γὰρ καὶ δεσμὸς οὗτος πάντα τῆς
οὐσίας ἐκπεπληρωκώς· ὁ δ᾽ εἴρας καὶ συνυφήνας
ἕκαστα πλήρης αὐτὸς ἑαυτοῦ κυρίως ἐστίν, οὐ
189 δεηθεὶς ἑτέρου τὸ παράπαν. XXXIX. εἰκότως
οὖν ἐρεῖ Μωυσῆς· " ὁ πλουτῶν οὐ προσθήσει, καὶ
ὁ πενόμενος οὐκ ἐλαττώσει ἀπὸ τοῦ ἡμίσους τοῦ
διδράχμου," ὅπερ ἐστίν, ὡς ἔφην, δραχμή τε καὶ

---

[1] My correction for τε in Wend.'s and Mangey's texts.

[a] Or, if we follow the parallel passage in *De Cher.* 73
where the children of mind are the various mental activities,

376

not the consecrated didrachmon portioned out on the same principle ? We are meant to consecrate one half of it, the drachma, and pay it as ransom for our own soul (Ex. xxx. 12, 13), which God who alone is truly free and a giver of freedom releases with a mighty hand from the cruel and bitter tyranny of passions and wrongdoings, if we supplicate him, sometimes too without our supplication. The other half we are to leave to the unfree and slavish kind of which he is a member who says " I have come to love my master," that is " the mind which rules within me," and my wife, that is " sense " the friend and keeper of the passion's household, " and the children," that is the evil offspring of the passions.[a] " I will not go out free " (Ex. xxi. 5). For 187 to such a kind, as its share in the didrachmon, must needs be given the lot which is no lot, the lot of dismissal which is the opposite of the dedicated drachma. The drachma is a unit, and a unit admits neither of addition nor subtraction, being the image of God who is alone in His unity and yet has fullness. Other things are in themselves without coherence, 188 and if they be condensed, it is because they are held tight by the divine Word, which is a glue and bond, filling up all things with His being.[b] He who fastens and weaves together each separate thing is in literal truth full of His own self, and needs nothing else at all. XXXIX. With reason then will Moses say, 189 " He that is rich shall not add, and he that is poor shall not diminish, from the half of the didrachmon " (Ex. xxx. 15). That half, as I said, is both a drachma

and those of sense the various sense processes, τούτων will refer to νοῦς and αἴσθησις. But κακά points rather to πάθη as the parents,   [b] See App. p. 571.

μονάς· ἧ πᾶς ἂν ἀριθμὸς εἴποι τὸ ποιητικὸν
ἐκεῖνο

> ἐν σοὶ μὲν λήξω, σέο δ' ἄρξομαι.

190 λήγει τε γὰρ ἀναλυόμενος ὁ κατὰ σύνθεσιν ἀπειράκις ἄπειρος ἀριθμὸς εἰς μονάδα, ἄρχεταί τε αὖ
πάλιν ἀπὸ μονάδος εἰς ἀπερίγραφον συντιθέμενος
πλῆθος. διόπερ οὐδ' ἀριθμόν, ἀλλὰ στοιχεῖον καὶ
ἀρχὴν ἀριθμοῦ ταύτην ἔφασαν, οἷς ζητεῖν ἐπι-
191 μελές.   ἔτι τοίνυν τὴν οὐράνιον τροφὴν—
σοφία δέ ἐστιν—τῆς ψυχῆς, ἢν καλεῖ μάννα,
διανέμει πᾶσι τοῖς χρησομένοις θεῖος λόγος ἐξ
[500] ἴσου, πεφροντικὼς | διαφερόντως ἰσότητος. μαρ-
τυρεῖ δὲ Μωυσῆς λέγων· " οὐκ ἐπλεόνασεν ὁ τὸ
πολύ, καὶ ὁ τὸ ἔλαττον οὐκ ἠλαττόνησεν," ἡνίκα
τῷ τῆς ἀναλογίας ἐχρήσαντο θαυμαστῷ καὶ περι-
μαχήτῳ μέτρῳ· δι' οὗ συνέβη μαθεῖν, ὅτι ἕκαστος
" εἰς τοὺς καθήκοντας " παρ' ἑαυτῷ συνέλεξεν οὐκ
ἀνθρώπους μᾶλλον ἢ λογισμοὺς καὶ τρόπους· ὁ
γὰρ ἐπέβαλεν ἑκάστῳ τοῦτ' ἀπεκληρώθη προ-
νοητικῶς, ὡς μήθ' ὑστερῆσαι μήτ' αὖ περιττεῦσαι.
192   XL. τὸ δὲ παραπλήσιον τῆς κατ'
ἀναλογίαν ἰσότητος ἔστιν εὑρεῖν καὶ ἐπὶ τοῦ λεγο-
μένου Πάσχα. Πάσχα δέ ἐστιν, ὅταν ἡ ψυχὴ τὸ
μὲν ἄλογον πάθος ἀπομαθεῖν μελετᾷ, τὴν δ'
193 εὔλογον εὐπάθειαν ἑκουσίως πάσχῃ· διείρηται γάρ,
" ἐὰν ὀλίγοι ὦσιν οἱ ἐν τῇ οἰκίᾳ, ὥστε μὴ ἱκανοὺς
εἶναι εἰς τὸ πρόβατον, τὸν πλησίον γείτονα προσ-

---

[a] Hom. *Iliad* ix. 97.
[b] *i.e.* all numbers are after all only so many units.
[c] See App. p. 571.
[d] Or, as Philo seems to understand the phrase, " those

and a unit, to which every number might well address the words of the poet,

> With thee I'll cease, with thee I will begin.[a]

For the whole series of numbers to infinity multi- 190 plied by infinity ends when resolved in the unit[b] and begins with the unit when arranged in an unlimited series. And therefore those who study such questions declare that the unit is not a number at all, but the element and source from which number springs.[c] Further, the heavenly food of 191 the soul, wisdom, which Moses calls " manna," is distributed to all who will use it in equal portions by the divine Word, careful above all things to maintain equality. Moses testifies to this in the words, " He that had much, had not too much, and he that had less did not lack " (Ex. xvi. 18), when they measured by the admirable and precious standard of proportion. And through this we come to understand how when each collected in his own store for his " belongings,"[d] these belongings are not human beings so much as thoughts and dispositions. For what fell to each was of set purpose so allotted, that there was neither short-coming nor superabundance.

XL. We may find a similar example of this pro- 192 portioned equality in what is called the Passover, which is held when the soul studies to unlearn irrational passion and of its own free will experiences the higher form of passion which reason sanctions. For it is laid down that " if there be few in the house, 193 so that they are not enough for the sheep, they shall

which were meet and right for him," connecting it no doubt with the Stoics' τὰ καθήκοντα. The E.V. is different —" They gathered every man according to his eating."

λαβεῖν, κατ' ἀριθμὸν ψυχῶν, ἵν' ἕκαστος τὸ
ἀρκοῦν αὐτῷ συναριθμῆται," μοῖραν, ἧς ἐστιν
ἐπάξιός τε καὶ χρεῖος, εὑρισκόμενος.

194 ἐπειδὰν δὲ καὶ τρόπον χώρας τὴν ἀρετὴν εἰς τοὺς
οἰκήτορας αὐτῆς ἐθελήσῃ διανέμειν, τοῖς πλείοσι
πλεονάζειν καὶ τοῖς ἐλάττοσιν ἐλαττοῦν τὴν κατά-
σχεσιν προστάττει, δικαιῶν μήτε τοὺς μείζους
ἐλαττόνων ἀξιοῦν—κενοὶ γὰρ ἐπιστήμης ἔσονται
—μήτε τοὺς ἐλάττους μειζόνων· χωρῆσαι γὰρ τὸ
195 μέγεθος αὐτῶν οὐ δυνήσονται.   XLI.
τῆς δὲ κατ' ἀριθμὸν ἰσότητος ἐναργέστατον δεῖγμά
ἐστι τά τε τῶν δώδεκα ἀρχόντων ἱερὰ δῶρα καὶ
ἔτι τὰ ἀπὸ τῶν δώρων διανεμόμενα τοῖς. ἱερεῦσιν·
" ἑκάστῳ " γάρ φησι " τῶν υἱῶν 'Ααρὼν ἔσται τὸ
196 ἴσον."   παγκάλη δὲ καὶ ἡ περὶ τὴν
σύνθεσιν τῶν ἐκθυμιωμένων ἐστὶν ἰσότης· λέγεται
γάρ· " λάβε σεαυτῷ ἡδύσματα, στακτήν, ὄνυχα
καὶ χαλβάνην ἡδυσμοῦ καὶ λίβανον διαφανῆ, ἴσον
ἴσῳ, καὶ ποιήσουσιν αὐτὸ θυμίαμα, μύρον μυρεψοῦ
ἔργον συνθέσεως καθαρᾶς, ἔργον ἅγιον." ἕκαστον
γὰρ τῶν μερῶν ἑκάστῳ φησὶ δεῖν ἴσον συνέρχεσθαι
197 πρὸς τὴν τοῦ ὅλου κρᾶσιν. ἔστι δ' οἶμαι τὰ
τέτταρα ταῦτα, ἐξ ὧν τὸ θυμίαμα συντίθεται,
σύμβολα τῶν στοιχείων, ἐξ ὧν ἀπετελέσθη σύμπας
ὁ κόσμος. στακτὴν μὲν γὰρ ὕδατι, γῇ δὲ ὄνυχα,
χαλβάνην δὲ ἀέρι, τὸν δὲ διαφανῆ λιβανωτὸν πυρὶ
ἀπεικάζει· στακτὴ μὲν γὰρ παρὰ τὰς σταγόνας
ὑδατῶδες, ξηρὸν δὲ ὄνυξ καὶ γεῶδες, τῇ δὲ
χαλβάνῃ τὸ ἡδυσμοῦ πρὸς τὴν ἀέρος ἔμφασιν

take in the next neighbour, according to the number of souls, that each may reckon what is sufficient for him " (Ex. xii. 4), thus gaining the portion which he deserves and needs. On the other hand, 194 when Moses would portion out virtue, like a country, to virtue's inhabitants he bids the more have more and the less to lessen their possession (Num. xxxv. 8), for he holds it right not to adjudge smaller shares to the greater, since then they will be devoid of knowledge, nor greater to the less, since they will not be able to contain the greatness of their shares.

XLI. Of numerical equality we have 195 the clearest example in the sacred gifts of the twelve rulers (Num. vii. 10 ff.) and further in the distributions made to the priests from the gifts. Each of the sons of Aaron, it says, shall have what is equal (Lev. vi. 40). We have also a splendid 196 example of equality in the composition of the frankincense offering. For we read " take to thyself sweet spices, oil drop of cinnamon, cloves and galbanum of sweetening and clear gum of frankincense, each in equal parts and they shall make of it incense, a perfume work of the perfumer of pure composition, a holy work " (Ex. xxx. 34, 35). Each of the parts, we see from his words, must be brought in equal measure, to make the combination of the whole. Now these 197 four, of which the incense is composed, are, I hold, a symbol of the elements, out of which the whole world was brought to its completion. Moses is likening the oil drop to water, the cloves to earth, the galbanum to air, and the clear gum to fire. For oil drop is watery because of its dripping, cloves are dry and earthy, and the words " of sweetening " are added to galbanum, to bring out the idea of air

προσετέθη—τὸ γὰρ εὐῶδες ἐν ἀέρι,—τῷ δὲ λιβα-
198 νωτῷ τὸ διαφανὲς πρὸς φωτὸς ἔνδειξιν. διὸ
καὶ τὰ βάρος ἔχοντα τῶν κούφων διεχώρισε, τὰ
μὲν τῷ συμπλεκτικῷ συνδέσμῳ ἑνώσας, τὰ δὲ
[501] διαλελυμένως ἐξενεγκών· | ἔφη γάρ· " λάβε σεαυτῷ
ἡδύσματα, στακτήν, ὄνυχα," ταῦτα ἀσύνδετα, τῶν
βάρος ἐχόντων, ὕδατός τε καὶ γῆς, σύμβολα, εἶτα
ἀφ' ἑτέρας ἀρχῆς μετὰ συμπλοκῆς " καὶ χαλβάνην
ἡδυσμοῦ καὶ λίβανον διαφανῆ," ταῦτα πάλιν καθ'
ἑαυτά, τῶν κούφων, ἀέρος καὶ πυρός, [τὰ] σημεῖα.
199 τὴν δὲ τούτων ἐμμελῆ σύνθεσίν τε καὶ κρᾶσιν τὸ
πρεσβύτατον καὶ τελειότατον ἔργον ἅγιον ὡς
ἀληθῶς εἶναι συμβέβηκε, τὸν κόσμον, ὃν διὰ
συμβόλου τοῦ θυμιάματος οἴεται δεῖν εὐχαριστεῖν
τῷ πεποιηκότι, ἵνα λόγῳ μὲν ἡ μυρεψικὴ τέχνη
κατασκευασθεῖσα σύνθεσις ἐκθυμιᾶται, ἔργῳ δὲ
ὁ θείᾳ σοφίᾳ δημιουργηθεὶς κόσμος ἅπας ἀνα-
200 φέρηται πρωὶ καὶ δειλινῆς ὁλοκαυτούμενος. βίος
γὰρ ἐμπρεπὴς κόσμῳ τῷ πατρὶ καὶ ποιητῇ
συνεχῶς καὶ ἀδιαστάτως εὐχαριστεῖν, μονονοὺκ
ἐκθυμιῶντι καὶ ἀναστοιχειοῦντι ἑαυτὸν πρὸς ἔνδειξιν τοῦ μηδὲν θησαυρίζεσθαι, ἀλλ' ὅλον ἑαυτὸν
ἀνάθημα ἀνατιθέναι τῷ γεγεννηκότι θεῷ.
201 XLII. θαυμάζω καὶ τὸν μετὰ σπουδῆς ἀ-
πνευστὶ δραμόντα συντόνως ἱερὸν λόγον, " ἵνα
στῇ μέσος τῶν τεθνηκότων καὶ τῶν ζώντων·
εὐθὺς " γάρ φησι Μωϋσῆς " ἐκόπασεν ἡ θραῦ-
σις." ἀλλ' οὐκ ἔμελλε κοπάσαι καὶ ἐπικουφίσαι
τὰ περιθρύπτοντα καὶ καταγνύντα καὶ συντρί-

since air has fragrance, and the word " clear " to
gum to indicate light. For the same reason he set 198
the heavy substances apart from the light, connecting the latter in a single phrase by means of the
conjunction " and," but stating the heavy in the
unconnected form. First he said " take to thyself
sweet spices, oil drop of cinnamon, cloves, both these
with the asyndeton, symbols of the heavy substances
earth and water." Then he makes a fresh beginning
using the conjunction, " and galbanum of sweetness
and clear gum of frankincense," and these two, which
indicate the light elements, air and fire, are also joined
by an " and." And the mixture thus harmoniously 199
compounded proves to be that most venerable and
perfect work, a work in very truth holy, even the
world, which he holds should under the symbol of
the incense offering give thanks to its Maker, so that
while in outward speech it is the compound formed
by the perfumer's art which is burnt as incense,
in real fact it is the whole world, wrought by divine
wisdom, which is offered and consumed morning
and evening in the sacrificial fire. Surely it is a 200
fitting life-work for the world, that it should give
thanks to its Maker continuously and without ceasing, wellnigh evaporating itself into a single elemental form, to shew that it hoards nothing as
treasure, but dedicates its whole being at the shrine
of God its Begetter. XLII. I marvel 201
too when I read of that sacred Word, which ran in
impetuous breathless haste " to stand between the
living and the dead." For at once, says Moses,
" the breaking was abated " (Num. xvi. 47, 48).
And indeed how could all that shatters and crushes
and ruptures our soul fail to be abated and lightened,

βοντα τὴν ἡμετέραν ψυχήν, διακρίναντος καὶ δια-
τειχίσαντος τοῦ θεοφιλοῦς τοὺς ὁσίους, οἳ ζῶσιν
ἀψευδῶς, ἀπὸ τῶν ἀνοσίων, οἳ τεθνήκασι πρὸς
202 ἀλήθειαν, λογισμῶν; τῷ γὰρ ἐγγὺς εἶναι πολλάκις
νοσούντων καὶ οἱ σφόδρα ὑγιαίνοντες ἐνδεξάμενοι
τὴν ἐκείνων νόσον ἐμέλλησαν τελευτῆσαι. τοῦτο
δ' ἀμήχανον ἔτι παθεῖν ἦν διαζευχθέντας ὅρῳ
μέσῳ παγέντι δυνατωτάτῳ, ὃς τὰς ἐφόδους καὶ
ἐπιδρομὰς τοῦ χείρονος μέρους ἀπὸ τοῦ βελτίονος
203 ἀπώσει. τεθαύμακα δὲ ἔτι μᾶλλον, ἐπειδὰν κατ-
ακούων τῶν λογίων ἀναδιδάσκωμαι, ὃν τρόπον
εἰσῆλθεν ἡ νεφέλη μέση τῆς τε Αἰγυπτιακῆς καὶ
τῆς Ἰσραηλιτικῆς στρατιᾶς· ὑπὸ γὰρ τοῦ φιλοπαθοῦς καὶ ἀθέου τὸ ἐγκρατὲς καὶ θεοφιλὲς γένος
οὐκέτ' εἴασε διώκεσθαι τὸ σκεπαστήριον καὶ
σωτήριον τῶν φίλων, ἀμυντήριον δὲ καὶ κολαστή-
204 ριον τῶν ἐχθρῶν ὅπλον, ἡ νεφέλη. διανοίαις μὲν
γὰρ ἀρετώσαις ἠρέμα σοφίαν ἐπιψεκάζει, τὴν ἀπαθῆ
φύσει παντὸς κακοῦ, λυπραῖς δὲ καὶ ἀγόνοις ἐπιστήμης ἀθρόας κατανίφει τιμωρίας, κατακλυσμὸν
205 φθορὰν οἰκτίστην ἐπιφέρουσα.   τῷ δὲ
ἀρχαγγέλῳ καὶ πρεσβυτάτῳ λόγῳ δωρεὰν ἔδωκεν
ἐξαίρετον ὁ τὰ ὅλα γεννήσας πατήρ, ἵνα μεθόριος
στὰς τὸ γενόμενον διακρίνῃ τοῦ πεποιηκότος. ὁ
δ' αὐτὸς ἱκέτης μέν ἐστι τοῦ θνητοῦ κηραίνοντος
ἀεὶ πρὸς τὸ ἄφθαρτον, πρεσβευτὴς δὲ τοῦ ἡγεμόνος
206 πρὸς τὸ ὑπήκοον. ἀγάλλεται δὲ ἐπὶ τῇ δωρεᾷ καὶ
[502] σεμνυνόμενος αὐτὴν | ἐκδιηγεῖται φάσκων· '' κἀγὼ
εἱστήκειν ἀνὰ μέσον κυρίου καὶ ὑμῶν,'' οὔτε
ἀγένητος ὡς ὁ θεὸς ὢν οὔτε γενητὸς ὡς ὑμεῖς,
ἀλλὰ μέσος τῶν ἄκρων, ἀμφοτέροις ὁμηρεύων,
παρὰ μὲν τῷ φυτεύσαντι πρὸς πίστιν τοῦ μὴ
384

when the God-beloved separates and walls off the consecrated thoughts, which veritably live, from the unholy which are truly dead? For often proximity 202 to the sick brings to the very healthiest the infection of their sickness and sure death in its train. But this fate was no longer possible to the consecrated, hedged in by the mightiest of pales, fixed in the midst to repel from the better sort the onslaught and inroads of the worse. Still more am I lost in admira- 203 tion, when I listen to the oracles and learn how the cloud entered in the midst between the hosts of Egypt and Israel (Ex. xiv. 20). For the further pursuit of the sober and God-beloved race by the passion-loving and godless was forbidden by that cloud, which was a weapon of shelter and salvation to its friends, and of offence and chastisement to its enemies. For on minds of rich soil that cloud sends 204 in gentle showers the drops of wisdom, whose very nature exempts it from all harm, but on the sour of soil, that are barren of knowledge, it pours the blizzards of vengeance, flooding them with a deluge of destruction most miserable.   To His 205 Word, His chief messenger, highest in age and honour, the Father of all has given the special pre- rogative, to stand on the border and separate the creature from the Creator. This same Word both pleads with the immortal as suppliant for afflicted mortality and acts as ambassador of the ruler to the subject. He glories in this prerogative and proudly 206 describes it in these words ' and I stood between the Lord and you ' (Deut. v. 5), that is neither uncreated as God, nor created as you, but midway between the two extremes, a surety to both sides ; to the parent, pledging the creature that it should never altogether

σύμπαν ἀφηνιάσαι ποτὲ καὶ ἀποστῆναι τὸ γεγονὸς
ἀκοσμίαν ἀντὶ κόσμου ἑλόμενον, παρὰ δὲ τῷ φύντι
πρὸς εὐελπιστίαν τοῦ μήποτε τὸν ἵλεω θεὸν περιιδεῖν τὸ ἴδιον ἔργον. ἐγὼ γὰρ ἐπικηρυκεύομαι τὰ
εἰρηναῖα γενέσει παρὰ τοῦ καθαιρεῖν πολέμους
ἐγνωκότος εἰρηνοφύλακος αἰεὶ θεοῦ.

207 XLIII. Διδάξας οὖν ἡμᾶς περὶ τῆς εἰς ἴσα
τομῆς ὁ ἱερὸς λόγος καὶ πρὸς τὴν τῶν ἐναντίων
ἐπιστήμην ἄγει φάσκων ὅτι τὰ τμήματα '' ἔθηκεν
ἀντιπρόσωπα ἀλλήλοις.'' τῷ γὰρ ὄντι πάνθ' ὅσα
ἐν κόσμῳ σχεδὸν ἐναντία εἶναι πέφυκεν, ἀρκτέον
208 δὲ ἀπὸ τῶν πρώτων· θερμὸν ἐναντίον ψυχρῷ καὶ
ξηρὸν ὑγρῷ καὶ κοῦφον βαρεῖ καὶ σκότος φωτὶ
καὶ νὺξ ἡμέρα, καὶ ἐν οὐρανῷ μὲν ἡ ἀπλανὴς τῇ
πεπλανημένῃ φορᾷ, κατὰ δὲ τὸν ἀέρα αἰθρία
νεφώσει, νηνεμία πνεύμασι, θέρει χειμών, ἔαρι
μετόπωρον—τῷ μὲν γὰρ ἀνθεῖ, τῷ δὲ φθίνει τὰ
[δ'] ἔγγεια,—πάλιν ὕδατος τὸ γλυκὺ τῷ πικρῷ καὶ
209 γῆς ἡ στεῖρα τῇ γονίμῳ. καὶ τἄλλα δὲ ἐναντία
πρόϋπτα, σώματα ἀσώματα, ἔμψυχα ἄψυχα, λογικὰ
ἄλογα, θνητὰ ἀθάνατα, αἰσθητὰ νοητά, κατα-
ληπτὰ ἀκατάληπτα, στοιχεῖα ἀποτελέσματα, ἀρχὴ
τελευτή, γένεσις φθορά, ζωὴ θάνατος, νόσος ὑγεία,
λευκὸν μέλαν, δεξιὰ εὐώνυμα, δικαιοσύνη ἀδικία,
φρόνησις ἀφροσύνη, ἀνδρεία δειλία, σωφροσύνη
ἀκολασία, ἀρετὴ κακία, καὶ τὰ τῆς ἑτέρας πάντα
210 εἴδη τοῖς τῆς ἑτέρας εἴδεσι πᾶσι· πάλιν γραμματικὴ ἀγραμματία, μουσικὴ ἀμουσία, παιδεία
ἀπαιδευσία, συνόλως τέχνη ἀτεχνία· καὶ τὰ ἐν ταῖς
τέχναις, φωνήεντα στοιχεῖα καὶ ἄφωνα, ὀξεῖς καὶ

rebel against the rein and choose disorder rather than order ; to the child, warranting his hopes that the merciful God will never forget His own work. For I am the harbinger of peace to creation from that God whose will is to bring wars to an end, who is ever the guardian of peace."

XLIII. Having taught us the lesson of equal 207 division the Scripture leads us on to the knowledge of opposites, by telling us that " He placed the sections facing opposite each other" (Gen. xv. 10). For in truth we may take it that everything in the world is by nature opposite to something else. Let us begin with what comes first. Hot is opposite to 208 cold, dry to wet, light to heavy, darkness to light, night to day. In heaven we have the course of the fixed stars opposite to the course of the planets, in the air cloudless to cloudy, calm to wind, summer to winter, spring when earth's growths bloom to autumn when they decay, again in water, sweet to bitter, and in land, barren to fruitful. And the other op- 209 posites are obvious : corporeal, incorporeal ; living, lifeless ; mortal, immortal ; sensible, intelligible ; comprehensible, incomprehensible ; elementary, completed ; beginning, end ; becoming, extinction ; life, death ; disease, health ; white, black ; right, left ; justice, injustice ; prudence, folly ; courage, cowardice ; continence, incontinence ; virtue, vice ; and all the species of virtue are opposite to all the species of vice. Again we have the opposite con- 210 ditions of the literary and the illiterate, the cultured and the uncultured, the educated and the un-educated, and in general the scientific and the un-scientific, and in the subject matter of the arts or sciences there are vocal sounds or vowels and non-

βαρεῖς φθόγγοι, εὐθεῖαι καὶ περιφερεῖς γραμμαί·
211 καὶ ἐν ζῴοις καὶ φυτοῖς ἄγονα γόνιμα, πολυτόκα
ὀλιγοτόκα, ᾠοτόκα ζῳοτόκα, μαλάκια[1] ὀστρακό-
212 δερμα, ἄγρια ἥμερα, μονωτικὰ ἀγελαῖα· καὶ πάλιν
πενία πλοῦτος, δόξα ἀδοξία, δυσγένεια εὐγένεια,
ἔνδεια περιουσία, πόλεμος εἰρήνη, νόμος ἀνομία, εὐ-
φυΐα ἀφυΐα, ἀπονία πόνος, νεότης γῆρας, ἀδυναμία
δύναμις, ἀσθένεια ῥώμη. καὶ τί δεῖ τὰ καθ' ἕκαστον ἀναλέγεσθαι ἀπερίγραφα καὶ ἀπέρατ'[2] ὄντα
213 τῷ πλήθει;   παγκάλως οὖν ὁ τῶν τῆς
φύσεως ἑρμηνεὺς πραγμάτων, τῆς ἀργίας καὶ
ἀμελετησίας ἡμῶν λαμβάνων οἶκτον ἑκάστοτ'
ἀφθόνως[3] ἀναδιδάσκει, καθὰ καὶ νῦν, "τὴν ἀντι-
πρόσωπον" ἑκάστων θέσιν οὐχ ὁλοκλήρων, ἀλλὰ
[503] τμημάτων ὑπαρχόντων· | ἓν γὰρ τὸ ἐξ ἀμφοῖν τῶν
214 ἐναντίων, οὗ τμηθέντος γνώριμα τὰ ἐναντία. οὐ
τοῦτ' ἐστίν, ὅ φασιν Ἕλληνες τὸν μέγαν καὶ
ἀοίδιμον παρ' αὐτοῖς Ἡράκλειτον κεφάλαιον τῆς
αὑτοῦ προστησάμενον φιλοσοφίας αὐχεῖν ὡς ἐφ'
εὑρέσει καινῇ; παλαιὸν γὰρ εὕρεμα Μωυσέως[a]
ἐστὶ τὸ ἐκ τοῦ αὐτοῦ τὰ ἐναντία τμημάτων λόγον
ἔχοντα ἀποτελεῖσθαι, καθάπερ ἐναργῶς ἐδείχθη.
215   XLIV. Ταῦτα μὲν οὖν καὶ ἐν ἑτέροις ἀκριβώσομεν. ἄξιον δὲ καὶ ἐκεῖνο μὴ παρησυχασθῆναι·
τὰ γὰρ λεγόμενα διχοτομήματα τριῶν ζῴων δίχα
διαιρεθέντων[4] ἐξ ἐγένετο, ὡς ἕβδομον τὸν τομέα

---

[1] Or μαλακά as mss. Wend prints μαλάκεια (presumably
from Pap.), but μαλάκια is the ordinary form.
[2] mss. ἀπέραν(σ)τα : Pap. απορατ. See App. p. 572.
[3] mss. ἕκαστον ἀφανῶς (Pap. αφονως).
[4] mss. διαιρεθέντων : Pap. διχα αιρεθεντων.

[a] Probably Moses rather than God.

vocal sounds or consonants, high notes and low
notes, straight lines and curved lines. In animals 211
and plants there are barren and productive, prolific
and unprolific, viviparous and oviparous, soft-skinned
and shell-skinned, wild and tame, solitary and
gregarious. In another class there are poverty and 212
riches ; eminence and obscurity ; high birth and
low birth ; want and abundance ; war, peace ;
law, lawlessness ; gifted nature, ungifted nature ;
labour, inaction ; youth, age ; impotence, power ;
weakness, strength. Why attempt to ennumerate
all and each of them, when their number is infinite
and illimitable ? How excellent then is 213
this lesson, which the interpreter [a] of Nature's facts
in his pity for our sluggishness and carelessness
lavishes on us always and everywhere, as he does in
this passage, that in every case it is not where things
exist as wholes, but where they exist as divisions or
sections, that they must be " set facing opposite
each other." For the two opposites together form
a single whole, by the division of which the opposites are known. Is not this the truth which 214
according to the Greeks Heracleitus, whose greatness they celebrate so loudly, put in the fore front
of his philosophy and vaunted it as a new discovery ?
Actually, as has been clearly shewn, it was Moses
who long ago discovered the truth that opposites
are formed from the same whole, to which they
stand in the relation of sections or divisions.

XLIV. This point will be discussed in detail else- 215
where. But there is another matter which should
not be passed over in silence. What are called the
half-pieces of the three animals when they are
divided into two made six altogether and thus the

εἶναι λόγον, διαστέλλοντα τὰς τριάδας, μέσον
216 αὐτὸν ἱδρυμένον. τὸ παραπλήσιόν μοι δοκεῖ σαφέ-
στατα μεμηνῦσθαι καὶ ἐπὶ τῆς ἱερᾶς λυχνίας· δε-
δημιούργηται γὰρ ἐξ καλαμίσκους ἔχουσα, τρεῖς
ἑκατέρωθεν, ἑβδόμη δὲ αὐτὴ μέση, διαιροῦσα καὶ
διακρίνουσα τὰς τριάδας. " τορευτὴ " γάρ ἐστι,
τεχνικὸν καὶ δόκιμον θεῖον ἔργον, " ἐξ ἑνὸς
χρυσίου καθαροῦ "· τὸ γὰρ ἓν καὶ μόνον καὶ
καθαρὸν ὄντως ἑβδομάδα τὴν ἀμήτορα γεγέννηκεν
ἐξ ἑαυτοῦ μόνου, μὴ προσχρησάμενον ὕλῃ τὸ
217 παράπαν.   χρυσὸν δ᾽ οἱ ἐγκωμιάζοντες
πολλὰ μὲν καὶ ἄλλα λέγουσι τῶν εἰς ἔπαινον, δύο
δὲ τὰ ἀνωτάτω, ἓν μέν, ὅτι ἰὸν οὐ παραδέχεται,
ἕτερον δέ, ὅτι εἰς ὑμένας λεπτοτάτους ἀρραγὴς
διαμένων ἐλαύνεταί τε καὶ χεῖται. σύμβολον οὖν
εἰκότως μείζονος φύσεως γέγονε, ἢ ταθεῖσα καὶ
κεχυμένη καὶ φθάσασα πάντη πλήρης ὅλη δι᾽
ὅλων ἐστίν, εὐαρμόστως καὶ τὰ ἄλλα συνυφήνασα.
218   περὶ τῆς προειρημένης λυχνίας ὁ
τεχνίτης διαλεγόμενος πάλιν φησίν, ὅτι " ἐκ τῶν
καλαμίσκων εἰσὶν οἱ βλαστοὶ ἐξέχοντες, τρεῖς
ἑκατέρωθεν, ἐξισούμενοι ἀλλήλοις· καὶ τὰ λαμπάδια
αὐτῶν, ἅ ἐστιν ἐπὶ τῶν ἄκρων, καρυωτὰ ἐξ
αὐτῶν· καὶ τὰ ἀνθέμια καὶ ἐν αὐτοῖς, ἵν᾽ ὦσιν ἐπ᾽
αὐτῶν οἱ λύχνοι καὶ τὸ ἀνθέμιον τὸ ἔβδομον ἐπ᾽
ἄκρου τοῦ λαμπαδίου ἐπὶ τῆς κορυφῆς ἄνωθεν,
στερεὸν ὅλον χρυσοῦν· καὶ ἑπτὰ λύχνους ἐπ᾽
219 αὐτῆς[1] χρυσοῦς "· ὥστε διὰ πολλῶν ἤδη κατα-
σκευάζεσθαι, ὅτι ἑξὰς εἰς δύο τριάδας ὑπὸ μέσου
τοῦ ἑβδόμου λόγου διῄρηται, καθάπερ ἔχει νυνί·

---

[1] mss. and Pap. αὐτοῖς: Wend. supports his correction by
§ 221 (lxx. αὐτῆς, i.e. λυχνίας).

Severer, the Word, who separates the two sets of three and stationed himself in their midst, was the seventh. The same is clearly shewn, I think, in 216 the holy candlestick also, which is wrought with six branches, three on each side, and itself in the middle makes the seventh, dividing and separating the threes. It is " chased," a work of art, approved and divine, made " of one piece of pure gold " (Ex. xxv. 36). For the One, alone and absolutely pure, has begotten the Seven, whom no mother bore, begotten her by himself alone, and employing no other medium whatsoever.   Now those who sound the praises 217 of gold, among its many laudable qualities, place these two highest, first that it is proof against rust, secondly that when it is beaten and fused into the thinnest possible sheets, it remains unbroken. Thus it naturally becomes the symbol of a higher nature, which when stretched and fused and reaching out on every side, is still complete in its fullness throughout and weaves everything else into a harmonious whole.   Again, of the aforesaid 218 candlestick the Master-craftsman says in his discourse that " there are branchlets jutting out from the branches, three on each side, equal to each other, and their lamps at the end of them come out from them in nut shape, and the flower-patterns in them, that the candle-bearers may be on them, and the seventh flower-pattern at the end of the lamp, on the top above, all of solid gold, and seven golden candle-bearers on it "[a] (Ex. xxxviii. 15-17). Thus 219 by many proofs it is now established that the Six is divided into two Threes by the Word, the Seventh in their midst, just as we find in the present passage.

[a] See App. p. 572.

πᾶσα γὰρ ἡ λυχνία σὺν τοῖς ὁλοσχερεστάτοις
μέρεσιν αὐτῆς, ἃ ἕξ ἐστιν, ⟨ἐξ ἑπτὰ⟩[1] ἐπάγη,
λαμπαδίων ἑπτά, ἀνθεμίων ἑπτά, λύχνων ἑπτά.
220 διαιροῦνται δὲ οἱ μὲν ἓξ λύχνοι τῷ ἑβδόμῳ, τὰ δὲ
ἀνθέμια ὁμοίως τῷ μέσῳ καὶ τὰ λαμπάδια τὸν
αὐτὸν τρόπον ὑπὸ τοῦ ἑβδόμου καὶ μέσου, οἱ δὲ
ἓξ καλαμίσκοι καὶ οἱ ἐκπεφυκότες ἴσοι βλαστοὶ
[504] ὑπ' αὐτοῦ τοῦ | στελέχους τῆς ⟨λυχνίας οὔσης⟩[2]
221 ἑβδόμης.   XLV. πολὺν δ' ὄντα τὸν
περὶ ἑκάστου λόγον ὑπερθετέον εἰσαῦθις. τοσοῦτο
δὲ αὐτὸ μόνον ὑπομνηστέον, ὅτι τῆς κατ' οὐρανὸν
τῶν ἑπτὰ πλανήτων χορείας μίμημά ἐστιν ἡ ἱερὰ
222 λυχνία καὶ οἱ ἐπ' αὐτῆς ἑπτὰ λύχνοι. πῶς;
ἐρήσεταί τις ἴσως· ὅτι, φήσομεν, ὅνπερ τρόπον οἱ
λύχνοι, οὕτως καὶ τῶν πλανήτων ἕκαστος φωσ-
φορεῖ· λαμπρότατοι γὰρ ὄντες αὐγοειδεστάτας ἄχρι
γῆς ἀποστέλλουσιν ἀκτῖνας, διαφερόντως δ' ὁ
223 μέσος τῶν ἑπτά, ἥλιος. μέσον δ' αὐτὸν οὐ μόνον
ἐπεὶ μέσην ἐπέχει χώραν, ὡς ἠξίωσάν τινες, καλῶ,
ἀλλ' ὅτι καὶ θεραπεύεσθαι καὶ δορυφορεῖσθαι πρὸς
ὑπασπιζόντων ἑκατέρωθεν ἀξιώματος ἕνεκα καὶ
μεγέθους καὶ ὠφελειῶν, ἃς τοῖς ἐπιγείοις ἅπασι
224 παρέχει, δίκαιος ἄλλως ἐστί. τὴν δὲ τῶν πλανήτων τάξιν ἄνθρωποι παγίως μὴ κατειληφότες—τί
δ' ἄλλο τῶν κατ' οὐρανὸν ἴσχυσαν κατανοῆσαι
βεβαίως;—εἰκοτολογοῦσιν, ἄριστα δ' ἐμοὶ στοχάζε-
σθαι δοκοῦσιν οἱ τὴν μέσην ἀπονενεμηκότες ἡλίῳ

[1] ⟨ἐξ ἑπτὰ⟩ is my insertion: Wend. notes the corruption
in the mss., since the genitives λαμπαδίων etc. have no
construction.
[2] My insertion; τῆς ἑβδόμης clearly needs a noun. Mangey

For the whole candlestick with its principal parts, six in number, consists of sevens, seven lamps, seven flower-patterns, seven candle-bearers. The six 220 candle-bearers are divided by the seventh, and so also the flower-patterns by the middle one, and the lamps in the same way by their seventh in the middle, and the six branches and the six branchlets which grow out of them by the main-stalk of the candlestick, which is seventh to them. XLV. On 221 each of these there is much to say, but it must be postponed to another occasion. Only thus much should be noted. The holy candlestick and the seven candle-bearers on it are a copy of the march of the choir of the seven planets.[a] How so? perhaps we 222 shall be asked. Because, we shall reply, each of the planets is a light-bringer, as the candle-bearers are. For they are supremely bright and transmit the great lustre of their rays to the earth, especially the central among the seven, the sun. I call it central, 223 not merely because it holds the central position, which some give as the reason, but because apart from this it has the right to be served and attended by its squires on either side, in virtue of its dignity and magnitude and the benefits which it provides for all that are on the earth. Now the order of the planets 224 is a matter of which men have no sure apprehension —indeed is there any other celestial phenomenon which can be known with real certainty?—and therefore they fall back on probabilities. But the best conjecture, in my opinion, is that of those who

---

[a] This explanation of the candlestick is also given by Josephus, *Ant.* iii. 6, 7.

proposed τῆς ἐβδόμης ⟨λυχνίας⟩. I suggest that the similarity of οὔσης to ους τῆς caused the omission.

τάξιν, τρεῖς μὲν ὑπὲρ αὐτὸν καὶ μετ' αὐτὸν τοὺς
ἴσους εἶναι λέγοντες, ὑπὲρ αὐτὸν μὲν φαίνοντα,
φαέθοντα, πυρόεντα, εἶθ' ἥλιον, μετ' αὐτὸν δὲ
στίλβοντα, φωσφόρον, τὴν ἀέρος γείτονα σελήνην.
225 ἐπίγειον οὖν βουληθεὶς ἀρχετύπου τῆς κατ'
οὐρανὸν σφαίρας ἑπταφεγγοῦς μίμημα παρ' ἡμῖν
ὁ τεχνίτης γενέσθαι πάγκαλον ἔργον προσέταξε,
τὴν λυχνίαν, δημιουργηθῆναι. δέδεικται δὲ καὶ ἡ
πρὸς ψυχὴν ἐμφέρεια αὐτῆς· ψυχὴ γὰρ τριμερὴς
μέν ἐστι, δίχα δὲ ἕκαστον τῶν μερῶν, ὡς ἐδείχθη,
τέμνεται, μοιρῶν δὲ γενομένων ἐξ ἕβδομος εἰκότως
τομεὺς ἦν ἁπάντων ὁ ἱερὸς καὶ θεῖος λόγος.
226   XLVI. ἄξιον δὲ μηδ' ἐκεῖνο παρ-
ησυχασθῆναι· τριῶν ὄντων ἐν τοῖς ἁγίοις σκεύῶν,
λυχνίας, τραπέζης, θυμιατηρίου, τὸ μὲν θυμιατήριον
εἰς τὴν ὑπὲρ τῶν στοιχείων εὐχαριστίαν ἀνάγεται,
ὡς ἐδείχθη πρότερον, ἐπεὶ καὶ αὐτὸ μοίρας ἔχει
τῶν τεττάρων, γῆς μὲν τὰ ξύλα, ὕδατος δὲ τὰ
ἐπιθυμιώμενα—πρότερον γὰρ τηκόμενα εἰς λιβάδας
αὖθις ἀναλύεται,—τὸν δὲ ἀτμὸν ἀέρος, πυρὸς δὲ τὸ
ἐξαπτόμενον—καὶ ἡ σύνθεσις δὲ λιβανωτοῦ καὶ
χαλβάνης ὄνυχός τε καὶ στακτῆς τῶν στοιχείων
σύμβολον,—ἡ δὲ τράπεζα εἰς τὴν ὑπὲρ τῶν θνητῶν
ἀποτελεσμάτων εὐχαριστίαν—ἄρτοι γὰρ καὶ σπονδεῖα
ἐπιτίθενται αὐτῇ, οἷς ἀνάγκη χρῆσθαι τὰ τῆς
τροφῆς δεόμενα,—ἡ δὲ λυχνία εἰς τὴν ὑπὲρ τῶν

Elsewhere (*e.g. De Conf.* 21) this tripartite division is
into νοῦς, θῦμος and ἐπιθυμία. But we nowhere have any
suggestion of these being subdivided, and the ὡς ἐδείχθη
leaves no doubt that the reference is to the classification
given in § 132, where the three parts were ψυχή, λόγος (as
speech) and αἴσθησις. The best we can make of it is that

assign the middle place to the sun and hold that there are three above him and the same number below him. The three above are Saturn, Jupiter and Mars, and the three below are Mercury, Venus and the Moon, which borders on the lower region of air. So the Master-craftsman, wishing that we should 225 possess a copy of the archetypal celestial sphere with its seven lights, commanded this splendid work, the candlestick, to be wrought. We have shewn, too, its resemblance to the soul. For the soul is tripartite, and each of its parts, as has been shewn, is divided into two,[a] making six parts in all, to which the holy and divine Word, the All-severer, makes a fitting seventh. XLVI. Another point too 226 should not be passed over in silence. The furniture of the sanctuary is threefold, candlestick, table and altar of incense. In the altar, as was shewn above,[b] we have the thought of thanksgiving for the elements, for the altar itself contains parts of the four elements. Its wood is of earth, the incense offered on it of water, since it is first melted and then resolved into drops, while the perfume is of air and the part which is ignited of fire ; moreover the compound made of frankincense, galbanum, cloves and oil of cinnamon (Ex. xxx. 34) is a symbol of the elements. In the table we have thanksgiving for the mortal creatures framed from these elements, since loaves and libations, which creatures needing food must use, are placed on it. In the candlestick we have thanksgiving for all the celestial world,

---

here ψυχή is the whole ψυχή in its wider sense, there in the sense of the mind or ψυχὴ ψυχῆς (cf. § 55). But even so we shall not get consistency. See note on § 125.

[b] i.e. in § 199, though there it is the θυμίαμα only and not the θυμιατήριον which gives thanks.

κατ' οὐρανὸν ἁπάντων, ἵνα μηδὲν μέρος τοῦ
[505] κόσμου | δίκην ἀχαριστίας ὄφλῃ, ἀλλ' εἰδῶμεν ὅτι
πάντα τὰ μέρη τὰ κατ' αὐτὸν εὐχαριστεῖ, τὰ
στοιχεῖα, τὰ ἀποτελέσματα, οὐ τὰ ἐπὶ γῆς μόνον,
227 ἀλλὰ καὶ τὰ ἐν οὐρανῷ.   XLVII. ἄξιον
δὲ σκέψασθαι, διὰ τί τῆς τραπέζης καὶ τοῦ θυμιατηρίου τὰ μέτρα δηλώσας τῆς λυχνίας οὐδὲν
ἀνέγραψε· μήποτε δι' ἐκεῖνο, ὅτι τὰ μὲν στοιχεῖα
καὶ τὰ θνητὰ ἀποτελέσματα, ὧν ἡ τράπεζα καὶ τὸ
θυμιατήριον σύμβολα, μεμέτρηται περατωθέντα
ὑπ' οὐρανοῦ—ἀεὶ γὰρ τὸ περιέχον τοῦ περιεχομένου
μέτρον,—ὁ δ' οὐρανός, οὗ σύμβολόν ἐστιν ἡ
228 λυχνία, ἀπειρομεγέθης ἐστί. περιέχεται γὰρ ὑπ'
οὐδενὸς σώματος, οὔτε ἰσομεγέθους αὐτῷ οὔτε
ἀπείρου, ἀλλ' οὐδ' ὑπὸ κενοῦ κατὰ Μωυσῆν[1] διὰ τὴν
ἐν τῇ ἐκπυρώσει[2] μυθευομένην τερατολογίαν· ἔστι
δὲ ὅρος αὐτοῦ ὁ θεός, ἡνίοχος καὶ κυβερνήτης
229 αὐτοῦ. ὥσπερ οὖν ἀπερίληπτον τὸ ὄν, οὕτως καὶ
τὸ ὁριζόμενον ὑπ' αὐτοῦ μέτροις τοῖς εἰς τὴν
ἡμετέραν ἐπίνοιαν ἥκουσιν οὐ μεμέτρηται, καὶ
τάχα ἐπεὶ κυκλοτερὴς ὢν καὶ ἄκρως εἰς σφαῖραν
ἀποτετορνευμένος μήκους καὶ πλάτους οὐ μετέχει.
230   XLVIII. Εἰπὼν οὖν τὰ πρέποντα περὶ τούτων
ἐπιλέγει· " τὰ δὲ ὄρνεα οὐ διεῖλεν," ὄρνεα καλῶν
τοὺς πτηνοὺς καὶ πεφυκότας μετεωροπολεῖν δύο

---

[1] ἀλλ' . . . Μωυσῆν comes in Pap. after σώματος in the
previous line, and in the mss. which do not omit it after
περιέχεται γάρ. But see App. p. 572.
[2] Some mss. and Pap. πυρώσει, others πυργώσει, which
Mangey adopted, rejecting ἀλλ' . . . Μωυσῆν and supposing
a reference to the tower of Babel.

---

[a] The connexion of the Stoic theory of the general con-

that so no part of the universe may be guilty of un-
thankfulness and we may know that all its parts
give thanks, the elements and the creatures framed
from them, not only those on earth, but those in
heaven. XLVII. A question worth con- 227
sideration is why the writer states the measurements
of the table and the altar but says nothing about the
measurements of the candlestick. Probably the
reason is that the four elements and the mortal
creatures framed from them, which are symbolized
by the table and the altar, are measured and defined
within limits by heaven, since that which contains
is the measurement of that which is contained. On
the other hand heaven, which is symbolized by the
candlestick, is of infinite magnitude, not compre- 228
hended by any material substance either equal in
size to it or infinite, nor again, as Moses shews, by
a void, the existence of which is implied in the
marvelmongers' fable of the general conflagration.[a]
God is its boundary, God who guides and steers it. 229
And so just as the Existent is incomprehensible, so
also that which is bounded by Him is not measured
by any standards which come within our powers of
conception. Perhaps too it is immeasurable in the
sense that being circular and rounded off into a
perfect sphere it possesses neither length nor breadth.

XLVIII. Having said what was fitting on these 230
matters, Moses continues, " the birds He did not
divide " (Gen. xv. 10). He gives the name of birds
to the two words or forms of reason, both of which are

flagration, ἐκπύρωσις, with that of the void is explained in *De
Aet.* 102. Fire implies expansion, and so when the world
is thus immensely expanded it must expand into a void. In
the same sense *S.V.F.* li. 537. There still remain, however,
difficulties in the passage. See App. p. 572.

λόγους, ἕνα μὲν ἀρχέτυπον ⟨τὸν⟩ ὑπὲρ ἡμᾶς,
231 ἕτερον δὲ μίμημα τὸν καθ' ἡμᾶς ὑπάρχοντα. καλεῖ
δὲ Μωυσῆς τὸν μὲν ὑπὲρ ἡμᾶς εἰκόνα θεοῦ, τὸν δὲ
καθ' ἡμᾶς τῆς εἰκόνος ἐκμαγεῖον. " ἐποίησε "
γάρ φησιν " ὁ θεὸς τὸν ἄνθρωπον " οὐχὶ εἰκόνα
θεοῦ, ἀλλὰ " κατ' εἰκόνα "· ὥστε τὸν καθ' ἕκαστον
ἡμῶν νοῦν, ὃς δὴ κυρίως καὶ πρὸς ἀλήθειαν
ἄνθρωπός ἐστι, τρίτον εἶναι τύπον ἀπὸ τοῦ πεποιηκότος, τὸν δὲ μέσον παράδειγμα μὲν τούτου,
232 ἀπεικόνισμα δὲ ἐκείνου.   φύσει δὲ ἄτμη-
τος ὁ ἡμέτερος γέγονε νοῦς. τὸ μὲν γὰρ ἄλογον
ψυχῆς μέρος ἑξαχῆ διελὼν ὁ δημιουργὸς ἑπτὰ
μοίρας εἰργάζετο, ὅρασιν, ἀκοήν, γεῦσιν, ὄσφρησιν,
ἀφήν, φωνήν, γόνιμον, τὸ δὲ λογικόν, ὃ δὴ νοῦς
ὠνομάσθη, ἄσχιστον εἴασε κατὰ τὴν τοῦ παντὸς
233 ὁμοιότητα οὐρανοῦ. καὶ γὰρ ἐν τούτῳ λόγος ἔχει
τὴν μὲν ἐξωτάτω[1] καὶ ἀπλανῆ σφαῖραν ἄτμητον
φυλαχθῆναι, τὴν δ' ἐντὸς ἑξαχῆ τμηθεῖσαν ἑπτὰ
κύκλους τῶν λεγομένων πλανήτων ἀποτελέσαι·
ὃ γάρ, οἶμαι, ἐν ἀνθρώπῳ ψυχή, τοῦτο οὐρανὸς ἐν
κόσμῳ. τὰς οὖν νοερὰς καὶ λογικὰς δύο φύσεις,
τήν τε ἐν ἀνθρώπῳ καὶ τὴν ἐν τῷ παντί, συμβέβηκεν ὁλοκλήρους καὶ ἀδιαιρέτους εἶναι. διὸ λέγεται
[506] " τὰ δὲ ὄρνεα οὐ | διεῖλε."   περιστερᾷ
234 μὲν ⟨οὖν⟩ ὁ ἡμέτερος νοῦς, ἐπειδὴ τιθασὸν καὶ
σύντροφον ἡμῖν ἐστι τὸ ζῷον, εἰκάζεται, τῷ δὲ
τούτου παραδείγματι ἡ τρυγών· ὁ γὰρ θεοῦ λόγος
φιλέρημος καὶ μονωτικός, ἐν ὄχλῳ τῷ τῶν γεγονότων καὶ φθαρησομένων οὐχὶ φυρόμενος, ἀλλ'

---

[1] mss. ἐξωτάτην: Pap. ανωτατω (ἐξωτάτω in De Cher. 22).

[a] See De Op. 117 and note.

winged and of a soaring nature. One is the archetypal reason above us, the other the copy of it which
we possess. Moses calls the first the " image of 231
God," the second the cast of that image. For God,
he says, made man not " the image of God " but
" after the image " (Gen. i. 27). And thus the mind
in each of us, which in the true and full sense is the
" man," is an expression at third hand from the
Maker, while between them is the Reason which
serves as model for our reason, but itself is the
effigies or presentment of God. Our 232
mind is indivisible in its nature. For the irrational
part of the soul received a sixfold division from its
Maker who thus formed seven parts, sight, hearing,
taste, smell, touch, voice and reproductive faculty.[a]
But the rational part, which was named mind, He
left undivided. In this he followed the analogy of
the heaven taken as a whole. For we are told that 233
there the outermost sphere of the fixed stars is kept
unsevered, while the inner sphere by a sixfold
division produces the seven circles of what we call
the wandering stars.[b] In fact I regard the soul as
being in man what the heaven is in the universe.
So then the two reasoning and intellectual natures,
one in man and the other in the all, prove to be
integral and undivided and that is why we read " He
did not divide the birds." Our mind is 234
likened to a pigeon, since the pigeon is a tame and
domesticated creature, while the turtle-dove stands
as the figure of the mind which is the pattern of
ours. For the Word, or Reason of God, is a lover of
the wild and solitary, never mixing with the medley
of things that have come into being only to perish,

[b] *Cf. Timaeus* 36 D and *De Cher.* 22 f.

ἄνω φοιτᾶν εἰθισμένος ἀεὶ καὶ ἑνὶ ὀπαδὸς εἶναι
μόνῳ μεμελετηκώς. ἄτμητοι μὲν οὖν αἱ δύο
φύσεις, ἥ τε ἐν ἡμῖν τοῦ λογισμοῦ καὶ ἡ ὑπὲρ
ἡμᾶς τοῦ θείου λόγου, ἄτμητοι δὲ οὖσαι μυρία
235 ἄλλα τέμνουσιν. ὅ τε γὰρ θεῖος λόγος τὰ ἐν τῇ
φύσει διεῖλε καὶ διένειμε πάντα, ὅ τε ἡμέτερος
νοῦς, ἅττ᾽ ἂν παραλάβῃ νοητῶς πράγματά τε καὶ
σώματα, εἰς ἀπειράκις ἄπειρα διαιρεῖ μέρη καὶ
236 τέμνων οὐδέποτε λήγει. τοῦτο δὲ συμβαίνει διὰ
τὴν πρὸς τὸν ποιητὴν καὶ πατέρα τῶν ὅλων
ἐμφέρειαν. τὸ γὰρ θεῖον ἀμιγές, ἄκρατον, ἀμερέ-
στατον ὑπάρχον ἅπαντι τῷ κόσμῳ γέγονεν αἴτιον
μίξεως, κράσεως, διαιρέσεως, πολυμερείας· ὥστε
εἰκότως καὶ τὰ ὁμοιωθέντα, νοῦς τε ὁ ἐν ἡμῖν καὶ
ὁ ὑπὲρ ἡμᾶς, ἀμερεῖς καὶ ἄτμητοι ὑπάρχοντες
διαιρεῖν καὶ διακρίνειν ἕκαστα τῶν ὄντων ἐρρωμένως δυνήσονται.

237 XLIX. Λαλήσας οὖν περὶ τῶν ἀτμήτων καὶ
ἀδιαιρέτων ὀρνέων φησὶν ἑξῆς· "κατέβη δὲ ὄρνεα
ἐπὶ τὰ σώματα, τὰ διχοτομήματα," ὁμωνυμίᾳ
μὲν χρησάμενος, τὴν δὲ πραγματικὴν διαμάχην
ἐναργέστατα τοῖς ὁρᾶν δυναμένοις διασυνιστάς·
παρὰ φύσιν γάρ ἐστι τὸ καταβαίνειν ὄρνεα,
238 τοῦ μετεωροπολεῖν ἕνεκα πτερωθέντα. καθάπερ
γὰρ τοῖς χερσαίοις οἰκειότατον χωρίον γῆ καὶ
μάλιστα τοῖς ἑρπετοῖς, ἃ μηδ᾽ ὑπὲρ αὐτῆς ἰλυ-
σπώμενα ἀνέχεται, φωλεοὺς δὲ καὶ καταδύσεις
ζητεῖ τὸν ἄνω χῶρον ἀποδιδράσκοντα διὰ τὴν
πρὸς τὰ κάτω συγγένειαν, τὸν αὐτὸν τρόπον καὶ

---

[a] The Hebrew has a different word for these birds, which

but its wonted resort is ever above and its study is to wait on One and One only. So then the two natures, the reasoning power within us and the divine Word or Reason above us, are indivisible, yet indivisible as they are they divide other things without number. The divine Word separated and apportioned all that 235 is in nature. Our mind deals with all the things material and immaterial which the mental process brings within its grasp, divides them into an infinity of infinities and never ceases to cleave them. This is 236 the result of its likeness to the Father and Maker of all. For the Godhead is without mixture or infusion or parts and yet has become to the whole world the cause of mixture, infusion, division and multiplicity of parts. And thus it will be natural that these two which are in the likeness of God, the mind within us and the mind above us, should subsist without parts or severance and yet be strong and potent to divide and distinguish everything that is.

XLIX. After speaking of the birds which were 237 left unsevered and undivided, he continues " and the birds came down to the carcasses, the half-pieces " (Gen. xv. 11). He employs the same word " birds." [a] but shews very clearly to those who have eyes to see the contrast in fact between the two kinds of birds. For it is against nature that birds whose wings were given them to soar on high should come down. Just as earth is the most suitable place for creatures 238 of the land, particularly reptiles, which in their wriggling course cannot even bear to be above ground, but make for holes and crannies and, since their natural place is below, avoid what is above,

the A.V. translates by "fowls," the R.V. by "birds of prey."

τοῖς πτηνοῖς ὁ ἀὴρ ἐνδιαίτημα οἰκεῖον, κούφοις
διὰ τὴν πτέρωσιν ὁ φύσει κοῦφος. ὅταν οὖν τὰ
ἀεροπόρα αἰθεροβατεῖν ὀφείλοντα καταβαίνῃ, πρὸς
χέρσον ἀφικνούμενα τῷ κατὰ φύσιν ἀδυνατεῖ
239 χρῆσθαι βίῳ.   τοὐναντίον δὲ Μωυσῆς
καὶ ὅσα τῶν ἑρπετῶν ἄνω δύναται πηδᾶν οὐ
μετρίως ἀποδέχεται· φησὶ γοῦν· " ταῦτα φάγεσθε
ἀπὸ τῶν ἑρπετῶν τῶν πετεινῶν, ἃ πορεύεται ἐπὶ
τεσσάρων, ἃ ἔχει σκέλη ἀνωτέρω τῶν ποδῶν,
ὥστε πηδᾶν ἐν αὐτοῖς ἀπὸ τῆς γῆς." ταῦτα
δ' ἐστὶ σύμβολα ψυχῶν, ὅσαι τρόπον ἑρπετῶν
προσερριζωμέναι τῷ γηΐνῳ σώματι καθαρθεῖσαι
μετεωροπολεῖν ἰσχύουσιν, οὐρανὸν ἀντικαταλλαξά-
240 μεναι γῆς καὶ φθορᾶς ἀθανασίαν.   πάσης οὖν
βαρυδαιμονίας ἀναπεπλῆσθαι νομιστέον ἐκείνας,
αἵτινες ἐν ἀέρι καὶ αἰθέρι τῷ καθαρωτάτῳ τρα-
φεῖσαι μετανέστησαν τὸν θεῖον ἀγαθῶν κόρον οὐ |
[507] δυνηθεῖσαι φέρειν ἐπὶ τὸ θνητῶν καὶ κακῶν χωρίον
γῆν. ἐπιφοιτῶσι δ' ἔννοιαι μυρίαι περὶ μυρίων
πραγμάτων ὅσων, αἱ μὲν ἑκούσιοι, αἱ δὲ κατ'
ἄγνοιαν, οὐδὲν διαφέρουσαι πτηνῶν, αἷς τὰ κατιόντα
241 ἐξωμοίωσεν ὄρνεα.   τῶν δὲ ἐννοιῶν ἡ
μὲν ἄνω φορὰ τὴν ἀμείνω τάξιν ἔλαχε συνοδοι-
πορούσης ἀρετῆς τῆς πρὸς τὸν οὐράνιον[1] καὶ θεῖον
χῶρον[2] ἀγούσης, τὴν χείρω δὲ ἡ κάτω κακίας
ἀφηγουμένης καὶ ἀντισπώσης βίᾳ. δηλοῖ δὲ καὶ

---

[1] mss. οὐρανὸν: Pap. θειων ουρανιων.
[2] So mss.: Wend. from Pap. χορον. While χορὸς θεῖος is
common in Philo (cf. Phaedrus 247 A), we have in a passage
similar to this, De Som. i. 151, σοφοὶ μὲν γὰρ τὸν ὀλύμπιον καὶ

so too the air is the suitable habitat for the birds, its natural lightness matching with the lightness which the wings give them. So when the denizens of the air, who should rather be explorers of the realm of ether, " descend," it is to the land that they come and there they cannot live their natural life.

Conversely Moses gives high approval 239 to those reptiles which can leap upwards. Thus he says, " These shall ye eat of the flying reptiles which go on four legs, which have legs above their feet, so as to leap with them from the earth " (Lev. xi. 21). These are symbols of the souls which though rooted like reptiles to the earthly body have been purified and have strength to soar on high, exchanging earth for heaven, and corruption for immortality. Surely 240 then we must suppose that misery wholesale and all-pervading must be the lot of those souls which reared in air and ether at its purest have left that home for earth the region of things mortal and evil, because the good things of God bred in them an intolerable satiety. And here they become the resort of thoughts and notions, numberless as the subjects with which they are concerned, some willingly admitted, some in mere ignorance. These thoughts are just like winged creatures and it is to them that he likens " the birds which come down."

Some of our thoughts fly up, others 241 down. To the upward flight falls the better lot, for it has for its fellow-traveller virtue leading it to the divine and heavenly region ; to the downward flight the worse lot falls, since vice goes in front and pulls it with might and main if it resists. How

---

οὐράνιον χῶρον ἔλαχον οἰκεῖν, where χορὸν is impossible, and χῶρον suits τόπων better.

τὰ ὀνόματα οὐχ ἥκιστα τὴν τῶν τόπων ἐναντιότητα· ἀρετὴ μὲν γὰρ οὐ μόνον παρὰ τὴν αἵρεσιν ὠνομάσθη, ἀλλὰ καὶ παρὰ τὴν ἄρσιν—αἴρεται γὰρ καὶ μετεωρίζεται διὰ τὸ αἰεὶ τῶν ὀλυμπίων ἐρᾶν,— κακία δὲ ἀπὸ τοῦ κάτω κεχωρηκέναι καὶ κατα-
242 πίπτειν τοὺς χρωμένους αὐτῇ βιάζεσθαι. τὰ γοῦν πολέμια τῆς ψυχῆς ἐννοήματα ἐπιποτώμενα καὶ ἐπιφοιτῶντα κάτεισι μὲν αὐτά, καταβάλλει δὲ καὶ τὴν διάνοιαν αἰσχρῶς ἐπιφερόμενα σώμασιν οὐ πράγμασιν,[1] αἰσθητοῖς οὐ νοητοῖς, ἀτελέσιν οὐχ ὁλοκλήροις, ἐφθαρμένοις οὐχὶ τοῖς ζῶσιν. οὐ γὰρ μόνον σώμασιν, ἀλλὰ καὶ σωμάτων δίχα διαιρεθέντων τμήμασιν ἐπιφοιτᾷ· τὰ δ' οὕτως διαιρεθέντα ἀμήχανον ἁρμονίαν δέξασθαι καὶ ἕνωσιν, τῶν πνευματικῶν τόνων, οἳ συμφυέστατος δεσμὸς
243 ἦσαν, διακοπέντων. L. εἰσηγεῖται δὲ γνώμην ἀληθεστάτην διδάσκων, ὅτι δικαιοσύνη μὲν καὶ πᾶσα ἀρετὴ ψυχῆς, ἀδικία δὲ καὶ πᾶσα κακία σώματος ἐρῶσι, καὶ ὅτι τὰ τῷ ἑτέρῳ φίλα τῷ ἑτέρῳ πάντως ἐχθρά ἐστι, καθὰ καὶ νῦν· αἰνιττόμενος γὰρ τοὺς ψυχῆς πολεμίους ὄρνεα εἰσήγαγε γλιχόμενα ἐμπλέκεσθαι καὶ ἐμφύεσθαι σώμασι καὶ σαρκῶν ἐμφορεῖσθαι, ὧν τὰς ἐφόδους καὶ ἐπιδρομὰς ἐπισχεῖν βουληθεὶς ὁ ἀστεῖος λέγεται αὐτοῖς συγκαθίσαι,[2] οἷα πρόεδρός τις ἢ πρόβουλος

---

[1] So mss. and Pap.: Wend. σώμασι καὶ πράγμασι. See App. p. 573.

[2] So lxx.: mss. and Pap. ἐγκαθίσαι.

[a] *i.e.* κακία is derived from the two words κάτω κεχωρηκέναι, the consonants in the second word being supposed to supply the second κ in κακία.

[b] For this use of πνεῦμα *cf.* πνεύματος ἐνωτικοῦ δυνάμει *De Op.* 131, and the definition of ἕξις in *Quod Deus* 35 as

404

opposite are the climes to which these two belong is shewn most clearly by their names. Virtue is so named not only because we choose it (αἵρεσις) but also from its uplifting (ἄρσις), for it is lifted up and soars on high, because it ever yearns for the celestial. Vice is so called because it has "gone down"[a] and compels those who have to do with it to fall down likewise. Thus thoughts hostile to the soul, 242 when they hover over it or perch upon it, not only come down themselves, but also bring downfall to the understanding, when in hideous fashion they pounce upon things material, not immaterial; which are of the senses, not of the intelligence; of imperfection, not of soundness; of corruption not of life. For they perch not only on bodies, but on sections of bodies divided in two. And it is impossible that bodies so divided should admit of joining or unifying, since the currents of spirit force,[b] which were their congenital ligament, have been broken into. L. Moses also brings before 243 us a thought of profound truth in teaching us that justice and every virtue love the soul, while injustice and every vice love the body; that what is friendly to the one is utterly hostile to the other—a lesson given in this passage as elsewhere. For in a figure he pictures the enemies of the soul as birds, eager to intertwine and ingraft themselves in bodies and to glut themselves with flesh, and it is to restrain the onsets and inroads of such that the man of worth is said to sit down in their company (Gen. xv. 11), like a chairman or president of a council.

πνεῦμα ἀναστρέφον ἐφ' ἑαυτό. In fact the three terms πνεῦμα, ἕξις, τόνος for a permeating and binding force seem more or less convertible. See the sections headed πνεῦμα, ἕξις, τόνος in S.V.F. ii. 439-462.

244 ὤν.   ἐπειδὴ γὰρ καὶ τὰ οἰκεῖα ὑπὸ ἐμφυλίου
στάσεως διειστήκει καὶ τὰ ἐχθρὰ στίφη διεφέρετο,
βουλὴν ἁπάντων συναγαγὼν ἐσκόπει περὶ τῶν
διαφόρων, ἵν᾽, εἰ δύναιτο, πειθοῖ χρώμενος καὶ τὸν
ξενικὸν πόλεμον καταλῦσαι καὶ τὴν ἐμφύλιον
ταραχὴν ἀνέλοι. τοὺς μὲν γὰρ ὥσπερ νέφος ἐπιρ-
ράξαντας ἀκαταλλάκτως ἔχοντας λυσιτελὲς ἦν ἀπο-
σκεδάσαι, τοῖς δὲ τὴν παλαιὰν συγγένειαν οἰκειώσα-
245 σθαι.   δυσμενεῖς μὲν οὖν ἄσπονδοι καὶ
ἀκατάλλακτοι γράφονται ψυχῆς ἀφροσύναι καὶ
ἀκολασίαι δειλίαι τε καὶ ἀδικίαι καὶ ὅσαι ἄλλαι
ἐκ πλεοναζούσης ὁρμῆς εἰώθασι φύεσθαι ἄλογοι
ἐπιθυμίαι, σκιρτῶσαι καὶ ἀπαυχενίζουσαι καὶ τὸν
εὐθὺν δρόμον τῆς διανοίας ἐπέχουσαι, πολλάκις
[509] | δὲ καὶ τὸ σύμπαν αὐτῆς σχῆμα σπαράττουσαί
246 τε καὶ καταβάλλουσαι.   τὰ δὲ τῶν
ἐνσπόνδων εἶναι δυναμένων προσκρούσματα τοιαῦτά
ἐστιν, ὁποίας εἶναι συμβέβηκε τὰς σοφιστῶν
δογματικὰς ἔριδας· ᾗ μὲν γὰρ πρὸς ἓν ἀπονεύουσι
τέλος, θεωρίαν τῶν τῆς φύσεως πραγμάτων,
λέγοιντ᾽ ἂν εἶναι φίλοι, ᾗ δ᾽ οὐχ ὁμογνωμονοῦσιν
ἐν ταῖς κατὰ μέρος ζητήσεσιν, ἐμφυλίῳ στάσει
χρῆσθαι, ὥσπερ οἱ ἀγένητον εἶναι λέγοντες τὸ
πᾶν τοῖς γένεσιν εἰσηγουμένοις αὐτοῦ, καὶ πάλιν
οἱ φθαρήσεσθαι τοῖς φθαρτὸν μὲν εἶναι φύσει,
μηδέποτε δὲ φθαρησόμενον διὰ τὸ κραταιοτέρῳ
δεσμῷ, τῇ τοῦ πεποιηκότος βουλήσει, συνέχεσθαι,
καὶ οἱ μηδὲν εἶναι ὁμολογοῦντες ἀλλὰ πάντα

---

[a] This seems to be the force of the imperfects. Philo is
falling back upon his reading and no doubt the conditions
described in the following sections belong rather to a past
time than to his own.

History tells us [a] how when discord reigned at home 244
through civil faction, or hostile bands were at
variance, such a one would summon a council of
all concerned and investigate the points of difference,
that if possible he might by his powers of persuasion
make an end of the external war or put down the
civil commotion. In the one case he would scatter
abroad the foes who rushed in irreconcilable hatred
like a storm cloud, in the other he would restore the
old feeling of intimate kinship—each a useful work.

   Now the list of deadly and irreconcilable 245
enemies of the soul comprises its follies, its acts of
cowardice and injustice and all the other irrational
lusts so constantly born of over-abundant appetite,[b]
which prance and struggle against the yoke and
hinder the straight onward course of the understanding, and often rend and overthrow its whole
frame.   But with those who might be 246
allies the causes of offence are such as we find in the
wranglings of the sophists on questions of dogma.
In so far as their minds are fixed on one end to dis-
cover the facts of nature, they may be said to be
friends, but in that they do not agree in their solu-
tions of particular problems they may be said to be
engaged in civil strife. Thus those who declare the
universe to be uncreated are at strife with those who
maintain its creation ; those who say that it will be
destroyed with those who declare that though by
nature destructible it will never be destroyed, being
held together by a bond of superior strength, namely
the will of its Maker ; those who maintain that
nothing is, but all things become, with those who
hold the opposite opinion ; those who argue at

[b] *Cf. De Conf.* 90 and note.

γίνεσθαι τοῖς ὑπολαμβάνουσι τἀναντία, καὶ οἱ
πάντων χρημάτων ἄνθρωπον μέτρον εἶναι διεξιόντες
τοῖς τὰ αἰσθήσεως καὶ τὰ διανοίας κριτήρια
συγχέουσι, καὶ συνόλως οἱ πάντα ἀκατάληπτα
εἰσηγούμενοι τοῖς γνωρίζεσθαι πάμπολλα φάσκου-
247 σιν. καὶ ἥλιος μέντοι καὶ σελήνη καὶ ὁ σύμπας
οὐρανός, γῆ τε καὶ ἀὴρ καὶ ὕδωρ, τά τε ἐξ αὐτῶν
σχεδὸν πάντα τοῖς σκεπτικοῖς ἔριδας καὶ φιλο-
νεικίας παρεσχήκασιν, οὐσίας καὶ ποιότητας,
μεταβολάς τε αὖ καὶ τροπὰς καὶ γενέσεις, ἔτι δὲ
φθορὰς αὐτῶν ἀναζητοῦσιν· μεγέθους τε πέρι καὶ
κινήσεως τῶν κατ᾽ οὐρανὸν οὐ πάρεργον ποιούμενοι τὴν ἔρευναν ἑτεροδοξοῦσιν οὐ συμφερόμενοι,
μέχρις ἂν ὁ μαιευτικὸς ὁμοῦ καὶ δικαστικὸς ἀνὴρ
συγκαθίσας θεάσηται τὰ τῆς ἑκάστου γεννήματα
ψυχῆς καὶ τὰ μὲν οὐκ ἄξια τροφῆς ἀπορρίψῃ, τὰ
δ᾽ ἐπιτήδεια διασώσῃ καὶ προνοίας τῆς ἁρμοτ-
248 τούσης ἀξιώσῃ. τὰ δὲ κατὰ τὴν φιλοσοφίαν μεστὰ
διαφωνίας γέγονε τὸν πιθανὸν καὶ στοχαστικὸν
νοῦν τῆς ἀληθείας ἀποδιδρασκούσης· τὸ γὰρ δυσ-
εύρετον καὶ δυσθήρατον αὐτῆς τὰς λογικάς, ὡς
οἶμαι, στάσεις ἐγέννησε.
249 LI. " Περὶ δὲ ἡλίου " φησί " δυσμὰς ἔκστασις
ἐπέπεσεν[1] τῷ Ἀβραάμ, καὶ ἰδοὺ φόβος σκοτεινὸς
μέγας ἐπιπίπτει αὐτῷ." ἔκστασις ἡ μέν ἐστι
λύττα μανιώδης παράνοιαν ἐμποιοῦσα κατὰ γῆρας
ἢ μελαγχολίαν ἤ τινα ὁμοιότροπον ἄλλην αἰτίαν,
ἡ δὲ σφοδρὰ κατάπληξις ἐπὶ τοῖς ἐξαπιναίως καὶ

---

[1] So LXX: MSS. ἔπεσε: Pap. ἐπεστησε.

---

^a For the philosophical opinions mentioned in this section
see App. p. 574.

ength that man is the measure of all things with
those who make havoc of the judgement-faculty of
both sense and mind ; and, to put it generally,
those who maintain that everything is beyond our
apprehension with those who assert that a great
number of things are cognizable.[a] And indeed sun 247
and moon and the whole heaven, also earth and air
and water and practically all that they produce,
have been the cause of strife and contention to the
inquirers when they probe into their essential
natures and qualities, their changes and phases,
the processes by which they come into being and
finally cease to be. For as to the magnitude and
movement of the heavenly bodies with all their
absorbing research they come to different and conflicting opinions, until the man-midwife[b] who is also
the judge takes his seat in their midst and observes
the brood of each disputant's soul, throws away all
that is not worth rearing, but saves what is worth
saving and approves it for such careful treatment as
is required. The history of philosophy is full of 248
discordance, because truth flees from the credulous
mind which deals in conjecture. It is her nature to
elude discovery and pursuit, and it is this which in my
opinion produces these scientific quarrellings.

LI. " About sunset " it continues, " an ' ecstasy ' 249
fell upon Abraham and lo a great dark terror falls
upon him " (Gen. xv. 12). Now " ecstasy " or
" standing out " takes different forms. Sometimes
it is a mad fury producing mental delusion due to old
age or melancholy or other similar cause. Sometimes it is extreme amazement at the events which

[b] Cf. Socrates' use of the figure in *Theaetetus* 151 c and
elsewhere.

PHILO

[509] ἀπροσδοκήτως | συμβαίνειν εἰωθόσιν, ἡ δὲ ἠρεμία
διανοίας, εἰ δὴ πέφυκέ ποτε ἡσυχάζειν, ἡ δὲ
πασῶν ἀρίστη ἔνθεος κατοκωχή τε καὶ μανία, ᾗ
250 τὸ προφητικὸν γένος χρῆται.   τῆς μὲν
οὖν πρώτης ἐν ταῖς ⟨ἐν⟩ Ἐπινομίδι γραφείσαις
ἀραῖς διαμέμνηται—παραπληξίαν γάρ φησι καὶ
ἀορασίαν καὶ ἔκστασιν διανοίας καταλήψεσθαι τοὺς
ἀσεβοῦντας, ὡς μηδὲν διοίσειν τυφλῶν ἐν μεσημ-
βρίᾳ καθάπερ ἐν βαθεῖ σκότῳ ψηλαφώντων,—
251   τῆς δὲ δευτέρας πολλαχοῦ—" ἐξέστη "
γάρ φησιν " Ἰσαὰκ ἔκστασιν μεγάλην, καὶ εἶπε·
τίς οὖν ὁ θηρεύσας μοι θήραν καὶ ἐνεγκών
μοι, καὶ ἔφαγον ἀπὸ πάντων πρὸ τοῦ σὲ ἐλθεῖν,
καὶ εὐλόγησα αὐτόν; καὶ εὐλογημένος ἔστω,"
καὶ ἐπὶ τοῦ Ἰακὼβ ἀπιστοῦντος τοῖς λέγουσιν, ὅτι
" ζῇ Ἰωσὴφ καὶ ἄρχει πάσης γῆς Αἰγύπτου "·
" ἐξέστη " γάρ φησι " τῇ διανοίᾳ, οὐ γὰρ ἐπίστευσεν αὐτοῖς," καὶ ἐν Ἐξαγωγῇ κατὰ τὴν ἐκκλη-
σίαν· " τὸ γὰρ ὄρος " φησί " τὸ Σινᾶ ἐκαπνίζετο
ὅλον διὰ τὸ καταβεβηκέναι τὸν θεὸν ἐπ' αὐτὸ ἐν
πυρί, καὶ ἀνέβαινεν ὁ καπνὸς ὡσεὶ ἀτμὶς καμίνου·
καὶ ἐξέστη πᾶς ὁ λαὸς σφόδρα," καὶ ἐν τῷ Λευι-
τικῷ κατὰ τὴν τῶν ἱερῶν τελείωσιν ἡμέρᾳ τῇ
ὀγδόῃ, ὁπότε " ἐξῆλθε πῦρ ἀπ' οὐρανοῦ καὶ κατ-
έφαγε τὰ ἐπὶ τοῦ θυσιαστηρίου, τά τε ὁλοκαυτώ-
ματα καὶ τὰ στέατα"· λέγεται γὰρ εὐθύς· " καὶ
εἶδε πᾶς ὁ λαὸς καὶ ἐξέστη, καὶ ἔπεσαν ἐπὶ πρόσωπον." ἡ γὰρ τοιαύτη ἔκστασις πτόησιν καὶ
δεινὴν κατάπληξιν ἐμποιεῖ—
252 Ἀλλ' οὐκ ἄξιον θαυμάσαι καὶ ἐπὶ τοῦ Ἠσαῦ,

410

so often happen suddenly and unexpectedly. Sometimes it is passivity of mind, if indeed the mind can ever be at rest ; and the best form of all is the divine possession or frenzy [a] to which the prophets as a class are subject.   The first form is mentioned 250 in the curses described in Deuteronomy, where he says that madness and loss of sight and " ecstasy " of mind will overtake the impious, so that they shall differ in nought from blind men groping at noonday as in deep darkness (Deut. xxviii. 28, 29).

The second we have in several places. Isaac was 251 astonished with a great ecstasy and said, " who is it then who has made a hunting and brought to me, and I have eaten of all before thou camest and I blessed him, and let him be blessed " (Gen. xxvii. 33).   And again when Jacob disbelieved those who told him that " Joseph lives and is ruler over all Egypt," he was in an " ecstasy," we are told, " in his mind, for he did not believe them " (Gen. xlv. 26). Also in Exodus, in the account of the congregation, it says, " for Mount Sinai was all covered with smoke, because God came down to it in fire and the smoke rose up like vapour of a furnace, and all the people were in a great ' ecstasy ' " (Ex. xix. 18).   Also in Leviticus at the completion of the sacrifices on the eighth day, when " fire came out from heaven and devoured what was on the altar, both the whole burnt offerings and the fats "; for the next words are, " and all the people saw it and were in an ' ecstasy,' and fell upon their faces " (Lev. ix. 24) : a natural consequence, for an " ecstasy " in this sense produces great agitation and terrible consternation.

Incidentally in the story of Jacob and Esau there 252

[a] See App. p. 574.

ὅτι εἰδὼς κυνηγεῖν ἀεὶ θηρεύεται καὶ πτερνίζεται
τὴν τέχνην ἐπὶ βλάβῃ κτησάμενος, οὐκ ὠφελείᾳ,
θηρεύειν δὲ οὐδέποτε ἐσπούδασε, καὶ ἐπὶ τοῦ
Ἰακώβ, ὅτι θηρεύει μὴ μαθών, ἀλλὰ φύσει κινού-
μενος, τὸ πάθος, καὶ φέρει τῷ δοκιμαστῇ, ὃς εἰ
δοκιμόν ἐστι διαγνώσεται, διὸ ἀπὸ πάντων φάγε-
253 ται;[1] πάντα γὰρ τὰ τῆς ἀσκήσεως ἐδώδιμα καθέστηκεν, ἡ ζήτησις, ἡ σκέψις, ἡ ἀνάγνωσις, ἡ ἀκρόα-
σις, ἡ προσοχή, ἡ ἐγκράτεια, ἡ ἐξαδιαφόρησις τῶν
ἀδιαφόρων. ἀπὸ πάντων δὲ τὰς ἀπαρχὰς δήπου-
θεν ἔφαγεν, ἀλλ᾽ οὐ πάντα· ἔδει γὰρ ὑπολείπεσθαι καὶ τῷ ἀσκητῇ τροφὰς οἰκείας ὡς ἆθλα.
254 "πρὸ τοῦ σε ἐλθεῖν" φυσικῶς· ἐὰν
γὰρ ἔλθῃ τὸ πάθος εἰς τὴν ψυχήν, οὐκ ἀπο-
λαύσομεν ἐγκρατείας· ἐλέγχει δὲ καὶ τὸν φαῦλον
ὡς βραδὺν καὶ ὀκνηρὸν καὶ μελλητὴν πρὸς τὰ
παιδείας ἔργα, ἀλλ᾽ οὐ πρὸς τὰ ἀκολασίας.
255 ἐργοδιώκτας οὖν Αἴγυπτος ἔχει πρὸς τὴν τῶν
παθῶν ἐπισπεύδοντας ἀπόλαυσιν, Μωυσῆς δ᾽

---

[1] Wend. does not put a mark of interrogation. If this is
not a mere misprint, he must have understood οὐκ ἄξιον
θαυμάσαι as "there is no need to wonder."

---

[a] The irrelevance of these five sections to the disquisition
on "ecstasy" led Mangey to consider them an interpolation
from another treatise. But the irrelevance does not differ
in kind from Philo's other ramblings, and we have a sort of
apology for it in § 256. The remarks are based on the texts
quoted to illustrate the second sense of "ecstasy" in § 251.
He feels that though they were quoted for that purpose,
they each have their moral which he does not wish to omit.
[b] See App. p. 574.
[c] The allegory of §§ 252-254 is very confused. Jacob

are thoughts well worthy of our admiration.[a] Esau, though he has the knowledge needed for the chase, is ever hunted and supplanted, because he has acquired his skill not to do good but harm, and moreover is never quick or zealous in his hunting. Jacob hunts passion not through teaching, but moved to it by nature, and brings the game to the tester who will decide whether it will stand the test. For this purpose the tester will eat of all that he brings. For all the elements of practice are food fit for eating, 253 inquiry, examination, reading, listening to instruction, concentration, perseverance, self-mastery, and power to treat things indifferent as indeed indifferent.[b] Of all these the tester naturally eats samples [b] only, not the whole. For the Practiser must have his proper food left to him, like prizes for his efforts.

Another lesson. The words " before 254 thou camest " are true to nature. For if passion has entered the soul we shall not get enjoyment from self-mastery. Secondly, they convict the bad of sloth and slackness and backwardness to the tasks of instruction, though not to those of incontinence.[c] And so it is Egypt which has its " task-drivers " 255 (Ex. v. 6) who urge others to the enjoyment of the

---

" hunts," *i.e.* supplants, πάθος symbolized by Esau (though elsewhere Esau is rather folly). But the game he brings so quickly (a sign as in *De Sac.* 64 and elsewhere of gifts sent direct from nature and God) turns out to be the qualities of the " Practiser." These qualities are submitted to the testing soul before πάθος can enter it, otherwise their flavour would be lost. Here Esau is still πάθος, but the next moment he is rather the worthless man hunting in a sense for the good, but failing through procrastination and slackness, and thus a contrast to the zeal of the man of worth. This zeal for the good implies an equal zeal to flee from evil, and the texts in § 255 illustrate this.

413

ἔμπαλιν μετὰ σπουδῆς παραγγέλλει τὸ Πάσχα
ἐσθίειν, τὴν ἀπὸ τούτων διάβασιν εὐωχεῖσθαι.
καὶ ὁ Ἰούδας φησίν· " εἰ μὴ γὰρ ἐβραδύναμεν, |
[510] ἤδη ἂν ὑπεστρέψαμεν δίς," οὔ φησι κατέβημεν εἰς
Αἴγυπτον, ἀλλ' ἐκεῖθεν ἐπανεσώθημεν.

256 εἰκότως καὶ Ἰακὼβ τεθαύμακεν, εἰ ἔτι ὁ ἐν
σώματι νοῦς, Ἰωσήφ, ζῇ πρὸς ἀρετὴν καὶ ἄρχει
τοῦ σώματος, ἀλλ' οὐκ ἄρχεται πρὸς αὐτοῦ.

Καὶ τἄλλα ἐπιὼν ἄν τις ὑποδείγματα τἀληθὲς
ἰχνεύειν δυνηθείη. πρόκειται δ' οὐ περὶ τούτων
νῦν ἀκριβολογεῖσθαι, διὸ ἐπὶ τὰ ἑξῆς τρεπτέον·
257 τῆς δὲ τρίτης ἐν οἷς τὰ περὶ τὴν τῆς γυναικὸς
γένεσιν φιλοσοφεῖ—" ἐπέβαλε γὰρ ὁ θεὸς " φησίν
" ἔκστασιν ἐπὶ τὸν Ἀδάμ, καὶ ὕπνωσεν," ἔκστασιν τὴν ἡσυχίαν καὶ ἠρεμίαν τοῦ νοῦ παραλαμ-
βάνων· ὕπνος γὰρ νοῦ ἐγρήγορσίς ἐστιν αἰσθήσεως,
καὶ γὰρ ἐγρήγορσις διανοίας αἰσθήσεως ἀπραξία,—

258 LII. τῆς δὲ τετάρτης ὃ νῦν σκο-
ποῦμεν· " περὶ δὲ ἡλίου δυσμὰς ἔκστασις ἐπέπεσεν τῷ Ἀβραάμ" ἐνθουσιῶντος καὶ θεοφορήτου
τὸ πάθος. ἀλλ' οὐχὶ τοῦτο μόνον διασυνίστησιν[1]
αὐτὸν προφήτην, ἀλλὰ καὶ γράμμα ῥητὸν ἐστηλι-
τευμένον ⟨ἐν⟩ ἱεραῖς βίβλοις, ἡνίκα τις ἐπεχεί-
ρησε τὴν ἐκ φύσεως ἄρχουσαν ἀρετήν, Σάρραν,
αὐτοῦ διοικίζειν, ὡς οὐκ ἴδιον σοφοῦ καὶ μόνου
κτῆμα, ἀλλὰ παντὸς τοῦ φρόνησιν ἐπιμορφάζοντος.

---

[1] mss. ἀλλὰ συνίστησι: Pap. (?) συνίστησι.

---

[a] For the interpretation of the tasks as lower pleasures cf.
De Conf. 93.
[b] Of course the first is what the Judah of the story did

414

passions;[a] it is Moses who bids eat the Passover and celebrate the crossing from passion " with haste " (Ex. xii. 11). So too Judah, " for if we had not delayed, we should already have returned twice over " (Gen. xliii. 10). He does not mean " we should have gone down twice to Egypt," but " we should have come up thence in safety."[b] Natural too is the wonder of Jacob that the mind within the body still lives to virtue and rules that body (Gen xlv. 26), instead of being ruled by it. 256

In the same way if we went through the other examples we should be able to trace the truth they teach, but the task before us now is not to work these out in detail, and therefore we must turn to the next point. We have the third sort of ecstasy when Moses finds a lesson of wisdom in the story of the creation of woman. God " cast," he says, " an ecstasy on Adam and he slept " (Gen. ii. 21). Here by ecstasy he means passivity and tranquillity of mind. For sleep of mind is waking of sense, since waking of the understanding is inaction of sense. 257

LII. The fourth kind of ecstasy we find in the passage we are now examining. " About sunset there fell upon Abraham an ecstasy," that is, what the inspired and God-possessed experience. Yet it is not merely this experience which proves him a prophet, but we have also the actual word written and recorded in the holy Scriptures, when another tried to take Sarah from his home, Sarah the virtue whose nature is to rule, as though that virtue was not the peculiar possession of the wise and of him alone, but belonged to any who counterfeits good 258

mean, but the delay which the Judah-mind, as Philo sees it, regrets can only be delay in escaping from Egypt.

415

" ἀπόδος " γάρ φησι " τὴν γυναῖκα τῷ ἀνθρώπῳ,
ὅτι προφήτης ἐστὶ καὶ προσεύξεται περὶ σοῦ, καὶ
259 ζήσεις."   παντὶ δὲ ἀστείῳ προφητείαν ὁ
ἱερὸς λόγος μαρτυρεῖ· προφήτης γὰρ ἴδιον μὲν
οὐδὲν ἀποφθέγγεται, ἀλλότρια δὲ πάντα ὑπ-
ηχοῦντος ἑτέρου· φαύλῳ δ' οὐ θέμις ἑρμηνεῖ γενέσθαι θεοῦ, ὥστε κυρίως μοχθηρὸς οὐδεὶς ἐνθουσιᾷ,
μόνῳ δὲ σοφῷ ταῦτ' ἐφαρμόττει, ἐπεὶ καὶ μόνος
ὄργανον θεοῦ ἐστιν ἠχεῖον, κρουόμενον καὶ πλητ-
260 τόμενον ἀοράτως ὑπ' αὐτοῦ. πάντας γοῦν ὁπό-
σους ἀνέγραψε δικαίους κατεχομένους καὶ προ-
φητεύοντας εἰσήγαγεν.   ὁ Νῶε δίκαιος·
ἆρ' οὐ καὶ εὐθὺς προφήτης; ἢ τὰς εὐχὰς καὶ
κατάρας ἃς ἐπὶ ταῖς αὖθις γενεαῖς ἐποιήσατο
ἔργων ἀληθείᾳ βεβαιωθείσας οὐ κατεχόμενος
261 ἐθέσπισε;   τί δὲ Ἰσαάκ; τί δὲ Ἰακώβ;
καὶ γὰρ οὗτοι διά τε ἄλλων πολλῶν καὶ μάλιστα
διὰ τῶν εἰς τοὺς ἐκγόνους προσρήσεων ὁμο-
λογοῦνται προφητεῦσαι.   τὸ γὰρ " συνάχθητε, ἵνα
ἀπαγγείλω τί ἀπαντήσεται ὑμῖν ἐπ' ἐσχάτῳ τῶν
ἡμερῶν " ἐνθουσιῶντος ἦν· ἡ γὰρ τῶν μελλόντων
262 κατάληψις ἀνοίκειος ἀνθρώπῳ.   τί δὲ |
[511] Μωυσῆς; οὐ προφήτης ᾄδεται πανταχοῦ; λέγει
γάρ· " ἐὰν γένηται ὑμῶν προφήτης κυρίου, ἐν
ὁράματι αὐτῷ γνωσθήσομαι, Μωυσῇ δὲ ἐν εἴδει,
καὶ οὐ δι' αἰνιγμάτων," καὶ πάλιν " οὐκ ἀνέστη
ἔτι προφήτης ὡς Μωυσῆς, ὃν ἔγνω κύριος αὐτὸν
263 πρόσωπον πρὸς πρόσωπον."   παγκάλως

416

sense. For the text runs, " restore the woman to the
man, because he is a prophet and shall pray for thee,
and thou shalt live " (Gen. xx. 7). Now 259
with every good man it is the holy Word which
assures him his gift of prophecy. For a prophet
(being a spokesman) has no utterance of his own, but
all his utterance came from elsewhere, the echoes of
another's voice. The wicked may never be the
interpreter of God, so that no worthless person is
" God-inspired " in the proper sense. The name
only befits the wise, since he alone is the vocal instrument of God, smitten and played by His invisible
hand. Thus, all whom Moses describes as just are 260
pictured as possessed and prophesying.
Noah was just. Is he not in the same breath shewn
as a prophet ? Were not the curses which he called
down on subsequent generations, the prayers which
he made on their behalf, all of which the actual
event confirmed, uttered by him under divine possession ? What of Isaac ? What of Jacob ? 261
They too are confessed as prophets by many other
evidences, but particularly by their speeches addressed to their children. For " Gather ye together
that I may proclaim what shall happen to you at the
end of the days " (Gen. xlix. 1) were the words of one
inspired. For apprehension of the future does not
belong to man. What of Moses ? Is he 262
not everywhere celebrated as a prophet ? For it
says, " if a prophet of the Lord arise among you, I will
be known to him in vision, but to Moses in actual
appearance and not through riddles " (Num. xii.
6, 8), and again " there no more rose up a prophet
like Moses, whom the Lord knew face to face "
(Deut. xxxiv. 10). Admirably then 263

417

οὖν τὸν ἐνθουσιῶντα μηνύει φάσκων '' περὶ ἡλίου δυσμὰς ἔκστασις ἐπέπεσεν.'' LIII. ἥλιον διὰ συμβόλου τὸν ἡμέτερον καλῶν νοῦν· ὅπερ γὰρ ἐν ἡμῖν λογισμός, τοῦτο ἐν κόσμῳ ἥλιος, ἐπειδὴ φωσφορεῖ ἑκάτερος, ὁ μὲν τῷ παντὶ φέγγος αἰσθητὸν ἐκπέμπων, ὁ δὲ ἡμῖν αὐτοῖς τὰς νοητὰς
264 διὰ τῶν καταλήψεων αὐγάς. ἕως μὲν οὖν ἔτι περιλάμπει καὶ περιπολεῖ ἡμῶν ὁ νοῦς μεσημβρινὸν οἷα φέγγος εἰς πᾶσαν τὴν ψυχὴν ἀναχέων, ἐν ἑαυτοῖς ὄντες οὐ κατεχόμεθα· ἐπειδὰν δὲ πρὸς δυσμὰς γένηται, κατὰ τὸ εἰκὸς ἔκστασις καὶ ἡ ἔνθεος ἐπιπίπτει κατοκωχή τε καὶ μανία. ὅταν μὲν γὰρ φῶς τὸ θεῖον ἐπιλάμψῃ, δύεται τὸ ἀνθρώπινον, ὅταν δ' ἐκεῖνο δύηται, τοῦτ' ἀνίσχει
265 καὶ ἀνατέλλει. τῷ δὲ προφητικῷ γένει φιλεῖ τοῦτο συμβαίνειν· ἐξοικίζεται μὲν γὰρ ἐν ἡμῖν ὁ νοῦς κατὰ τὴν τοῦ θείου πνεύματος ἄφιξιν, κατὰ δὲ τὴν μετανάστασιν αὐτοῦ πάλιν εἰσοικίζεται· θέμις γὰρ οὐκ ἔστι θνητὸν ἀθανάτῳ συνοικῆσαι. διὰ τοῦτο ἡ δύσις τοῦ λογισμοῦ καὶ τὸ περὶ αὐτὸν σκότος ἔκστασιν καὶ θεοφόρητον μανίαν ἐγέννησε.
266 τὸ δὲ ἀκόλουθον προσυφαίνει τῇ γραφῇ φάσκων '' ἐρρέθη πρὸς Ἀβραάμ''· ὄντως γὰρ ὁ προφήτης, καὶ ὁπότε λέγειν δοκεῖ, πρὸς ἀλήθειαν ἡσυχάζει, καταχρῆται δὲ ἕτερος αὐτοῦ τοῖς φωνητηρίοις ὀργάνοις, στόματι καὶ γλώττῃ, πρὸς μήνυσιν ὧν ἂν θέλῃ· τέχνῃ δὲ ἀοράτῳ καὶ παμμούσῳ ταῦτα κρούων εὔηχα καὶ παναρμόνια καὶ γέμοντα συμφωνίας τῆς πάσης ἀποτελεῖ.
267 LIV. Τίνα δ' ἐστὶν ἃ ἐρρέθη προθεσπισθέντα,

---

[a] Philo apparently finds in the impersonal ἐρρέθη a sug-

does he describe the inspired when he says " about sunset there fell on him an ecstasy." LIII. " Sun " is his name under a figure for our mind. For what the reasoning faculty is in us, the sun is in the world, since both of them are light-bringers, one sending forth to the whole world the light which our senses perceive, the other shedding mental rays upon ourselves through the medium of apprehension. So 264 while the radiance of the mind is still all around us, when it pours as it were a noonday beam into the whole soul, we are self-contained, not possessed. But when it comes to its setting, naturally ecstasy and divine possession and madness fall upon us. For when the light of God shines, the human light sets ; when the divine light sets, the human dawns and rises. This is what regularly befalls the fellowship of 265 the prophets. The mind is evicted at the arrival of the divine Spirit, but when that departs the mind returns to its tenancy. Mortal and immortal may not share the same home. And therefore the setting of reason and the darkness which surrounds it produce ecstasy and inspired frenzy. To connect 266 what is coming with what is here written he says " it was said to Abraham "[a] (Gen. xv. 3). For indeed the prophet, even when he seems to be speaking, really holds his peace, and his organs of speech, mouth and tongue, are wholly in the employ of Another, to shew forth what He wills. Unseen by us that Other beats on the chords with the skill of a master-hand and makes them instruments of sweet music, laden with every harmony.

LIV. It is well to hear what these predictions 267

gestion that the prophetic inspiration comes to the prophet in a mysterious way, which he does not understand.

PHILO

καλὸν ἀκοῦσαι· πρῶτον μέν, ὅτι τῷ φιλαρέτῳ κατοικεῖν οὐ δίδωσιν ὁ θεὸς ὡς ἐν οἰκείᾳ γῇ τῷ σώματι, ἀλλὰ παροικεῖν ὡς ἐν ἀλλοδαπῇ μόνον ἐπιτρέπει χώρᾳ. '' γινώσκων '' γάρ φησι '' γνώσῃ, ὅτι πάροικον ἔσται τὸ σπέρμα σου ἐν γῇ οὐκ ἰδίᾳ.'' παντὸς δὲ φαύλου συγγενὲς τὸ σώματος χωρίον, ἐν ᾧ μελετᾷ κατοικεῖν, οὐ παροικεῖν.

268 ἐν μὲν δὴ παίδευμα τοῦτο· ἕτερον δέ, ὅτι τὰ δουλείαν καὶ κάκωσιν καὶ δεινήν, ὡς αὐτὸς ἔφη, ταπείνωσιν ἐπάγοντα τῇ ψυχῇ τὰ κατὰ γῆν ἐστιν '' οὐκ ἰδία[1] ''· νόθα γὰρ καὶ ξένα διανοίας τὰ σώματος ὡς ἀληθῶς πάθη, σαρκὸς ἐκπεφυκότα, ᾗ προσ-
269 ερρίζωται.   τετρακόσια δὲ ἔτη γίνεται ἡ δουλεία κατὰ τὰς τῶν τεττάρων παθῶν δυνάμεις. ἀρχούσης μὲν γὰρ ἡδονῆς μετεωρίζεται καὶ φυσᾶται
[512] τὸ φρόνημα, χαύνῳ | κουφότητι ἐξαιρόμενον· ὅταν δὲ ἐπιθυμία κρατήσῃ, ἔρως ἐγγίνεται τῶν ἀπόντων καὶ τὴν ψυχὴν ὥσπερ ἀπ' ἀγχόνης ἐλπίδος ἀτελοῦς ἐκρέμασε· διψῇ μὲν γὰρ ἀεί, πιεῖν δὲ ἀδυνατεῖ
270 ταντάλειον τιμωρίαν ὑπομένουσα. κατὰ δὲ τὴν τῆς λύπης δυναστείαν συνάγεται καὶ συστέλλεται φυλ-λορροούντων καὶ ἀφαναινομένων τρόπον δένδρων· τὸ γὰρ εὐθαλὲς αὐτῆς καὶ πῖον ἰσχναίνεται. φόβου γε μὴν τυραννήσαντος οὐδεὶς ἔτι μένειν ἀξιοῖ, δρασμῷ δὲ καὶ φυγῇ χρῆται, μόνως ἂν οὕτως σωθήσεσθαι προσδοκῶν· ἐπιθυμία μὲν γὰρ ὁλκὸν ἔχουσα

---

[1] οὐκ ἴδια] so two mss.; Pap. apparently doubtful, for Wend. gives '' Pap. (οικιδ)ια.'' The other mss. have οἰκίδια, which Mangey, Wend., and apparently all editors and translators read. But apart from οἰκίδιον not occurring elsewhere in Philo, οὐκ ἴδια is wanted as a lesson on the last two words of the text, the former lesson being on πάροικον, and this second lesson is further emphasized by νόθα καὶ ξένα.

were, which were thus said to him. First that God does not grant as a gift to the lover of virtue that he should dwell in the body as in homeland, but only permits him to sojourn there, as in a foreign country. For " knowing thou shalt know," he says, " that thy seed shall be sojourners in a land[a] which is not their own " (Gen. xv. 3). But every fool takes the body for the place of his nativity and studies to dwell there, not to sojourn. This is one lesson. 268 Another is that the things of earth which bring slavery and ill-treatment and dire humiliation,[b] to use his own words, are " not our own." For the passions of the body are truly bastards, outlanders to the understanding, growths of the flesh in which they have their roots. " And the slavery is for 269 four hundred years " ; thus he shews the powers exercised by the four passions. When pleasure rules, the temper is high flown and inflated, uplifted with empty levity. When desire is master, a yearning for what is not arises and suspends the soul on unfulfilled hope as on a noose. For the soul is ever athirst yet never able to drink, suffering the torments of a Tantalus. Under the sovereignty of grief it is 270 pinched and shrinks, like trees which shed their leaves and wither ; for its bloom and richness turn into leanness. Finally when fear has made itself lord no one thinks it good to stand his ground, but abandons himself to flight, expecting that in this alone will safety be found. For while desire has a power of attraction and forces us to the pursuit of the

[a] Or " earth," as Philo interprets it below.
[b] An allusion to the unquoted part of the text καὶ δουλώσουσιν αὐτοὺς καὶ κακώσουσιν αὐτοὺς καὶ ταπεινώσουσιν αὐτούς.

δύναμιν, κἂν φεύγῃ τὸ ποθούμενον, διώκειν ἀναγκάζει, φόβος δ' ἔμπαλιν ἀλλοτριότητα ἐμποιῶν
διοικίζει καὶ μακρὰν τοῦ φαινομένου διίστησιν.
271 LV. αἱ δὲ τῶν λεχθέντων ἡγεμονίαι
παθῶν βαρεῖαν τοῖς ἀρχομένοις ἐπάγουσι δουλείαν,
ἄχρις ἂν ὁ βραβευτὴς καὶ δικαστὴς θεὸς διακρίνῃ
τὸ κακούμενον ἀπὸ τοῦ κακοῦντος καὶ τὸ μὲν εἰς
ἐλευθερίαν ἐξέληται παντελῆ, τῷ δὲ τἀπίχειρα ὧν
272 ἐξήμαρτεν ἀποδῷ. λέγεται γάρ· " τὸ δὲ ἔθνος
ᾧ ἂν δουλεύσωσι κρινῶ ἐγώ· μετὰ δὲ ταῦτα ἐξ-
ελεύσονται ὧδε μετὰ ἀποσκευῆς πολλῆς." ἀνάγκη
γὰρ θνητὸν ὄντα τῷ τῶν παθῶν ἔθνει πιεσθῆναι
καὶ τὰς οἰκείους τῷ γενομένῳ κῆρας ἀναδέξασθαι,
βούλημα δὲ θεοῦ τὰ σύμφυτα κακὰ τοῦ γένους
273 ἡμῶν ἐπικουφίζειν· ὥστε καὶ ἡμεῖς ἐν ἀρχῇ τὰ
οἰκεῖα πεισόμεθα ὠμῶν[a] γενόμενοι δεσποτῶν δοῦλοι,
καὶ ὁ θεὸς τὸ οἰκεῖον ἐργάσεται ἑαυτῷ, ἄφεσιν καὶ
ἐλευθερίαν ταῖς ἱκέτισιν αὐτοῦ ψυχαῖς προκηρύξας,
οὐ μόνον λύσιν δεσμῶν καὶ ἔξοδον ἐκ τῆς περι-
πεφρουρημένης εἱρκτῆς παρασχόμενος, ἀλλὰ καὶ
ἐφόδια δούς, ἅπερ ἀποσκευὴν ἐκάλεσε. τί δὲ τοῦτ'
274 ἐστίν; ἐπειδὰν ἄνωθεν ἀπ' οὐρανοῦ καταβὰς ὁ
νοῦς ἐνδεθῇ ταῖς σώματος ἀνάγκαις, εἶτα ὑπὸ
μηδεμιᾶς δελεασθεὶς οἷα ἀνδρόγυνος ἢ γύνανδρος
τὰ ἡδέα ἀσπάσηται κακά, μείνας δὲ ἐπὶ τῆς ἑαυτοῦ
φύσεως ἀνὴρ ὄντως τραχηλίζειν μᾶλλον ἢ τρα-
χηλίζεσθαι δύνηται, τοῖς τῆς ἐγκυκλίου μουσικῆς

---

[a] ἀνάγκαις echoes the δουλώσουσι of the text just quoted,
as κακά echoes the κακώσουσι.

desired object even though it flee from our grasp, fear on the other hand creates a sense of estrangement and sunders and removes us far from the sight we dread.　　　　　LV. The sovereignties of the 271 passions here named entail a grievous slavery on their subjects, until God the arbiter and judge makes a separation between the ill-treater and the ill-treated, brings forth the one to full liberty and renders to the other the recompense for his misdeeds. For we read, " the nation whom they shall 272 serve I will judge, and after this they shall come out hither with much stock " (Gen. xv. 14). It must needs be that mortal man shall be oppressed by the nation of the passions and receive the calamities which are proper to created being, but it is God's will to lighten the evils which are inherent in our race. So while we shall suffer at first such things as 273 are proper to ourselves, enslaved as we are to cruel masters, God will accomplish the work which is proper to Himself in proclaiming redemption and liberty to the souls which are His suppliants, and not only will He provide release from bonds and an issue from the closely-guarded prison, but give us also the viaticum which he here calls " stock." What is the meaning of this ? It is when the mind 274 which has come down from heaven, though it be fast bound in the constraints [a] of the body, nevertheless is not lured by any of them to embrace like some hybrid, man-woman or woman-man,[b] the pleasant-seeming evils, but holding to its own nature of true manhood has the strength to be victor instead of victim in the wrestling-bout. Reared in all the lore of the schools, it acquires therefrom

[b] See App. p. 574.

ἐντραφεὶς[1] ἅπασιν,[2] ἐξ ὧν θεωρίας λαβὼν ἵμερον
ἐγκράτειαν καὶ καρτερίαν, ἐρρωμένας ἀρετάς,
ἐκτήσατο, μετανιστάμενος καὶ κάθοδον τὴν εἰς
τὴν πατρίδα εὑρισκόμενος πάντ' ἐπάγεται τὰ
παιδείας, ἅπερ ἀποσκευὴ καλεῖται.

275 LVI. Τοσαῦτα καὶ περὶ τούτων εἰπὼν ἐπιλέγει·
" σὺ δὲ ἀπελεύσῃ πρὸς τοὺς πατέρας σου μετ'
εἰρήνης τραφεὶς ἐν γήρᾳ καλῷ." οὐκοῦν οἱ μὲν |
[513] ἀτελεῖς καὶ πολεμούμεθα καὶ δουλεύομεν καὶ μόλις
ἀπαλλαγὴν τῶν ἐπικρεμασθέντων φοβερῶν εὑρισκό-
μεθα, τὸ δὲ τέλειον γένος ἀδούλωτον, ἀπολέμητον,
εἰρήνῃ καὶ ἐλευθερίᾳ βεβαιοτάτῃ ἐντρεφόμενον.

276 δογματικῶς δὲ τὸν ἀστεῖον οὐκ ἀπο-
θνήσκοντα, ἀλλ' ἀπερχόμενον εἰσήγαγεν, ἵν' ἄσβε-
στον καὶ ἀθάνατον τὸ τῆς κεκαθαρμένης ἄκρως
ψυχῆς ἀποφανῇ γένος, ἀποδημίᾳ τῇ ἐνθένδε πρὸς
οὐρανὸν χρησόμενον, οὐ διαλύσει καὶ φθορᾷ, ἣν
277 ἐπάγειν θάνατος δοκεῖ.   μετὰ δὲ τὸ
" ἀπελεύσῃ " γέγραπται τὸ " πρὸς τοὺς πατέρας
σου "· ποίους πατέρας, ἄξιον σκέψασθαι. τοὺς
μὲν γὰρ ἐν τῇ Χαλδαίων χώρᾳ βεβιωκότας, οἷς
μόνοις ἐχρήσατο συγγενέσιν, οὐκ ἂν λέγοι, διὰ
τὸ χρησμῷ τῶν ἀφ' αἵματος ἁπάντων διῳκίσθαι.
" εἶπε " γάρ φησι " κύριος τῷ Ἀβραάμ· ἄπελθε
ἐκ τῆς γῆς σου καὶ ἐκ τῆς συγγενείας σου καὶ ἐκ
τοῦ οἴκου τοῦ πατρός σου εἰς τὴν γῆν ἣν σοι δείξω·
278 καὶ ποιήσω σε εἰς ἔθνος μέγα." τὸν γὰρ ἀλλο-

---

[1] mss. and Pap. ἐγγραφεὶς.
[2] A noun seems to be wanted either as a substitute for or
in addition to ἅπασι. Wend. suggests προπαιδεύμασι or
παιδεύμασι (or perhaps μαθήμασι).

a longing for the higher contemplation, and wins the sturdy virtues of self-mastery and perseverance ; and thus when the pilgrim wins his return to his native land, he takes with him all these fruits of instruction, which are here called " stock." [a]

LVI. Having said thus much on these points also 275 he continues, " but thou shalt depart to thy fathers nourished with peace, in a goodly old age " [b] (Gen. xv. 15). So then we who are imperfect are victims both of war and slavery, and hard-won is our release from the terrors which menace us. But the perfect are a race subject neither to war nor slavery, but nourished in peace and freedom sure and secure.

And when he represents the good man as not dying 276 but departing, there is sound doctrine in the words. He would have the nature of the fully purified soul shewn as unquenchable and immortal, destined to journey from hence to heaven, not to meet with dissolution and corruption, which death appears to bring.　　　　　　After " thou shalt depart " come 277 the words " to thy fathers." What fathers? This is worth inquiring. For Moses could not mean those who had lived in the land of the Chaldeans, who were the only kinsfolk Abraham had, seeing that the oracle had set his dwelling away from all those of his blood. For we read, " the Lord said unto Abraham ' depart from thy land and from thy kinsfolk and from the house of thy father unto the land which I shall shew thee, and I will make thee into a great nation ' " (Gen. xii. 1, 2). Was it 278 reasonable that he should again have affinity with the

---

[a] See App. p. 575.
[b] The μετ᾽ εἰρήνης or ἐν εἰρήνῃ of the lxx is of course intended to go with ἀπελεύσῃ.

τριωθέντα ἐπιφροσύνῃ θείᾳ πῶς ἦν τοῖς αὐτοῖς
εὔλογον οἰκειοῦσθαι πάλιν; πῶς δὲ τὸν ἔθνους
καὶ γένους ἑτέρου μέλλοντα ἡγεμόνα ἔσεσθαι
προσκληροῦσθαι τῷ παλαιῷ; οὐ γὰρ ἂν ἐχαρίζετο
καινὸν τρόπον τινὰ καὶ νέον ἔθνος καὶ γένος αὐτῷ
ὁ θεός, εἰ μὴ τοῦ ἀρχαίου κατὰ τὸ παντελὲς
279 ἀπεσχοίνιζεν. ἐθνάρχης γὰρ καὶ γενάρχης ὡς
ἀληθῶς ἐστιν οὗτος, ἀφ' οὗ καθάπερ ἀπὸ ῥίζης
τὸ σκεπτικὸν καὶ θεωρητικὸν τῶν τῆς φύσεως
πραγμάτων ἀνέβλαστεν ἔρνος, ὄνομα Ἰσραήλ·
ἐπεὶ καὶ " τὰ παλαιὰ ἐκ προσώπου νέων ἐκφέρειν "
διείρηται. ποῦ γὰρ ἀρχαιολογίας ἔτι καὶ παλαιῶν
καὶ κατημαξευμένων ἐθῶν ὄφελος, οἷς ἐξαπιναίως
οὐ προσδοκήσασιν ἀθρόα καὶ νέα ὤμβρησεν ἀγαθά;
280   LVII. πατέρας οὖν οὐχ ὧν μετ-
ανάστατος ἐγένετο ἡ ψυχὴ καλεῖ τοὺς ἐν τοῖς
Χαλδαϊκοῖς κατορωρυγμένους μνήμασιν, ἀλλ' ὡς
μὲν ἔνιοί φασιν, ἥλιον καὶ σελήνην καὶ τοὺς ἄλλους
ἀστέρας—τὴν γὰρ τῶν κατὰ γῆν ἁπάντων γένεσιν
διὰ τούτων λόγος ἔχει συνίστασθαι,—ὡς δέ τινες
νομίζουσι, τὰς ἀρχετύπους ἰδέας, τὰ νοητὰ καὶ
ἀόρατα ἐκεῖνα τῶν αἰσθητῶν καὶ ὁρωμένων τούτων
παραδείγματα, πρὸς ἃ τὴν τοῦ σοφοῦ διάνοιαν
281 μετοικίζεσθαι.   τινὲς δὲ πατέρας ὑπ-
ετόπασαν εἰρῆσθαι τὰς τέτταρας ἀρχάς τε καὶ
δυνάμεις, ἐξ ὧν συνέστηκεν ὁ κόσμος, γῆν ὕδωρ
ἀέρα καὶ πῦρ· εἰς γὰρ ταύτας ἕκαστον τῶν γενο-
282 μένων φασὶν ἀναλύεσθαι δεόντως. καθάπερ γὰρ

ᵃ See note on *De Sac.* 79.
ᵇ Mangey took this to mean " whose souls have departed,"
" quorum animae demigrarunt," and he might have alleged
in support *De Sac.* 10 τὴν πρὸς τὸν ὄντα μετανάστασιν ψυχῆς of

very persons from whom he had been alienated by the
forethought of God ? Or that he who was to be the
captain of another race and nation should be associated with that of a former age ? God would not
bestow on him a fresh and in a sense a novel race and
nation, if he were not cutting him right adrift from
the old. Surely he is indeed the founder of the nation 279
and the race, since from him as root sprang the young
plant called Israel, which observes and contemplates
all the things of nature. So we are told to bear out
the old from the face of the new (Lev. xxvi. 10).[a]
Rightly, for how shall they on whom the rain of new
blessings has fallen in all its abundance, sudden and
unlooked for, still find profit in old-world lore and the
ruts of ancient customs ? LVII. No ; by 280
" fathers " he does not mean those whom the
pilgrim soul has left behind,[b] those who lie buried in
the sepulchres of Chaldaea, but possibly, as some say,
the sun, moon and other stars to which it is held that
all things on earth owe their birth and framing, or,
as others think, the archetypal ideas which, invisible
and intelligible *there*, are the patterns of things visible
and sensible *here*—the ideas in which, as they say, the
mind of the Sage finds its new home.
Others again have surmised that by " fathers " are 281
meant the four first principles and potentialities, from
which the world has been framed, earth, water, air
and fire. For into these, they say, each thing that has
come into being is duly resolved. Just as nouns and 282

Moses' death. But apart from the singular ψυχή, such a
description of the death of the " fathers " would be pointless
here, and the allegorical use of μετανίστασθαι and kindred
words throughout this meditation (*e.g.* § 274) leaves no doubt
that the words are to be taken as in the translation.

ὀνόματα καὶ ῥήματα καὶ τὰ λόγου μέρη πάντα
συνέστηκε μὲν ἐκ τῶν τῆς γραμματικῆς στοιχείων,
ἀναλύεται δὲ πάλιν εἰς ἔσχατα ἐκεῖνα, τὸν αὐτὸν
τρόπον ἕκαστος ἡμῶν συγκριθεὶς ἐκ τῶν τεττάρων
καὶ δανεισάμενος ἀφ' ἑκάστης οὐσίας μικρὰ
[514] μόρια, | καθ' ὡρισμένας περιόδους καιρῶν ἐκτίνει
τὸ δάνειον, εἰ μέν τι ξηρὸν εἴη, ἀποδιδοὺς γῇ, εἰ
δέ τι ὑγρόν, ὕδατι, εἰ δὲ ψυχρόν, ἀέρι, εἰ δ' ἔν-
283 θερμον, πυρί. τὰ μὲν σωματικὰ ταῦτα, τὸ δὲ
νοερὸν καὶ οὐράνιον τῆς ψυχῆς γένος πρὸς αἰθέρα
τὸν καθαρώτατον ὡς πατέρα ἀφίξεται. πέμπτη
γάρ, ὡς ὁ τῶν ἀρχαίων λόγος, ἔστω τις οὐσία
κυκλοφορητική, τῶν τεττάρων κατὰ τὸ κρεῖττον
διαφέρουσα, ἐξ ἧς οἵ τε ἀστέρες καὶ ὁ σύμπας
οὐρανὸς ἔδοξε γεγενῆσθαι, ἧς κατ' ἀκόλουθον
θετέον καὶ τὴν ἀνθρωπίνην ψυχὴν ἀπόσπασμα.

284 LVIII. Τὸ δὲ " μετ' εἰρήνης τραφεὶς " οὐκ
ἀπὸ σκοποῦ προσδιώρισται, ἀλλ' ὅτι σχεδὸν τὸ
πλεῖστον ἀνθρώπων γένος ἐπὶ πολέμῳ καὶ τοῖς
ἐκ πολέμου κακοῖς πᾶσι τρέφεται. πόλεμος δ' ὁ
μὲν ἀπὸ τῶν ἐκτός ἐστιν, ὃν ἀδοξία καὶ πενία καὶ
δυσγένεια καὶ τὰ ὁμοιότροπα ἐπάγουσιν, ὁ δ' ἀπὸ
τῶν ἐμφυλίων, κατὰ μὲν τὸ σῶμα ἀσθένειαι, λῶβαι,
πηρώσεις παντελεῖς καὶ κηρῶν σωρὸς ἄλλων
ἀμυθήτων, κατὰ δὲ τὴν ψυχὴν πάθη, νοσήματα,
ἀρρωστήματα, αἱ[1] ἀφροσύνης καὶ ἀδικίας καὶ τῶν
ὁμοτυράννων χαλεπαὶ καὶ βαρύταται ἐπαναστάσεις
285 καὶ ἀκαθαίρετοι δυναστεῖαι. " μετ' εἰρήνης οὖν

---

[1] My correction for ms. and Pap.? δι': Wend. proposed
ἔτι δ'.

---

[a] στοιχεῖα being the regular term for the letters of the
alphabet.   [b] See App. p. 575.

verbs and all parts of speech which are composed of the " elements " in the grammatical sense [a] are finally resolved into the same, so too each of us is composed of the four mundane elements, borrowing small fragments from the substance of each, and this debt he repays when the appointed time-cycles are completed, rendering the dry in him to earth, the wet to water, the cold to air, and the warm to fire.[b] These all 283 belong to the body, but the soul whose nature is intellectual and celestial will depart to find a father in ether, the purest of the substances.[c] For we may suppose that, as the men of old declared, there is a fifth substance, moving in a circle,[b] differing by its superior quality from the four. Out of this they thought the stars and the whole of heaven had been made and deduced as a natural consequence that the human soul also was a fragment thereof.

LVIII. The words " nourished with peace " are 284 not a pointless addition, but mean that the greater part of the human race are with little exception " nourished " for war and all its attendant evils. Now war sometimes arises from things outside us, waged against us by ill-repute and poverty and mean birth and the like. Sometimes it arises from intestine enemies—in the body, sicknesses, maimings, complete disablements of the senses and numberless other calamities piled on each other; in the soul, passions, diseases and infirmities of mind, the fierce and bitter insurrections, the inexpugnable despotisms of folly and injustice and their fellow usurpers. So, then, if a man be " nourished with peace " he 285

[c] *i.e.* Philo is willing to accept this explanation of " fathers," if with the four elements for the body is coupled the fifth for the soul.

τραφεὶς '' γαληνὸν καὶ εὔδιον κτησάμενος βίον,
εὐδαίμον' ὡς ἀληθῶς καὶ μακάριον . . . [1]
πότε οὖν τοῦτο συμβήσεται; ὅταν εὐοδῇ μὲν τὰ
ἐκτὸς πρὸς εὐπορίαν καὶ εὐδοξίαν, εὐοδῇ δὲ τὰ
σώματος πρὸς ὑγίειάν τε καὶ ἰσχύν, εὐοδῇ δὲ τὰ
286 ψυχῆς πρὸς ἀπόλαυσιν ἀρετῶν. χρῄζει γὰρ ἕκαστον
οἰκείων δορυφόρων· δορυφορεῖται δὲ σῶμα μὲν
εὐδοξίᾳ καὶ περιουσίᾳ καὶ ἀφθονίᾳ πλούτου, ψυχὴ
δὲ τῷ τοῦ σώματος ὁλοκλήρῳ καὶ κατὰ πάντα
ὑγιεινῷ, ὁ δὲ νοῦς ὑπὸ τῶν ἐν ταῖς ἐπιστήμαις
θεωρημάτων· ἐπεὶ ὅτι γε εἰρήνης οὐχ ἦν αἱ πόλεις
ἄγουσι μέμνηται, σαφές ἐστι τοῖς ἐντυγχάνουσι
ταῖς ἱεραῖς γραφαῖς· μεγάλους ⟨γὰρ⟩ καὶ βαρεῖς
πολέμους Ἀβραὰμ ἀνεδέξατο, οὓς καθῃρηκὼς
287 φαίνεται. καὶ ἡ τῆς πατρῴας μέντοι γῆς ἀπόλειψις
μετανισταμένῳ καὶ πάλιν οἰκῆσαι μὴ δυναμένῳ,
φορουμένῳ δὲ ὧδε κἀκεῖσε καὶ ἐρήμους καὶ
ἀτριβεῖς ὁδοὺς ἀλωμένῳ τῷ μὴ θεοπροπίοις καί
τισι θεσφάτοις πεπιστευκότι βαρὺς ἦν πόλεμος.
ἀλλ' ἔδει γὰρ καὶ τρίτον τι τῶν φοβερῶν προσ-
επιδαψιλεύσασθαι, λιμόν, μεταναστάσεως καὶ
288 πολέμου κακὸν χεῖρον. ποίαν οὖν εἰρήνην ἤγαγεν;
τὸ γάρ, οἶμαι, μετανίστασθαι καὶ ἀνίδρυτον εἶναι
καὶ βασιλέων ἀμάχοις ἐναντιοῦσθαι δυνάμεσι[2] καὶ
λιμῷ πιέζεσθαι πόλεμον οὐχ ἕνα, πολλοὺς δὲ καὶ
289 πολυτρόπους ἔοικε μηνύειν. ἀλλ' ἔν γε ταῖς δι'
ὑπονοιῶν ἀποδόσεσιν εἰρήνης ἀκράτου δεῖγμα
ἕκαστον αὐτῶν εἶναι συμβέβηκε· παθῶν γὰρ |

[1] The sentence seems imperfect as it stands; either read
as Mangey ⟨ὁ⟩ γαληνὸν κτλ. sc. ἐστι or more likely a verb has
been lost: Wend. ἀπελεύσεται (or perhaps ἄπεισι after τραφεὶς).
[2] MSS. and Pap. δυνάμενον or μὴ δυνάμενον: Mangey's text
has βασιλεῦσιν . . . μὴ δυνάμενον.

will depart, having gained a calm, unclouded life, a life of true bliss and happiness.   When will this be found? When there is welfare outside us, welfare in the body, welfare in the soul, the first bringing ease of circumstance and good repute, the second health and strength, the third delight in virtues. For each part needs its own proper guards.[a] 286 The body is guarded by good repute and unstinted abundance of wealth, the soul by the complete health and soundness of the body, the mind by the acquired lore of the various forms of knowledge. Such is the meaning of the text. For that he is thinking of a peace other than that which states enjoy is clear to those who are versed in the holy Scriptures. For Abraham underwent great and severe wars, which he is shewn to have fought to the finish. And 287 further, the mere leaving of his fatherland, to emigrate without any possibility of dwelling there again, to be borne hither and thither and to wander over desolate and untrodden roads were in itself a grievous war for one who had no divine message or promise wherein to trust. Still more he had, to crown this profusion of terrors, a third, famine (Gen. xii. 10), an evil worse than migration and war. What kind 288 of peace, then, was his? For surely to be a homeless emigrant, to be confronted by kings with overwhelming forces and to feel the stress of famine would seem to indicate not one war only, but many and manifold. But if we turn to the allegorical exposi- 289 tion of the words, each of these three proves to be an evidence of peace pure and simple. For dearth and

---

[a] *Cf. De Conf.* 18 f.

[515] ἔνδεια καὶ λιμὸς καὶ καθαίρεσις ἐχθρῶν ἀδικημάτων
καὶ μετανάστασις ἀπὸ Χαλδαϊκῆς δόξης πρὸς τὴν
φιλόθεον, τουτέστιν ἀπὸ τοῦ γεγονότος αἰσθητοῦ
πρὸς τὸ νοητὸν καὶ πεποιηκὸς αἴτιον, εὐνομίαν καὶ
εὐστάθειαν κατασκευάζουσιν.

290 Ὑπισχνεῖται δὲ τῷ τοιαύτην ἄγοντι εἰρήνην
καλὸν γῆρας, οὐ δήπου τὴν πολυχρόνιον ἀλλὰ τὴν
μετὰ φρονήσεως ζωήν· τὸ γὰρ εὐήμερον πολυετίας
κρεῖττον, ὅσῳ καὶ βραχύτερον φῶς σκότους αἰωνίου.
μίαν γὰρ ἡμέραν ὑγιῶς εἶπέ τις προφητικὸς ἀνὴρ
βούλεσθαι βιῶναι μετ' ἀρετῆς ἢ μυρία ἔτη ἐν σκιᾷ
θανάτου, θάνατον[1] μέντοι τῶν φαύλων αἰνιττόμενος
291 βίον. τὸ δὲ αὐτὸ καὶ νῦν ἔργοις μᾶλλον ἢ ῥήμασι[2]
διασυνίστησι Μωυσῆς· ὃν γὰρ ἀναγράφει γήρᾳ
χρησόμενον καλῷ, τῶν πρὸ αὐτοῦ σχεδὸν ἁπάντων
ὀλιγοχρονιώτατον εἰσήγαγε, φιλοσοφῶν καὶ διδάσκων ἡμᾶς, τίς ὁ πρὸς ἀλήθειαν εὐγήρως ἐστίν,
ἵνα μὴ πολὺν[3] τῦφον ἐπὶ τοῦ φανεροῦ σώματός
ποτε ἀποδεξώμεθα γέμοντα αἰσχύνης καὶ πολλῶν
ὀνειδῶν, ἀλλ' εὐβουλίαν καὶ σταθερότητα ψυχῆς
ἰδόντες τὸ γέρως ἀδελφὸν καὶ παρώνυμον καλὸν
292 γῆρας ἐπιφημίσωμέν τε καὶ μαρτυρήσωμεν. δογματικῶς οὖν ἄκουε κατὰ τὸν νομοθέτην μόνον τὸν
ἀστεῖον εὐγήρων καὶ μακροβιώτατον, ὀλιγοχρονιώ-

---

[1] Pap. θανατον: mss. σκιὰν: perhaps θανάτου σκιὰν.
[2] Pap. εν τοις . . ῥημασι: mss. ἔργον . . . ῥῆμα.
[3] Pap. πολυ: mss. παλαιὸν (πολιὸν). See App. p. 575.

famine of passions, the rout of enemies in the shape of wrongdoings, the migration from the creed of the Chaldeans to the creed of the lovers of God, that is, from the created and sensible to the intelligible and creative Cause—these build up the fabric of good order and stability.

To him who enjoys a peace like this Moses 290 promises a goodly old age, not meaning, we may be sure, the life of long duration, but the life lived wisely. For the welfare of a day ranks as far above multitude of years, as the briefer daylight above an eternity of darkness. It was a wholesome saying of a man of prophetic gifts that he would rather live a single day with virtue than ten thousand years in the shadow of death (Ps. lxxxiv. [lxxxiii.] 11)[a] where under the figure of death he indicates the life of the wicked. And Moses in the present instance shews 291 the same by the facts he records rather than by words. For this Abraham, whom he here describes as destined to a goodly old age, is represented by him as more short-lived than practically all who went before him. Thus he shews to us, who are his scholars in wisdom, who it is whose old age is happy, to the end that we should not look with favour on all the abounding vanity of the outward body, a vanity full of shame and rich in reproaches, but recognizing in right judgement and stability of soul that goodly old age, which both in name and nature is twin brother of " reward,"[b] give it its rightful title and testify to its truth. Learn then thy lesson and hear 292 how the lawgiver tells us that happy old age and longest span of life is only for the good, but briefest

---

[a] See App. p. 575.
[b] For the play on γῆρας and γέρας cf. De Sobr. 16.

τατον δὲ τὸν φαῦλον, ἀποθνῄσκειν ἀεὶ μανθάνοντα,
μᾶλλον δὲ τὴν ἀρετῆς ζωὴν ἤδη τετελευτηκότα.

293 LIX. Λέγεται δ' ἑξῆς· " τετάρτη δὲ γενεᾷ
ἀποστραφήσονται ὧδε," οὐχ ἵνα αὐτὸ μόνον
μηνυθῇ χρόνος, ἐν ᾧ τὴν ἱερὰν οἰκήσουσι γῆν, ἀλλὰ
καὶ ὑπὲρ τοῦ τελείαν ἀποκατάστασιν ψυχῆς παραστῆσαι. γίνεται δὲ ὡσανεὶ τετάρτῃ γενεᾷ· ὃν
294 δὲ τρόπον, ἄξιον συνδιασκέψασθαι. ἀποκυηθὲν τὸ
βρέφος ἄχρι τῆς πρώτης ἑπταετίας ἐν ἡλικίᾳ τῇ
παιδικῇ ψυχῆς ἀκραιφνοῦς μεμοίραται, λείῳ
μάλιστα ἐμφεροῦς κηρῷ, τοῖς ἀγαθῶν καὶ κακῶν
χαρακτῆρσι μήπω τετυπωμένης· καὶ γὰρ ὅσα
γράφεσθαι δοκεῖ, ὑγρότητι ἐπαλειφόμενα συγχεῖται.
295 πρώτη μὲν ἥδε ὡσανεὶ γενεὰ ψυχῆς· δευτέρα δέ,
ἥτις μετὰ τὴν παιδικὴν ἡλικίαν κακοῖς ἄρχεται
συζῆν, ἅ τε ἐξ ἑαυτῆς εἴωθε γεννᾶν ψυχὴ καὶ ὅσα
παρὰ τῶν ἄλλων ἀσμένη δέχεται. διδάσκαλοί τε
γὰρ ἁμαρτημάτων μυρίοι, τίτθαι καὶ παιδαγωγοὶ
καὶ γονεῖς καὶ οἱ κατὰ πόλεις γεγραμμένοι καὶ
ἄγραφοι νόμοι θαυμάζοντες ἃ χρὴ γελᾶσθαι, καὶ
ἄνευ τῶν διδαξόντων αὐτομαθής ἐστιν αὐτὴ πρὸς
τὰ ὑπαίτια, ὡς ὑπ' εὐφορίας ἀεὶ κακῶν βρίθειν.
296 " ἔγκειται " γάρ φησι Μωυσῆς " ἡ διάνοια τοῦ
[516] ἀνθρώπου | ἐπιμελῶς ἐπὶ τὰ πονηρὰ ἐκ νεότητος."
ἥδ' ἐστὶν ἡ ἐπαρατοτάτη γενεὰ μὲν συμβολικῶς,
κυρίως δὲ ἡλικία, καθ' ἣν τό τε σῶμα ἡβᾷ καὶ ἡ
ψυχὴ πεφύσηται, τῶν ἐντυφομένων ἀναρριπιζο-

---

[a] The phrase is apparently intended to be the converse of
the Platonic thought of the wise man studying to die to the
body, *cf. De Gig.* 14. But it seems strange, and Mangey
suggested λανθάνοντα. Possibly φθάνοντα, which would carry
on the thought of ὀλιγοχρονιώτατον.

is the life of the wicked, since he is ever studying to die[a] or rather has died already to the life of virtue.

LIX. Next we have " but in the fourth generation 293 they shall come back hither " (Gen. xv. 16). These words are meant not only to state the date at which they should inhabit the holy land, but to bring before us the thought of the complete restoration of the soul. That restoration may be said to come in the fourth generation. How it comes deserves our careful consideration. The infant from the day of its 294 birth for the first seven years, that is through the age of childhood, possesses only the simplest elements of soul, a soul which closely resembles smooth wax and has not yet received any impression of good or evil, for such marks as it appears to receive are smoothed over and confused by its fluidity. This is 295 what we may call the first generation of the soul. The second is that which follows childhood and begins to associate with evils, both these engendered by the soul of its own motion, and those which are willingly accepted at the hands of others. For the instructors to sin are legion, nurses and " pedagogues "[b] and parents and the laws of cities, written and unwritten, which extol what should be derided ; and apart from and before such instruction, the soul is its own pupil in the school of guilt, so that it is throughout weighed down by its capacity for producing ills. " The mind 296 of man," says Moses, " is carefully intent upon wickedness from youth " (Gen. viii. 21). The curse is heaviest on this " generation," to use the figurative term for the literal " age," in which the body is in its bloom and the soul inflated, when the smouldering passions are being fanned into a flame, consuming

[b] Or " home-tutors."

μένων παθῶν, '' ἅλως τε καὶ ἀστάχυς καὶ πεδία ''
297 καὶ ὅσα ἂν τύχῃ καταπιμπράντων. ταύτην τὴν
ἐπίνοσον γενεὰν ἢ ἡλικίαν ὑπό τινος τρίτης οἷα
ὑπὸ ἰατρικῆς φιλοσοφίας νοσηλευθῆναι χρή, κατ-
επασθεῖσαν λόγοις ὑγιεινοῖς καὶ σωτηρίοις, δι' ὧν
κένωσιν μὲν ἐνδέξεται τῆς ἀμέτρου τῶν ἁμαρτημάτων πλησμονῆς, πλήρωσιν δὲ λιμηρᾶς κενώσεως
τῶν κατορθωμάτων καὶ ἐρημίας δεινῆς.

298 μετὰ τὴν θεραπείαν οὖν ταύτην γενεᾷ τετάρτῃ
φύεται ψυχῇ δύναμίς τε καὶ ῥώμη κατὰ τὴν τῆς
φρονήσεως βεβαιοτάτην ἀνάληψιν καὶ τὸ ἐν ἁπάσαις
ἀρεταῖς ἀκλινές τε καὶ πάγιον. τοῦτ' ἐστὶ τὸ
λεγόμενον· '' τετάρτῃ δὲ γενεᾷ ἀποστραφήσονται
ὧδε.'' κατὰ γὰρ τὸν δειχθέντα τέταρτον ἀριθμὸν
ἀποστραφεῖσα τοῦ διαμαρτάνειν ἡ ψυχὴ κληρονόμος
299 ἀποδείκνυται σοφίας. πρῶτος μὲν γὰρ ἀριθμός,
καθ' ὃν οὔτε ἀγαθῶν οὔτε κακῶν λαβεῖν ἔννοιαν
ἔστιν, ἀτυπώτου τῆς ψυχῆς ὑπαρχούσης· δεύτερος
δέ, καθ' ὃν φορᾷ τῶν ἁμαρτημάτων χρώμεθα·
τρίτος δέ, ἐν ᾧ θεραπευόμεθα, τὰ νοσερὰ δι-
ωθούμενοι καὶ τὴν ἀκμὴν τῶν παθῶν ἀφηβῶντες·
τέταρτος δέ, ἐν ᾧ παντελοῦς ὑγιείας καὶ ῥώσεως
μεταποιούμεθα, ὁπότε ἀποστρεφόμενοι τὰ φαῦλα
τοῖς καλοῖς ἐγχειρεῖν δοκοῦμεν, πρότερον δὲ οὐκ
ἔξεστι.

300 LX. Τὸ δὲ ἄχρι τίνος, αὐτὸς μηνύσει λέγων·
'' οὔπω γὰρ ἀναπεπλήρωνται αἱ ἀνομίαι τῶν
Ἀμορραίων.'' δίδωσι δὲ ἀφορμὴν τοῖς ἀσθενε-
στέροις τὰ τοιαῦτα, ὡς ὑπολαμβάνειν, ὅτι Μωυσῆς
εἱμαρμένην καὶ ἀνάγκην ὡς αἰτίας τῶν γινομένων

" threshing-floor and standing corn and fields " (Ex. xxii. 6) and whatever lies in their path. This 297 stricken generation or age must be tended on its sickbed by a third, taking the form of philosophy with its healing art, and put under the spell of sound and salutary reasonings. Through these it will be able to void the vast overload of sins and to fill its void, its starvation, its fearful emptiness of right actions.   So after this healing treatment 298 there grows in the fourth generation within the soul power and vigour, because it has fully and firmly apprehended good sense and is immovably established in all virtues. This is what is meant by the saying " in the fourth generation they shall turn back hither." For under that fourth number, to which he points, the soul turns back from sinning and is declared the heir of wisdom. The first number is 299 that under which it is impossible to form any conception of good or ill and the soul receives no impressions. Under the second we experience the onrush of sin. The third is that in which we receive the healing treatment, when we cast off the elements of sickness and the crisis of passion is reached and passed. The fourth is that in which we make good our claim to complete health and strength, when we feel that we are turning back from wickedness and laying our hands to the good. Till then we may not do so.[a]

LX. How that "until" is fixed he will himself 300 shew us, when he says " for the iniquities of the Amorites are not yet fulfilled " (Gen. xv. 16). Such words as these give weaker minds a handle for supposing that Moses represents fate and necessity as

---

[a] For the thought of §§ 293-299 cf. De Sacr. 18 f. and note.

301 ἁπάντων εἰσάγει. χρὴ δὲ μὴ ἀγνοεῖν, ὅτι
ἀκολουθίαν μὲν καὶ εἱρμὸν καὶ ἐπιπλοκὰς αἰτιῶν
ἅτε φιλόσοφος καὶ θεοφράδμων ἀνὴρ οἶδε, τούτοις δ' οὐκ ἀνάπτει τὰς τῶν γινομένων αἰτίας.
ἐφαντασιώθη γὰρ πρεσβύτερον ἄλλο ἐποχούμενον
τοῖς ὅλοις ἡνιόχου τρόπον ἢ κυβερνήτου· πηδαλιουχεῖ γὰρ τὸ κοινὸν τοῦ κόσμου σκάφος, ᾧ τὰ
πάντα ἐμπλεῖ, καὶ τὸ πτηνὸν ἅρμα, τὸν σύμπαντα
οὐρανόν, ἡνιοχεῖ χρώμενον αὐτεξουσίῳ καὶ αὐτο-
302 κράτορι βασιλείᾳ. τί οὖν καὶ περὶ
τούτων λεκτέον; ἑρμηνεύονται Ἀμορραῖοι λα-
λοῦντες, τὸ δὲ μέγιστον ἀγαθὸν ἀνθρώπῳ δωρηθὲν
ὑπὸ φύσεως, τὸν λόγον, μυρίοι τῶν λαβόντων
διέφθειραν ἀχαρίστως καὶ ἀπίστως τῇ δούσῃ
προσενεχθέντες. οὗτοι δέ εἰσιν οἱ γόητες, οἱ
κόλακες, οἱ πιθανῶν σοφισμάτων εὑρεταί, |
[517] φενακίσαι καὶ παρακρούσασθαι μόνον εὖ εἰδότες,
τοῦ ἀψευδεῖν οὐ πεφροντικότες. ἐπιτηδεύουσι
μέντοι καὶ ἀσάφειαν, ἀσάφεια δὲ βαθὺ σκότος ἐν
303 λόγῳ, κλέπταις δὲ συνεργὸν τὸ σκότος. οὗ χάριν
Μωυσῆς τὸν ἀρχιερέα δηλώσει καὶ ἀληθείᾳ δια-
κεκόσμηκεν, ἀρίδηλον ἀξιῶν εἶναι καὶ ἀληθῆ τὸν
τοῦ σπουδαίου λόγον. οἱ δὲ πολλοὶ τὸν ἄδηλον καὶ
ψευδῆ μεταδιώκουσιν, ᾧ συνεπιγράφεται πᾶς ὁ
τῶν ἀγελαίων καὶ ἠμελημένων ἀνθρώπων ἀπατώ-
304 μενος ὄχλος. ἕως μὲν οὖν " οὐκ ἀναπεπλήρωται
τὰ ἁμαρτήματα τῶν Ἀμορραίων," τουτέστι τῶν
σοφιστικῶν λόγων διὰ τὸ ἀνεξέλεγκτον, ἀλλ' ἔτι

ᵃ Presumably the critics meant that the text represented
God as wishing to bring the people to the Holy Land
earlier, but unable to do so till some other event had taken
place.

the cause of all events.[a] But we should recognize 301
that while as a philosopher and interpreter of God he
understood that causes have their sequence, connexion and interplay, he did not ascribe the causation of events to these subsidiary factors. He en-
visaged something else higher than and antecedent
to these, a Someone who is borne on the universe
like a charioteer or pilot. He steers the common
bark of the world, in which all things sail ; He guides
that winged chariot, the whole heaven, exerting an
absolute sovereignty which knows no authority
but its own.   What then must be our 302
explanation of these particular words ? This.—The
name Amorites is by interpretation " talkers."
Now speech is the greatest boon given by nature to
mankind, but the gift has been marred by thousands
of the recipients who have dealt ungratefully and
faithlessly with the power which gave it. Such are
impostors, flatterers, inventors of cunning plausibilities, who know well how to cheat and mislead, but
that only, and have no thought for honest truth.
And further, they practise a lack of clearness, which
in speech is profound darkness, and darkness is the
fellow-worker of thieves. It is for this reason that 303
Moses adorned the high priest with Manifestation and
Truth[b] (Ex. xxviii. 26), judging that the speech of the
man of worth should be transparent and true. But
the speech which most aim at is obscure and false,
and this is accepted by all the deluded multitude of
common and unmeritable men. So long then as 304
" the sins of the Amorites," that is of sophistical
arguments, " are not fulfilled," because they have

---

[b] The Urim and Thummim of the E.V. (Ex. xxviii. 30), *cf.*
Leg. All. iii. 123 f.

ολκὸν[1] ἔχοντα δύναμιν ταῖς πιθανότησιν ἡμᾶς
ἐπάγεται, [καὶ] ἀποστραφῆναι καὶ καταλιπεῖν
αὐτὰ οὐ δυνάμενοι τῷ δελεάζεσθαι καταμένομεν.
305 ἐὰν δὲ πᾶσαι αἱ ψευδεῖς πιθανότητες
διελεγχθῶσιν ὑπὸ τῶν ἀληθῶν πίστεων καὶ πλήρεις
αὐτῶν καὶ ἐπιχειλεῖς αἱ ἁμαρτίαι περιφανῶσιν,
ἀποδρασόμεθα ἀμεταστρεπτὶ καὶ μονονοὺ τὰ
ἀπόγαια ἀράμενοι τῆς τῶν ψευσμάτων καὶ σοφισμάτων χώρας ἐξαναχθησόμεθα, τοῖς ἀληθείας
ναυλοχωτάτοις ὑποδρόμοις καὶ λιμέσιν ἐνορμί-
306 σασθαι ἐπειγόμενοι. τοιοῦτον δὴ τὸ δηλούμενον
ὑπὸ τῆς προτάσεως· ἀμήχανον γὰρ ἀποστραφῆναι
καὶ μισῆσαι καὶ καταλιπεῖν τὸ πιθανὸν ψεῦδος, εἰ
μὴ τὸ περὶ αὐτὸ ἁμάρτημα πλῆρες ἀναφανείη καὶ
τέλειον· ἀναφανεῖται δὲ ἐκ τοῦ μὴ περιέργως[2]
διελεγχθῆναι κατὰ τὴν τοῦ ἀληθοῦς ἀντίταξιν καὶ
βεβαίωσιν.

307 LXI. Λέγει δὲ ἑξῆς· " ἐπεὶ δὲ ἐγίνετο ὁ ἥλιος
πρὸς δυσμαῖς, φλὸξ ἐγένετο," δηλῶν ὅτι ἀρετὴ
πρᾶγμά ἐστιν ὀψίγονον καὶ μήν, ὡς ἔφασάν τινες,
πρὸς αὐταῖς ταῖς τοῦ βίου δυσμαῖς βεβαιούμενον.
ἀρετὴν δὲ ἀπεικάζει φλογί· καθάπερ γὰρ ἡ φλὸξ
καίει μὲν τὴν παραβληθεῖσαν ὕλην, φωτίζει δὲ τὸν
γείτονα ἀέρα, τὸν αὐτὸν τρόπον ἐμπίπρησι μὲν τὰ
ἁμαρτήματα ἡ ἀρετή, φέγγους δὲ τὴν ὅλην ἀνα-
308 πίμπλησι διάνοιαν. ἀλλὰ γὰρ ἔτι τῶν
ἀδιαιρέτων καὶ ἀμερίστων λόγων ἐπικρατούντων
ταῖς πιθανότησιν, οὓς Ἀμορραίους ἀνακαλεῖ,
περιφανεστάτην καὶ ἄσκιον αὐγὴν ἰδεῖν οὐ δυνά-

---

[1] mss. and Pap. ἔτι ἐνδίολκον, a word otherwise unknown,
though retained in the lexica. It is difficult to see on what
principles it is formed.

not been refuted, but still in virtue of their powers of attraction seduce us with their plausibilities, while their enticements make us powerless to turn from and leave them, we remain where we are.[a]

But if ever all the plausible fallacies are refuted by 305 true beliefs, and thus the cup is filled to the brim and their sins appear in their true light, we shall run for our lives without a backward glance, or (shall we say ?) slip our cable and sail clean away from the land of falsehood and sophistry, eager to find an anchorage in the most secure of all roadsteads, the haven of truth. Such is the lesson expressed in the 306 problem here presented. For it is impossible to turn back from, to hate, to leave the plausible falsehood, unless the sin involved in it be revealed complete and consummated. And this revelation will be made when, confronted by the firm evidence of truth, it receives the much-needed [b] refutation.

LXI. He continues, " but when the sun was at its 307 setting a flame arose " (Gen. xv. 17). Thus he shews that virtue is a late birth and indeed, as some have said, established firmly only at the very close of life's day. He likens virtue to a flame, for just as the flame consumes the fuel which lies at hand but gives light to the air in its neighbourhood, so virtue burns up the sins but fills the whole mind with its beam.

But while those unanalysed and un- 308 classified ways of thinking, which he calls Amorites, govern us with their plausibilities, we cannot see the

---

[a] Or " remain unable," etc.
[b] Lit. " not unnecessarily." Or, if we read παρέργως (see crit. note), " thoroughly and carefully."

---

[2] So Pap. and some mss.: others μὴ παρέργως, a very common collocation in Philo, cf. (e.g.) § 40. So Mangey.

μεθα· κλιβάνου δ' εἰλικρινὲς πῦρ οὐκ ἔχοντος, ἀλλ'
ὡς αὐτὸς ἔφη καπνιζομένου τρόπον διακείμεθα,
σπινθῆρσι μὲν τῆς ἐπιστήμης ὑποτυφόμενοι, μήπω
δὲ καθαρῷ πυρὶ δοκιμασθῆναι καὶ κραταιωθῆναι
309 δυνάμενοι. πολλὴ δὲ τῷ σπείραντι τοὺς σπινθῆρας
χάρις, ἵνα μὴ νεκρῶν τρόπον σωμάτων ὁ νοῦς ὑπὸ
παθῶν καταψυχθῇ, ἀλλ' ἔνθερμος ὢν καὶ χλιαινό-
μενος ὑπεκκαύμασιν ἀρετῆς ζωπυρῆται μέχρι τοῦ
τὴν εἰς πῦρ ἱερόν, ὡς ὁ Ναδὰβ καὶ Ἀβιούδ,
310 δέξασθαι μεταβολήν.   καπνὸς δὲ γίνεται
[518] μὲν πρὸ πυρός, | δακρύειν δὲ βιάζεται τοὺς
πλησιάζοντας. ἀμφότερα δὲ φιλεῖ συμβαίνειν·
τοῖς τε γὰρ ἀρετῆς ἀγγελοῖς προσχωροῦντες[1]
τελειότητα ἐλπίζομεν, καὶ εἰ μήπω δυναίμεθα
τυχεῖν αὐτῆς, οὐκ ἀδακρυτὶ διάγομεν ἀνιώμενοι.
πολὺς γὰρ ὅταν ἵμερος ἐντακῇ, πρὸς τὴν τοῦ
ποθουμένου θήραν ἐπισπεύδει καὶ ἄχρι τοῦ συλ-
311 λαβεῖν κατηφεῖν ἀναγκάζει.   κλιβάνῳ
δὲ νῦν ἐξωμοίωσε τὴν ψυχὴν τοῦ φιλομαθοῦς καὶ
ἐλπίδα τελειώσεως ἔχοντος, ἐπειδὴ τροφῆς πεττο-
μένης[2] ἑκάτερον ἀγγεῖόν ἐστιν, ὁ μὲν τῆς διὰ σιτίων
φθαρτῶν, ἡ δὲ τῆς δι' ἀφθάρτων ἀρετῶν.
αἱ δὲ λαμπάδες τοῦ πυρὸς αἱ δαδουχούμεναι τοῦ

---

[1] τοῖς . . ἀγγέλοις mss. and Pap.: Wend. corrects to ταῖς
. . . αὐγαῖς. For προσχωροῦντος (so Wend.) the mss. have
προσχορεύοντες or προχορεύοντες (Pap.?): Mangey ἐγχορεύοντες.
See App. p. 575.

[2] Wend. inserts συγκραταιοῦν from Pap. which apparently
has κραταιουν preceded by a space, or illegibility, of some
kind, which he regards as representing three letters. But
συγκραταιόω is unknown to the lexica, and if it exists must
be transitive, and we should expect τροφήν rather than
τροφῆς. If Pap. is to be followed, I should suggest ὡσεὶ (or

rays in their full unshadowed brightness. We are in the same plight as the furnace which has no clear fire, but to use his own word (Gen. xv. 17) is " smoking." The flickerings of knowledge are smouldering within us, but we cannot as yet bear the strengthening test of pure fire. Yet great thanks are due to 309 Him who sowed these flickering sparks, to the end that the mind should not be chilled by passion like dead bodies, but, warmed and heated by the glowing coals of virtue, be quickened into flame, till it finds its full conversion into sacred fire, like Nadab and Abihu ^a (Lev. x. 2).   Now smoke comes 310 before fire and forces those who approach it to shed tears. Both these, in the moral sphere, are a common experience. When we draw near to the forerunners of virtue we hope for its consummation, and if we cannot yet attain it our days are spent in sorrow and tears. For when some strong absorbing yearning has sunk into us, it urges us on to the quest of the desired object and forces us to be heavy of heart, until it is within our grasp.   Again in this 311 passage he compares the soul of him who loves learning and hopes for its consummation to a furnace or oven, because each serves as a vessel wherein is prepared nourishing food, in the one case the food of corruptible meats, in the other that of incorruptible virtues.   Again the torches of fire borne as in the mystic torch-rite are the judgements of

^a For the construing of the fate of Nadab and Abihu as an exaltation by fire to heaven *cf. Leg. All.* ii. 58.

οἷα) κραταιὸν. But, as in § 76, I have thought it better to omit it.

δαδούχου θεοῦ κρίσεις[1] εἰσίν, αἱ λαμπραὶ καὶ διαυγεῖς,
αἷς ἔθος μέσον τῶν διχοτομημάτων, λέγω δὲ τῶν
ἐναντιοτήτων, ἐξ ὧν ἅπας ὁ κόσμος συνέστηκε,
312 διάγειν. λέγεται γάρ· " λαμπάδες πυρός, αἳ
διῆλθον μέσον τῶν διχοτομημάτων," ἵνα γνῶς,
ὅτι αἱ θεῖαι δυνάμεις διὰ μέσων καὶ πραγμάτων
καὶ σωμάτων ἰοῦσαι φθείρουσι μὲν οὐδέν—μένει
γὰρ ἀπαθῆ τὰ διχοτομήματα,—διαιροῦσι δὲ καὶ
διαστέλλουσι σφόδρα καλῶς τὰς ἑκάστων φύσεις.
313 LXII. Τῆς οὖν τῶν εἰρημένων ἐπιστήμης κληρονόμος δεόντως ἀποδείκνυται ὁ σοφός· " ἐν γὰρ τῇ
ἡμέρᾳ " φησίν " ἐκείνῃ διέθετο κύριος τῷ Ἀβραὰμ
διαθήκην λέγων· τῷ σπέρματί σου δώσω τὴν γῆν
314 ταύτην." ποίαν γῆν δηλοῖ, εἰ μὴ τὴν προειρη-
μένην, ἐφ' ἣν ποιεῖται τὴν ἀναφοράν; ἧς ἐστιν
ὁ καρπὸς κατάληψις ἀσφαλὴς καὶ βεβαία τῆς τοῦ
θεοῦ σοφίας, καθ' ἣν τὰ σύμπαντα τοῖς τομεῦσιν
ἑαυτοῦ διαφυλάττει ἀπαθῆ τὰ ἀγαθὰ κακοῦ κατὰ
315 τὰ ἐπὶ τοῖς τὴν γένεσιν ἀφθάρτοις.[2]   εἶτ'
ἐπιλέγει· " ἀπὸ τοῦ ποταμοῦ Αἰγύπτου ἕως τοῦ
ποταμοῦ τοῦ μεγάλου [ποταμοῦ] Εὐφράτου,"
δηλῶν ὅτι οἱ τέλειοι τὰς μὲν ἀρχὰς ἔχουσιν ἀπὸ
σώματος καὶ αἰσθήσεως καὶ τῶν ὀργανικῶν μερῶν,
ὧν ἄνευ ζῆν οὐκ ἔνεστι—χρήσιμα γὰρ πρὸς τὴν
ἐν τῷ μετὰ σώματος βίῳ παιδείαν,—τὰ δὲ τέλη
ἐπὶ τὴν τοῦ θεοῦ σοφίαν, τὸν μέγαν ὡς ἀληθῶς

---

[1] κρίσεις is the reading of the mss. (Pap. not stated): Wend.
unreasonably, as it seems to me, even if he finds it in Pap.,
corrects to κρίσις.

[2] The last part of this sentence is noted by Wend. as
corrupt. I suggest and have translated καθ' ἣν τὰ σύμπαντα
τοῖς τομεῦσιν ἑαυτοῦ δια⟨κρίνας⟩ φυλάττει ἀπαθῆ τὰ ἀγαθὰ κακοῦ
καθὰ πρέπει τοῖς τὴν γένεσιν ἀφθάρτοις. See App. p. 576.

444

God the torch-bearer, judgements bright and radiant, whose wont it is to range between the half-pieces, that is between the opposites of which the whole world is composed. For we read " torches of fire 312 which passed through between the half-pieces " (Gen. xv. 17). Thus you may know how highly excellent is the work of the Potencies of God as they pass through the midst of material and immaterial things. They destroy nothing—for the half-pieces remain unharmed—but divide and distinguish the nature of each.

LXII. Rightly then is the Sage declared to be the 313 heir of the knowledge of the truths here mentioned. For " on that day," says Moses, " God made a covenant with Abraham, saying, " to thy seed will I give this land " (Gen. xv. 18). What land does he 314 mean, but that which was mentioned before to which he now refers,[a] the land whose fruit is the sure and stedfast apprehension of the wisdom of God, by which through His dividing powers He separates all things and keeps untouched by evil those that are good, as it is meet they should be kept for those who are born to life imperishable?[b] Then 315 he continues, " from the river of Egypt to the great river Euphrates " (Gen. xv. 18). Here he shews how it stands with the perfected. Their perfecting begins with the body and sense and the parts which serve as organs, without which we cannot live, since they are needed for our training while in the life of the body. It ends in the attainment of the wisdom of God, that truly great river, brimming over with

---

[a] *i.e.* in Gen. xv. 17, which was interpreted as wisdom in §§ 98 and 99.

[b] See App. p. 576.

ποταμόν, χαρᾶς καὶ εὐφροσύνης καὶ τῶν ἄλλων
316 πλημμυροῦντα ἀγαθῶν. οὐ γὰρ ἀπὸ τοῦ ποταμοῦ
Εὐφράτου ἕως τοῦ Αἰγύπτου ποταμοῦ τὴν χώραν
περιέγραψεν—οὐ[1] γὰρ ἂν ἀρετὴν εἰς τὰ σωματικὰ
πάθη κατεβίβασεν,—ἀλλ᾽ ἔμπαλιν " ἀπὸ τοῦ
Αἰγύπτου ἕως τοῦ μεγάλου Εὐφράτου." ἀπὸ γὰρ
τῶν θνητῶν αἱ βελτιώσεις γίνονται πρὸς τὰ
ἄφθαρτα.

[1] Perhaps, as Mangey, οὕτως, " for that would have been
to " etc.

joy and gladness [a] and all other blessings.   For note 316
that he does not fix the limits of the land as stretch-
ing from the river Euphrates to the river of Egypt [b]—
he would never have made virtue take a downward
course into the bodily passions—but in the opposite
order, from the river of Egypt to the great Euphrates.
For all progress in good begins with the mortal and
proceeds to the imperishable.

[a] There is evidently a play on the resemblance of Εὐφράτης
and εὐφροσύνη; cf. its description as εὐφραίνοντα τὴν διανοίαν
Leg. All. i. 72.

[b] Or " the river Aegyptus." In the Quaestiones (Gen. iii. 5)
Philo, commenting on this passage, quotes Odyssey xiv. 255
to shew that the old name for the Nile was Egyptus.

ON MATING WITH
THE PRELIMINARY STUDIES

(DE CONGRESSU QUAERENDAE
ERUDITIONIS GRATIA) [a]

[a] I have thought it better not to attempt to alter the traditional Latin title (which is given by Wendland without *quaerendae*), absurd as it is. The subject of the treatise is the training of the mind by the school subjects, the training being termed " mating," or " intercourse," because the union of Abraham with Hagar is the allegorical form in which it is set. The Greek would be better expressed, though possibly not in the best Latin, by " De coniugio cum primordiis erudiendi."

ANALYTICAL INTRODUCTION

THE subject of this treatise is Gen. xvi. 1-6 with some omissions.

1. Now Sarai, Abram's wife, was not bearing to him, and she had a handmaiden, an Egyptian, named Hagar.

2. And Sarai said to Abram : " Behold the Lord hath shut me out from bearing. Go in therefore unto my handmaiden that I may have children from her." And Abram hearkened to the voice of Sarai.

3. And Sarai the wife of Abram, after Abram had dwelt ten years in the land of Canaan, took Hagar, the Egyptian, her handmaid, and gave her to Abram her husband as a wife.

4. And he went in unto Hagar, and she conceived, and she saw that she was with child, and her mistress was dishonoured before her.

5. And Sarai said to Abram, " I am wronged at thy hands. I have given my handmaiden to thy bosom. But seeing that she was with child, I was dishonoured before her. The Lord judge between thee and me."

6. And Abram said to Sarai, " Behold thy hand-maid is in thy hands. Do with her as is pleasing to thee." And Sarai afflicted her.

This treatise, though it has little of the eloquence and spirituality which brighten most of the others, has a special interest of its own. Nowhere else in

451

Philo nor, so far as I know, in any other Greek writer do we find so full a treatment of the Stoic doctrine, that the accepted school course or Encyclia was the proper preparation for philosophy.[a] Apart from this there are many remarks on the value of the different subjects and the relations of teacher and pupil, which are both sensible and acute, however fantastical we may think their allegorical setting.

Philo begins by pointing out that while Virtue or Wisdom which are represented by Sarah is never barren, she is at this stage in the story Sarai (Σάρα not Σάρρα), that is wisdom in the individual, who is as yet incapable of begetting by her. Stress therefore is to be laid on " she was not bearing for him " (1-12), and when in Sarah's own words this limitation is not mentioned, we must ascribe it to the delicacy of feeling which true wisdom shews for others (13). The immature soul must therefore resort to the hand-maid, the Encyclia, and the list of these is given with some remarks on the educational value of each (14-19). The first thing we note about the handmaid of the story is her race. She is an Egyptian, of the body that is, and the Encyclia depend on the senses in a way in which the higher philosophy does not (20-21). Secondly her name—Hagar, means a sojourner, and the relation of the sojourner to the full citizen expresses that of the Encyclia to philosophy (22-23).

The thought that Abraham, the soul which learns by teaching, needs Hagar, naturally leads to the consideration of the case of Jacob, the soul which progresses through practice. He has two wives and

[a] For some remarks on this and Philo's attitude in general towards "secular" education see General Introduction, Vol. I, pp. xvi ff.

two concubines, and the functions of these four are described in a long and difficult allegory [a] (24-33). On the other hand Isaac has but one wife and no concubine. Thus again he appears in his regular part as the " self-taught," the " gifted by nature," for such a soul has not the need of the extraneous aids which the other two require (34-38). Thence we pass to remarks on other cases of wives and concubines, a short one on Manasseh (39-43), and a more elaborate one on Nahor, Abraham's brother [b] (44-53). Finally comes the thought that the bad also has a wife in the mind, which bears vice, and a concubine in the body, which bears passion. This is founded on the notice of Esau's son's concubine and passes into a denunciation of the Esau-mind itself, as the nature which represents both hardness and fiction (54-62).

" He hearkened to the voice of Sarah." This raises the thought how little real attention there is in the people who attend lectures and the like, how little memory even if they attend, and how little practice even if they remember (63-68). But further, the phrase "listened to her voice," instead of "listened to her," suggests the natural attitude of the Abraham-mind, as against the Jacob-mind which " practises " and thus thinks more of personal example than of what is said (69-70).

" Sarai the *wife* of Abram took Hagar and *gave* her to Abram." Virtue (or philosophy) is actively willing to give to the immature soul its preparation through the Encyclia (71, 72), while on the other hand the seemingly unnecessary repetition of the word " wife " shews the stress which philosophy justly lays on her status. She is always the wife and the

other only the handmaid (73). Philo illustrates this
from his personal experience. He tells how he
delighted as a youth in literature, mathematics and
music, yet always recognized that they were but
stepping-stones to the higher study of ethics, which
teaches us to control the lower nature, and how thus
he avoided the error of those who treat these inferior
studies as an occupation for life (74-80).

Abraham had "dwelt ten years in the land of
Canaan" when he took Hagar. Even for the
Encyclia the soul is not at first fit. Childhood, in
which we are dominated by bodily things, and early
boyhood, in which we learn the difference between
right and wrong, are both too early. While Egypt
signifies the body and its passions, Canaan stands for
vice, and it is only after we have passed some time
in the stage in which vice is possible that we have the
ability for these solid studies (81-88). But the
number ten is not to be pressed. It is just the perfect
number (89), and Philo takes the opportunity to
descant on the prominence of it in the Pentateuch.
Noah as tenth from Adam (90); Abraham as tenth
combatant against the nine kings, a number which
signifies hostility (91-93); the offering of tithes on
various occasions, followed by the familiar insistence
on the duty to offer of everything mental as well as
bodily (94-106); the passover in which the lamb is
killed on the tenth day (106); the Atonement and
the proclamation of the Jubilee also on that day
(107-108). Other examples follow, most of which,
as for instance the account of the presents with which
Isaac wooed Rebecca, and the ten curtains of the
tabernacle, whose four colours represented the four
elements, digress into morals and fancies drawn from

the content of these passages, quite apart from the Ten interest (109-119). He concludes with the remarks that after all these examples were unnecessary, since the Ten Commandments in themselves are enough to prove his point (120).

After reiterating the necessity of postponing school instruction to a suitable age, Philo proceeds to the words " He went in unto her." This indicates the right attitude of the scholar to the teacher (121-122), but the teacher also will often do well to make the advances, as Leah did to Jacob (122-123), though again Knowledge may sometimes veil her face to try the sincerity of her pupils, as Tamar did before she gave herself to Judah (124-125). So too the word συνέλαβε, " she conceived " (lit. " she took "), has in Greek no mark of the gender, and thus in our allegory we may interpret that the " taking " is mutual (126).

Contrasted with this right view of the relation of the two is the arrogance of many teachers who think that the progress of their gifted pupils is due to themselves (127). When knowledge takes this attitude it may be described by the phrase " to have in the womb," used of Hagar's pregnancy, whereas Rebecca was said to " receive in the womb," for the " receive " and " have " represent respectively reverent humility and self-conceit (128-130). He finds " received " used in the story of Moses' birth and this leads to an eulogy of Moses and the tribe of Levi (131-134). Somewhat loosely connected with this is a short interpretation of a law by which the man who struck a woman and caused a premature birth was punished by a fine or death, according as the child born dead was fully formed or not. To destroy the fruits of another's mind is always a crime, but a greater

455

when the idea is fully formed, than when it is not (135-138).

"When she saw that she was pregnant." Philo is confident that the first "she" is Sarah because philosophy sees into the nature of the "arts" which make up the Encyclia better than the arts see themselves. He gives the accepted definitions of "art" and "knowledge" and likens their relation to each other to that of sense to mind (139-145). Then follows a remarkable illustration of this, shewing that at the back of geometry lie the definitions of point, line and the like, which come from philosophy, and similarly that though the *grammaticus* may expound literature, he must go to philosophy for the nature of the parts of speech and the logic of sentences (146-150).

Philosophy rightly resents the ignoring of her claims which is represented in the words "I was dishonoured before her," and to her complaints the true student will answer with Abraham's words: "She is in thy hands," and leave the lower knowledge to the treatment expressed in "and she afflicted or ill-treated her," always remembering however that by this word (ἐκάκωσε) only admonishing or correcting is meant (151-157).

What form the admonishing would take Philo does not discuss, but passes off into a justification of his giving this meaning to ἐκάκωσεν and this takes up the rest of the treatise. Consideration of the demoralizing effects of luxury shews that affliction if regulated by law is beneficial (158-160), and the use of the unleavened bread, called in Deuteronomy bread of affliction, and of bitter herbs at the Paschal Feast agree with this, for feasts are things of joy and the ordinance must mean that chastening toil is a joy to the earnest soul (161-162). So too at the end of the story of the bitter water of Marah we read that at Marah God gave Israel laws—the law of justice (163). The same text says that at Marah God tried Israel, tried them that is with the test of toil to which so many succumb (164-165). Yet again the waters of Marah became sweet, that is the toil is sweetened by the love of toil (166). The lesson of the unleavened bread at the Passover is confirmed by the unleavened shewbread and the prohibition of leaven in the sacrifices (167-169). So when we find in Deuteronomy " He afflicted thee and made thee weak with hunger " coupled with " He fed thee with Manna "—the word of God—we understand that the affliction is one of discipline and the famine a dearth of passion and vice (170-174). So too when Isaac blesses Jacob, even slavery is part of the blessing, and in Proverbs " the Lord chastens whom He loves "(175-177). Philo concludes the argument with what he thinks a clinching proof, that if the law speaks of " ill-treating or afflicting with evil," it implies that afflicting may exist without evil (178-179).[a]

The last section reiterates the necessity of giving the passage an allegorical sense, and implies, if it does not actually say so, that on the literal view the story would be nothing more than an unworthy record of women's jealousies.

[a] See note on § 178.

ΠΕΡΙ ΤΗΣ ΠΡΟΣ ΤΑ
ΠΡΟΠΑΙΔΕΥΜΑΤΑ ΣΥΝΟΔΟΥ

1
[519] **I.** '' Σάρα δὲ ἡ γυνὴ Ἀβραὰμ οὐκ ἔτικτεν αὐτῷ. ἦν δὲ αὐτῇ παιδίσκη Αἰγυπτία, ᾗ ὄνομα Ἄγαρ. εἶπε δὲ Σάρα πρὸς Ἀβραάμ· ἰδού, συνέκλεισέ με κύριος τοῦ μὴ τίκτειν, εἴσελθε πρὸς τὴν παιδίσκην

2 μου, ἵνα τεκνοποιήσῃς ἐξ αὐτῆς.'' τὸ Σάρας ὄνομα μεταληφθέν ἐστιν '' ἀρχή μου''· φρόνησις δὲ ἡ ἐν ἐμοὶ καὶ σωφροσύνη ἡ ἐν ἐμοὶ καὶ ἡ ἐπὶ μέρους δικαιοσύνη καὶ ἑκάστη τῶν ἄλλων ἀρετῶν, ἣν περὶ ἐμὲ μόνον εἶναι συμβέβηκεν, ἀρχή ἐστιν ἐμοῦ μόνου· ἐπιστατεῖ γάρ μου καὶ ἡγεμονεύει πειθαρχεῖν ἐγνωκότος, βασιλὶς ἐκ φύσεως ὑπάρ-

3 χουσα. ταύτην Μωυσῆς, τὸ παραδοξό- τατον, καὶ στεῖραν ἀποφαίνει καὶ πολυγονωτάτην, εἴ γε τὸ πολυανθρωπότατον τῶν ἐθνῶν ἐξ αὐτῆς ὁμολογεῖ γενέσθαι. τῷ γὰρ ὄντι ἡ ἀρετὴ πρὸς μὲν τὰ φαῦλα πάντα ἐστείρωται, τῶν δὲ ἀγαθῶν εὐτοκίᾳ χρῆται τοιαύτῃ, ὡς μηδὲ μαιευτικῆς

4 τέχνης—φθάνει γὰρ ἀποτίκτουσα—δεῖσθαι. τὰ μὲν οὖν ζῷα καὶ φυτὰ διαλείποντα τὸν πλείω χρόνον ἅπαξ ἢ δὶς τὸ πλεῖστον τοὺς οἰκείους δι᾽ ἐνιαυτοῦ φέρει καρπούς, καθ᾽ ὃν ἔταξεν ἀριθμὸν ἑκάστοις ἡ φύσις ἐναρμοζόμενον ταῖς ἐτησίοις

---

[a] For the thought *cf. De Cher.* 5.

ON MATING WITH
THE PRELIMINARY STUDIES

I. " Now Sarah the wife of Abraham was not bearing **1**
him children, but she had an Egyptian handmaiden
named Hagar, and Sarah said to Abraham, ' Behold
the Lord hath closed me that I should not bear. Go
in unto my handmaid and beget children from her ' "
(Gen. xvi. 1, 2). Now Sarah's name is, by interpre- **2**
tation, " sovereignty of me," and the wisdom in me,
the self-control in me, the individual righteousness
and each of the other virtues whose place is confined
to the " me," are a sovereignty over me only.[a] That
sovereignty rules and dominates me, who have willed
to render obedience to it, in virtue of its natural
queenship.   This ruling power Moses **3**
represents as at once barren and exceedingly prolific,
since he acknowledges that from her sprang the most
populous of nations. A startling paradox, yet true.
For indeed virtue is barren as regards all that is bad,
but shews herself a fruitful mother of the good ; a
motherhood which needs no midwifery, for she bears
before the midwife comes.[b] Animals and plants bear **4**
the fruit proper to them only after considerable intervals, once or twice at most in the year, the number
being determined for each by nature and adjusted

---

[b] An allusion to Ex. i. 19 ; *cf. De Mig.* 142.

ὥραις· ἀρετὴ δὲ οὐ διαλείπουσα ἀνελλιπῶς δὲ καὶ
ἀδιαστάτως κατὰ τοὺς ἀμερεῖς χρόνους ἀεὶ γεννᾷ,
βρέφη μὲν οὐδαμῶς, λόγους δὲ ἀστείους καὶ
[520] βουλὰς | ἀνεπιλήπτους καὶ ἐπαινετὰς πράξεις.
5   II. ἀλλ' οὔτε πλοῦτος, ᾧ μὴ δυνατόν
ἐστι χρῆσθαι, τοὺς κεκτημένους ὠφελεῖ οὔτε ἡ
φρονήσεως εὐτοκία, ἐὰν μὴ καὶ ἡμῖν αὐτοῖς τὰ
ὠφέλιμα τίκτῃ. τοὺς μὲν γὰρ εἰσάπαν ἀξίους
ἔκρινε τῆς συμβιώσεως αὐτῆς, οἱ δ' οὔπω ⟨τὴν⟩
ἡλικίαν ἔδοξαν ἔχειν, ὡς ἐπαινετῆς καὶ σώφρονος
οἰκουρίας ἀνέχεσθαι· οἷς τὰ προτέλεια τῶν γάμων
ἐφῆκε ποιεῖσθαι, ἐλπίδα καὶ τοῦ θύσειν τοὺς γάμους
6 παρασχοῦσα.   Σάρα οὖν, ἡ ἄρχουσά μου
τῆς ψυχῆς ἀρετή, ἔτικτε μέν, ἐμοὶ δ' οὐκ ἔτικτε·
οὐ γὰρ ἠδυνάμην πω νέος ὢν τὰ γεννήματα αὐτῆς
παραδέχεσθαι, τὸ φρονεῖν, τὸ δικαιοπραγεῖν, τὸ
εὐσεβεῖν, διὰ τὸ πλῆθος τῶν νόθων παίδων, οὓς
ἀπεκύησάν μοι αἱ κεναὶ δόξαι. τροφαὶ γὰρ αἱ
τούτων καὶ συνεχεῖς ἐπιμέλειαι καὶ φροντίδες
ἄληκτοι[1] τῶν γνησίων καὶ ὡς ἀληθῶς ἀστῶν
7 ὀλιγωρεῖν ἠνάγκασαν. καλὸν οὖν εὔχεσθαι τὴν
ἀρετὴν μὴ μόνον τίκτειν, ἣ καὶ δίχα εὐχῆς
εὐτοκεῖ, ἀλλὰ καὶ ἡμῖν αὐτοῖς τίκτειν, ἵνα
τῶν σπερμάτων καὶ γεννημάτων αὐτῆς μεταλαγ-
χάνοντες εὐδαιμονῶμεν. εἴωθε γὰρ θεῷ μόνῳ
τίκτειν, τὰς ἀπαρχὰς ὧν ἔτυχεν ἀγαθῶν εὐχαρίστως
ἀποδιδοῦσα τῷ τὴν ἀειπάρθενον μήτραν, ὥς φησι
8 Μωυσῆς, ἀνοίξαντι.   καὶ γὰρ τὴν λυχνίαν, τὸ ἀρχέτυπον τοῦ μιμήματος παράδειγμα, ἐκ

---

[1] MSS. ἄλεκτοι.

[a] i.e. in Ex. xxv. 37, in the "pattern shewn to Moses in
the mount" (v. 40), the lamps are to give light ἐξ ἑνὸς προ-

to the seasons of the year. But virtue has no such intervals. She bears ceaselessly, successively, from moment to moment, and her offspring are no infants, but honest words, innocent purposes and laudable acts. II. But as wealth which one cannot use 5 does not profit the owner, so the motherhood of virtue profits not if the offspring be not profitable for ourselves. Some she judges quite worthy to share her life, but others she thinks have not yet reached the age to submit to her admirable and chaste and sober domesticity. Such she allows to celebrate the preliminaries of marriage, and holds out hopes of consummating the full rite in the future. So Sarah, the 6 virtue which rules my soul, was a mother, but not a mother for me. For young as I was I could not yet receive her offspring, wisdom, justice, piety, because of the multitude of bastard children whom vain imaginations had borne to me. The nurture of these, the constant supervision, the ceaseless anxiety, compelled me to take little thought of the genuine, the truly free-born. It is well then to pray that virtue 7 may not only bear (she does that in abundance without our prayers), but also may bear for ourselves, that we, by sharing in what she sows and genders, may enjoy happiness. For in ordinary course she bears for God only, thankfully rendering the first-fruits of the blessings bestowed upon her to Him who, as Moses says, opens the womb which yet loses not its virginity (Gen. xxix. 31). In confirmation of 8 this we read that the candlestick, that is the original pattern of the later copy,[a] gives light from one part

σώπου (E.V. " over against it"). In the narrative of the making of the candlestick, Ex. xxxviii. 5 f. (xxxvii. 17), this point is not repeated.

461

τοῦ ἑνὸς μέρους φησὶ φαίνειν, δηλονότι τοῦ πρὸς
θεόν· ἑβδόμη γὰρ οὖσα καὶ μέση τῶν ἓξ καλαμίσκων δίχα διῃρημένων εἰς τριάδας, ἑκατέρωθεν
δορυφορούντων, ἄνω τὰς αὐγὰς ἀποστέλλει πρὸς
τὸ ὄν,[1] λαμπρότερον ἡγουμένη τὸ φέγγος ἢ ὡς
δύνασθαι θνητὴν αὐτῷ προσβάλλειν ὄψιν.

9 III. διὰ τοῦτο οὔ φησι μὴ τίκτειν τὴν Σάραν, ἀλλ'
αὐτῷ τινι μὴ τίκτειν. οὐ γάρ ἐσμεν ἱκανοὶ δέξα-
σθαί πω γονὰς ἀρετῆς, εἰ μὴ πρότερον ἐντύχοιμεν
αὐτῆς τῇ θεραπαινίδι· θεραπαινὶς δὲ σοφίας ἡ διὰ
10 τῶν προπαιδευμάτων ἐγκύκλιος μουσική.[2] ὥσπερ
γὰρ ἐν μὲν οἰκίαις αὔλειοι πρόκεινται κλισιάδων,
ἐν δὲ πόλεσι τὰ προάστεια, δι' ὧν εἴσω βαδίζειν
ἔνεστιν, οὕτως καὶ ἀρετῆς πρόκειται τὰ ἐγκύκλια·
ταῦτα γὰρ ὁδός ἐστιν ἐπ' ἐκείνην φέρουσα.

11 Χρὴ δ' εἰδέναι, ὅτι τῶν μεγάλων ὑποθέσεων
μεγάλα καὶ τὰ προοίμια εἶναι συμβέβηκε. μεγίστη
δὲ ὑπόθεσις ἀρετή· καὶ γὰρ περὶ μεγίστην ὕλην
καταγίνεται, τὸν σύμπαντα ἀνθρώπων βίον. εἰκότως οὖν οὐ βραχέσι χρήσεται προοιμίοις, ἀλλὰ
γραμματικῇ, γεωμετρίᾳ, ἀστρονομίᾳ, ῥητορικῇ,
[521] μουσικῇ, τῇ | ἄλλῃ λογικῇ θεωρίᾳ πάσῃ, ὧν
ἐστι σύμβολον ἡ Σάρας θεραπαινὶς Ἄγαρ, ὡς
12 ἐπιδείξομεν. '' εἶπε '' γάρ φησι '' Σάρα πρὸς
Ἀβραάμ· ἰδοὺ συνέκλεισέ με κύριος τοῦ μὴ τίκ-
τειν· εἴσελθε πρὸς τὴν παιδίσκην μου, ἵνα τεκνοποιήσῃς ἐξ αὐτῆς.'' τὰς σωμάτων πρὸς σώματα
μίξεις καὶ ὁμιλίας ἡδονὴν ἐχούσας τὸ τέλος ὑπεξ-

---

[1] mss. ἕν.
[2] Some mss. add καὶ ἡ λογικὴ σοφισμάτων γεῦσις (νεῦσις), the
last word being evidently a corruption for εὕρεσις. *Cf.* § 29.
The interpolators did not understand that μουσική is here
used in the more general sense.

only, that is the part where it looks towards God. For being seventh in position, and placed between the six branches, divided as they are into triplets which guard it on either side, it sends its rays upwards towards the Existent, as though feeling that its light were too bright for human sight to look upon it (Ex. xxv. 37, 31).   III. This is why Moses 9 does not say that Sarah did not bear, but only that she did not bear for some particular person. For we are not capable as yet of receiving the impregnation of virtue unless we have first mated with her handmaiden, and the handmaiden of wisdom is the culture gained by the primary learning of the school course. For, just as in houses we have outer doors in front of 10 the chamber doors, and in cities suburbs through which we can pass to the inner part, so the school course precedes virtue ; the one is a road which leads to the other.

Now we must understand that great themes need 11 great introductions ; and the greatest of all themes is virtue, for it deals with the greatest of materials, that is the whole life of man. Naturally, then, virtue will employ no minor kind of introduction, but grammar, geometry, astronomy,[a] rhetoric, music, and all the other branches of intellectual study. These are symbolized by Hagar, the handmaid of Sarah, as I shall proceed to shew. For Sarah, we are told, said 12 to Abraham : " Behold, the Lord has shut me out from bearing. Go in unto my handmaid, that thou mayest beget children from her." In the present discussion, we must eliminate all bodily unions or

See App. p. 577.

αιρετέον τοῦ παρόντος λόγου· νοῦ γὰρ πρὸς ἀρετὴν
ἐστι σύνοδος ἐξ αὑτῆς ἐφιεμένου παιδοποιεῖσθαι,
εἰ δὲ μὴ δύναιτο εὐθύς, ἀλλά τοι τὴν θεραπαινίθα
αὑτῆς, τὴν μέσην παιδείαν, ἐγγυᾶσθαι διδασκο-
13 μένου.   IV. ἄξιον δὲ τῆς αἰδοῦς κατα-
πλαγῆναι σοφίαν, ἥτις τὸ βραδὺ πρὸς γένεσιν ἢ
τελέως ἄγονον οὐκ ἠξίωσεν ἡμῖν ὀνειδίσαι, καίτοι
τοῦ χρησμοῦ τἀληθὲς εἰπόντος, ὅτι '' οὐκ ἔτικτεν,''
οὐ διὰ φθόνον, ἀλλὰ διὰ τὴν ἡμῶν αὐτῶν ἀνεπι-
τηδειότητα· '' συνέκλεισε '' γάρ φησι '' μὲ κύριος
τοῦ μὴ τίκτειν,'' καὶ οὐκέτι προστίθησιν '' ὑμῖν,''
ἵνα μὴ προφέρειν ἀτυχίαν καὶ ὀνειδίζειν ἑτέροις
14 δοκῇ.   '' εἴσελθε '' οὖν φησι '' πρὸς τὴν
παιδίσκην μου,'' τὴν τῶν μέσων καὶ ἐγκυκλίων
ἐπιστημῶν μέσην παιδείαν, '' ἵνα τεκνοποιήσῃ
πρότερον ἐξ αὐτῆς''· αὖθις γὰρ δυνήσῃ καὶ τῶν
πρὸς τὴν δέσποιναν ὁμιλιῶν ⟨ἐπὶ⟩ γενέσει παίδων
15 γνησίων ἀπόνασθαι.   γραμματικὴ μὲν
γὰρ ἱστορίαν τὴν παρὰ ποιηταῖς καὶ συγγραφεῦσιν
ἀναδιδάξασα[1] νόησιν καὶ πολυμάθειαν ἐργάσεται
καὶ καταφρονητικῶς ἔχειν ἀναδιδάξει τῶν ὅσα αἱ
κεναὶ δόξαι τυφοπλαστοῦσι, διὰ τὰς κακοπραγίας,
αἷς τοὺς ἀδομένους παρ' αὐτοῖς ἥρωάς τε καὶ
16 ἡμιθέους λόγος ἔχει χρήσασθαι.   μουσικὴ δὲ τὸ μὲν ἄρρυθμον [ἐν] ῥυθμοῖς, τὸ δ' ἀνάρμοστον ἁρμονίᾳ, τὸ δ' ἀπῳδὸν καὶ ἐκμελὲς μέλει
κατεπᾴδουσα τὸ ἀσύμφωνον εἰς συμφωνίαν ἄξει.
γεωμετρία δ' ἰσότητος καὶ ἀναλογίας ἐμβαλ-

---

[1] Or perhaps, as Wendland conjectures, ἀναπτύξασα. See
§ 148 and note.

[a] Or "delicate feeling." The genitive is one of cause, a
common construction with θαυμάζω and similar verbs.

intercourse which has pleasure as its object. What is meant is a mating of mind with virtue. Mind desires to have children by virtue, and, if it cannot do so at once, is instructed to espouse virtue's handmaid, the lower instruction. IV. Now we may 13 well feel profound admiration for the discretion[a] shewn by Wisdom. She refrains from reproaching us with our backwardness or complete impotence in generation, though, as the text truly stated, it was through our unfitness that she was not bearing, and not because she grudged us offspring. Thus she says, " The Lord has shut me out from bearing," and does not go on to add, " for you." She does not wish to seem to upbraid and reproach others for their misfortune. " Go in, then," she says, " to 14 my handmaid, the lower instruction given by the lower branches of school lore, that first you may have children by her," for afterwards you will be able to avail yourself of the mistress's company to beget children of higher birth. For grammar 15 teaches us to study literature in the poets and historians, and will thus produce intelligence and wealth of knowledge. It will teach us also to despise the vain delusions of our empty imagination by shewing us the calamities which heroes and demi-gods who are celebrated in such literature are said to have undergone.[b] Music will charm away the 16 unrhythmic by its rhythm, the inharmonious by its harmony, the unmelodious and tuneless by its melody,[c] and thus reduce discord to concord. Geometry will sow in the soul that loves to learn the seeds of equality

[b] See App. p. 577.
[c] The accepted division of music was into rhythm, harmony, and melody; cf. De Agr. 137.

λομένη τὰ σπέρματα εἰς ψυχὴν φιλομαθῆ γλα-
φυρότητι συνεχοῦς θεωρίας δικαιοσύνης ζῆλον
17 ἐμποιήσει.   ῥητορικὴ δὲ καὶ τὸν νοῦν πρὸς
θεωρίαν ἀκονησαμένη καὶ πρὸς ἑρμηνείαν γυμ-
νάσασα τὸν λόγον καὶ συγκροτήσασα λογικὸν
ὄντως ἀποδείξει τὸν ἄνθρωπον ἐπιμεληθεῖσα τοῦ
ἰδίου καὶ ἐξαιρέτου, ὃ μηδενὶ τῶν ἄλλων ζῴων ἡ
18 φύσις δεδώρηται. διαλεκτικὴ δὲ ἡ ῥητορικῆς
ἀδελφὴ καὶ δίδυμος, ὡς εἶπόν τινες, τοὺς ἀληθεῖς
τῶν ψευδῶν λόγους διακρίνουσα καὶ τὰς τῶν
σοφισμάτων πιθανότητας ἐλέγχουσα μεγάλην νόσον
ψυχῆς, ἀπάτην, ἀκέσεται.   τούτοις οὖν
καὶ τοῖς παραπλησίοις ἐνομιλῆσαι καὶ ἐμπρο-
μελετῆσαι λυσιτελές· ἴσως γάρ, ἴσως, ὃ πολλοῖς
συνέβη, διὰ τῶν ὑπηκόων ταῖς βασιλίσιν ἀρεταῖς
19 γνωρισθησόμεθα.   οὐχ ὁρᾷς, ὅτι καὶ τὸ σῶμα
[522] ἡμῶν οὐ πρότερον πεπηγυίαις | καὶ πολυτελέσι
χρῆται τροφαῖς, πρὶν ἢ ταῖς ἀποικίλοις καὶ γαλα-
κτώδεσιν ἐν ἡλικίᾳ τῇ βρεφώδει; τὸν αὐτὸν δὴ
τρόπον καὶ τῇ ψυχῇ παιδικὰς μὲν νόμισον εὐτρε-
πίσθαι τροφὰς τὰ ἐγκύκλια καὶ τὰ καθ' ἕκαστον
αὐτῶν θεωρήματα, τελειοτέρας δὲ καὶ πρεπούσας
ἀνδράσιν ὡς ἀληθῶς τὰς ἀρετάς.
20   V. Οἱ δὲ πρῶτοι τῆς μέσης παιδείας χαρακτῆρες
διὰ δυεῖν παρίστανται συμβόλων, τοῦ τε γένους
καὶ τοῦ ὀνόματος.   γένος μέν ἐστιν Αἰγυπτία,
καλεῖται δὲ Ἅγαρ, τοῦτο δὲ ἑρμηνευθέν ἐστι
παροίκησις· ἀνάγκη γὰρ τὸν ἐγχορεύοντα ταῖς
ἐγκυκλίοις θεωρίαις καὶ πολυμαθείας ἑταῖρον ὄντα
τῷ γεώδει καὶ Αἰγυπτίῳ προσκεκληρῶσθαι σώ-

and proportion, and by the charm of its logical continuity will raise from those seeds a zeal for justice.

Rhetoric, sharpening the mind to the observation of facts, and training and welding thought to expression,[a] will make the man a true master of words and thoughts, thus taking into its charge the peculiar and special gift which nature has not bestowed on any other living creature. Dialectic, the sister and twin,[b] as some have said, of Rhetoric, distinguishes true argument from false, and convicts the plausibilities of sophistry, and thus will heal that great plague of the soul, deceit. It is profitable then to take these and the like for our associates and for the field of our preliminary studies. For perhaps indeed it may be with us, as it has been with many, that through the vassals we shall come to the knowledge of the royal virtues. Observe too that our body is not nourished in the earlier stages with solid and costly foods. The simple and milky foods of infancy come first. Just so you may consider that the school subjects and the lore which belongs to each of them stand ready to nourish the childhood of the soul, while the virtues are grown-up food, suited for those who are really men.

V. The primary characteristic marks of the lower education are represented by two symbols giving its race and its name. In race it is Egypt, but its name is Hagar, which is by interpretation " sojourning." [c] The votary of the school studies, the friend of wide learning, must necessarily be associated with the earthly and Egyptian body ; since he needs eyes

17

18

19

20

---

[a] The θεωρία represents the technical εὕρεσις. See on *De Mig.* 35.   [b] See App. p. 577.

[c] See note on *Leg. All.* iii. 244.

ματι, χρῄζοντα καὶ ὀφθαλμῶν, ὡς ἰδεῖν καὶ
ἀναγνῶναι, καὶ ὤτων, ὡς προσσχεῖν τε καὶ
ἀκοῦσαι, καὶ τῶν ἄλλων αἰσθήσεων, ὡς ἕκαστον
21 τῶν αἰσθητῶν ἀναπτύξαι. δίχα γὰρ τοῦ κρίνοντος
τὸ κρινόμενον οὐ πέφυκε καταλαμβάνεσθαι· κρίνει
δὲ τὸ αἰσθητὸν αἴσθησις, ὥστ' ἀκριβωθῆναί τι τῶν
κατὰ τὸν αἰσθητὸν κόσμον, ἐν οἷς ἡ πλείων μοῖρα
τοῦ φιλοσοφεῖν, οὐκ ἐνῆν ἄνευ αἰσθήσεως. αἴσθησις δέ, τὸ σωματοειδέστερον ψυχῆς μέρος, τῷ τῆς
ὅλης ψυχῆς ἀγγείῳ προσερρίζωται, τὸ δὲ τῆς ψυχῆς
ἀγγεῖον Αἴγυπτος διὰ συμβόλου προσονομάζεται.
22   Χαρακτὴρ μὲν εἷς ὁ ἀπὸ τοῦ γένους οὗτος, ὃν
ἡ θεραπαινὶς ἀρετῆς ἔλαχεν· ὁ δὲ ἀπὸ τοῦ ὀνόματος
ποῖός ἐστιν, ἐπισκεψώμεθα. τὴν μέσην παιδείαν
παροίκου λόγον ἔχειν συμβέβηκεν· ἐπιστήμη μὲν
γὰρ καὶ σοφία καὶ ἀρετὴ πᾶσα αὐθιγενὴς καὶ
αὐτόχθων καὶ πολῖτις ὡς ἀληθῶς ἐστι μόνη τοῦ
παντός, αἱ δὲ ἄλλαι παιδεῖαι δευτέρων καὶ τρίτων
καὶ ὑστάτων ἄθλων τυγχάνουσαι μεθόριοι ξένων
καὶ ἀστῶν εἰσιν· οὐδετέρου τε γὰρ γένους ἀκράτου
καὶ πάλιν ἀμφοῖν κατά τινα κοινωνίαν ἐφάπτονται.
23 πάροικος γὰρ τῷ μὲν ἐνδιατρίβειν ἀστοῖς, τῷ δὲ
μὴ κατοικεῖν ἀλλοδαποῖς ἰσοῦται· καθάπερ, οἶμαι,
καὶ οἱ θετοὶ παῖδες, ᾗ μὲν κληρονομοῦσι τὰ τῶν
θεμένων, τοῖς γνησίοις, ᾗ δ' οὐ γεγέννηνται πρὸς
αὐτῶν, τοῖς ὀθνείοις. ὃν δὴ λόγον ἔχει δέσποινα
μὲν πρὸς θεραπαινίδα, γυνὴ δὲ ἀστὴ πρὸς παλ-
λακήν, τοῦτον ἕξει τὸν λόγον ἀρετὴ Σάρρα πρὸς
παιδείαν Ἄγαρ· ὥστ' εἰκότως τοῦ θεωρίαν καὶ
ἐπιστήμην ἐζηλωκότος, Ἀβραὰμ ὄνομα, γένοιτ'
ἂν ἡ μὲν ἀρετή, Σάρρα, γυνή, παλλακὴ δὲ Ἄγαρ,
ἡ ἐγκύκλιος μουσικὴ πᾶσα.

to see and read, ears to listen and hear, and the other senses to unveil the several objects of sense. For the 21 thing judged cannot be apprehended without one to judge it, and it is sense which judges the sensible, and therefore without sense it is always impossible to obtain accurate knowledge of any of the phenomena in the sensible world which form the staple of philosophy. Sense being the bodily part of the soul is riveted to the vessel of the soul as a whole, and this soul-vessel is symbolically called Egypt.

This, then, is one of the marks of the handmaid of 22 virtue, namely that of race. Let us now consider the nature of the other mark, that of name. The lower education is in the position of a sojourner. For knowledge and wisdom and every virtue are native born, indigenous, citizens in the truest sense, and in this they are absolutely alone; but the other kinds of training, which win second or third or last prizes, are on the border-line between foreigners and citizens. For they belong to neither kind in its pure form, and yet in virtue of a certain degree of partnership they touch both. The sojourner in so far as he is staying in the 23 city is on a par with the citizens, in so far as it is not his home, on a par with foreigners. In the same way, I should say, adopted children, in so far as they inherit from their adopters, rank with the family ; in so far as they are not their actual children, with outsiders. Sarah, virtue, bears, we shall find, the same relation to Hagar, education, as the mistress to the servant-maid, or the lawful wife to the concubine, and so naturally the mind which aspires to study and to gain knowledge, the mind we call Abraham, will have Sarah, virtue, for his wife, and Hagar, the whole range of school culture, for his concubine.

469

24 Ὧτινι μὲν οὖν φρόνησις ἐκ διδασκαλίας περιγίνεται, τὴν Ἄγαρ οὐκ ἂν ἀποδοκιμάζοι· πάνυ γὰρ
ἀναγκαία ἡ τῶν προπαιδευμάτων κτῆσις. VI. εἰ
δέ τις τοὺς ὑπὲρ ἀρετῆς ἄθλους ἐγνωκὼς δια-
πονεῖν μελέταις χρῆται συνεχέσιν ἀνενδότως ἔχων
πρὸς ἄσκησιν, δύο μὲν ἀστάς, παλλακὰς δὲ τὰς
[523] ἴσας, τῶν ἀστῶν | θεραπαινίδας, ἄξεται. φύσιν
25 δὲ καὶ ἰδέαν ἔλαχεν αὐτῶν ἑκάστη διάφορον.
αὐτίκα τῶν ἀστῶν ἡ μέν ἐστιν ὑγιεινοτάτη καὶ
εὐσταθεστάτη καὶ εἰρηνικωτάτη κίνησις, ἣν ἀπὸ
τοῦ συμβεβηκότος ὠνόμασε Λείαν. ἡ δὲ ἔοικεν
ἀκόνῃ, καλεῖται δὲ Ῥαχήλ, πρὸς ἣν ὁ φίλαθλος
καὶ φιλογυμναστὴς νοῦς παραθηγόμενος ὀξύνεται·
ἑρμηνεύεται δὲ ὄρασις βεβηλώσεως, οὐκ ἐπειδὴ
βεβήλως ὁρᾷ, ἀλλὰ τοὐναντίον, ὅτι τὰ ὁρατὰ καὶ
αἰσθητὰ παρὰ τὴν ἀκήρατον φύσιν τῶν ἀοράτων
καὶ νοητῶν οὐκ εὐαγῆ βέβηλα δὲ εἶναι νομίζει.
26 τῆς γὰρ ψυχῆς ἡμῶν διμεροῦς ὑπαρχούσης καὶ τὸ
μὲν λογικὸν τὸ δὲ ἄλογον ἐχούσης, ἀρετὴν ἑκατέρῳ
ὑπάρχειν συμβέβηκε, Λείαν μὲν τῷ λογικῷ, τῷ δὲ
27 ἀλόγῳ[1] Ῥαχήλ.   γυμνάζει γὰρ ἡμᾶς ἡ
μὲν διὰ τῶν αἰσθήσεων καὶ τῶν τοῦ ἀλόγου μερῶν
πάντων καταφρονητικῶς ἔχειν ὧν ἀλογεῖν ἄξιον,
δόξης καὶ πλούτου καὶ ἡδονῆς, ἃ περίβλεπτα καὶ

[1] mss. τὸ λογικὸν καὶ τὸ ἄλογον, which might be kept, if with
some mss. we read ἑκάτερον ἔχειν above for ἑκατέρῳ ὑπάρχειν.

[a] The allegory of §§ 24-33 is in some ways difficult and very
different from Philo's usual way of treating the two wives of
Jacob. Elsewhere Rachel is αἴσθησις or σώματος εὐμορφία.
Here no doubt she is connected with τὸ ἄλογον and trains us
through the senses and so far is entitled to have the bodily
function of "swallowing" as her handmaid, but her function
is to teach us the inferiority of sense, while Leah is no longer
the virtue which "refuses" vice and is "weary" with effort

He then who gains wisdom by instruction will not 24 reject Hagar, for the acquisition of these preliminary subjects is quite necessary, (VI.) but, anyone whose mind is set on enduring to the end the weary contest in which virtue is the prize, who practises continually for that end, and is unflagging in self-discipline, will take to him two lawful wives and as handmaids to them two concubines.[a] And to each of them is given a different 25 nature and appearance. Thus one of the lawful wives is a movement, sound, healthy and peaceful, and to express her history Moses names her Leah or "smooth."[b] The other is like a whetstone. Her name is Rachel, and on that whetstone the mind which loves effort and exercise sharpens its edge. Her name means "vision of profanation," not because her way of seeing is profane, but on the contrary, because she judges the visible world of sense to be not holy but profane, compared with the pure and undefiled nature of the invisible world of mind. For 26 since our soul is twofold, with one part reasoning and the other unreasoning, each has its own virtue or excellence, the reasoning Leah, the unreasoning Rachel. The virtue we call Rachel, acting 27 through the senses and the other parts of our unreasoning nature, trains us to despise all that should be held of little account, reputation and wealth and

(see note on *De Cher.* 41), but the virtue which proceeds to noble life without a conflict. In fact, she is rather akin to the αὐτομαθής Isaac, and Rachel to the ἀσκητής Jacob. Why this Leah needs oratorical power for her handmaid is not clear to me.

[b] Philo here and in § 31 adopts the Epicurean term λεία κίνησις, which he has used with disparagement in *De Post.* 79, and with a qualification in *De Agr.* 142 (see notes). The name is also derived from the Greek instead of the Hebrew in *Leg. All.* ii. 59, but in a somewhat different sense.

PHILO

περιμάχητα ὁ πολὺς καὶ ἀγελαῖος ἀνθρώπων ὄχλος
κρίνει δεδεκασμέναις μὲν ἀκοαῖς, δεδεκασμένῳ δὲ
28 καὶ τῷ ἄλλῳ τῶν αἰσθήσεων δικαστηρίῳ· ἡ δὲ
ἀναδιδάσκει τὴν ἀνώμαλον καὶ τραχεῖαν ὁδὸν
ἄβατον φιλαρέτοις ψυχαῖς ἐκτρέπεσθαι, λείως δὲ
διὰ τῆς λεωφόρου βαίνειν ἄνευ πταισμάτων καὶ
29 τῶν ἐν ποσὶν ὀλίσθων.   ἀναγκαίως οὖν
τῆς μὲν προτέρας ἔσται θεραπαινὶς ἡ διὰ τῶν
φωνητηρίων ὀργάνων ἑρμηνευτικὴ δύναμις καὶ ἡ
λογική¹ σοφισμάτων εὕρεσις εὐστόχῳ πιθανότητι
καταγοητεύουσα, τῆς δὲ ἀναγκαῖαι τροφαί, πόσις τε
30 καὶ βρῶσις. ὀνόματα δὲ ἡμῖν τῶν δυεῖν θεραπαινίδων ἀνέγραψε, Ζέλφαν τε καὶ Βάλλαν. ἡ μὲν
οὖν Ζέλφα μεταληφθεῖσα πορευόμενον καλεῖται
στόμα, τῆς ἑρμηνευτικῆς καὶ διεξοδικῆς σύμβολον δυνάμεως, ἡ δὲ Βάλλα κατάποσις, τὸ πρῶτον καὶ ἀναγκαιότατον θνητῶν ζῴων ἔρεισμα·
καταπόσει γὰρ τὰ σώματα ἡμῶν ἐνορμεῖ, καὶ τὰ
τοῦ ζῆν πείσματα ἐκ ταύτης ὡς ἀπὸ κρηπῖδος
31 ἐξῆπται.   πάσαις οὖν ταῖς εἰρημέναις
δυνάμεσιν ὁ ἀσκητὴς ἐνομιλεῖ, ταῖς μὲν ὡς ἐλευθέ-
ραις καὶ ἀσταῖς, ταῖς δὲ ὡς δούλαις καὶ παλλακίσιν.
ἐφίεται μὲν γὰρ τῆς Λείας κινήσεως—λεία δὲ
κίνησις ἐν μὲν σώματι γινομένη ὑγείαν, ἐν δὲ ψυχῇ
καλοκἀγαθίαν καὶ δικαιοσύνην ἂν ἐργάσαιτο—,
Ῥαχὴλ δὲ ἀγαπᾷ πρὸς τὰ πάθη παλαίων καὶ πρὸς

¹ I suspect a lacuna between λογικὴ and σοφισμάτων. See
App. p. 577.

ᵃ See App. p. 577.
ᵇ In the interpretation of Zilpah's name διεξοδικῆς represents πορευόμενον and ἑρμηνείας (-ευτικῆς) represents στόμα. The
former corresponds to the εὕρεσις of technical rhetoric and
472

pleasure, which the vulgar mass of ordinary men who accept the verdict of dishonest hearsay and the equally dishonest court of the other senses, judge worthy of their admiration and their efforts. Leah 28 teaches us to avoid the rough and uneven path, impassable to virtue-loving souls, and to walk smoothly along the level highway where there are no stumbling-blocks or aught that can make the foot to slip.

Necessarily then Leah will have for her 29 handmaid the faculty of expression by means of the vocal organs, and on the side of thought the art of devising clever arguments whose easy persuasiveness is a means of deception,[a] while Rachel has for her's the necessary means of sustenance, eating and drinking. Moses has given us, as the names of these 30 two handmaidens, Zilpah and Bilhah (Gen. xxx. 3, 9). Zilpah by interpretation is " a walking mouth,"[b] which signifies the power of expressing thought in language and directing the course of an exposition, while Bilhah is "swallowing," the first and most necessary support of mortal animals. For our bodies are anchored on swallowing, and the cables of life are fastened on to it as their base. With all 31 these aforesaid faculties the Man of Practice mates, with one pair as free-born legitimate wives, with the other pair as slaves and concubines. For he desires the smooth, the Leah movement, which will produce health in the body, noble living and justice in the soul. He loves Rachel when he wrestles with the passions and when he goes into training to gain self-control,

thus appears in § 33 as ἡ κατὰ διάνοιαν πηγή. διέξοδος, a rather vague word, signifying a fully worked out narrative or disquisition, is used because the ὅδος in it corresponds to πορευόμενον. Hence the use of the word "course" in the translation.

PHILO

ἐγκράτειαν ἀλειφόμενος καὶ τοῖς αἰσθητοῖς πᾶσιν
32 ἀντιταττόμενος. διττοὶ μὲν γὰρ ὠφελείας τρόποι,
ἢ κατὰ ἀπόλαυσιν ἀγαθῶν ὡς ἐν εἰρήνῃ ἢ κατὰ
[524] ἀντίταξιν καὶ ὑφαίρεσιν κακῶν ὡς ἐν | πολέμῳ.
Λεία μὲν οὖν ἐστι, καθ' ἣν συμβαίνει τὰ πρεσβύτερα καὶ ἡγεμονεύοντα ἀγαθὰ καρποῦσθαι,
Ῥαχὴλ δέ, καθ' ἣν τὰ ὡς ἂν ἐκ πολέμου λάφυρα·
33 τοιαύτη μὲν ἡ πρὸς τὰς ἀστὰς συμβίωσις. χρῄζει
δὲ ὁ ἀσκητὴς Βάλλας μέν, καταπόσεως, ἀλλὰ ὡς
δούλης καὶ παλλακίδος—ἄνευ γὰρ τροφῆς καὶ ζωῆς
οὐδ' ἂν τὸ εὖ ζῆν περιγένοιτο, ἐπειδὴ τὰ μέσα τῶν
ἀμεινόνων ἀεὶ θεμέλιοι,—χρῄζει δὲ καὶ Ζέλφας,
διεξοδικῆς ἑρμηνείας, ἵνα τὸ λογικὸν αὐτῷ διχόθεν
συνερανίζηται πρὸς τελείωσιν, ἔκ τε τῆς κατὰ
διάνοιαν πηγῆς καὶ ἐκ τῆς περὶ τὸ φωνητήριον
ὄργανον ἀπορροῆς.

34   VII. Ἀλλ' οὗτοι μὲν καὶ πλειόνων γυναικῶν καὶ
παλλακίδων, οὐκ ἀστῶν μόνον, ἄνδρες ἐγένοντο,
ὡς αἱ ἱεραὶ μηνύουσι γραφαί· τῷ δὲ Ἰσαὰκ οὔτε
πλείους γυναῖκες οὔτε συνόλως παλλακή, μόνη δ'
35 ἡ κουρίδιος ἄχρι παντὸς συνοικεῖ. διὰ τί; ὅτι
καὶ ἡ διδακτικὴ ἀρετή, ἣν Ἀβραὰμ μέτεισι,
πλειόνων δεῖται, γνησίων μὲν τῶν κατὰ φρόνησιν,
νόθων δὲ τῶν κατὰ τὰ ἐγκύκλια προπαιδεύματα
θεωρημάτων, καὶ ἡ δι' ἀσκήσεως τελειουμένη, περὶ
ἣν Ἰακὼβ ἐσπουδακέναι φαίνεται· διὰ πλειόνων
γὰρ καὶ διαφερόντων αἱ ἀσκήσεις δογμάτων, ἡγου-
μένων ἑπομένων, προαπαντώντων ὑστεριζόντων,
πόνους τοτὲ μὲν ἐλάττους τοτὲ δὲ μείζους ἐχόντων.
474

and takes his stand to oppose all the objects of sense. For help may take two forms. It may act by giving 32 us enjoyment of the good, the way of peace, or by opposing and removing ill, the way of war. So it is Leah through whom it comes to pass that he reaps the higher and dominant blessings, Rachel through whom he wins what we may call the spoils of war. Such is his life with the legitimate wives. But the 33 Practiser needs also Bilhah, " swallowing," though only as the slave and concubine, for without food and the life which food sustains we cannot have the good life either, since the less good must always serve as foundation for the better. He needs Zilpah too, the gift of language giving expression to the course of an exposition, that the element of words and thoughts may make its twofold contribution to the perfecting process, through the fountain of thought in the mind and the outflow through the tongue and lips.

VII. Now Abraham and Jacob, as the Holy Scrip- 34 tures tell us, became the husbands of several women, concubines as well as legitimate wives, but Isaac had neither more wives than one nor any concubine at all, but his lawful wife is the one who shares his home throughout. Why is this ? It is because the virtue 35 that comes through teaching, which Abraham pursues, needs the fruits of several studies, both those born in wedlock, which deal with wisdom, and the base-born, those of the preliminary lore of the schools. It is the same with the virtue which is perfected through practice, which Jacob seems to have made his aim. For many and different are the truths in which practice finds its exercising ground, truths which both lead and follow, hasten to meet it and lag behind, and entail sometimes greater, sometimes less

36 τὸ δὲ αὐτομαθὲς γένος, οὗ κεκοινώνηκεν Ἰσαάκ, ἡ
εὐπαθειῶν ἀρίστη χαρά, φύσεως ἁπλῆς καὶ ἀμιγοῦς
καὶ ἀκράτου μεμοίραται, μήτε ἀσκήσεως μήτε
διδασκαλίας δεόμενον, ἐν οἷς παλλακίδων ἐπιστημῶν, οὐκ ἀστῶν μόνον, ἐστὶ χρεία. θεοῦ γὰρ τὸ
αὐτομαθὲς καὶ αὐτοδίδακτον ἄνωθεν ἀπ᾽ οὐρανοῦ
καλὸν ὀμβρήσαντος ἀμήχανον ἦν ἔτι δούλαις καὶ
παλλακαῖς συμβιῶναι τέχναις, νόθων δογμάτων οἷα
37 παίδων ὀρεχθέντα. δεσποίνης γὰρ καὶ βασιλίδος
ἀρετῆς ὁ τούτου λαχὼν τοῦ γέρως ἀνὴρ ἀνα-
γράφεται· καλεῖται δὲ παρὰ μὲν Ἕλλησιν ὑπομονή,
παρὰ δὲ Ἑβραίοις Ῥεβέκκα. ζητεῖ γὰρ ὁ ἄπονον
καὶ ἀταλαίπωρον εὑράμενος σοφίαν δι᾽ εὐμοιρίαν
φύσεως καὶ εὐτοκίαν ψυχῆς οὐδὲν τῶν εἰς βελτίω-
38 σιν. ἔχει γὰρ ἐν ἑτοίμῳ τέλεια τὰ τοῦ θεοῦ δῶρα
χάρισι ταῖς πρεσβυτέραις ἐπιπνευσθέντα, βούλεται
δὲ καὶ εὔχεται ταῦτα ἐπιμεῖναι. παρό μοι δοκεῖ
καὶ ὁ εὐεργέτης, ἵνα διαιωνίζωσιν αἱ χάριτες αὐτοῦ
τῷ λαβόντι, γυναῖκα τὴν ἐπιμονὴν ἐγγυῆσαι.

39   VIII. Ἀνάμνησίς γε μὴν μνήμης τὰ δευτερεῖα
φέρεται καὶ ὁ ἀναμιμνησκόμενος τοῦ μεμνημένου·
[525] ὁ μὲν | γὰρ ἔοικε τῷ συνεχῶς ὑγιαίνοντι, ὁ δὲ τῷ
ἐκ νόσου ἀναλαμβάνοντι· λήθη γὰρ νόσος μνήμης.
40 ἀνάγκη δὲ τὸν ὑπομνήσει χρώμενον ἐκλαθέσθαι
πρότερον ὧν ἐμέμνητο. τὴν μὲν οὖν μνήμην
Ἐφραΐμ, ἑρμηνευόμενον καρποφορίαν, ὁ ἱερὸς ὀνομάζει λόγος, τὴν δὲ ἀνάμνησιν ἐκ λήθης Μανασσῆν
476

labour. But the self-learnt kind, of which Isaac is a 36 member, that joy which is the best of the good emotions, is endowed with a simple nature free from mixture and alloy, and wants neither the practice nor the teaching which entails the need of the concubine as well as the legitimate forms of knowledge. When God rains down from heaven the good of which the self is a teacher and learner both, it is impossible that that self should still live in concubinage with the slavish arts, as though desiring to be the father of bastard thoughts and conclusions. He who has obtained this prize is enrolled as the husband of the queen and mistress virtue. Her name in the Greek means " constancy " ; in the Hebrew it is Rebecca. He who has gained the wisdom that comes without 37 toil and trouble, because his nature is happily gifted and his soul fruitful of good, does not seek for any means of betterment : for he has ready beside him in 38 their fulness the gifts of God, conveyed by the breath of God's higher graces, but he wishes and prays that these may remain with him constantly. And therefore I think his Benefactor, willing that His graces once received should stay for ever with him, gives him Constancy for his spouse.

VIII. Again, reminiscence takes the second place 39 to memory, and so with the reminded and the rememberer. The conditions of these two resemble respectively continuous health and recovery from disease, for forgetting is a disease of memory. The 40 man who is reminded must necessarily have forgotten what he remembered before. So the holy word names memory Ephraim, which by interpretation is " fruit-bearing," while reminding or reminiscence is called in the Hebrew Manasseh, that is " from

41 προσαγορεύουσιν Ἑβραῖοι. ὄντως γὰρ ἡ μὲν τοῦ
μεμνημένου ψυχὴ καρποφορεῖ ἃ ἔμαθεν οὐδὲν
ἀποβάλλουσα αὐτῶν, ἡ δὲ τοῦ ἀναμνήσει χρωμένου
ἔξω λήθης γίνεται, ᾗ πρὶν ὑπομνησθῆναι κατέσχητο.
μνημονικῷ μὲν οὖν ἀνδρὶ ἀστὴ συμβιοῖ γυνή,
μνήμη, ἐπιλανθανομένῳ δὲ παλλακίς, ἀνάμνησις,
Σύρα τὸ γένος, ἀλαζὼν καὶ ὑπέραυχος· Συρία γὰρ
42 ἑρμηνεύεται μετεωρία.[1] τῆς δὲ παλλακίδος ταύτης,
ἀναμνήσεως, υἱός ἐστι Μαχείρ, ὡς Ἑβραῖοι καλοῦσιν, ὡς δὲ Ἕλληνες, πατρός·[2] νομίζουσι γὰρ οἱ
ἀναμιμνησκόμενοι τὸν πατέρα νοῦν αἴτιον εἶναι τοῦ
ὑπομνησθῆναι, καὶ οὐ λογίζονται, ὅτι ὁ αὐτὸς
οὗτος ἐχώρησέ ποτε καὶ λήθην, οὐκ ἂν δεξάμενος
43 αὐτήν, εἰ παρ' αὐτὸν ἦν τὸ μεμνῆσθαι. λέγεται
γάρ· " ἐγένοντο υἱοὶ Μανασσῆ, οὓς ἔτεκεν αὐτῷ
ἡ παλλακὴ ἡ Σύρα, τὸν Μαχείρ· Μαχεὶρ δὲ ἐγέννησε τὸν Γαλαάδ."

Καὶ Ναχὼρ μέντοι, ὁ ἀδελφὸς Ἀβραάμ, ἔχει δύο
γυναῖκας, ἀστήν τε καὶ παλλακήν· ὄνομα δὲ τῆς
μὲν ἀστῆς Μελχά, Ῥουμὰ δὲ τῆς παλλακίδος.
44 ἀλλ' οὐχ ἱστορικὴ γενεαλογία ταῦτ' ἐστὶν ἀναγρα-
φεῖσα παρὰ τῷ σοφῷ νομοθέτῃ—μηδεὶς τοῦτ' εὖ
φρονῶν ὑπονοήσειεν,—ἀλλὰ πραγμάτων ψυχὴν
ὠφελῆσαι δυναμένων διὰ συμβόλων ἀνάπτυξις.
τὰ δ' ὀνόματα μεταβαλόντες εἰς τὴν ἡμετέραν
διάλεκτον εἰσόμεθα τὴν ὑπόσχεσιν ἀληθῆ. φέρ'
οὖν ἕκαστον αὐτῶν ἐρευνήσωμεν.

[1] So mss.: Wendland μετέωρα, which the mss. have in
Leg. All. iii. 18. The neuter plural seems strange; μετεωρία,
however, is only quoted from Latin writers and in the sense
of " forgetfulness."

[2] Cohn suggested ⟨ἐγρήγορσις⟩ πατρός, from " Onomastica,
ed. Lag. 195. 68." This I have not been able to see.

forgetfulness." For it is quite true that the soul of 41 the rememberer has the fruits of what he learned and has lost none of them, whereas the soul of the reminded comes out of forgetfulness which possessed him before he was reminded. The man of memory then is mated to a legitimate wife, memory ; the forgetful man to a concubine, reminiscence, Syrian by race, boastful and arrogant, for Syria is by interpretation " loftiness." This concubine has for a son, in the 42 Hebrew, Machir, meaning with us " the father's," for people who recall to memory think that the father mind was the cause of their being reminded, and do not reflect that this same mind also contained the forgetfulness, for which it would not have had room, if memory were present with it. We read, " The 43 sons of Manasseh were those whom the Syrian concubine bore to him, Machir, and Machir begat Gilead " (Gen. xlvi. 20).[a]

Nahor too, the brother of Abraham, has two wives, legitimate and concubine, and the name of the legitimate wife was Milcah, and the name of the concubine Reumah (Gen. xxii. 23, 24). Now let no 44 sane man suppose that we have here in the pages of the wise legislator an historical pedigree. What we have is a revelation through symbols of facts which may be profitable to the soul. And if we translate the names into our own tongue, we shall recognize that what is here promised is actually the case. Let us inquire then into each of them.

[a] This verse is not in the Hebrew here, but the substance of it appears in both Hebrew and LXX in 1 Chron. vii. 14.

PHILO

45 IX. Ναχὼρ ἑρμηνεύεται φωτὸς ἀνάπαυσις, Μελχὰ
δὲ βασίλισσα, Ῥουμὰ δὲ ὁρῶσά τι. τὸ μὲν οὖν
φῶς ἔχειν κατὰ διάνοιαν ἀγαθόν, τὸ δὲ ἀναπαυό-
μενον καὶ ἠρεμοῦν καὶ ἀκίνητον οὐ τέλειον ἀγαθόν·
ἡσυχίᾳ μὲν γὰρ τὰ κακὰ χρῆσθαι λυσιτελές, τὰ
46 δὲ ἀγαθὰ κινήσει συμφέρον. τίς γὰρ ὄνησις
εὐφώνου ἡσυχάζοντος ἢ μὴ αὐλοῦντος αὐλητοῦ ἢ
κιθαριστοῦ μὴ κιθαρίζοντος ἢ συνόλως τεχνίτου τὰ
κατὰ τὴν τέχνην μὴ ἐνεργοῦντος; ἢ γὰρ ἄνευ
πράξεώς θεωρία ψιλὴ πρὸς οὐδὲν ὄφελος τοῖς
ἐπιστήμοσιν· οὐ γὰρ ὁ παγκρατιάζειν ἢ πυκτεύειν
ἢ παλαίειν εἰδὼς ἐξαγκωνισθεὶς ἀπόναιτ' ἂν
ἀθλήσεως ἢ ὁ τὴν τοῦ τρέχειν ἐπιστήμην ἐκμαθών,
εἰ ποδαγρικῷ χρήσαιτο πάθει ἤ τινα ἄλλην περὶ
47 τὰς βάσεις κῆρα ἀναδέξαιτο. φῶς δὲ ψυχῆς
ἡλιοειδέστατον ἐπιστήμη· καθάπερ γὰρ τὰ ὄμματα
αὐγαῖς, καὶ ἡ διάνοια σοφίᾳ περιλάμπεται καὶ |
[526] ὀξυδερκέστερα ἐμβλέπειν ἐγχριομένη καινοῖς ἀεὶ
48 θεωρήμασιν ἐθίζεται. φωτὸς οὖν ἀνάπαυσις ἑρμηνεύεται Ναχὼρ εἰκότως· ᾗ μὲν γὰρ Ἀβραάμ ἐστι
τοῦ σοφοῦ συγγενής, φωτὸς τοῦ κατὰ σοφίαν
μετέσχηκεν· ᾗ δ' οὐ συναποδεδήμηκεν αὐτῷ τὴν
ἀπὸ τοῦ γενομένου πρὸς τὸ ἀγένητον καὶ τὴν ἀπὸ
τοῦ κόσμου πρὸς τὸν κοσμοπλάστην ἀποδημίαν,
χωλὴν καὶ ἀτελῆ τὴν ἐπιστήμην ἐκτήσατο, ἀνα-
παυομένην καὶ μένουσαν, μᾶλλον δ' ἀνδριάντος
49 ἀψύχου τρόπον πεπηγυῖαν. τῆς γὰρ Χαλδαϊκῆς

ᵃ In the allegory of §§ 45-53, Nahor represents any
philosophy which does not rise to the acknowledgement of
God, not merely astrology, though for a moment in § 49 it
seems to be identified with it. Rather its highest study is
astrology, a science for which, so far as it recognizes the
harmony of the heavens, Philo has considerable respect, cf.

IX. Nahor means "rest of light"[a]; Milcah, "queen"; 45
and Reumah, "seeing something." Now to have light
in the mind is good, yet what is at rest, quiet and
immovable, is not a perfect good ; it is well that
things evil should be in a state of stillness ; motion
on the other hand is the proper condition for the good.
For what use is the flute-player, however fine a per- 46
former he may be, if he remain quiet and does not
play, or the harpist if he does not use his harp, or in
general any craftsman if he does not exercise his
craft ? No knowledge is profitable to the possessors
through the mere theory if it is not combined with
practice : a man may know how to contend in the
pancratium, to box or to wrestle, yet if his hands be
tied behind his back he will get no good from his
athletic training ; so too with one who has mastered
the science of running, if he suffers from gout or from
any other affliction of the feet. Now knowledge is 47
the great sunlight of the soul. For as our eyes are
illuminated by the sun's rays, so is the mind by
wisdom, and anointed with the eyesalve of ever fresh
acquisitions of knowledge it grows accustomed to
see with clearer vision. Nahor is therefore properly
called " rest of light " : in so far as he is wise Abra- 48
ham's kinsman, he has obtained a share in wisdom's
light ; but in so far as he has not accompanied him
abroad in his journey from the created to the uncreated, and from the world to the world's Framer,
the knowledge he has gained is halting and incomplete, resting and staying where it is, or rather standing stockstill, like a lifeless statue. For he does not 49

De Mig. 178 ff. Its lower study is sceptical quibbling, and
these two represent respectively the lawful wife and the
concubine.

PHILO

οὐ μετανίσταται χώρας, τουτέστι τῆς περὶ ἀστρονομίαν θεωρίας οὐ διαζεύγνυται, τὸ γενόμενον πρὸ
τοῦ πεποιηκότος καὶ κόσμον πρὸ θεοῦ τετιμηκώς,
μᾶλλον δὲ τὸν κόσμον αὐτὸν θεὸν αὐτοκράτορα
νομίζων, οὐκ αὐτοκράτορος ἔργον θεοῦ.

50 X. Μελχὰν δὲ ἄγεται γυναῖκα, οὐκ ἀνθρώπων ἢ
πόλεων ἀφηγουμένην, ⟨ἣν⟩ τύχῃ, βασιλίδα, ἀλλ'
ὁμώνυμον αὐτὸ μόνον ἐκείνη. καθάπερ γὰρ τὸν
οὐρανόν, ἅτε κράτιστον ὄντα τῶν γεγονότων,
βασιλέα τῶν αἰσθητῶν εἴποι τις ἂν οὐκ ἀπὸ σκοποῦ,
οὕτως καὶ τὴν περὶ αὐτὸν ἐπιστήμην, ἣν μετίασιν
οἱ ἀστρονομοῦντες καὶ Χαλδαῖοι διαφερόντως,

51 βασιλίδα τῶν ἐπιστημῶν. γυνὴ μὲν οὖν ἥδε ἀστή,
παλλακὴ δὲ ἡ ἔν τι τῶν ὄντων ὁρῶσα, κἂν εἰ
πάντων εὐτελέστατον ὑπάρχοι. τῷ μὲν οὖν ἀρίστῳ
γένει τὸ ἄριστον ὁρᾶν, τὸ ὄντως ὄν, συμβέβηκεν—Ἰσραὴλ γὰρ ὁρῶν θεὸν ἑρμηνεύεται,—τῷ δὲ
δευτερείων ἐφιεμένῳ τὸ δεύτερον, τὸν αἰσθητὸν
οὐρανὸν καὶ τὴν ἐν αὐτῷ τῶν ἀστέρων ἐναρμόνιον
τάξιν καὶ πάμμουσον ὡς ἀληθῶς χορείαν.

52 τρίτοι δέ εἰσιν οἱ σκεπτικοί, τῶν μὲν ἐν τῇ φύσει
κρατίστων, αἰσθητῶν τε καὶ νοητῶν, οὐκ ἐφ-
απτόμενοι, περὶ μικρὰ μέντοι σοφίσματα τριβόμενοι
καὶ γλισχρολογούμενοι. τούτοις ἡ ὁρῶσά τι κἂν[1]
τὸ μικρότατον παλλακὶς Ῥουμὰ συνοικεῖ μὴ
δυναμένοις πρὸς τὴν τῶν ἀμεινόνων ἐλθεῖν ἔρευναν,

53 ἐξ ὧν τὸν ἑαυτῶν βίον ὀνήσουσιν. ὥσπερ γὰρ ἐν
ἰατροῖς ἡ λεγομένη λογιατρεία πολὺ τῆς τῶν
καμνόντων ὠφελείας ἀποστατεῖ—φαρμάκοις γὰρ
καὶ χειρουργίαις καὶ διαίταις, ἀλλ' οὐ λόγοις,
αἱ νόσοι θεραπεύονται,—οὕτω καὶ ἐν φιλοσοφίᾳ

---

[1] mss. καί.

remove from the land of Chaldaea, that is he does not sever himself from the study of astrology ; he honours the created before the creator, and the world before God, or rather he holds that the world is not the work of God but is itself God absolute in His power. X. But in Milcah he marries 50 a queen, not a ruler of men or perhaps cities, but one who merely bears the same name with a different meaning. For just as heaven, being the best and greatest of created things, may be rightly called the king of the world of our senses, so the knowledge of heaven, which the star-gazers and the Chaldaeans especially pursue, may be called the queen of sciences. Milcah, then, is the legitimate wife, but the concubine 51 is she who sees one thing of what is, though it be but the meanest of all. Now to see the best, that is the truly existing, is the lot of the best of races, Israel, for Israel means seeing God. The race or kind that strives for the second place sees the second best, that is the heaven of our senses, and therein the well-ordered host of the stars, the choir that moves to the fullest and truest music. Third are the 52 sceptics, who do not concern themselves with the best things in nature, whether perceived by the senses or the mind, but spend themselves on petty quibbles and trifling disputes. These are the house-mates of Reumah, who " sees something," even the smallest, men incapable of the quest for the better things which might bring profit to their lives. In 53 the case of physicians what is called word-medicine is far removed from assistance to the sick, for diseases are cured by drugs and surgery and prescriptions of diet, but not with words ; and so too in philosophy

λογοπῶλαι καὶ λογοθῆραί τινες αὐτὸ μόνον εἰσί,
τὸν ἀρρωστημάτων γέμοντα βίον θεραπεύειν οὔτε
ἐθέλοντες οὔτε ἐπιτηδεύοντες, ἐκ πρώτης δὲ
ἡλικίας ἄχρι γήρως ἐσχάτου γνωσιμαχοῦντές τε
[527] καὶ συλλαβομαχοῦντες οὐκ ἐρυθριῶσιν, | ὥσπερ
τῆς εὐδαιμονίας ἐπʼ ὀνομάτων καὶ ῥημάτων [καὶ]
ἀπεράντῳ καὶ ἀνηνύτῳ περιεργίᾳ κειμένης, ἀλλʼ
οὐκ ἐν τῷ τὸ ἦθος, τὴν τοῦ ἀνθρωπείου ⟨βίου⟩
πηγήν, ἄμεινον καταστήσασθαι, τὰς μὲν κακίας
ὑπερορίους φυγαδεύσαντα αὐτοῦ, τὰς δὲ ἀρετὰς
εἰσοικίσαντα.[1]

54 XI. Παλλακὰς μέντοι [ἢ][2] δόξας καὶ δόγματα
προσίενται καὶ οἱ φαῦλοι. φησὶ γοῦν ὅτι Θαμνά,
ἡ παλλακὴ Ἐλιφὰς τοῦ υἱοῦ Ἡσαῦ, ἔτεκε τῷ
Ἐλιφὰς τὸν Ἀμαλήκ. ὢ τῆς τοῦ ἀπογόνου
λαμπρᾶς δυσγενείας· ὄψει δὲ αὐτοῦ τὴν δυσ-
γένειαν, ἐὰν ἀποστὰς τοῦ περὶ ἀνθρώπων ταῦτα
εἰρῆσθαι νομίζειν τὴν ψυχὴν ὥσπερ ἐξ ἀνατομῆς
55 ἐπισκέπτῃ. τὴν μὲν τοίνυν ἄλογον καὶ ἄμετρον
ὁρμὴν τοῦ πάθους Ἀμαλὴκ προσαγορεύει· μεταληφθεὶς γάρ ἐστι λαὸς ἐκλείχων· καθάπερ γὰρ ἡ
τοῦ πυρὸς δύναμις τὴν παραβληθεῖσαν ὕλην ἀνα-
λίσκει, τὸν αὐτὸν τρόπον καὶ τὸ πάθος ἀναζέον τὰ
ἐν ποσὶ πάντα ἐπιλιχμᾶται καὶ διαφθείρει.

56 τούτου τοῦ πάθους πατὴρ Ἐλιφὰς ἀναγράφεται
δεόντως· ἑρμηνεύεται γάρ· θεός με διέσπειρεν.
ἀλλʼ οὐχ ὅταν ἀνασκεδάσῃ ἢ διασπείρῃ καὶ σκορα-

---

[1] τινα must be understood as subject to καταστήσασθαι;
otherwise grammar will require φυγαδεύσαντας (-ες?) and
εἰσοικίσαντας (-ες?).

[2] Perhaps read παλλακὰς μέντοι ⟨καὶ ἀστάς⟩, δόξας κτλ.
See App. p. 578.

there are men who are merely word-mongers and word-hunters, who neither wish nor practise to cure their life, brimful of infirmities as it is, but from their earliest years to extreme old age contend in battles of argument[a] and battles of syllables and blush not to do so. They act as though happiness depended on the endless fruitless hypercriticism of words as such,[b] instead of on establishing on a better basis character, the fount of human life,[c] by expelling the vices from its borders and planting there the virtues as settlers in their stead.

XI. The wicked, too, take to them as concubines, 54 opinions and doctrines. Thus he says that Timna, the concubine of Eliphaz, the son of Esau, bore Amalek to Eliphaz (Gen. xxxvi. 12). How distinguished is the misbirth of him whose descent is here given ! What the misbirth is you will see, if you cast away all thought that these words refer to men and turn your attention to what we may call the anatomy of soul-nature.[d] It is then the unreasoning and un- 55 measured impulse or appetite of passion which he calls Amalek, for the word by translation means " people licking up." For as the force of fire consumes the fuel laid before it, so too the boiling of passion licks up and destroys all that stands in its way. This passion is rightly declared to 56 have Eliphaz for its father, for Eliphaz means " God hath dispersed me." And is it not true that when God scatters and disperses the soul and ejects

---

[a] See App. p. 577.
[b] Lit. " nouns and verbs," see note on *De Mig.* 49.
[c] See App. p. 578.
[d] Lit. " observe the soul as it were by anatomy."

κίσῃ τὴν ψυχὴν ἀφ' ἑαυτοῦ ὁ θεός, τὸ ἄλογον
εὐθὺς γεννᾶται πάθος; τὴν μὲν γὰρ ὁρατικὴν
αὐτοῦ φιλόθεον ὄντως διάνοιαν, κληματίδα εὐγενῆ,
καταφυτεύει ῥίζας ἀποτείνων πρὸς ἀιδιότητα καὶ
εὐφορίαν καρπῶν διδοὺς πρὸς κτῆσιν καὶ ἀπό-
57 λαυσιν ἀρετῶν. διὸ καὶ Μωυσῆς εὔχεται φάσκων·
" εἰσαγαγὼν καταφύτευσον αὐτούς," ἵνα μὴ ἐφ-
ήμερα ἀλλ' ἀθάνατα καὶ μακραίωνα γένηται τὰ
θεῖα βλαστήματα. τὴν δὲ ἄδικον καὶ ἄθεον ψυχὴν
φυγαδεύων ἀφ' ἑαυτοῦ πορρωτάτω διέσπειρεν εἰς
τὸν ἡδονῶν καὶ ἐπιθυμιῶν καὶ ἀδικημάτων χῶρον.
ὁ δὲ χῶρος οὗτος προσφυέστατα ἀσεβῶν καλεῖται,
οὐχ ὁ μυθευόμενος ἐν Ἅιδου· καὶ γὰρ ὁ πρὸς
ἀλήθειαν Ἅιδης ὁ τοῦ μοχθηροῦ βίος ἐστίν, ὁ
ἀλάστωρ καὶ παλαμναῖος καὶ πάσαις ἀραῖς ἔνοχος.
58   XII. ἔστι δὲ καὶ ἑτέρωθι τὸ γράμμα
τοῦτο ἐστηλιτευμένον· " ἡνίκα διεμέριζεν ὁ ὕψι-
στος ἔθνη, ὡς διέσπειρεν υἱοὺς Ἀδάμ," τοὺς γηΐνους
ἅπαντας τρόπους οὐράνιον οὐδὲν ἀγαθὸν ἐσπουδα-
κότας ἰδεῖν ἤλασεν, ἀοίκους καὶ ἀπόλιδας καὶ
σποράδας ὄντως ἐργασάμενος. οὐδενὶ γὰρ τῶν
φαύλων οὐκ οἶκος, οὐ πόλις, οὐκ ἄλλο τῶν εἰς
κοινωνίαν οὐδὲν διασῴζεται, ἀλλ' ἀνίδρυτος ὢν
σπείρεται, πάντῃ φορούμενος καὶ μετανιστάμενος
ἀεὶ καὶ μηδαμόθι στηριχθῆναι δυνάμενος.
59 γίνεται οὖν τῷ φαύλῳ ἐξ ἀστῆς μὲν κακία, τὸ δὲ
πάθος ἐκ παλλακῆς. λογισμοῦ γὰρ ἡ μὲν ὅλη
[528] ψυχὴ καθάπερ ἀστὴ σύμβιος | —ψυχὴ δὲ ἐπίληπτος
τίκτει κακίας,—ἡ δὲ τοῦ σώματος φύσις παλλακή,

---

[a] Or "graft."   [b] Or simply "recorded."
[c] i.e. including the ἄλογον part of the soul as well as the
"soul's soul" or mind. Cf. Quis Rerum 55.

it with contumely from His presence unreasoning passion is at once engendered? The mind which truly loves God, that has the vision of Him, He " plants in," as a branch [a] of goodly birth, and He deepens its roots to reach to eternity and gives it fruitfulness for the acquisition and enjoyment of virtue. That is why Moses prays in these words, 57 " Bring them in and plant them in " (Ex. xv. 17), that the saplings of God's culture may not be for a day but age-long and immortal. On the other hand he banishes the unjust and godless souls from himself to the furthest bounds, and disperses them to the place of pleasures and lusts and injustices. That place is most fitly called the place of the impious, but it is not that mythical place of the impious in Hades. For the true Hades is the life of the bad, a life of damnation and blood-guiltiness, the victim of every curse.

XII. And elsewhere we have this text, 58 graven as on a stone,[b] " When the Highest divided the nations, when He dispersed the sons of Adam " (Deut. xxxii. 8), that is, when He drove away all the earthly ways of thinking which have no real desire to look on any heaven-sent good, and made them homeless and cityless, scattered in very truth. For none of the wicked have preserved for them home or city, nor aught else that tends to fellowship, but they are scattered without settlement, driven about on every side, ever changing their place, nowhere able to hold their ground. So then the wicked man 59 begets vice by his legitimate wife and passion by his concubine. For the soul as a whole [c] is the legitimate life-mate of reason, and if it be a soul of guilt it brings forth vices. The bodily nature is the concubine, and

PHILO

δι᾽ ἧς ἡ γένεσις τοῦ πάθους θεωρεῖται· ἡδονῶν γὰρ
60 καὶ ἐπιθυμιῶν χώρα τὸ σῶμα. καλεῖται δὲ
Θαμνά, ἧς μεταληφθέν ἐστι τοὔνομα ἔκλειψις
σαλευομένη· ἐκλείπει γὰρ καὶ ἀδυνατεῖ ἡ ψυχὴ τῷ
πάθει, σάλον καὶ κλύδωνα πολὺν ἀπὸ σώματος
ἐνδεξαμένη διὰ τὸν καταρραγέντα βαρὺν χειμῶνα
61 ἐξ ἀμετρίας ὁρμῆς.   κεφαλὴ δὲ ὡς ζῴου
πάντων τῶν λεχθέντων μερῶν ὁ γενάρχης ἐστὶν
Ἠσαῦ, ὃς τοτὲ μὲν ποίημα, τοτὲ δὲ δρῦς ἑρμηνεύεται, δρῦς μέν, παρόσον ἀκαμπὴς καὶ ἀνένδοτος
ἀπειθής τε καὶ σκληραύχην φύσει, συμβούλῳ
χρώμενος ἀνοίᾳ, δρύινος ὄντως, ποίημα δέ, παρόσον πλάσμα καὶ μῦθός ἐστιν ὁ μετὰ ἀφροσύνης
βίος, τραγῳδίας καὶ κενοῦ κόμπου καὶ πάλιν
γέλωτος καὶ κωμικῆς χλεύης ἀνάπλεως, ὑγιὲς ἔχων
οὐδέν, κατεψευσμένος, ἐκτετοξευκὼς ἀλήθειαν, τὴν
ἄποιον καὶ ἀνείδεον καὶ ἄπλαστον φύσιν ἐν οὐδενὶ
62 λόγῳ τιθέμενος, ἧς ὁ ἀσκητὴς ἐρᾷ. μαρτυρεῖ δὲ
Μωυσῆς φάσκων, ὅτι " ἦν Ἰακὼβ ἄπλαστος,
οἰκῶν οἰκίαν," ὥστε ὁ ἐναντίος τούτῳ ἄοικος ἂν
εἴη, πλάσματος καὶ ποιήματος καὶ μυθικῶν λήρων
ἑταῖρος, μᾶλλον δὲ σκηνὴ καὶ μῦθος αὐτός.
63 XIII. Ἡ μὲν δὴ λογισμοῦ φιλοθεάμονος πρὸς
ἀστὰς καὶ παλλακίδας δυνάμεις σύνοδος, ὡς οἷόν
τε ἦν, εἴρηται· τὸν δ᾽ εἱρμὸν τοῦ λόγου συνυφαν-

---

^a Cf. note on De Sac. 17.

^b Throughout these sections there is a play upon the
technical literary use of ποίημα and πλάσμα. While ποίημα
in this sense is a poem in general, πλάσμα is used of fictitious
but possible material such as was used in comedy, while
μῦθος gives the legendary matter which formed the staple of
tragedy. The double use of ποίημα in Quod Det. 125 is
somewhat similar.

we see that through it passion is generated, for the body is the region of pleasures and lusts. This 60 concubine is called Timna, whose name translated is " tossing faintness." For the soul faints and loses all power through passion when it receives from the body the flood of tossing surge caused by the storm wind which sweeps down in its fury, driven on by unbridled appetite.　　　　And of all the mem- 61 bers of the clan here described Esau is the progenitor, the head as it were of the whole creature,—Esau whose name we sometimes interpret as " an oak," sometimes as " a thing made up." [a] He is an oak because he is unbending, unyielding, disobedient and stiff-necked by nature, with folly as his counsellor, oak-like in very truth ; he is a thing made up because the life that consorts with folly is just fiction and fable, full of the bombast of tragedy on the one hand and of the broad jesting of comedy on the other ; [b] it has nothing sound about it, is utterly false and has thrown truth overboard ; it makes no account of the nature which is outside qualities [c] and forms and fashionings, the nature which the Man of Practice loves. To this Moses testifies when he says, " Jacob 62 was a plain or unfashioned man, living in a house " (Gen. xxv. 27). And therefore Esau his opposite must be houseless, and the friend of fiction and make-up and legendary follies, or rather himself the actor's stage and the playwright's legend.

XIII. We have now to the best of our ability 63 described the mating of the reason which yearns to see and learn with the faculties both of the lawful and the concubine type. We must now continue the thread of our discourse by examining the words

[c] Again a play (not translatable) on ποίημα.

τέον τἀκόλουθα διερευνῶντας. '' ὑπήκουσε '' φησίν
'' Ἀβραὰμ τῆς φωνῆς Σάρρας''· ἀναγκαῖον γὰρ
τοῖς παραγγέλμασιν ἀρετῆς τὸν μανθάνοντα πειθ-
64 αρχεῖν. οὐ πάντες δὲ πειθαρχοῦσιν, ἀλλ' ὅσοις
σφοδρὸς ἔρως ἐντέτηκεν ἐπιστήμης· ἐπεὶ καθ'
ἑκάστην σχεδὸν ἡμέραν τά τε ἀκροατήρια καὶ τὰ
θέατρα πληροῦται, διεξέρχονται δὲ ἀπνευστὶ συνείροντες τοὺς περὶ ἀρετῆς λόγους οἱ φιλοσοφοῦντες.
65 ἀλλὰ τί τῶν λεγομένων ὄφελος; ἀντὶ γὰρ τοῦ
προσέχειν ἑτέρωσε τὸν νοῦν ἀποστείλαντες οἱ μὲν
πλοῦ καὶ ἐμπορίας, οἱ δὲ προσόδων καὶ γεωργίας,
οἱ δὲ τιμῶν καὶ πολιτείας, οἱ δὲ τῶν ἀφ' ἑκάστης
τέχνης καὶ ἐπιτηδεύσεως κερδῶν, ἄλλοι δὲ τιμωρίας ἐχθρῶν, οἱ δὲ τῶν ἐν ταῖς ἐρωτικαῖς ἐπιθυμίαις ἀπολαύσεων καὶ συνόλως ἑτέρων ἕτεροι
διαμέμνηνται, ὡς ἕνεκα τῶν ἐπιδεικνυμένων κεκω-
φῆσθαι, τοῖς μὲν σώμασι παρεῖναι μόνον, ταῖς δὲ
διανοίαις ἀπηλλάχθαι, εἰδώλων καὶ ἀνδριάντων
66 διαφέρειν μηδέν.   εἰ δέ τινες καὶ προσ-
έχουσι, τοσοῦτον χρόνον καθέζονται μόνον ἀκούοντες, ἀπαλλαγέντες δ' οὐδενὸς τῶν εἰρημένων διαμέμνηνται, καὶ ἧκον τερφθῆναι δι' ἀκοῆς μᾶλλον
ἢ ὠφεληθῆναι· ὥστε οὐδὲν αὐτῶν ἴσχυσεν ἡ ψυχὴ
συλλαβεῖν καὶ κυοφορῆσαι, ἀλλ' ἅμα τὸ κινοῦν τὴν
[529] ἡδονὴν αἴτιον | ἡσύχασε καὶ ἡ προσοχὴ κατεσβέσθη.
67   τρίτοι δέ εἰσιν οἷς ἔναυλα μὲν τὰ
λεχθέντα ὑπηχεῖ, σοφισταὶ δὲ ἀντὶ φιλοσόφων
ἀνευρίσκονται. τούτων ὁ μὲν λόγος ἐπαινετός, ὁ
δὲ βίος ψεκτός ἐστι· δυνατοὶ μὲν γὰρ εἰπεῖν,
68 ἀδύνατοι δέ εἰσι πράττειν τὰ βέλτιστα. μόλις οὖν

which follow. Abraham, it says, " hearkened to the voice of Sarah " (Gen. xvi. 2), for the learner must needs obey the commands of virtue. Yet not all do 64 obey, only those in whom the strong longing for knowledge has become ingrained. Hardly a day passes but the lecture-halls and theatres are filled with philosophers discoursing at length, stringing together without stopping to take breath their disquisitions on virtue. Yet what profit is there in their 65 talk ? For instead of attending, the audience dismiss their minds elsewhither, some occupied with thoughts of voyaging and trading, some with their farming and its returns, others with honours and civic life, others on the profits they get from their particular trade and business, others with the vengeance they hope to wreak on their enemies, others with the enjoyments of their amorous passions, the class of thought in fact differing with the class of person. Thus, as far as what is being demonstrated is concerned, they are deaf, and while they are present in the body are absent in mind, and might as well be images or statues. And any who 66 do attend sit all the time merely hearing, and when they depart they remember nothing that has been said, and in fact their object in coming was to please their sense of hearing rather than to gain any profit ; thus their soul is unable to conceive or bring to the birth, but the moment the cause which stirred up pleasure is silent their attention is extinguished too.

There is a third class, who carry away 67 an echo of what has been said, but prove to be sophists rather than philosophers. The words of these deserve praise, but their lives censure, for they are capable of saying the best, but incapable of doing it.

ἔστιν εὑρεῖν προσεκτικὸν καὶ μνημονικόν, τὸ πράττειν τοῦ λέγειν προτιμῶντα, ἃ δὴ μαρτυρεῖται τῷ
φιλομαθεῖ διὰ τοῦ " ὑπήκουσε τῆς φωνῆς Σάρρας."
οὐ γὰρ ἀκούων ἀλλ' ὑπακούων εἰσάγεται· τὸ δέ
ἐστι τοῦ συναινεῖν καὶ πειθαρχεῖν εὐθυβολώτατον
69 ὄνομα.   οὐκ ἀπὸ σκοποῦ δὲ πρόσκειται
τὸ " τῆς φωνῆς," ἀλλὰ μὴ τῆς φωνούσης Σάρρας
ὑπακοῦσαι. ἴδιον γὰρ τοῦ μανθάνοντος φωνῆς καὶ
λόγων ἀκροᾶσθαι, διδάσκεται γὰρ τούτοις μόνοις·
ὁ δὲ ἀσκήσει τὸ καλὸν ἀλλὰ μὴ διδασκαλίᾳ κτώ-
μενος οὐ τοῖς λεγομένοις ἀλλὰ τοῖς λέγουσι προσ-
έχει, μιμούμενος τὸν ἐκείνων βίον ἐν ταῖς κατὰ
70 μέρος ἀνεπιλήπτοις πράξεσι. λέγεται γὰρ ἐπὶ τοῦ
Ἰακώβ, ἡνίκα εἰς τὸν συγγενικὸν γάμον πέμπεται·
" εἰσήκουσεν Ἰακὼβ τοῦ πατρὸς καὶ τῆς μητρὸς
αὐτοῦ, καὶ ἐπορεύθη εἰς τὴν Μεσοποταμίαν," οὐ
τῆς φωνῆς οὐδὲ τῶν λόγων—τοῦ γὰρ βίου μιμητὴν
ἔδει τὸν ἀσκητήν, οὐκ ἀκροατὴν λόγων εἶναι·
τοῦτο μὲν γὰρ ἴδιον τοῦ διδασκομένου, ἐκεῖνο δὲ
τοῦ διαθλοῦντος,—ἵνα κἀνταῦθα διαφορὰν ἀσκητοῦ
καὶ μανθάνοντος καταλάβωμεν, τοῦ μὲν κοσμου-
μένου κατὰ τὸν λέγοντα, τοῦ δὲ κατὰ τὸν ἐκείνου
λόγον.
71 XIV. " Λαβοῦσα " οὖν φησι " Σάρρα ἡ γυνὴ
Ἀβραὰμ Ἄγαρ τὴν Αἰγυπτίαν, τὴν ἑαυτῆς παιδίσκην, μετὰ δέκα ἔτη τοῦ οἰκῆσαι Ἀβραὰμ ἐν γῇ
Χαναάν, ἔδωκε τῷ Ἀβραὰμ τῷ ἀνδρὶ αὐτῆς αὐτῷ
γυναῖκα." βάσκανον μὲν καὶ πικρὸν καὶ κακόηθες
φύσει κακία, ἥμερον δὲ καὶ κοινωνικὸν καὶ εὐμενὲς

Rarely then shall we find one who combines attention, 68
memory and the valuing of deeds before words, which
three things are vouched for in the case of Abraham,
the lover of learning, in the phrase " He hearkened to
the voice of Sarah," for he is represented not as hearing, but as hearkening, a word which exactly expresses assent and obedience.   There is a 69
point, too, in the addition " to the voice," instead of
" he hearkened to Sarah speaking." For it is a
characteristic mark of the learner that he listens to a
voice and to words, since by these only is he taught,
whereas he who acquires the good through practice,
and not through teaching, fixes his attention not on
what is said, but on those who say it, and imitates
their life as shewn in the blamelessness of their
successive actions. Thus we read in the case of 70
Jacob, when he was sent to marry into his mother's
family, " Jacob heard his father and mother, and went
to Mesopotamia " (Gen. xxviii. 7). " Heard *them*,"
it says, not their voice or words, for the practiser must
be the imitator of a life, not the hearer of words, since
the latter is the characteristic mark of the recipient
of teaching, and the former of the strenuous self-
exerciser. Thus this text too is meant as a lesson to
us that we may realize the difference between a
learner and a practiser, how the course of one is
determined by what a person says, the other by the
person himself.

XIV. The verse continues, " So Sarah the wife of 71
Abraham, ten years after Abraham dwelt in Canaan,
took Hagar the Egyptian her handmaid and gave
her to Abraham her husband as his wife " (Gen.
xvi. 3). Now vice is malignant and sour and ill-
minded by nature, while virtue is gentle and sociable

PHILO

ἀρετή, πάντα τρόπον τοὺς εὐφυῶς ἔχοντας ὠφελεῖν
72 ἢ δι' αὐτῆς ἢ δι' ἑτέρων ἐθέλουσα. νυνὶ γοῦν μήπω
δυναμένοις ἡμῖν ἐκ φρονήσεως παιδοποιεῖσθαι τὴν
ἑαυτῆς ἐγγυᾷ θεραπαινίδα, τὴν ἐγκύκλιον, ὡς ἔφην,
παιδείαν, καὶ μονονοὺ προξενεῖν καὶ νυμφοστολεῖν
ὑπομένει· αὐτὴ γὰρ λέγεται λαβοῦσα διδόναι τῷ
73 ἀνδρὶ αὐτῆς γυναῖκα ταύτην.   ἄξιον δὲ
διαπορῆσαι, διὰ τί νυνὶ πάλιν γυναῖκα τοῦ 'Αβραὰμ
εἶπε τὴν Σάρραν, πολλάκις ἤδη πρότερον μεμηνυ-
κώς· οὐ γὰρ μακρολογίας τὸ φαυλότατον εἶδος,
ταυτολογίαν, ἐπιτετήδευκε. τί οὖν λεκτέον; ἐπειδὴ
μέλλει τὴν θεραπαινίδα φρονήσεως, τὴν ἐγκύκλιον
παιδείαν, ἐγγυᾶσθαι, φησὶν ὅτι οὐκ ἐξελάθετο τῶν
πρὸς τὴν δέσποιναν αὐτῆς ὁμολογιῶν, ἀλλ' οἶδε μὲν
ἐκείνην ἑαυτοῦ νόμῳ καὶ γνώμῃ γυναῖκα, ταύτην δὲ
ἀνάγκῃ καὶ βίᾳ καιροῦ. τοῦτο δὲ παντὶ συμβαίνει
φιλομαθεῖ· μάρτυς δ' ὁ πεπονθὼς γένοιτ' ἂν ἀψευ-
74 δέστατος. | ἐγὼ γοῦν ἡνίκα πρῶτον
[530] κέντροις φιλοσοφίας πρὸς τὸν πόθον αὐτῆς ἀν-
ηρεθίσθην, ὡμίλησα κομιδῇ νέος ὢν μιᾷ τῶν θεραπαινίδων αὐτῆς, γραμματικῇ, καὶ ὅσα ἐγέννησα ἐκ
ταύτης, τὸ γράφειν, τὸ ἀναγινώσκειν, τὴν ἱστορίαν
75 τῶν παρὰ ποιηταῖς, ἀνέθηκα τῇ δεσποίνῃ. καὶ
πάλιν ἑτέρᾳ συνελθών, γεωμετρίᾳ, καὶ τοῦ κάλλους
ἀγάμενος—εἶχε γὰρ συμμετρίαν καὶ ἀναλογίαν ἐν
τοῖς μέρεσι πᾶσι—τῶν ἐγγόνων οὐδὲν ἐνοσφισάμην,
76 ἀλλὰ τῇ ἀστῇ φέρων ἐδωρησάμην. ἐσπούδασα καὶ
τρίτῃ συνελθεῖν—ἦν δὲ εὔρυθμος, εὐάρμοστος, ἐμ-

494

and kindly, willing in every way, either by herself
or others, to help those whom nature has gifted.
Thus in the case before us, since as yet we are unable 72
to beget by wisdom, she gives us the hand of her
maiden, who is, as I have said, the culture of the
schools; and she does not shrink, we may almost say,
to carry out the wooing and preside over the bridal
rites; for she herself, we are told, took Hagar and
gave her as wife to her husband.   Now 73
it is worth considering carefully why in this place
Moses again calls Sarah the wife of Abraham, when
he has already stated the fact several times; for
Moses did not practise the worst form of prolixity,
namely tautology. What must we say then? This.
When Abraham is about to wed the handmaid of
wisdom, the school culture, he does not forget, so
the text implies, his faith plighted to her mistress,
but knows that the one is his wife by law and deliberate choice, the other only by necessity and the force
of occasion. And this is what happens to every lover
of learning; personal experience will prove the most
infallible of testimonies.   For instance 74
when first I was incited by the goads of philosophy
to desire her I consorted in early youth with one of
her handmaids, Grammar, and all that I begat by
her, writing, reading and study of the writings of the
poets, I dedicated to her mistress. And again I kept 75
company with another, namely Geometry, and was
charmed with her beauty, for she shewed symmetry
and proportion in every part. Yet I took none of
her children for my private use, but brought them as
a gift to the lawful wife. Again my ardour moved 76
me to keep company with a third; rich in rhythm,
harmony and melody was she, and her name was

μελής, μουσικὴ δὲ ἐκαλεῖτο—καὶ ἐγέννησα ἐξ αὐτῆς
διατονικὰ χρώματα καὶ ἐναρμόνια, συνημμένα,
διεζευγμένα μέλη, τῆς διὰ τεττάρων, τῆς διὰ
πέντε, τῆς διὰ πασῶν συμφωνίας ἐχόμενα, καὶ
πάλιν οὐδὲν αὐτῶν ἀπεκρυψάμην, ἵνα πλουσία μοι
γένηται ἡ ἀστὴ γυνή, μυρίων οἰκετῶν ὑπηρετου-
77 μένη πλήθει.   τινὲς γὰρ τοῖς φίλτροις τῶν
θεραπαινίδων δελεασθέντες ὠλιγώρησαν τῆς δεσποίνης, φιλοσοφίας, καὶ κατεγήρασαν οἱ μὲν ἐν
ποιήμασιν, οἱ δὲ ἐν γραμμαῖς, οἱ δὲ ἐν χρωμάτων
κράσεσιν, οἱ δὲ ἐν ἄλλοις μυρίοις, οὐ δυνηθέντες
78 ἐπὶ τὴν ἀστὴν ἀναδραμεῖν. ἔχει γὰρ ἑκάστη τέχνη
γλαφυρότητας, ὁλκούς τινας δυνάμεις, ὑφ᾽ ὧν ἔνιοι
ψυχαγωγούμενοι καταμένουσιν, ἐκλελησμένοι τῶν
πρὸς φιλοσοφίαν ὁμολογιῶν. ὁ δὲ ἐμμένων ταῖς
συνθήκαις πορίζει πάντα πανταχόθεν πρὸς τὴν
ἀρέσκειαν αὐτῆς. εἰκότως οὖν τῆς πίστεως αὐτὸν
ἀγάμενος ὁ ἱερὸς λόγος φησίν, ὅτι καὶ νῦν ἦν αὐτῷ
γυνὴ Σάρρα, ὅτε τὴν θεραπαινίδα πρὸς τὴν ἐκείνης
79 ἀρέσκειαν ἠγάγετο. καὶ μὴν ὥσπερ τὰ ἐγκύκλια
συμβάλλεται πρὸς φιλοσοφίας ἀνάληψιν, οὕτω καὶ
φιλοσοφία πρὸς σοφίας κτῆσιν. ἔστι γὰρ φιλοσοφία ἐπιτήδευσις σοφίας, σοφία δὲ ἐπιστήμη
θείων καὶ ἀνθρωπίνων καὶ τῶν τούτων αἰτίων.
γένοιτ᾽ ἂν οὖν ὥσπερ ἡ ἐγκύκλιος μουσικὴ φιλο-
80 σοφίας, οὕτω καὶ φιλοσοφία δούλη σοφίας. φιλοσοφία δὲ ἐγκράτειαν μὲν γαστρός, ἐγκράτειαν δὲ

Music, and from her I begat diatonics, chromatics and enharmonics, conjunct and disjunct melodies, conforming with the consonance of the fourth, fifth or octave intervals.[a]   And again of none of these did I make a secret hoard, wishing to see the lawful wife a lady of wealth with a host of servants ministering to her.   For some have been ensnared by the **77** love lures of the handmaids and spurned the mistress, and have grown old, some doting on poetry, some on geometrical figures, some on the blending of musical " colours,"[b] and a host of other things, and have never been able to soar to the winning of the lawful wife.[c] For each art has its charms, its powers of attraction, **78** and some beguiled by these stay with them and forget their pledges to Philosophy. But he who abides by the covenants he has made provides from every quarter everything he can to do her service. It is natural, then, that the holy word should say in admiration of his faithfulness that even then was Sarah his wife when he wedded the handmaid to do her service. And indeed just as the school subjects **79** contribute to the acquirement of philosophy, so does philosophy to the getting of wisdom.   For philosophy is the practice or study of wisdom, and wisdom is the knowledge of things divine and human and their causes.[d] And therefore just as the culture of the schools is the bond-servant of philosophy, so must philosophy be the servant of wisdom. Now philo- **80** sophy teaches us the control of the belly and the

---

[a] *Cf. Leg. All.* iii. 122, *De Post.* 104, *De Agr.* 137.

[b] See App. p. 578.

[c] For the tendency to prolong the study of the Encyclia beyond what Philo considered the proper time *cf. De Ebr.* 51.

[d] See App. p. 579.

τῶν μετὰ γαστέρα, ἐγκράτειαν δὲ καὶ γλώττης
ἀναδιδάσκει. ταῦτα λέγεται μὲν εἶναι δι᾽ αὐτὰ
αἱρετά, σεμνότερα δὲ φαίνοιτ᾽ ⟨ἄν⟩, εἰ θεοῦ τιμῆς
καὶ ἀρεσκείας ἕνεκα ἐπιτηδεύοιτο. μεμνῆσθαι οὖν
δεῖ τῆς κυρίας, ὁπότε μέλλοιμεν αὐτῆς ⟨τὰς⟩
θεραπαινίδας μνᾶσθαι· καὶ λεγώμεθα μὲν ἄνδρες
εἶναι τούτων, ὑπαρχέτω δ᾽ ἡμῖν ἐκείνη πρὸς
81 ἀλήθειαν γυνή, μὴ λεγέσθω.

[531]   XV. | Δίδωσι δ᾽ οὐκ εὐθὺς εἰς τὴν Χαναναίων
γῆν ἀφικομένῳ, ἀλλὰ μετὰ δεκαετίαν τῆς ἐκεῖ
διατριβῆς. τί δὲ τοῦτ᾽ ἐστίν, οὐκ ἀμελῶς ἐπι-
σκεπτέον· ἐν ἀρχῇ μὲν τῆς γενέσεως ἡμῶν ἡ ψυχὴ
συντρόφοις τοῖς πάθεσι μόνοις χρῆται, λύπαις,
ἀλγηδόσι, πτόαις, ἐπιθυμίαις, ἡδοναῖς, ἃ διὰ τῶν
αἰσθήσεων ἐπ᾽ αὐτὴν ἔρχεται, μήπω τοῦ λογισμοῦ
βλέπειν δυναμένου τά τε ἀγαθὰ καὶ κακὰ καὶ
ᾗ διαφέρει ταῦτα ἀλλήλων ἀκριβοῦν, ἀλλ᾽ ἔτι
νυστάζοντος καὶ ὡς ἐν ὕπνῳ βαθεῖ καταμεμυκότος.
82 χρόνου δὲ προϊόντος ὅταν ἐκβαίνοντες τῆς παιδικῆς ἡλικίας μειρακιοῦσθαι μέλλωμεν, τὸ δίδυμον
στέλεχος εὐθὺς ἐκ μιᾶς, ἀρετὴ καὶ κακία, φύεται
ῥίζης· καὶ ποιούμεθα μὲν τὴν κατάληψιν ἀμφοῖν,
αἱρούμεθα δὲ πάντως τὴν ἑτέραν, οἱ μὲν εὐφυεῖς
83 ἀρετήν, κακίαν δ᾽ οἱ ἐναντίοι.   τούτων
προϋποτυπωθέντων εἰδέναι χρή, ὅτι παθῶν μὲν
Αἴγυπτος σύμβολόν ἐστι, κακιῶν δὲ ἡ Χαναναίων
γῆ· ὥστ᾽ εἰκότως ἀναστήσας ἀπ᾽ Αἰγύπτου τὸν
84 λεὼν εἰς τὴν Χαναναίων εἰσάγει χώραν. ἄνθρωπος
γάρ, ὡς ἔφην, ἅμα μὲν τῇ γενέσει τὸ Αἰγύπτιον
πάθος ἔλαχεν οἰκεῖν ἡδοναῖς καὶ ἀλγηδόσι προσ-
ερριζωμένος, αὖθις δ᾽ ἀποικίαν στέλλεται τὴν πρὸς

parts below it, and control also of the tongue. Such powers of control are said to be desirable in themselves, but they will assume a grander and loftier aspect if practised for the honour and service of God. So when we are about to woo the handmaids we must remember the sovereign lady, and let us be called their husbands, but let her be not called but be in reality our true wife.

XV. Next Sarah gives Hagar to Abraham, not at 81 once after his arrival in the land of the Canaanites, but after he has stayed there for ten years. The meaning of this requires careful consideration. In the first stage of our coming into existence the soul is reared with none but passions to be its comrades, griefs, pains, excitements, desires, pleasures, all of which come to it through the senses, since the reason is not yet able to see good and evil and to form an accurate judgement of the difference between them, but is still slumbering, its eyes closed as if in deep sleep. But as time goes on, when we leave 82 the stage of boyhood and are adolescent, there springs from the single root the twofold stalk, virtue and vice, and we form an apprehension of both, but necessarily choose one or the other, the better-natured choosing virtue, the opposite kind vice.

Following on this preliminary sketch 83 we must know that Egypt symbolizes sense, and the land of the Canaanites vice, and thus it is natural that when Moses brings the people out of Egypt he should lead them into the country of the Canaanites. The man, as I have said, at his first coming into being 84 receives for his habitation Egyptian passion, and his roots are fixed in pleasures and pains ; but after awhile he emigrates to a new home, vice. The

κακίαν, ἤδη τοῦ λογισμοῦ πρὸς τὸ ὀξυωπέστερον
ἐπιδεδωκότος καὶ καταλαμβάνοντος μὲν ἀμφότερα,
ἀγαθόν τε αὖ καὶ κακόν, τὸ δὲ χεῖρον αἱρουμένου
διὰ τὸ πολὺ μετέχειν τοῦ θνητοῦ, ᾧ τὸ κακὸν
οἰκεῖον, ἐπεὶ καὶ τοὐναντίον τῷ θείῳ, τὸ ἀγαθόν.

85   XVI. ἀλλ' αἱ μὲν φύσει πατρίδες
αὗται, παιδικῆς μὲν ἡλικίας τὸ πάθος, Αἴγυπτος,
ἡβώσης δὲ κακία, ἡ Χανανῖτις. ὁ δὲ ἱερὸς λόγος,
καίτοι σαφῶς ἐπιστάμενος τὰς τοῦ θνητοῦ γένους
πατρίδας ἡμῶν, ὑποτίθεται τὰ πρακτέα καὶ συν-
οίσοντα παραγγέλλων μισεῖν τὰ ἔθη καὶ τὰ νόμιμα
86 καὶ τὰ ἐπιτηδεύματα αὐτῶν ἐν οἷς φησι· " καὶ εἶπε
κύριος πρὸς Μωυσῆν λέγων· λάλησον τοῖς υἱοῖς
Ἰσραὴλ καὶ ἐρεῖς πρὸς αὐτούς· ἐγὼ κύριος ὁ θεὸς
ὑμῶν· κατὰ τὰ ἐπιτηδεύματα γῆς Αἰγύπτου, ἐν ᾗ
κατοικήσατε ἐπ' αὐτῆς, οὐ ποιήσετε· καὶ κατὰ τὰ
ἐπιτηδεύματα γῆς Χαναάν, εἰς ἣν ἐγὼ εἰσάγω ὑμᾶς
ἐκεῖ, οὐ ποιήσετε· καὶ τοῖς νομίμοις αὐτῶν οὐ
πορεύσεσθε· τὰ κρίματά μου ποιήσετε, καὶ τὰ
προστάγματά μου φυλάξεσθε, πορεύεσθε ἐν αὐτοῖς·
ἐγὼ κύριος ὁ θεὸς ὑμῶν. καὶ φυλάξεσθε πάντα τὰ
προστάγματά μου καὶ τὰ κρίματά μου, καὶ ποιήσετε αὐτά. ὁ ποιήσας αὐτὰ ζήσεται ἐν αὐτοῖς·
87 ἐγὼ κύριος ὁ θεὸς ὑμῶν." οὐκοῦν ἡ πρὸς ἀλήθειαν
ζωὴ περιπατοῦντός[1] ἐστιν ἐν ταῖς τοῦ θεοῦ κρίσεσι
[532] καὶ προστάξεσιν, | ὥστε θάνατος ἂν εἴη τὰ τῶν
ἀθέων ἐπιτηδεύματα. τίνα δὲ τὰ ἀθέων εἴρηται·

                 [1] MSS. περὶ παντός.

reason has by this time advanced to a higher degree of vision, and while it apprehends both alternatives, good and evil, chooses the worst, because mortality is so large an ingredient in the reason, and evil is native to mortality as its opposite, good, is to the divine. XVI. Now according to nature 85 these are the native-lands of the two ages : Egypt, that is passion, of the age of childhood ; Canaan, that is vice, of the age of adolescence. But the holy word, though it knows full well what are the native-lands of our mortal race, sets before us what we should do and what will be for our good, by bidding us hate the habits and the customs and the practices of those lands. It does so in the following words, " And the 86 Lord spake unto Moses, saying : ' Speak unto the sons of Israel, and thou shalt say unto them " I am the Lord your God. According to the practices of the land of Egypt, in which ye dwelt therein, ye shall not do ; and according unto the practices of the land of Canaan, into which I bring you there, you shall not do, and by their customs ye shall not walk. Ye shall do My judgements and ye shall keep My ordinances, walk in them. I am the Lord your God. And ye shall keep all My ordinances and My judge-ments, and ye shall do them. He that doeth them shall live in them. I am the Lord your God ' " (Lev. xviii. 1-5). So then the true life is the life of him 87 who walks in the judgements and ordinances of God, so that the practices of the godless must be death. And what the practices of the godless are we have been told. They are the practices of passion and

τὰ πάθους καὶ κακιῶν ἐστιν,[1] ἐξ ὧν τὰ ἀσεβῶν καὶ
ἀνοσιουργῶν[2] πλήθη φύεται.

88 Μετὰ δεκαετίαν οὖν τῆς πρὸς Χαναναίους μετ-
οικίας ἀξόμεθα τὴν Ἄγαρ, ἐπειδήπερ εὐθὺς μὲν
γενόμενοι λογικοὶ τῆς φύσει βλαβερᾶς ἀμαθίας καὶ
ἀπαιδευσίας μεταποιούμεθα, χρόνῳ δ' ὕστερον καὶ
ἐν ἀριθμῷ τελείῳ, δεκάδι, νομίμου[3] παιδείας τῆς
ὠφελεῖν δυναμένης εἰς ἐπιθυμίαν ἐρχόμεθα.

89 XVII. Τὸν δὲ περὶ δεκάδος λόγον ἐπιμελῶς μὲν
ἠκρίβωσαν μουσικῶν παῖδες, ὕμνησε δὲ οὐ μετρίως
ὁ ἱερώτατος Μωυσῆς, ἀναθεὶς αὐτῇ τὰ κάλλιστα,
τὰς ἀρχάς,[4] τὰς ἀπαρχάς, τὰ τῶν ἱερέων ἐνδελεχῆ
δῶρα, τὴν τοῦ Πάσχα διατήρησιν, τὸν ἱλασμόν, τὴν
διὰ πεντηκονταετίας ἄφεσίν τε καὶ εἰς τὰς ἀρχαίας
λήξεις ἐπάνοδον, τὴν κατασκευὴν τῆς ἀδιαλύτου
σκηνῆς, ἄλλα μυρία, ὧν μακρὸν ἂν εἴη μεμνῆσθαι.

90 τὰ δὲ καίρια οὐ παρετέον.[5]   αὐτίκα τὸν
Νῶε ἡμῖν—πρῶτος δ' οὗτος δίκαιος ἐν ταῖς ἱεραῖς
ἀνερρήθη γραφαῖς—ἀπὸ τοῦ διαπλασθέντος ἐκ γῆς
εἰσάγει δέκατον, οὐκ ἐνιαυτῶν πλῆθος παραστῆσαι

---

[1] MSS. τινὰ δὲ ἀθεώρητα πάθους καὶ κακιῶν ἐστιν.—The text
printed is my conjecture. Mangey retains the MS. text
and translates, ignoring the neuter τινὰ, "quidam non per-
pendunt affectus et vitia." Markland's ἅτινα δή is an improvement, but still leaves ἀθεώρητα in the unnatural sense
of "regardless of" (and therefore "practising"). Moreover,
the words are quite pointless. With the correction the
argument proceeds quite logically. The later part of the
quotation tells us that he who does God's ordinances will
live. It follows that the practices of the godless are death.
If you ask what are the practices of the godless, the first
part of the text has told us (εἴρηται) that they are the practices
of Egypt and Canaan, that is (see § 85) passion and vice.
We might perhaps get even nearer to the MSS. by omitting
τὰ before ἀθέων.

502

vices, from which spring the many multitudes of the impious and the workers of unholiness.

So then ten years after our migration to the Canaanites we shall wed Hagar, since as soon as we have become reasoning beings we take to ourselves the ignorance and indiscipline whose nature is so mischievous [a] and only after a time and under the perfect number ten do we reach the desire for the lawful discipline which can profit us. 88

XVII. Now the lore of the decad has been carefully discussed in detail in the schools of the musicians, and is extolled in no ordinary degree by the holiest of men, Moses, who connects with it things of special excellence, governments, the first-fruits, the recurrent gifts of the priests, the observation of the passover, the atonement, the liberation and return to the old possessions in the fiftieth year, the furnishing of the permanent tabernacle, and others without number. These it would take too long to mention, but crucial examples must not be omitted. 89

For instance, he represents Noah, the first man recorded as just in holy scriptures, as the tenth descendant from the man who was moulded from the earth ; and in doing so he does not wish to set before 90

---

[a] Or perhaps "the natural (and harmful) ignorance," which, though a less obvious way of taking the words, agrees better with the thought that ignorance is the πατρίς of the man.

---

[2] Perhaps read ἀνοσίων ἔργων; general practices are the progenitors of particular deeds.

[3] MSS. νομίμω (-ως).

[4] So one MS.: the rest εὐχάς, which Mangey preferred, but see beginning of § 92, and the thought of ἀρχάς recurs in § 110.　　　[5] MSS. παρεατέον or παριτέον.

βουλόμενος, ἀλλὰ διδάξαι σαφῶς, ὅτι ὥσπερ δεκὰς
ἀριθμῶν τῶν ἀπὸ μονάδος ἐστὶ πέρας τελειότατον,
οὕτω τὸ δίκαιον ἐν ψυχῇ τέλειον καὶ πέρας ὄντως
91 τῶν κατὰ τὸν βίον πράξεων.   τὴν μὲν
γὰρ πολλαπλασιαζομένην ἐφ' ἑαυτὴν τριάδα πρὸς
ἐνάτου γένεσιν ἀριθμοῦ πολεμιωτάτην ἐξεῖπον οἱ
χρησμοί, τὴν δὲ ἐπιβεβηκυῖαν μονάδα πρὸς ἐκπλή-
92 ρωσιν δεκάδος ὡς φίλην ἀπεδέξαντο. σημεῖον δέ·
τὰς ἐννέα τῶν βασιλέων ἀρχάς, ἡνίκα ἡ ἐμφύλιος
ἀνερριπίσθη στάσις, τῶν τεττάρων παθῶν πρὸς τὰς
πέντε αἰσθήσεις κονισαμένων καὶ πόρθησιν καὶ
κατασκαφὴν κινδυνευούσης τρόπον πόλεως τῆς
ὅλης[1] ἀναδέχεσθαι ψυχῆς, ἐκστρατεύσας ὁ σοφὸς
93 Ἀβραὰμ κατέλυσε δέκατος ἐπιφανείς. οὗτος ἀντὶ
χειμῶνος γαλήνην καὶ ὑγείαν ἀντὶ νόσου καὶ ζωήν,
εἰ δεῖ τἀληθὲς εἰπεῖν, ἀντὶ θανάτου παρεσκεύασε,
τοῦ νικηφόρου θεοῦ τροπαιοφόρον αὐτὸν ἀναδεί-
ξαντος, ᾧ καὶ τὰς δεκάτας χαριστήρια τῆς νίκης
94 ἀνατίθησι.   καὶ παντὸς μέντοι τοῦ ἐλθόν-
τος "ὑπὸ τὴν ῥάβδον," λέγω δὲ τὴν παιδείαν,
ἡμέρου καὶ τιθασοῦ θρέμματος τὸ δέκατον ἀποκρίνεται, νόμου προστάξει γινόμενον "ἅγιον," ἵν' ἐκ
πολλῶν διδασκώμεθα τὴν δεκάδος πρὸς θεὸν
οἰκειότητα καὶ τὴν τοῦ ἐννέα ἀριθμοῦ πρὸς τὸ
95 θνητὸν ἡμῶν γένος.   XVIII. ἀλλὰ γὰρ
[533] οὐκ ἀπὸ ζῴων | μόνον ἀπάρχεσθαι δεκάτας, ἀλλὰ
καὶ ἀπὸ τῶν ὅσα ἐκ γῆς βλαστάνει διείρηται.
"πᾶσα" γάρ φησι "δεκάτη τῆς γῆς ἀπὸ τοῦ

---

[1] Some mss. αὐλῆς: Wend. conjectures ἀλούσης.

---

[a] See note on § 59. Here the phrase seems to be used of
the animal or unreasoning nature, ignoring the mind. For
the "city" of the story is Sodom, which is a "soul blind of

us any particular number of years, but to shew us clearly that, just as ten is the end of the numbers which start from one and most perfect, so justice in the soul is perfect and the true end of our life's actions. For when three is multiplied by 91 itself and thus produces the number nine, the oracles pronounce it to be a number of great hostility, while the added one which completes the ten they approve of as friendly. This is shewn in the incident of 92 Abraham and the nine kings. When the civil war burst into flames, and the four passions prepared for combat with the five senses, when the whole soul*a* was on the point to suffer sacking and razing like a city, wise Abraham took the field, and appearing as the tenth, made an end of all nine governments (Gen. xiv.). He provided calm in the place of storm, health for 93 sickness, and life we may truly say for death, being declared the winner of the trophies by God the victory-giver, to whom too he dedicated the tenths as thank-offerings for his victory (Gen. xiv. 20). Further, everything that comes " under the rod," the 94 rod of discipline,*b* that is every tame and docile creature, has a tenth set apart from it which by the ordinance of the law becomes " holy " (Lev. xxvii. 32), that so through many reminders we may learn the close connexion of ten with God and of nine with our mortal race. XVIII. But indeed it is 95 commanded to offer tenths as first-fruits, not only from animals, but from all that springs from the earth. " Every tenth of the earth," it says, " from the seed

reason " (§ 109). Wendland's ἀλούσης (agreeing with πόλεως) may be right.

b Cf. Leg. All. iii. 89 f., De Post. 97. For ten as the number of παιδεία cf. note on De Sac. 122.

σπέρματος καὶ τοῦ καρποῦ τοῦ ξυλίνου ἐστὶν ἅγιον
τῷ κυρίῳ· καὶ πᾶσα δεκάτη βοῶν καὶ προβάτων,
καὶ πᾶν ὃ ἂν διέλθῃ ἐν τῷ ἀριθμῷ ὑπὸ τὴν ῥάβδον,
96 τὸ δέκατον ἔσται ἅγιον τῷ κυρίῳ." ὁρᾷς ὅτι καὶ
ἀπὸ τοῦ περὶ ἡμᾶς ὄγκου σωματικοῦ, ὃς γεώδης καὶ
ξύλινος ὄντως ἐστίν, οἴεται δεῖν ἀπάρχεσθαι; ἡ
γὰρ ζωὴ καὶ διαμονὴ καὶ αὔξησις καὶ ὑγίεια αὐτῷ
θείᾳ γίνεται χάριτι. ὁρᾷς δ' ὅτι καὶ ἀπὸ τῶν ἐν
ἡμῖν αὐτοῖς ζῴων ἀλόγων—ταῦτα δ' εἰσὶν αἰσθήσεις
—πάλιν ἀπάρχεσθαι διείρηται; τὸ γὰρ ὁρᾶν καὶ
ἀκούειν καὶ ὀσφραίνεσθαι καὶ γεύεσθαι, ἔτι δὲ
ἅπτεσθαι δωρεαὶ θεῖαι, ὑπὲρ ὧν εὐχαριστητέον.
97   ἀλλὰ γὰρ οὐ μόνον ἐπὶ τοῖς ξυλίνοις
καὶ γηίνοις σώματος ὄγκοις[1] οὐδ' ἐπ' ἀλόγοις ζῴοις,
ταῖς αἰσθήσεσι, τὸν εὐεργέτην ἐπαινεῖν διδα-
σκόμεθα, ἀλλὰ καὶ ἐπὶ τῷ νῷ, ὃς κυρίως εἰπεῖν
ἄνθρωπός ἐστιν ἐν ἀνθρώπῳ, κρείττων ἐν χεί-
98 ρονι καὶ ἀθάνατος ἐν θνητῷ. διὰ τοῦτο οἶμαι τὰ
πρωτότοκα καθιέρωσε πάντα, τὴν δεκάτην, λέγω
Λευιτικὴν φυλήν, ἀντικαταλλαξάμενος πρὸς διατήρησιν καὶ φυλακὴν ὁσιότητος καὶ εὐσεβείας καὶ
λειτουργιῶν, αἳ πρὸς τὴν τοῦ θεοῦ τιμὴν ἀνα-
φέρονται. τὸ γὰρ πρῶτον καὶ ἄριστον ἐν ἡμῖν αὐτοῖς
ὁ λογισμός ἐστι, καὶ ἄξιον τὰς συνέσεως καὶ
ἀγχινοίας καταλήψεώς τε καὶ φρονήσεως καὶ τῶν
ἄλλων δυνάμεων, ὅσαι περὶ αὐτόν εἰσιν, ἀπαρχὰς
ἀνατιθέναι θεῷ τῷ τὴν εὐφορίαν τοῦ διανοεῖσθαι
99 παρασχόντι. ἐνθένδε ὁ μὲν ἀσκητικὸς ὁρμηθεὶς
εὐχόμενος εἶπε· " πάντων ὧν ἄν μοι δῷς, δεκάτην
ἀποδεκατώσω σοί," ὁ δὲ χρησμὸς ὁ μετὰ τὰς
ἐπινικίους εὐχὰς ἀναγραφείς, ἃς ὁ τὴν αὐτομαθῆ

[1] MSS. σωματικοῖς.

and from the fruit of wood, and every tenth of oxen and sheep, and everything that passes through in the number under the rod the tenth shall be holy unto the Lord " (Lev. xxvii. 30, 32). Observe that he thinks 96 that first-fruits are due from our body, the cumbersome mass which is indeed of earth and of wood. For its life and survival, growth and health, come to it by the grace of God. Note too that we are also bidden to give first-fruits of the unreasoning creatures within us, the senses, for sight and hearing and smell and taste and touch also are gifts of God for which we must give thanks.   Yet not only for the 97 wooden and earthen mass of the body, not only for the unreasoning creatures, the senses, are we taught to praise the Benefactor, but also for the mind which may be truly called the man within the man, the better part within the worse, the immortal within the mortal. This is why, I believe, He sanctified all the 98 first-born, and took as their ransom the tenth, that is the tribe of Levi, that they should observe and maintain holiness and piety and the rites which are offered for the honour of God. For the first and best thing in us is the reason, and it is only right that from its intelligence, its shrewdness, its apprehension, its prudence and the other qualities which belong to it, we should offer first-fruits to God, who gave to it its fertility of thinking. It was this feeling which 99 prompted the Man of Practice when he vowed thus, " Of all that thou givest me, I will give a tenth to thee " (Gen. xxviii. 22) ; which prompted the oracle that follows the blessing given to the victor by Melchisedek the holder of that priesthood, whose

καὶ αὐτοδίδακτον λαχὼν ἱερωσύνην ποιεῖται Μελ-
χισεδέκ, '' ἔδωκε γὰρ αὐτῷ '' φησίν '' δεκάτην ἀπὸ
πάντων,'' ἀπὸ τῶν κατ' αἴσθησιν τὸ καλῶς αἰσθάνεσθαι, ἀπὸ τῶν κατὰ λόγον τὸ εὖ λέγειν, ἀπὸ τῶν
100 κατὰ νοῦν τὸ εὖ διανοεῖσθαι.   παγκάλως
οὖν καὶ ἀναγκαίως ἅμα ἐν εἴδει παραδιηγήματος,
ἡνίκα τῆς οὐρανίου καὶ θείας τροφῆς τὸ μνημεῖον
ἐν στάμνῳ χρυσῷ καθιεροῦτο, φησὶν ὡς ἄρα '' τὸ
γομὸρ τὸ δέκατον τῶν τριῶν μέτρων ἦν.'' ἐν ἡμῖν
γὰρ αὐτοῖς τρία μέτρα εἶναι δοκεῖ, αἴσθησις, λόγος,
νοῦς· αἰσθητῶν μὲν αἴσθησις, ὀνομάτων δὲ καὶ
ῥημάτων καὶ τῶν λεγομένων ὁ λόγος, νοητῶν δὲ
101 νοῦς. ἀφ' ἑκάστου δὴ τῶν τριῶν μέτρων τούτων
ἀπαρκτέον ὥσπερ τινὰ ἱερὰν δεκάτην, ἵνα καὶ τὸ
λέγειν καὶ τὸ αἰσθάνεσθαι καὶ τὸ καταλαμβάνειν
ἀνυπαιτίως καὶ ὑγιεινῶς κατὰ θεὸν ἐξετάζηται· τὸ
[534] γὰρ ἀληθινὸν καὶ | δίκαιον μέτρον τοῦτ' ἐστί, τὰ δὲ
102 καθ' ἡμᾶς ψευδῆ τε καὶ ἄδικα. XIX. εἰκότως οὖν
καὶ ἐπὶ τῶν θυσιῶν τὸ μὲν δέκατον τοῦ μέτρου τῆς
σεμιδάλεως τοῖς ἱερείοις ἐπὶ τὸν βωμὸν συναν-
ενεχθήσεται, ὁ δὲ ἔνατος ἀριθμός, τὸ λείψανον τοῦ
δεκάτου, παρ' ἡμῖν αὐτοῖς παραμενεῖ.
103 τούτοις συνᾴδει καὶ ἡ τῶν ἱερέων ἐνδελεχὴς θυσία·
τὸ γὰρ δέκατον τὸ τοῦ οἶφι σεμιδάλεως ἀεὶ διείρηται προσφέρειν αὐτοῖς. ἔμαθον γὰρ τὸν ἔνατον
ὑπερβαίνοντες αἰσθητὸν δοκήσει θεὸν τὸν δέκατον
καὶ μόνον ὄντα ἀψευδῶς προσκυνεῖν. ἐννέα γὰρ
ὁ κόσμος ἔλαχε μοίρας, ἐν οὐρανῷ μὲν ὀκτώ, τήν
τε ἀπλανῆ καὶ ἑπτὰ τὰς πεπλανημένας ἐν τάξεσι

---

[a] Or "Him who is tenth and alone truly exists"; or
"Him who is truly tenth and alone" (cf. § 105), referring to
the mystical identity of the Ten and the One.

tradition he had learned from none other but himself. For " he gave him," it runs, " a tenth from all " (Gen. xiv. 20) ; from the things of sense, right use of sense ; from the things of speech, good speaking ; from the things of thought, good thinking.

Admirable then, and demanded by the facts, are the 100 words added as a sort of side utterance, when while telling us how the memorial of the divine and heaven-sent food was enshrined in a golden jar he continues, " the omer was the tenth part of three measures " (Ex. xvi. 36). For we seem to contain three measures, sense, speech, mind ; sense measuring the objects of sense, speech the parts of speech and what we say, and mind the things of mind. Of each of these three 101 measures we must offer as it were a holy tenth, that speech, sense perception and apprehension may be judged soundly and blamelessly according to God's standard, for this is the true and just measure, while our measures are false and unjust. XIX. So too it 102 is only natural that in the matter of sacrifices the tenths of the measure of fine flour should be brought with the victims to the altar (Ex. xxix. 40), while the numbers up to nine, what is left by the tenth, remain with ourselves. And the recurrent obla-tion of the priests is in agreement with this ; they 103 are commanded to offer always the tenth of the ephah of fine flour (Lev. vi. 20), for they have learned to rise above the ninth, the seeming deity, the world of sense, and to worship Him who is in very truth God, who stands alone as the tenth.[a] For to the 104 world belong nine parts, eight in heaven, one of the stars which wander not and seven of those that wander, though the order of their wandering is ever

φερομένας ταῖς αὐταῖς, ἐνάτην δὲ γῆν σὺν[1] ὕδατι
καὶ ἀέρι· τούτων γὰρ μία συγγένεια τροπὰς καὶ
105 μεταβολὰς παντοίας δεχομένων. οἱ μὲν οὖν πολλοὶ
τὰς ἐννέα ταύτας μοίρας καὶ τὸν παγέντα κόσμον ἐξ
αὐτῶν ἐτίμησαν, ὁ δὲ τέλειος τὸν ὑπεράνω τῶν
ἐννέα, δημιουργὸν αὐτῶν, δέκατον θεὸν· ὅλον γὰρ
ὑπερκύψας τὸ ἔργον ἐπόθει τὸν τεχνίτην, καὶ
ἱκέτης καὶ θεραπευτὴς ἐσπούδαζεν αὐτοῦ γενέσθαι·
διὰ τοῦτο δεκάτην ἐνδελεχῆ τῷ δεκάτῳ καὶ μόνῳ
106 καὶ αἰωνίῳ ὁ ἱερεὺς ἀνατίθησι.   τοῦτ᾽
ἐστὶ κυρίως εἰπεῖν τὸ ψυχικὸν Πάσχα, ἡ ⟨ἀπὸ⟩
παντὸς πάθους καὶ παντὸς αἰσθητοῦ διάβασις πρὸς
τὸ δέκατον, ὃ δὴ νοητόν ἐστι καὶ θεῖον· λέγεται
γάρ· '' δεκάτῃ τοῦ μηνὸς τούτου λαβέτωσαν ἕκαστος πρόβατον κατ᾽ οἰκίαν,'' ἵνα ἀπὸ τῆς δεκάτης τῷ
δεκάτῳ καθιερωθῇ τὰ θύματα διατηρηθέντα ἐν τῇ
ψυχῇ κατὰ δύο μοίρας ἐκ τριῶν πεφωτισμένῃ,
μέχρις ἂν ὅλη δι᾽ ὅλων γενομένη φέγγος οὐράνιον,
οἷα πλησιφαὴς σελήνη κατὰ δευτέρας ἑβδομάδος
παραύξησιν, μὴ μόνον φυλάττειν ἀλλὰ καὶ ἱερουργεῖν ἤδη δύνηται τὰς ἀσινεῖς καὶ ἀμώμους προ-
107 κοπάς.   τοῦτ᾽ ἐστὶν ἱλασμός[2]—καὶ γὰρ
οὗτος δεκάτῃ τοῦ μηνὸς βεβαιοῦται, τὸν δέκατον
ἱκετευούσης θεὸν ψυχῆς καὶ τὴν ταπεινότητα καὶ

---

[1] mss. τὴν σὺν (ἐν).   [2] mss. ἱλασμούς.

---

[a] The imperfects are difficult. The translation suggests
that though " gnomic " like the aorist ἐτίμησαν, and not
referring specially to the past, they differ from the aorist in
expressing continuity. *Cf. Quis Rerum* 17.
[b] The thought of the section is that the sheep taken on the
tenth day, when the moon is two thirds on its way to fullness,
is an allegory of a soul which has reached a certain stage of

the same, while earth with water and air make the ninth, for the three form a single family, subject to changes and transformations of every kind. Now 105 the mass of men pay honour to these nine parts and to the world which is formed from them, but he that has reached perfection honours Him that is above the nine, even their maker God, who is the tenth. For he continues to soar above all the artificer's work and desire *a* the artificer Himself, ever eager to be His suppliant and servant. That is why the priest offers recurrently a tenth to Him who is tenth and alone and eternal. We find this " ten " plainly 106 stated in the story of the soul's passover, the crossing from every passion and all the realm of sense to the tenth, which is the realm of mind and of God; for we read " on the tenth day of this month let everyone take a sheep for his house " (Ex. xii. 3), and thus beginning with the tenth day we shall sanctify to Him that is tenth the offering fostered in the soul whose face has been illumined through two parts out of three, until its whole being becomes a brightness, giving light to the heaven like a full moon by its increase in the second week. And thus it will be able not only to keep safe, but to offer as innocent and spotless victims its advances on the path of progress.*b* We find the same in the pro- 107 pitiation which is established on the tenth day of the month (Lev. xxiii. 27), when the soul is suppliant to God the tenth, and is schooled to know the humilia-

progress and preserves (or increases?) it till it reaches its consummation, when it offers itself to God. For the connexion of the sheep with moral progress *cf. De Sac.* 112 προκοπῆς δὲ πρόβατον, ὡς καὶ αὐτὸ δηλοῖ τοὔνομα (derived from προβαίνω) σύμβολον. φωτισμός and παραύξησις are the regular terms for the "lighting up" and increasing of the moon.

οὐδένειαν τοῦ γενητοῦ περίνοια[1] λογισμοῦ πεποιθυίας καὶ τὰς ἐν ἅπασι τοῖς καλοῖς ὑπερβολὰς καὶ
ἀκρότητας τοῦ ἀγενήτου δεδιδαγμένης. ἵλεως οὖν
καὶ ἄνευ ἱκετείας ἵλεως εὐθὺς γίνεται τοῖς ἑαυτοὺς
κακοῦσι καὶ συστέλλουσι καὶ μὴ καυχήσει καὶ
108 οἰήσει φυσωμένοις.   τοῦτ' ἐστὶν ἄφεσις,
τοῦτ' ἐλευθερία παντελὴς ψυχῆς ὃν ἐπλανήθη τε
πλάνον ἀποσειομένης καὶ πρὸς τὴν ἀπλανῆ φύσιν
μεθορμιζομένης καὶ ἐπὶ τοὺς κλήρους ἐπανιούσης,
[535] οὓς ἔλαχεν, ἡνίκα λαμπρὸν | ἔπνει καὶ τοὺς περὶ
τῶν καλῶν πόνους ἤθλει.[2] τότε γὰρ αὐτὴν τῶν
ἄθλων ἀγάμενος ὁ ἱερὸς λόγος ἐτίμησε, γέρας
ἐξαίρετον δούς, κλῆρον ἀθάνατον, τὴν ἐν ἀφθάρτῳ
109 γένει τάξιν.   τοῦτο καὶ Ἀβραὰμ ὁ σοφὸς
ἱκετεύει, μελλούσης ἐμπίπρασθαι λόγῳ μὲν τῆς
Σοδομίτιδος γῆς, ἔργῳ δὲ τῆς ἐστειρωμένης τὰ
καλὰ καὶ τυφλῆς τὸν λογισμὸν ψυχῆς, ἵν', ἐὰν
εὑρεθῇ τὸ δικαιοσύνης μνημεῖον, ἡ δεκάς, ἐν αὐτῇ,
τύχῃ τινὸς ἀμνηστίας· ἄρχεται μὲν οὖν τῆς ἱκεσίας
ἀπὸ τοῦ τῆς ἀφέσεως ἀριθμοῦ, πεντηκοντάδος,
λήγει δὲ εἰς δεκάδα, τὴν τελευταίαν ἀπολύτρωσιν.
110   XX. ἀφ' οὗ μοι δοκεῖ καὶ Μωυσῆς
μετὰ τὴν χιλιάρχων καὶ ἑκατοντάρχων καὶ πεντη-
κοντάρχων αἵρεσιν ἐπὶ πᾶσι δεκαδάρχους χειρο-
τονεῖν, ἵν', εἰ μὴ δύναιτο διὰ τῶν πρεσβυτέρων
τάξεων βελτιοῦσθαι ὁ νοῦς, ἀλλά τοι διὰ τῶν

---

[1] mss. περινοίαν (-ας): Mangey adopted περινοίᾳ, but took
it as "having learnt by sagacity of reason the nothingness,"
etc., a sense which πεποιθυίας cannot, I think, bear. The
translation given above is just grammatical, but awkward in
the extreme. For conjectures see Appendix, p. 579.

[2] mss. ἤνθει.

[a] Though 50 (see § 109) is the leading number in the

tion and nothingness of its trust in the sagacity of a created reason, and how transcendent and supreme is the Uncreated in all that is good. And so He becomes propitious, and propitious even at once without their supplication, to those who afflict and belittle themselves and are not puffed up by vaunting and self-pride. We find it in the 108 "release"[a] (Lev. xxv. 9 ff.), in the perfect freedom of soul which shakes off the wandering of its past and finds a new harbour in the nature which wanders not, and returns to the heritages which it received in the years when the breath of its spirit was fresh and strong, and travail which has the good for its prize exercised its energy. For then the holy word, in admiration of its efforts, honoured it, and gave it a special guerdon, an undying heritage, its place in the order of the imperishable.

We find it in the suppliant prayer of wise Abraham, 109 who when fire was about to consume what is called the land of Sodom, but is in reality a soul barren of good and blind of reason, prayed that if there should be found in it that token of righteousness, the ten, it might receive some remission of punishment (Gen. xviii. 32). He begins indeed his supplication with fifty, the number of release, but ends with ten, which closes the possibility of redemption.

XX. It is on the same principle, as it seems to me, 110 that Moses, after choosing rulers of thousands and hundreds and fifties, appointed rulers of tens last of all (Ex. xviii. 25), so that if the mind could not be bettered through the work of the senior ranks, it might get purification through the hindermost.

institution of the Jubilee year, Philo refers to its proclamation on the 10th day of the month.

111 ὑστάτων καθαίρηται.   πάγκαλον δὲ δόγμα
καὶ ὁ τοῦ φιλομαθοῦς παῖς ἔμαθεν, ἡνίκα τὴν
θαυμαστὴν ἐκείνην ἐπρέσβευε πρεσβείαν, αὐτο-
μαθεῖ σοφῷ προξενῶν οἰκειοτάτην ἀρετήν, ἐπιμονήν.
" δέκα γὰρ καμήλους λαμβάνει," τὴν δεκάδος,
λέγω δὲ παιδείας ὀρθῆς, ἀνάμνησιν, ἀπὸ πολλῶν
112 ἀπείρων μὲν οὖν τοῦ κυρίου μνημῶν. λαμβάνει δὲ
καὶ " τῶν ἀγαθῶν ἐκείνου " δῆλον ὡς οὐκ ἄργυρον
οὐδὲ χρυσὸν ἤ τινα ἄλλα τῶν ἐν ὕλαις φθαρταῖς—
τὴν γὰρ ἀγαθοῦ πρόσρησιν οὐδέποτε τούτοις ἐπεφήμισε Μωυσῆς,—ἀλλὰ τὰ γνήσια, ἃ δὴ ψυχῆς
ἐστι μόνα, ἐφοδιάζεται καὶ ἐμπορεύεται, διδασκαλίαν, προκοπήν, σπουδήν, πόθον, ζῆλον, ἐνθου-
113 σιασμούς, προφητείας, τοῦ κατορθοῦν ἔρωτα· οἷς
ἐμμελετῶν καὶ ἐνασκούμενος, ὅταν ὥσπερ ἐκ
πελάγους ἐνορμίζεσθαι λιμένι μέλλῃ, λήψεται δύο
μὲν ἐνώτια, ἀνὰ δραχμὴν ὁλκήν, ψέλια δὲ δέκα
χρυσῶν ἐπὶ τὰς χεῖρας τῆς προξενουμένης. ὦ
θεοπρεποῦς κόσμου, δραχμὴν μίαν[1] εἶναι τὸ ἄκουσμα
καὶ μονάδα ἀρραγῆ καὶ ὁλκὸν φύσει—ἀκοὴν γὰρ
οὐδενὶ σχολάζειν ἐμπρεπές, ὅτι μὴ λόγῳ ἑνί, ὃς
ἂν τὰς τοῦ ἑνὸς ἀρετὰς καὶ μόνου θεοῦ καλῶς
διεξέρχηται,—δέκα δὲ χρυσῶν τὰ ἐγχειρήματα·
πράξεις γὰρ αἱ κατὰ σοφίαν τελείοις ἀριθμοῖς
βεβαιοῦνται, καὶ ἔστιν ἑκάστη τιμιωτέρα χρυσοῦ.
114   XXI. τοιαύτη τίς ἐστι καὶ ἡ ἀριστίνδην ἐπικριθεῖσα τῶν ἀρχόντων εἰσφορά, ἣν

[1] mss. μέν: perhaps, as Wendland conjectures, μὲν μίαν.

And that is the high truth, too, which 111
the servant of the lover of learning had mastered
when he went as ambassador on that splendid errand,
wooing for the man of self-taught wisdom the bride
most suited to him, constancy (Gen. xxiv. 10); for
out of the many or rather countless memories of his
lord, he takes "ten camels," that is the "reminding"[a]
which right instruction figured by the ten produces.
He takes too of "his goods," clearly meaning not 112
gold or silver or any others which are found in perishable materials, for Moses never gave the name of
good to these; but genuine goods, which are soul-
goods only, he takes for his journey's provisions and
his trading wares,—teaching, progress, earnestness,
longing, ardour, inspiration, prophecy, and the love of
high achievement. By practice and exercising him- 113
self in these, when the time comes for him to leave
the seas, so to speak, and anchor in harbour, we shall
find that he takes two ear-rings, drawing a weight[b] of a
drachma, and bracelets of ten weights of gold for the
hands of the bride, whom he courts for his master
(Gen. xxiv. 22). Truly a glorious adorning, first that
the thing heard should be a single drachma, a unit
without fractions whose nature is to draw, for it is
not well that hearing should devote itself to aught
save one story only, a story which tells in noble words
the excellences of the one and only God; secondly,
that the undertakings of the hands should be of
ten weights of gold, for the actions of wisdom rest
firmly on perfect numbers and each of them is more
precious than gold. XXI. Such too is that 114
tribute of the princes, chosen as the best that they

[a] For the symbolism of camels = memory, and Philo's
reasons for it, cf. De Post. 148 f.
[b] For the play on ὀλκή, ὀλκός, see De Mig. 202.

ἐποιήσαντο, ἡνίκα ἡ ψυχὴ κατασκευασθεῖσα ὑπὸ
φιλοσοφίας ἱεροπρεπῶς τὰ ἐγκαίνια ἦγεν αὐτῆς
εὐχαριστοῦσα τῷ διδασκάλῳ καὶ ὑφηγητῇ θεῷ.
" θυΐσκην γὰρ δέκα χρυσῶν πλήρη θυμιάματος
ἀνατίθησιν," ἵνα τὰς ὑπὸ φρονήσεως καὶ πάσης
ἀρετῆς ἀναδιδομένας αὔρας ὁ μόνος ἐπικρίνῃ σοφός.
115 ἐπειδὰν δὲ δόξωσιν εἶναι προσηνεῖς, τὸ ἐφύμνιον |
[536] ᾄσεται Μωυσῆς λέγων· " ὠσφράνθη κύριος ὀσμὴν
εὐωδίας," τὸ ὀσφρανθῆναι τιθεὶς ἐπὶ τοῦ συν-
αινέσαι· οὐ γὰρ ἀνθρωπόμορφος οὐδὲ μυκτήρων
ἤ τινων ἄλλων ὀργανικῶν μερῶν χρεῖος.
116 προϊὼν δὲ καὶ τὸ θεῖον ἐνδιαίτημα, τὴν σκηνήν,
" δέκα αὐλαίας " ἐρεῖ· τὸ γὰρ τῆς ὅλης πῆγμα
σοφίας ἀριθμὸν τέλειον εἴληχε, δεκάδα· σοφία δὲ
αὐλὴ καὶ βασίλειόν ἐστι τοῦ πανηγεμόνος καὶ
117 μόνου βασιλέως αὐτοκράτορος. ὁ μὲν δὴ νοητὸς
οἶκος οὗτος, αἰσθητὸς δ᾽ ὁ κόσμος ἐστίν, ἐπεὶ καὶ
τὰς αὐλαίας ἐκ τοιούτων συνύφηνεν, ἃ τῶν τεττάρων στοιχείων σύμβολά ἐστιν· ἐκ γὰρ βύσσου
καὶ ὑακίνθου καὶ πορφύρας καὶ κοκκίνου δημιουρ-
γοῦνται, τεττάρων, ὡς ἔφην, ἀριθμῷ.[1] σύμβολον
δὲ γῆς μὲν ἡ βύσσος—φύεται γὰρ ἐκ ταύτης,—
ἀέρος δὲ ὁ ὑάκινθος—μέλας γὰρ οὗτος φύσει,—
ὕδατος δὲ ἡ πορφύρα—τὸ γὰρ τῆς βαφῆς αἴτιον ἐκ

---

[1] So Mangey : mss. and Wendland ἀριθμῶν.

---

[a] Or "chosen (by God) in virtue of the princes' special
rank or merit"; cf. Plato, Legg. 855 c τὸ τῶν περυσινῶν
ἀρχόντων ἀριστίνδην ἀπομερισθὲν δικαστήριον. Mangey's translation, "per optimates viritim facta collatio," gives no
adequate sense to ἀριστίνδην.

[b] There is an obvious play on αὐλή and αὐλαίας which
cannot be reproduced in English.

[c] Or "the adornment (i.e. the curtains) is perceived by

had,[a] which they offered when the soul, equipped by the love of wisdom, celebrated its dedication in right holy fashion, giving thanks to the God who was its teacher and guide. For the worshipper offers " a censer of ten gold weights, full of incense " (Num. vii. 14, 20, etc.), that God who alone is wise might choose the perfumes exhaled by wisdom and every virtue. And when these perfumes are pleasant in 115 His judgement, Moses will celebrate them in a hymn of triumph in the words " The Lord smelt a scent of sweet fragrance " (Gen. viii. 21). Here he uses smell in the sense of accept, for God is not of human form, nor has need of nostrils or any other parts as organs. And further on he will speak of 116 God's dwelling-place, the tabernacle, as being " ten curtains " (Ex. xxvi. 1), for to the structure which includes the whole of wisdom the perfect number ten belongs, and wisdom is the court[b] and palace of the All-ruler, the sole Monarch, the Sovereign Lord. This dwelling is a house perceived by the mind, yet 117 it is also the world of our senses,[c] since he makes the curtains to be woven from such materials as are symbolical of the four elements ; for they are wrought of fine linen, of dark red,[d] of purple and of scarlet, four in number as I said. The linen is a symbol of earth, since it grows out of earth ; the dark red of air, which is naturally black ; the purple of water, since the means by which the dye is produced, the shell-fish

sense." The translation above is given in the belief that the thought is something less obvious. Philo finding the tabernacle apparently identified with the curtains (ποιήσεις σκηνὴν δέκα αὐλαίας) infers the mystical identity of the two worlds, cf. De Mig. 205. But it is difficult to extract this sense from the words as they stand. Perhaps read αἰσθητὸς δὲ καὶ κόσμος.   [d] Or " dark blue."

θαλάττης, ἡ ὁμωνυμοῦσα κόγχη,—πυρὸς δὲ τὸ
κόκκινον· ἐμφερέστατον γὰρ φλογί.

118 πάλιν γε μὴν Αἴγυπτον ἀφηνιάσασαν, ἡνίκα τὸν
ἀντίθεον[1] ἀπεσέμνυνε νοῦν τὰ παράσημα τῆς βασιλείας ἀναδοῦσα αὐτῷ, τὸν θρόνον, τὸ σκῆπτρον, τὸ
διάδημα, δέκα πληγαῖς καὶ τιμωρίαις ὁ τῶν ὅλων
119 ἐπίτροπος καὶ κηδεμὼν νουθετεῖ.   τὸν
αὐτὸν δὲ τρόπον καὶ Ἀβραὰμ ὑπισχνεῖται τῷ
σοφῷ οὔτε πλειόνων οὔτε ἐλαττόνων, ἀλλὰ αὐτὸ
μόνον δέκα ἐθνῶν ἀπώλειαν καὶ παντελῆ φθορὰν
ἐργάσεσθαι καὶ τὴν τῶν ἀναιρεθέντων χώραν
δώσειν τοῖς ἐγγόνοις αὐτοῦ, πανταχοῦ δεκάδι καὶ
πρὸς ἔπαινον καὶ πρὸς ψόγον καὶ πρὸς τιμὴν καὶ
πρὸς κόλασιν καταχρῆσθαι δικαιῶν.

120 καίτοι τί τούτων μεμνήμεθα; τὴν γὰρ ἱερὰν
καὶ θείαν νομοθεσίαν[2] δέκα τοῖς σύμπασι λόγοις
Μωυσῆς ἀναγέγραφεν· οὗτοι δέ εἰσι θεσμοί, τῶν
κατὰ μέρος ἀπείρων νόμων γενικὰ κεφάλαια, ῥίζαι
καὶ ἀρχαὶ ⟨καὶ⟩ πηγαὶ ἀέναοι διαταγμάτων προσ-
τάξεις καὶ ἀπαγορεύσεις περιεχόντων ἐπ' ὠφελείᾳ
121 τῶν χρωμένων.   XXII. εἰκότως οὖν
μετὰ δεκαετίαν τῆς εἰς Χαναναίων γῆν[3] ἀφίξεως ἡ
πρὸς τὴν Ἅγαρ κοινωνία γίνεται· οὐ γὰρ εὐθὺς
λογικοὶ γενόμενοι πλαδώσης ἔτι τῆς διανοίας
ὀρεχθῆναι παιδείας τῆς ἐγκυκλίου δυνάμεθα, ἀλλ'
ἐπειδὰν σύνεσιν καὶ ἀγχίνοιαν κραταιωσάμενοι
μηκέτι κούφῃ καὶ ἐπιπολαίῳ, ἀλλὰ βεβαίᾳ καὶ
παγίᾳ γνώμῃ περὶ ἁπάντων χρώμεθα.

[1] mss. ἀντίθετον.
[2] mss. ἐκκλησίαν—a very drastic alteration, for which,
however, there seems no alternative; unless indeed we substituted ἀναδεδίδαχεν for ἀναγέγραφεν. But the congregation
though often called " holy " could hardly be called " divine."

which bears the same name, comes from the sea ; and the scarlet of fire, since it closely resembles flame. Again rebellious Egypt, when it 118 glorified the mind which usurps the place of God, and bestowed on it the emblems of sovereignty, the throne, the sceptre, the diadem, is admonished through ten plagues and punishments by the Guardian and Ruler of all. In the same way He promises 119 to wise Abraham that He will work the ruin and complete destruction of just ten nations, neither more nor less, and will give the land of the victims to his descendants (Gen. xv. 18-20). Thus everywhere he thinks well to extend the meaning of the ten, to cover both praise and blame, honour and chastisement. But why note such examples as 120 these, when the holy and divine law is summed up by Moses in precepts which are ten in all, statutes which are the general heads, embracing the vast multitude of particular laws, the roots, the sources, the perennial fountains of ordinances containing commandments positive and prohibitive for the profit of those who follow them ?

XXII. It is quite natural, then, that the mating with 121 Hagar should take place when ten years have elapsed from the arrival in the land of the Canaanites ; for we cannot desire the training of the schools the moment we become reasoning beings, as the understanding is still soft and flaccid. That only comes when we have hardened our intelligence and quickness of mind and possess about all things a judgement which is no longer light and superficial, but firm and steady.

---

³ All mss. but one γῆς, which points to Mangey's conjecture τῆς εἰς Χαναναίων ⟨ἐκ Χαλδαίων⟩ γῆς.

122
[537] Διὸ τἀκόλουθον προσυφαίνεται | τὸ " εἰσῆλθε
πρὸς "Αγαρ"· ἦν γὰρ ἁρμόττον τῷ μανθάνοντι
πρὸς ἐπιστήμην διδάσκαλον φοιτᾶν, ἵνα ἀναδιδαχθῇ
τὰ προσήκοντα ἀνθρώπου φύσει παιδεύματα. νυνὶ
μὲν ὁ γνώριμος εἰς διδασκάλου βαδίζων εἰσάγεται·
προεκτρέχει δὲ πολλάκις ἐξοικίσασα φθόνον ἀφ'
123 ἑαυτῆς καὶ τοὺς ἔχοντας εὐφυῶς ἐπισπᾶται. τὴν
γοῦν ἀρετήν, Λείαν, ἔστιν ἰδεῖν προαπαντῶσαν καὶ
λέγουσαν τῷ ἀσκητῇ· " πρὸς μὲ εἰσελεύσῃ σήμε-
ρον," ἡνίκα ἐκεῖνος ἀγρόθεν ἐπανῄει. ποῖ[1] γὰρ
ὤφειλεν <εἰσ>ελθεῖν ὁ τῶν ἐπιστήμης σπερμάτων
καὶ φυτῶν ἐπιμελητής, ὅτι μὴ πρὸς τὴν γεωρ-
124 γηθεῖσαν ἀρετήν ;   XXIII. ἔστι δ' ὅτε
καὶ ἀποπειρωμένη τῶν φοιτητῶν, ὡς ἔχουσι προ-
θυμίας καὶ σπουδῆς, οὐχ ὑπαντᾷ μέν, ἐγκαλυψα-
μένη δὲ τὸ πρόσωπον ὥσπερ Θάμαρ ἐπὶ τριόδου
καθέζεται, πόρνης δόξαν παρασχοῦσα τοῖς ὁδῷ
βαδίζουσιν, ἵνα οἱ περιέργως ἔχοντες ἀνακαλύ-
ψαντες ἀναφήνωσι καὶ καταθεάσωνται τὸ ἄψαυστον
καὶ ἀμίαντον καὶ παρθένιον ὄντως αἰδοῦς καὶ
125 σωφροσύνης ἐκπρεπέστατον κάλλος. τίς οὖν ὁ
ἐξεταστικὸς καὶ φιλομαθὴς καὶ μηδὲν ἄσκεπτον
καὶ ἀδιερεύνητον τῶν ἐγκεκαλυμμένων πραγμάτων
παραλιπεῖν ἀξιῶν ἐστιν, ὅτι μὴ ὁ ἀρχιστράτηγος
καὶ βασιλεὺς καὶ ταῖς πρὸς θεὸν ὁμολογίαις ἐμμένων τε καὶ χαίρων, ὄνομα Ἰούδας ; " ἐξέκλινε "
γάρ φησι " πρὸς αὐτὴν τὴν ὁδὸν καὶ εἶπεν· ἔασόν
με εἰσελθεῖν πρὸς σέ "—ἀλλ' οὐκ ἔμελλε παρα-
βιάζεσθαι—καὶ σκοπεῖν, τίς τε ἡ ἐγκεκαλυμμένη
126 δύναμίς ἐστι καὶ ἐπὶ τί παρεσκεύασται. μετὰ τοίνυν

---

[1] Some mss. and Wendland ποῦ.

That is why the text continues with the words that 122
follow, " He went in unto Hagar " (Gen. xvi. 4), for
it was well that the learner should resort to knowledge as his teacher, to be instructed in the lessons
suited to human nature. In the present case the
pupil is represented as going to the teacher's school,
but often knowledge rids herself of grudging pride,
runs out to meet the gifted disciples, and draws them
into her company. And so we may see that Leah, 123
or virtue, goes forth to meet the Man of Practice
when he was returning from the field, and says to
him, " Thou shalt come in unto me to-day " (Gen.
xxx. 16) ; for whither indeed should he go in, he who
is tending the seeds and saplings of knowledge, save
to virtue, the field of his husbandry ?

XXIII. But sometimes she makes trial of her scholars, 124
to test their zeal and earnestness ; and then she does
not meet them, but veils her face and sits like Tamar
at the cross-roads, presenting the appearance of a
harlot to the passers-by (Gen. xxxviii. 14, 15). Her
wish is that inquiring minds may unveil and reveal
her and gaze upon the glorious beauty, inviolate,
undefiled and truly virginal, of her modesty and
chastity. Who then is he, the investigator, the lover 125
of learning, who refuses to leave aught of the things
that are veiled, unexamined and unexplored ? He
can only be the chief captain, the king, whose name
is Judah, who persists and rejoices in confessing and
praising God. " He turned aside his path to her "
(Gen. xxxviii. 16) it says, and said " Suffer me to come
in unto thee." " Suffer me," he means (for he would
not use force to her), " suffer me to see what is the
virtue which veils its face from me, and what purpose
it is prepared to serve." And so then after he went 126

521

τὸ εἰσελθεῖν γέγραπται " καὶ συνέλαβε " καὶ τὸ
" τίς " ῥητῶς οὐ μεμήνυται· συλλαμβάνει γὰρ καὶ
συναρπάζει ἡ μὲν τέχνη τὸν μανθάνοντα ἐρωτικῶς
ἔχειν ἀναπείθουσα ἑαυτῆς, ὁ δὲ μανθάνων τὴν διδά-
σκουσαν, ὁπότε φιλομαθὴς εἴη.

127 Πολλάκις δέ τις τῶν μέσας ἐπιστήμας[1] ὑφηγου-
μένων γνωρίμου τυχὼν εὐφυοῦς ηὔχησεν ἐπὶ τῇ
διδασκαλίᾳ μόνος ὑπολαβὼν τῷ φοιτητῇ γεγονέναι
τῆς εὐμαθίας αἴτιος, καὶ μετεωρίσας καὶ φυσήσας
ἑαυτὸν ὑψαυχενεῖ καὶ τὰς ὀφρῦς εὖ μάλα ἀνα-
σπάσας τετύφωται καὶ παρὰ τῶν βουλομένων συν-
διατρίβειν πάμπολλα αἰτεῖ· οὓς δ' ἂν αἴσθηται
πένητας μέν, διψῶντας δὲ παιδείας, ἀποστρέφεται,
ὥσπερ θησαυρόν τινα σοφίας μόνος ἀνευρηκώς.

128   τοῦτ' ἐστὶ τὸ " ἐν γαστρὶ ἔχειν," οἰδεῖν
καὶ τετυφῶσθαι καὶ ὄγκον πλείονα τοῦ μετρίου
περιβεβλῆσθαι, δι' ὧν καὶ τὴν κυρίαν τῶν μέσων
ἐπιστημῶν, ἀρετήν, ἔδοξάν τινες ἀτιμάζειν, ἐπί-
129 τιμον οὖσαν ἐξ ἑαυτῆς. ὅσαι μὲν οὖν ψυχαὶ μετὰ
φρονήσεως κυοφοροῦσι ⟨μετὰ⟩[2] πραγμάτων τικ-
τουσιν ὅμως, τὰ συγκεχυμένα διακρίνουσαι καὶ |

---

[1] mss. πολλάκις δέ τινα τῶν μέσων ἐπιστημῶν ὑφηγουμένου(-η),
which Mangey keeps with ὑφηγούμενος.

[2] ⟨μετὰ⟩ is my insertion: Mangey takes πραγμάτων as
object of κυοφοροῦσι (surely impossible) and reads ὁμοίως for
ὅμως (i.e. all these souls bear in the same way): Wendland
proposed ⟨ἄνευ⟩ πραγμάτων . . . ἀπόνως. I understand Philo
to mean that these souls, before they attain their εὐτοκία,
have to go through the pains suggested by διαστέλλουσαι τὰ
συγκεχυμένα. I have not found the combination μετὰ πραγμάτων as antithesis to the common ἄνευ, but σὺν πράγμασι and
μετὰ πραγματείας are quoted.

in to her, we read of a conceiving or taking[a] (Gen. xxxviii. 18). Who it is who conceives or takes we are not told in so many words. For the art or science that is studied does seize and take hold of the learner and persuades him to be her lover, and in like manner the learner takes his instructress, when his heart is set on learning.

Often on the other hand some teacher of the lower 127 subjects, who has chanced to have a gifted pupil, boasts of his own teaching power, and supposes that his pupil's high attainments are due to him alone. So he stands on tiptoe, puffs himself out, perks up his neck and raises high his eyebrows, and in fact is filled with vanity, and demands huge fees from those who wish to attend his courses ; but when he sees that their thirst for education is combined with poverty, he turns his back on them as though there were some treasures of wisdom which he alone has discovered. That is the condition called 128 " having in the womb," a swollen, vanity-ridden condition, robed in a vesture of inordinate pride, which makes some people appear to dishonour virtue, the essentially honourable mistress in her own right of the lower branches of knowledge. The souls then 129 whose pregnancy is accompanied with wisdom, though they labour, do bring their children to the birth, for they distinguish and separate what is in con-

---

[a] *i.e.* grammatically the subject of συνέλαβε may be either. Philo must not be thought to deny that in the literal story the subject must be Tamar, but spiritually both learner and teacher may be said συλλαμβάνειν in its original sense of to seize or take, and he considers himself entitled to find this secondary thought in the text.

[538] διαστέλλουσαι, καθάπερ ἡ Ῥεβέκκα—λαβοῦσα γὰρ
ἐν γαστρὶ τῶν διττῶν διανοίας[1] ἐθνῶν ἐπιστήμην,
ἀρετῆς τε καὶ κακίας, εὐτοκίᾳ χρωμένη τὴν ἑκατέρου φύσιν διαστέλλει τε καὶ διακρίνει·—ὅσαι δὲ
ἄνευ φρονήσεως, ἢ ἀμβλίσκουσιν ἢ δύσεριν καὶ
σοφιστὴν βάλλοντα καὶ τοξεύοντα ἢ βαλλόμενον
130 καὶ τοξευόμενον ἀποκύουσι. καὶ μήποτε εἰκότως·
αἱ μὲν γὰρ λαμβάνειν, αἱ δὲ ἔχειν ἐν γαστρὶ οἴονται,
παμμεγέθους <οὔσης> διαφορᾶς. αἱ μὲν γὰρ
ἔχειν νομίζουσαι τὴν αἵρεσιν[2] καὶ γένεσιν ἑαυταῖς
ἐπιγράφουσαι σεμνομυθοῦσιν, αἱ δὲ λαμβάνειν ἀξιοῦ-
σαι τὸ μὲν μηδὲν οἰκεῖον ἐξ ἑαυτῶν ἔχειν συν-
ομολογοῦσι, τὰ δὲ σπέρματα καὶ τὰς γονὰς ἔξωθεν
ἀρδομένας καταλαμβάνουσαι καὶ θαυμάζουσαι[3] τὸν
διδόντα κακὸν μέγιστον, φιλαυτίαν, ἀγαθῷ τελείῳ,
131 θεοσεβείᾳ, διωθοῦνται.   XXIV. τοῦτον
τὸν τρόπον καὶ τὰ νομοθετικῆς τῆς παρὰ ἀνθρώποις κατεβλήθη σπέρματα· "ἦν γάρ τις" φησίν
" ἐκ τῆς φυλῆς Λευί, ὃς ἔλαβε τῶν θυγατέρων τῶν
Λευί, καὶ ἔσχεν αὐτήν. καὶ ἐν γαστρὶ ἔλαβε καὶ
ἔτεκεν ἄρρεν· ἰδόντες δὲ αὐτὸ ἀστεῖον ὂν ἐσκέπασαν
132 αὐτὸ μῆνας τρεῖς." οὗτός ἐστι Μωυσῆς, ὁ καθαρώτατος νοῦς, ὁ ἀστεῖος ὄντως, ὁ νομοθετικὴν
ὁμοῦ καὶ προφητείαν ἐνθουσιώσῃ καὶ θεοφορήτῳ
σοφίᾳ λαβών, ὃς γένος ὢν τῆς Λευιτικῆς φυλῆς καὶ

---

[1] mss. διανοίαις.
[2] The word hardly makes sense: ? ἄροσιν.
[3] mss. καταλαμβάνουσι καὶ θαυμάζουσι.

fusion within them, just as Rebecca, receiving in her womb the knowledge of the two nations of the mind, virtue and vice, distinguished the nature of the two and found therein a happy delivery (Gen. xxv. 23). But where its pregnancy is without wisdom, the soul either miscarries or the offspring is the quarrelsome sophist [a] who shoots with the bow (Gen. xxi. 20), or is the target of the bowman. And this contrast is to 130 be expected. For the one kind of soul thinks that it receives in the womb, and the other that it has in the womb, and that is a mighty difference. The latter, supposing that they " have," with boastful speech ascribe the choice and the birth to themselves. The former claim but to receive, and confess that they have of themselves nothing which is their own. They accept [b] the seeds of impregnation that are showered on them from outside, and revere the Giver, and thus by honouring God they repel the love of self, repel, that is, the greatest of evils by the perfect good. XXIV. In this way 131 too were sown the seeds of the legislative art which we men enjoy. " There was," says the Scripture, " a man of the tribe of Levi who took one of the daughters of Levi and had her to wife, and she received in her womb and bore a male child, and seeing that he was goodly they guarded him for three months " (Ex. ii. 1, 2). This is Moses, the mind of purest quality, 132 the truly " goodly," [c] who, with a wisdom given by divine inspiration, received the art of legislation and prophecy alike, who being of the tribe of Levi both

---

[b] Or " seize upon." The word expresses something less passive than λαμβάνειν but escapes the thought of self-satisfaction which he finds in ἔχειν.

[c] See note on *De Conf.* 106.

τὰ πρὸς πατρὸς καὶ τὰ πρὸς μητρὸς ἀμφιθαλὴς τῆς
133 ἀληθείας ἔχεται.   μέγιστον δὲ ἐπάγγελμα
τοῦ γενάρχου τῆς φυλῆς ἐστι ταύτης· θαρρεῖ γὰρ
λέγειν, ὅτι αὐτός μοι μόνος ἐστὶ θεὸς τιμητέος,
ἄλλο δ' οὐδὲν τῶν μετ' αὐτόν, οὐ γῆ, οὐ θάλασσα,
οὐ ποταμοί, οὐκ ἀέρος φύσις, οὐ πνευμάτων οὐχ
ὡρῶν[1] μεταβολαί, οὐ ζῴων οὐ φυτῶν ἰδέαι, οὐχ
ἥλιος, οὐ σελήνη, οὐκ ἀστέρων πλῆθος ἐν τάξεσιν
ἐναρμονίοις περιπολούντων, οὐχ ὁ σύμπας οὐρανός
134 τε καὶ κόσμος. μεγάλης καὶ ὑπερφυοῦς ψυχῆς τὸ
αὔχημα, γένεσιν ὑπερκύπτειν καὶ τοὺς ὅρους αὐτῆς
ὑπερβάλλειν καὶ μόνου τοῦ ἀγενήτου περιέχεσθαι
κατὰ τὰς ἱερὰς ὑφηγήσεις, ἐν αἷς διείρηται " ἔχε-
σθαι αὐτοῦ." τοιγάρτοι τοῖς ἐχομένοις καὶ ἀδιαστάτως θεραπεύουσιν ἀντιδίδωσι κλῆρον αὐτόν.
ἐγγυᾶται δέ μου τὴν ὑπόσχεσιν λόγιον, ἐν ᾧ
135 λέγεται· " κύριος αὐτὸς κλῆρος αὐτοῦ." οὕτως
ἐν γαστρὶ λαμβάνουσαι μᾶλλον ἢ ἔχουσαι[2] αἱ ψυχαὶ
τίκτειν πεφύκασι.   καθάπερ δ' οἱ σώματος ὀφθαλμοὶ πολλάκις μὲν ἀμυδρῶς πολλάκις δὲ
τηλαυγῶς ὁρῶσι, τὸν αὐτὸν τρόπον καὶ τὸ τῆς
ψυχῆς ὄμμα τοτὲ μὲν ὑποσυγκεχυμένας καὶ ἀδήλους
τοτὲ δὲ καθαρὰς καὶ τρανὰς δέχεται τὰς ἀπὸ τῶν
[539]
136 πραγμάτων | ἰδιότητας. ἡ μὲν οὖν ἀσαφὴς καὶ ἀδη-
λουμένη προσβολὴ ἔοικε τῷ μήπω κατὰ γαστρὸς
ἐμβρύῳ διατυπωθέντι, ἡ δὲ ἐναργὴς καὶ τρανὴ

___

[1] MSS. ἀέρων or καίρων.
[2] MSS. ἔχουσαι μᾶλλον ἢ λαμβάνουσαι.

___

[a] Or "being of the tribe of Levi and equally fortunate
both on his father's and his mother's side, holds fast to
truth." But the point of the last words is not clear in this
rendering.

on the father's and the mother's side has a double link *a* with truth.   Great indeed is the profession of the founder of this tribe.*b* He has the ₁₃₃ courage to say, God and God alone must I honour, not aught of what is below God, neither earth nor sea nor rivers, nor the realm of air, nor the shiftings of the winds and seasons, nor the various kinds of animals and plants, nor the sun nor the moon nor the host of the stars, performing their courses in ranks of ordered harmony, no, nor yet the whole heaven and universe. A great and transcendent soul does ₁₃₄ such a boast bespeak, to soar above created being, to pass beyond its boundaries, to hold fast to the Uncreated alone, following the sacred admonitions in which we are told to cling to Him (Deut. xxx. 20), and therefore to those who thus cling and serve Him without ceasing He gives Himself as portion, and this my affirmation is warranted by the oracle which says, " The Lord Himself is his portion " (Deut. x. 9). Thus *c* we see the capacity to bear comes to souls by ₁₃₅ " receiving " rather than by " having in the womb."

But just as the eyes of the body often see dimly and often clearly, so the distinguishing characteristics which things present sometimes reach the eye of the soul in a blurred and confused, sometimes in a clear and distinct form. When the vision thus presented is indistinct and ill-defined, it ₁₃₆ is like the embryo not yet fully formed in the depths of the womb ; when it is distinct and definite, it bears

b Levi, not Moses as Wendland seems to think. See App. p. 579.
c οὕτως takes us back to the argument, interrupted in § 133 by the meditation on the tribe of Levi, and, as often, marks the conclusion of the argument. In §§ 138-139 we have a different point, though suggested by it.

μάλιστα τῷ διαπεπλασμένῳ καὶ καθ' ἕκαστον τῶν
ἐντός τε καὶ ἐκτὸς μερῶν τετεχνιτευμένῳ καὶ τὴν
137 ἁρμόττουσαν ἰδέαν ἀπειληφότι.   νόμος
δὲ ἐπὶ τούτοις ἐγράφη πάνυ καλῶς καὶ συμφερόντως
τεθεὶς οὗτος· " ἐὰν μαχομένων ἀνδρῶν δύο πατάξῃ
τις γυναῖκα ἐν γαστρὶ ἔχουσαν καὶ ἐξέλθῃ τὸ παιδίον
αὐτῆς μὴ ἐξεικονισμένον, ἐπιζήμιον ζημιωθήσεται·
καθ' ὅ τι ἂν ἐπιβάλῃ ὁ ἀνὴρ τῆς γυναικός, δώσει
μετὰ ἀξιώματος· ἐὰν δὲ ἐξεικονισμένον ᾖ, δώσει
ψυχὴν ἀντὶ ψυχῆς." οὐ γὰρ ἦν ὅμοιον, τέλειόν τε
καὶ ἀτελὲς διανοίας ἔργον διαφθεῖραι, οὐδὲ εἰκα-
ζόμενον καὶ καταλαμβανόμενον, οὐδὲ ἐλπιζόμενον
138 καὶ ἤδη ὑπάρχον. διὰ τοῦτο ὅπου μὲν ἐπιτίμιον
ἄδηλον ἐπ' ἀδήλῳ πράγματι, ὅπου δὲ ὡρισμένον
ἐπὶ τελείῳ νομοθετεῖται, τελείῳ δὲ οὐχὶ τῷ πρὸς
ἀρετήν, ἀλλὰ τῷ κατά τινα τέχνην τῶν ἀνεπιλήπτων γενομένῳ· κυοφορεῖ γὰρ αὐτὸ[1] οὐχ ἡ λαβοῦσα,
ἀλλ' ἡ ἐν γαστρὶ ἔχουσα, οἴησιν πρὸ ἀτυφίας ἐπ-
αγγελλομένη. καὶ γὰρ ἀμήχανον ἀμβλίσκειν τὴν ἐν
γαστρὶ λαβοῦσαν, ἐπεὶ τὸ φυτὸν ὑπὸ τοῦ σπείραν-
τος ἐμπρεπὲς τελεσφορεῖσθαι· τὴν δὲ ἔχουσαν οὐκ
ἀνοίκειον, ἅτε νόσῳ χωρὶς ἰατροῦ κατεσχημένην.
139   XXV. Μὴ νομίσῃς δὲ τὴν Ἄγαρ λέγεσθαι ἑαυτὴν

---

[1] mss. αὑτόν.

---

[a] Philo means that " perfected " or " fully grown " is here
used of things on a lower plane. Since the woman of the
enactment is said " to have in the womb," the allegory
cannot mean that the perfected work of the mind is one of
moral perfection. It refers rather to the fully formed ideas
produced by " a system of conceptions coordinated for some
useful end " (see the definition of " art " in § 141). Such arts
have nothing wrong about them (ἀνεπιλήπτων), but cannot
rank with the study of virtue. For this reduced sense of
ἀνεπίληπτος see note on De Mig. 207.

a close analogy to the same embryo when fully shaped, with each of its parts inward and outward elaborated, and thus possessed of the form suited to it.

Now there is a law well and suitably enacted to deal 137 with this subject which runs thus : " When two men are fighting if one strikes a woman who has in the womb, and her child comes forth not fully formed, he shall be surely fined : according as the husband of the woman shall lay upon him he shall be fined with a valuation, but if the child be fully formed he shall give life for life " (Ex. xxi. 22, 23). This was well said, for it is not the same thing to destroy what the mind has made when it is perfect as when it is imperfect, when it is guesswork as when it is apprehended, when it is but a hope as when it is a reality. Therefore in one the thing in question and the 138 penalty are alike indefinite, in the other there is a specified penalty for a thing perfected. Note however that by " perfected " we do not mean perfected in virtue, but that it has attained perfection in some one of the arts to which no exception can be taken.[a] For the child in this case is the fruit of one who has in the womb, not has received in the womb, one whose attitude is that of self-conceit rather than of modesty. And indeed miscarriage is impossible for her who " has received in the womb," for it is to be expected that the Sower should bring the plant to its fulness : for her who " has in the womb " it is natural enough ; she is the victim of her malady, and there is no physician to help her.[b]

XXV. Do not suppose that by the words " When 139

[b] Or "if there is no physician." Philo, that is, may not intend to deny the possibility of a better fate for those " who have in the womb."

ὁρᾶν ἐν γαστρὶ ἔχουσαν διὰ τοῦ " ἰδοῦσα[1] ὅτι ἐν
γαστρὶ ἔχει," ἀλλὰ τὴν κυρίαν αὐτῆς Σάρραν. καὶ
γὰρ ὕστερον αὕτη περὶ ἑαυτῆς φησιν· " ἰδοῦσα ὅτι
140 ἐν γαστρὶ ἔχει, ἠτιμάσθην[2] ἐνώπιον αὐτῆς." διὰ
τί; ὅτι αἱ μέσαι τέχναι, καὶ εἰ τὰ καθ' αὑτάς, ὧν
εἰσιν ἐγκύμονες, ὁρῶσιν, ἀλλά τοι πάντως ἀμυδρῶς
ὁρῶσιν, ἀλλ' ἐπιστῆμαι τηλαυγῶς καὶ σφόδρα
ἐναργῶς καταλαμβάνουσιν· ἐπιστήμη γὰρ πλέον
ἐστὶ τέχνης, τὸ βέβαιον καὶ ἀμετάπτωτον ὑπὸ
141 λόγου προσειληφυῖα. τέχνης μὲν γὰρ ὅρος οὗτος·
σύστημα ἐκ καταλήψεων συγγεγυμνασμένων[3] πρός
τι τέλος εὔχρηστον, τοῦ εὐχρήστου διὰ τὰς κακο-
τεχνίας ὑγιῶς προστιθεμένου· ἐπιστήμης δέ· κατάληψις ἀσφαλὴς καὶ βέβαιος, ἀμετάπτωτος ὑπὸ
142 λόγου.   μουσικὴν μὲν οὖν καὶ γραμ-
ματικὴν καὶ τὰς συγγενεῖς καλοῦμεν τέχνας—καὶ
γὰρ οἱ ἀποτελούμενοι δι' αὐτῶν τεχνῖται λέγονται
μουσικοί τε καὶ γραμματικοί,—φιλοσοφίαν δὲ καὶ
τὰς ἄλλας ἀρετὰς ἐπιστήμας καὶ τοὺς ἔχοντας αὐτὰς
[540] ἐπιστήμονας· | φρόνιμοι γάρ εἰσι καὶ σώφρονες καὶ
φιλόσοφοι, ὧν οὐδὲ εἷς ἐν τοῖς τῆς διαπεπονημένης
ἐπιστήμης σφάλλεται δόγμασι, καθάπερ οἱ προ-
ειρημένοι ἐν τοῖς τῶν μέσων τεχνῶν θεωρήμασιν.

---

[1] LXX εἶδεν, which perhaps should be read here.
[2] So LXX: MSS ἠτ(ο)ιμάσθη.
[3] MSS. ἐγγεγυμνασμένων (-ον), which may be right. See
App. p. 580.

---

[a] See App. 580.
[b] Or "apprehensions" as below. But the word seems to
be used in a slightly different sense in the two definitions.
[c] Or perhaps "results arrived at," in contrast to principles
(δόγματα). That is to say, the difference between δόγματα

she saw that she had in the womb "(Gen. xvi. 4), it
is meant that Hagar saw that it was so with herself.
It is her mistress Sarah who saw, for afterwards Sarah
says of herself, " Seeing that she had in the womb, I
was dishonoured before her " (Gen. xvi. 5). Why is 140
this ? Because the lower arts, even if they see their
own products, which are carried in their · womb,
necessarily see them but dimly, while they are clearly
and very distinctly apprehended by knowledge in its
various forms. For knowledge is something more
than art, as it has in addition a stability which no
argument can shake. The definition of art is as 141
follows : [a] a system of conceptions [b] co-ordinated to
work for some useful end, " useful " being a very
proper addition to exclude mischievous arts. Knowledge on the other hand is defined as a sure and
certain apprehension which cannot be shaken by
argument.[a]   We give the name of arts 142
therefore to music, grammar and the kindred arts,
and accordingly those who by means of them reach
fulness of accomplishment are called artists, whether
they are musicians or grammarians ; but we give the
name of knowledge to philosophy and the other
virtues, and that of men of knowledge to those who
possess these virtues. Those only are prudent and
temperate and philosophers who without exception
do not err in the dogmatic conclusions belonging to
that form of knowledge which they have mastered by
their diligence in the way that the above-mentioned
err in the more theoretical conclusions [c] of the lower

and θεωρήματα, which are often combined by Philo, lies not
so much in that the latter are uncertain (Euclid did not
consider his θεωρήματα uncertain), as in that they are slighter,
and do not rise to the status of an important principle.

143 ὥσπερ γὰρ ὀφθαλμοὶ μὲν ὁρῶσιν, ὁ δὲ νοῦς δι᾽
ὀφθαλμῶν τηλαυγέστερον, καὶ ἀκούει μὲν ὦτα, ὁ
δὲ νοῦς δι᾽ ὤτων ἄμεινον, καὶ ὀσφραίνονται μὲν
οἱ μυκτῆρες, ἡ δὲ ψυχὴ διὰ ῥινῶν ἐναργέστερον,
καὶ αἱ ἄλλαι αἰσθήσεις τῶν καθ᾽ αὑτὰς ἀντι-
λαμβάνονται, καθαρώτερον δὲ καὶ εἰλικρινέστερον
ἡ διάνοια—κυρίως γὰρ εἰπεῖν ἥδ᾽ ἐστὶν ὀφθαλμὸς
μὲν ὀφθαλμῶν, ἀκοὴ δὲ ἀκοῆς καὶ ἑκάστης τῶν
αἰσθήσεων αἴσθησις εἰλικρινεστέρα, χρωμένη μὲν
ἐκείναις ὡς ἐν δικαστηρίῳ ὑπηρέτισι, δικάζουσα
δ᾽ αὐτὴ τὰς φύσεις τῶν ὑποκειμένων, ὡς τοῖς μὲν
συναινεῖν, τὰ δὲ ἀποστρέφεσθαι,—οὕτως αἱ μὲν
λεγόμεναι μέσαι τέχναι ταῖς κατὰ τὸ σῶμα δυνάμεσιν ἐοικυῖαι τοῖς θεωρήμασιν ἐντυγχάνουσι κατά
τινας ἁπλᾶς ἐπιβολάς, ἀκριβέστερον δὲ ἐπιστῆμαι
144 καὶ σὺν ἐξετάσει περιττῇ. ὃ γὰρ νοῦς πρὸς αἴσθησιν, τοῦτ᾽ ἐπιστήμη πρὸς τέχνην ἐστί· καθάπερ
γὰρ αἴσθησίς τις αἰσθήσεων, ὡς ἐλέχθη πρότερον,
ἐστὶν ἡ ψυχή * * *[1] ἐκείνων μὲν οὖν ἑκάστη μικρὰ
ἄττα τῶν ἐν τῇ φύσει παρεσπάσατο, περὶ ἃ πο-
νεῖται καὶ πραγματεύεται, γραμμὰς μὲν γεωμετρία,
φθόγγους δὲ μουσική, φιλοσοφία δὲ πᾶσαν τὴν τῶν
ὄντων φύσιν· ὕλη γάρ ἐστιν αὐτῆς ὅδε ὁ κόσμος καὶ
145 πᾶσα ἡ τῶν ὄντων ὁρατή τε καὶ ἀόρατος οὐσία. τί
οὖν θαυμαστόν, εἰ ἡ τὰ ὅλα καθορῶσα θεᾶται καὶ
τὰ μέρη, καὶ ἄμεινον ἐκείνων, ἅτε ὀφθαλμοῖς
μείζοσι καὶ ὀξυδερκεστέροις ἐνομματωθεῖσα ; εἰκότως οὖν ἡ κυρία φιλοσοφία τὴν μέσην παιδείαν, τὴν

---

[1] Wendland supplies οὕτως τέχνη τις τεχνῶν ἐπιστήμη.

[a] Lit. "through simple applications (of the mind)." *Cf.*
note on *De Post.* 79.

arts. The following illustration may serve. The 143
eyes see, but the mind through the eyes sees further
than the eyes. The ears hear, but the mind through
the ears hears better than the ears. The nostrils
smell, but the soul through the nose smells more
vividly than the nose, and while the other senses
apprehend the objects proper to them, the understanding apprehends with more purity and clarity.
For we may say quite properly that the mind is the
eye's eye and the hearing's hearing and the purified
sense of each of the senses ; it uses them as ushers in
its tribunal, but itself passes judgement on the natures
of the objects presented, giving its assent to some
and refusing it to others. In the same way, what we
call the lower or secondary arts, resembling as they do
the bodily faculties, handle the questions which they
answer without involved consideration,[a] but knowledge in each case does so with greater accuracy and
minute examination. What the mind is to sense, 144
that knowledge is to art ; for just as, to repeat the
statement, the soul is the sense of the senses, [so
knowledge is the art of arts.] So each of the arts has
detached and annexed some small items from the
world of nature which engage its efforts and attention : geometry has its lines, and music its notes, but
philosophy takes the whole nature of existing things ;
for its subject matter is this world and every form of
existence visible and invisible. Why wonder, then, 145
if when it surveys the whole of things it sees also the
parts, and sees them better than those others, furnished as it is with stronger eyes and more penetrat-
ing sight ? Naturally then will the pregnancy of the
handmaid, the lower instruction, be more visible to

θεραπαινίδα αὐτῆς, ἐγκύμονα θεάσεται μᾶλλον ἢ
146 ἑαυτὴν ἐκείνη.   XXVI. καίτοι γ' οὐδὲ
τοῦτό τις ἀγνοεῖ, ὅτι πάσαις ταῖς κατὰ μέρος τὰς
ἀρχὰς καὶ τὰ σπέρματα, ἐξ ὧν ἀναβλαστεῖν ἔδοξε
τὰ θεωρήματα, φιλοσοφία δεδώρηται. ἰσόπλευρα
γὰρ καὶ σκαληνὰ κύκλους τε καὶ πολυγώνια καὶ τὰ
ἄλλα σχήματα γεωμετρία προσεξεῦρε, σημείου δὲ
καὶ γραμμῆς καὶ ἐπιφανείας καὶ στερεοῦ φύσιν, ἃ
δὴ ῥίζαι καὶ θεμέλιοι τῶν λεχθέντων εἰσίν, οὐκέτι
147 γεωμετρία. πόθεν γὰρ αὐτῇ λέγειν ὁριζομένῃ, ὅτι
σημεῖον μέν ἐστιν οὗ μέρος οὐδέν, γραμμὴ δὲ
μῆκος ἀπλατές, ἐπιφάνεια δὲ ὃ μῆκος καὶ πλάτος
μόνον ἔχει, στερεὸν δὲ ὃ τὰς τρεῖς ἔχει διαστάσεις,
μῆκος, πλάτος, βάθος; ταῦτα γὰρ ἀνάκειται
φιλοσοφίᾳ καὶ ἡ περὶ ὅρων πραγματεία πᾶσα τῷ
148 φιλοσόφῳ.   τό γε μὴν γράφειν καὶ
ἀναγινώσκειν γραμματικῆς τῆς ἀτελεστέρας ἐπάγγελμα, ἣν παρατρέποντές τινες γραμματιστικὴν
καλοῦσι, τῆς δὲ τελειοτέρας ἀνάπτυξις τῶν παρὰ
[541] ποιηταῖς τε καὶ συγγραφεῦσιν. | ἐπειδὰν οὖν περὶ
τῶν τοῦ λόγου διεξέρχωνται μερῶν, τότε οὐ τὰ
φιλοσοφίας εὑρήματα παρασπῶνταί τε καὶ παρ-
149 εργολαβοῦσι; ταύτης γὰρ ἴδιον ἐξετάζειν, τί σύν-
δεσμος, τί ὄνομα, τί ῥῆμα, τί κοινὸν ὄνομα, τί
ἴδιον, τί ἐλλιπὲς ἐν λόγῳ, τί πλῆρες, τί ἀποφαντόν,
τί ἐρώτημα, τί πύσμα, τί περιεκτικόν, τί εὐκτικόν,

---

[a] Or "prose-writers" in general. On the definition of
γραμματική here given see App. p. 580.

[b] The word (παρεργολαβεῖν) is not known elsewhere.
L. & S. translate "take as an accessory." Stephanus
(impossibly) "quaestum ex aliqua re facere." I understand
the word, in accordance with the common use of πάρεργον for

the mistress philosophy than it is to the handmaid herself.   XXVI. And indeed this too is 146 general knowledge that all the particular arts have their origins and the germs from which the conclusions they reach seem to spring, as a gift from philosophy. For such further matters as isosceles and scalene triangles, and circles and polygons and the other figures are the discovery of geometry ; but when we come to the nature of the point, the line, the superficies and the solid which are the roots and foundations of those named above, we leave geometry behind. For whence does she obtain the 147 definition of a point as that which has no parts, of a line as length without breadth, of superficies as that which has length and breadth only, and of a solid as that which has three dimensions, length, breadth, and depth ? For these belong to philosophy, and the whole subject of definitions is the philosopher's province.   Again the lower stage of grammar, 148 sometimes by a slight modification of γραμματική called γραμματιστική, undertakes to teach reading and writing, while the task of the higher stage is the elucidation of the writings of the poets and historians.[a] When therefore they discourse on the parts of speech, are they not encroaching on, and casually appropriating[b] the discoveries of philosophy ? For it is the 149 exclusive property of philosophy to examine what a conjunction is, or a noun, or a verb, or a common as distinguished from a proper noun, or in the sentence what is meant by defective or complete or declaratory or inquiry, or question, or comprehensive, or pre-

a thing of secondary importance, to imply that they adopt these terms without any thought of how they are arrived at or any conception of their importance.

τί ἀρατικόν[1]· τὰς γὰρ περὶ αὐτοτελῶν καὶ ἀξιωμά-
των καὶ κατηγορημάτων πραγματείας ἥδ' ἐστὶν ἡ
150 συνθεῖσα. ἡμίφωνον δὲ ἢ φωνῆεν ἢ παντελῶς
ἄφωνον στοιχεῖον ἰδεῖν, καὶ πῶς ἕκαστον τούτων
εἴωθε λέγεσθαι, καὶ πᾶσα ἡ περὶ φωνῆς καὶ στοιχείων καὶ τῶν τοῦ λόγου μερῶν ἰδέα οὐ φιλοσοφίᾳ
πεπόνηται καὶ κατήνυσται; βραχείας δ' ὥσπερ
ἀπὸ χειμάρρου σπάσαντες λιβάδας καὶ βραχυτέραις
ταῖς ἑαυτῶν ψυχαῖς ἐναποθλίψαντες τὸ κλαπὲν οἱ
φῶρες οὐκ ἐρυθριῶσι προφέροντες ὡς ἴδιον.

151 XXVII. Οὗ χάριν φρυαττόμενοι τῆς κυρίας, ᾗ
τὸ κῦρος ὄντως καὶ ἡ τῶν θεωρουμένων ἀνάκειται
βεβαίωσις, ἀλογοῦσι. συναισθομένη δὲ αὕτη τῆς
ὀλιγωρίας τούτων ἐλέγξει καὶ μετὰ παρρησίας
φήσει· ἀδικοῦμαι καὶ παρασπονδοῦμαι τό γε ἐφ'
152 ὑμῖν ὁμολογίας παραβαίνουσιν. ἀφ' οὗ γὰρ ἐνεκολ-
πίσασθε τὰ προπαιδεύματα, τῆς ἐμῆς θεραπαινίδος
τὰ ἔγγονα, τὴν μὲν ὡς γαμετὴν ἐξετιμήσατε, ἐμὲ
δὲ οὕτως ἀπεστράφητε, ὡς μηδὲ πώποτε ἐς ταυτὸν
ἐλθόντες. ἀλλ' ἴσως ἐγὼ μὲν ταῦτα περὶ ὑμῶν
ὑπείληφα, ἐκ τῆς φανερᾶς πρὸς τὴν οἰκέτιν ὁμιλίας
τὴν ἄδηλον πρὸς ἐμὲ αὐτὴν ἀλλοτρίωσιν τεκμαιρο-
μένη· εἰ δ' ὑμεῖς ἐναντίως ἢ ὡς ὑπείληφα διά-
κεισθε, γνῶναι μὲν ἀμήχανον ἑτέρῳ, ῥᾴδιον δὲ
153 μόνῳ θεῷ. διόπερ οἰκείως ἐρεῖ· '' κρίναι ὁ θεὸς
ἀνὰ μέσον ἐμοῦ καὶ σοῦ,'' οὐ προκατεγνωκυῖα ὡς

---

[1] τί εὐκτικόν, τί ἀρατικόν is deduced by Wendland from
εὐκτικόν M, ὁρατικόν A, εὖ τί κακὸν ἄρα SF, εὖ κακὸν δὲ τί H.
For ἀρατικόν cf. De Agr. 140.

[a] For the explanation of these terms, where they have not

catory, or imprecatory. For to her is due the system
which embraces the study of complete sentences and
propositions and predicates.[a] Again, the observation 150
of the semi-vowel, the vowel and the completely voiceless or consonant, and the usage of each, and the whole
field of phonetics and the elements of sound and the
parts of speech, have been worked out and brought
to its consummation by philosophy. From this, as
from a torrent, the plagiarists have drawn a few small
drops, squeezed them into their still smaller souls,
and do not blush to parade what they have filched as
their own.

XXVII. So in their insolence they neglect the mis- 151
tress to whom the lordship really belongs, to whom is
due the firm foundation of their studies. And she,
conscious of their neglect, will rebuke them and
speak with all boldness. " I am wronged and betrayed, in so far as you have broken faith with me.
For ever since you took to your arms the lower forms 152
of training, the children of my handmaid, you have
given her all the honour of the wedded wife, and
turned from me as though we had never come together. And yet perhaps, in thinking this of you, I
may be but inferring from your open company with
her my servant a less certain matter, your alienation
from me. But to decide whether your feelings are as
I have supposed, or the opposite, is a task impossible
for any other, but easy for God alone," and therefore 153
Sarah will say quite properly, " God judge between
you and me " (Gen. xvi. 5). She does not hastily

been already explained in the note to the parallel passage
De Agr. 140, 141, see App. p. 580. It is a good example of
Philo's capacity for looking at things from opposite points of
view, that there these distinctions are scoffed at as superfluous
refinements, here they belong to true philosophy.

ἠδικηκότος, ἀλλ' ἐνδοιάζουσα ὡς τάχ' ἂν ἴσως καὶ
κατορθοῦντος· ὅπερ ἀψευδῶς οὐκ εἰς μακρὰν
ἀναφαίνεται δι' ὧν ἀπολογούμενος καὶ τὸν ἐνδοιασμὸν αὐτῆς ἐξιώμενός φησιν· '' ἰδοὺ ἡ παιδίσκη ἐν
ταῖς χερσί σου, χρῶ αὐτῇ, ὡς ἄν σοι ἀρεστὸν ᾖ.''
154 καὶ γὰρ ὁ παιδίσκην εἰπὼν ἀμφότερα ὁμολογεῖ, τό
τε δούλην καὶ τὸ νηπίαν¹ εἶναι—τὸ γὰρ τῆς παιδί-
σκης ὄνομα ἑκατέρῳ τούτων ἐφαρμόζει,—συνομο-
λογεῖ δὲ πάντως εὐθὺς καὶ τἀναντία, τῇ μὲν νηπίᾳ
τὴν τελείαν, τῇ δὲ δούλῃ τὴν κυρίαν, μονονοὺ βοῶν
ἄντικρυς, ὅτι τὴν μὲν ἐγκύκλιον παιδείαν καὶ ὡς
νεωτέραν καὶ ὡς θεραπαινίδα ἀσπάζομαι, τὴν δὲ
ἐπιστήμην καὶ φρόνησιν ὡς τελείαν καὶ δέσποιναν
155 ἐκτετίμηκα.   τὸ δὲ '' ἐν ταῖς χερσί σου ''
δηλοῖ μὲν τὸ ὑποχείριός ἐστί σοι. σημαίνει δὲ καὶ
τοιοῦτον ἕτερον· τὰ μὲν τῆς δούλης εἰς χεῖρας |
[542] ἀφικνεῖται σώματος—σωματικῶν γὰρ ὀργάνων καὶ
δυνάμεων τὰ ἐγκύκλια χρεῖα,—τὰ δὲ τῆς κυρίας εἰς
ψυχὴν ἔρχεται· λογισμοῖς γὰρ τὰ κατά τε φρόνησιν
156 καὶ ἐπιστήμην ἀνατίθεται. ὥσθ' ὅσῳ δυνατώτερον
καὶ δραστικώτερον καὶ τοῖς ὅλοις κρεῖττον διάνοια
χειρός² ἐστι, τοσούτῳ τῆς ἐγκυκλίου μουσικῆς ἐπιστήμην καὶ φρόνησιν θαυμασιωτέραν εἶναι νενόμικα
καὶ διαφερόντως ἐκτετίμηκα. λαβοῦσα οὖν, ὦ καὶ
ὑπάρχουσα καὶ πρὸς ἐμοῦ νομιζομένη κυρία, τὴν
ἐμὴν ἅπασαν παιδείαν ὡς θεραπαινίδι χρῶ, '' ὡς
157 εὐάρεστόν σοι.'' τὸ δὲ σοὶ εὐάρεστον οὐκ ἀγνοῶ

---

¹ MSS. νήπιον.   ² MSS. χρεῖος.

ᵃ The argument implies that "thy hands" refers to the
body, a natural thought if the address was to the soul, but
not so appropriate when addressed to philosophy. For
another suggestion see App. p. 581.

condemn Abraham as a wrongdoer, but expresses a doubt as though perhaps his heart may be true and upright. That it is so is shewn unmistakably soon after, when he makes his defence and thereby heals her doubts. " Behold," he says, " the servant girl is in thy hands. Deal with her as is pleasing to thee " (Gen. xvi. 6). Indeed in calling her a servant girl 154 he makes a double admission, that she is a slave and that she is childish, for the name suits both of these. At the same time the words involve necessarily and absolutely the acknowledgment of the opposites of these two, of the full-grown as opposed to the child, of the mistress as opposed to the slave. They amount almost to a loud and emphatic confession : I greet the training of the schools, he implies, as the junior and the handmaid, but I have given full honour to knowledge and wisdom as the full-grown and the mistress. And the words "in thy hands" 155 mean no doubt " she is subject to thee," but they also signify something more, namely that while what is implied by the slave belongs to the domain of the hands in the bodily sense, since the school subjects require the bodily organs and faculties, what is implied by the mistress reaches to the soul, for wisdom and knowledge and their implications are referred to the reasoning faculties.[a] " And so," says Abraham, " in 156 the same degree as the mind is more powerful, more active and altogether better than the hand, I hold knowledge and wisdom to be more admirable than the culture of the schools and have given them full and special honour. Do thou then, who both art the mistress and art held as such by me, take all my training and deal with it as thy handmaid, ' even as is well-pleasing to thee.' And what is well-pleasing

ὅτι πάντως ἐστὶν ἀγαθόν, εἰ καὶ μὴ προσηνές, καὶ
ὠφέλιμον, εἰ καὶ μακρὰν τοῦ ἡδέος ἀφέστηκεν.

Ἀγαθὸν δὲ καὶ ὠφέλιμον τοῖς ἐλέγχου δεομένοις
νουθεσία, ὃ ἑτέρῳ ὀνόματι κάκωσιν ὁ ἱερὸς μηνύει
158 λόγος. XXVIII. διόπερ ἐπιφέρει· " καὶ ἐκάκωσεν
αὐτήν," ἴσον τῷ ἐνουθέτησε καὶ ἐσωφρόνισε.
λυσιτελὲς γὰρ σφόδρα τοῖς ἐν ἀδείᾳ καὶ ἐκεχειρίᾳ,
καθάπερ ἵπποις ἀφηνιασταῖς, ὀξὺ κέντρον, ἐπεὶ
μάστιγι μόλις καὶ ἀγωγῇ δαμασθῆναι καὶ τιθα-
159 σευθῆναι δύνανται. ἢ τὰ προκείμενα ἆθλα οὐχ
ὁρᾷς τοῖς ἀνεπιπλήκτοις[1]; λιπῶσιν, εὐρύνονται,
πιαίνονται, λαμπρὸν πνέουσιν· εἶτα αἴρονται τὰ
ἀσεβείας, οἱ πανάθλιοι καὶ βαρυδαίμονες, οἰκτρὰ
βραβεῖα, ⟨ἐπ'⟩ ἀθεότητι κηρυττόμενοι καὶ στεφα-
νούμενοι. διὰ γὰρ τὴν λείως ῥέουσαν εὐτυχίαν
ὑπέλαβον ἑαυτοὺς εἶναι τοὺς ὑπαργύρους καὶ
ὑποχρύσους θεούς, νομίσματος κεκιβδηλευμένου
τὸν τρόπον, τοῦ ἀληθινοῦ καὶ ὄντως ὄντος ἐκλαθό-
160 μενοι. μαρτυρεῖ δὲ καὶ Μωυσῆς ἐν οἷς φησιν·
" ἐλιπάνθη, ἐπαχύνθη, ἐπλατύνθη καὶ ἐγκατέλιπε
θεὸν τὸν ποιήσαντα αὐτόν"· ὥστε εἰ ἡ ἐπὶ πλέον
ἄνεσις τὸ μέγιστον κακόν, ἀσέβειαν, ὠδίνει,
τοὐναντίον ἡ μετὰ νόμου κάκωσις ἀγαθὸν τέλειον
ἀποτίκτει, τὴν ἀοίδιμον νουθεσίαν.
161 ἐνθένδε ὁρμηθεὶς καὶ τῆς πρώτης ἑορτῆς τὸ σύμ-

---

[1] mss. τοῖς ἀνεπιπλήκτως or τοὺς ἀνεπιπλήκτους. The former
may perhaps suggest τοῖς ἀνεπιπλήκτως ⟨ζῶσι⟩.

---

[a] See App. p. 581.
[b] The article is difficult. The translation assumes that
τοὺς ... ὑποχρύσους is a belated epithet to ἑαυτούς like οἱ
πανάθλιοι above. But this is very awkward. Perhaps better
"they think themselves to be gods, these gods (of the
pagans) whose very gold and silver is unreal." There is an

to thee I know full well is altogether good, even if
it be not agreeable, and profitable even if it be far
removed from pleasant."

Yes, good and profitable. And such to those who
need convincing of their errors is the admonishing
which the holy text indicates under its other name
of affliction. XXVIII. Therefore he adds "and 158
she afflicted her" (Gen. xvi. 6), which means she
admonished and chastised her. For the sharp spur
is indeed profitable to those who live in security and
ease, just as it is to unruly horses, since it is difficult
to master or break them in merely with the whip or
guiding hand. Or do you fail to see the rewards 159
which await the unrebuked?[a] They grow sleek and
fat, they expand themselves, and the breath of their
spirit is lusty and strong, and then to their utter
sorrow and misery they win the woeful prizes of
impiety, proclaimed and crowned as victors in the
contest of godlessness. For because of the smooth
flow of their prosperity, veneered as they are with
gold and silver,[b] like base coin, they fancy themselves
to be gods, forgetting Him who is the true coin, the
really Existent. I have Moses' testimony when he 160
says, " He waxed fat, grew thick, was widened, and
abandoned the God who made him " (Deut. xxxii.
15). It follows that if increased laxity is the parent
of that greatest of ills, impiety, contrariwise affliction, regulated by law, breeds a perfect good, that
most admirable thing, admonition.[c]   On 161
this same principle he calls the unleavened bread,

---

allusion to Ex. xx. 23 θεοὺς ἀργυροῦς καὶ θεοὺς χρυσοῦς οὐ
ποιήσετε. For the use of the prefix ὑπ- see App. p. 581.

[c] As κάκωσις μετὰ νόμου has been stated to be another
name for νουθεσία, this remark is extraordinarily weak. See
App. p. 582.

βολον " ἄρτον κακώσεως " εἶπε, τὰ ἄζυμα. καίτοι
τίς οὐκ οἶδεν, ὅτι ἑορταὶ καὶ θαλίαι περιποιοῦσιν
ἱλαρὰς εὐφροσύνας καὶ εὐθυμίας, οὐ κακώσεις;
ἀλλὰ δῆλον, ὡς ὀνόματι κατακέχρηται πόνου, τοῦ
162 σωφρονιστοῦ. τὰ γὰρ πλεῖστα καὶ μέγιστα τῶν
ἀγαθῶν ἀσκητικαῖς ἀθλήσεσι καὶ ἡβῶσι πόνοις
εἴωθε περιγίνεσθαι· ψυχῆς δὲ ἑορτὴ ζῆλος ὁ τῶν
ἀρίστων καὶ τελεσφορούμενος πόνος. οὗ χάριν
διείρηται καὶ " ἐπὶ πικρίδων τὰ ἄζυμα ἐσθίειν "
οὐχ ὡς προσεψήματος, ἀλλ' ἐπειδὴ τὸ μὴ οἰδεῖν καὶ
ἀναζεῖν ταῖς ἐπιθυμίαις, ἐστάλθαι δὲ καὶ συνῆχθαι
πρὸς ἀηδίας οἱ πολλοὶ τίθενται, πικρὸν ἡγούμενοι
[543] τὸ | ἀπομαθεῖν τὸ πάθος, ὅπερ ἐστὶν εὐφροσύνη καὶ
163 ἑορτὴ διανοίᾳ φιλάθλῳ.   XXIX. ταύτης
ἕνεκά μοι δοκεῖ τῆς αἰτίας ἐν χωρίῳ, ὃ κέκληται
πικρία, τὰ νόμιμα ἀναδιδαχθῆναι· ἡδὺ μὲν γὰρ
τὸ ἀδικεῖν, ἐπίπονον δὲ τὸ δικαιοπραγεῖν· τοῦτο
δέ ἐστιν ὁ ἀψευδέστατος νόμος. ἐξελθόντες γάρ,
φησιν, ἐκ τῶν Αἰγυπτιακῶν παθῶν " ἦλθον εἰς
Μερρά, καὶ οὐκ ἠδύναντο πιεῖν ὕδωρ ἐκ Μερρῶν·
πικρὸν γὰρ ἦν. διὰ τοῦτο ἐπωνομάσθη τὸ ὄνομα
τοῦ τόπου ἐκείνου πικρία. καὶ διεγόγγυζεν ὁ λαὸς
κατὰ Μωυσῆ λέγοντες· τί πιόμεθα ; ἐβόησε δὲ
Μωυσῆς πρὸς κύριον, καὶ ἔδειξεν αὐτῷ κύριος
ξύλον, καὶ ἐνέβαλεν αὐτὸ εἰς τὸ ὕδωρ, καὶ ἐγλυκάνθη τὸ ὕδωρ. ἐκεῖ ἔθετο αὐτῷ δικαιώματα καὶ
164 κρίσεις,   κἀκεῖ αὐτὸν ἐπείραζεν." ἡ γὰρ
ἄδηλος ἀπόπειρα καὶ δοκιμασία τῆς ψυχῆς ἐστιν ἐν

---

[a] Or " at the height of its vigour." But the word is strange
and perhaps to be suspected.
[b] Though these words run on in the LXX, there is really a
stop at " judgements," which brings to an end the proof of

the symbol of the first feast, " bread of affliction."
And yet we all know that feasts and highdays produce
cheerfulness and gladness, not affliction. Clearly he 162
is extending the meaning of the word as a name for
the chastener, toil, for the most numerous and most
important of goods are wont to result from repeated
strenuous contention and keen ^{a} toiling, and the soul's
feast is ardour for the best, and the consummation
of toil. That is why we also have the command to
" eat the unleavened bread with bitter herbs "
(Ex. xii. 8), not as a relish, but because the mass of
men hold that when they no longer swell and boil
with desires, but are confined and compressed, they
are in a state of discomfort ; and they think that the
unlearning of passion is a bitterness, though to a
mind that welcomes effort that same is a joy and a
feast.   XXIX. For this cause I believe 163
the lesson of the statutes of the law was given in
a place whose name is bitterness, for injustice is
pleasant and just-dealing is troublesome, and this is
the most infallible of laws. For when they had gone
out of the passions of Egypt, says the text, " they
came to Marah, and they could not drink water from
Marah, for it was bitter. Therefore the name of that
place was called bitterness, and the people murmured
against Moses, saying what shall we drink ? And
Moses called aloud to the Lord, and the Lord shewed
him a tree ; and he threw it into the water, and the
water was sweetened. There He laid down for him
ordinances and judgements "(Ex. xv. 23-25).
" And there He tried him " ^{b} (ibid.), the text con- 164
tinues. Yes, for the trial and proving of the soul,

---

the connexion of κάκωσις and its bitterness with law. The
final words raise a new point, its connexion with " trial."

τῷ πονεῖν καὶ πικραίνεσθαι· ὅπῃ γὰρ ταλαντεύσει,
χαλεπὸν διαγνῶναι. οἱ μὲν γὰρ προκαμόντες
ἀνέπεσον, βαρὺν ἀντίπαλον ἡγησάμενοι τὸν πόνον,
καὶ τὰς χεῖρας ὑπ' ἀσθενείας ὥσπερ ἀπειρηκότες
ἀθληταὶ καθῆκαν, παλινδρομεῖν εἰς Αἴγυπτον ἐπὶ
165 τὴν ἀπόλαυσιν τοῦ πάθους ἐγνωκότες. οἱ δὲ τὰ
φοβερὰ καὶ δεινὰ τῆς ἐρήμης πάνυ τλητικῶς καὶ
ἐρρωμένως ἀναδεχόμενοι τὸν ἀγῶνα τοῦ βίου
διήθλησαν ἀδιάφθορον καὶ ἀήττητον φυλάξαντες
καὶ τῶν τῆς φύσεως ἀναγκαίων κατεξαναστάντες,
ὡς πεῖναν, δίψος, [ῥῖγος,] κρύος, θάλπος, ὅσα τοὺς
ἄλλους εἴωθε δουλοῦσθαι, κατὰ πολλὴν ἰσχύος
166 περιουσίαν ὑπάγεσθαι.   αἴτιον δὲ ἐγένετο οὐ ψιλὸς ὁ πόνος, ἀλλὰ σὺν τῷ γλυκανθῆναι·
λέγει γάρ· " ἐγλυκάνθη τὸ ὕδωρ," γλυκὺς δὲ καὶ
ἡδὺς πόνος ἑτέρῳ ὀνόματι φιλοπονία καλεῖται. τὸ
γὰρ ἐν πόνῳ γλυκὺ ἔρως ἐστὶ καὶ πόθος καὶ ζῆλος
167 καὶ φιλία τοῦ καλοῦ. μηδεὶς οὖν τὴν τοιαύτην
κάκωσιν ἀποστρεφέσθω, μηδ' " ἄρτον κακώσεως "
νομισάτω ποτὲ λέγεσθαι τὴν ἑορτῆς καὶ εὐφροσύνης
τράπεζαν ἐπὶ βλάβῃ μᾶλλον ἢ ὠφελείᾳ· τρέφεται
γὰρ τοῖς παιδείας δόγμασιν ἡ νουθετουμένη ψυχή.

168   XXX. τὸ ἄζυμον πέμμα τοῦτο οὕτως
ἐστὶν ἱερόν, ὥστε χρησμοῖς προστέτακται δώδεκα
ἄρτους ἀζύμους ταῖς φυλαῖς ἰσαρίθμους προτιθέναι
ἐπὶ τῆς ἐν τοῖς ἀδύτοις χρυσῆς τραπέζης, καὶ
169 καλοῦνται προθέσεως. καὶ νόμῳ δὲ ἀπείρηται
πᾶσαν ζύμην καὶ πᾶν μέλι προσφέρειν τῷ βωμῷ·
χαλεπὸν γὰρ ἢ τὰς γλυκύτητας τῶν κατὰ τὸ σῶμα

with all its uncertainty, lies in toil and bitterness of heart, and it is uncertain because it is hard to discern which way the balance will incline. Some faint ere the struggle has begun, and lose heart altogether, counting toil a too formidable antagonist, and like weary athletes they drop their hands in weakness and determine to speed back to Egypt to enjoy passion. But there 165 are others who, facing the terrors and dangers of the wilderness with all patience and stoutness of heart, carry through to its finish the contest of life, keeping it safe from failure and defeat, and take a strong stand against the constraining forces of nature, so that hunger and thirst, cold and heat, and all that usually enslave the rest, are made their subjects by their preponderating fund of strength.

But this result is brought about not by toil unaided, 166 but by toil with sweetening. He says " the water was sweetened," and another name for the toil that is sweet and pleasant is love of labour. For what is sweet in toil is the yearning, the desire, the fervour, in fact the love of the good. Let no one, 167 then, turn away from affliction such as this, or think that, when the table of joy and feasting is called the bread of affliction, harm and not benefit is meant. No, the soul that is admonished is fed by the lessons of instruction's doctrine. XXX. So holy 168 is this unleavened bake-meat, that the oracles ordain that twelve unleavened loaves, corresponding to the number of the tribes, be set forth on the golden table in the inmost shrine, and these are called the loaves of setting forth (Ex. xxv. 29). And further it is 169 forbidden by law to bring any leaven or any honey to the altar (Lev. ii. 11). For it is a hard matter to consecrate as holy the sweet flavours of bodily

ἡδονῶν ἢ τὰς τῆς ψυχῆς ἀραιὰς καὶ χαύνους ἐπάρσεις καθιεροῦν ὡς ἅγια, τὰ φύσει βέβηλα καὶ
170 ἀνίερα ἐξ αὐτῶν. ἆρ᾽ οὖν οὐκ εἰκότως ἐπισεμνυνόμενος ὁ προφήτης λόγος, ὄνομα Μωυσῆς, ἐρεῖ· "μνησθήσῃ πᾶσαν τὴν ὁδὸν ἣν ἤγαγέ σε κύριος ὁ θεὸς ἐν ἐρήμῳ, ὅπως ἂν κακώσῃ σε καὶ ἐκπειράσῃ σε καὶ διαγνωσθῇ τὰ ἐν καρδίᾳ σου, εἰ
[544] φυλάξεις ἐντολὰς αὐτοῦ ἢ | οὔ· καὶ ἐκάκωσέ σε καὶ ἐλιμαγχόνησέ σε καὶ ἐψώμισέ σε τὸ μάννα, ὃ οὐκ ᾔδεισαν οἱ πατέρες σου, ἵνα ἀναγγείλῃ σοι, ὅτι οὐκ ἐπ᾽ ἄρτῳ μόνῳ ζήσεται ὁ ἄνθρωπος, ἀλλ᾽ ἐν παντὶ
171 ῥήματι ἐκπορευομένῳ διὰ στόματος θεοῦ·" τίς οὖν οὕτως ἀνόσιός ἐστιν, ὡς ὑπολαβεῖν κακωτὴν τὸν θεὸν καὶ λιμόν, οἴκτιστον ὄλεθρον, ἐπάγοντα τοῖς ἄνευ τροφῆς ζῆν μὴ δυναμένοις; ἀγαθὸς γὰρ καὶ ἀγαθῶν αἴτιος, εὐεργέτης, σωτήρ, τροφεύς, πλουτοφόρος, μεγαλόδωρος, κακίαν ὁρῶν ἱερῶν ἀπεληλακώς· οὕτω γὰρ τὰ γῆς ἄχθη, τόν τε Ἀδὰμ καὶ Εὖαν,[1] ἐφυγάδευσεν ἐκ τοῦ παραδείσου.
172 μὴ παραγώμεθα οὖν ταῖς φωναῖς, ἀλλὰ τὰ δι᾽ ὑπονοιῶν σημαινόμενα σκοπῶμεν καὶ λέγωμεν, ὅτι τὸ μὲν "ἐκάκωσε" ἴσον ἐστὶ τῷ ἐπαίδευσε καὶ ἐνουθέτησε καὶ ἐσωφρόνισε, τὸ δὲ "λιμῷ παρέβαλεν" οὐ σιτίων καὶ ποτῶν εἰργάσατο ἔνδειαν, ἀλλ᾽ ἡδονῶν καὶ ἐπιθυμιῶν φόβων τε καὶ λύπης καὶ ἀδικημάτων καὶ συνόλως ἁπάντων ὅσα ἢ κακιῶν
173 ἐστιν ἢ παθῶν ἔργα. μαρτυρεῖ δὲ τὸ ἐπιλεγόμενον ἑξῆς· "ἐψώμισέ σε τὸ μάννα." ἆρά γε τὸν τὴν ἄπονον καὶ ἀταλαίπωρον τροφὴν δίχα σπουδῆς

---

[1] So Mangey: mss. and Wendland Κάιν.

[a] See App. p. 582.

pleasures or the risings of the soul in their leaven-like thinness and sponginess, so profane and unholy are they by their very nature. Is it not, then, 170 with legitimate pride that the prophet-word called Moses says, as we shall find, " Thou shalt remember all the way which the Lord thy God led thee in the wilderness, that He might afflict thee and prove thee and the thoughts in thy heart might be tested, whether thou wilt keep His commandments or not, and He afflicted thee and made thee weak by famine and fed thee with manna which thy fathers knew not, that He might proclaim to thee that not alone on bread shall man live, but on every word that goeth forth through the mouth of God " (Deut. viii. 2). Who then is so impious as to suppose that God is 171 an afflictor, or evil-entreater, and that He sends famine, death in its most miserable form, on those who cannot live without food ? For God is good and the cause of what is good, the benefactor, the saviour, the nourisher, the enricher, the bountiful giver, and He has expelled evil-mindedness from the holy boundaries. For so He banished those cumberers of the earth, both Adam and Eve,[a] from Paradise.

Let us not, then, be misled by the actual 172 words, but look at the allegorical meaning that lies beneath them, and say that " afflicted " is equivalent to " disciplined and admonished and chastened," and that " subjected to famine " does not mean that He brought about a dearth of food and drink, but a dearth of pleasures and desires and fears and grief and wrong-doings, and in general all the works of the vices or the passions. And this is confirmed by the words that 173 follow, " He fed thee with the manna." He who provided the food that costs no toil or suffering, the

547

τῶν ἀνθρώπων οὐκ ἐκ γῆς, ὡς ἔθος, ἀναδοθεῖσαν,
ἀπ' οὐρανοῦ δέ, τεράστιον ἔργον, ἐπ' εὐεργεσίᾳ τῶν
χρησομένων παρασχόμενον ἄξιον λέγειν λιμοῦ καὶ
κακώσεως ἢ τοὐναντίον εὐθηνίας καὶ εὐετηρίας
174 ἀδείας τε καὶ εὐνομίας αἴτιον; ἀλλ' οἱ πολλοὶ καὶ
ἀγελαῖοι νομίζουσι τοὺς λόγοις θείοις τρεφομένους
ἀθλίως καὶ ταλαιπώρως ζῆν—ἄγευστοι γάρ εἰσι
τοῦ παντρόφου γεύματος σοφίας,—οἱ δ' ⟨ἐν⟩ ταῖς
εὐπαθείαις καὶ εὐφροσύναις λελήθασι διάγοντες.
175   XXXI. οὕτω τοίνυν ἡ ποιά κάκωσις
ὠφέλιμόν ἐστιν, ὥστε καὶ τὸ ταπεινότατον αὐτῆς,
ἡ δουλεία, μέγα ἀγαθὸν νενόμισται. καὶ ταύτην
ηὔξατό τις ἐν ταῖς ἱεραῖς ἀναγραφαῖς πατὴρ υἱῷ,
τῷ ἄφρονι Ἡσαῦ ὁ ἄριστος Ἰσαάκ. εἶπε γάρ που·
176 "ἐπὶ μαχαίρᾳ σου ζήσεις, καὶ τῷ ἀδελφῷ σου
δουλεύσεις," λυσιτελέστατον κρίνων τῷ πόλεμον
ἀντ' εἰρήνης αἱρουμένῳ καὶ ὥσπερ ἐν μάχαις
ὁπλοφοροῦντι διὰ τὴν ἐν τῇ ψυχῇ στάσιν καὶ
ταραχὴν ὑπηκόῳ γενέσθαι καὶ δουλεῦσαι καὶ
ἐπιτάγμασιν, ἅττ' ἂν ὁ σωφροσύνης ἐραστὴς
177 ἐπικελεύσῃ, πᾶσι πειθαρχεῖν.   ἐνθένδε
μοι δοκεῖ τις τῶν φοιτητῶν Μωυσέως, ὄνομα εἰ-
ρηνικός, ὃς πατρίῳ γλώττῃ Σαλομὼν καλεῖται,
φάναι· "παιδείας θεοῦ, υἱέ, μὴ ὀλιγώρει, καὶ μὴ
ἐκλύου ὑπ' αὐτοῦ ἐλεγχόμενος· ὃν γὰρ ἀγαπᾷ
κύριος ἐλέγχει, μαστιγοῖ δὲ πάντα υἱὸν ὃν παραδέχεται." οὕτως ἄρα ἡ ἐπίπληξις καὶ νουθεσία
[545] καλὸν νενόμισται, | ὥστε δι' αὐτῆς ἡ πρὸς θεὸν

ᵃ Or "agreement," "covenant," words which describe the
normal relation of God and Israel. Wendland, suspecting
the word, conjectures ὁμολογεῖται συγγένεια γίνεσθαι.

food which without the cares and pains of men came not from the earth in the common way, but was sent, a wonder and a marvel from heaven for the benefit of those who should use it—can we rightly speak of Him as the author of famine and affliction ? Should we not on the contrary call Him the author of thriving and prosperity and secure and ordered living ? But 174 the multitude, the common herd, who have never tasted of wisdom, the one true food of us all, think that those who feed on the divine words live in misery and suffering, and little know that their days are spent in continued well-being and gladness.

XXXI. Thus so profitable a thing is affliction of one 175 sort, that even its most humiliating form, slavery, is reckoned a great blessing. Such slavery we read of in the holy scriptures as invoked by a father on his son, by the most excellent Isaac on the foolish Esau. There is a place where he says, " Thou shalt live on 176 thy sword and shalt be a slave to thy brother " (Gen. xxvii. 40). He judges it most profitable for him who chooses war instead of peace, who by reason of his inward tumult and rebellion is armed as it were with the weapons of war, that he should become a subject and a slave and obey all the orders that the lover of self-control may impose. Therefore, I think, 177 did one of Moses' disciples, who is named a man of peace, which is in our ancestral tongue Solomon, say as follows : " My son, despise not the discipline of God, nor faint when thou art rebuked by Him, for whom the Lord loveth He rebukes and scourges every son whom He receiveth " (Prov. iii. 11, 12). So we see that reproaching and admonition are counted so excellent a thing, that they turn our acknowledgment[a] of God into kinship with Him, for what relation

549

ὁμολογία συγγένεια γίνεται. τί γὰρ οἰκειότερον
178 υἱῷ πατρὸς ἢ υἱοῦ πατρί;   ἀλλ' ἵνα μὴ
λόγον ἐκ λόγου συνείροντες μηκύνειν δοκῶμεν,
ἐναργεστάτην δίχα τῶν εἰρημένων πίστιν παρεξό-
μεθα τοῦ τὴν ποιὰν κάκωσιν ἀρετῆς ἔργον εἶναι·
νόμος γάρ ἐστι τοιοῦτος· " πᾶσαν χήραν καὶ
ὀρφανὸν οὐ κακώσετε· ἐὰν δὲ κακίᾳ κακώσητε
αὐτούς." τί λέγει; ἆρ' ὑπό τινος ἔστιν ἄλλου
κακοῦσθαι; εἰ γὰρ κακίας ἔργα μόνης αἱ κακώσεις,
περιττὸν τὸ ὁμολογούμενον γράφειν, ὃ καὶ δίχα
179 προσθήκης ἀνομολογηθήσεται. φήσει δὲ πάντως·
οἶδα καὶ ὑπὸ ἀρετῆς ἐλεγχόμενον καὶ ὑπὸ φρονήσεως παιδευόμενον. διόπερ οὐ πᾶσαν κάκωσιν ἐν
αἰτίᾳ τίθεμαι, ἀλλὰ τὴν μὲν δικαιοσύνης καὶ
νομοθετικῆς ἔργον οὖσαν—ἐπιπλήξει γὰρ σωφρονί-
ζει—μάλιστα θαυμάζω, τὴν δὲ ἀφροσύνης καὶ
κακίας, βλαβερὰν ὑπάρχουσαν, ἀποστρέφομαι καὶ
κακίζω δεόντως.
180 Ὅταν οὖν τὴν Ἄγαρ κακουμένην ὑπὸ Σάρρας
ἀκούσῃς, μηδὲν τῶν ἐν ταῖς γυναικείαις ζηλο-
τυπίαις εἰωθότων γίνεσθαι ὑπονοήσῃς· οὐ γὰρ περὶ
γυναικῶν ἐστιν ὁ λόγος, ἀλλὰ διανοιῶν, τῆς μὲν
γυμναζομένης ἐν τοῖς προπαιδεύμασι, τῆς δὲ τοὺς
ἀρετῆς ἄθλους διαθλούσης.

---

[a] The argument in these sections depends, as often, on
Philo's failure to understand the well-known Hebrew idiom.
Cf., e.g., his treatment of βρώσει φάγῃ (Gen. ii. 16) in Leg. All.
i. 97 and of θανάτῳ ἀποθανεῖσθε of the same text in Leg. All.
i. 105.

can be closer than that of a father to a son, or a son to a father? But lest the series of argu- 178 ment following argument should seem tedious and prolix, I will add but one proof, and that the clearest, to those here given, to shew that affliction or ill-usage of a kind is a work of virtue.[a] There is a law in the following terms: "Ye shall not evil-entreat any widow or orphan, but if ye evil-entreat them with evil[b]" (Ex. xxii. 22). What does he mean? Is it that one can be evil-entreated by some other thing than evil? For if evil-treatments are the work of evil and nothing else, it is superfluous to add what is a matter of agreement and will be admitted even without any further words. No doubt he means to say, " I know that one 179 may be rebuked by virtue and disciplined by wisdom, and therefore I do not hold all afflicting or evil-entreating to be blameworthy." When it is the work of justice and the power of the law which chastens by reproof I am filled with admiration. When it is the work of folly and vice and therefore harmful, I turn away from it and call it by the evil names that are its due.

When, then, you hear of Hagar as afflicted or evil- 180 entreated by Sarah, do not suppose that you have here one of the usual accompaniments of women's jealousy. It is not women that are spoken of here; it is minds—on the one hand the mind which exercises itself in the preliminary learning, on the other, the mind which strives to win the palm of virtue and ceases not till it is won.

[b] Or "evil-mindedness," and so throughout for κακία.

PHILO

VOLUME IV

WITH AN ENGLISH TRANSLATION BY

F. H. COLSON

AND

G. H. WHITAKER

HARVARD UNIVERSITY PRESS

CAMBRIDGE, MASSACHUSETTS

LONDON, ENGLAND

First published 1932
Revised and reprinted 1939
Reprinted 1949, 1958, 1968, 1985, 1996

ISBN 0-674-99287-3

Printed in Great Britain by St Edmundsbury Press Ltd,
Bury St Edmunds, Suffolk, on acid-free paper.
Bound by Hunter & Foulis Ltd, Edinburgh, Scotland.

CONTENTS

PREFACE TO VOLUME IV

As was stated in the Preface to the last volume, Mr. Whitaker's versions of the treatises he had agreed to take in this volume and the fifth were in existence at his death. As it happens, however, his part in this volume was confined to one treatise of the four, viz. the *De Migratione*. This had reached the typescript stage, and just before his death I had sent him some corrections or suggestions which he had accepted. Since then, however, I have made a good many further alterations in that treatise. On the *De Confusione* he had sent me only a few suggestions, and my versions of the other two treatises he had not seen at all. Altogether I feel that, for good or for ill, I must take the final responsibility for this volume, and I have therefore ceased to use such phrases as "The Translators think" and used the first person singular instead. That the work has suffered by his absence, and that there are sure to be many things which I should have altered or modified if I had had his advice, need hardly be said.

A misunderstanding shewn by a reviewer makes me think that it would be well to say something about the textual notes. My own view has always been that, while it would be beyond the scope of a work of this kind to indicate the variants in the mss., places in which the text printed has no ms. authority should be recorded. Mr. Whitaker did not altogether

vii

agree with me, and consequently in the first two volumes there was no consistent attempt to give this information, though the reproduction of the angular and square brackets did indicate insertions and omissions in the text. In the third volume and this, however, I have made it a rule to note all cases (except such as are merely orthographical) where the text printed is purely conjectural, however certain the conjectures may be.[a] Further, it is to be understood that, unless it is stated otherwise, the text printed is that of Wendland. It does not follow, however, that any particular emendation of the text is due to Wendland, as I have not thought it necessary to distinguish between his emendations and those of Mangey, Markland and Turnebus, so long as he himself has adopted them. I also note all cases where I have not followed Wendland's text, and, where the emendation is our own, have stated the fact. Of these last there are not many. But there are a good many more noted in footnotes or appendix where I feel fairly confident that the reading we have suggested is right, but have not that degree of certitude which would justify my printing it in the text itself. As to Wendland's corrections, while I accept without question the facts of his *apparatus criticus*, I do not, as the work progresses, feel the same confidence in his judgement. He does not seem to me to consider sufficiently how the text which he adopts came to be corrupted to the form which it has in the MSS. On the whole, however, the principle laid down in the preface of the first volume, that where hesitation does not amount to conviction the

---

[a] Omissions and insertions are of course not noted in the footnotes, as the brackets speak for themselves.

APPENDIX TO *DE CONFUSIONE*

§ 5. *All of whom are agreed that the earth is the centre of the universe.* Cf. Aristot. *De Caelo*, ii. 13, 293 a τῶν πλείστων ἐπὶ τοῦ μέσου κεῖσθαι (sc. τὴν γῆν) λεγόντων. The contrary opinion, that the centre is fire, was held by the Pythagoreans. Cf. also Diog. Laert. ix. 57.

§ 24. *Creeping and flying . . . beasts.* Evidently these represent the θυμός and ἐπιθυμία in the whole ψυχή, though Philo does not show which is which, cf. § 21. Judging from that we may suppose that the "flying" are the ἐπιθυμίαι.

§ 27. *Veiled under their name of Sodomite.* The phrase κατὰ γλῶτταν does not imply a Hebrew word, for the other two examples in the index (αἴθειν 156 below, Ἄρης from ἀρήγειν, *Leg. ad Gaium* 112) are both Greek. A γλῶσσα is often an obscure word which requires explanation (hence our *glossary*). So ἡμεῖς δὲ οὐδὲ ποιητὰς ἐπαινοῦμεν τοὺς κατὰ γλῶσσαν γράφοντας ποιήματα, Lucian, *Lexiph.* 25. Cf. "lingua secretior, quas Graeci γλῶσσας vocant," Quintilian, i. 35.

§ 44. *Jer. xv. 10.* Other mss. of the lxx have οὐκ ὠφέλησα οὐδὲ ὠφέλησάν με, and so some of the mss. of Philo. Origen, however, remarks that while most of the copies of the lxx have ὠφελ-, the best and those most conforming to the Hebrew have ὠφειλ-. Wendland adopted ὠφειλ- on the grounds (1) that the better mss. of Philo have it, (2) that it is supported by the interpretation given in § 50. This last seems to me very doubtful, and altogether there is little or nothing to choose between the two.

§ 46. *Fullest peace.* The epithet ἀπόλεμος is applied to εἰρήνη in *De Fug.* 174, but in the sense of the true (inward) peace, and in somewhat the same way in *De Op.* 142. Here it seems pointless, unless we suppose that εἰρήνη conveys to

Philo something short of an unbroken peace. The first half of this sentence almost repeats *De Gig.* 51.

§ 52. *The touch*, etc. The sentence as taken in the translation is extremely awkward. Further, the analogy of *De Plant.* 133, where ἀφή is called ἡ ἀνὰ πᾶν τὸ σῶμα σκιδναμένη δύναμις, suggests that τῶν ἐν τοῖς σώμασι δυνάμεων is the faculty of touch. This might be obtained if we omit the second τῶν and transpose κατὰ τὰς προσπιπτούσας to after δυνάμεων, *i.e.* "about the faculties or sensations residing in our bodies corresponding to the particular substances which come in contact with them."

§ 55. τροφόν. This reading, which personifies Midian, fits better with τὸν ἔκγονον αὐτῆς than τροφήν. On the other hand, the latter might be regarded as an allusion to Num. xxv. 2 "the people ate of their sacrifices," and Ps. cv. (cvi.) 28 καὶ ἐτελέσθησαν τῷ Βεελφεγὼρ καὶ ἔφαγον τὰς θυσίας νεκρῶν. To suppose an allusion to the Psalm will give extra point to νεκρῶν. Philo may have understood it to refer to the worshippers instead of to the idols.

Ibid. ὑμνοῦντα. This alteration of one letter will enable the sentence to be translated without any other change, though it is true that it would be more natural to take ἄφωνον καὶ νεκρόν as predicate after ἀποδεῖξαι rather than, as it is taken in the translation, as a further attribute to χορόν. If ὑπνοῦντα is retained with Wendland (and his suggestion that it is an antithesis to ὁρῶντος has some support from *De Mig.* 222 τυφλὸν γὰρ ὕπνος), some other alteration is required. Wendland himself suggested γελάσαντες or ἀγαπήσαντα for γελασθέντα. Mangey's suggestion of τελεσθέντα is very tempting, *cf. De Mut.* 196. But I see no way of fitting it into the construction. It can hardly be supposed that the idiom of τελεῖσθαι τελετήν can be extended to τελεῖσθαι Μαδιάμ.

§ 70. *Submerged.* Or "have taken refuge in." *Cf.* the use of ὑπόδρομος *Quod Deus* 156. Philo reads this sense into the LXX. ἔφυγον ὑπὸ τὸ ὕδωρ, which meant presumably "fled with the water over or threatening them." E.V. "fled against it."

§ 90. *The other members of that fraternity and family.* This passage follows the Stoic classification. The four passions and the four vices mentioned are those of the Stoics, who added, as secondary to the primary four, incontinence (ἀκρασία), stupidity (βραδύνοια), ill-advisedness (δυσβουλία),

APPENDICES

Diog. Laert. vii. 93. It is these last three which presumably are meant here.

§ 99. *An appearance of brick.* Wendland was inclined to correct εἶδος to ἔργον, in accordance with the quotation of the text above, and εἶδος might well be a slip of the scribe induced by the preceding εἶδει. But on the other hand εἶδος seems to be needed to represent the δοκεῖ of the interpretation. It seems to me safer to regard it as a slip of Philo himself, who for the moment thought that the εἶδος of the quotation went with πλίνθου instead of with στερεώματος.

§ 103. *The asphalt was clay.* In the original quotation in § 2 the mss. shew, as the LXX itself, ἄσφαλτος ἐγένετο ὁ πηλός. The question naturally arises whether we should amend the text there to bring it into conformity with this, as Wendland suggests (see footnote there). On the whole it seems to me better to leave it and to suppose that Philo here rests his argument on the order of the words. He seems sometimes to attribute an extraordinary value to order, *cf. Quod Deus* 72 and *De Mig.* 140.

§ 106. It is impossible to reproduce in translation the thoughts which the ἀστεῖος of Ex. ii. 2 suggests here to Philo. Struck, like the writer of the Epistle to the Hebrews (xi. 23), with the word applied to the infant Moses in the sense of a fine child, on which he also comments in *De Congressu* 132, he naturally enough connects it with the Stoic use for "virtuous." But he also remembers its connexion with ἄστυ, and this enables him to identify the ἀστεῖον παιδίον with another ideal of the Stoics, the "world-citizen"; see *De Op.* 3 and note. The same play on the double meaning of ἀστεῖος appears in § 109 ἀστεῖοι . . . πολιτεύματι.

§ 108. θεοῦ δὲ ὕμνος. In support of the emendation suggested in the footnote, it may be noted that Ps. xlv. (xlvi.) 4 is actually interpreted in a way very similar to what I suggest here in *De Som.* ii. 246 ff. There we are told that the "city of God" signifies in one sense the world, in another, the soul of the Sage.

It is no objection, I think, that ἡ τοιάδε naturally, though not necessarily, refers to πολιτεία rather than πόλις. If the city is God's, its πολιτεία must be God's also.

§ 111. ὁ νοῦς. While the use of "the mind" in the sense of an evil mind is quite Philonic, it does not occur elsewhere in this passage, and just above we have ὁ ἄφρων.

The very easy correction to ἄνους seems to me therefore very probable.

§ 115. I have not been able to find elsewhere this argument or statement that the apparent examples of a providential administration of the world are sufficiently explained by τὸ αὐτόματον, and are not frequent enough to amount to even human, much less divine, providence. Philo does not repeat it in the arguments adduced by the inquirer in *De Prov.* 11. The sections of the *De Nat. Deorum* in which Cotta discusses "deorumne providentia mundus regatur" are lost.

§ 124. *The causes which come higher*, etc. *I.e.* apparently, mind and sense, which are nearer to the original Cause than the circumstances which we often call "causes." The word seems to be introduced to interpret the "firstlings" in Abel's offering. But a more natural sense would be obtained if we suppose that the scribe by a not unnatural slip wrote πρεσβυτέρας for νεωτέρας.

Philo seems to use αἰτία for secondary causes in preference to αἴτιον. He only uses it of God when contrasting Him with other αἰτίαι.

§ 137. περιττεύειν, κτλ. For my suggestion of πέρα τοῦ εἶναί που for περιττεύειν οὐ cf. Aristotle, *Phys.* iv. 1, p. 208 b 29 διὰ τὸ νομίζειν, ὥσπερ οἱ πολλοί, πάντα εἶναί που καὶ ἐν τόπῳ. For πέρα cf. πέρα μνήμης καὶ νοήσεως ἱστάμενον, *De Mut.* 12.

Ibid. In accordance with the derivation of that name. I.e. θεός from τίθημι. Philo always uses ἔτυμον and ἐτύμως in this technical way, cf. *e.g.* De Vita Mos. i. 17 δίδωσιν ὄνομα θεμένη Μωυσῆν ἐτύμως διὰ τὸ ἐκ τοῦ ὕδατος αὐτὸν ἀνελέσθαι· τὸ γὰρ ὕδωρ μῶν ὀνομάζουσι Αἰγύπτιοι. The one example of those given in the index which at first sight appears to be an exception shews the rule most clearly. In *Quod Omn. Prob.* 73 we have οἱ ἐτύμως ἑπτὰ σοφοὶ προσονομασθέντες, which we might naturally suppose to mean that they were truly called wise. But examination shews that the allusion is to the supposed derivation of σοφός from σεβασμός, from which also ἑπτά is, according to Philo, derived (*De Op.* 127).

§ 141. ἀκοὴν μὴ μαρτυρεῖν. This is the form in which the MSS. give the phrase in a similar passage in *De Spec. Leg.* iv. 61, and which is regularly used by Demosthenes and Isaeus. Wendland on that passage notes that here ἀκοῇ should be corrected to ἀκοὴν.

APPENDICES

Philo is no doubt alluding to the Attic orators, particularly to Dem. *Contra Eubuliden* p. 1300 πᾶσι προσήκειν . . . μηδεμίαν προσάγειν ἀκοὴν πρὸς τὸν τοιοῦτον ἀγῶνα. οὕτω γὰρ τοῦτ' ἄδικον καὶ σφόδρα πάλαι κέκριται, ὥστ' οὐδὲ μαρτυρεῖν ἀκοὴν ἐῶσιν οἱ νόμοι, οὐδ' ἐπὶ τοῖς πάνυ φαύλοις ἐγκλήμασι. So too in ps.-Dem. *Contra Steph.* ii. p. 1130, *Contra Leoch.* p. 1027, where exception is made if the person who was heard is dead. See *Dict. of Ant.* art. "Akoēn Marturein." In *De Spec. Leg.* Philo definitely says, what he perhaps implies here, that the Attic legislators took the principle from Moses.

§ 149. Ryle, *Philo and Holy Scripture*, p. xxvi, supposes the reference to be to Ezra viii. 2. This is quite unnecessary. Ezra is nowhere else quoted by Philo, and Ryle's idea, that the use of βασιλικαί instead of the usual βασίλειαι points to a different group from the books of Kings, is fanciful.

§ 151. ἐπὶ τῆς πολίτιδος τὸ κατασκευαστόν. While the general sense of this is clear, the text is very doubtful. κατασκευαστόν ("artificial") for the regularity which *seems* artificial is strange but not impossible, and τὸ παραπλήσιον may be used as an adverb. But the word πολῖτις, only known as the feminine of πολίτης, is impossible here, where fever or malaria is clearly meant.

I suggest very hesitatingly that τῆς πολίτιδος may be a corruption of τῆς σπληνίτιδος. The word σπληνῖτις for a disease of the spleen is not found in the medical writers, but they constantly insist on the enlargement of the spleen as a regular symptom of malaria (see W. H. S. Jones, *Malaria*, index).

Wendland would correct to ἐπὶ τῆς πυρετοῦ καταβολῆς τὸ παραπλήσιον, which bears little resemblance to the text.

Mangey thought that the whole passage was an irrelevant interpolation. On the contrary, as an illustration of Philo's point, that we find harmony and regularity in things evil, it seems very appropriate.

Ibid. εἰς αὐτά. The phrase is, as it stands, unintelligible. I suggest and have translated εἰς αὐτὰς or εἰς αὐτὰς αὐτήν (with regard to themselves, *i.e.* each other). I understand Philo to mean that while the attacks recur at the same hour, they vary somewhat in nature, but the varieties also have a regular order. Whether this is medically untrue, or whether if it is, Philo is likely to have thought it true, I do not know.

PHILO

Wendland suggested αὐτὴν αἰεί. Mangey read εἰς τὰ αὐτά. I think ἰσότητα might be worth considering.

§ 154. ἅς τι τῶν ὄντων. This seems to me less unsatisfactory than Wendland's reading. But τι=ὁτιοῦν in this position is strange. Possibly οὔ τι (adverbial). Also ἔθος, for which Wendland would substitute θέμις, is odd. Altogether the text is unsatisfactory.

§ 164. *The fortunes of tyrants.* Philo doubtless has in mind the description of the miserable condition of tyrants in *Republic*, Bk. ix., particularly 576 B.

§ 165. *Free licence to sin.* This use of ἐκεχειρία (*cf.* τὴν ἐς τὸ ἁμαρτάνειν ἐκεχειρίαν, *De Jos.* 254) seems peculiar to Philo. It suggests that when it occurs without such explanatory phrases, as in *De Cher.* 92 and *De Sac.* 23, the meaning is rather licence in general, than, as it was translated there, "freedom from stress of business."

§ 173. *Each of them as a whole.* Did anyone deify the νοητὸς κόσμος? Philo perhaps means that the deification of the visible world *ipso facto* involved that of the invisible.

§ 174. ἑκάστων. I retain this, supposing that the army of the subordinates are regarded as formed of three kinds, (1) the Potencies who as agents in the creation of the two worlds stand above the rest, (2) the divine natures in heaven, *i.e.* the heavenly bodies, (3) the "souls" or angels in the lower air.

§§ 184-187. The sense of these sections is given also by Stobaeus, as from Chrysippus (*S. V.F.* ii. 471), with the same illustrations from the wine and water and oiled sponge, and much the same language throughout. There is, however, a complete difference in his use of the term μῖξις, which he distinguishes from παράθεσις and applies to the ἀντιπαρέκτασις δι' ὅλων in dry substances while κρᾶσις is reserved for the same in liquids. His example of μῖξις is the mixture of fire and iron in heated iron. It does not follow that Philo made a mistake; the use of terms seems to have varied. *Cf. ibid.* 473.

§ 186. *Resolved.* Or "expanded." Some MSS. ἀναπληροῦσθαι. See on the word Liddell & Scott (1927). The suggestion there that the word suggests "resolving into *simple* elements" is unnecessary.

§ 187. *Confusion is the annihilation. Cf. S.V.F.* 473 (also from Chrysippus) τὰς δέ τινας (*sc.* μίξεις γίνεσθαι) συγχύσει,

APPENDICES

δι' ὅλων τῶν τε οὐσιῶν αὐτῶν καὶ τῶν ἐν αὐταῖς ποιοτήτων συμφθει-
ρομένων ἀλλήλαις, ὡς γίνεσθαί φησιν ἐπὶ τῶν ἰατρικῶν φαρμάκων,
κατὰ σύμφθαρσιν τῶν μιγνυμένων ἄλλου τινὸς ἐξ αὐτῶν γεννωμένου
σώματος.

§ 198. Heinemann in a note added to Stein's translation considers that πεφορημένος is unsuitable here and suggests πεφυρημένος. But this comes from φυράω, which will not give any suitable meaning, and the word of which he is thinking is no doubt πεφυρμένος, from φύρω, which is certainly often combined with συγχέω, cf. particularly *Spec. Leg.* iv. 77 διαιρείτω καὶ διακρινέτω τὰς φύσεις τῶν πραγμάτων ἵνα μὴ φύρηται συγχεόμενα τοῖς παρασήμοις τὰ δόκιμα. However, the explanation of πεφορημένος given in the footnote seems to me satisfactory, cf. the combination of πεφορημένος with ἄσωτος to indicate the profligate in *De Fug.* 28, and πάντῃ φορούμενος associated with σπείρεται in the sense of διασπείρεται in *De Cong.* 58.

APPENDIX TO *DE MIGRATIONE*

§ 5. *Soul as soul.* This phrase, which occurred in *Quod Det.* 9, belongs, as Posner points out, to Stoic usage. See Sext. Emp. *Adv. Math.* vii. 233. The Stoics call the φαντασία a τύπωσις ἐν ψυχῇ ὡς ἂν ἐν ψυχῇ, because "impression on the soul" might in itself be applied to a pain felt in any part of the living organism. The addition, ὡς ἂν ἐν ψυχῇ signifies that it is "no chance part" which is affected, but the mind or dominant principle.

§ 17. *Untouched by corruption and worthy of perpetual memory.* What is the distinction between ἀξιομνημόνευτα and ἄφθαρτα or ἀδιάφθορα? Apparently the former are Joseph's vision of, or hope for, the future, while the latter are the record of his life, so far as it is good. Philo may mean that while the record remains in the background as an example, the hope becomes the inspiring principle of the succeeding generations. If so, "ever to be borne in mind" might perhaps give better the sense of ἀξιομνημόνευτα.

§ 21. *He derided lusts*, etc. Neither Mangey nor Wendland give the reference to Gen. xxxix. 14 and 17, where Potiphar's wife says "Lo, he hath brought in a Hebrew servant to mock at us" (ἐμπαίζειν ἡμῖν). Presumably they supposed the words to be a general description of Joseph's continence. But the form shews that it is a separate item in Joseph's virtues, each based on a separate text. "Us" is interpreted as meaning "all the passions." That in the story the "mocking" referred to Joseph's alleged misconduct matters little or nothing to Philo.

§ 23. ἀνέχεται . . . ἐνθάπτεται . . . παρέπεται. I have no hesitation in rejecting Mangey's and Wendland's emendation of these to infinitives. Not only would these require, as Wendland indeed saw, the insertion of τὸ (or rather οἷον τὸ to agree with πολλά), and perhaps the change of οὐ to μή, but

APPENDICES

the sense seems to me quite inferior. This particular "trait" has already been given as one of the ἀξιομνημόνευτα in § 18. I understand the sentence to sum up all that has been said and to assert that the good deeds and words are the "bones," which themselves cry to be taken from Egypt, and in fact never have been buried at all, a phrase quite inapplicable to Joseph himself. There would of course from this point of view be no objection to reading ἐνθάπτεσθαι dependent on ἀνέχεται, but no sufficient reason for the alteration.

§ 24. διακρίνει παρελθών. The text is very perplexing. As H has παρελθόντα, Wendland suggests as a possibility διακρίνεται παρ' ἐλπίδα. This seems to me out of place. Mangey suggested διακρίνεται παραλυθέντα. The reading which Wendland actually prints, and which has been reproduced here, is not satisfactory, as the παρελθών is very pointless. I should hesitatingly suggest either διακρίνει παρελών, "removes" and "separates," or better, as retaining the διακρίνεται of all mss., διακρίνεται παρεισελθόντων, "is separated from adventitious accretions." παρεισέρχομαι in the sense of "invading surreptitiously" is used by Philo, De Op. 150, De Ebr. 157.

§ 32. Release. An allusion to the ordinance by which in the sabbatical year the land (here compared to the mind) was to be left fallow, Ex. xxxiii. 11 τῷ δὲ ἑβδόμῳ ἄφεσιν ποιήσεις καὶ ἀνήσεις αὐτήν, καὶ ἔδονται οἱ πτωχοὶ τοῦ ἔθνους σου. In Lev. xxv. 4-7 we have the same ordinance, but with ἀνάπαυσις for ἄφεσις. Philo understands that the land by divine grace will bear plentifully of itself. Compare his φορὰ τῶν αὐτοματιζομένων ἀγαθῶν with τὰ αὐτόματα ἀναβαίνοντα of Lev. He may also be thinking of the somewhat similar ordinance of the Jubilee year, ἐνιαυτὸς ἀφέσεως, though there ἄφεσις means release for the people rather than for the land. On ὥσπερ τῶν ἐκουσίων Mangey wrote "omnino male" and proposed ὡς φόρτων τῶν ἐτησίων. But ἑκούσιος is in Philo's thought the direct antithesis of αὐτόματος.

§ 35. ἔσχον γὰρ ἑρμηνείαν, εὕρεσιν. I have adopted Markland's ἔσχον for σχεδόν, but see every reason against changing εὕρεσιν. The five elements of composition are εὕρεσις, τάξις or οἰκονομία, ἑρμηνεία (otherwise called φράσις, λέξις, ἀπαγγελία), μνήμη, ὑπόκρισις. Philo enumerates them in De Som. i. 205. Of these terms the two last belong entirely to spoken oratory, and τάξις would be out of place. When inspiration comes, the two things that come are "ideas" and "language."

561

PHILO

These two (in Latin *inventio* and *elocutio*) are often given as the kernel of composition, *e.g.* Quintilian, Pr. 12 "omnia inventione atque elocutione explicanda sunt." See note on *De Cher.* 105.

§ 42. *Insight.* The not very common word εἴδησιν is evidently introduced with reference to εἶδεν. So in the other place where Philo uses it (*De Plant.* 36), it is connected with the tree of knowledge, which in Gen. ii. 9 is the tree τοῦ εἰδέναι.

Ibid. To give teaching . . . to the ignorant, etc. Or it might be taken "to give teaching . . . is proper not for the ignorant, but only for the One who knows." Mangey translates the reading he adopted (see critical note), "decebat igitur ignorantes docere, commonstrareque illis singula, non vero scientem," apparently meaning that it is right to teach the ignorant, but not to teach God who knows. But apart from the question whether εἶχε εὐπρεπές can mean "decebat," this has no bearing on the proof that it is God who "shews."

§ 49. *The various parts of speech.* By Philo's time the primitive division into verbs, nouns, and conjunctions (the first two often standing alone in popular language) had been greatly developed and this is recognized in the συνόλως of § 48. The phrase οἱ εἰς ὀνομάτων καὶ ῥημάτων ἰδέας μεριζόμενοι may recur to the primitive division and suggest that there are only two main ἰδέαι (so the translation), or he may mean that verbs and nouns have their various ἰδέαι or subdivisions, the pronoun being a form of the noun and the adverb of the verb. See the *loci classici* in Quintilian, i. 4. 18, and Dion. Hal. *De Comp.* 2.

§ 54. *Both in conduct of life and in principle.* Philo's conception of moral "greatness," as shewn by his illustrations in § 55, is a full development and intensification of each particular virtue, and this he equates with the power to understand and know. Possibly, therefore, here τὰ περὶ τὸν βίον κατορθώματα = πλῆθος, and τὰ περὶ λόγον = μέγεθος. If so, the former will represent the καθήκοντα or "daily duties" of the Stoics, and the latter their κατορθώματα proper, which connoted to them inwardness and sustained moral purpose. See note on *Quod Deus* 100.

§ 69. ἐπιγραφόμενος. This correction of Wendland's for αἰνιττόμενος is based on the close imitation of the passage in Clem. Alex. *Protrept.* 25 αἰνίττεται δὲ . . . τὸν πολλοὺς ἐπι-

APPENDICES

γραφόμενον ψευδωνύμους θεοὺς ἀντὶ τοῦ μόνου ὄντος θεοῦ, ὥσπερ ὁ ἐκ τῆς πόρνης τοὺς πολλοὺς ἐπιγράφεται πατέρας ἀγνοίᾳ τοῦ πρὸς ἀλήθειαν πατρός. Mangey suggested ἀναπλαττόμενος, which is not as good sense, though nearer to the MSS.

§ 79. *Mints them . . . before.* The paraphrastic translation is an attempt to bring out Philo's play upon ἄσημος and ἐπίσημος as signifying (1) uncoined and coined money, (2) obscure and clear or conspicuous.

Ibid. In it. Philo quotes Ex. iv. 14 in three other places. In *De Mut.* 168 the MSS. have as here ἐν αὐτῷ. In *Quod Det.* 126 and 135, they have, as the LXX itself, ἐν ἑαυτῷ and the comment on the latter of these shews that this is what Philo wrote. While printing ἐν αὐτῷ I feel very doubtful as to its correctness here and in *De Mut.*

§ 94. *Realities.* For the philosophical use of ὑπαρκτά *cf.* τεκμήριον τοῦ ὑπαρκτὴν εἶναι τὴν ἀρετήν, Diog. Laert. vii., and ἔστι μὲν ὑπαρκτὸν πρᾶγμα σοφία, *De Mut.* 37. Compare the same point in *De Sac.* 43, where the force of ὑπαρκτά was unfortunately not properly recognized in the translation. Similarly in *Leg. All.* iii. 197 Ἀβραὰμ . . . τὰ μὲν ὑπάρχοντα . . . κατέχει, ἀποπέμπεται δὲ τὴν ἵππον τοῦ βασιλέως Σοδόμων ὡς καὶ τὰ ὑπαρκτὰ τῶν παλλακῶν, it now seems clear to me that we should read τὰ ⟨μὴ⟩ ὑπαρκτά, perhaps also τῶν ⟨υἱων τῶν⟩ παλλακῶν.

§ 125. *The threefold divisions of eternity.* Or "time." This curious interpretation of the three patriarchs is perhaps explained in § 154. "The clear sight of things present," and the "expectation of things to come," fit in fairly well with the αὐτομαθής and the προκόπτων, the characters regularly assigned to Isaac and Jacob, while the "memory of the past" suits, though not so well, the διδακτικὴ ἀρετή of Abraham. He may also be thinking of Ex. iii. 15, where "God of Abraham, Isaac, and Jacob" is God's αἰώνιον ὄνομα.

§ 138. *Spin your airy fables.* The word ἀερομυθεῖτε need not mean more than talk windily, *cf.* the use of ἀερόμυθος in the list of vices in *De Sacr.* 33. But there may be a special significance in it here, as the moon at any rate bordered on the ἀήρ (*S.V.F.* ii. 527).

§ 140. *It does not say,* etc. This amazing argument admits of no satisfactory explanation. It clearly demands that παιδίον *may* be nominative, but Mangey's suggestion to

PHILO

read Σάρραν is out of the question. Apart from other difficulties, the natural negation would be οὐχὶ Σάρρα. Nor can Philo be supposed to have really thought that Σάρρα was indeclinable, seeing that he uses Σάρρας in the same sentence and elsewhere Σάρραν itself. The least unsatisfactory explanation I can give is that he means that Σάρρα, like other O.T. names, which though capable of being declined in Greek are not declined, e.g. Ἀαρών, might conceivably be undeclinable and that therefore Moses, wishing to suggest that, though literally Sarah suckles Isaac, spiritually Isaac suckles Sarah, uses this form rather than the passive, in which no ambiguity would be possible. Possibly also he puts some reliance on παιδίον preceding Σάρρα. See on De Conf. 102.

§ 150. The allusions in this section are (1) to Lot's settling in Sodom (Gen. xii. 32), which naturally signifies his "old complaint" of ἀμαθία, cf. De Conf. 27, (2) to his capture (xiv. 12) by the Four Kings, signifying the four passions, cf. De Congressu 22, (3) the quarrel between the shepherds of Lot and Abraham (xiii. 7), which Philo unfairly turns into a conflict between the two men.

§ 160. *The idol of Egyptian vanity.* The meaning of this is not clear. In the other places where Philo uses Αἰγυπτιακὸς τῦφος it is with reference to the Golden Calf as being a return to Egyptian idolatry. The meaning therefore here may be that by riding behind Pharaoh he acknowledges him as a god. But in De Som. ii. 46, where this incident is referred to, Joseph himself is ὑποτυφόμενος, and ibid. 16 we have ἀναβαίνει ἐπὶ τὴν κενὴν δόξαν ὡς ἐφ' ἅρμα. This suggests that ἱδρύεται here may mean "seats himself on," but no real parallel is forthcoming. Mangey suggested ἐνδύεται.

§ 164. μελιττῶν. The μὲν αὐτῶν of the mss. seems to me to break down in two ways. There is no antithesis for the μέν. Philo's μέν indeed is occasionally not followed by δέ, but in these cases there is, wherever I have noted them, an antithesis to something which has gone before. Again, the plural αὐτῶν is quite out of place where both the people concerned are in the singular, and the one cannot be supposed to have any share in the labours of the other. It will be admitted that μελιττῶν makes excellent sense. Textually the ΛΙ of ΜΕΛΙΤΤΩΝ passes very easily into Ν, and Τ with no great difficulty into Τ, and when ΜΕΝΤΤΩΝ had

APPENDICES

thus been obtained the insertion of **A** to make sense would naturally follow.

§ 165. ὑπ' εὐθυμίας. It is not clear what cheerfulness has to do with the φιλοθεάμων or why it opens the eyes of the soul. As all mss. (except H²) have ὑπὲρ εὐθυμίας, it is possible, I think, that the true reading may be ὑπ' ἐρεύνης θείας, which exactly describes the φιλοθεάμων. Compare τῆς τῶν θείων ἐρεύνης, *Leg. All.* iii. 71 and (for the objective use of θεῖος) τῆς θείας θεωρίας, § 150 above, and θεῖος ἵμερος, § 157.

§ 167. *Arts copying Nature's works*, etc. *Cf. De Ebr.* 90, where art is the μίμημα and ἀπεικόνισμα of nature, on which Adler remarks that, as the context shews, it does not mean that art imitates natural objects, but that it follows Nature's methods. So here ἔργων may be "ways of working," or "processes."

§ 174. ὑποστείληταί σε . . . The Hebrew and E.V. have "will not pardon thy transgression." Did the LXX. mean much the same "he will not shrink (from punishing)"? At any rate Philo would seem to have taken it in some such sense, for where the text is quoted in the *Quaestiones* (in Exod. ii. 13) the Latin version of the Armenian has "non enim verebitur te."

§ 180. *For if it came into being and is one*, etc. Philo takes ἕν in the full sense of the Stoic ἡνωμένον (*cf.* note on *Quod Det.* 49) and argues that if the world is ἡνωμένον, it must be composed of the same elements throughout and this, it is implied, will in itself effect συμπάθεια. Sext. Emp. *Adv. Math.* ix. 78 (*S.V.F.* ii. 1013) puts the Stoic argument in much the same way but in reverse order. Only ἡνωμένα exhibit συμπάθεια, and since there is συμπάθεια between the parts of the Cosmos, the Cosmos must be an ἡνωμένον σῶμα.

§ 206. διανιστάμενον. My suggestion of διανεσταμένον is made provisionally subject to better knowledge as to this perfect passive in the compounds of ἵστημι. In *Timaeus* 81 D there is at any rate some authority for διεσταμένοι. So the LXX in Num. xxxi. 48 καθεσταμένοι. Here a few mss. have διενιστάμενον. The present must mean "waking up," as in *Quod Deus* 97. Cohn's suggestion of διασυνιστάμενον (presumably meaning "proved to be such," *i.e.* μνημονικόν) does not give much point to ἄτε.

§ 207. *That does not call for our censure.* The application of the adjective ἀνεπίληπτον, which usually denotes high

PHILO

praise, to the hybrid number seventy-five is at first sight strange, and Mangey's proposal ⟨οὐκ⟩ ἀνεπιλήπτου is textually, considering our experience of the omissions of the negative in Philo, quite sound. But it would really give an inferior sense. The stress is here laid on the virtues of seventy-five, not on its shortcomings, and if we give ἀνεπίληπτος a somewhat reduced sense as in the translation (*cf.* ταμιείας ἀνεπιλήπτου § 89, and *De Cong.* 138), that stress is well brought out. Midway between Joseph and Moses stands the Jacob soul, ὁ προκόπτων, and in its progress the seventy-five is a necessary and therefore "blameless" stage. This is immediately illustrated by §§ 208 ff., where Jacob even in victory is well-advised to return to Haran, that is, to the world of sense and even (§ 209), of opportunism.

§ 210. ζωοτροφεῖ. Mr. Whitaker was inclined to adopt Mangey's suggestion of ζωπυρεῖ, which is in accordance with ζέον καὶ πεπυρωμένον. On the other hand ζωοτροφεῖ serves to carry on the parable in which the passions are the wild cattle reared by the κτηνοτρόφοι of Haran.

§§ 210, 211 (footnote). *De Som.* ii. 85 ff. looks as if the advice to temporize with angry people is to be taken more literally than I have suggested in the note.

§ 221. τῇ ἑτέρᾳ. Further consideration shews beyond doubt that in *De Sac.* 37 where we printed, following Cohn and Mangey, οὐ τῇ ῥαστώνῃ ταῦτα ληπτά we should have put τῇ ἑτέρᾳ or θατέρᾳ. There one ms. has ῥαστώνη, others οὐ τη and οὐχ ἁπλῶς, while by far the best authority, the Papyrus, has ουθετερα, the origin of which is obvious. The phrase seems for some reason to have puzzled the scribes. It is strange that the two German scholars also failed to understand it, for even the old editions of Liddell & Scott record τῇ ἑτέρᾳ λαμβάνειν "'to get with little trouble,' a proverb," and give the reference to Plato.

APPENDIX TO
QUIS RERUM DIVINARUM HERES

§ 14. *A spherical shape.* *Cf.* Diog. Laert. vii. 158 ἀκούειν δὲ τοῦ μεταξὺ τοῦ τε φωνοῦντος καὶ τοῦ ἀκούοντος ἀέρος πληττομένου σφαιροειδῶς, εἶτα κυματουμένου καὶ ταῖς ἀκοαῖς προσπίπτοντος, ὡς κυματοῦται τὸ ἐν τῇ δεξαμένῃ ὕδωρ κατὰ κύκλους ὑπὸ τοῦ ἐμβληθέντος λίθου, " we hear when the air between the sonant body and the organ of hearing suffers concussion, a vibration which spreads spherically and then forms waves and strikes upon the ears, just as the water in a reservoir forms wavy circles when a stone is thrown into it " (Hicks's translation). So too Plut. *Epit.* iv. 20 (Diels, *Dox.* p. 409), where contrasting the effect of the stone in the pool, he adds καὶ αὕτη μὲν (the pool) κυκλικῶς κινεῖται, ὁ δ' ἀὴρ σφαιρικῶς.

§ 17. *Tense of . . . completed action.* The Greek grammarians named the four tenses of past time (χρόνος παρεληλυθώς) as follows: imperfect, παρατατικός; aorist, ἀόριστος; perfect, παρακείμενος; pluperfect, ὑπερσυντελικός. The name συντελικός for the aorist is sometimes, but rarely, found (see *Greek Gramm.* Part II. vol. iii. p. 85), but its use, perhaps to cover both aorist and perfect, is reflected in the name for the pluperfect and in the Latin term, *perfectum tempus.*

§ 25. *Thou hast given me a tongue of instruction*, etc. The reference for this almost verbatim quotation from Isaiah is given by J. Cohn. It seems to have escaped previous editors.

§ 29. ἀνεστοιχειωμένος. The word, which recurs in §§ 184 and 200, seems to mean " reduced to a single element "; *cf.* *De Vit. Mos.* ii. 288 ὃς αὐτὸν δυάδα ὄντα, σῶμα καὶ ψυχήν, εἰς μονάδος ἀνεστοιχείου φύσιν. L. & S. " into its elements."

§ 36. ἔφεσιν (MSS. φύσιν). I have ventured on this correction because the MS. reading seems to me untranslatable.

PHILO

Mangey has "sinere ut naturae meae bonum intereat";
Yonge, "to be indifferent to the sight of my own nature
separated from the good"; J. Cohn, "wenn mein Wesen
untergehen und nicht mehr die Schönheit schauen würde."
I do not see how any of these can be got out of the Greek.
Though not common, ἔφεσις in the sense of "desire" is
sufficiently authenticated and, if right, was of course intended to echo ἐφίεμαι. At the same time, τὴν ἐμαυτοῦ φύσιν
makes a good antithesis to γένος, and the corruption may
lie in τοῦ καλοῦ (as I have alternatively suggested), or in
καταλυθεῖσαν.

§ 46. *And when the better life*, etc. The metaphor is not
very clear. It would be made clearer (though at the expense
of some awkwardness) if we take συνεπισπασθέν to agree with
βάρος instead of with τοῦθ'. In that case the meaning would
be that when that part of the mixed which belongs to the
better life preponderates in its side of the scales, the base
life in the other scale is pulled up and kicks the beam.

§ 52. *Gave the name*, etc. I do not see much sense in
this expression, even if ὠνόμασεν can be taken (as by J. Cohn),
as merely meaning "he described as." I am inclined to
think that the ἐκείνην of Pap. is right. Though grammatically
superfluous after ἥν, so much so as to be almost ungram-
matical, it may be partly accounted for by the desire to
emphasize the antithesis to ἑαυτοῦ, and it gives a clear sense:
"he gave to her who was his own death the name of Life."

§ 75. πάνθειον. It is curious that the Lexica have not
noticed the occurrence of this word in Philo, here and in
De Aet. 10. Otherwise, apart from definite notices of the
Pantheon at Rome, the only example given is a passage in
Aristotle quoted by a scholiast and referring to the Pantheon
at Olympia.

§ 76. As νοητῶν, added by the Papyrus after ἡμῶν, cannot
be translated as it stands, I have not inserted it. It may be
a mere slip induced by the νοητός above. Cohn suggested
ἔξω γηίνων ⟨καὶ ἐφιέμενος⟩ νοητῶν. The phrase ὑπεξελθὼν ἐξ
ἡμῶν for ἐξ ἑαυτοῦ is certainly strange, but may be modelled
on the ὃς ἐξελεύσεται ἐκ σοῦ of the text.

§ 81. ἀλλὰ σωμάτων ⟨καὶ⟩ τὰς ἐν τούτοις. Wendland's text
makes the ἐν τούτοις almost unintelligible, unless we may
suppose that ταῦτα stands for the phenomenal world; *cf.*
§280 and *De Ebr.* 132 (and note). The insertion of καί and

APPENDICES

change of punctuation removes the difficulty satisfactorily, though ἐν is hardly the preposition we should expect. Mangey's suggestion of ἐν τόποις gets some support from *De Sac.* 68.

§ 115. σπέρματα καὶ καταβολαί. It is hard to decide between this reading and Wendland's ("Are the seed-droppings of the plants the works of agriculture or invisible works of invisible nature?"). My preference for the former chiefly rests on a feeling that while σπέρματα may well be thought of as nature's work (*cf.* § 121), this cannot be said of the human agency expressed in καταβολαί.

§ 132. *Where the object,* etc. For the difference between φαντασία καταληπτική and ἀκατάληπτος see Diog. Laert. vii. 46 τῆς δὲ φαντασίας τὴν μὲν καταληπτικήν, τὴν δὲ ἀκατάληπτον· καταληπτικὴν μὲν . . . τὴν γινομένην ἀπὸ ὑπάρχοντος κατ' αὐτὸ τὸ ὑπάρχον ἐναπεσφραγισμένην καὶ ἐναπομεμαγμένην· ἀκατάληπτον δὲ τὴν μὴ ἀπὸ ὑπάρχοντος, ἢ ἀπὸ ὑπάρχοντος μέν, μὴ κατ' αὐτὸ δὲ τὸ ὑπάρχον· τὴν μὴ τρανῆ μηδὲ ἔκτυπον, "there are two species of presentation, the one apprehending a real object, the other not. The former . . . is defined as that which proceeds from a real object, agrees with that object itself, and has been imprinted seal-fashion and stamped upon the mind; the latter, or non-apprehending, that which does not proceed from any real object, or, if it does, fails to agree with the reality itself, not being clear or distinct" (Hicks's translation).

§ 136. *Fire . . . heaven.* The doctrine of the two kinds of fire is Stoic. See *S.V.F.* i. 120 where the "useful" fire is called ἄτεχνον (non-creative?), and the other τεχνικόν. The best parallel to Philo's language is in Cic. *De natura deorum,* ii. 40 from Cleanthes where of one he says, "ignis, quem usus vitae requirit, confector est et consumptor omnium idemque, quocumque invasit, cuncta disturbat ac dissipat": of the other, "contra ille corporeus vitalis et salutaris omnia conservat, alit, auget, sustinet sensuque adficit."

§ 144. *Other things are equal in capacity,* etc. Wendland's punctuation (a comma after μεγέθει) suggests that he understood the words as Mangey, Cohn, and Yonge all do, "cubit compared with cubit is equal in magnitude, but different in power" (Mangey "gravitate"). But this is hardly sense. It is quite easy to understand ἴσα from the preceding ἴσα μεγέθει, and we thus get the third form of equality, of which

569

PHILO

weights and measures of capacity are a natural example, and which is referred to again in § 151.

§ 145. *One essential form is the proportional*, etc. Wendland refers to Aristot. *Pol.* viii. 1, p. 1301 b, where proportional equality is called λόγῳ or κατ' ἀξίαν. But there is no need to suppose any definite reference. The idea of ἀναλογία runs through all Greek arithmetic.

§ 156. *No heightening or lowering of intensity.* A Stoic phrase. The Stoics laid down that Virtue and the Good admitted neither of ἐπίτασις nor ἄνεσις (*S.V.F.* iii. 92), and in this differed from the τέχναι which did admit of such variations and gradations (*ibid.* 525). Thus Philo's words are a way of saying that God's art is like the Good and not like human art. For the antithesis of ἐπίτασις and ἄνεσις in a rather different sense *cf. Quod Deus* 162.

§ 165. *The three which followed the sun's creation.* This may no doubt mean that the fourth day, on which the sun was created, divided the first, second and third from the fifth, sixth and seventh. But the stress so constantly laid on the ἑξάς of creation, and equality (not the fourth day) being given as the divider, make it more probable that the three μεθ' ἥλιον are the fourth, fifth and sixth. If so, it is strange that the fourth should be called "*after* the sun." Should we read μεθ' ἥλιον in both places?

§ 169. *From his commonwealth.* Or "from his own commonwealth." On a similar passage, *De Gig.* 59, I suggested that Philo was hinting at a comparison between the πολιτεία of Moses and that of Plato, which expelled some forms of poetry for the same reasons as are here given for expelling painting and sculpture, viz. their tendency to produce illusion and deception. No such reason, however, is given here, and further observation of Philo's usage inclines me to think that his use of the reflexive pronoun in such phrases is not to be pressed.

§ 170. ⟨οὐ τοῦ⟩ ὃ κτλ. That the negative has fallen out is evident. Mangey however proposed ⟨οὐχ⟩ ὃ, which is quite possible, though οὐ τοῦ ὃ is more strictly grammatical. If, as suggested in the footnote, we read. τοῦ κυρίου ⟨τοῦ θεοῦ⟩, it would certainly be preferable to follow it by οὐχ ὃ. That Philo should have written six ου's in succession is hardly credible.

Ibid. The number Seven. The definite use by Philo of

APPENDICES

ἐβδομάς for the seventh day (ἐβδόμη) is certainly rare, but is difficult to avoid here, or in *De Vit. Mos.* i. 205. For the epithets applied to the ἐβδομάς cf. *De Op.* 100, and *Leg. All.* i. 15. In the first of them the idea is ascribed to philosophers other than the Pythagoreans, in the second to the Pythagoreans themselves.

§ 182. *The high priest Moses.* As Moses in the history is not high priest, Mangey thought this should be corrected to ἀρχιπροφήτης. But Moses' function here is that of high priest, and he is actually given the title in *De Vit. Mos.* ii. 75 and elsewhere.

§ 185. νοῦ θείαις or νουθεσίαις. How is the latter to be translated? "Following the admonitions in its revolutions"? Mangey, who suggested and perhaps intended to translate προόδοις for περιόδοις, has "sequendo castigationis ductum"; Yonge, "following the guidance of admonition"; J. Cohn, "zu bestimmter Zeit den Mahnungen Folge leistet." There is no suggestion that any of these adopted νουθεσίας, which is given by one ms. and would make the phrase more tolerable. I accept Wendland's conjecture with confidence, and suggest that νοῦ περιόδοις is taken from *Timaeus* 47 B ἵνα τὰς ἐν οὐρανῷ κατιδόντες τοῦ νοῦ περιόδους χρησαίμεθα ἐπὶ τὰς περιφορὰς τὰς τῆς παρ' ἡμῖν διανοήσεως, and again (*ibid.* D) ταῖς ἐν ἡμῖν τῆς ψυχῆς περιόδοις. We have already had the combination θείαις περιόδοις in § 88, where the general sense of the passage is in close agreement with *Timaeus* 47, and though there is less analogy between that and the context here, Philo's love of the dialogue will account for his here introducing the phrase.

§ 188. *Filling . . . being.* J. Cohn and Leisegang (*Index*) take this as "filled all existing things." But is πάντα τῆς οὐσίας for πᾶσαν τὴν οὐσίαν Greek? On the other hand it seems doubtful whether ἐκπληροῦν is, like πληροῦν, followed by the genitive. Perhaps read πάντα ⟨τὰ⟩ τῆς οὐσίας.

§ 190. *And therefore those who study such questions,* etc. Cf. Diog. Laert. viii. 25 of the Pythagorean tenets: ἀρχὴν μὲν ἁπάντων μονάδα· ἐκ δὲ τῆς μονάδος ἀόριστον δυάδα ὡς ἂν ὕλην τῇ μονάδι αἰτίῳ ὄντι ὑποστῆναι· ἐκ δὲ τῆς μονάδος καὶ τῆς ἀορίστου δυάδος τοὺς ἀριθμούς, "the principle of all things is the monad or unit; arising from this monad the undefined dyad or two serves as material substratum to the monad, which is cause; from the monad and the undefined dyad spring numbers" (Hicks's translation).

PHILO

§ 212. ἀπέρατα or ἀπέραντα. If, as would appear from Liddell & Scott (1927), the evidence for the existence of ἀπέρατος in the sense of "unlimited" depends mainly or entirely on Philo, it seems doubtful whether it is worth much. Two examples of ἀπέρατος are given in the index apart from this passage. In one of these ἀπέρατος φλόξ, De Mig. 100, the natural meaning is "impassable." In the other, De Fug. 57, we have ἀπέρατος αἰών in all MSS. Here, as stated in the footnote, the MSS. are all for ἀπέραντα, though the Papyrus may be said to favour the other. Unless better evidence is forthcoming, there would seem to be good grounds for following the MSS. here, and correcting to ἀπέραντος, as Mangey wished, in De Fug. 57.

§ 218. Lamps . . . candle-bearers. I do not vouch for the accuracy of the translation of these terms, which concern the study of the LXX rather than that of Philo. Mangey gives "cauliculi" for λαμπάδια (but also for καλαμίσκοι), and "lucernae" for λύχνοι. J. Cohn translates the two by "Kelche" and "Lampen." When he gives "Kelche" (cups) he is presumably equating λαμπάδια with κρατῆρες in the parallel account of the chandelier in Ex. xxv. 31. The received text of the LXX has ἐνθέμια (sockets?) for ἀνθέμια.

§ 228. The general conflagration. While the general sense of the section is made perfectly clear by the passages referred to in the footnote, there remain the following questions:

(a) The position of the words ἀλλὰ . . . Μωυσῆν. Wendland was confident that these words had been written in the margin of the archetype and inserted in different places by different scribes, and omitted by others, and only at last placed in their right position by himself. This is probable enough, but is it quite certain that the Papyrus erred in placing them between σώματος and οὔτε ἰσομεγέθους, since in De Aet. 102 the void, as postulated by the Stoics, is said to be ἄπειρον (and so too S. V.F. ii. 536-540)? Is it impossible that Philo while quoting this should safeguard his statement by adding ἰσομεγέθους?

(b) How did Moses disprove the void? Does Philo mean that since in De Aet. 19 Moses is said to have asserted the eternity of the world in Gen. viii. 22, he thereby denied the ἐκπύρωσις, and consequently the void also? If so, the meaning of διά will differ somewhat from that given in the translation, i.e. "nor does the fable of the ἐκπύρωσις, if we

572

follow Moses, justify us in postulating the existence of the void."

(c) The chief difficulty of the passage is that διά must be unnaturally strained to yield either meaning. I am inclined to think there is a corruption somewhere. I suggest, very tentatively of course, a lacuna after διά, e.g. διαⱯφερόμενον τοῖς εἰσηγουμένοις⟩ τὴν ἐν τῇ κτλ.; cf. De Mig. 180.

§ 242. σώμασιν οὐ πράγμασιν. I feel little doubt that Wendland was wrong in changing οὐ to καί. The balance of the sentence and the stress laid on σώματα throughout the passage, which is a meditation on τὰ σώματα τὰ διχοτομήματα of his text, in themselves support the ms. reading. Wendland may have taken πράγματα to be an interpretation of διχοτομήματα. But surely Philo's interpretation of the word (an interpretation of course entirely opposed to that which he has given in the earlier chapters) is that "bodies cut in two" signify the lifelessness and incompleteness of material things. The question, however, must be decided by the other passages where σώματα and πράγματα are set in antithesis. These are as follows:

(a) De Mut. 60 ἔνιοι μὲν οὖν τῶν . . . μώμους ἀεὶ τοῖς ἀμώμοις προσάπτειν ἐθελόντων οὐ σώμασι μᾶλλον ἢ πράγμασι. (The πράγματα attacked by these cavillers are the allegorical explanations of literal difficulties.)

(b) Ibid. 173 Πεντεφρῆ τὸν . . . ἀρχιμάγειρον . . . ἐν ἀψύχοις καὶ νεκροῖς καλινδούμενον οὐ σώμασι μᾶλλον ἢ πράγμασι. I.e., the chief cook in the spiritual sense lives in an environment of dead ideas.

(c) De Som. ii. 101 εὐξαίμην ἂν οὖν καὶ αὐτὸς δυνηθῆναι τοῖς γνωσθεῖσιν ὑπὸ τούτων ἐμμεῖναι βεβαίως· ὀπτῆρες γὰρ καὶ κατάσκοποι καὶ ἔφοροι πραγμάτων οὐ σωμάτων εἰσὶν ἀκριβοδίκαιοι. This is said of the sons of Jacob representing the wise, and rebuking the empty dreams of Joseph.

In all these apparently πράγματα signifies things belonging to the mental world, ideas in fact, though they need not necessarily be good, as in (b), just as the νοῦς of Egypt is an evil mind. But the antithesis becomes clearer in

(d) Ibid. 134 τὸν μὲν γὰρ φρονήσεως ἀσκητὴν ὑπολαμβάνομεν ἥλιον, ἐπειδήπερ ὁ μὲν τοῖς σώμασιν ὁ δὲ τοῖς κατὰ ψυχὴν πράγμασιν ἐμπαρέχει φῶς. Here πράγματα is definitely connected with νοητά as opposed to αἰσθητά, and the sense is exactly in agreement with our passage, as I understand it.

PHILO

§ 246. The different opinions mentioned in this section represent problems which Philo would constantly have heard disputed in contemporary discussions. In so far as they refer to the historic schools, we may say (1) that the creation of the universe was maintained by the Stoics and Epicureans and denied by the Peripatetics; (2) the words about the eternity of the universe and the reason given for it are almost a quotation from *Timaeus* 41 в, though there it is the "lesser gods," not the universe, which are spoken of; (3) "becoming" and "being" may be assigned respectively to Heracleitus and the Eleatic school, but Philo was familiar with the antithesis in Plato, *e.g. Theaetetus* 152, where also (4) he found the famous saying of Protagoras that "man is the measure of all things." He takes it in what may have been its original, though perhaps not the generally accepted, meaning, as opposed to the sceptical view that our mind and senses are untrustworthy, and so also in the other two places where he quotes it (*De Post.* 35 and *De Som.* ii. 193), though there it is its profanity as claiming for man what belongs only to God which is stressed. (5) "Those who maintain that everything is beyond our apprehension" are the sceptics, both those of the school of Pyrrho and the later Academy, while "those who assert that a great number of things are cognizable" are the non-sceptical philosophers in general, none of whom would assert more than that knowledge was generally, but not universally, attainable.

§ 249. *Divine possession or frenzy.* Philo in this description of prophetic "ecstasy" evidently has in mind *Phaedrus* 244 ε and 245 ʌ in which the words κατοκωχή τε καὶ μανία occur (followed at once by the phrase ἀπαλὴν καὶ ἄβατον ψυχήν which he has already used in § 38). *Cf.* § 264.

§ 253. *To treat things indifferent as indeed indifferent.* So in *Quod Det.* 122 it is the characteristic of justice ἐξαδιαφορεῖν τὰ μεθόρια κακίας καὶ ἀρετῆς, such as wealth, reputation and office, while on the other hand in *De Post.* 81, if Mangey's emendation is accepted, the misuser of natural gifts ἐξαδιαφορεῖ τὰ διάφορα. The words ἐξαδιαφορεῖν and -ησις are not quoted from any other writer than Philo.

Ibid. ἀπαρχάς is used here in a general sense, as there is no thought of offering to a god; *cf.* Dion. Hal. *De Comp.* iii. λόγων ἀπαρχάς, "specimen passages."

§ 274. *Or woman-man.* This addition is strange. In the

APPENDICES

other two places recorded, where Philo uses the word, it is as here coupled with ἀνδρόγυνος, but in contrast with it of a woman who adopts masculine dress or habits—an idea which is quite alien here. I suspect that it is an interpolation.

Ibid. Stock. See General Introduction, vol. i. p. xvi, though the statement there requires some correction. The ἀποσκευή is not the Encyclia, but the whole fruits of παιδεία of which the Encyclia are the first stage.

§ 282. The phraseology of the section is taken from *Timaeus* 42 E πυρὸς καὶ γῆς ὕδατός τε καὶ ἀέρος ἀπὸ τοῦ κόσμου δανειζόμενοι μόρια, ὡς ἀποδοθησόμενα πάλιν.

§ 283. *Moving in a circle.* Cf. Aristot. *De Caelo*, i. 2 and 3, where it is laid down that while the four elements have a rectilineal, the ether or fifth element has a circular movement. So also Philo of the heaven in *De Somn.* i. 21. See also *Quod Deus* 46 and note.

§ 290. *In the shadow of death.* The lxx actually has (like the Hebrew) ἐπὶ σκηνώμασι ἁμαρτωλῶν. This curious slip of memory was no doubt partly due to the sound σκ in both phrases.

§ 291. πολύν. This reading of Wendland's, based on the πολύ of Pap., does not seem to me satisfactory. Wendland himself, while noting the πολιόν of G, says " fortasse recte." Yet " grey-haired vanity " also seems strange. I should prefer to read πολιῶν (fem.) or πολιᾶς, both well-known terms for old age.

§ 310. τοῖς . . . ἀγγέλοις. While I retain and translate this, I do not think it satisfactory. The use of ἄγγελος is strange and only distantly paralleled by *De Mut.* 162 αὐγὴ γὰρ αὐγῆς ἄγγελος. But though Wendland accepted Mangey's ταῖς . . . αὐγαῖς as certain, it seems to me even less satisfactory, at any rate when coupled with Wendland's προσχωροῦντες or Mangey's ἐγχορεύοντες. There is no great likeness of form, and the sense is poor. The clause evidently interprets κάπνος γίνεται πρὸ πυρός. At this stage there are no " rays," and while " hope " may fairly stand for " smoke," to say " when we approach the rays we hope," is a poor equivalent to " smoke comes before fire," and Mangey's " as we move amid the rays we hope " is none at all. It would, however, be much improved if we read πρὼ (πρωὶ) ἐγχορεύοντες, *i.e.* " in our *first* stage of experiencing the rays, we hope " (and nothing more).

575

PHILO

Perhaps we might bring it still nearer to the mss. by putting ἀγγείοις for ἀγγέλοις. The oven or furnace is actually called an ἀγγεῖον ἀρετῆς a few lines below, and though there, as well as in § 308, we are the furnace, not in it, such a variation of the figure is not impossible. After all it is not really the furnace which smokes, but the fuel in it, and if we read τοῖς τε γὰρ ἀρετῆς ἀγγείοις πρὼ (πρωὶ) ἐγχορεύοντες τελειότητα ἐλπίζομεν, we have a text almost identical with that of the mss. and Pap., and giving a sense intelligible in itself (though not in complete agreement with its environment), that " when we are in the early stage of playing the part of fuel in the furnaces in which virtue is produced, we emit only the smoke of hoping for the full flame." (This general use of χορεύω and ἐγχορεύω is common enough in Philo, see *e.g. De Fug.* 45 ὁ ἔτι χορεύων ἐν τῷ θνητῷ βίῳ.)

§ 314. καθ' ἣν . . . ἀφθάρτοις. The text suggested in the footnote, which might be varied by ⟨διακρίνας⟩ διαφυλάττει for δια⟨κρίνας⟩ φυλάττει, and κατὰ τὰ ἅ for καθά, is fairly near to the mss. and seems to me to give a satisfactory sense. Mangey strangely accepted Markland's feeble suggestion of τοῖς τιμῶσιν αὐτόν for τοῖς τομεῦσιν ἑαυτοῦ.

Ibid. Who are born to life imperishable. With the change of ἐπί to πρέπει (or perhaps to ἔδει), these words present no difficulty. I understand them to be an interpretation, which in fact is needed, of τῷ σπέρματί σου. That the "seed of Abraham" should be called "those who in their origin are incorruptible" is natural enough.

APPENDIX TO *DE CONGRESSU*

§ 11. *Astronomy*. Astronomy of an elementary kind was regularly included among the Encyclia, but is not named by Philo in his other lists of the subjects, doubtless because, as often in other writers, it is regarded as a branch of geometry. *Cf.* Quintilian, i. 10. 46 " quid quod se eadem geometria tollit ad rationem usque mundi ? in qua siderum certos constitutosque cursus numeris docet."

§ 15. *The calamities . . . undergone*. This thought of the ethical value of history and poetry (epic and tragic) has already been brought out in *De Sac.* 78 f. See also *De Abr.* 23.

§ 18. *Sister and twin*. Though ὡς εἶπόν τινες indicates that this is a definite quotation from some writer or writers, the close relation of dialectic to rhetoric, though much discussed by the Stoics (see *S.V.F.* i. 75, ii. 294), is not described by this phrase in any source known to us. Aristotle speaks of rhetoric as being (1) ἀντίστροφον (counterpart), (2) παραφυές (offshoot), (3) μόριον (part), (4) ὁμοίωμα (copy), of rhetoric (Aristot. *Rhet.* i. 1. 1, i. 2. 7).

§ 29. *On the side of thought . . deception*. It seems to me almost incredible that Leah's handmaid, oratory or rhetoric, should on the side of ideas be limited to sophistical rhetoric, though one might understand this sort being admitted with the other, as indeed we find in *De Agr.* 13. Below in § 33 there is no such disparagement. I am strongly inclined to suspect a lacuna such as ἡ λογική *sc.* δύναμις ⟨τῆς διανοίας, οὐχ⟩ ἡ κτλ. Or for τῆς διανοίας we might conjecture τῶν πραγμάτων (facts), in which case ἡ λογική would still agree with εὕρεσις.

§ 53. *Battles of argument*. Elsewhere in Philo this word and γνωσιμαχία seem to be used generally for contention, without any particular meaning attaching to γνωσι-. Here, however, in combination with συλλαβομαχοῦντες, it seems

577

necessary to give the γνωσι- a more definite meaning, such as "of argument" or "as to knowledge."

§ 54. *The fount of human life.* Cf. *S.V.F.* i. 205 ἦθός ἐστι πηγὴ βίου, ἀφ᾽ ἧς αἱ κατὰ μέρος πράξεις ῥέουσι.

Ibid. ⟨ἀστάς⟩. That ἀστάς has been lost, as suggested in the footnote, seems to me very probable, though possibly a better form of the sentence, preserving the first ἤ of all mss., and the ἤ before δόγματα of some, would be παλλακὰς μέντοι ἤ ἀστάς, δόξας ἤ δόγματα. It is true that no Biblical example of the ἀστή of the wicked man is given, but in § 59 her existence as the mother of κακία, while the παλλακή is the mother of πάθος, is assumed. If we make this insertion, the conjunction of δόξα (= παλλακή) with δόγμα (= ἀστή) gets a clear meaning. As it stands, this conjunction, which is not recorded elsewhere, is otiose. But in *De Sac.* 5 we have them contrasted, the καλὸν δόγμα, Abel, with the ἄτοπος δόξα, Cain, and in general δόγμα, though, as in this case, it may be bad, is associated with principles and convictions arrived at by reason in contrast to unreasoning δόξα. That the former should produce vicious principles (κακία) and the latter fleeting passion is quite in keeping.

§ 77. *Doting on poetry . . . musical colours.* Clem. Al. (*Strom.* i. p. 332) reproduces these words as κατεγήρασαν οἱ μὲν αὐτῶν ἐν μουσικῇ, οἱ δὲ ἐν γεωμετρίᾳ, ἄλλοι δὲ ἐν γραμματικῇ, οἱ πλεῖστοι δὲ ἐν ῥητορικῇ. Hence Mangey strangely thought that γραμμαῖς should be corrected to γραμματικῇ, though in his translation he retains it as "delineationibus." But Philo's ποιήμασι gives Clement's γραμματικῇ, as his γραμμαῖς gives γεωμετρίᾳ. γραμμαῖς cannot mean "drawing," as Yonge certainly and Mangey presumably supposed. It is a regular term for geometrical figures, and γραμμικαὶ ἀποδείξεις for geometrical proofs (Quintilian i. 10. 38.) Mangey translates χρωμάτων κράσεσι by "temperaturis colorum," which leaves it doubtful whether he thought, as Yonge did, that it meant painting. There can be no reasonable doubt that it refers to the χρώματα of music. Though Aristotle laid stress on γραφική as a means of education, it never appears among the Encyclia. On the other hand the χρώματα, as shown in § 76, are an important element in music. Aristides Quintilianus (p. 18) gives this explanation of the name: χρῶμα, τὸ διὰ ἡμιτονίων συντεινόμενον· ὡς γὰρ τὸ μεταξὺ λευκοῦ καὶ μέλανος χρῶμα καλεῖται, οὕτω τὸ διὰ μέσων ἀμφοῖν θεωρούμενον

APPENDICES

χρῶμα καλεῖται. This suggests that κράσεις χρωμάτων may mean blendings which constitute χρώματα rather than blendings of them, but I leave this to the experts.

§ 79. *For philosophy*, etc. For this Stoic definition *cf.* S.V.F. ii. 36 τὴν φιλοσοφίαν φασὶν ἐπιτήδευσιν εἶναι σοφίας, τὴν δὲ σοφίαν ἐπιστήμην θείων τε καὶ ἀνθρωπίνων πραγμάτων. Cicero gives it in a form nearer to Philo, *De Off.* ii. 5 " nec quicquam aliud est philosophia . . . praeter studium sapientiae. Sapientia autem est, ut a veteribus philosophis definitum est, rerum divinarum et humanarum causarumque, quibus eae res continentur, scientia."

§ 107. περινοίᾳ λογισμοῦ πεποιθυίας. The translation given assumes (1) that πεποιθυίας (of a soul trusting) is not co-ordinate with the other participles, (2) that γενητοῦ agrees with λογισμοῦ; neither of which seems likely, though grammatically possible. Moreover, Philo would probably have written τοῦ πεποιθέναι instead of πεποιθυίας. Wendland conjectured περὶ πάντα λογισμῷ μεμαθηκυίας. This seems very arbitrary. Cohn suggested περινοίᾳ καὶ λογισμῷ πεπονθυίας. But if this means " experiencing through reasoning the nothingness of creation," it does not seem to me Greek. I suggest as slightly better to transfer περ. λογ. πεπ. and read ἱκετευούσης θεὸν ψυχῆς περινοίᾳ λογισμοῦ ⟨οὐ⟩ πεποιθυίας καὶ τὴν ταπεινότητα καὶ οὐδενείαν τοῦ γενητοῦ καὶ τὰς ἐν ἅπασι τοῖς καλοῖς ὑπερβολὰς καὶ ἀκρότητας τοῦ ἀγενήτου δεδιδαγμένης. This will make good sense and run smoothly, and it seems more likely that Philo thinks that human sagacity (περίνοια) or even human reason proves worthless in this supreme abasement, than that it is the agent by which the soul is schooled to humiliate itself, as Cohn's and Wendland's suggestions imply. Textually the loss of οὐ after λογισμοῦ is negligible and the departure from the mss., apart from the slight change of -αν to -ᾳ, lies in the transference of the three difficult words. I shall not be surprised however if it does not give general satisfaction.

§ 133. *The founder of this tribe.* Wendland gives as reference for the saying " God alone must I honour " Ex. xx. 3, *i.e.* the First Commandment, and therefore presumably took the γενάρχης to be Moses. But the reference is, I think, to the Blessing of Levi (Deut. xxxiii. 9) " who saith to his father and his mother I have not seen thee, and his brothers he knew not and his sons he disclaimed." In *Leg.*

PHILO

All. ii. 51 Philo has made a very similar use of this text
(though there the father and the mother are mind and body),
inferring from it that the Levi-mind rejects all such things
for the sake of having God as his portion, in accordance
with the words of Deut. x. 9, which he again quotes here.
And the same interpretation of Deut. xxxiii. 9 is given in
De Fug. 89, where Levi is called ὁ ἀρχηγέτης τοῦ θιάσου τούτου.

§ 141. *A system of conceptions*, etc. For this Stoic definition *cf. S.V.F.* i. 73, ii. 93 f. Sometimes in a longer form,
συγγεγυμνασμένων καὶ ἐπὶ τέλος εὔχρηστον τῷ βίῳ λαμβανόντων
(ἐχόντων) τὴν ἀναφόραν, where the masculine λαμβανόντων
shews that συγγ. also is masculine and that not the conceptions but the things conceived of are coordinated. As
ἐγγεγυμνασμένων appears in some examples (see *S.V.F.* i. 73),
Wendland is perhaps somewhat rash in altering to συγγ. If
ἐγγ. is retained, translate "exercised upon."

Ibid. For the definition of ἐπιστήμη, given in practically
the same words as here, see *S.V.F.* i. 68.

§ 148. *Elucidation of the . . . poets and historians.* This
definition with minor variations was the accepted one. In
the grammar of Dionysius Thrax, which furnished the model
for the later grammarians, both Greek and Latin, it appears
in the form ἐμπειρία τῶν παρὰ ποιηταῖς τε καὶ συγγραφεῦσι ὡς
ἐπὶ τὸ πολὺ λεγομένων. The definition brings out the important fact that γραμματική originally suggested literary study
rather than what we call grammar.

§ 149. The only terms in this list which either need explanation or have not had it on *De Agr.* 140, 141 are ἀποφαντόν
and περιεκτικόν. From Diog. Laert. vii. 65 it appears that
ἀποφαντόν which I have rendered by "declaratory" = ἀξίωμα,
i.e. a statement which must be either true or false, which
cannot be said of the forms of speech (ἐρώτημα, etc.) which
follow. While D. L. himself defines ἀξίωμα as πρᾶγμα αὐτο-
τελὲς ἀποφαντὸν ὅσον ἐφ' ἑαυτῷ, he has confused his inter-
preters by quoting Chrysippus: ἀξίωμά ἐστι τὸ ἀποφαντὸν ἢ
καταφαντὸν ὅσον ἐφ' ἑαυτῷ, οἷον Ἡμέρα ἐστί, Δίων περιπατεῖ.
This has led Hicks to translate ἀποφαντόν "capable of being
denied," as opposed to καταφαντόν. But this is surely to
confuse ἀποφαντός from ἀποφαίνω with ἀποφατικός from
ἀπόφημι. Liddell & Scott both in the earlier and in the
recent edition make the confusion worse, as while giving
ἀποφ. as = "asserting," they say under καταφ. "to be affirmed,

580

opposed to ἀποφαντός." I feel no doubt that ἀποφ. is "affirming" or "capable of being affirmed," and I should explain the καταφαντόν of Chrysippus as a synonym, which some preferred, unless indeed he means that ἀποφ. is used of such sentences as ἡμέρα ἐστί, and καταφ. of such as Δίων περιπατεῖ. Also it might easily be a gloss.

It should be added that as to ἀποφαντικός, sometimes used for the indicative mood, the examples shew that no doubt is possible, and ἀποφαντικός can hardly be separated from ἀποφαντός.

As for περιεκτικόν, it is most probably a mistake for προστακτικόν (imperative), which appears in D. L.'s list. At any rate if it is genuine, it must have some meaning unknown to us. The only sense in which we meet the word is for a place in which a number of things or persons are collected, e.g. ἀμπελών, παρθενών. Stephanus, indeed, has a statement, which L. & S. have copied, that περιεκτικὸν ῥῆμα is a verb in the middle voice, but no authority is given. And both these meanings are impossible in a list which contains different forms of sentences.

§ 155. "*In thy hands*." I suspect that Philo suggests in this section that the Greek of the text quoted may mean not only "The handmaid is in thy hands (or power)," but *also* "Thy handmaid is in the hands." It must be remembered that when he gives two alternative meanings for a passage, he does not think, as we should, that one *must* be the right one. To his mind they may both be intended. If we suppose that he is here commenting on "Thy handmaid is in the hands," the argument will become much clearer. The supposition will involve reading here ἐν ταῖς χερσί for ἐν ταῖς χερσί σου, but there is not much difficulty in this. A scribe failing to see the point might very naturally add σου.

§ 159. *Unrebuked*. Or "whose licence is unchecked." Mangey suspected ἀνεπίπληκτος in this sense, and perhaps it more generally means "not liable to rebuke," "blameless." But see Plato, *Legg.* 695 B, where it is applied to the undisciplined boyhood of Cyrus's sons, who left to women and eunuchs became οἵους ἦν εἰκὸς αὐτοὺς γενέσθαι τροφῇ ἀνεπιπλήκτῳ τραφέντας. So too in manhood they are τρυφῆς μεστοὶ καὶ ἀνεπιπληξίας.

Ibid. ὑπαργύρους καὶ ὑποχρύσους. These adjectives, which Mangey translated by "aureos et argenteos," ignoring the

PHILO

ὑπο-, are at first sight very difficult. All the evidence in the dictionaries hitherto given goes to prove that the prefix indicates not that the silver or gold conceals some other metal, but that it is covered or concealed by it. Thus while ὑπάργυρος may suggest a base coin, because the silver is coated with gold, ὑπόχρυσος would only suggest gold concealed by some baser metal. An article, however, by A. Körte in *Hermes*, 1929, pp. 262 f., to which Dr. Rouse called my attention, brings considerable evidence from inscriptions of the third century, as well as a line from Menander, 170 ff. (ὑπόχρυσος δακτύλιός τις οὑτοσί, αὐτὸς σιδηροῦς), to shew that ὑποχ. is used of iron rings or the like gilded over. Körte does not deal with ὑπάργυρος, but the same principle will apply. He connects the prefix with the common use of ὑπο- in adjectives, particularly in medical language, to indicate " somewhat," *e.g.* ὑπόλευκος " whitish." While he translates ὑπόχρυσος " gilded," it need not be inferred, I think, that the word in itself means this. Rather the two words are opposed to ὁλόχρυσος, ὁλάργυρος, and indicate that the gold and silver are not the predominant, or at least not the sole elements. But since, as a matter of fact, the admixture of gold or silver would regularly take the form of a coating, " veneered " or " plated " may stand.

§ 160. *Admonition.* I do not think that Philo can have written νουθεσίαν. Apart from the absurdity pointed out in the footnote, the ὥστε demands something inferred from the text, which has stated that those who live without κάκωσις forsake God. The inference must be that those who are under κάκωσις cleave to Him. I think Philo must have written εὐσέβειαν or θεοσέβειαν, which by some blunder was changed to νουθεσίαν as νομοθεσίαν to ἐκκλησίαν in § 120.

§ 171. *Eve.* Here again one can only suppose a similar blunder, possibly assisted by the similarity of **KAIETAN** to **KAIN**. Though Wendland retains the ms. text, it seems to me incredible that Philo should have thought that Cain was expelled from Paradise. At any rate, even if Philo wrote Cain, he meant to write Eve.